RACING IN AUSTRALIA
GUIDE TO SEASON 2018/19

www.slatterymedia.com

The Slattery Media Group
Level 39/385 Bourke Street, Melbourne
Victoria, Australia, 3000
Visit slatterymedia.com

Copyright © The Slattery Media Group 2018
First edition published by The Slattery Media Group in 2008. Second edition 2016. Third edition 2017.
Fourth edition 2018.

All rights reserved. No part of this publication may be reproduced, stored in a retrieval system
or transmitted in any form by any means without the prior permission of the copyright owner.
Inquiries should be made to the publisher.

Images reproduced with permission.

 A catalogue record for this book is available from the National Library of Australia

Group publisher: Geoff Slattery
Editor: Danny Power
Designer: Kate Slattery

On the cover:
Champion mare Winx and jockey Hugh Bowman after winning their third consecutive
Cox Plate at Moonee Valley last year

Back cover (from the top):
Australia's champion trainer of winners in 2017/18, Darren Weir, who set a record of 490.
Trainer Joseph O'Brien and jockey Corey Brown celebrate Rekindling's win in the Melbourne Cup.
Chris Waller, who trained a season-topping 13 Group 1 winners.

Printed and bound in Australia by Griffin Press

www.slatterymedia.com

RACING IN AUSTRALIA
GUIDE TO SEASON 2018/19

EDITED BY DANNY POWER

CONTENTS

THE RACES

Race index 6
Group 1 races 8
Group 2 races 172

GROUP 1 LISTS

Jockeys all time 284
Jockeys current 284
Trainers all time 285
Trainers current 285

THE PREMIERSHIPS

JOCKEYS

New South Wales 287
Queensland 289
South Australia 291
Tasmania 292
Victoria 293
Western Australia 296

TRAINERS

New South Wales 298
Queensland 299
South Australia 300
Tasmania 301
Victoria 302
Western Australia 304

Tommy's and Bart's Group 1 tallies downgraded

Last year there was a bit of a stir when we announced in *Racing In Australia* that the long-held belief that champion jockey George Moore's 119 Group 1 wins was an Australian record was wrong.

In reality, Moore's tally was only 105, which means current champion jockey Damien Oliver is on top of the all-time Group 1 list with 109. Roy Higgins' tally also has been significantly downgraded to 92.

Moore's and Higgins' totals had come from the research of noted racing historian, journalist and editor of Turf Monthly, the late Warwick Hobson, who delved into records in 1998.

It was discovered that Hobson's research had a number of flaws, in particular that he rewarded the past champions with Group 1 wins for races that were Group 1 in 1998, when in fact quite a few, such as the Flight Stakes and Lightning Stakes, started "life" as Group 2s when Pattern racing was introduced in Australia for the 1979/80 season.

We have now done some work on the leading trainers, and again Hobson's work over-rated some of Australia's great trainers. He had Tommy Smith on 282 Group 1 wins—a world record until Ireland's Aidan O'Brien knocked him off—and Bart Cummings was credited with 268 (including two in

BART ON TOP: a revision of the Group 1 list for Australia's trainers see Bart Cummings, pictured here with Saintly, overtaking Tommy Smith. Photo: VRC collection

partnership with his grandson James), and Colin Hayes on 98.

The revised list (see pages 284-285), using the 1979-80 Pattern-race formula, has Cummings ahead of Smith, 246 to 243, followed by Gai Waterhouse 139, Lee Freedman 125, John Hawkes 111 and Hayes now on 91.

Racing In Australia's figures might differ slightly from historians who are also applying that formula to the historical Group 1 list because I regard the Merson Cooper Stakes, which seamlessly transferred to the Blue Diamond Stakes in 1980 as a Group 1 race.

It's a case I am happy to argue.

IN THIS EDITION

Racing In Australia features an extensive analysis of Australia's 167 Group 1 and Group 2 races.

It's much more than a list of past winners of some of Australia's famous races; not only does it focus on the impact of each race, but also the path on which the past winners trod and to where it led them in the future.

Champion trainers Lee Freedman, Gai Waterhouse and Murray Baker have used this historical data to help map spring and autumn carnival programs for their horses. Bookie and noted form analyst Robbie Waterhouse finds the information invaluable to his research.

A unique feature of *Racing In Australia* is a complete study of the leading past-winning jockeys and trainers, as well as all the current winners, for each race.

Racing In Australia's aim is to develop the ultimate guide and reference for racing media and broader racing fans, and we are working on the Group 3 races for next year.

This edition includes lists of the Group 1-winning statistics of Australia's leading and current jockeys and trainers, and the historical premiership winners in each state, some going back to 1900.

I hope you enjoy the fourth edition of *Racing In Australia*, which is the product of hours of painstaking research that began in 2006, and never seems to stop.

Danny Power
Editor

RACE INDEX

Group 1, 2018/19

AUGUST 2018
Page Race
8   ATC Winx Stakes (1400m)—Randwick

SEPTEMBER 2018
10   MRC Memsie Stakes (1400m)—Caulfield
12   VRC Makybe Diva Stakes (1600m)—Flemington
14   ATC George Main Stakes (1600m)—Randwick
16   ATC Golden Rose Stakes (1400m)—Rosehill
18   MRC Sir Rupert Clarke Stakes (1400m)—Caulfield
20   MVRC Moir Stakes (1000m)—Moonee Valley
22   ATC Epsom Handicap (1600m)—Randwick
24   ATC The Metropolitan (2400m)—Randwick
26   ATC Flight Stakes (1600m)—Randwick
28   MRC Underwood Stakes (1800m)—Caulfield

OCTOBER 2018
30   VRC Turnbull Stakes (2000m)—Flemington
32   ATC Spring Champion Stakes (2000m)—Randwick
34   MRC Caulfield Guineas (1600m)—Caulfield
37   MRC Thousand Guineas (1600m)—Caulfield
39   MRC Toorak Handicap (1600m)—Caulfield
41   MRC Caulfield Stakes (2000m)—Caulfield
43   MRC Stella Artois Caulfield Cup (2400m)—Caulfield
46   MVRC Manikato Stakes (1200m)—Moonee Valley
48   MVRC Ladbrokes Cox Plate (2040m)—Moonee Valley

NOVEMBER 2018
52   VRC Coolmore Stud Stakes (1200m)—Flemington
54   VRC Kennedy Mile (1600m)—Flemington
56   VRC Myer Classic (1600m)—Flemington
58   VRC AAMI Victoria Derby—Flemington
61   VRC Lexus Melbourne Cup—Flemington
64   VRC Kennedy Oaks (2500m)—Flemington
67   VRC Darley Classic (1200m)—Flemington
69   VRC Seppelts Wines Stakes (2000m)—Flemington
71   WATC Railway Stakes (1600m)—Ascot

DECEMBER 2018
73   WATC Winterbottom Stakes (1200m)—Ascot
75   WATC Kingston Town Classic (1800m)—Ascot

FEBRUARY 2019
77   MRC Orr Stakes (1400m)—Caulfield
79   VRC Black Caviar Lightning Stakes (1000)—Flemington
81   MRC Blue Diamond Stakes (1200m)—Caulfield
84   MRC Futurity Stakes (1400m)—Caulfield
87   MRC Oakleigh Plate (1100m)—Caulfield

MARCH 2019
89   ATC Chipping Norton Stakes (1600m)—Randwick
91   ATC Surround Stakes (1200m)—Warwick Farm
93   VRC Australian Guineas (1600m)—Flemington
95   ATC Randwick Guineas (1600m)—Randwick
97   ATC Canterbury Stakes (1300m)—Randwick
99   VRC Australian Cup (2000m)—Flemington
101   VRC Newmarket Handicap (1200m)—Flemington
104   ATC Coolmore Classic (1500m)—Rosehill
106   MVRC William Reid Stakes (1200m)—Moonee Valley
108   ATC Golden Slipper Stakes (1200m)—Rosehill
111   ATC George Ryder Stakes (1500m)—Rosehill
113   ATC Ranvet Stakes (2000m)—Rosehill
115   ATC The Galaxy (1100m)—Rosehill
117   ATC Rosehill Guineas (2000m)—Rosehill
120   ATC Tancred (2400m)—Rosehill
122   ATC Vinery Stud Stakes (2000m)—Rosehill

APRIL 2019
124   ATC Doncaster Handicap (1600m)—Randwick
127   ATC TJ Smith Stakes (1200m)—Randwick
129   ATC Australian Derby (2400m)—Randwick
132   ATC Sires' Produce Stakes (1400m)—Randwick
135   ATC Queen Elizabeth Stakes (2000m)—Randwick
138   ATC Sydney Cup (3200m)—Randwick
140   ATC Australian Oaks (2400m)—Randwick
142   ATC Queen Of The Turf Stakes (1600m)—Randwick
144   ATC All Aged Stakes (1400m)—Randwick
146   ATC Champagne Stakes (1600m)—Randwick

MAY 2019
148   SAJC Schweppes Oaks (2000m)—Morphettville
150   SAJC Robert Sangster Stakes (1200m)—Morphettville
152   SAJC South Australian Derby (2500m)—Morphettville
154   BRC Doomben 10,000 (1200m)—Doomben
156   SAJC The Goodwood (1200m)—Morphettville
158   BRC Doomben Cup (2000m)—Doomben
160   BRC Kingsford Smith Cup (1300m)—Doomben

JUNE 2019
162   BRC Queensland Oaks (2400m)—Eagle Farm
164   BRC Stradbroke Handicap (1400m)—Eagle Farm
166   BRC JJ Atkins (1600m)—Eagle Farm
168   BRC Queensland Derby (2400m)—Eagle Farm
170   Tatts RC Tattersall's Tiara (1400m)—Eagle Farm

Group 2, 2018/19

AUGUST 2018
172   ATC Missile Stakes (1200m)—Randwick
173   MRC PB Lawrence Stakes (1400m)—Caulfield
174   ATC Silver Shadow Stakes (1200m)—Randwick

SEPTEMBER 2018
175 Tattersalls Chelmsford Stakes (1600m)—Randwick
176 Tattersalls Furious Stakes (1200m)—Randwick
177 Tattersalls Tramway Stakes (1400m)—Randwick
178 ATC The Run To The Rose (1200m)—Rosehill
179 ATC Theo Marks Quality (1300m)—Rosehill
181 ATC Stan Fox Stakes (1500m)—Rosehill
182 MVRC McEwen Stakes (1000m)—Moonee Valley
183 MVRC Dato' Tan Chin Nam Stakes (1600m)—M. Valley
184 VRC Danehill Stakes (1200m)—Flemington
185 VRC Let's Elope Stakes (1400m)—Flemington
186 VRC Bobbie Lewis Quality (1200m)—Flemington
187 ATC The Shorts (1100m)—Randwick
189 ATC Tea Rose Stakes (1400m)—Randwick
190 ATC Golden Pendant (1400m)—Rosehill
191 ATC Shannon Stakes (1500m)—Rosehill
192 MVRC W.H. Stock Stakes (1600m)—Moonee Valley
194 MVRC Stutt Stakes (1600m)—Moonee Valley
195 ATC Hill Stakes (1800m)—Randwick
197 ATC Premiere Stakes (1200m)—Randwick
198 MRC Thousand Guineas Prelude (1400m)—Caulfield

OCTOBER 2018
199 ATC Roman Consul Stakes (1200m)—Randwick
200 VRC Edward Manifold Stakes (1600m)—Flemington
201 VRC Gilgai Stakes (1200m)—Flemington
203 VRC Rose Of Kingston Stakes (1400m)—Flemington
204 MRC Schillaci Stakes (1100m)—Caulfield
205 MRC Herbert Power Stakes (2400m)—Caulfield
206 MRC Caulfield Sprint (1100m)—Caulfield
207 MRC Tristarc Stakes (1400m)—Caulfield
208 MVRC The MV Vase (2040m)—Moonee Valley
208 MVRC MV Fillies Classic (1600m)—Moonee Valley
211 MVRC Crystal Mile (1600m)—Moonee Valley
212 MVRC Moonee Valley Gold Cup (2500m)—Moonee Valley

NOVEMBER 2018
213 VRC Wakeful Stakes (2000m)—Flemington
214 VRC Linlithgow Stakes (1200m)—Flemington
216 VRC Matriarch Stakes (2000m)—Flemington
217 WATC Lee Steere Stakes (1400m)—Ascot
218 MRC Sandown Guineas (1600m)—Sandown Hillside
219 MRC Zipping Classic (2400m)—Sandown Hillside
221 WATC WA Guineas (1600m)—Ascot

DECEMBER 2018
222 ATC Villiers Stakes (1600m)—Randwick
223 WATC Ted Van Heemst Stakes (2100m)—Ascot

JANUARY 2019
224 WATC Perth Cup (2400m)—Ascot
226 MVRC Australia Stakes (1200m)—Moonee Valley

FEBRUARY 2019
227 ATC Expressway Stakes (1200m)—Rosehill
228 ATC Breeders' Classic (1200m)—Randwick
229 MRC Autumn Stakes (1400m)—Caulfield
230 MRC Rubiton Stakes (1100m)—Caulfield
231 MRC Blue Diamond Prelude Fillies (1100m)—Caulfield
233 ATC Apollo Stakes (1400m)—Randwick
234 ATC Light Fingers Stakes (1200m)—Randwick
235 ATC Hobartville Stakes (1400m)—Rosehill
236 ATC Silver Slipper Stakes (1100m)—Rosehill
237 ATC Millie Fox Stakes (1300m)—Rosehill
238 MRC Peter Young Stakes (1800m)—Caulfield
240 MRC Caulfield Autumn Classic (1800m)—Caulfield
241 MRC Angus Armanasco Stakes (1400m)—Caulfield

MARCH 2019
242 ATC Skyline Stakes (1200m)—Warwick Farm
243 ATC Sweet Embrace Stakes (1200m)—Warwick Farm
244 ATC Guy Walter Stakes (1400m)—Warwick Farm
245 ATC Challenge Stakes (1000m)—Randwick
247 ATC Reisling Stakes (1200m)—Randwick
248 ATC Todman Stakes (1200m)—Randwick
249 VRC A.V. Kewney Stakes (1600m)—Flemington
250 VRC Sires' Produce Stakes (1400m)—Flemington
252 SAJC Adelaide Cup (3200m)—Morphettville
253 MVRC Alister Clark Stakes (2040m)—Moonee Valley
254 VRC Blamey Stakes (1600m)—Flemington
256 ATC Phar Lap Stakes (1500m)—Rosehill
257 ATC Ajax Stakes (1500m)—Rosehill
258 MVRC Sunline Stakes (1600m)—Moonee Valley
259 ATC Tulloch Stakes (2000m)—Rosehill
260 ATC Emancipation Stakes (1500m)—Rosehill

APRIL 2019
262 ATC Chairman's Handicap (2600m)—Randwick
263 WATC Karrakatta Plate (1200m)—Ascot
264 ATC Arrowfield 3YO Sprint (1200m)—Randwick
265 ATC Sapphire Stakes (1200m)—Randwick
266 ATC Percy Sykes Stakes—Randwick
268 W.A.T.C. Derby (2400m)—Ascot
269 BRC Victory Stakes (1200m)—Eagle Farm

MAY 2019
271 GCTC A.D. Hollindale Stakes (1800m)—Gold Coast
272 SAJC Euclase Stakes (1200m)—Morphettville
273 SAJC Queen Of The South Stks (1600m)—Morphettville
274 BRC Champagne Classic (1200m)—Doomben
275 BRC The Roses (2000m)—Doomben
276 BRC Sires' Produce (1400m)—Eagle Farm

JUNE 2019
277 BRC PJ O'Shea Stakes (2200m)—Eagle Farm
279 BRC Moreton Cup (1300m)—Eagle Farm
280 BRC Queensland Guineas (1600m)—Eagle Farm
281 BRC Brisbane Cup (2400m)—Eagle Farm
282 BRC Dane Ripper Stakes (1400m)—Eagle Farm

ATC Winx Stakes (1400m)—Randwick

$500,000 Group 1 3YO&Up WFA. August 18, 2018.

2017-18 RESULT: Time: 1:21.8 (Good 3)

FP	NO	HORSE	TRAINER	JOCKEY	MARGIN	BAR.	WGT	SP
1	6	WINX	Chris Waller	Hugh Bowman		4	57kg	$1.24F
2	2	HARTNELL	John O'Shea	James McDonald	3.5L	3	59kg	$21
3	4	REBEL DANE	Gary Portelli	Tommy Berry	4.3L	2	59kg	$11
4	7	LUCIA VALENTINA	Kris Lees	Kerrin McEvoy	4.4L	1	57kg	$11
5	5	VANBRUGH	Chris Waller	Glyn Schofield	8.9L	6	58.5kg	$31
6	1	WHO SHOT THEBARMAN	Chris Waller	Brenton Avdulla	10.1L	7	59kg	$81
7	3	GRAND MARSHAL	Chris Waller	Jason Collett	11.1L	5	59kg	$201

PAST WINNERS

YEAR	WINNER	JOCKEY	TRAINER	2ND	3RD	TIME
2017	Winx	Hugh Bowman	Chris Waller	Foxplay	Ecuador	1:21.8
2016	Winx	Hugh Bowman	Chris Waller	Hartnell	Rebel Dane	1:23.8
2015	Royal Descent	Hugh Bowman	Chris Waller	Pornichet	Messene	1:21.5
2014	Tiger Tees	Glyn Schofield	Joseph Pride	Royal Descent	Criterion	1:27.7
2013	Veyron	Christian Reith	Linda Laing	Streama	Rain Affair	1:21.5
2012	Pinwheel	Kerrin McEvoy	Peter Snowden	Secret Admirer	Danleigh	1:22.5
2011	Pinwheel	Kerrin McEvoy	Peter Snowden	Ilovethiscity	Startsmeup	1:25.8
2010	Metal Bender	Tim Clark	Chris Waller	Triple Honour	Danleigh	1:24.2
2009	Trusting	Chris Munce	Jason Coyle	O'lonhro	Mr Baritone	1:21.5
2008	Racing to Win	Hugh Bowman	John O'Shea	Gallant Tess	Danzippo	1:24.5
2007	Race not run					
2006	Courts In Session	Danny Beasley	Guy Walter	Racing To Win	Desert War	1:23.3
2005	Sir Dex	Zac Purton	Gregory Hickman	Dizelle	Sportsman	1:22.8
2004	Private Steer	Glen Boss	John O'Shea	So Assertive	Niello	1:22.7
2003	Lonhro	Darren Beadman	John Hawkes	Clangalang	Defier	1:24.3
2002	Defier	Chris Munce	Guy Walter	Lonhro	Republic Lass	1:22.8
2001	Lonhro	Darryl McLellan	John Hawkes	Diamond Dane	Shogun Lodge	1:17.3

BACKGROUND

First run: 1923 (won by Sunburst). Group 2 1979-2017, Group 1 from 2018. Run over 1600m before 1938. Run over 1400m 1938, 1942, 1949 & 1951. Run over 1300m 2000 & 2001. Run at Warwick Farm 1923-39, 1951-68, 1970, 1972-79, 1982-92, 1994-99, 2001-02, 2004, 2008, 2010-12. Run at Canterbury 2000. Run at Randwick 1940-50, 1969, 1971, 1980, 1981, 1993 & 2003; 2005-06, from 2013. Formerly the Warwick Stakes. Renamed the Winx Stakes in 2018. Not held in 2007 due to the Equine Influenza outbreak.

Most recent mare to win: Winx (2017).

Most recent 3YO to win: C&G—Lonhro (2001); Filly—Silver Shadow (1975).

Multiple winners: 13—Winx (2017, 2016); Pinwheel (2012, 2011); Lonhro (2003, 2001); Filante (1997, 1996); Super Impose (1992, 1991); Kingston Town (1982, 1981, 1980); Gay Gauntlet (1967, 1965); Sky High (1962, 1961); Tarien (1954, 1953); San Domenico (1951, 1950); Chatham (1934, 1933); Johnnie Jason (1932, 1931); Limerick (1929, 1928, 1927).

Fastest time (1400m): Filante (1997) 1:21.06.

Notable winners: Winx (2017, 2016); Lonhro (2003, 2001); Sunline (1999); Filante (1997, 1996); Shaftesbury Avenue (1992); Super Impose (1991, 1990); Kingston Town (1982, 1981, 1980); Sky High (1962, 1961); Tulloch (1957); Flight (1944); Chatham (1934, 1933); Amounis (1930); Limerick (1929, 1928, 1927); Windbag (1926); Whittier (1925).

Warwick Stakes winners won the lead-up races:
Missile Stakes: 1—Pinwheel (2012).

Warwick Stakes winners went on to win in the same preparation:
Chelmsford Stakes: 13—Winx (2017); Lonhro (2003); Filante (1996); March Hare (1994); Kingston Town (1981, 1980); Purple Patch (1976); Longfella (1973); Bernborough (1946); Beaulivre (1940); Defaulter (1939); Limerick (1928, 1927).
George Main Stakes: 11—Winx (2017, 2016); Lonhro (2003); Kingston Town (1982, 1981); Party's Pride (1978); Purple Patch (1976); Nippon (1972); Tarien (1953); San Domenico (1950); The Groom (1949).
Epsom Handicap: 5—Filante (1996); Super Impose (1991, 1990); Sky High (1961); Chatham (1933).
Cox Plate: 7—Winx (2017, 2016); Sunline (1999); Kingston Town (1982, 1981, 1980); Chatham (1934).
Caulfield Cup: 4—Tulloch (1957); Beaulivre (1940); Amounis (1930); Whittier (1925).

Victoria Derby: 3—Tulloch (1957); Talking (1936); Johnnie Jason (1931).
Leading winning jockeys: 6 wins Darby Munro (Tarien 1954, Removal 1945, Katanga 1943, Beaulivre 1940, Allunga 1937, Rogilla 1935).
4 wins Hugh Bowman (Winx 2017, 2016, Royal Descent 2015, Racing To Win 2008); Kevin Langby (Gypsy Kingdom 1979, Silver Shadow 1975, Longfella 1973, Royal Show 1970); Neville Sellwood (Up And Coming 1959, El Khobar 1956, Prince Cortauld 1955, The Groom 1949).
Current winning jockeys: 4 wins Hugh Bowman (Winx 2017, 2016, Royal Descent 2015, Racing To Win 2008).
2 wins Kerrin McEvoy (Pinwheel 2012, 2011).
1 win Glen Boss (Private Steer 2004); Larry Cassidy (Sunline 1999); Tim Clark (Metal Bender 2010); Grant Cooksley (Star Dancer 1994); Damien Oliver (Groucho 1990); Zac Purton (Sir Dex 2005); Christian Reith (Veyron 2013); Glyn Schofield (Tiger Tees 2104).
Leading winning trainers: 9 wins Tommy Smith (Kingston Town 1982, 1981, 1980, Silver Shadow 1975, Longfella 1973, Royal Show 1970, Tulloch 1957, Tarien 1954, 1953).
4 wins Jack Denham (Filante 1997, 1996, Flotilla 1988, Purple Patch 1976); Chris Waller (Winx 2017, 2016, Royal Descent 2015, Metal Bender 2010).
3 wins Jack Green (Reveille 1964, Sky High 1962, 1961); Fred Jones (Limerick 1929, 1928, 1927); Fred Williams (Talking 1936, Chatham 1934, 1933).
Current winning trainers: 4 wins Chris Waller (Winx 2017, 2016, Royal Descent 2015, Metal Bender 2010).
2 wins Lee Freedman (Super Impose 1991, 1990); John Hawkes (Lonhro 2003, 2001); John O'Shea (Racing To Win 2008, Private Steer 2004); Peter Snowden (Pinwheel 2012, 2011); Bruce Wallace (Star Dancer 1995, Prince Of Praise 1993).
1 win Jason Coyle (Trusting 2009); Greg Hickman (Sir Dex 2005); Linda Laing (Veyron 2013); Joe Pride (Tiger Tees 2014); John Size (Al Mansour 2000); Jenny Vance (What Can I Say 1998).
Points of interest: Racing To Win, second in 2006, went on to win the Group 1 Epsom Handicap (1600m) at Randwick in October.
Maurice McCarten rode Limerick in his three wins (1929, 1928, 1927) and trained Prince Cortauld to win in 1955.

Winx (2017, 2016) recorded her 18th consecutive win in 2017—after missing the start by four lengths.

MRC Memsie Stakes (1400m)—Caulfield

Of $1,000,000. Group 1, WFA, 3YO&Up. September 1, 2018

2017-18 RESULT: Time: 1:23.36 (Good 3)

FP	NO	HORSE	TRAINER	JOCKEY	MARGIN	BAR.	WGT	SP
1	5	VEGA MAGIC	David & Ben Hayes & Tom Dabernig	Craig Williams		2	59kg	$2.25F
2	1	BLACK HEART BART	Darren Weir	Brad Rawiller	1.75L	4	59kg	$6
3	3	TOSEN STARDOM	Darren Weir	Blake Shinn	1.85L	3	59kg	$15
4	8	HEY DOC	Tony McEvoy	Luke Currie	2.6L	1	58.5kg	$6.50
5	2	LE ROMAIN	Kris Lees	Ben Melham	2.8L	5	59kg	$8.50
6	7	JON SNOW	Murray Baker & Andrew Forsman	Stephen Baster	3.1L	9	58.5kg	$71
7	11	I AM A STAR	Shane Nichols	Luke Nolen	5.35L	6	56.5kg	$18
8	4	HUMIDOR	Darren Weir	Mark Zahra	5.45L	10	59kg	$26
9	12	YANKEE ROSE	Dean Yendall	David Vandyke	5.95L	7	56.5kg	$17
10	10	SINGLE GAZE	Nick Olive	Kathy O'Hara	8.2L	8	57kg	$81
11	9	SEABURGE	David & Ben Hayes & Tom Dabernig	Regan Bayliss	9.45L	11	58.5kg	$71

PAST WINNERS

YEAR	WINNER	JOCKEY	TRAINER	2ND	3RD	TIME
2017	Vega Magic	Craig Williams	David & Ben Hayes & Tom Dabernig	Black Heart Bart	Tosen Stardom	1:23.3
2016	Black Heart Bart	Brad Rawiller	Darren Weir	Rising Romance	Mahuta	1:23.9
2015	Boban	Glyn Schofield	Chris Waller	Entirely Platinum	Stratum Star	1:24.6
2014	Dissident	Ben Melham	Peter Moody	Sweet Idea	Puissance De Lune	1:22.7
2013	Atlantic Jewel	Michael Rodd	Mark Kavanagh	Ferlax	Super Cool	1:24.4
2012	Sincero	Michael Rodd	Stephen Farley	Happy Trails	Second Effort	1:23.2
2011	King's Rose	Luke Nolen	Peter Moody	Heart Of Dreams	Red Colossus	1:23.4
2010	So You Think	Steven Arnold	Bart Cummings	Whobegotyou	Shoot Out	1:26.6
2009	Mic Mac	Danny Nikolic	Greg Eurell	Whobegotyou	Zarita	1:24.4
2008	Weekend Hussler	Brad Rawiller	Ross McDonald	Maldivian	Pompeii Ruler	1:23.2
2007	Miss Finland	Craig Williams	David Hayes	Haradasun	Tipungwuti	1:24.2
2006	El Segundo	Darren Gauci	Colin Little	Casual Pass	Apache Cat	1:23.2
2005	Makybe Diva	Steven King	Lee Freedman	Barely A Moment	Regal Roller	1:26.7
2004	Regal Roller	Mark Flaherty	Clinton McDonald	Pacific Dancer	Delzao	1:23.0
2003	Le Zagaletta	Brett Prebble	Lee Freedman	Super Elegant	Out Of Options	1:25.2
2002	Magical Miss	Steven Arnold	Bart Cummings	Fields Of Omagh	Dash For Cash	1:24.0
2001	Sunline	Greg Childs	Trevor Mckee	Plavonic	Rum	1:25.5
2000	Sunline	Greg Childs	Trevor Mckee	Umrum	Oliver Twist	1:25.4
1999	Sir Boom	Greg Hall	Mel Hutchins	The Message	Londolozi	1:24.8
1998	Dane Ripper	Damien Oliver	Bart Cummings	Willoughby	La Volta	1:22.8
1997	Tarnpir Lane	Gavin Eades	Cliff Brown	Bradson	Doriemus	1:23.9
1996	Sir Boom	Jason Patton	Mel Hutchins	Seascay	Poetic King	1:23.9
1995	Island Morn	Peter Knuckey	Peter Hayes	Station Hand	Blevic	1:23.2

BACKGROUND

First run in 1899 (won by Veneda). Group 2 1979 to 2012. Group 1 from 2013. Run over 1600m 1899, 1971-79; 1800m 1890-1970; 1400m from 1980.
Most recent mare to win: Atlantic Jewel (2013).
Most recent 3YO to win: C&G—Battle Sign (1975). Note: No 3YO filly has won.
Multiple winners: 10—Sunline (2001, 2000); Sir Boom (1999, 1996); Yangtze (1966, 1965); Coppice (1955, 1954); Comic Court (1950, 1949); Waltzing Lily (1934, 1933); Heroic (1926, 1925); Lord (1961, 1960, 1959, 1958); Ajax (1940, 1939, 1938); Eurythmic (1922, 1921, 1920).
Fastest time (1400m): Dane Ripper (1998) 1:22.80.
Notable winners: Black Heart Bart (2016); Boban (2015); So You Think (2010); Weekend Hussler (2008); Makybe Diva (2005); Sunline (2001, 2000); Dane Ripper (1998); Rancho Ruler (1988); Rubiton (1987); Manikato (1982); Plush (1976); Zambari (1973); Galilee (1968); Lord (1961, 1960, 1959, 1958); Rising Fast (1956); Comic Court (1950, 1949); Tranquil Star (1945); Ajax (1940, 1939, 1938); Hall Mark (1935); Waltzing Lily (1933, 1934); Phar Lap (1931); Heroic (1926, 1925); Eurythmic (1922, 1921, 1920); Artilleryman (1919); Bobadil (1905); Hymettus (1901).

Memsie Stakes winners won the lead-up races:
Bletchingly Stakes: None.
Regal Roller Stakes: 1—Vega Magic (2017)
PB Lawrence Stakes (Liston Stakes): 4—Regal Roller (2004), Zambari (1973); Lord (1958), Syntax (1957).
Note: Regal Roller (2004) is the only winner of the double since it became a 1400m event in 1980.
Memsie Stakes winners went on to win in the same preparation:
Makybe Diva Stakes: 5—Dissident (2014); Weekend Hussler (2008); Lord (1961); Comic Court (1949); Lungi (1948).
Stocks Stakes: 2—Atlantic Jewel (2013); King's Rose (2011).
Dato Tan Chin Nam Stakes: 5—Sunline (2000); Palace Reign (1993); Naturalism (1992); Rubiton (1987); Dazzling Duke (1986).
Underwood Stakes: 16—Black Heart Bart (2016); So You Think (2010); Weekend Hussler (2008); El Segundo (2006); Rubiton (1987); Lord (1960, 1958); Syntax (1957); Attley (1947); Ajax (1940, 1939, 1938); Phar Lap (1931); Highland (1929); Royal Charter (1927); Heroic (1926).Caulfield Stakes: 16—Atlantic Jewel (2013); So You Think (2010); Lord (1960, 1959, 1958); Comic Court (1950); Lawrence (1944); Ajax (1938); Gothic (1928); Royal Charter (1927); Heroic (1925); Maid Of The Mist (1923); Eurythmic (1922, 1921, 1920); Traquette (1915).
Underwood Stakes & Caulfield Stakes (Caulfield WFA spring treble): 5—So You Think (2010); Lord (1960, 1958); Ajax (1938); Royal Charter (1927). Note: No horse has completed the treble since the Memsie became a G1 races in 2013.
Caulfield Cup: 4—Silver Bounty (1981); Peshawar (1952); Eurythmic (1920); Hymettus (1901).
Cox Plate: 7—So You Think (2010); Makybe Diva (2005); Sunline (2000); Rubiton (1987); Ajax (1938); Phar Lap (1931); Heroic (1926).
Melbourne Cup: 3—Makybe Diva (2005); Comic Court (1950); Artilleryman (1919).
Leading winning jockeys:
5 wins Jack Purtell (Comic Court 1950, 1949, Lungi 1948, Attley 1947, Sun Valley 1943); Bill Williamson (Syntax 1957, Rising Fast 1956, Peshawar 1952, Noble Prince 1946, Lawrence 1944).
4 wins Geoff Lane (Coppelius 1963, Lord 1960, 1959, 1958).
Current winning jockeys:
2 wins Steven Arnold (So You Think 2010, Magical Miss 2002); Brad Rawiller (Black Heart Bart 2016, Weekend Hussler 2008); Michael Rodd (Atlantic Jewel 2013, Sincero 2012); Craig Williams (Vega Magic 2017, Miss Finland 2007).
1 win Grant Cooksley (The Phantom 1990); Peter Knuckey (Island Morn 1995); Ben Melham (Dissident 2014); Luke Nolen (King's Rose 2011); Damien Oliver (Dane Ripper 1998); Brett Prebble (Le Zagaletta 2003); Glyn Schofield (Boban 2015).
Leading winning trainers:
11 wins Jack Holt (Noble Prince 1946, Hall Mark 1935, High Brae 1932, Highland 1929, Royal Charter 1927, Heroic 1926, 1925, Englefield 1924, Eurythmic 1922, 1921, 1920).
8 wins Ken Hilton (Future 1964, Lord 1961, 1960, 1959, 1958, Coppice 1955, 1954, Ellerslie 1951).
4 wins Bart Cummings (So You Think 2010, Magical Miss 2002, Dane Ripper 1998, Galilee 1968); Frank Musgrave (Ajax 1940, 1939, 1938, Aleconner 1914).
Current winning trainers:
3 wins Lee Freedman (Makybe Diva 2005, Le Zagaletta 2003, Naturalism 1992); David Hayes (Vega Magic 2017, Miss Finland 2007, Palace Reign 1993).
1 win Murray Baker (The Phantom 1990); Cliff Brown (Tarnpir Lane 1997); Gary Carson (Silver Bounty 1981); Greg Eurell (Mic Mac 2009); Steve Farley (Sincero 2012); John Hawkes (Tolhurst 1980); David & Ben Hayes & Tom Dabernig (Vega Magic 2017); Mark Kavanagh (Atlantic Jewel 2013); Colin Little (El Segundo 2006); Clinton McDonald (Regal Roller 2004); Chris Waller (Boban 2015); Darren Weir (Black Heart Bart 2016).
Points of interest:
The most recent Melbourne Cup winners to contest the Memsie are: Prince Of Penzance (2015), Green Moon (2012), Efficient (2007), Makybe Diva (2004-05) and Doriemus (1995).
Valiant Chief and Charles Fox dead-heated in 1936. Eirisdale and Massinissa dead-heated in 1900.
No horse has won the Caulfield spring "Big 4"—Memsie Stakes, Underwood Stakes, Caulfield Stakes and Caulfield Cup. The closest is Eurythmic, who won the Memsie, Caulfield Stakes and Caulfield Cup, but missed on the Underwood Stakes.
Gary Carson rode Ahjay to win in 1970, and trained Silver Bounty to success in 1981.

VRC Makybe Diva Stakes (1600m)—Flemington
Of $750,000. Group 1. Weight for Age, 3YO&Up. September 15, 2018.

2017-18 RESULT: Time: 1:35.35   (Good 4)

FP	NO	HORSE	TRAINER	JOCKEY	MARGIN	BAR.	WGT	SP
1	6	HUMIDOR	Darren Weir	Damian Lane		10	59kg	$17
2	1	HARTNELL	James Cummings	Kerrin McEvoy	3.25L	8	59kg	$1.70 fav
3	2	BLACK HEART BART	Darren Weir	Brad Rawiller	3.75L	7	59kg	$8.50
4	5	GAILO CHOP	Darren Weir	Mark Zahra	4.05L	1	59kg	$18
5	12	SINGLE GAZE	Nick Olive	Kathy O'Hara	5.05L	11	57kg	$101
6	7	VENTURA STORM	David & Ben Hayes & Tom Dabernig	Regan Bayliss	5.35L	4	59kg	$91
7	4	TAVAGO	Trent Busuttin & Natalie Young	Damien Oliver	5.45L	6	59kg	$81
8	8	JON SNOW	Murray Baker & Andrew Forsman	Stephen Baster	5.95L	3	58.5kg	$21
9	10	INFERENCE	Michael, Wayne & John Hawkes	Dwayne Dunn	6.25L	9	58.5kg	$51
10	9	HEY DOC	Tony McEvoy	Luke Currie	7.75L	12	58.5kg	$8.50
11	3	LE ROMAIN	Kris Lees	Ben Melham	12.75L	5	59kg	$14
12	11	SEABURGE	David & Ben Hayes & Tom Dabernig	Craig Williams	20.75L	2	58.5kg	$81

PAST WINNERS

YEAR	WINNER	JOCKEY	TRAINER	2ND	3RD	TIME
2017	Humidor	Damian Lane	Darren Weir	Hartnell	Black Heart Bart	1:35.3
2016	Palentino	Mark Zahra	Darren Weir	Black Heart Bart	He or She	1:36.2
2015	Fawkner	Damien Oliver	Robert Hickmott	Rising Romance	Entirely Platinum	1:37.9
2014	Dissident	Ben Melham	Peter Moody	Fawkner	Puissance De Lune	1:36.9
2013	Foreteller	Craig Newitt	Chris Waller	Puissance De Lune	Moudre	1:37.0
2012	Southern Speed	Craig Williams	Leon Macdonald & Andrew Gluyas	Manighar	Moudre	1:37.8
2011	Littorio	Craig Williams	Nigel Blackiston	Glass Harmonium	Midas Touch	1:37.8
2010	Shocking	Michael Rodd	Mark Kavanagh	Heart Of Dreams	Vigor	1:41.7
2009	Vigor	Damien Oliver	Danny O'Brien	Typhoon Tracy	Master O'Reilly	1:35.8
2008	Weekend Hussler	Brad Rawiller	Ross McDonald	Zarita	Littorio	1:38.6
2007	Marasco	Darren Beadman	Fred Kersley	Apache Cat	Zipping	1:36.7
2006	Pompeii Ruler	Craig Newitt	Mick Price	Sphenophyta	Zipping	1:38.5
2005	Confectioner	Craig Williams	David Hayes	Free At Last	Our Smoking Joe	1:35.8
2004	Hugs Dancer	Greg Childs	Tony Mc Evoy	Elvstoem	Zagalia	1:38.2
2003	Pentastic	Steven Arnold	David Hall	Walk On Air	Mummify	1:37.2
2002	Northerly	Greg Childs	Fred Kersley	Le Zagaletta	Silver Baron	1:37.9
2001	Native Jazz	Brett Prebble	Myles Plumb	Aka Bilk	Universal Prince	1:37.4
2000	Go Flash Go	Neville Wilson	John Blakey	Oliver Twist	Showella	1:42.1
1999	Sky Heights	Damien Oliver	Colin Alderson	Laebeel	What Can I Say	1:37.3
1998	Umrum	Danny Nikolic	Leon Macdonald	Darazari	Our Unicorn	1:35.7
1997	Marble Halls	Damien Oliver	Cliff Brown	Count Chivas	Istidaad	1:37.6

BACKGROUND

First run: 1948 (won by Lungi). Group 2 1979-2012. Group 1 from 2013. Run over 2000m 1948-64. Until 2006 known as the Craiglee Stakes. Registered as the Makybe Diva Stakes.
Most recent mare to win: Southern Speed (2012). 13 mares have won the Makybe Diva Stakes.
Most recent 3YO to win: C&G—Acramitis (1954) is the only 3YO to win the Makybe Diva Stakes.
Multiple winners: 2—Sailor's Guide (1957, 1956); Chicquita (1951, 1950).
Fastest time (1600m): Dual Choice (1971) 1:34.90
Notable winners: Fawkner (2015); Dissident (2014); Southern Speed (2012); Shocking (2010); Weekend Hussler (2008); Northerly (2002); Sky Heights (1999); Jeune (1995); Mahogany (1994); Mannerism (1993); Durbridge (1991); Zabeel (1990); Rose Of Kingston (1982); Sovereign Red (1981); Dulcify (1979); Family Of Man (1978); Ming Dynasty (1977); How Now (1976); Gay Icarus (1973); Rain Lover (1969); Tobin Bronze (1966); Light Fingers (1965); Aquanita (1962); Lord (1961); Sailor's Guide (1957, 1956); Chicquita (1951, 1950); Comic Court (1949).

Makybe Diva Stakes winners won the lead-up races:
Peter Lawrence (JJ Liston) Stakes: 8—Pompeii Ruler (2006); Mahogany (1994); Military Plume (1987); Pleach (1983); Sovereign Red (1981); Stellar Belle (1967); Tobin Bronze (1966); Cromis (1955).
Memsie Stakes: 5—Dissident (2014); Weekend Hussler (2008); Lord (1961); Comic Court (1949); Lungi (1948).
Makybe Diva Stakes winners went on to win in the same preparation:
Underwood Stakes: 10—Weekend Hussler (2008); Northerly (2002); Sovereign Red (1981); How Now (1976); Rain Lover (1969); Lowland (1968); Tobin Bronze (1966); Havelock (1963); Aquanita (1962); Cromis (1955).
Turnbull Stakes: 9—Northerly (2002); Sky Heights (1999); Marble Halls (1997); Dulcify (1979); Stellar Belle (1967); Tobin Bronze (1966); Sir Dane (1964); Aquanita (1962); Comic Court (1949).
Caulfield Stakes: 2—How Now (1976); Gay Poss (1970).
Caulfield Cup: 4—Northerly (2002); Sky Heights (1999); Ming Dynasty (1977); How Now (1976).
Cox Plate: 5—Northerly (2002); Dulcify (1979); Tobin Bronze (166); Sir Dane (1964); Aquanita (1962).
Melbourne Cup: 2—Rain Lover (1969); Light Fingers (1965).
Leading winning jockeys:
6 wins Roy Higgins (Tontonan 1975, Gay Poss 1979, Lowland 1968, Light Fingers 1965, Sir Dane 1964, Aquanita 1962).
4 wins Geoff Lane (Stellar Belle 1967, Havelock 1963, Nilarco 1960, Vogel 1959); Damien Oliver (Fawkner 2015, Vigor 2009, Sky Heights 1999, Marble Halls 1997); Jack Purtell (Cromis 1955, Chicquita 1951, Comic Court 1949, Lungi 1948).
Current winning jockeys:
4 wins Damien Oliver (Fawkner 2015, Vigor 2009, Sky Heights 1999, Marble Halls 1997).
3 wins Craig Williams (Southern Speed 2012, Littorio 2011, Confectioner 2005).
2 wins Craig Newitt (Foreteller 2013, Pompeii Ruler 2006).
1 win Steven Arnold (Pentastic 2003); Damian Lane (Humidor 2017); Ben Melham (Dissident 2014); Brett Prebble (Native Jazz 2001); Brad Rawiller (Weekend Hussler 2008); Michael Rodd (Shocking 2010); Mark Zahra (Palentino 2016).
Leading winning trainers:
6 wins Bart Cummings (Prolific 1984, Ming Dynasty 1977, Tontonan 1975, Gay Poss 1970, Lowland 1968, Light Fingers 1965).
4 wins Colin Hayes (Military Plume 1987, Fine Offer 1985, Dulcify 1979, How Now 1976).
3 wins Lee Freedman (Marble Halls 1997, Mahogany 1994, Mannerism 1993); David Hayes (Confectioner 2005, Jeune 1995, Zabeel 1990).
Current winning trainers:
3 wins Lee Freedman (Marble Halls 1997, Mahogany 1994, Mannerism 1993); David Hayes (Confectioner 2005, Jeune 1995, Zabeel 1990).
2 wins Fred Kersley (Marasco 2007, Northerly 2002); Leon Macdonald (Southern Speed 2012, Umrum 1998); Darren Weir (Humidor 2017, Palentino 2016).
1 win Nigel Blackiston (Littorio 2011); David Hall (Pentastic 2003); Robert Hickmott (Fawkner 2015); Pat Hyland (Saleous 1996); Mark Kavanagh (Shocking 2010); Leon Macdonald & Andrew Gluyas (Southern Speed 2012); Tony McEvoy (Hugs Dancer 2004); John Meagher (Star Of The Realm 1992); Danny O'Brien (Vigor 2009); Mick Price (Pompeii Ruler 2006); Chris Waller (Foreteller 2013).
Point of interest:
Mongolian Khan (7th behind Boban in 2015) and Elvstroem (2nd behind Hugs Dancer in 2004) are the most recent Caulfield Cup winners to contest the Makybe Diva Stakes in the same year.

ATC George Main Stakes (1600m)—Randwick
Of $500,000. Group 1. Weight for Age, 3YO&Up. September 15, 2018.

2017-18 RESULT: Time: 1:33.65 (Good 3)

FP	NO	HORSE	TRAINER	JOCKEY	MARGIN	BAR.	WGT	SP
1	7	WINX	Chris Waller	Hugh Bowman		1	57kg	$1.12
2	1	HAPPY CLAPPER	Patrick Webster	Blake Shinn	1.3L	7	59kg	$15
3	9	FOXPLAY	Chris Waller	Brenton Avdulla	5.8L	3	56.5kg	$21
4	4	MCCREERY	Chris Waller	Michael Walker	7.6L	8	59kg	$151
5	5	MACKINTOSH	Chris Waller	Glyn Schofield	7.7L	2	59kg	$101
6	8	HEAVENS ABOVE	Tim Martin	Tye Angland	8.1L	6	57kg	$91
7	3	RED EXCITEMENT	Gerald Ryan	Joshua Parr	9.3L	4	59kg	$26
8	2	ECUADOR	Gai Waterhouse & Adrian Bott	Adam Hyeronimus	9.5L	5	59kg	$81

PAST WINNERS

YEAR	HORSE	JOCKEY	TRAINER	2ND	3RD	TIME
2017	Winx	Hugh Bowman	Chris Waller	Happy Clapper	Foxplay	1:33.6
2016	Winx	Hugh Bowman	Chris Waller	Hauraki	It's Somewhat	1:36.1
2015	Kermadec	Glyn Schofield	Chris Waller	Royal Descent	Pornichet	1:37.7
2014	Sacred Falls	Zac Purton	Chris Waller	Royal Descent	Laser Hawk	1:35.6
2013	Streama	Blake Shinn	Guy Walter	Royal Descent	Veyron	1:34.7
2012	Shoot Out	Hugh Bowman	Chris Waller	Rangirangdoo	Secret Admirer	1:36.4
2011	Sincero	Chris O'Brien	Stephen Farley	Ilovethiscity	Triple Elegance	1:28.5
2010	More Joyous	Corey Brown	Gai Waterhouse	Trusting	Empires Choice	1:35.6
2009	Road to Rock	Glyn Schofield	Anthony Cummings	Black Piranha	Onemorenomore	1:35.5
2008	Mentality	Corey Brown	John Hawkes	Theseo	Gallant Tess	1:34.6
2007	Race Not Run					
2006	Racing To Win	Glen Boss	John O'Shea	Red Dazzler	Desert War	1:33.8
2005	Mr Celebrity	Len Beasley	Gai Waterhouse	Shania Dane	Outback Prince	1:34.6
2004	Grand Armee	Danny Beasley	Gai Waterhouse	King's Chapel	Shamekha	1:36.9
2003	Lonhro	Darren Beadman	John Hawkes	Grand Armee	Defier	1:37.5
2002	Defier	Chris Munce	Guy Walter	Excellerator	Sunline	1:38.3
2001	Viscount	Kerrin McEvoy	John Hawkes	Shogun Lodge	Courvoisier	1:36.7
2000	Adam	Justin Sheehan	Ray Brock	Mr. Innocent	Al Mansour	1:35.3
1999	Shogun Lodge	Shane Dye	Bob Thomsen	Sunline	Adam	1:35.0
1998	Dracula	Larry Cassidy	John Hawkes	Tycoon Lil	Des's Dream	1:35.1
1997	Encounter	Shane Dye	Clarry Conners	Filante	Juggler	1:36.0

BACKGROUND

First run: 1945 (won by Modulation). Group 1 since 1980. Run at Warwick Farm 1983 & 2001. Not held in 2007.
Most recent mare to win: Winx (2017).
Most recent 3YO to win: Viscount (2001); No filly has won. Note: 10 3YOs have won the George Main (from 1988 to 2001, seven 3YOs won the WFA race).
Multiple winners: 5—Winx (2017, 2016); Kingston Town (1982, 1981); Regal Rhythm (1968, 1967); Count Radiant (1965, 1964); Shannon (1947, 1946).
Fastest time (1600m): Winx (2017) 1:33.65
Notable winners: Winx (2017, 2016); Shoot Out (2012); More Joyous (2010); Mentality (2008); Racing To Win (2006); Grand Armee (2004); Lonhro (2003); Shogun Lodge (1999); Juggler (1996); Durbridge (1994); Shaftesbury Avenue (1990); Campaign King (1987); Emancipation (1983); Kingston Town (1982, 1981); All Shot (1973); Baguette (1971); Wenona Girl (1963); Martello Towers (1961); Kingster (1956); San Domenico (1950); Shannon (1947, 1946).
George Main Stakes winners won the lead-up races:
Warwick Stakes: 10—Winx (2017, 2016); Lonhro (2003); Defier (2002); Kingston Town (1982, 1981); Party's Pride (1978); Nippon (1972); Tarien (1953); San Domenico (1950).
Chelmsford Stakes: 6—Winx (2017); Lonhro (2003); Campaign King (1987); Emancipation (1983); Kingston Town (1981); Purple Patch (1976).
Tramway Handicap: 5—Sincero (2011); Shaftesbury Avenue (1990); Tullmax (1980); Imposing (1979); Landy (1957).
Theo Marks Stakes: 7—More Joyous (2010); Racing To Win (2006); Defier (2002); Inspired (1984); Ricochet (1970); Martello Towers (1961); Shannon (1946).

George Main Stakes winners went on to win in the same preparation:
Epsom Handicap: 4—Racing To Win (2006); Imposing (1979); Ricochet (1970); Chantal (1966).
Theo Marks Stakes & Epsom Handicap: 1—Racing To Win (2006).
Spring Champion Stakes: 1—Coronation Day (1992).
Caulfield Stakes: 6—Winx (2016); Lonhro (2003); Juggler (1996); Kingston Town (1982, 1981); De La Salle (1948).
Cox Plate: 4—Winx (2017, 2016); Kingston Town (1982, 1981).
Caulfield Stakes & Cox Plate: 3—Winx (2016); Kingston Town (1982, 1981).
Leading winning jockeys:
9 wins George Moore (Baguette 1971, Zephyrus 1969, Chantal 1966, Count Radiant 1965, 1964, Martello Towers 1961, Landy 1957, Tarien 1953, The Groom 1949).
4 wins Shane Dye (Shogun Lodge 1999, Encounter 1997, Gennaker 1988, Ma Chiquita 1986).
Current winning jockeys:
3 wins Hugh Bowman (Winx 2017, 2016, Shoot Out 2012); Larry Cassidy (Dracula 1998, March Hare 1993, Coronation Day 1992).
2 wins Glen Boss (Racing To Win 2006, Juggler 1996); Corey Brown (More Joyous 2010, Mentality 2008).
1 win Kerrin McEvoy (Viscount 2001); Chris O'Brien (Sincero 2011); Zac Purton (Sacred Falls 2014); Glyn Schofield (Road To Road 2009); Blake Shinn (Streama 2013); Cyril Small (Vo Rogue 1989).
Leading winning trainer:
12 wins Tommy Smith (Kingston Town 1982, 1981, Imposing 1979, Hartshill 1975, Zephyrus 1969, Regal Rhythm 1968, 1967, Count Radiant 1965, 1964, Martello Towers 1961, Landy 1957, Tarien 1953).
Current winning trainers:
4 wins John Hawkes (Mentality 2008, Lonhro 2003, Viscount 2001, Dracula 1998); Gai Waterhouse (More Joyous 2010, Mr. Celebrity 2005, Grand Armee 2004, Juggler 1996); Chris Waller (Winx 2017, 2016, Sacred Falls 2014, Shoot Out 2012).
1 win Clarry Conners (Encounter 1997); Anthony Cummings (Road To Rock 2009); Garry Frazer (Turridu 1995); Michael, Wayne, John Hawkes (Mentality 2008); David Hayes (Planet Ruler 1991); Steve Farley (Sincero 2011); John O'Shea (Racing To Win 2006).
Points of interest:
Grey Boots was runner-up in three consecutive years—1950 (to San Domenico); 1951 (Oversight); 1952 (Montana).
Inspired (1984) won the 1984 Golden Slipper. Baguette (1972) won the 1971 Golden Slipper.
No horse has won a Warwick Stakes, George Main Stakes and Epsom Handicap in the same year.
Winx (2016) completed a winning sequence of 11; when she won in 2017, her winning sequence had grown to 20.

ATC Golden Rose Stakes (1400m)—Rosehill
Of $1,000,000. Group 1. Set Weights, 3YO. September 22, 2018.

2017-18 RESULT: Time: 1:22.41 (Good 3)

FP	NO	HORSE	TRAINER	JOCKEY	MARGIN	BAR.	WGT	SP
1	5	TRAPEZE ARTIST	Gerald Ryan	Tye Angland		14	56.5kg	$41
2	14	CHAMPAGNE CUDDLES	Bjorn Baker	Jason Collett	4.3L	8	54.5kg	$17
3	2	MENARI	Gerald Ryan	Joshua Parr	4.5L	11	56.5kg	$2.40
4	4	GOLD STANDARD	Gai Waterhouse & Adrian Bott	Tommy Berry	4.6L	10	56.5kg	$10
5	10	ASSIMILATE	Peter & Paul Snowden	Hugh Bowman	5.6L	9	56.5kg	$10
6	6	CHAUFFEUR	Michael, Wayne & John Hawkes	Brenton Avdulla	6.2L	7	56.5kg	$26
7	12	PERAST	Paul Perry	Adam Hyeronimus	6.4L	5	56.5kg	$101
8	9	DRACARYS	Peter & Paul Snowden	Tim Clark	6.9L	1	56.5kg	$20
9	3	PARIAH	Peter & Paul Snowden	Blake Shinn	7.6L	12	56.5kg	$8.50
10	7	MERCHANT NAVY	Ciaron Maher	Mark Zahra	8.6L	2	56.5kg	$7
11	13	FORMALITY	David & Ben Hayes & Tom Dabernig	Kerrin McEvoy	9.4L	13	54.5kg	$20
12	11	SHOGUN SUN	Kelly Schweida	Christian Reith	13.8L	6	56.5kg	$26
13	1	THE MISSION	Paul Perry	Corey Brown	15.1L	3	56.5kg	$101
14	8	DIAMOND TATHAGATA	Mark Newnham	Glyn Schofield	15.3L	4	56.5kg	$201

PAST WINNERS

YEAR	WINNER	JOCKEY	TRAINER	2ND	3RD	TIME
2017	Trapeze Artist	Tye Angland	Gerald Ryan	Champagne Cuddles	Menari	1:22.4
2016	Astern	James McDonald	John O'Shea	Omei Sword	Impending	1:23.9
2015	Exosphere	James McDonald	John O'Shea	Speak Fondly	Sebring Sun	1:21.8
2014	Hallowed Crown	Hugh Bowman	Bart & James Cummings	Scissor Kick	Shooting To Win	1:24.0
2013	Zoustar	Jim Cassidy	Chris Waller	Dissident	Bull Point	1:22.5
2012	Epaulette	Tommy Berry	Peter Snowden	Albrecht	Ashokan	1:22.3
2011	Manawanui	Glyn Schofield	Ron Leemon	Smart Missile	Helmet	1:23.3
2010	Toorak Toff	Damien Oliver	Rick Hore-Lacy	Squamosa	Ilovethiscity	1:21.9
2009	Denman	Kerrin McEvoy	Peter Snowden	Trusting	Stryker	1:22.8
2008	Forensics	Hugh Bowman	Anthony Cummings	El Cambio	Kingda Ka	1:22.4
2008	Duporth	Danny Nikolic	Peter Snowden	Stripper	Desuetude	1:23.8
2007	Race not run					
2006	Court Command	Darryl McLellan	Darren Smith	Empires Choice	Mentality	1:23.1
2005	Paratroopers	Darren Beadman	John Hawkes	Racing To Win	Pendragon	1:23.5
2004	Doonan	Hugh Bowman	Helen Page	Al Maher	Lieutenant	1:23.1
2003	In Top Swing	Hugh Bowman	Noel Mayfield-Smith	Handsome Ransom	Ashenti	1:24.0

BACKGROUND

First run: 2003 (won by In Top Swing). Listed 2005. Group 3 from 2006. Group 2 2008 (run twice in 2008, autumn and spring). Group 1 from 2009. Run as a restricted 3YO race in 2003-04. Moved from the spring 2007 to March 2008 (won by Duporth) due to the Equine Influenza outbreak.
Most recent filly to win: Forensics (autumn 2008). Note: Forensics (2008) is the only filly to win.
Fastest time (1400m): Exosphere (2015) 1:21.83
Notable winners: Trapeze Artist (2017); Astern (2016); Exosphere (2015); Hallowed Crown (2014); Zoustar (2013); Toorak Toff (2010); Denman (2009); Duporth (spring 2008); Forensics (autumn 2008); Paratroopers (2005); In Top Swing (2003).
Sydney autumn 2YO Group 1 features and the Golden Rose:
Golden Slipper: 1—Forensics (2008, autumn).
ATC Sires' Produce Stakes: None.
Champagne Stakes: None.

Golden Rose winners have won the lead-up races:
Up And Coming Stakes: 2—Manawanui (2011); Court Command (2006).
Vain Stakes: 1—Toorak Toff (2010).
The Rosebud (first run 2011): None.
The Run To The Rose (first run 2006): 4—Astern (2016); Exosphere (2015); Hallowed Crown (2014); Denman (2009).
Golden Rose winners went on to win in the same preparation:
Theo Marks Stakes: 1—Paratroopers (2005).
MRC Guineas Prelude: 1—Epaulette (2009);
Roman Consul Stakes: 2—Exosphere (2015); Zoustar (2013).
Stan Fox Stakes: 4—Manawanui (2011); Denman (2009); Court Command (2006); Paratroopers (2005).
Caulfield Guineas: 1—In Top Swing (2003).
Moonee Valley Vase: 1—Manawanui (2011).
Coolmore Stud Stakes: 1—Zoustar (2013).
Leading winning jockeys:
4 wins Hugh Bowman (Hallowed Crown 2014, Duporth 2008, Doonan 2004; In Top Swing 2003).
2 wins James McDonald (Astern 2016, Exosphere 2015).
Current winning jockeys:
4 wins Hugh Bowman (Hallowed Crown 2014, Duporth 2008, Doonan 2004; In Top Swing 2003).
2 wins James McDonald (Astern 2016, Exosphere 2015).
1 win Tye Angland (Trapeze Artist 2017); Tommy Berry (Epaulette 2012); Damien Oliver (Toorak Toff 2010); Glyn Schofield (Manawanui 2011).
Leading winning trainers:
2 wins John O'Shea (Astern 2016, Exosphere 2015); Peter Snowden (Epaulette 2012, Forensics 2008).
Current winning trainers:
2 wins John O'Shea (Astern 2016, Exosphere 2015); Peter Snowden (Epaulette 2012, Forensics 2008).
1 win Anthony Cummings (Duporth 2008); James Cummings (Hallowed Crown 2014; in partnership with Bart Cummings); John Hawkes (Paratroopers 2005); Ron Leemon (Manawanui 2011); Noel Mayfield-Smith (In Top Swing 2003); Helen Page (Doonan 2004); Gerald Ryan (Trapeze Artist 2017); Chris Waller (Zoustar 2013).
Point of interest:
The Golden Rose is judged by the Australian Pattern Racing Committee to be a new race, and it does not replace the Group 2 Peter Pan Stakes that was last run in 2002 (won by Sportsman).
Run twice in 2008 due to cancellation of 2007 (EI outbreak). Forensics won in March; Duporth won in August.

MRC Sir Rupert Clarke Stakes (1400m)—Caulfield
Of $500,000. Group 1. Handicap, Minimum Weight 52kg. September 22, 2018.

2017-18 RESULT: Time: 1:22.28 (Good 3)

FP	NO	HORSE	TRAINER	JOCKEY	MARGIN	BAR.	WGT	SP
1	9	SANTA ANA LANE	Anthony Freedman	Dean Yendall		6	52KG	$26
2	14	MR SNEAKY	Anthony Freedman	Brenton Avdulla	0.75L	4	52kg	$8
3	11	SO SI BON	Robbie Laing	Craig Newitt	2L	2	52kg	$26
4	7	SOVEREIGN NATION	David & Ben Hayes & Tom Dabernig	Regan Bayliss	2.1L	7	52kg	$21
5	10	THEANSWERMYFRIEND	Robert Smerdon	Kerrin McEvoy	2.4L	9	52kg	$4
6	4	TOSEN STARDOM	Darren Weir	Blake Shinn	2.6L	14	55.5kg	$6
7	3	SCALES OF JUSTICE	Lindsey Smith	Brad Rawiller	2.7L	5	56kg	$3.60f
8	16	LAND OF PLENTY	Grahame Begg	Linda Meech	3L	12	52kg	$41
9	5	GRANDE ROSSO	David & Ben Hayes & Tom Dabernig	Corey Brown	3.75L	8	52.5kg	$21
10	1	IT'S SOMEWHAT	James Cummings	Hugh Bowman	3.95L	11	58kg	$21
11	13	ATTENTION	Peter & Paul Snowden	Ben Thompson	5.2L	1	52kg	$41
12	15	ROYAL TUDOR	Rodney Ollerton	Chris Symons	5.95L	3	52.5kg	$101
13	2	LUCKY HUSSLER	Darren Weir	Mark Zahra	8.2L	10	56.5kg	$51
14	8	CANNYESCENT	David & Ben Hayes & Tom Dabernig	Beau Mertens	11.7L	13	52kg	$31

PAST WINNERS

YEAR	WINNER	JOCKEY	TRAINER	2ND	3RD	TIME
2017	Santa Ana Lane	Dean Yendall	Anthony Freedman	Mr Sneaky	So Si Bon	1:22.2
2016	Bon Aurum	Kerrin McEvoy	Ciaron Maher	Voodoo Lad	Fast 'N' Rocking	1:23.4
2015	Stratum Star	Craig Williams	Darren Weir	Disposition	Under The Louvre	1:22.0
2014	Trust In A Gust	Damian Lane	Darren Weir	Dissident	Bull Point	1:23.0
2013	Rebel Dane	Glen Boss	Gary Portelli	Fontelina	Solzhenitsyn	1:23.8
2012	Moment Of Change	Luke Nolen	Peter Moody	We're Gonna Rock	Solzhenitsyn	1:22.1
2011	Toorak Toff	Craig Williams	Rick Hore-Lacy	Pinnacles	Master Of Design	1:21.9
2010	Response	Craig Williams	Mathew Ellerton & Simon Zahra	No Evidence Needed	Woorim	1:22.2
2009	Turffontein	Glen Boss	Anthony Cummings	Stickpin	Raffaello	1:25.3
2008	Orange County	Damien Oliver	Brian Mayfield-Smith	Bon Hoffa	Turffontein	1:24.3
2007	Bon Hoffa	Vlad Duric	Wendy Kelly	Niconero	Wonderful World	1:22.5
2006	Rewaaya	Craig Williams	David Hayes	Miss Andretti	Undue	1:23.4
2005	Barely A Moment	Craig Williams	David Hayes	Super Kid	Sky Cuddle	1.25.7
2004	Regal Roller	Mark Flaherty	Clinton McDonald	Our Egyptian Raine	Alinghi	1.24.2
2003	Exceed And Excel	Corey Brown	Tim Martin	Reactive	Titanic Jack	1.21.2
2002	Pernod	Kerrin McEvoy	Michael Moroney	Bel Esprit	Royal Code	1.22.6
2001	Mr Murphy	Damien Oliver	Lee Freedman	Fubu	Umrum	1.23.5
2000	Testa Rossa	Brett Prebble	Dean Lawson	Camarena	Porto Roca	1.21.9
1999	Testa Rossa	Damien Oliver	Dean Lawson	Nina Haraka	Redoutes Choice	1.22.1
1998	Lord Luskin	Stephen Baster	Leon Corstens	Theatre	Haltemann	1.23.3
1997	Cut Up Rough	Steven King	Peter C Hayes	Tampir Lane	Delsole	1.22.9

BACKGROUND

First run: 1951 (won by Jovial Lad). Group 1 from 1979. Run as the Invitation Stakes (for invited jockeys) from 1951 to 1974. Also known as the Marlboro Cup, Show Day Cup, VicHealth Cup, Eat Well Live Well Cup and Dubai Racing Club Cup.
Note: Statistics start from 1975, when the race was opened to all jockeys—previously the Invitation Stakes for invited jockeys representing each state.
Most recent mare to win: Response (2010). Note: 11 mares have won.
Most recent 3YO to win: C&G—Exceed And Excel (2003); No 3YO filly has won.
Multiple winners: 2—Testa Rossa (2000, 1999); Private Talk (1979, 1976).
Fastest time (1400m): Exceed And Excel (2003) 1:21.20
Notable winners: Santa Ana Lane (2018); Exceed And Excel (2003); Testa Rossa (2000, 1999); Encosta De Lago (1997); Our Maizcay (1995); Poetic King (1994); Mannerism (1992); Rancho Ruler (1988); Canny Lass (1986); Magari (1982); Torbek (1980); Raffindale (1977); Cap d'Antibes (1975).

Sir Rupert Clarke Stakes winners won the lead-up races:
Bobbie Lewis Quality: 3—Bon Hoffa (2007); Magari (1982); Soldier Of Fortune (1981).
Let's Elope Stakes: 2—Rewaaya (2006); Mannerism (1992).
Tontonan Stakes (from 2011): 1—Bon Aurum (2016).

Sir Rupert Clark Stakes winners went on to win in the same preparation:
Toorak Handicap: 9—Trust In A Gust (2014); Barely A Moment (2005); Regal Roller (2004); Canny Lass (1986); Magari (1982); Torbek (1980); Tauto (1970); Anonyme (1961); Jovial Lad (1951).
Manikato Stakes: None, but won by Manikato (1979); Winfreux (1968) when Manikato Stakes was run before the Sir Rupert Clarke (moved in 2012).
Coolmore Stud Stakes: None, but Encosta De Lago (1996); Our Maizcay (1995); Manikato (1978) won the double when Coolmore Stud Stakes was run before the Sir Rupert Clarke Stakes. Moved in 2006.
Caulfield Guineas: 2—Our Maizcay (1995); Manikato (1978).
Emirates Stakes: 2—Testa Rossa (2000); Magari (1982).
Toorak Handicap & Emirates Stakes: 1—Magari (1982).

Leading winning jockeys:
6 wins Damien Oliver (Orange County 2008; Mr Murphy 2001; Testa Rossa 1999; Poetic King 1994; Mannerism 1992; Submariner 1990). Note: Submariner is Oliver's first G1 winner.
5 wins Craig Williams (Stratum Star 2015, Toorak Toff 2011, Response 2010, Rewaaya 2006, Barely A Moment 2005).

Current winning jockeys:
6 wins Damien Oliver (Orange County 2008; Mr Murphy 2001; Testa Rossa 1999; Poetic King 1994; Mannerism 1992; Submariner 1990).
5 wins Craig Williams (Stratum Star 2015, Toorak Toff 2011, Response 2010, Rewaaya 2006, Barely A Moment 2005).
2 wins Glen Boss (Rebel Dane 2013, Turffontein 2009); Kerrin McEvoy (Bon Aurum 2016, Pernod 2002).
1 win Stephen Baster (Lord Luskin 1998); Corey Brown (Exceed And Excel 2003); Vlad Duric (Bon Hoffa 2007); Damian Lane (Trust In A Gust 2014); Luke Nolen (Moment Of Change 2012); Brett Prebble (Testa Rossa 2000); Dean Yendall (Santa Ana Lane 2017).

Leading winning trainer:
4 wins Lee Freedman (Mr Murphy 2001; Encosta de Lago 1996; Poetic King 1994; Mannerism 1992).

Current trainers:
4 wins Lee Freedman (Mr Murphy 2001; Encosta de Lago 1996; Poetic King 1994; Mannerism 1992).
2 wins David Hayes (Rewaaya 2006, Barely A Moment 2005); Darren Weir (Stratum Star 2015, Trust In A Gust 2014).
1 win Leon Corstens (Lord Luskin 1998); Anthony Cummings (Turffontein 2009); Mat Ellerton & Simon Zahra (Response 2010); Anthony Freedman (Santa Ana Lane 2017); Wendy Kelly (Bon Hoffa 2007); Ciaron Maher (Bon Aurum 2016); Tim Martin (Exceed And Excel 2003); Clinton McDonald (Regal Roller 2004); John Meagher (Ranger's Son 1983); Wally Mitchell (Western Pago 1987); Michael Moroney (Pernod 2002); Gary Portelli (Rebel Dane 2013); Grant Searle (Our Maizcay 1995); Wayne Walters (Torbek 1980); Allan Williams (Black Rouge 1993).

Points of interest:
Mannerism (1992) is the only Rupert Clarke winner to win a Caulfield Cup. She did it in the same preparation in 1992.
Raffindale (1977) won the Sir Rupert Clarke, and finished second to Family Of Man in the 1977 Cox Plate.
Submariner (1990) is jockey Damien Oliver's first Group 1 winner.
Barely A Moment (2005) is the sire of Moment Of Change (2012).
Bon Hoffa (2007) is the sire of Bon Aurum (2016).

MVRC Moir Stakes (1000m)—Moonee Valley
Of $500,000. Group 1. Weight for Age, 3YO&Up. September 28, 2018.

2017-18 RESULT: Time: 58.30 (Good 3)

FP	NO	HORSE	TRAINER	JOCKEY	MARGIN	BAR.	WGT	SP
1	13	SHE WILL REIGN	Gary Portelli	Kerrin McEvoy		8	50kg	$4.40
2	10	VIDDORA	Lloyd Kennewell	Joe Bowditch	0.1L	7	56.5kg	$31
3	9	SHEIDEL	David & Ben Hayes & Tom Dabernig	Joao Moreira	0.85L	4	56.5kg	$9
4	4	ROCK MAGIC	Chris Gangemi	Jarrad Noske	1.6L	6	58.5kg	$21
5	3	VOODOO LAD	Darren Weir	Blake Shinn	1.8L	12	58.5kg	$11
6	8	FAATINAH	David & Ben Hayes & Tom Dabernig	Regan Bayliss	1.9L	1	58.5kg	$18
7	2	MALAGUERRA	Peter Gelagotis	Ben Melham	2L	13	58.5kg	$20
8	7	JUNGLE EDGE	Mick Bell	Kevin Forrester	2.4L	9	58.5kg	$201
9	12	SWEET SHERRY	Brent Stanley	Luke Currie	2.5L	3	56.5kg	$61
10	1	TERRAVISTA	Joseph Pride	Corey Brown	4L	5	58.5kg	$17
11	6	DERRYN	David & Ben Hayes & Tom Dabernig	Mark Zahra	4.2L	2	58.5kg	$21
12	5	RUSSIAN REVOLUTION	Peter & Paul Snowden	Hugh Bowman	7.7L	11	58.5kg	$3f
13	11	HEATHERLY	Mathew Ellerton & Simon Zahra	Damian Lane	7.9L	10	56.5kg	$12

PAST WINNERS

YEAR	WINNER	JOCKEY	TRAINER	2ND	3RD	TIME
2017	She Will Reign	Kerrin McEvoy	Gary Portelli	Viddora	Sheidel	58.3
2016	Extreme Choice	Craig Newitt	Mick Price	Heatherly	Wild Rain	58.7
2015	Buffering	Damian Browne	Robert Heathcote	Ball Of Muscle	Angelic Light	57.2
2014	Buffering	Damian Browne	Robert Heathcote	Lankan Rupee	Rebel Dane	1:10.9
2013	Samaready	Craig Newitt	Mick Price	Buffering	Le Bonsir	1:11.2
2012	Buffering	Hugh Bowman	Robert Heathcote	Ready To Rip	Thankgodyou'rehere	1:10.9
2011	Black Caviar	Luke Nolen	Peter Moody	Doubtful Jack	Here De Angels	1:10.1
2010	Black Caviar	Luke Nolen	Peter Moody	Hot Danish	True Persuasion	1:11.0
2009	Apache Cat	Damien Oliver	Greg Eurell	Mic Mac	Bank Robber	1:10.0
2008	Lucky Secret	Danny Brereton	Tony Vasil	Bel Mer	Mr Baritone	1:09.9
2007	Miss Andretti	Craig Newitt	Lee Freedman	Gold Edition	Let Go Thommo	1:10.6
2006	California Dane	Kieren Fallon	Lee Freedman	Let Go Thommo	Poets Voice	58.0
2005	Virage De Fortune	Craig Williams	Bruce Mclachlan	Miss Mooney Mooney	Imprisoned	59.1
2004	Bomber Bill	Steven Arnold	Robert Smerdon	Regimental Gal	Dance The Waves	58.4
2003	Our Egyptian Raine	Nash Rawiller	Grahame Begg	Spinning Hill	Dantana	57.7
2002	Spinning Hill	Frankie Dettori	Guy Walter	Bomber Bill	Mistegic	57.7
2001	Mistegic	Glen Boss	Lee Curtis	Regal Shot	Appoint	58.7
2000	Falvelon	Damien Oliver	Danny J Bougoure	Notoire	Super Elegant	59.8
1999	Magic Music	Damien Oliver	John Sadler	Paint	Spargo	57.5
1998	Show No Emotion	Nash Rawiller	Tony Noonan	Appoint	Dance Beat	58.0
1997	Al Mansour	Larry Cassidy	Bruce Mclachlan	Spartacus	Ossie Cossie	57.4

BACKGROUND

First run: 1976 (won by Scamanda). Group 2 from 1979. Group 1 from 2013. Run over 1000m 1976-2006; from 2015. 1200m 2007-2014 Registered name is the A.J. Moir Stakes. Also known as the Schweppes Stakes or Schweppervesence Stakes
Most recent mare to win: Samaready (2013).
Most recent 3YO to win: Filly—She Will Reign (2017); C&G—Extreme Choice (2016). Note: 13 3YOs have won.
Multiple winners: 4—Buffering (2015, 2014, 2012); Black Caviar (2011, 2010); With Me (1991, 1990); The Judge (1979, 1978). Note: The Judge dead-heated with Grey Sapphire in 1979.
Fastest time (1000m Strathayr from 1995): Buffering (2015) 57.26
Notable winners: She Will Reign (2017); Extreme Choice (2016); Buffering (2015, 2014, 2012), Black Caviar (2011, 2010); Apache Cat (2009); Miss Andretti (2007); Virage De Fortune (2005); Bomber Bill (2004); Spinning Hill (2002); Falvelon (2000); Al Mansour (1997); Spartacus (1996); Sequalo (1994); Placid Ark (1987); Special (1986); Manikato (1982); The Judge (1978 & 1979); Scamanda (1976).

Note: The Moir Stakes moved from Cox Plate day to late September in 2013. Swapped with the Manikato Stakes (now run on Cox Plate eve).
Moir Stakes winners won the lead-up races:
Ian McEwen Stakes: None.
Moir Stakes winners also won in the same preparation:
Manikato Stakes: 3—Spinning Hill (2002); Manikato (1982); Scamanda (1976).
Schillaci Stakes: 9—Buffering (2012); Black Caviar (2011, 2010); Spinning Hill (2002); Mistegic (2001); Falvelon (2000); Magic Music (1999); Show No Emotion (1998); The Judge (1978).
Linlithgow Stakes: 5—Our Egyptian Raine (2003); Al Mansour (1997); Sequalo (1994); Placid Ark (1987); Scamanda (1976).
Darley Classic: 3—Black Caviar (2011, 2010); Miss Andretti (2007). Note: VRC Sprint Classic (WFA) before 2007 was known as the Salinger Stakes and run as a handicap.
Moir Stakes & William Reid Stakes (Jan.) (same season): 4—Black Caviar (season 2010-11); Virage De Fortune (2005-06); Spartacus (1996-97); Manikaro (1981-82).
Leading winning jockeys:
4 wins Damien Oliver (Apache Cat 2009, Falvelon 2000, Magic Music 1999, Schillaci 1992).
3 wins Shane Dye (Spartacus 1996, Quality Gold 1995, Clay Hero 1989); Roy Higgins (Bold Prospect 1981, The Judge 1979, Tetranate 1977); Craig Newitt (Extreme Choice 2016, Samaready 2013, Miss Andretti 2007); Harry White (Bold Jet 1983, Grey Sapphire 1979, The Judge 1978).
Current winning jockeys:
4 wins Damien Oliver (Apache Cat 2009, Falvelon 2000, Magic Music 1999, Schillaci 1992).
3 wins Craig Newitt (Extreme Choice 2016, Samaready 2013, Miss Andretti 2007).
2 wins Damian Browne (Buffering 2015, 2014); Luke Nolen (Black Caviar 2011, 2010); Nash Rawiller (Our Egyptian Raine 2003, Show No Emotion 1998).
1 win Steven Arnold (Bomber Bill 2004); Glen Boss (Mistegic 2001); Hugh Bowman (Buffering 2012); Larry Cassidy (Al Mansour 1997); Frankie Dettori (Spinning Hill 2002); Kerrin McEvoy (She Will Reign 2017); Craig Williams (Virage De Fortune 2005).
Leading winning trainers:
4 wins Angus Armanasco (Victoria Peak 1980, The Judge 1979, 1978, Tetranate 1977); Bruce McLachlan (Virage De Fortune 2005, Al Mansour 1997, With Me 1991, 1990).
3 wins Lee Freedman (Miss Andretti 2007, California Dane 2006, Schillaci 1992); Rob Heathcote (Buffering 2015, 2014, 2012).
Current winning trainers:
3 wins Lee Freedman (Miss Andretti 2007, California Dane 2006, Schillaci 1992); Rob Heathcote (Buffering 2015, 2014, 2012).
2 wins Mick Price (Extreme Choice 2016, Samaready 2013).
1 win Grahame Begg (Our Egyptian Raine 2003); Danny Bougoure (Falvelon 2000); Leon Corstens (Magic Music 1999); Lee Curtis (Mistegic 2001); Greg Eurell (Apache Cat 2009); John Hawkes (Sports Works 1993); Wally Mitchell (Placid Ark 1987); Tony Noonan (Show No Emotion 1998); Gary Portelli (She Will Reign 2017); Grant Searle (Quality Gold 1995); Robert Smerdon (Bomber Bill 2004); Tony Vasil (Lucky Secret 2008).
Points of interest:
Clay Hero and Good Old Ted dead-heated in 1989. The Judge and Grey Sapphire dead-heated in 1979.
The race was to be first run in 1975, but the meeting was abandoned due to rain. The Judge (1979, 1978) and Victoria Peak (1980) are brother and sister. Both are by Showdown from Bellition. The Judge is the great grandsire of Mistegic (2001). Mistegic is by Strategic, by The Judge's best son Zeditave.
Buffering (2015, 2014, 2012) went on to win the 2015 G1 Winterbottom Stakes at Ascot in Perth in the same preparation. He also won the Winterbottom in 2013. He was retired after finishing fifth in the 2016 Moir Stakes.
Irish jockey Kieron Fallon won the Moir Stakes on California Dane in 2006; Italian born, England-based Frankie Dettori won on Spinning Hill in 2002.

ATC Epsom Handicap (1600m)—Randwick
Of $1,000,000. Group 1. Handicap, Min Weight 52kg. 3YO&Up. September 29, 2018.

2017-18 RESULT: Time: 1:33.17 (Good 3)

FP	NO	HORSE	TRAINER	JOCKEY	MARGIN	BAR.	WGT	SP
1	1	HAPPY CLAPPER	Patrick Webster	Blake Shinn		2	57kg	$2.40F
2	9	TOM MELBOURNE	Chris Waller	Glen Boss	0.5L	9	52kg	$8
3	13	SNITZSON	David & Ben Hayes & Tom Dabernig	Cory Parish	3L	3	50.5kg	$26
4	2	FOXPLAY	Chris Waller	Hugh Bowman	3.1L	10	54.5kg	$8
5	3	SOUND PROPOSITION	Kris Lees	Corey Brown	3.4L	7	54kg	$12
6	11	COMIN' THROUGH	Chris Waller	Joao Moreira	4.4L	8	51kg	$5
7	6	MCCREERY	Chris Waller	Tommy Berry	4.9L	4	53kg	$26
8	5	RED EXCITEMENT	Gerald Ryan	Brenton Avdulla	5.8L	1	53.5kg	$18
9	12	SAVILE ROW	Michael Moroney	Jay Ford	7.1L	5	51kg	$31
10	8	ZANBAGH	John P Thompson	Damian Lane	7.9L	6	53kg	$31

PAST WINNERS

YEAR	WINNER	JOCKEY	TRAINER	2ND	3RD	TIME
2017	Happy Clapper	Blake Shinn	Pat Webster	Tom Melbourne	Snitzson	1:33.1
2016	Hauraki	James McDonald	John O'Shea	Dibayani	Mackintosh	1:33.8
2015	Winx	Hugh Bowman	Chris Waller	Ecuador	Sons Of John	1:34.5
2014	He's Your Man	Joao Moreira	Chris Waller	Royal Descent	Hooked	1:33.3
2013	Boban	Glyn Schofield	Chris Waller	Streama	Toydini	1:34.4
2012	Fat Al	Tommy Berry	Gai Waterhouse	Ambidexter	Rolling Pin	1:34.5
2011	Secret Admirer	Brenton Avdulla	Grahame Begg	Pinker Pinker	Red Tracer	1:35.5
2010	Captain Sonador	Glen Boss	Roger Milne	Trusting	Sacred Choice	1:34.1
2009	Rock Kingdom	Blake Shinn	Gai Waterhouse	Rangirangdoo	Road To Rock	1:38.6
2008	Theseo	Zac Purton	Gai Waterhouse	Bank Robber	Gallant Tess	1:36.2
2007	Race Not Run					
2006	Racing To Win	Glen Boss	John O'Shea	Desert War	Malcolm	1:35.1
2005	Desert War	Larry Cassidy	Gai Waterhouse	Johan's Toy	Lotteria	1:34.5
2004	Desert War	Scott Seamer	Gai Waterhouse	Our Egyptian Raine	Tsuimai	1:37.2
2003	Clangalang	Corey Brown	Gerald Ryan	Grand Armee	Forum Floozie	1:35.2
2002	Excellerator	Jim Cassidy	Gai Waterhouse	Kingsgate	Gordo	1:35.5
2001	Final Fantasy	Mark De Montfort	Bruce Cross	Kingsgate	Crawl	1:22.5
2000	Shogun Lodge	Glen Boss	Bob Thomsen	Landsighting	Chinhoyi	1:33.5
1999	Allez Suez	John Marshall	Bart Cummings	Referral	Zastov	1:33.7
1998	Dodge	Larry Cassidy	John Hawkes	Super Slew	Iron Horse	1:34.0
1997	Iron Horse	Chris Munce	Gai Waterhouse	Tarnpir Lane	Blazing Steel	1:33.5

BACKGROUND

First run: 1865 (won by Dundee). Group 1 since 1979. Run over 1800m 1879-83. Run at Warwick Farm in 1983. Not held in 2007 due equine influenza.
Mares To Win: 14—Winx (2015); Secret Admirer (2001); Chantal (1966); Ma Cherie (1960); De La Salle (1948); Capris (1936); Maximize (1906); Air Motor (1902); Alemene (1898); Novice (1889); Folly (1885); Evangeline (1875); Deceptive (1870); Phoebe (1868).
3YO winners: 2—Noholme (1959); Espiegle (1884).
Multiple Winners: 7—Desert War (2005, 2004); Super Impose (1992, 1991); Toi Port (1964, 1963); Chatham (1933, 1932); Amounis (1928, 1926); Melodrama (1908, 1907); Masquerade (1883, 1882).
Fastest time (1600m): Happy Clapper (2017) 1:33.17
Epsom Handicap winners won the lead-up races:
Warwick Stakes: 5—Filante (1996); Super Impose (1991, 1990); Sky High (1961); Chatham (1933).
Chelmsford Stakes: 1—Filante (1996).
Theo Marks Stakes: 6—Winx (2015); Racing To Win (2006); From The Planet (1989); Ricochet (1970); Cabochon (1967); Hans (1955).
Tramway Handicap: 13—Happy Clapper (2017); Hauraki (2016); Chanteclair (1986); Imposing (1979); High Law (1952); De La Salle (1948); Shannon (1945); Chatham (1932); Amounis (1928); Rostrum (1922); Beauford (1921); Wolario (1919); Melodrama (1908).
Cameron Handicap: 1—Excellerator (2002). Note: Denali (1950) won the 1949 Epsom Hcp.

George Main Stakes & Epsom Handicap: 4—Racing To Win (2006); Imposing (1979); Chantal (1966); De La Salle (1948).
Kingston Town Stakes: 1—He's Your Man (2014).
Hill Stakes: 8—Desert War (2005); Super Impose (1991); Imposing (1979); Toi Port (1964, 1963); Noholme (1959); Shannon (1945); Chatham (1933).
Bill Ritchie Stakes: 1—Boban (2013).
Epsom Handicap winners went on to win in the same preparation:
Caulfield Cup: No horse has won the Epsom Handicap and Caulfield Cup in the same year. However, Amounis won the Epsom in 1926 & 1928 and the Caulfield Cup in 1930.
Caulfield Stakes: 5—Sky High (1961); De La Salle (1948); High Caste (1940); Chatham (1933); Marvel (1891).
Toorak Handicap: 2—Golden Sword (1993); Gunsynd (1971).
Cox Plate: 4—Winx (2015); Noholme (1959); Chatham (1932); Nightmarch (1929).
Mackinnon Stakes: 3—Theseo (2008); Sky High (1961); Marvel (1891)
Longines Mile (Cantala Stakes): 7—Boban (2013); Chanteclair (1986); Riverdale (1984); Gunsynd (1971); Vaals (1927); Amounis (1926); Claro (1923).
The Randwick "mile" double:
Epsom Handicap & Doncaster Handicap (same season): 7—Happy Clapper (2017-18 season); Winx (2015-16); Super Impose (1990-91); Gunsynd (1971-72); Chatham (1933-34); Marvel (1891-82); Dundee (1865-66).
Epsom Handicap & Doncaster Handicap (same year): 4—Racing To Win (2006); Super Impose (1991, 1990); Hyman (1909).
Leading winning jockeys:
5 wins Donald Nicholson (Espiegle 1884, Masquerade 1883, 1882, Waxy 1881, Master Avenel 1880).
4 wins Jim Munro (Silver Ring 1934, Amounis 1928, 1926, Boaster 1925); Neville Sellwood (Noholme 1959, Knave 1956, Silver Phantom 1953, Titanic 1947).
Current winning jockeys:
3 wins Glen Boss (Captain Sonador 2010); Racing To Win 2006, Shogun Lodge 2000); Larry Cassidy (Desert War 2005, Dodge 1998, Golden Sword 1993).
2 wins Blake Shinn (Happy Clapper 2017; Rock Kingdom 2009).
1 win Brenton Avdulla (Secret Admirer 2011); Tommy Berry (Fat Al 2012); Hugh Bowman (Winx 2015); Corey Brown (Clangalang 2003); Grant Cooksley (From The Planet 1989); James McDonald (Hauraki 2016); Joao Moreira (He's Your Man 2014); Zac Purton (Theseo 2008); Glyn Schofield (Boban 2013).
Leading winning trainers:
7 wins Tommy Smith (Chanteclair 1986, Bold Diplomat 1980, Imposing 1979, Authentic Heir 1975, Lord Nelson 1973, Gunsynd 1971, Speed Of Sound 1968); Gai Waterhouse (Fat Al 2012, Rock Kingdom 2009, Theseo 2008, Desert War 2005, 2004, Excellerator 2002, Iron Horse 1997).
5 wins Fred Williams (Chatham 1933, 1932, Vaals 1972, Claro 1923, Greenstead 1920).
Current winning trainers:
7 wins Gai Waterhouse (Fat Al 2012, Rock Kingdom 2009, Theseo 2008, Desert War 2005, 2004, Excellerator 2002, Iron Horse 1997).
3 wins Chris Waller (Winx 2015, He's Your Man 2014, Boban 2013).
2 wins John O'Shea (Hauraki 2016, Racing To Win 2006).
1 win Grahame Begg (Secret Admirer 2011); Bruce Cross (Final Fantasy 2001); Noel Doyle (Kinjite 1992); John Hawkes (Dodge 1998); John Meagher (Golden Sword 1993); Roger Milne (Captain Sonador 2010); Paul Perry (Navy Seal 1994); Gerald Ryan (Clangalang 2003); Pat Webster (Happy Clapper 2017).
Points of interest:
Dead-heat for first—Metellus & Boaster (1925); Atalanta & Kingfisher (1873). Gay Lover was first past the post in 1936, but lost on protest to Capris. Champion mare Wenona Girl carried 56.5kg when second to Rochdale in 1962. Imposera (1988) finished second in the Epsom Handicap to Regal Native, and then won the 1988 Caulfield Cup. Galilee finished second to Chantal in 1966 before winning the 1966 Caulfield and Melbourne Cups.
Heaviest winning weights: Marvel (1891) 64.5kg; Chatham (1933) 61.5kg; Super Impose (1991) 61kg; Wolaroi (1919) 61kg; Amounis (1928) 60.5kg; Silver Ring (1934) 60kg; *Chantal (1966) 52.5kg. *Heaviest winning weight carried by a mare.
Donald Nicholson, who won five Epsom Handicaps in consecutive years from 1880 to 1884, died in a race fall, aged 24, in the 1885 Caulfield Cup.

ATC The Metropolitan (2400m)—Randwick

Of $750,000. Group 1. Handicap, Min Weight 52kg, 3YO&Up. September 29, 2018.

2017-18 RESULT: Time: 2:27.73 (Good 3)

FP	NO	HORSE	TRAINER	JOCKEY	MARGIN	BAR.	WGT	SP
1	10	FOUNDRY	Robert Hickmott	Michael Dee		8	50.5kg	$10
2	5	BIG DUKE	Darren Weir	Brenton Avdulla	0.5L	6	55kg	$5
3	7	CHOCANTE	Stephen Marsh	Corey Brown	1.8L	1	54.5kg	$21
4	2	WHO SHOT THEBARMAN	Chris Waller	Hugh Bowman	2.6L	2	57kg	$16
5	8	BROADSIDE	Gai Waterhouse & Adrian Bott	Tim Clark	3L	9	52kg	$6.50
6	1	LIBRAN	Chris Waller	Glyn Schofield	3.6L	3	57kg	$8.50
7	6	ANTONIO GIUSEPPE	Chris Waller	Joao Moreira	3.7L	4	54.5kg	$6.50
8	12	MY DIAMANTINE	Brian Smith	Andrew Spinks	4.1L	5	50kg	$91
9	9	LIFE LESS ORDINARY	Chris Waller	Kerrin McEvoy	5L	10	51kg	$4.20f
10	3	DESTINY'S KISS	Joseph Pride	Jason Collett	5.7L	7	55.5kg	$41

PAST WINNERS

YEAR	WINNER	JOCKEY	TRAINER	2ND	3RD	TIME
2017	Foundry	Michael Dee	Robert Hickmott	Big Duke	Chocante	2:27.7
2016	Sir John Hawkwood	Blake Spriggs	John Thompson	Antonio Guiseppe	Allergic	2:30.4
2015	Magic Hurricane	James McDonald	John O'Shea	Beaten Up	Havana Cooler	2:28.5
2014	Junoob	Tye Angland	Chris Waller	Opinion	Araldo	2:26.5
2013	Seville	Hugh Bowman	Robert Hickmott	Julienas	Sneak A Peek	2:32.0
2012	Glencadam Gold	Tommy Berry	Gai Waterhouse	Kelinni	Reuben Percival	2:29.7
2011	The Verminator	Craig Newitt	Chris Waller	Hawk Island	Lamasery	2:33.4
2010	Herculian Prince	Nash Rawiller	Gai Waterhouse	Mourayan	No Wine No Song	2:29.9
2009	Speed Gifted	Corey Brown	Lee Freedman	Lodge The Deeds	Fiumicino	2:35.1
2008	Newport	Peter Wells	Paul Perry	Bianca	Get Up Jude	2:33.0
2007	Race Not Run					
2006	Tawqeet	Dwayne Dunn	David Hayes	Activation	Vanquished	2:31.1
2005	Railings	Darren Beadman	John Hawkes	Run Rita Run	Men At Work	2:28.4
2004	County Tyrone	Corey Brown	Kris Lees	Itemise	Don Raphael	2:33.6
2003	Bedouin	Glen Boss	John O'Shea	Daneborogh	Bodie	2:34.4
2002	Victory Smile	Danny Beasley	Donna Logan	Piachay	Dress Circle	2:31.3
2001	Dress Circle	Len Beasley	Gai Waterhouse	Danyon	Homewrecker	2:29.4
2000	Coco Cobanna	Chris Munce	Gai Waterhouse	Pasta Express	Citra's Prince	2:44.3
1999	Vita Man	Brian York	Maurice Campbell	Able Master	Ask The Waiter	2:48.4
1998	In Joyment	Larry Cassidy	Gai Waterhouse	Doriemus	Joss Sticks	2:45.7
1997	Heart Ruler	Jim Cassidy	Jack Denham	Linesman	Court Of Honour	2:41.6

BACKGROUND

First run: 1866 (won by Bylong). Group 1 since 1979. Run over 3200m 1866-91; 2400m 1892-1919; 2600m 1920-2000, except for 1933 when run at Warwick Farm (2400m). Not held in 2007 due to EI outbreak.
Most recent mare to win: Coco Cobanna (2000).
Most recent 3YO to win: C&G—Marvel Loch (1903); No filly has won. Note: Imported galloper St. Spasa (GB) (1914) was a 3YO to Northern Hemisphere time, but considered a 4YO in Australia.
Multiple winners: 5—Hayai (1984, 1983); Tails (1970, 1969); Murray Stream (1947, 1945); Cagou (1917, 1913); Mooltan (1908, 1907).
Fastest time (2400m): Foundry (2017) 2:27.73
Notable winners: Tawqeet (2006); Railings (2005); Natski (1988); Hayai (1983 & 1984); Belmura Lad (1981); Ming Dynasty (1978); Battle Heights (1976); Analie (1973); Tails (1969 & 1970); General Command (1967); Macdougal (1959); Straight Draw (1957); Carioca (1953); Dalray (1952); Delta (1951); Beau Vite (1940); Rebus (1919); Marvel Loch (1903); The Barb (1868); Tim Whiffler (1867).

The Metropolitan winners won the lead-up races:
ATC JRA Plate: 1—Herculian Prince (2010).
Wyong Gold Cup: 1—The Verminator (2011).
Kingston Town Stakes: 7—Herculian Prince (2010); Vita Man (1999); Lord Revenir (1991); Analie (1973); Tails (1969); Piper's Son (1964); Monte Carlo (1958). Note: Dress Circle (2001) won the 2002 Kingston Town. Tails also won the 1970 Metropolitan.
ATC Premier's Cup: 3—Magic Hurricane (2015); Glencadam Gold (2012); Railings (2005).
Newcastle Cup: 5—Glencadam Gold (2012); Hunter (1989); Duo (1966); Conductor (1950); Strength (1931).
Colin Stephen Quality Handicap: 21—Railings (2005); Dress Circle (2001); Coco Cobanna (2000); Vita Man (1999); In Joyment (1998); Heart Ruler (1997); Hula Flight (1996); Zamination (1993); Natski (1988); Nicholas John (1982); Piper's Son (1964); Redcraze (1956); Dalray (1952); Delta (1951); Beau Vite (1940); Royal Chief (1938); St. Carwyne (1915); Mooltan (1908); San Fran (1901); Abercorn (1889); Dagworth (1872).
Hill Stakes: 3—Junoob (2014); Redcraze (1956); Beau Vite (1940).
The Metropolitan winners went on to win in the same preparation:
Caulfield Cup: 4—Tawqeet (2006); Railings (2005); Hayai (1983); Redcraze (1956).
Melbourne Cup: 5—Macdougal (1959); Straight Draw (1957); Dalray (1952); Delta (1951); Tim Whiffler (1867).
The Metropolitan winners and the Sydney Cup:
The Metropolitan & Sydney Cup (same season): 4—General Command (season 1967-68); Straight Draw (1957-58); Rebus (1918-19); The Barb (1868-69).
Leading winning jockeys:
5 wins Kevin Langby (Ming Dynasty 1978; Bon Teint 1975; Analie 1973; Oncidon 1971; Striking Force 1965).
4 wins Ted Bartle (Main Topic 1943, Royal Chief 1938, Strength 1931, Murillo 1927); Jim Cassidy (Heart Ruler 1997, Zamination 1993, Hunter 1989, Spritely Native 1985).
Current winning jockeys:
3 wins Grant Cooksley (Glastonbury 1994, Lord Revenir 1991, Donegal Mist 1990).
2 wins Glen Boss (Bedouin 2003, Electronic 1995); Corey Brown (Speed Gifted 2009, County Tyrone 2004).
1 win Tommy Berry (Glencadam Gold 2012); Hugh Bowman (Seville 2013); Larry Cassidy (In Joyment 1998); Michael Dee (Foundry 2017); Dwayne Dunn (Tawqeet 2006); James McDonald (Magic Hurricane 2015); Craig Newitt (The Verminator 2011); Nash Rawiller (Herculian Prince 2010); Blake Shinn (Junoob 2014); Blake Spriggs (Sir John Hawkwood 2016); Peter Wells (Newport 2008).
Leading winning trainers:
8 wins Gai Waterhouse (Glencadam Gold 2012, Herculian Prince 2010, Dress Circle 2001, Coco Cobanna 2000, In Joyment 1998, Hula Flight 1996, Electronic 1995, Te Akau Nick 1992).
7 wins Tommy Smith (Sir Serene 1977, Bon Teint 1975, Passetreul 1974, Analie 1973, Oncidon 1971, Wiedersehen 1968, Redcraze 1956).
Current winning trainers:
8 wins Gai Waterhouse (Glencadam Gold 2012, Herculian Prince 2010, Dress Circle 2001, Coco Cobanna 2000, In Joyment 1998, Hula Flight 1996, Electronic 1995, Te Akau Nick 1992).
2 wins David Hayes (Tawqeet 2006, Glastonbury 1994); Robert Hickmott (Foundry 2017, Seville 2013); Jim Lee (Hayai 1984, 1983); John O'Shea (Magic Hurricane 2015, Bedouin 2003); Chris Waller (Junoob 2014, The Verminator 2011).
1 win John Hawkes (Railings 2005); Kris Lees (County Tyrone 2004); Donna Logan (Victory Smile 2002); Paul Perry (Newport 2008); John Thompson (Sir John Hawkwood 2016); Bruce Wallace (Lord Revenir 1991).
Points of interest:
Straight Draw (1957) won the AJC The Metropolitan and Melbourne Cup, and in 1958 won the Sydney Cup.
Oro (1935) won on protest from High Cross.
Trainer Jim Cummings won The Metropolitan in 1962 with The Dip. His son, Bart, won it twice with Belmura Lad 1981 and Ming Dynasty 1978.
Father-daughter trainers, Tommy Smith (dec) and Gai Waterhouse, have won 15 of the past 63 The Metropolitans between them.

ATC Flight Stakes (1600m)—Randwick
Of $500,000. Group 1. Set Weights, 3YO Fillies. September 29, 2018.

2017-18 RESULT: Time: 1:34.83 (Good 3)

FP	NO	HORSE	TRAINER	JOCKEY	MARGIN	BAR.	WGT	SP
1	2	ALIZEE	James Cummings	Glyn Schofield		10	56kg	$2.90F
2	1	CHAMPAGNE CUDDLES	Bjorn Baker	Jason Collett	2.3L	11	56kg	$3.80
3	4	CELLARGIRL	Kelly Schweida	Michael Walker	4.6L	4	56kg	$10
4	3	ONE MORE HONEY	John P Thompson	Blake Shinn	4.7L	2	56kg	$9
5	9	SMOOTH LANDING	John P Thompson	Damian Lane	5.3L	1	56kg	$91
6	10	LUVALUVA	John Sargent	Ms Rachel King (a)	5.7L	9	56kg	$81
7	6	I AM EXCITED	David Pfieffer	Kerrin McEvoy	6.2L	8	56kg	$18
8	5	SWEET DEAL	John P Thompson	Hugh Bowman	7.3L	5	56kg	$16
9	8	PANDEMONIUM	Gai Waterhouse & Adrian Bott	Joao Moreira	7.9L	3	56kg	$7
10	7	LEGAL GIRL	Clarry Conners	Corey Brown	9.5L	7	56kg	$31
11	11	COLLEGE ROMANCE	Anthony & Edward Cummings	Tim Clark	16.2L	6	56kg	$151

PAST WINNERS

YEAR	WINNER	JOCKEY	TRAINER	2ND	3RD	TIME
2017	Alizee	Glyn Schofield	James Cummings	Champagne Cuddles	Cellargirl	1:34.8
2016	Global Glamour	Tim Clark	Gai Waterhouse & Adrian Bott	Yankee Rose	Sezanne	1:34.7
2015	Speak Fondly	Tommy Berry	Gai Waterhouse	Honesta	Perignon	1:35.9
2014	First Seal	Blake Shinn	John P Thompson	Winx	Thinking Of You	1:34.7
2013	Guelph	Kerrin McEvoy	Peter Snowden	Sensibility	Bound For Earth	1:36.2
2012	Norzita	Hugh Bowman	Bart Cummings	Longport	Dear Demi	1:36.0
2011	Streama	Hugh Bowman	Guy Walter	Hallowell Belle	Dowager Queen	1:36.7
2010	Secret Admirer	Brenton Avdulla	Grahame Begg	More Strawberries	Parables	1:34.6
2009	More Joyous	Nash Rawiller	Gai Waterhouse	Sister Madly	Hurtle Myrtle	1:40.0
2008	Samantha Miss	Hugh Bowman	Kris Lees	Portillo	Kamillsy	1:38.4
2007	Race Not Run					
2006	Cheeky Choice	Hugh Bowman	Gai Waterhouse	My Lady's Chamber	Fleur Royale	1:36.0
2005	Fashions Afield	Danny Beasley	Gai Waterhouse	Beauty Watch	Mnemosyne	1:37.2
2004	Lotteria	Jim Cassidy	Gai Waterhouse	Cincinnati Gal	Covertly	1:37.6
2003	Unearthly	Corey Brown	David Payne	Santissima	Classy Dane	1:36.6
2002	Royal Purler	Patrick Payne	Gregory Hickman	Victory Vein	Private Steer	1:37.4
2001	Ha Ha	Jim Cassidy	Gai Waterhouse	Moonflute	Hosannah	1:36.2
2000	Unworldly	Larry Cassidy	John Hawkes	Picholine	Lady Mulan	1:34.5
1999	Danglissa	Chris Munce	Gai Waterhouse	The Golden Dane	Miss Zoe	1:34.4
1998	Sunline	Larry Cassidy	Trevor Mckee	Camarena	Confer	1:34.8
1997	Only A Lady	Grant Cooksley	Clarry Conners	Bonanova	On Air	1:34.2

BACKGROUND

First run: 1947 (won by Nizam's Ring). Group 2 1979-84. Group 1 since 1985. Not held in 2007 due to EI.
Fastest time (1600m): Only A Lady (1997) 1:34.23.
Notable winners: Alizee (2018); Global Glamour (2017); First Seal (2014); Guelph (2013); Streama (2011); More Joyous (2009); Samantha Miss (2008); Lotteria (2004); Ha Ha (2001); Sunline (1998); Slight Chance (1992); Triscay (1990); Research (1988); Bounding Away (1986); Goleen (1984); Cap d'Antibes (1974); Flying Gauntlet (1967); Wenona Girl (1960); Nizam's Ring (1947).
Sydney autumn 2YO Triple Crown and the Flight Stakes:
Golden Slipper: 2—Ha Ha (2001); Bounding Away 1986).
ATC Sires' Produce: 3—Guelph (2013); Fashions Afield (2005); Wenona Girl (1960);
Champagne Stakes: 5—Guelph (2013), Samantha Miss (2008); Triscay (1990); Bounding Away (1986); Wattle (1948).
Flight Stakes winners won the lead-up races:
Silver Shadow Stakes: 5—Speak Fondly (2015); Samantha Miss (2008); Ha Ha (2001); Angst (1993); Triscay (1990).
Golden Rose: None.

Furious Stakes: 11—Speak Fondly (2015); Streama (2011); Samantha Miss (2008); Unworldly (2000); Danglissa (1999); Sunline (1998); Dashing Eagle (1996 dead-heat); Danarani (1994); Angst (1993); Research (1988); Tingo Tango (1985).
Tea Rose Stakes: 15—Alizee (2017); First Seal (2014); Guelph (2013); Streama (2011); More Joyous (2009); Samantha Miss (2008); Cheeky Choice (2006); Ha Ha (2001); Unworldly (2000); Danglissa (1999); Sunline (1998); Assertive Lass (1996); Pontal Lass (1995); Danarani (1994); Angst (1993).
Furious Stakes & Tea Rose Stakes: 5—Streama (2011); Samantha Miss (2008); Danglissa (1999); Sunline (1998); Angst (1993).
Silver Shadow Stakes, Furious Stakes & Tea Rose Stakes: 2—Samantha Miss (2008); Angst (1993).
Flight Stakes winners went on to win in same preparation:
Thousand Guineas: 6—Global Glamour (2016); Guelph (2013); Dashing Eagle (1996); Goleen (1984); Wenona Girl (1960); Nizam's Ring (1947).
VRC Oaks: 4—Samantha Miss (2008); Slight Chance (1992); Research (1988); Nizam's Ring (1947).
Thousand Guineas & VRC Oaks: 1—Nizam's Ring (1947).
Flight Stakes winners won in the following autumn:
Vinery Stud Stakes: 3—Norzita (Vinery 2013); Slight Chance (1993); Research (1989).
Australian Oaks: 6—Streama (Oaks 2011); Triscay (1991); Research (1989); Bounding Away (1987); Flying Fable (1969); Wenona Girl (1961).
Vinery Stud Stakes & Australian Oaks: 1—Research (1989).
Leading winning jockeys:
8 wins George Moore (Better Gleam 1971, Natal lass 1969, Flying Fable 1968, Candy Floss 1966, Reveille 1964, Jan's Image 1962, Hoa Hine 1961, Redeswood 1953).
4 wins Hugh Bowman (Norzita 2012, Streama 2011, Samantha Miss 2008, Cheeky Choice 2006); Neville Sellwood (Wenona Girl 1960, Weeamera 1959, Straightlaced 1958, Putoko 1950).
Current winning jockeys:
4 wins Hugh Bowman (Norzita 2012, Streama 2011, Samantha Miss 2008, Cheeky Choice 2006).
2 wins Larry Cassidy (Unworldly 2000, Sunline 1998); Grant Cooksley (Only A Lady 1997, Slight Chance 1992).
1 win Brenton Avdulla (Secret Admirer 2010); Tommy Berry (Speak Fondly 2015); Glen Boss (Pontal Lass 1995); Corey Brown (Unearthly 2003); Kerrin McEvoy (Guelph 2013); Nash Rawiller (More Joyous 2009); Glyn Schofield (Alizee 2017); Blake Shinn (First Seal 2014).
Leading winning trainers:
13 wins Tommy Smith (A Little Kiss 1989, Bounding Away 1986, Gelsomino 1982, Snowing 1979, Jubilee Walk 1978, Siduri 1972, Better Gleam 1971, Natal Lass 1969, Flying Fable 1968, Flying Gauntlet 1967, Candy Floss 1966, Jan's Image 1962, Hoa Hine 1961).
9 wins Gai Waterhouse (Global Glamour 2016, Speak Fondly 2015, More Joyous 2009, Cheeky Choice 2006, Fashions Afield 2005, Lotteria 2004, Ha Ha 2001, Danglissa 1999, Assertive Lass 1996).
6 wins Bart Cummings (Norzita 2012, Dashing Eagle 1996, Danarani 1994, Sun Sally 1977 Apollua 1976, Cap d'Antibes 1974).
Leading current trainers:
9 wins Gai Waterhouse (Global Glamour 2016, Speak Fondly 2015, More Joyous 2009, Cheeky Choice 2006, Fashions Afield 2005, Lotteria 2004, Ha Ha 2001, Danglissa 1999, Assertive Lass 1996).
3 wins Clarry Conners (Only A Lady 1997, Pontal Lass 1995, Research 1988).
1 win Grahame Begg (Secret Admirer 2010); James Cummings (Alizee 2017); John Hawkes (Unworldly 2000); Greg Hickman (Royal Purler 2002); Kris Lees (Samantha Miss 2008); Noel Mayfield-Smith (Angst 1993); David Payne (Unearthly 2003); Peter Snowden (Guelph 2013); John Thompson (First Seal 2014); Gai Waterhouse & Adrian Bott (Global Glamour 2016).
Point of interest:
Judyann (1987) and Goleen (1984) are sisters—by Gosh from Baleen.
Alizee (2017) is a great, great granddaughter of Triscay (1990)

MRC Underwood Stakes (1800m)—Caulfield

Of $750,000. Group 1. Weight for Age, 3YO&Up. September 30, 2018.

2017-18 RESULT: Time: 1:48.41   (Good 3)

FP	NO	HORSE	TRAINER	JOCKEY	MARGIN	BAR.	WGT	SP
1	8	BONNEVAL	Murray Baker & Andrew Forsman	Hugh Bowman		3	56kg	$4.40
2	1	HARTNELL	James Cummings	Kerrin McEvoy	1L	7	59kg	$2.10f
3	3	GAILO CHOP	Darren Weir	Mark Zahra	1.1L	1	59kg	$11
4	6	SINGLE GAZE	Nick Olive	Ms Kathy O'Hara	1.85L	4	57kg	$26
5	2	BLACK HEART BART	Darren Weir	Brad Rawiller	1.95L	8	59kg	$6
6	5	INFERENCE	Michael, Wayne & John Hawkes	Dwayne Dunn	2.35L	5	58kg	$51
7	9	SAMOVARE	David & Ben Hayes & Tom Dabernig	Damian Lane	2.85L	6	56kg	$14
8	4	HE'S OUR ROKKII	David & Ben Hayes & Tom Dabernig	Regan Bayliss	7.35L	2	59kg	$51

PAST WINNERS

YEAR	HORSE	JOCKEY	TRAINER	2ND	3RD	TIME
2017	Bonneval	Hugh Bowman	Murray Baker & Andrew Forsman	Hartnell	Gailo Chop	1:48.4
2016	Black Heart Bart	Brad Rawiller	Darren Weir	He or She	Lucia Valentina	1:50.6
2015	Mourinho	Vlad Duric	Peter Gelagotis	Fawkner	The Cleaner	1:48.8
2014	Foreteller	Glen Boss	Chris Waller	Happy Trails	Crackerjack King	1:50.2
2013	It's A Dundeel	James McDonald	Murray Baker	Atlantic Jewel	Dear Demi	1:54.7
2012	Ocean Park	Glen Boss	Gary Hennessy	Voila Ici	December Draw	1:51.4
2011	Lion Tamer	Michael Rodd	Murray Baker	Southern Speed	Midas Touch	1:50.0
2010	So You Think	Steven Arnold	Bart Cummings	Dariana	Metal Bender	1:49.5
2009	Heart Of Dreams	Craig Newitt	Mick Price	Whobegotyou	Predatory Pricer	1:49.5
2008	Weekend Hussler	Brad Rawiller	Ross McDonald	Pompeii Ruler	Littorio	1:49.8
2007	Rubiscent	Danny Nikolic	Mick Price	Miss Finland	Marasco	1:49.0
2006	El Segundo	Darren Gauci	Colin Little	Polar Bear	Molotov	1:49.5
2005	Perlin	Danny Nikolic	Graeme Rogerson	Our Smoking Joe	Shes Justa Tad	1.52.7
2004	Elvstroem	Nash Rawiller	Tony Vasil	Shes Archie	Delzao	1:50.0
2003	Mummify	Danny Nikolic	Lee Freedman	Grey Song	Aint Seen Nothing	1:49.5
2002	Northerly	Greg Childs	Fred Kersley	Magical Miss	Don Eduardo	1:48.9
2001	Northerly	Damien Oliver	Fred Kersley	Universal Prince	Kaapstad Way	1:50.2
2000	Oliver Twist	Greg Childs	Brian Mayfield-Smith	Skoozi Please	Kaapstad Way	1:47.6
1999	Intergaze	Craig Carmody	Rod Craig	Sky Heights	Inaflury	1:48.5
1998	Tie The Knot	Shane Dye	Guy Walter	Jezabeel	Umrum	1:49.5
1997	Always Aloof	Danny Nikolic	Lee Freedman	Istidaad	Marble Halls	1:49.6

BACKGROUND

First run: 1924 (won by Whittier). Group 1 since 1979. Run over 1600m 1924-41 & 1944-48; Run over 1400m in 1942. 2000m 1954-93; 1800m 1949-53 and since 1994. Also known as the Williamstown Stakes (run at Williamstown 1924-38); Run at Moonee Valley 1946 & 1947; Flemington 1943-45. Not held in 1942. Run twice in 1994 (April & September).
Most recent mare to win: Bonneval (2017). Only six mares have won the Underwood.
Most recent 3YO to win: C&G—Sobar (1972). Only four 3YOs have won the Underwood (the others were: Young Idea 1935, Hall Mark 1933, Liberal 1932). No filly has won.
Multiple winners: 12—Northerly (2002, 2001); Future (1967, 1965); Aquanita (1962, 1961); Lord (1960, 1958); Flying Halo (1954, 1953); Beau Gem (1950, 1949); Attley (1947, 1946); Ajax (1940, 1939, 1938); Young Idea (1937, 1935); Hall Mark (1934, 1933); Highland (1929, 1928); Whittier (1925, 1924).
Fastest time (1800m): Oliver Twist (2000) 1:47.60
Notable winners: Bonneval (2017); Black Heart Bart (2016); It's A Dundeel (2013); Ocean Park (2012); So You Think (2010); Weekend Hussler (2008); Northerly (2002, 2001); Intergaze (1999); Tie The Knot (1998); Octagonal (1996); Jeune (1994); Rubiton (1987); Bonecrusher (1986); So Called (1978); Sobar (1972); Rain Lover (1970); Tobin Bronze (1966); Lord (1960, 1958); Royal Gem (1948); Attley (1947, 1946); Ajax (1940, 1939 & 1938); Young Idea (1937, 1935); Hall Mark (1934, 1933); Phar Lap (1931); Heroic (1926); Young Idea (1937, 1935); Hall Mark (1934, 1933); Highland (1929, 1928); Heroic (1926); Whittier (1925, 1924).

Underwood Stakes winners won the lead-up races:
PB Lawrence Stakes (JJ Liston): 7—Mourinho (2015); So Called (1978); Tobin Bronze (1966); Lord (1958); Syntax (1957); Cromis (1955); Ellerslie (1952).
Memsie Stakes: 16—Black Heart Bart (2016); So You Think (2012); Weekend Hussler (2008); El Segundo (2006); Rubiton (1987); Lord (1960, 1958); Syntax (1957); Attley (1947); Ajax (1940, 1939, 1938); Phar Lap (1931); Highland (1929); Royal Charter (1927); Heroic (1926).
Dato Tan Chin Nam (Feehan) Stakes: 4—Bonneval (2017); Northerly (2001); Rubiton (1987); So Called (1978).
Makybe Diva Stakes: 10—Weekend Hussler (2008); Northerly (2002); Sovereign Red (1981); How Now (1976); Rain Lover (1969); Lowland (1968); Tobin Bronze (1966); Havelock (1963); Aquanita (1962); Cromis (1955).
Underwood Stakes winners went on to win in same preparation:
Turnbull Stakes (since 1948): 5—Elvstroem (2004); Northerly (2002); Tobin Bronze (1966); Aquanita (1962); Syntax (1957). Note: Beau Gem (Turnbull 1948) won the Underwood in 1949 & 1950.
Makybe Diva & Turnbull (since 1948): 3—Northerly (2002); Tobin Bronze (1966); Aquanita (1962).
Caulfield Stakes: 13—Ocean Park (2012); So You Think (2010); Northerly (2001); Bonecrusher (1986); Tristarc (1985); How Now (1976); Gay Icarus (1971); Comtempler (1964); Lord (1960, 1958); Ajax (1938); Hall Mark (1934); Royal Charter (1927).
Caulfield Cup: 7—Elvstroem (2004); Mummify (2003); Northerly (2002); Tristarc (1985); How Now (1976); Sobar (1972); Gay Icarus (1971).
Cox Plate: 16—Ocean Park (2012); So You Think (2010); Northerly (2002, 2001); Almaarad (1989); Rubiton (1987); Bonecrusher (1986); So Called (1978); Tobin Bronze (1966); Aquanita (1962); Ray Ribbon (1956); Ajax (1938); Young Idea (1937); Phar Lap (1931); Highland (1928); Heroic (1926).
Caulfield Stakes & Cox Plate: 5—Ocean Park (2012); So You Think (2010); Northerly (2001); Bonecrusher (1986); Ajax (1938).
Mackinnon Stakes: 8—So You Think (2010); Rubiton (1987); Bounty Hawk (1984); Tobin Bronze (1966); Aquanita (1962); Trellios (1959); Ajax (1938); Phar Lap (1931).
Caulfield Stakes, Cox Plate & Mackinnon Stakes: 2—So You Think (2010), Ajax (1938).
Melbourne Cup: 2—Jeune (1994); Rain Lover (1969).
Leading winning jockeys:
5 wins Harold Badger (Attley 1946, Sun Valley 1941, Ajax 1940, 1939, 1938).
4 wins Bill Duncan (Highland 1929, 1928, Royal Charter 1927, Whittier 1925); Danny Nikolic (Rubiscent 2007; Perlin 2005; Mummify 2003; Always Aloof 1997); Harry White (Rubiton 1987; Bounty Hawk 1984; Trissaro 1983; Sobar 1972).
Current winning jockeys:
2 wins Glen Boss (Foreteller 2014, Ocean Park 2012); Brad Rawiller (Black Heart Bart 2016, Weekend Hussler 2008).
1 win Steven Arnold (So You Think 2010); Hugh Bowman (Bonneval 2017); Grant Cooksley (The Phantom 1990); Vlad Duric (Mourinho 2015); James McDonald (It's A Dundeel 2013); Craig Newitt (Heart Of Dreams 2009); Damien Oliver (Northerly 2001); Nash Rawiller (Elvstroem 2004); Michael Rodd (Lion Tamer 2011).
Leading winning trainers:
7 wins Ken Hilton (Sobar 1972; Future 1965, 1967; Havelock 1963; Lord 1960, 1958; Ellerslie 1952); Jack Holt (Young Idea 1937, Hall Mark 1934, 1933, Highland 1929, 1928, Royal Charter 1927, Heroic 1926).
6 wins Bart Cummings (So You Think 2010, Bounty Hawk 1984, Trissaro 1983, Big Philou 1970, Lowland 1968; Trellios 1959).
4 wins Murray Baker (Bonneval 2017, It's A Dundeel 2013, Lion Tamer 2011, The Phantom 1990); Lee Freedman (Mummify 2003, Always Aloof 1997; Sharscay 1995, Runyon 1993).
Current winning trainers:
4 wins Murray Baker (Bonneval 2017, It's A Dundeel 2013, Lion Tamer 2011, The Phantom 1990); Lee Freedman (Mummify 2003, Always Aloof 1997; Sharscay 1995, Runyon 1993).
2 wins Fred Kersley (Northerly 2002, 2001); Mick Price (Heart Of Dreams 2009, Rubiscent 2007).
1 win Murray Baker & Andrew Forsman (Bonneval 2018); Rod Craig (Intergaze 1999); Peter Gelagotis (Mourinho 2015); John Hawkes (Octagonal 1996); David Hayes (Jeune 1994); Gary Hennessy (Ocean Park 2012); Colin Little (El Segundo 2006); Frank Ritchie (Bonecrusher 1986); Graeme Rogerson (Perlin 2005); Tony Vasil (Elvstroem 2004); Chris Waller (Foreteller 2014); Darren Weir (Black Heart Bart 2016).
Points of interest:
Waitangirua and My Brown Jug dead-heated for first in 1980.
Royal Gem (1948)—Dhoti-French Gem—and Beau Gem (1950, 1949)—Helios-French Gem—are half-brothers.
In 2015, the first three horses across the line were 8YOs (geldings)—Mourinho, Fawkner and The Cleaner.
Mourinho is the equal oldest winner of the Underwood with Highland (1929).

VRC Turnbull Stakes (2000m)—Flemington
Of $500,000. Group 1. Set Weights plus Penalties, 4YO&Up. October 6, 2018.

2017-18 RESULT: Time: 2:02.07 (Good4)

FP	NO	HORSE	TRAINER	JOCKEY	MARGIN	BAR.	WGT	SP
1	2	WINX	Chris Waller	Hugh Bowman		2	57kg	$1.20F
2	3	VENTURA STORM	David & Ben Hayes & Tom Dabernig	Regan Bayliss	6.5L	5	56.5kg	$17
3	1	HUMIDOR	Darren Weir	Damian Lane	7.25L	4	59kg	$7.50
4	4	ASSIGN	Robert Hickmott	Katelyn Mallyon	9L	6	56.5kg	$51
5	6	SIR ISAAC NEWTON	Robert Hickmott	Damien Oliver	11.25L	7	54.5kg	$31
6	5	MAGICOOL	Tony Romeo	Christopher Brown	26.25L	1	54.5kg	$201
7	7	SKYFIRE	Amy Johnston	Dwayne Dunn	26.45L	3	54.5kg	$201

PAST WINNERS

YEAR	WINNER	JOCKEY	TRAINER	2ND	3RD	TIME
2017	Winx	Hugh Bowman	Chris Waller	Ventura Storm	Humidor	2:02.0
2016	Hartnell	James McDonald	John O'Shea	Jameka	Tally	2:01.0
2015	Preferment	Hugh Bowman	Chris Waller	Royal Descent	Set Square	2:01.3
2014	Lucia Valentina	Kerrin McEvoy	Kris Lees	Lidari	Brambles	2:01.8
2013	Happy Trails	Dwayne Dunn	Paul Beshara	Puissance De Lune	Fawkner	2:02.9
2012	Green Moon	Craig Williams	Robert Hickmott	Seville	December Draw	2:02.1
2011	December Draw	Michael Rodd	Mark Kavanagh	Glass Harmonium	Playing God	2:03.9
2010	Zipping	Nicholas Hall	Robert Hickmott	Shocking	Shoot Out	2:03.2
2009	Efficient	Nicholas Hall	John Sadler	Predatory Pricer	Scenic Shot	2:01.6
2008	Littorio	Steven King	Nigel Blackiston	Master O'Reilly	Zipping	2:02.4
2007	Devil Moon	Corey Brown	Mark Kavanagh	Scenic Shot	Haradasun	2:03.4
2006	Sphenophyta	Danny Nikolic	Lee Freedman	Our Smoking Joe	Aqua D Amore	2:01.9
2005	Makybe Diva	Steven King	Lee Freedman	Lad Of The Manor	Confectioner	2:01.5
2004	Elvstroem	Nash Rawiller	Tony Vasil	Mummify	Confectioner	2:00.4
2003	Studebaker	Stephen Baster	John Hawkes	Pentastic	Strasbourg	2:04.0
2002	Northerly	Greg Childs	Fred Kersley	Dash For Cash	Fields Of Omagh	2:02.3
2001	Sunline	Greg Childs	Trevor Mckee	Universal Prince	Primrose Sands	2:03.9
2000	Fairway	Darren Beadman	Jack Denham	Sunline	Diatribe	2:02.2
1999	Sky Heights	Damien Oliver	Colin Alderson	Ruy Lopez	Inaflury	2:04.6
1998	Aerosmith	Greg Childs	Peter Hurdle	Gold Guru	Our Unicorn	2:05.8
1997	Marble Halls	Damien Oliver	Lee Freedman	Always Aloof	Seascay	2:03.1

BACKGROUND

First run: 1865 (The Sign). Group 2 1979-2005. Group 1 from 2006. Run as a handicap until 1993. WFA and penalties. WFA 1964-70. Run over 3200m 1865-82 & 1885-89; 2800m 1884; 2600m 1890-91; 2400m 1883, 1892-93, 1916-22 & 1948-70; 2000m 1895-1915 and 1923 & from 1971; 1800m 1924; 1600m 1925-47. Previous known as the Melbourne (8f) Stakes, October Stakes, September Stakes and Royal Park Stakes.
Most recent mare to win: Winx (2017). Note: 11 mares have won since 1948.
Most recent 3YO to win: John Wilkes (1937); No filly has won. Note: No 3YO has won since the Turnbull was changed to 2000m.
Multiple winners (since 1948): 2—Vo Rogue (1988, 1987); Comic Court (1950, 1949).
Fastest time (2000m): Elvstroem (2004) 2:00.40
Notable winners (since 1948): Winx (2017); Hartnell (2016); Green Moon (2012); Efficient (2009); Makybe Diva (2005); Elvstroem (2004); Northerly (2002); Sunline 2001); Doriemus (1996); Naturalism (1992); Let's Elope (1991); Better Loosen Up (199); Super Impose (1989); Vo Roge (1988, 1987); Dulcify (1979); Leilani (1974); Galilee (1968); Tobin Bronze (1966); Craftsman (1965); Sir Dane (1964); Sometime (1963); Aquanita (1962); Redcraze (1955); Rising Fast (1954); Comic Court (1950, 1949); Beau Gem (1948).
Note: the following statistics are from 1948.
Turnbull Stakes winners won the lead-up races:
Lawrence Stakes (JJ Liston): 3—Stellar Belle (1967); Tobin Bronze (1966); Syntax (1957).
Makybe Diva Stakes: 9—Northerly (2002); Sky Heights (1999); Marble Halls (1997); Dulcify (1979); Stellar Belle (1967); Tobin Bronze (1966); Sir Dane (1964); Aquanita (1962); Comic Court (1949).
Stocks Stakes: 1—Devil Moon (2007).
Underwood Stakes: 5—Elvstroem (2004); Northerly (2002); Tobin Bronze (1966); Aquanita (1962); Syntax

(1957). Note: Beau Gem (1948) won the Underwood in 1949 & 1950.
Makybe Diva Stakes & Underwood Stakes: 3—Northerly (2002); Tobin Bronze (1966); Aquanita (1962).
Chelmsford Stakes: 2—Winx (2017); Hartnell (2016).
Hill Stakes: 2—Hartnell (2016); Preferment (2015).
Turnbull Stakes winners went on to win in the same preparation:
Caulfield Stakes: 4—Arctic Symbol (1970); Sometime (1963); Rising Fast (1954); Comic Court (1950).
Caulfield Cup: 8—Elvstroem (2004); Northerly (2002); Sky Heights (1999); Let's Elope (1991); Analight (1975); Leilani (1974); Sometime (1963); Rising Fast (1954).
Cox Plate: 10—Winx (2018); Makybe Diva (2005); Northerly (2002); The Phantom Chance 1993); Better Loosen Up (1990); Dulcify (1979); Tobin Bronze (1966); Sir Dane (1964); Aquanita (1962); Rising Fast (1954).
Melbourne Cup: 5—Green Moon (2012); Makybe Diva (2005); Let's Elope (1991); Rising Fast (1954); Comic Court (1950).
Caulfield Cup & Melbourne Cup: 2—Let's Elope (1991); Rising Fast (1954).
Caulfield Cup, Cox Plate & Melbourne Cup: 1—Rising Fast (1954). Note: Rising Fast also won the Caulfield Stakes, Mackinnon Stakes and Queen Elizabeth Stakes in an unparalleled 1954 spring campaign.
Leading winning jockeys:
4 wins Roy Higgins (Denise's Joy 1976, Leilani 1974, Galilee 1968, Sir Dane 1964); Harry White (Just Now 1986, Birchwood 1982, No Peer 1981, Lefroy 1978).
3 wins Greg Childs (Northerly 2002; Sunline 2001; Aerosmith 1998); Steven King (Littorio 2008; Makybe Diva 2005; Let's Elope 1991); Bill Williamson (Aircraft 1960, Syntax 1957, Rising Fast 1954).
Current winning jockeys:
2 wins Hugh Bowman (Winx 2017, Preferment 2015); Nicholas Hall (Zipping 2009, Efficient 2008); Damien Oliver (Sky Heights 1999, Marble Halls 1997); Cyril Small (Vo Rogue 1988, 1987).
1 win Stephen Baster (Studebaker 2003); Corey Brown (Devil Moon 2007); Dwayne Dunn (Happy Trails 2013); James McDonald (Hartnell 2016); Kerrin McEvoy (Lucia Valentina 2014); Nash Rawiller (Elvstroem 2004); Michael Rodd (December Draw 2011); Craig Williams (Green Moon 2012).
Leading winning trainers:
6 wins Lee Freedman (Sphenophyta 2006; Makybe Diva 2005; Marble Halls 1997; Doriemus 1996, Naturalism 1992; Super Impose 1989).
Current winning trainers:
6 wins Lee Freedman (Sphenophyta 2006; Makybe Diva 2005; Marble Halls 1997; Doriemus 1996, Naturalism 1992; Super Impose 1989).
2 wins Robert Hickmott (Green Moon 2012, Zipping 2010); Mark Kavanagh (December Draw 2011, Devil Moon 2007); Chris Waller (Winx 2017, Preferment 2015).
1 win Paul Beshara (Happy Trails 2013); Nigel Blackiston (Littorio 2008); John Hawkes (Studebaker 2003); David Hayes (Better Loosen Up 1990); Peter Hurdle (Aerosmith 1998); Fred Kersley (Northerly 2002); Kris Lees (Lucia Valentina 2014); John O'Shea (Hartnell 2016); John Sadler (Efficient 2009); Tony Vasil (Elvstroem 2004); Gai Waterhouse (All Our Mob 1995).
Point of interest:
Redding (1994) beat Paris Lane on protest.
Winx (2017) recorded her first win at Flemington—it was her 21st consecutive win (14th Group 1).

ATC Spring Champion Stakes (2000m)—Randwick
Of $500,000. Group 1. Set Weights, 3YO. October 6, 2018.

2017-18 RESULT: Time: 2:03.94 (Good 3)

FP	NO	HORSE	TRAINER	JOCKEY	MARGIN	BAR.	WGT	SP
1	1	ACE HIGH	David Payne	Tye Angland		4	56.5kg	$3.10F
2	3	TANGLED	Chris Waller	Blake Shinn	0.1L	2	56.5kg	$5.50
3	7	SULLY	Trent Busuttin & Natalie Young	Brenton Avdulla	1.6L	9	56.5kg	$8.50
4	4	SANCTIONED	James Cummings	Kerrin McEvoy	2.1L	10	56.5kg	$4
5	2	ASTORIA	James Cummings	Glyn Schofield	3.9L	8	56.5kg	$10
6	6	DISSOLUTION	Michael, Wayne & John Hawkes	Sam Clipperton	4.6L	1	56.5kg	$13
7	5	COLESBERG	David Payne	Jason Collett	8.1L	3	56.5kg	$61
8	10	CORAL COAST	Stuart Webb	Tim Clark	8.8L	6	54.5kg	$26
9	9	SURPRISE BULLET	Barry Lockwood	Larry Cassidy	13.4L	5	56.5kg	$51
10	8	LANGLEY	John O'Shea	Christian Reith	23.4L	7	56.5kg	$31

PAST WINNERS

YEAR	WINNER	JOCKEY	TRAINER	2ND	3RD	TIME
2017	Ace High	Tye Angland	David Payne	Tangled	Sully	2:03.9
2016	Yankee Rose	Dean Yendall	David Vandyke	Swear	Prized Icon	2:02.4
2015	Vanbrugh	Glyn Schofield	Chris Waller	I'm Belucci	Man Of Choice	2:02.8
2014	Hampton Court	Josh Parr	Gai Waterhouse	First Seal	Sweynesse	2:00.1
2013	Complacent	Christian Reith	Peter Snowden	Criterion	Savvy Nature	2:03.3
2012	It's A Dundeel	James McDonald	Murray Baker	Proisir	Honorius	2:02.6
2011	Doctor Doom	Rod Quinn	Guy Walter	Darci Be Good	Sangster	2:05.8
2010	Erewhon	Hugh Bowman	Peter Snowden	Retrieve	Praecido/Shootoff	2:02.9
2009	Monaco Consul	Jay Ford	Michael Moroney	Gathering	Viking Legend	2:09.9
2008	Sousa	Corey Brown	Peter Snowden	Predatory Pricer	Excelltastic	2:06.2
2007	Race Not Run					
2006	Teranaba	Larry Cassidy	Anthony Cummings	All Black Gold	He's No Pie Eater	2:04.5
2005	Hotel Grand	Jay Ford	Anthony Cummings	Pendragon	Duelled	2:04.8
2004	Savabeel	Chris Munce	Graeme Rogerson	Outback Prince	Cedar Manor	2:07.2
2003	Niello	Corey Brown	John Hawkes	November Dreaming	Tsuimai	2:03.4
2002	Platinum Scissors	Jim Cassidy	Gai Waterhouse	Soprana	Maskerado	2:04.3
2001	Viking Ruler	Len Beasley	Clarry Conners	Evander	Silver Baron	1:49.5
2000	Universal Prince	Justin Sheehan	Bede Murray	Falls The Shadow	Go Bint	2:05.1
1999	Fairway	Brian York	Jack Denham	Shogun Lodge	Liberty Hall	2:02.3
1998	Dignity Dancer	Chris Munce	Bill Mitchell	Lawyer	Arena	2:00.4
1997	Tie The Knot	Darren Beadman	Guy Walter	Brave Prince	El Mirada	2:05.4

BACKGROUND

First run: 1971 (won by Gay Icarus). Group 1 since 1979. Run over 2100m (Warwick Farm) in 1983. Run over 2100m (Kensington inner track) 2001. Run in the autumn 1971-78. Not held in 2007 due to the EI outbreak.
Fillies to win: Yankee Rose (2016). Note: the only filly to win.
Fastest time (2000m): Hampton Court (2014) 2:00.19
Notable winners: Ace High (2017); Yankee Rose (2016); It's A Dundeel (2012); Monaco Consul (2009); Savabeel (2004); Niello (2003); Universal Prince (2000); Dignity Dancer (1998); Tie The Knot (1997); Nothin' Leica Dane (1995); Danewin (1994); Stylish Century (1989); Beau Zam (1987); Sir Dapper (1983); Best Western (1981); Kingston Town (1979); Cheyne Walk (1976); Taras Bulba (1975); Gay Icarus (1971).
Sydney autumn 2YO feature winners to win the Spring Champion Stakes:
Golden Slipper: 1—Sir Dapper (1983).
ATC Sires' Produce: 2—Yankee Rose (2016); Latin Knight (Sires' 1971; Spring Champion, autumn 1972).
ATC Champagne Stakes: None.
Spring Champion Stakes winners won the lead-up races:
Golden Rose Stakes: None. Note: three horses won the precursor to the Golden Rose, the Peter Pan Stakes: 3—Sir Dapper (1983); Best Western (1981); Kingston Town (1979).
NJC Spring Stakes: 5—Sousa (2008); Hotel Grand (2005); Universal Prince (2000); Coronation Day (1992); Easter (1985).

Gloaming Stakes: 10—Ace High (2017); Vanbrugh (2015); Complacent (2013); It's A Dundeel (2012); Fairway (1999); Tie The Knot (1997); Magic Of Sydney (1996); Sir Dapper (1983); Best Western (1981); Kingston Town (1979).
Dulcify Quality: 5—Hampton Court (2014); Tie The Knot (1997); Nothin' Leica Dane (1995); Danewin (1994); Sakana (1988).
Spring Champion Stakes winners went on to win in same preparation:
Caulfield Classic (former Norman Robinson Stakes): 2—Platinum Scissors (2002); Nothin' Leica Dane (1995).
Caulfield Guineas: None.
Moonee Valley Vase: None.
Cox Plate: 1—Savabeel (2004). Note: Yankee Rose (2016) finished third in the Cox Plate.
Victoria Derby: 4—Ace High (2017); Monaco Consul (2009); Nothin' Leica Dane (1995); Stylish Century (1989).
Spring Champion Stakes winners won in the following autumn:
Australian Derby (autumn, since 1978): 5—It's A Dundeel (Derby 2013); Universal Prince (2001); Fairway (2000); Beau Zam (1988); Kingston Town (1979).
Leading winning jockeys:
4 wins Ron Quinton (Easter 1985; Sir Dapper 1983; Veloso 1982; Gold Brick 1973).
3 wins Brian York (Fairway 1999, Fraternity 1993, St. Jude 1990).
Current winning jockeys:
2 wins Corey Brown (Sousa 2008, Niello 2003); Jay Ford (Monaco Consul 2009, Hotel Grand 2005).
1 win Tye Angland (Ace High 2017); Hugh Bowman (Erewhon 2010); Larry Cassidy (Teranaba 2006); James McDonald (It's A Dundeel 2012); Josh Parr (Hampton Court 2014); Christian Reith (Complacent 2013); Glyn Schofield (Vanbrugh 2015); Robert Thompson (Just A Steal 1978); Dean Yendall (Yankee Rose 2016).
Leading winning trainer:
4 wins Bart Cummings (Stylish Century 1989; Beau Zam 1987; Best Western 1981; Asgard 1974); Tommy Smith (Easter 1985, Luck's A Lottery 1984, Kingston Town 1979, Cheyne Walk 1976); Gai Waterhouse (Hampton Court 2014, Platinum Scissors 2002, Magic Of Sydney 1996, Nothin' Leica Dane 1995).
Current winning trainer:
4 wins Gai Waterhouse (Hampton Court 2014, Platinum Scissors 2002, Magic Of Sydney 1996, Nothin' Leica Dane 1995).
2 wins Anthony Cummings (Teranaba 2006, Hotel Grand 2005); Peter Snowden (Complacent 2013, Sousa 2008).
1 win Murray Baker (It's A Dundeel 2012); Les Bridge (Sir Dapper 1983); Clarry Conners (Viking Ruler 2001); John Hawkes (Niello 2003); Mike Moroney (Monaco Consul 2009); David Payne (Ace High 2017); Graeme Rogerson (Savabeel 2004); David Vandyke (Yankee Rose 2016); Chris Waller (Vanbrugh 2015).
Point of interest:
It's A Dundeel (2012) is the only horse to clean sweep Sydney's Group 1 features for open 3YOs (1600m or further)—Spring Champion Stakes in the spring, and the Randwick Guineas, Rosehill Guineas and Australian Derby in the autumn.
Dignity Dancer (1998) went on to win the Melbourne autumn treble (and bonus)—G2 Autumn Classic, G2 Alister Clark Stakes and G1 Australian Guineas.

MRC Caulfield Guineas (1600m)—Caulfield
Of $2,000,000. Group 1. Set Weights, 3YO. October 13, 2018.

2017-18 RESULT: Time: 1:36.04 (Good 3)

FP	NO	HORSE	TRAINER	JOCKEY	MARGIN	BAR.	WGT	SP
1	17	MIGHTY BOSS	Mick Price	Michael Walker		5	56.5kg	$101
2	11	KEMENTARI	James Cummings	Damian Lane	0.3L	10	56.5kg	$5.50
3	16	CATCHY	David & Ben Hayes & Tom Dabernig	Mark Zahra	1.3L	3	54.5kg	$4.40f
4	6	ROYAL SYMPHONY	Tony McEvoy	Dwayne Dunn	2.3L	9	56.5kg	$4.80
5	8	PERAST	Paul Perry	Ben Melham	3.55L	2	56.5kg	$11
6	14	LEVENDI	Peter Gelagotis	Anthony Darmanin	3.75L	7	56.5kg	$21
7	13	SALSAMOR	Trent Busuttin & Natalie Young	Brad Rawiller	4.5L	8	56.5kg	$26
8	9	SANCTIONED	James Cummings	Glyn Schofield	4.8L	15	56.5kg	$21
9	15	HOLY SNOW	Mick Price	Michael Dee	5.55L	14	56.5kg	$61
10	4	SIRCCONI	Peter Morgan	Linda Meech	5.75L	13	56.5kg	$71
11	5	SHOWTIME	Michael, Wayne & John Hawkes	Damien Oliver	7L	1	56.5kg	$12
12	1	THE MISSION	Paul Perry	Beau Mertens	10.25L	11	56.5kg	$51
13	7	GOLD STANDARD	Gai Waterhouse & Adrian Bott	Stephen Baster	10.65L	6	56.5kg	$8
14	10	AL PASSEM	Ken Keys	Ben Thompson	12.65L	12	56.5kg	$151
15	3	AZAZEL	Tony McEvoy	Luke Currie	37.65L	4	56.5kg	$51

PAST WINNERS

YEAR	WINNER	JOCKEY	TRAINER	2ND	3RD	TIME
2017	Mighty Boss	Michael Walker	Mick Price	Kementari	Catchy	1:36.0
2016	Divine Prophet	Dwayne Dunn	Michael, Wayne & John Hawkes	Seaburge	Hey Doc	1:36.5
2015	Press Statement	Hugh Bowman	Chris Waller	Lizard Island	Ready For Victory	1:36.4
2014	Shooting To Win	James McDonald	Peter & Paul Snowden	Rich Enuff	Wandjina	1:35.5
2013	Long John	Kerrin McEvoy	Peter Snowden	Divine Calling	Shamus Award	1:36.7
2012	All Too Hard	Dwayne Dunn	Michael, Wayne & John Hawkes	Pierro	Epaulette	1:36.0
2011	Helmet	Kerrin McEvoy	Peter Snowden	Manawanui	Huegill	1:35.3
2010	Anacheeva	Luke Nolen	Peter Moody	Run For Levi	Masquerader	1:37.0
2009	Starspangledbanner	Danny Nikolic	Leon Corstens	Carrara	Manhattan Rain	1:35.6
2008	Whobegotyou	Michael Rodd	Mark Kavanagh	Time Thief	Von Costa De Hero	1:36.4
2007	Weekend Hussler	Brad Rawiller	Ross McDonald	Scenic Blast	Marching	1:36.4
2006	Wonderful World	Luke Nolen	Bart Cummings	Excites	Court Command	1:35.9
2005	Gods Own	Glen Boss	Bart Cummings	Paratroopers	Primus	1:37.6
2004	Econsul	Chris Munce	Graeme Rogerson	Barely A Moment	Under Command	1:38.0
2003	In Top Swing	Noel Callow	Noel Mayfield-Smith	Face Value	Kempinsky	1:36.0
2002	Helenus	Steven King	Leon Corstens	Bel Esprit	Choisir	1:35.4
2001	Lonhro	Darren Gauci	John Hawkes	Ustinov	Pure Theatre	1:36.7
2000	Show A Heart	Steven King	Barry Miller	Fubu	Sale Of Century	1:35.8
1999	Redoutes Choice	Jim Cassidy	Rick Hore-Lacy	Testa Rossa	Commands	1:35.8
1998	Kenwood Melody	Shane Dye	Bill Mitchell	Lauries Lottery	Spectacular Gold	1:38.0
1997	Encounter	Shane Dye	Clarry Conners	Schubert	General Nediym	1:36.2

BACKGROUND

First run: 1881 (won by Wheatear). Group 1 since 1979. Run at Flemington 1940-43.

Most recent filly to win: Surround (1976). Note: 14 fillies have won the Caulfield Guineas. In the past 55 years, five winning fillies—Surround, Dual Choice (1970); Storm Queen (1966); Lady Sybil (1960) and Wiggle (1958).

Fastest time (1600m): Helmet (2011) 1:35.30

Notable winners: All Too Hard (2012); Starspangledbanner (2009); Weekend Hussler (2007); Lonhro (2001); Redoute's Choice (1999); Mahogany (1993); Red Anchor (1984); Grosvenor (1982); Sovereign Red (1980); Manikato (1978); Luskin Star (1977); Surround (1976); Sobar (1972); Vain (1969); Storm Queen (1966); Tulloch (1957); Royal Gem (1945 dead-heat); High Caste (1939); Ajax (1937); Heroic (1924); Patrobas (1915); Malt King (1909); Sweet Nell (1903); Bobadil (1898); Wallace (1895).

2YO feature winners and the Caulfield Guineas:
Blue Diamond Stakes: 2—Redoute's Choice (1999); Manikato (1978).
Golden Slipper Stakes: 4—Manikato (1978); Luskin Star (1977); Vain (1969); Storm Queen (1966).
VRC Sires' Produce Stakes: 14—All Too Hard (2011); Vain (1969); Tulloch (1957); Iron Duke (1949); High Caste (1939); Nuffield (1938); Rampion (1926); King Carnival (1923); Thrice (1917); Sweet Nell (1903); Aurum (1897); Patron (1893); Autonomy (1892); Maddelina (1886).
ATC Sires' Produce Stakes: 14—Helmet (2011); Encounter (1997); St. Covet (1994); Luskin Star (1977); Time And Tide (1963); Tulloch (1957); Nuffield (1938); Ajax (1937); Young Idea (1935); Ammon Ra (1931); Soorak (1922); Thrice (1917); Autonomy (1892); Rudolph (1889).
ATC Champagne Stakes (since 1600m in 1972): 4—Helmet (2011); Encounter (1997); Red Anchor (1984); Luskin Star (1977).
JJ Atkins Stakes: 4—Press Statement (2015); Show A Heart (2000); Mahogany (1993); Luskin Star (1977).
Caulfield Guineas winners won the lead-up races:
Vain Stakes: 1—Starspangledbanner (2009).
McNeil Stakes: 1—Starspangledbanner (2009).
Up And Coming Stakes: 3—Divine Prophet (2016); Our Maizcay (1995); Mahogany (1993).
Ming Dynasty Stakes: 2—Lonhro (2001); Kenwood Melody (1998).
Golden Rose: No horse has won a Golden Rose and Caulfield Guineas.
Guineas Prelude: 4—Helmet (2011); Anacheeva (2010); Wonderful World (2006); Alfa (1996).
Sir Rupert Clarke Stakes: 2—Our Maizcay (1995); Manikato (1978).
Stutt Stakes: 10—Whobegotyou (2008); Helenus (2002); Red Anchor (1984); Surround (1976); Beau Sovereign (1971); Storm Queen (1966); Star Affair (1965); Lady Sybil (1960); Phoibus (1948); Attley (1945).
Gloaming Stakes: 1—Grosvenor (1982).
Stan Fox Stakes: 4—Press Statement (2015); Shooting To Win (2014); Lonhro (2001); Kenwood Melody (1998).
Caulfield Guineas winners went on to win in the same preparation:
Coolmore Stud Stakes: 5—Weekend Hussler (2007); Our Maizcay (1995); Manikato (1978); Surround (1976); Vain (1969). Note: Before 2006, the Coolmore Stud Stakes (1200m) was run in September, before the Guineas.
The MV Vase: 2—Helenus (2002); Alfa (1996).
Victoria Derby: 16—Helenus (2002); Mahogany (1993); Red Anchor (1984); Grosvenor (1982); Sovereign Red (1980); Coppelius (1962); Tulloch (1957); Hydrogen (1951); Great Britain (1942); Lucrative (1940); Theo (1934); Liberal (1932); Rampion (1926); Eusebius (1918); Lady Wallace (1905); Wallace (1895). Note: Lady Wallace (1905) is the only filly to take the double against the colts and geldings.
VRC Oaks: 4—Surround (1976); Lady Sybil (1960); Lady Wallace (1905); Sweet Nell (1903).
Caulfield Cup: 4—Sobar (1972); Yangtze (1964); Tulloch (1957); Sweet Nell (1903). Note: Sweet Nell (1903) is the only filly to complete the double.
Cox Plate: 4—Red Anchor (1984); Surround (1976); Rajah Sahib (1968); Star Affair (1965).
Melbourne Cup: 2—Artilleryman (1919); Patrobas (1915).
Leading winning jockeys:
3 wins Scobie Breasley (Phoibus 1948, Royal Gem 1945, Kintore 1944); Tom Hales (Rudolph 1889, Volley 1888, Carlyon 1887); Roy Higgins (Luskin Star 1977, Star Affair 1965, Lady Sybil 1960); George Lambert (Ettefred 1916, Andelosia 1913, Burrawang 1912); Bobby Lewis (Thrice 1917, Booran 1906, Sweet Nell 1903); Maurice McCarten (Lucrative 1940, Ajax 1937, Ammon Ra 1931); George Moore (Tulloch 1957, King Brian 1961, Time And Tide 1963); Ashley Reed (Young Idea 1935, Green Wave 1930, Balmerino 1928); Brent Thomson (Vitalic 1988; Marwong 1987; Beechcraft 1983).
Current winning jockeys:
2 wins Dwayne Dunn (Divine Prophet 2016, All Too Hard 2012); Kerrin McEvoy (Long John 2013, Helmet 2011); Luke Nolen (Anacheeva 2010, Wonderful World 2006).
1 win Glen Boss (God's Own 2005); Hugh Bowman (Press Statement 2015); Noel Callow (In Top Swing 2003); James McDonald (Shooting To Win 2014); Damien Oliver (Centro 1990); Brad Rawiller (Weekend Hussler 2007); Michael Rodd (Whobegotyou 2008); Michael Walker (Mighty Boss 2017).
Leading winning trainers:
5 wins Bart Cummings (Wonderful World 2007; God's Own 2006; Alfa 1996; Kenmark 1974; Storm Queen 1966); Geoff Murphy (Marwong 1987, Grosvenor 1982, Sovereign Red 1980, Surround 1976, Beau Sovereign 1971).
4 wins Tom Payten (Autonomy 1892, Rudolph 1889, Valley 1888, Carlyon 1887); James Scobie (Thrice 1917, Demas 1904, Sweet Nell 1903, Annesley 1890).
Current winning trainers:
3 wins John Hawkes (Divine Prophet 2016, All Too Hard 2012, Lonhro 2001); Peter Snowden (Shooting To Win 2014, Long John 2013, Helmet 2011).
2 wins Leon Corstens (Starspangledbanner 2009, Helenus 2002); Lee Freedman (Mahogany 1993, Centro 1990); Michael, Wayne & John Hawkes (Divine Prophet 2016, All Too Hard 2012); David Hayes (St. Covet 1994, Palace Reign 1992).

1 win Les Bridge (Drawn 1985); Clarry Conners (Encounter 1997); Mark Kavanagh (Whobegotyou 2008); Noel Mayfield-Smith (In Top Swing 2003); Mick Price (Mighty Boss 2017); Graeme Rogerson (Econsul 2004); Grant Searle (Our Maizcay 1995); Peter & Paul Snowden (Shooting To Win 2014); Chris Waller (Press Statement 2015).

Points of interest:

Skalato was first past the post in 2000, but he was later disqualified after returning a positive swab. The race was awarded to Show A Heart.

Marwong (1987) won on protest from Our Poetic Prince. In 1979, Runaway Kid won on protest from Bold Diplomat. Royal Gem and Attley dead-heated for first in 1945.

Redoute's Choice (1999) is the sire of winner God's Own (2005); Beau Sovereign (1977), sire of Palace Reign (1992); Vain (1969), sire of Kenmark (1974); Heroic (1924), sire of Nuffield (1938) and Ajax (1937); Wallace (1895), sire of Patrobas (1915), Lady Wallace (1905) and Kinglike (1900); Bobadil (1898) sire of Blague (1914) and Danaus (1910).

Starspangledbanner (2009) won the 2010 G1 Golden Jubilee Stakes (1200m) at Royal Ascot and the 2010 G1 July Cup (1200m) at Newmarket when trained by Irishman Aidan O'Brien.

Champion jockey Scobie Breasley was suspended for a month for easing the favourite Chanak down in the shadows of the post in 1947, only to be caught on the line by 33/1 chance Hororata (Billy Briscoe).

MRC Thousand Guineas (1600m)—Caulfield
Of $500,000. Group 1. Set Weights, 3YO Fillies. October 13, 2018.

2017-18 RESULT: Time: 1:36.27 (Good 3)

FP	NO	HORSE	TRAINER	JOCKEY	MARGIN	BAR.	WGT	SP
1	5	ALOISIA	Aaron Purcell	Luke Nolen		1	55.5kg	$14
2	1	SHOALS	Anthony Freedman	Mark Zahra	1.25L	4	55.5kg	$4.40
3	2	ALIZEE	James Cummings	Glyn Schofield	2L	2	55.5kg	$2.15f
4	8	SHE'S SO HIGH	Mick Price	Damien Oliver	5.75L	5	55.5kg	$18
5	7	MINTHA	Tony McEvoy	Luke Currie	6.15L	6	55.5kg	$31
6	3	BOOKER	Mathew Ellerton & Simon Zahra	Dwayne Dunn	9.9L	8	55.5kg	$7
7	4	PURE SCOT	David & Ben Hayes & Tom Dabernig	Ben Melham	10.1L	3	55.5kg	$26
8	6	LEATHER'N'LACE	Darren Weir	Damian Lane	12.6L	7	55.5kg	$15

PAST WINNERS

YEAR	WINNER	JOCKEY	TRAINER	2ND	3RD	TIME
2017	Aloisia	Luke Nolen	Aaron Purcell	Shoals	Alizee	1:36.2
2016	Global Glamour	Kerrin McEvoy	Gai Waterhouse & Adrian Bott	I Am A Star	Whispering Brook	1:36.8
2015	Stay With Me	Dwayne Dunn	David Hayes & Tom Dabernig	Jameka	Badawiya	1:35.8
2014	Amicus	Hugh Bowman	Chris Waller	Traveston Girl	Sabatini	1:36.4
2013	Guelph	Kerrin McEvoy	Peter Snowden	May's Dream	Gregers	1:37.7
2012	Commanding Jewel	Damien Oliver	Leon Corstens	Dear Demi	Zydeco	1:37.1
2011	Atlantic Jewel	Michael Rodd	Mark Kavanagh	Mosheen	Sharnee Rose	1:35.8
2010	Yosei	Michelle Payne	Stuart Webb	Heartsareforlove	Brazilian Pulse	1:39.8
2009	Irish Lights	Glen Boss	David Hayes	Melito	Faint Perfume	1:38.8
2008	Gallica	Damien Oliver	Mick Price	Cats Whisker	Glowlamp	1:38.6
2007	Serious Speed	Danny Nikolic	Leon Macdonald	Extension of Time	Antarctic Miss	1:36.3
2006	Miss Finland	Craig Williams	David Hayes	Permaiscuous	Cheeky Choice	1:37.2
2005	Mnemosyne	Darren Beadman	John Hawkes	Rewaaya	Serenade Rose	1:36.3
2004	Alinghi	Damien Oliver	Lee Freedman	Hollow Bullet	Ballet Society	1:37.1
2003	Special Harmony	Damien Oliver	Lee Freedman	Hinting	Spurcent	1:36.4
2002	Macedon Lady	Steven King	John Symons	La Bella Dama	Fuji Dancer	1:36.4
2001	Magical Miss	Steven Arnold	Bart Cummings	Ha Ha	Li Lo Lill	1:37.0
2000	All Time High	Steven Arnold	Russell Cameron	Ponton Flyer	Tanith	1:36.3
1999	Shizu	Jim Cassidy	Michael Moroney	Danglissa	Beat The Fade	1:39.4
1998	Inaflury	Darren Gauci	Colin Alderson	Danelagh	St. Clemens Belle	1:38.3
1997	Lady Of The Pines	Darren Beadman	Peter C Hayes	Rose Of Danehill	Regal Sashay	1:35.9

BACKGROUND

First run: 1946 (Sweet Chime). Group 1 since 1979. Moved from Wednesday—middle of the Caulfield Carnival—to the first Saturday in 2014.
Fastest time (1600m): Arborea (1993) 1:35.60
Notable winners: Global Glamour (2016); Guelph (2013); Atlantic Jewel (2011); Miss Finland (2006); Alinghi (2004); Special Harmony (2003); Northwood Plume (1994); Richfield Lady (1991); Riverina Charm (1988); Rom's Stiletto (1982); Toy Show (1975); Toltrice (1972); Begonia Belle (1967); Cendrillon (1966); Gipsy Queen (1965); Indian Summer (1961); Wenona Girl (1960); But Beautiful (1958); True Course (1950); Chicquita (1949); Siren Song (1948); Nizam's Ring (1948); Sweet Chime (1946).
Thousand Guineas winners won the lead-up races:
Furious Stakes: 3—Mnemosyne (2005); Dashing Eagle (1996); Tristanagh (1989).
Tea Rose Stakes: 4—Guelph (2013); Mnemosyne (2005); Whisked (1990); Tristanagh (1989).
Flight Stakes: 6—Global Glamour (2016); Guelph (2013); Dashing Eagle (1996); Wenona Girl (1960); Brimses (1955); Nizam's Ring (1947).
Atlantic Jewel Stakes (new race 2015, 1200m at Caulfield): 1—Stay With Me (2015).
Edward Manifold Stakes: 14—Gallica (2008); Alinghi (2004); Special Harmony (2003), Inaflury (1998); Azzurro (1992); Richfield Lady (1991); Riverina Charm (1988); Princess Talaria (1977); Gipsy Queen (1965); Indian Summer (1961); Chicquita (1949); Goldenway (1957); Bendrum (1956); Siren Song (1948).
Tranquil Star Stakes (Guineas Prelude): 3—Irish Lights (2009); Miss Finland (2006); Bianco Flyer (1987).
Thousand Guineas winners went on to win in the same preparation:

Wakeful Stakes: 13—Atlantic Jewel (2011); Arborea (1993); Richfield Lady (1991); Tristanagh (1989); Brava Jeannie (1979); Just Topic (1973); Toltrice (1972); Indian Summer (1961); Wenona Girl (1960); True Course (1950); Chicquita (1949); Nizam's Ring (1947); Sweet Chime (1946).

VRC Oaks: 17—Miss Finland (2006); Special Harmony (2003); Magical Miss (2001); Northwood Plume (1994); Arborea (1993); Richfield Lady (1991); Tristanagh (1989); Toltrice (1972); Rom's Stiletto (1982); Brava Jeannie (1979); Gipsy Queen (1965); Indian Summer (1961); Lady Mogambo (1954); True Course (1950); Chicquita (1949); Nizam's Ring (1947); Sweet Chime (1946).

Wakeful Stakes & VRC Oaks: 10—Arborea (1993); Richfield Lady (1991); Tristanagh (1989); Brava Jeannie (1979); Toltrice (1972); Indian Summer (1961); True Course (1950); Chicquita (1949); Nizam's Ring (1947); Sweet Chime (1946).

Edward Manifold & VRC Oaks: 3—Richfield Lady (1991); Indian Summer (1961); Chicquita (1949).

Edward Manifold, Wakeful Stakes & VRC Oaks: 3—Richfield Lady (1991); Indian Summer (1961); Chicquita (1949).

Leading winning jockeys:
5 wins Damien Oliver (Commanding Jewel 2012, Gallica 2008; Alinghi 2004; Special Harmony 2003; Azzurro 1992).
3 wins Darren Beadman (Mnemosyne 2005; Lady Of The Pines 1997; Dashing Eagle 1996); Jim Cassidy (Shizu 1999; Tristanagh 1989; Magic Flute 1986); Pat Hyland (Rom's Stiletto 1982, What's The Verdict 1971, Begonia Belle 1967); Darren Gauci (Inaflury 1998; Shame 1995; Riverina Charm 1988); Bill Williamson (Goldenway 1957, Bendrum 1956, True Course 1950).

Current winning jockeys:
5 wins Damien Oliver (Commanding Jewel 2012, Gallica 2008; Alinghi 2004; Special Harmony 2003; Azzurro 1992).
2 wins Steven Arnold (Magical Miss 2001, All Time High 2000); Kerrin McEvoy (Global Glamour 2016, Guelph 2013).
1 win Glen Boss (Irish Lights 2009); Hugh Bowman (Amicus 2014); Dwayne Dunn (Stay With Me 2015); Luke Nolen (Aloisia 2017); Michelle Payne (Yosei 2010); Michael Rodd (Atlantic Jewel 2011); Craig Williams (Miss Finland 2006).

Leading winning trainers:
5 wins Bart Cummings (Magical Miss 2001; Dashing Eagle 1996; Richfield Lady 1991; Tristanagh 1989; Anna Rose 1963); Tommy Smith (Shankhill Lass 1985, Copperama 1981, Princess Talaria 1977, Toy Show 1975, Regal Peace 1962).
4 wins Lee Freedman (Alinghi 2004 Special Harmony 2003, Northwood Plume 1994, Azzurro 1992).

Current winning trainers:
4 wins Lee Freedman (Alinghi 2004 Special Harmony 2003, Northwood Plume 1994, Azzurro 1992).
3 wins John Hawkes (Mnemosyne 2005, Shame 1995, Toltrice 1972); David Hayes (Stay With Me 2015, Irish Lights 2009, Miss Finland 2006).
1 win Russell Cameron (All Time High 2000); Clarry Conners (Arborea 1993); Leon Corstens (Commanding Jewel 2012); David Hayes & Tom Dabernig (Stay With Me 2015); Mark Kavanagh (Atlantic Jewel 2011); Robbie Laing (Perfect Bliss 1983); Leon Macdonald (Serious Speed 2007); Michael Moroney (Shizu 1999); Mick Price (Gallica 2008); Aaron Purcell (Aloisia 2017); Peter Snowden (Guelph 2013); John Symons (Macedon Lady 2002); Chris Waller (Amicus 2014); Gai Waterhouse & Adrian Bott (Global Glamour 2016); Stuart Webb (Yosei 2010).

Points of interest:
Anna Rose & Heirloom dead-heated in 1963.
Miss Finland (2006) and Toy Show (1975) are the only two Golden Slipper winners to also win a Thousand Guineas.
Charlie Waymouth rode Chicquita to win in 1949, and trained Bendrum to win in 1956.
Commanding Jewel (2012), by Commands from Regard (by Zabeel), is a three-quarter sister to Atlantic Jewel (2011), by Fastnet Rock from Regard.
Golden Chariot (1951) is the dam of Wenona Girl (1960); Miss Finland (2006) is the dam of Stay With Me (2015).

MRC Toorak Handicap (1600m)—Caulfield
Of $500,000. Group 1. Handicap, Minimum Weight 52kg. October 13, 2018.

2017-18 RESULT: Time: 1:35.86   (Good 3)

FP	NO	HORSE	TRAINER	JOCKEY	MARGIN	BAR.	WGT	SP
1	1	TOSEN STARDOM	Darren Weir	Damian Lane		16	57.5kg	$10
2	14	SOVEREIGN NATION	David & Ben Hayes & Tom Dabernig	Beau Mertens	1L	17	52kg	$21
3	16	PETROLOGY	David & Ben Hayes & Tom Dabernig	Chris Parnham	2L	13	52kg	$101
4	19	MASK OF TIME	Hugo Palmer	Daniel Moor	2.2L	1	52kg	$91
5	3	SEABURGE	David & Ben Hayes & Tom Dabernig	Mark Zahra	2.3L	12	55kg	$81
6	4	TOM MELBOURNE	Chris Waller	Glen Boss	2.6L	15	55kg	$8.50
7	9	EGG TART	Chris Waller	Damien Oliver	3.1L	9	53.5kg	$5.50f
8	7	TURNITAROUND	Matthew Williams	Ben Thompson	3.3L	?	54.5kg	$51
9	17	JACQUINOT BAY	David & Ben Hayes & Tom Dabernig	Ben Allen (a)	3.4L	11	52kg	$41
10	18	WYNDSPELLE	Michael Kent	Nikita Beriman	4.4L	7	52kg	$26
11	11	OMEI SWORD	Chris Waller	Stephen Baster	4.5L	5	52kg	$14
12	10	MR SNEAKY	Anthony Freedman	Dean Yendall	4.8L	8	52.5kg	$6
13	5	HE OR SHE	David & Ben Hayes & Tom Dabernig	Dwayne Dunn	5L	18	54.5kg	$101
14	12	SNITZSON	David & Ben Hayes & Tom Dabernig	Cory Parish	5.1L	10	52kg	$31
15	8	COMIN' THROUGH	Chris Waller	Michael Walker	7.85L	4	53.5kg	$9
16	2	KASPERSKY	Jane Chapple-Hyam	Luke Nolen	7.95L	3	56kg	$31
17	15	THEANSWERMYFRIEND	Robert Smerdon	Michael Dee	11.2L	6	52kg	$7
18	6	I AM A STAR	Shane Nichols	Ben Melham	12.45L	14	54.5kg	$20

PAST WINNERS

YEAR	WINNER	JOCKEY	TRAINER	2ND	3RD	TIME
2017	Tosen Stardom	Damian Lane	Darren Weir	Sovereign Nation	Petrology	1:35.8
2016	He's Our Rokkii	Dwayne Dunn	David & Ben Hayes & Tom Dabernig	Great Esteem	Tivaci	1:36.1
2015	Lucky Hussler	Glen Boss	Darren Weir	Disposition	Stratum Star	1:34.5
2014	Trust In A Gust	Brad Rawiller	Darren Weir	Speediness	Desert Jeuney	1:35.2
2013	Solzhenitsyn	Nash Rawiller	Robert Heathcote	Trevieres	Blackie	1:36.4
2012	Solzhenitsyn	Corey Brown	Robert Heathcote	Spirit Song	Yosei	1:35.2
2011	King Mufhasa	Michael Rodd	Stephen McKee	King's Rose	Luen Yat Forever	1:36.2
2010	More Joyous	Nash Rawiller	Gai Waterhouse	We're Gonna Rock	Poor Judge	1:36.4
2009	Allez Wonder	Michelle Payne	Bart Cummings	Gold Salute	Rock Kingdom	1:35.0
2008	Alamosa	Craig Newitt	Mick Price	Rockwood	Pillar of Hercules	1:36.9
2007	Divine Madonna	Michael Rodd	Mark Kavanagh	Niconero	Wonderful World	1.37.3
2006	Red Dazzler	Jim Cassidy	Mick Price	Rewaaya	Niconero	1.37.5
2005	Barely A Moment	Craig Williams	David Hayes	Super Kid	Calveen	1.37.9
2004	Regal Roller	Mark Flaherty	Clinton McDonald	Osca Warrior	Infinite Grace	1.37.4
2003	Roman Arch	Luke Currie	Mick Whittle	Fields Of Omagh	Umrum	1.36.0
2002	Shot Of Thunder	Glen Boss	John O'Shea	Umrum	Pernod	1.36.1
2001	Show A Heart	Glen Boss	Barry Miller	La Zagaletta	Shot Of Thunder	1.35.8
2000	Umrum	Jim Cassidy	Leon Macdonald	Go Flash Go	Crawl	1.36.4
1999	Umrum	Eddie Wilkinson	Leon Macdonald	Nina Haraka	Go Flash Go	1.36.0
1998	Marble Halls	Jim Cassidy	Lee Freedman	Rustic Dream	Umrum	1.38.2
1997	Penghulu	Greg Childs	Peter C Hayes	Catalan Opening	Ravarda	1.35.2

BACKGROUND

First run: 1881 (won by Josephine). Group 1 since 1979. Run over 1700m 1931-35; 1800m 1891. Run at Flemington 1940-43. Run in two division in 1943.
Most recent mare to win: More Joyous (2010). Note: 10 mares have won in the past 44 years.
Most recent 3YO to win: C&G—K. Cid (1932); No filly has won. Seven 3YOs have won the Toorak.

Multiple winners: 5—Solzhenitsyn (2013, 2012); Umrum (2000, 1999); Nicopolis (1964, 1963); Desert Breeze (1953, 1952); Saxony (1949, 1948).

Fastest time (1600m): Allez Wonder (2009) 1:35.09.

Notable winners: King Mufhasa (2011), More Joyous (2010); Alamosa (2008); Roman Arch (2003); Show A Heart (2001); Umrum (1999 & 2000); Cole Diesel (1989); Canny Lass (1986); Magari (1982); Plush (1975); Leilani (1974); All Shot (1972); Gunsynd (1971); Tauto (1970); Tried And True (1968); Tobin Bronze 1967; Galilee (1966); Nicopolis (1964, 1963); Royal Gem (1946); The Trump (1937); Highland (1929).

Toorak Handicap winners won the lead-up races:
George Main Stakes: 1—More Joyous (2010)
Sir Rupert Clarke Stakes: 9—Trust In A Gust (2014); Barely A Moment (2005); Regal Roller (2004); Canny Lass (1986); Magari (1982); Torbek (1980); Tauto (1970); Anonyme (1961); Jovial Lad (1951).
Epsom Handicap: 3—Golden Sword (1993); Gunsynd (1971); Metellus (1925).

Toorak Handicap winners went on to win in the same preparation:
Caulfield Cup: 9—Cole Diesel (1989); Leilani (1974); Tobin Bronze (1967); Galilee (1966); Grey Boots (1950); Royal Gem (1946); The Trump (1937); Textile (1927); Uncle Sam (1912). Note: Leilani (1974) is the only mare to complete the double.
Cox Plate: 1—Tobin Bronze (1967).
Cantala Stakes: 4—Magari (1982); All Shot (1972); Gunsynd (1971); Burberry (1943); Gold Salute (1940).
Sir Rupert Clarke Stakes & Cantala Stakes: 1—Magari (1982).
Emirates (Mackinnon) Stakes: 3—Tosen Stardom (2017); Leilani (1974); The Trump (1937)

Leading winning jockey:
7 wins Reg Heather (Plato 1954, Desert Breeze 1953, Jovial Lad 1951, Grey Boots 1950, Don Pedro 1947, Royal Gem 1946, Burberry 1943).
4 wins Jim Cassidy (Red Dazzler 2006, Umrum 2000, Marble Halls 1998; Comrade 1991); Roy Higgins (Leilani 1974, All Shot 1972, Gunsynd 1971, Gabonia 1960).
3 wins Glen Boss (Lucky Hussler 2015, Shot Of Thunder 2002, Show A Heart 2001); Bill Duncan (Highland 1929, Kalloni 1928, Metellus 1925); Roy Higgins (All Shot 1972, Gunsynd 1971, Gabonia 1960); Ted Sullivan (Abdera 1926, Stare 1921, Miss Meadows 1915).

Leading current jockeys:
3 wins Glen Boss (Lucky Hussler 2015, Shot Of Thunder 2002, Show A Heart 2001).
2 wins Nash Rawiller (Solzhenitsyn 2013, More Joyous 2010) Michael Rodd (King Mufhasa 2011; Divine Madonna 2007).
1 win Corey Brown (Solzhenitsyn 2012); Luke Currie (Roman Arch 2003); Dwayne Dunn (He's Our Rokkii 2016); Michelle Payne (Allez Wonder 2009); Brett Prebble (Sober Suit 1995); Brad Rawiller (Trust In A Gust 2014); Craig Williams (Barely A Moment 2005).

Leading winning trainers:
3 wins Bart Cummings (Allez Wonder 2009; Leilani 1974, Galilee 1966); Ike Foulsham (Iolaire 1906, Massinissa 1898, Verdure 1882); Walter Hickenbotham (Miss Meadows 1915, True Scot 1907, Mostyn 1895); Jack Holt (Highland 1929, Metellus 1925, Sonora 1923); Darren Weir (Tosen Stardom 2017, Lucky Hussler 2015, Trust In A Gust 2014).

Current winning trainers:
3 wins Darren Weir (Tosen Stardom 2017, Lucky Hussler 2015, Trust In A Gust 2014).
2 wins David Hayes (He's Our Rokkii 2016, Barely A Moment 2005); Rob Heathcote (Solzhenitsyn 2013, 2012); Leon Macdonald (Umrum 2000, 1999); John Meagher (Golden Sword 1993, Ready To Expode 1992).
1 win David & Ben Hayes & Tom Dabernig (He's Our Rokkii 2016); Clinton McDonald (Regal Roller 2004); Peter McGregor (Ricochet Rose 1990); Stephen McKee (King Mufhasa 2011); John O'Shea (Shot Of Thunder 2002); Mick Price (Red Dazzler 2006); Gerald Ryan (Sober Suit 1995); Wayne Walters (Torbek 1980); Gai Waterhouse (More Joyous 2010).

Points of interest:
Galilee is the only horse to win a Toorak Handicap and Melbourne Cup. He did it in the same year, 1966.
Regal Roller (2004) won the Liston Stakes, Memsie Stakes and Sir Rupert Clarke Stakes before winning the Toorak Handicap.
Dead-heats: El Golea & Ena (1938); Journal & Epigram (1935).

MRC Caulfield Stakes (2000m)—Caulfield
Of $1,000,000. Group 1. Weight For Age, 3YO&Up. October 13, 2018.

2016-17 RESULT: Time: 2:03.42   (Good 3)

FP	NO	HORSE	TRAINER	JOCKEY	MARGIN	BAR.	WGT	SP
1	2	GAILO CHOP	Darren Weir	Mark Zahra		5	59kg	$5.50
2	3	JOHANNES VERMEER	Aidan O'Brien	Katelyn Mallyon	0.2L	6	59kg	$31
3	6	JON SNOW	Murray Baker & Andrew Forsman	Stephen Baster	2.7L	9	58kg	$8.50
4	8	SINGLE GAZE	Nick Olive	Kathy O'Hara	2.8L	1	57kg	$21
5	7	INFERENCE	Michael, Wayne & John Hawkes	Dwayne Dunn	4.05L	3	58kg	$21
6	11	BONNEVAL	Murray Baker & Andrew Forsman	Damian Lane	4.15L	11	56kg	$3.70f
7	4	RIVEN LIGHT	William Mullins	Glen Boss	4.65L	4	59kg	$21
8	9	ABBEY MARIE	Michael Kent	Beau Mertens	4.75L	10	57kg	$26
9	1	HARTNELL	James Cummings	Glyn Schofield	6L	7	59kg	$4.20
10	10	THE TAJ MAHAL	Aidan O'Brien	Damien Oliver	8L	2	56.5kg	$10
11	5	CALDERON	Tony McEvoy	Luke Currie	11L	8	59kg	$51

PAST WINNERS

YEAR	WINNER	JOCKEY	TRAINER	2ND	3RD	TIME
2017	Gailo Chop	Mark Zahra	Darren Weir	Johannes Vermeer	Jon Snow	2:02.1
2016	Winx	Hugh Bowman	Chris Waller	Black Heart Bart	He or She	2:03.4
2015	Criterion	Michael Walker	David Hayes & Tom Dabernig	Happy Trails	Mongolian Khan	2:02.0
2014	Fawkner	Nicholas Hall	Robert Hickmott	Criterion	Side Glance	2:01.6
2013	Atlantic Jewel	Michael Rodd	Mark Kavanagh	Foreteller	Super Cool	2:02.9
2012	Ocean Park	Glen Boss	Gary Hennessy	Alcopop	Sincero	2:04.7
2011	Descarado	Nash Rawiller	Gai Waterhouse	Avienus	Lights of Heaven	2:02.5
2010	So You Think	Steven Arnold	Bart Cummings	Alcopop	Whobegotyou	2:02.4
2009	Whobegotyou	Damien Oliver	Mark Kavanagh	Heart Of Dreams	Vision And Power	2:01.5
2008	Douro Valley	James Winks	Danny O'Brien	Pompeii Ruler	Guillotine	2:04.3
2007	Maldivian	Michael Rodd	Mark Kavanagh	Miss Finland	Anamato	2:01.9
2006	Casual Pass	Nash Rawiller	Mathew Ellerton	Pompeii Ruler	El Segundo	2:02.6
2005	El Segundo	Darren Gauci	Colin Little	Fields Of Omagh	Confectioner	2:04.8
2004	Mummify	Danny Nikolic	Lee Freedman	Grand Armee	Starcraft	2:03.2
2003	Lonhro	Darren Beadman	John Hawkes	Mummify	Defier	2:02.3
2002	Lonhro	Darren Beadman	John Hawkes	Sunline	Ustinov	2:00.6
2001	Northerly	Damien Oliver	Fred Kersley	Shogun Lodge	Ethereal	2:02.5
2000	Sky Heights	Glen Boss	Colin Alderson	Shogun Lodge	Tie The Knot	2:03.6
1999	Northern Drake	Grant Cooksley	Manfred Man	Tie The Knot	Aerosmith	2:02.1
1998	Might and Power	Jim Cassidy	Jack Denham	Tycoon Lil	Gold Guru	2:03.5
1997	Filante	Jim Cassidy	Jack Denham	Alfa	Tampir Lane	2:02.7

BACKGROUND
First run: 1886 (won by Isonomy). Group 1 since 1979. Run over 1800m 1886-1967 except for 1887 & 1888 when 2000m; Returned to 2000m in 1968. Previously known as the Yalumba Stakes. Registered name Caulfield Stakes.
Most recent mare to win: Winx (2016).
Most recent 3YO to win: C&G—Mighty Kingdom (1979); No 3YO filly has won.
Multiple winners: 10—Lonhro (2003, 2002); Kingston Town (1982, 1981); Winfreux (1967, 1966, 1965); Sky High (1962, 1961); Lord (1960, 1959, 1958); Lawrence (1945, 1944); High Caste (1940, 1939); Eurythmic (1922, 1921, 1920); Artillerie (1910, 1909); Wakeful (1902, 1901).
Fastest time (2000m): Shaftesbury Avenue (1991) 1:59.30
Notable winners: Winx (2016); Criterion (2015); Fawkner (2014); Atlantic Jewel (2013); So You Think (2010); Lonhro (2003, 2002); Northerly (2001); Might And Power (1998); Rough Habit (1994); Naturalism (1993); Bonecrusher (1986); Kingston Town (1982, 1981); Family Of Man (1977); Gunsynd (1972); Winfreux (1967, 1966, 1965); Sky High (1962, 1961); Lord (1960, 1959, 1958); Redcraze (1956); Rising Fast (1954); Comic Court (1950); Bernborough (1946); Tranquil Star (1942); Ajax (1938); Hall Mark (1934); Chatham (1933); Amounis (1930); Manfred (1926); Heroic (1925); Eurythmic (1922, 1921, 1920); Wakeful (1902, 1901).
Caulfield Stakes winners won the lead-up races:

Memsie Stakes: 17—Atlantic Jewel (2013); So You Think (2010); Lord (1960, 1959, 1958); Peshawar (1952); Comic Court (1950); Lawrence (1944); Ajax (1938); Royal Charter (1927); Heroic (1925); Maid Of The Mist (1923); Eurythmic (1922, 1921, 1920); Traquette (1915); Pink 'Un (1908).
Makybe Diva Stakes: 3—Whobegotyou (2009); How Now (1976); Gay Poss (1970).
Dato Tan Chin Nam Stakes: 3—Northerly (2001); Winfreux (1965); Rising Fast (1954).
George Main Stakes: 6—Winx (2016); Lonhro (2003); Juggler (1996); Kingston Town (1982, 1981); De La Salle (1948).
Underwood Stakes: 13—Ocean Park (2012); So You Think (2010); Northerly (2001); Bonecrusher (1986); Tristarc (1985); How Now (1976); Gay Icarus (1971); Comtempler (1964); Lord (1958, 1960); Ajax (1938); Hall Mark (1934); Royal Charter (1927).
JRA Cup: 2—Maldivian (2007); El Segundo (2005).
Turnbull Stakes (since 1948): 4—Arctic Symbol (1970); Sometime (1963); Rising Fast (1954); Comic Court (1950). Note: Since 1948 no horse has won the Underwood Stakes, Turnbull Stakes and Caulfield Stakes in the same season.

Caulfield Stakes winners went on to win in the same preparation:
Caulfield Cup: 14—Sydeston (1990); Tristarc (1985); Mighty Kingdom (1979); How Now (1976); Gay Icarus (1971); Sometime (1963); Redcraze (1956); Rising Fast (1954); Peshawar (1952); Columnist (1947); Tranquil Star (1942); Amounis (1930); Manfred (1926); Eurythmic (1920).
Cox Plate: 16—Winx (2016); Ocean Park (2012); So You Think (2010); Northerly (2001); Might And Power (1998); Almaarad (1989); Bonecrusher (1986); Kingston Town (1982, 1981); Family Of Man (1977); Gunsynd (1972); Rising Fast (1954); Amana (1943); Tranquil Star (1942); Ajax (1938); Young Idea (1936). Note: Tranquil Star (1942) is the only mare to complete the double.
Caulfield Cup & Cox Plate: 2—Rising Fast (1954); Tranquil Star (1942).
Melbourne Cup: 3—Rising Fast (1954); Comic Court (1950); Mentor (1888).
Mackinnon Stakes: 22—So Yo Think (2010); Lonhro (2002); Winfreux (1967); Sky High (1961); Rising Fast (1954); Comic Court (1950); Amana (1943); Tranquil Star (1942); Ajax (1938); Gothic (1928); Manfred (1926); Eurythmic (1921, 1920); Magpie (1918); Lavendo (1916); Traquette (1915); Solution (1906); Gladsome (1904); Wakeful (1902, 1901); Marvel (1891); Isonomy (1886).
Caulfield Cup, Cox Plate & Melbourne Cup: 1—Rising Fast (1954). Note: Rising Fast also won the Turnbull Stakes, Mackinnon Stakes and Queen Elizabeth Stakes in an unparalleled 1954 spring campaign.

Leading winning jockeys:
4 wins Frank Dempsey (Hall Mark 1934, Eurythmic 1922, 1921, 1920); Jim Johnson (Comtempler 1964, Winfreux 1965, 1966, 1967); Damien Oliver (Whobegotyou 2009, Northerly 2001, Danewin 1995, Naturalism 1993).

Current winning jockeys:
4 wins Damien Oliver (Whobegotyou 2009, Northerly 2001, Danewin 1995, Naturalism 1993).
2 wins Glen Boss (Ocean Park 2012, Sky Heights 2000); Nash Rawiller (Descarado 2011, Casual Pass 2006); Michael Rodd (Atlantic Jewel 2013, Maldivian 2007).
1 win Steven Arnold (So You Think 2010); Hugh Bowman (Winx 2016); Grant Cooksley (Northern Drake 1999); Nicholas Hall (Fawkner 2014); Michael Walker (Criterion 2015); James Winks (Douro Valley 2008); Mark Zahra (Gailo Chop 2017).

Leading winning trainers:
8 wins Jack Holt (Young Idea 1936, Hall Mark 1934, High Syce 1929, Royal Charter 1927, Heroic 1925, Eurythmic 1922, 1921, 1920); Tommy Smith (Alibhai 1984, Kingston Town 1982, 1981, Mighty Kingdom 1979, Zambari 1975, Igloo 1974, Gunsynd 1972, Redcraze 1956).
7 wins Lou Robertson (Iron Duke 1949, Lawrence 1945, 1944, Feldspar 1935, Cimbrian 1931, Gothic 1928, Lavendo 1916).
6 wins Bart Cummings (So You Think 2010, Shaftesbury Avenue 1991, Sky Chase 1988, Hyperno 1980, Lloyd Boy 1978, Gay Poss 1970).

Current winning trainers:
3 wins Mark Kavanagh (Atlantic Jewel 2013, Whobegotyou 2009, Maldivian 2007).
2 wins John Hawkes (Lonhro 2003, 2002); Gai Waterhouse (Descarado 2011, Juggler 1996).
1 win Paddy Busuttin (Castletown 1992); Mat Ellerton (Casual Pass 2006); David Hayes & Tom Dabernig (Criterion 2015); Gary Hennessy (Ocean Park 2012); Robert Hickmott (Fawkner 2014); Colin Little (El Segundo 2005); Fred Kersley (Northerly 2001); John Meagher (Drought 1987); Danny O'Brien (Douro Valley 2008); Frank Ritchie (Bonecrusher 1986); Chris Waller (Winx 2016); Darren Weir (Gailo Chop 2017); John Wheeler (Rough Habit 1994).

Points of interest:
Playboy was first past the post in 1950, but lost on protest to Comic Court. Redding (1994) beat Paris Lane on protest.
Dead heats: Zambari & Guest Star (1975); Arctic Symbol & Gay Poss (1970); Dhaulagiri & Lord (1960).
So You Think (2010) was partially sold to Coolmore Stud late in 2010, and won five G1 races in England and Ireland for trainer Aidan O'Brien. He was retired to stud in June 2012.
Criterion (2015) won the G1 ATC Queen Elizabeth Stakes (2000m, Randwick) in April 2015, and then raced in Hong Kong and England before returning to win the Caulfield Stakes through an "international" preparation through quarantine.

MRC Stella Artois Caulfield Cup (2400m)—Caulfield
Of $5,000,000. Group 1. Handicap, 3YO&Up. October 20, 2018.

2017-18 RESULT: Time: 2:27.66   (Good 3)

FP	NO	HORSE	TRAINER	JOCKEY	MARGIN	BAR.	WGT	SP
1	13	BOOM TIME	David & Ben Hayes & Tom Dabernig	Cory Parish		3	52kg	$51
2	10	SINGLE GAZE	Nick Olive	Kathy O'Hara	1.25L	12	53kg	$31
3	3	JOHANNES VERMEER	Aidan O'Brien	Ben Melham	1.45L	2	54.5kg	$5
4	17	LORD FANDANGO	Archie Alexander	Ben Allen (a)	1.85L	9	50kg	$21
5	1	HUMIDOR	Darren Weir	Damian Lane	2.6L	7	56kg	$6.50
6	2	MARMELO	Hughie Morrison	Hugh Bowman	2.7L	10	55.5kg	$16
6	14	ABBEY MARIE	Michael Kent	Beau Mertens	2.7L	5	51.5kg	$31
8	15	HARLEM	David & Ben Hayes & Tom Dabernig	Chad Schofield	3.45L	1	51.5kg	$9
9	4	JON SNOW	Murray Baker & Andrew Forsman	Stephen Baster	4.7L	6	54.5kg	$13
10	12	HARDHAM	David Brideoake	Craig Newitt	5.2L	8	52.5kg	$81
11	16	AMELIE'S STAR	Darren Weir	Craig Williams	5.3L	13	51kg	$9.50
12	8	WICKLOW BRAVE	William Mullins	Joao Moreira	5.4L	16	54kg	$71
13	7	VENTURA STORM	David & Ben Hayes & Tom Dabernig	Damien Oliver	6.4L	4	54kg	$12
14	11	BONNEVAL	Murray Baker & Andrew Forsman	Kerrin McEvoy	8.15L	14	52.5kg	$8
15	9	INFERENCE	Michael, Wayne & John Hawkes	Dwayne Dunn	8.65L	11	53.5kg	$26
16	5	HE'S OUR ROKKII	David & Ben Hayes & Tom Dabernig	Luke Nolen	15.65L	15	54kg	$101
17	6	SIR ISAAC NEWTON	Robert Hickmott	Katelyn Mallyon	20.15L	17	54kg	$71

PAST WINNERS

YEAR	WINNER	JOCKEY	TRAINER	2ND	3RD	TIME
2017	Boom Time	Cory Parish	David & Ben Hayes & Tom Dabernig	Single Gaze	Johannes Vermeer	2:27.6
2016	Jameka	Nick Hall	Ciaron Maher	Scottish	Exospheric	2:28.8
2015	Mongolian Khan	Opie Bosson	Murray Baker	Trip To Paris	Our Ivanhowe	2:27.7
2014	Admire Rakti	Zac Purton	Tomoyuki Umeda	Rising Romance	Lucia Valentina	2:32.1
2013	Fawkner	Nicholas Hall	Robert Hickmott	Dandino	Dear Demi	2:29.1
2012	Dunaden	Craig Williams	Mikel Delzangles	Alcopop	Lights Of Heaven	2:28.8
2011	Southern Speed	Craig Williams	Leon Macdonald & Andrew Gluyas	Green Moon	Tullamore	2:28.4
2010	Descarado	Chris Munce	Gai Waterhouse	Harris Tweed	Monaco Consul	2:35.6
2009	Viewed	Brad Rawiller	Bart Cummings	Roman Emperor	Vigor	2:29.7
2008	All The Good	Kerrin McEvoy	Saeed Bin Suroor	Nom Du Jeu	Barbaricus	2:27.4
2007	Master O'Reilly	Vlad Duric	Danny O'Brien	Douro Valley	Princess Coup	2.26.1
2006	Tawqeet	Dwayne Dunn	David Hayes	Aqua Damore	Delta Blues	2:27.6
2005	Railings	Greg Childs	John Hawkes	Eye Popper	Mummify	2:27.9
2004	Elvstroem	Nash Rawiller	Tony Vasil	Makybe Diva	Grey Song	2.31.3
2003	Mummify	Danny Nikolic	Lee Freedman	Grey Song	Distinctly Secret	2.25.9
2002	Northerly	Greg Childs	Fred Kersley	Fields Of Omagh	Republic Lass	2.30.3
2001	Ethereal	Scott Seamer	Sheila Laxon	Sky Heights	Celestial Show	2.30.9
2000	Diatribe	Glen Boss	George Hanlon	Kaapstad Way	Fairway	2.25.3
1999	Sky Heights	Grant Cooksley	Colin Alderson	Laebeel	Inaflury	2.30.1
1998	Taufans Melody	Jim Cassidy	Lady Herries	Lisas Game	Tie The Knot	2.30.1
1997	Might And Power	Jim Cassidy	Jack Denham	Doriemus	Catalan Opening	2.26.2

BACKGROUND

First run: 1879 (won by Newminster). The Caulfield Cup was run in the autumn 1879-1881; a second spring Cup was run in 1881 (won by Master Avenel). Run at Flemington 1940-1943.

Mares to win: 22—Jameka (2016): Southern Speed (2011); Ethereal (2001); Arctic Scent (1996); Mannerism (1992); Let's Elope (1991); Imposera (1988); Tristarc (1985); How Now (1976); How Now (1976); Analight (1975); Leilani (1974); Swell Time (1973); Regal Wench (1954); Tranquil Star (1942); Rivette (1939); Maple

(1923); Wynette (1917); Lady Medallist (1911); Sweet Nell (1903); Grace Darling (1885); Blink Bonny (1884).
3YOs to win: 15—Mighty Kingdom (1979); Sobar (1972); Yangtze (1964); Summer Fair (1961); Sir Blink (1958); Tulloch (1957); Palfresco (1935); Whittier (1922); Bronzetti (1917); Poseidon (1906); Sweet Nell (1903); Dewey (1899); Amberite (1897); Waterfall (1895); Little Jack (1882). Note: Sweet Nell (1903) is the only 3YO filly to win.
Multiple winners: 7—Ming Dynasty (1980, 1977); Rising Fast (1955, 1954); Whittier (1925, 1922); Uncle Sam (1914, 1912); Poseidon (1907, 1906); Hymettus (1901, 1898); Paris (1894, 1892).
Fastest time (2400m): Might And Power 2:26.20 (1997).
Caulfield Cup winners and the Derbys & Oaks:
Victoria Derby (as 4YO): 3—Elvstroem (2004); Manfred (1926); Poseidon (1907). Note: Poseidon won (3YO) in 1906.
ATC Australian Derby (as 4YO): 4—Mongolian Khan (2015); Sky Heights (1999); Manfred (1926); Poseidon (1907). Note: Only Sky Heights has won since the Derby moved to the autumn in 1979.
VRC Oaks: 2—Jameka (2016, as 4YO); Sweet Nell (1903). Note: Sweet Nell is the only 3YO filly to win.
ATC Australian Oaks (as 4YOs): 2—How Now (1976); Leilani (1974).
Caulfield Cup winners won the lead-up races:
Naturalism Stakes: 1—Jameka (2016).
Underwood Stakes: 7—Elvstroem (2004); Mummify (2003); Northerly (2002); Tristarc (1985); How Now (1976); Sobar (1972); Gay Icarus (1971).
Turnbull Stakes (since 1948): 8—Elvstroem (2004); Northerly (2002); Sky Heights (1999); Let's Elope (1991); Analight (1975); Leilani (1974); Sometime (1963); Rising Fast (1954).
The Metropolitan: 4—Tawqeet (2006); Railings (2005); Hayai (1983); Redcraze (1956).
Caulfield Stakes: 14—Sydeston (1990); Tristarc (1985); Mighty Kingdom (1979); How Now (1976); Gay Icarus (1971); Sometime (1963); Redcraze (1956); Rising Fast (1954); Peshawar (1952); Columnist (1947); Tranquil Star (1942); Amounis (1930); Manfred (1926); Eurythmic (1920).
Toorak Handicap: 9—Cole Diesel (1989); Leilani (1974); Tobin Bronze (1967); Galilee (1966); Grey Boots (1950); Royal Gem (1946); The Trump (1937); Textile (1927); Uncle Sam (1912). Note: Leilani (1974) is the only mare to complete the double.
Herbert Power Handicap: 6—Master O'Reilly (2007); Beer Street (1970); Rising Fast (1955); My Hero (1953); Poseidon (1907); Marvel Loch (1905).
Caulfield Cup winners went on to win in same preparation:
Cox Plate: 4—Northerly (2002); Tobin Bronze (1967); Rising Fast (1954); Tranquil Star (1942).
Melbourne Cup: 11—Ethereal (2001); Might And Power (1997); Doriemus (1995); Let's Elope (1991); Gurner's Lane (1982); Galilee (1966); Even Stevens (1962); Rising Fast (1954); Rivette (1939); The Trump (1937); Poseidon (1906).
Note: Melbourne Cup (different years): 3—Viewed (CC 2009; MC 2008); Rising Fast (CC 1955, MC 1954); Skipton (CC 1943, MC 1941).
Caulfield Cup, Cox Plate & Melbourne Cup (same year): 1—Rising Fast (1954).
Northern Hemisphere-trained starters:

YEAR	HORSE	COUNTRY	TRAINER	JOCKEY	PLACINGS
2017	Johannes Vermeer	IRE	Aidan O'Brien	Ben Melham	3rd
	Marmelo	UK	Hughie Morrison	Hugh Bowman	6th
	Wicklow Brave	IRE	Willie Mullins	Joao Moreira	12th
2016	Scottish	UK	Charlie Appleby	Kerrin McEvoy	2nd
	Sir Isaac Newton	IRE	Aidan O'Brien	Colm O'Donoghue	7th
	Articus	GER	Andreas Wohler	Zac Purton	13th
2015	Trip To Paris	UK	Ed Dunlop	Tom Berry	2nd
	Snow Sky	UK	Sir Michael Stoute	Damien Oliver	5th
	Fame Game	JPN	Yoshitada Manukata	Zac Purton	6th
	Hokko Brave	JPN	Yasutoshi Matsunaga	Craig Williams	10th
2014	Admire Rakti	JPN	Tomoyuki Umeda	Zac Purton	1st
	Seismos	IRE	Marco Botti	Craig Newitt	15th
2013	Dandino	UK	Marco Botti	Craig Williams	2nd
2012	Dunaden	FR	Mikel Delzangles	Craig Williams	1st
	Americain	FR	Alain de Royer Dupre	Gerald Mosse	4th
	My Quest For Peace	UK	Luca Cumani	Corey Brown	5th
	Jakkalberry	UK	Marco Botti	Colm O'Donoghue	13th
2011	Manighar	UK	Luca Cumani	Damien Oliver	4th
	Drunken Sailor	UK	Luca Cumani	Dwayne Dunn	7th
	Saptapadi	UK	Brian Ellison	Mark Zahra	14th
2010	Manighar	UK	Luca Cumani	Damien Oliver	5th
	Mr Medici	HK	Peter Ho	Gerald Mosse	6th
	Tokai Trick	JPN	Kenji Nonaka	Shinji Fujita	12th
2009	Kirklees	UAE	Saeed Bin Suroor	Kerrin McEvoy	7th
	Cima De Triopmem	UK	Luca Cumani	Damien Oliver	13th
2008	All The Good	UAE	Saeed Bin Suroor	Kerrin McEvoy	1st
	Mad Rush	UK	Luca Cumani	Damien Oliver	4th
2007	Purple Moon	UK	Luca Cumani	Kerrin McEvoy	6th
2006	Delta Blues	JPN	Katsuhiko Sumii	Nash Rawiller	3rd

	Pop Rock	JPN	Katsuhiko Sumii	Damien Oliver	7th
	Land N Stars	UK	Jamie Poulton	Nick Ryan	18th
2005	Eye Opener	JPN	Izumi Shimizu	Shinji Fujita	2nd
	Carte Diamond	UK	Brian Ellison	Weichong Marwing	9th
	Razkalla	UAE	Saeed Bin Suroor	Kerrin McEvoy	16th
2003	Hugs Dancer	UK	James Given	Dean McKeown	7th
	In Time's Eye	IRE	Dermot Weld	Damien Oliver	10th
2002	Beekeeper	UAE	Saeed Bin Suroor	Kerrin McEvoy	6th
	Helene Vitality	HK	David Hayes	Dwayne Dunn	12th
2000	Mont Rocher	FR	John Hammond	John Marshall	11th
	All The Way	UAE	Saeed Bin Suroor	Greg Hall	16th
1998	Taufan's Melody	UK	Lady Herries	Ray Cochrane	1st
	Faithful Son	UAE	Saeed Bin Suroor	Damien Oliver	4th

Leading winning jockeys:
5 wins Scobie Breasley (Peshawar 1952, St Fairy 1945, Counsel 1944; Skipton 1943, Tranquil Star 1942).
4 wins Damien Oliver (Sky Heights 1999, Doriemus 1995, Paris Lane 1994, Mannerism 1992).
3 wins Frank Dempsey (Eurythmic 1920, Bronzetti 1917, Lavendo 1915); Mick Mallyon (Bunratty Castle 1968, Gay Icarus 1971, Leilani 1974); Neville Sellwood (Tulloch 1957, Basha Felika 1951, Grey Boots 1950).

Current winning jockeys:
4 wins Damien Oliver (Sky Heights 1999, Doriemus 1995, Paris Lane 1994, Mannerism 1992).
2 wins Nick Hall (Jameka 2016, Fawkner 2013); Craig Williams (Dunaden 2012, Southern Speed 2011).
1 win Opie Bosson (Mongolian Khan 2015); Dwayne Dunn (Tawqeet 2006); Vlad Duric (Master O'Reilly 2007); Kerrin McEvoy (All The Good 2008); Cory Parish (Boom Time 2017); Zac Purton (Admire Rakti 2014); Brad Rawiller (Viewed 2009); Nash Rawiller (Elvstroem 2004).

Leading winning trainers:
7 wins Bart Cummings (Viewed 2009, Let's Elope 1991, Ming Dynasty 1980, 1977, Leilani 1974, Big Philou 1969, Galilee 1966).
4 wins Lee Freedman (Mummify 2003, Doriemus 1995, Paris Lane 1994, Mannerism 1992); Tommy Smith (Mighty Kingdom 1979, Taksan 1978, Tulloch 1957, Redcraze 1956).

Current winning trainers:
4 wins Lee Freedman (Mummify 2003, Doriemus 1995, Paris Lane 1994, Mannerism 1992).
3 wins David Hayes (Boom Time 2017, Tawqeet 2006, Fraar 1993).
1 win Murray Baker (Mongolian Khan 2015); Saeed Bin Suroor (All The Good 2008); Mikel Delzangles (Dunaden 2013); John Hawkes (Railings 2005); David & Ben Hayes & Tom Dabernig (Boom Time 2017); Robert Hickmott (Fawkner 2013); Fred Kersley (Northerly 2002); Sheila Laxon (Ethereal 2001); Leon Macdonald (Southern Speed 2011); Ciaron Maher (Jameka 2016); Danny O'Brien (Master O'Reilly 2007); Tomoyuki Umeda (Admire Rakti 2014); Tony Vasil (Elvstroem 2004); Gai Waterhouse (Descarado 2010).

Points of interest
Heaviest winning weights: Redcraze (1956) 9st 13lbs (63kg); Rising Fast (1954) 9.10 (61.5kg); Tobin Bronze (1967) 9.10 (61.5kg).
Lightest winning weight: Oakleigh (1887) 6st 9lbs (42kg),
The odds: Shortest priced winner: Tulloch (1957) 4/6 ($1.66); Shortest priced loser: Tobin Bronze (1966) 8/11 ($1.72)—6th behind Galilee.
Longest priced winner: Saint Warden (1943) 100/1 ($101)
Longest priced placegetter: Father's Day (1978) 200/1 ($201)—3rd behind Taksan.
Highest attendance: 52,009 (2005, won by Railings). Last year's attendance: 30,000.
Biggest winning margin: 7.5 lengths—Might And Power (1997).
From 1879, 1880 and 1881, the Caulfield Cup was run in the autumn. A second CC was run in the 1881.
Dead-heats (for first): Aborigine and Blue Book (1909); (placings) Baghdad Note and Royal Show (third, 1970).
The Caulfield Cup has been postponed only once—1937—from Saturday (Oct. 16) to Wednesday (Oct. 20) due to heavy rain and the state of the track.
Caulfield was used as a troop base during WWII—run at Flemington 1940-41-42-43 (two divisions in 1943).
Big Philou (Roy Higgins) won on protest from Nausori (Des Lake) in 1969—alleged interference at the 200m.
Tim Swiveller was first past the post in 1893, but disqualified for boring out. Sainfoin was elevated to first.
The first $1 million Caulfield Cup was run in 1996, won by Arctic Scent.

MVRC Manikato Stakes (1200m)—Moonee Valley
Of $1,000,000. Group 1. Weight for Age. October 26, 2018.

2017-18 RESULT: Time: 1:09.96 (Good 3)

FP	NO	HORSE	TRAINER	JOCKEY	MARGIN	BAR.	WGT	SP
1	5	REBEL DANE	Gary Portelli	Ben Melham		4	58.5kg	$61
2	8	FELL SWOOP	Matthew Dale	Hugh Bowman	0.2L	3	58.5kg	$7.50
3	7	JAPONISME	Chris Waller	Glyn Schofield	1.2L	7	58.5kg	$16
4	6	THE QUARTERBACK	Robbie Griffiths	Matthew Allen	1.3L	10	58.5kg	$16
5	4	UNDER THE LOUVRE	Robert Smerdon	Chris Parnham	1.8L	5	58.5kg	$19
6	1	BUFFERING	Robert Heathcote	Damian Browne	1.9L	2	58.5kg	$9
7	2	CHAUTAUQUA	Michael, Wayne & John Hawkes	Dwayne Dunn	2.0L	8	56.5kg	$12
8	10	ENGLISH	Gai Waterhouse & Adrian Bott	Mark Zahra	2.0L	1	58.5kg	$2.45f
9	3	LUCKY HUSSLER	Darren Weir	Brad Rawiller	3.5L	9	58.5kg	$16
10	9	HOLLER	John O'Shea	James McDonald	3.6L	6	58.5kg	$9.50

PAST WINNERS

YEAR	WINNER	JOCKEY	TRAINER	2ND	3RD	TIME
2017	Hey Doc	Luke Currie	Tony McEvoy	In Her Time	Malaguerra	1:09.9
2016	Rebel Dane	Ben Melham	Gary Portelli	Fell Swoop	Japonisme	1:10.9
2015	Chautauqua	Tommy Berry	Michael, Wayne & John Hawkes	Srikandi	Rebel Dane	1:09.5
2014	Lankan Rupee	Craig Newitt	Mick Price	Angelic Light	Famous Seamus	1:10.3
2013	Buffering	Damian Browne	Robert Heathcote	Lucky Nine	Sessions	1:11.4
2012	Sea Siren	Jim Cassidy	John O'Shea	Mental	We're Gonna Rock	1:11.3
2011	Sepoy	Kerrin McEvoy	Peter Snowden	Sister Madly	More Joyous	1:11.0
2010	Hay List	Glyn Schofield	John Mcnair	True Persuasion	Eagle Falls	1:09.9
2009	Danleigh	Kerrin McEvoy	Chris Waller	Phelan Ready	Nicconi	1:12.5
2008	Typhoon Zed	Nash Rawiller	Tim Martin	Absolut Glam	Kaphero	1:10.6
2007	Gold Edition	Stathi Katsidis	Ron Maund	Vormista	Dr Nipandtuck	1:10.6
2006	Miss Andretti	Craig Newitt	Lee Freedman	Dance Hero	Sassbee	1:09.2
2005	Spark Of Life	Glen Boss	Allan Denham	Perfectly Ready	Our Egyptian Raine	1:11.5
2004	Spark Of Life	Danny Nikolic	Allan Denham	Yell	Dilly Dally	1:13.3
2003	Spinning Hill	Patrick Payne	Guy Walter	True Glo	The Big Chill	1:11.2
2002	Spinning Hill	Patrick Payne	Guy Walter	Bel Esprit	Mistegic	1:10.5
2001	Piavonic	Nash Rawiller	Tony Noonan	Sunline	Falvelon	1:12.9
2000	Sunline	Greg Childs	Trevor Mckee	Honour The Name	Miss Pennymoney	1:11.6
1999	Redoutes Choice	Jim Cassidy	Rick Hore-Lacy	Marstic	Flavour	1:14.5
1998	Dane Ripper	Damien Oliver	Bart Cummings	Sir Boom	Theatre	1:12.3
1997	Spartacus	Darren Beadman	Rick Hore-Lacy	Poetic King	Cut Up Rough	1:11.3

BACKGROUND

First run: 1968 (won by Winfreux). Group 2 1979-89. Run at Flemington 1976 & 1995. Known as the Freeway Stakes until 1984.
Most recent mare to win: Sea Siren (2012). Note: 10 mares have won.
Most recent 3YO to win: C&G—Sepoy (2011); Filly—Dual Choice (1970). Note: Dual Choice is the only 3YO filly to win. Note: seven 3YOs have won.
Multiple winners: 5—Spark Of Life (2005, 2004); Spinning Hill (2003, 2002); Manikato (1982, 1979); Tauto (1974, 1973); Dual Choice (1971, 1970).
Fastest time (1200m): Miss Andretti (2007) 1:09.29
Notable winners: Chautauqua (2015); Lankan Rupee (2014); Buffering (2013); Sepoy (2011); Hay List (2010); Miss Andretti (2006); Sunline (2000); Redoute's Choice (1999); Dane Ripper (1998); Rancho Ruler (1988); Rubiton (1987); Strawberry Road (1983); Manikato (1979, 1982); Century (1972); Tauto (1974, 1973); Dual Choice (1971, 1970); Vain (1969).
Blue Diamond winners also won lead-up races:
Bletchingly Stakes : 1—You Remember (1995).
Ian McEwen Stakes: 2—Chautauqua (2015); Miss Andretti (2006).
Moir Stakes: (no horse has won the double since the Moir was moved from after to before the Manikato Stakes

in 2012. Three horses won it before the move—Spinning Hill (2002); Manikato (1982); Scamanda (1976).
Manikato Stakes winners went on to win same preparation:
VRC Sprint Classic: 3—Buffering (2013); Dual Choice (1970); Vain (1969). Note: Dual Choice and Vain were 3YOs.
Coolmore Stud Stakes: 3—Sepoy (2011); Century (1972); Vain (1969).
Cox Plate (currently irrelevant as the Manikato was moved to race on Cox Plate eve in 2012): 3—Sunline (2000); Rubiton (1987); Strawberry Road (1983).
Winterbottom Stakes: 1—Buffering (2013).
Manikato Stakes winners went on to win in the autumn that season:
William Reid Stakes: 2—Miss Andretti (Manikato 2006), Dual Choice (1971).
Lightning Stakes: 3—Chautauqua (Manikato 2015); Lankan Rupee (2014); Dual Choice (1970).
Oakleigh Plate: 2—Dual Choice (Manikato 1970 and 1971)
Newmarket Handicap: 1—Miss Andretti (Manikato 2006).
TJ Smith Stakes: 2—Chautauqua (Manikato 2015); Spinning Hill (2002).
Manikato Stakes winners had previously won:
Blue Diamond Stakes (same year): 2—Sepoy (2011); Redoute's Choice (1999);
Golden Slipper Stakes (same year): 1—Sepoy (2011).
William Reid Stakes (same year): 3—Spartacus (1997); Manikato (1979); Winfreux (1968).
Leading winning jockey:
4 wins Frank Reys (Tauto 1974, 1973, Dual Choice 1971, 1970).
3 wins Gary Willetts (Strawberry Road 1983; Manikato 1982, 1979).
Current winning jockeys:
2 wins Kerrin McEvoy (Sepoy 2011, Danleigh 2009); Craig Newitt (Lankan Rupee 2014, Miss Andretti 2006); Damien Oliver (Dane Ripper 1998, Sonic Express 1991); Nash Rawiller (Typhoon Zed 2008, Piavonic 2001).
1 win Tommy Berry (Chautauqua 2015); Glen Boss (Spark Of Life 2005); Damian Browne (Buffering 2013); Luke Currie (Hey Doc 2017); Ben Melham (Rebel Dane 2016); Glyn Schofield (Hay List 2010); Brian Werner (Lockley's Tradition 1986).
Leading winning trainers:
4 wins Bart Cummings (Dane Ripper 1998; Never Undercharge 1993; Lord Dudley 1975; Century 1972); Bob Hoysted (Touch Of Genius 1985, Manikato 1982, 1979, Scamanda 1976).
Current winning trainers:
2 wins Allan Denham (Spark Of Life 2005, 2004); John Hawkes (Chautauqua 2015, Spanish Mix 1994).
1 win Gary Carson (Silver Bounty 1981); Rob Heathcote (Buffering 2013); Michael, Wayne & John Hawkes (Chautauqua 2015); Tim Martin (Typhoon Zed 2008); Tony McEvoy (Hey Doc 2017); John McNair (Hay List 2010); Tony Noonan (Piavonic 2001); John O'Shea (Sea Siren 2012); Gary Portelli (Rebel Dane 2016); Mick Price (Lankan Rupee 2014); Peter Snowden (Sepoy 2011); Chris Waller (Danleigh 2009).
Point of interest:
Three horses have won the Moonee Valley's "big three" spring races—Manikato Stakes (1200m), Dato Tan Chin Nam Stakes (1600m) and Cox Plate (2040m)—in the same spring campaign: Sunline (2000); Rubiton (1987); Strawberry Road (1983). Of course, the Manikato was run earlier in the spring at that time

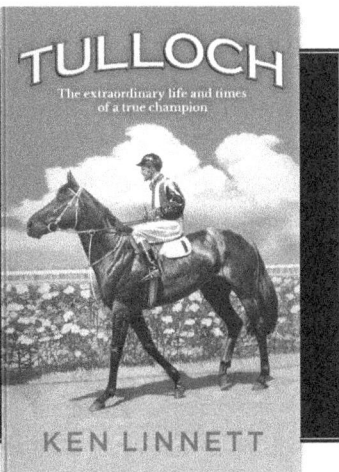

MVRC Ladbrokes Cox Plate (2040m)—Moonee Valley

Of $4,000,000. Group 1. Weight for Age, 3YO&Up. October 29, 2018.

2017-18 RESULT: Time: 2:02.94 (Good 3)

FP	NO	HORSE	TRAINER	JOCKEY	MARGIN	BAR.	WGT	SP
1	8	WINX	Chris Waller	Hugh Bowman		5	57kg	$1.18
2	3	HUMIDOR	Darren Weir	Blake Shinn	0.4L	7	59kg	$31
3	5	FOLKSWOOD	Charlie Appleby	Kerrin McEvoy	4.65L	4	59kg	$26
4	9	ROYAL SYMPHONY	Tony McEvoy	Dean Yendall	6.15L	6	49.5kg	$19
5	2	GAILO CHOP	Darren Weir	Mark Zahra	6.25L	3	59kg	$21
6	1	HAPPY CLAPPER	Patrick Webster	Damien Oliver	6.55L	8	59kg	$31
7	6	SEABURGE	David & Ben Hayes & Tom Dabernig	Regan Bayliss	13.55L	1	57.5kg	$101
8	7	HARDHAM	David Brideoake	Luke Nolen	14.8L	2	57.5kg	$101

PAST WINNERS

YEAR	WINNER	JOCKEY	TRAINER	2ND	3RD	TIME
2017	Winx	Hugh Bowman	Chris Waller	Humidor	Folkswood	2:02.9
2016	Winx	Hugh Bowman	Chris Waller	Hartnell	Yankee Rose	2:06.3
2015	Winx	Hugh Bowman	Chris Waller	Criterion	Highland Reel	2:02.9
2014	Adelaide	Ryan Moore	Aidan O'Brien	Fawkner	Silent Achiever	2:03.7
2013	Shamus Award	Chad Schofield	Danny O'Brien	Happy Trails	Fiorente	2:05.2
2012	Ocean Park	Glen Boss	Gary Hennessy	All Too Hard	Pierro	2:04.1
2011	Pinker Pinker	Craig Williams	Greg Eurell	Jimmy Choux	Rekindled Interest	2:05.3
2010	So You Think	Steven Arnold	Bart Cummings	Zipping	Whobegotyou	2:07.4
2009	So You Think	Glen Boss	Bart Cummings	Manhattan Rain	Zipping	2:03.9
2008	Maldivian	Michael Rodd	Mark Kavanagh	Zipping	Samantha Miss	2:06.9
2007	El Segundo	Luke Nolen	Colin Little	Wonderful World	Haradasun	2:06.3
2006	Fields Of Omagh	Craig Williams	David Hayes	El Segundo	Pompeii Ruler	2:06.9
2005	Makybe Diva	Glen Boss	Lee Freedman	Lotteria	Fields Of Omagh	2:09.3
2004	Savabeel	Chris Munce	Graeme Rogerson	Fields Of Omagh	Starcraft	2:06.9
2003	Fields Of Omagh	Steven King	Tony Mcevoy	Defier	Lonhro	2:07.6
2002	Northerly	Patrick Payne	Fred Kersley	Defier	Grandera	2:06.3
2001	Northerly	Damien Oliver	Fred Kersley	Sunline	Viscount	2:05.8
2000	Sunline	Greg Childs	Trevor Mckee	Diatribe	Referral	2:07.7
1999	Sunline	Greg Childs	Trevor Mckee	Tie The Knot	Sky Heights	2:05.4
1998	Might And Power	Jim Cassidy	Jack Denham	Northern Drake	Tycoon Lil	2:03.5
1997	Dane Ripper	Damien Oliver	Bart Cummings	Filante	Vialli	2:07.7

BACKGROUND

First run: 1922 (won by Violoncello (GB)). 1922-1942 1900m; 1943-1972 2000m; 1973 abt 2000m; 1974-1985 2050m; from 1986 2040m. Race divided in 1946.

3YOs to win: 20—Shamus Award (2013); So You Think (2009); Savabeel (2004); Octagonal (1995); Red Anchor (1984); Surround (1976); Taj Rossi (1973); Abdul (1970); Daryl's Joy (1969); Rajah Sahib (1968); Star Affair (1965); Noholme (1959); Kingster (1955); Bronton (1951); Alister (1950); Delta (1949); Carbon Copy (1948); Chanak (1947); Garrio (1935); Manfred (1925).

Note: Surround (1976) is the only filly. Makybe Diva and Lotteria (2005) are the only mares to quinella the Cox Plate. The most recent 3YO filly to place in the Cox Plate is Samantha Miss (2008)—third behind Maldivian.

Fillies and mares to win: 8 individuals for 13 wins—Winx (2017, 2016, 2015); Pinker Pinker (2011); Makybe Diva (2005); Sunline (2000, 1999); Dane Ripper (1997); Surround (1976); Flight (1946, 1945); Tranquil Star (1944, 1942).

Note: Surround is the only 3YO filly.

Multiple winners: 10—Winx (2017, 2016, 2015); So You Think (2010, 2009); Fields Of Omagh (2006, 2003); Northerly (2002, 2001); Sunline (2000, 1999); Kingston Town (1983, 1982, 1981); Tobin Bronze (1967, 1966); Hydrogen (1953, 1952); Flight (1946, 1945); Tranquil Star (1944, 1942);

Fastest time (2040m): Winx (2017) 2:02.94. Note: the fastest time before Strathayr was Better Loosen Up (1990, 2:01.50).

Cox Plate winners have won the lead-up races:
Makybe Diva Stakes: 5—Northerly (2002); Dulcify (1979); Tobin Bronze (1966); Sir Dane (1964); Aquanita (1962).
Dato Tan Chin Nam Stakes: 9—El Segundo (2007); Northerly (2001); Sunline (2000); Better Loosen Up (1990); Our Poetic Prince (1988); Rubiton (1987); Strawberry Road (1983); So Called (1978); Rising Fast (1954).

Underwood Stakes: 16—Ocean Park (2012); So You Think (2010); Northerly (2002, 2001); Almaarad (1989); Rubiton (1987); Bonecrusher (1986); So Called (1978); Tobin Bronze (1966); Aquanita (1962); Ray Ribbon (1956); Ajax (1938); Young Idea (1937); Phar Lap (1931); Highland (1928); Heroic (1926).
Epsom Handicap: 4—Winx (2015); Noholme (1959); Chatham (1932); Nightmarch (1929).
Turnbull Stakes (since 1948): 10—Winx (2017); Makybe Diva (2005); Northerly (2002); The Phantom Chance 1993); Better Loosen Up (1990); Dulcify (1979); Tobin Bronze (1966); Sir Dane (1964); Aquanita (1962); Rising Fast (1954).
Caulfield Guineas: 4—Red Anchor (1984); Surround (1976); Rajah Sahib (1968); Star Affair (1965).
Note 1: The most recent 3YO to run in the Caulfield Guineas and win the Cox Plate is Shamus Award (2013), who was third behind Long John in the Guineas; before that it was So You Think (2009), who finished fifth behind Starspangledbanner in the Guineas.
Note 2: In 2012, All Too Hard won the Guineas and finished second behind Ocean Park in the Cox Plate; Pierro was second behind All Too Hard and third in the Cox Plate.
Caulfield Stakes: 16—Winx (2016); Ocean Park (2012); So You Think (2010); Northerly (2001); Might And Power (1998); Almaarad (1989); Bonecrusher (1986); Kingston Town (1982, 1981); Family Of Man (1977); Gunsynd (1972); Rising Fast (1954); Amana (1943); Tranquil Star (1942); Ajax (1938); Young Idea (1936).
Note: Tranquil Star (1942) is the only mare to complete the double.
Underwood Stakes & Caulfield Stakes: 5—Ocean Park (2012); So You Think (2010); Northerly (2001); Bonecrusher (1986); Ajax (1938).
Turnbull Stakes, Caulfield Cup & Melbourne Cup (since 1948): 1—Rising Fast (1954). Note: Rising Fast also won the Caulfield Stakes, Mackinnon Stakes and Queen Elizabeth Stakes in an unparalleled 1954 spring campaign.
Mackinnon (Emirates) Stakes: 20—So You Think (2010); Better Loosen Up (1990); Rising Prince (1985); Dulcify (1979); Tobin Bronze (1966); Sir Dane (1964); Aquanita (1962); Tulloch (1960); Rising Fast (1954); Hydrogen (1953); Flight (1946); Tranquil Star (1944, 1942); Amana (1943); Beau Vite (1941, 1940); Ajax (1938); Rogilla (1933); Phar Lap (1931, 1930).
Caulfield Stakes & Mackinnon: 5—So You Think (2010); Rising Fast (1954); Amana (1943); Tranquil Star (1942); Ajax (1938).

Past placegetters to win a Cox Plate:
Cox Plate minor placegetter to win the following year: 7—most recent are El Segundo (won 2007, 2nd in 2006); Fields Of Omagh (2006, 3rd in 2005); Solvit (1994, 2nd in 1993); Super Impose (1992, 2nd in 1991); Our Poetic Prince (1988, 2nd in 1987).

Cox Plate and the Caulfield Cup:
Caulfield Cup (same year): 4—Northerly (2002); Tobin Bronze (1967); Rising Fast (1954); Tranquil Star (1942).
Caulfield Cup (different years): 8—Might And Power (CP 1998; CC 1997); Tulloch (CP 1960; CC 1957); Redcraze (CP 1957; CC 1956); Rising Fast (CP 1954; CC 1955); Rogilla (CP 1933; CC 1932); Amounis (CP 1927; CC 1930); Manfred (CP 1925; CC 1926); Violoncello (CP 1922; CC 1921).

Cox Plate winners and the Melbourne Cup:
Melbourne Cup: 5—Makybe Diva (2005); Saintly (1996); Rising Fast (1954); Phar Lap (1930); Nightmarch (1929).
Note: the most recent Cox Plate winner to run in the Melbourne Cup is So You Think (2010), who finished third behind Americain.
The most recent Melbourne Cup winner to run in the Cox Plate as a lead-up is Fiorente (2013), who finished third behind Shamus Award.
Rising Fast (1954) is the only horse to win by Caulfield Cup, Cox Plate and Melbourne Cup in the same year. He was ridden by Arthur Ward in the Caulfield Cup and Jack Purtell in the Cox Plate and Melbourne Cup. (Note: no jockey has won all three in the same year).

Cox Plate winners won the autumn features:
Australian Cup (same year, since 1964 when Australian Cup reduced to 2000m): 3—Makybe Diva (2005); Northerly (2001); Saintly (1986).
Australian Cup (same season, since 1964): 5—Northerly (Cox Plate 2002); Dane Ripper (1998); Better Loosen Up (1990); Bonecrusher 1986); Family Of Man (1977).
Tancred Stakes (same year): 4—Makybe Diva (2005); Mighty And Power (1998); Bonecrusher (1986); Kingston Town (1980).
Tancred Stakes (same season): 2—Octagonal (Cox Plate 1995); Our Poetic Prince (1988).
ATC Queen Elizabeth Stakes (same year): 5—Winx (2017); Might And Power (1998); Rising Prince (1985); Battle Heights (1974); Tulloch (1960).
ATC Queen Elizabeth Stakes (same season): 4—Winx (Cox Plate 2017, 2016); Our Poetic Prince (1988); Tulloch (1960).

Cox Plate winners and the Derbys:
Victoria Derby (same year): 6—Red Anchor (1984); Taj Rossi (1973); Daryl's Joy (1969); Alister (1950); Delta (1949); Manfred (1925).
Note: the most recent 3YO to run in the Cox Plate and back up a week later in the Derby is Savabeel—he won the Cox Plate before finishing second behind Plastered in the Derby.

Victoria Derby (Cox Plate as 4YOs): 4—Dulcify (1979); Tobin Bronze (1966); Hydrogen (1952); Phar Lap (1930). No horse has won the Cox Plate and ATC Australian Derby as 3YOs since the Derby was moved from spring to autumn in 1979.

ATC Australian Derby (Cox Plate as 4YOs): 5—Bonecrusher (1986); Strawberry Road (1983); Kingston Town (1981); Dulcify (1979); Phar Lap (1930).

Internationals: Adelaide (IRE), 2014, is the only northern hemisphere-trained horse to win the Cox Plate.

The internationals to compete are:

1999 won by Sunline
Make No Mistake (IRE) (trained by Dermot Weld, Ireland; ridden by Pat Smullen) 8th
2001 won by Northerly
Silvano (GER) (Andreas Wolher, Germany; Andreas Suborics) 4th
Caitano (GER) (Andreas Schultz, Germany; Andrasch Starke) 7th behind Northerly.
2002 won by Northerly
Grandera (UK) (Saeed bin Suroor, UK; Frankie Dettori) third.
2003 won by Fields Of Omagh
Paraca (ARG) (Andrew Balding, UK; Nash Rawiller) 8th
2004 won by Savabeel
Elegant Fashion (David Hayes, Hong Kong; Gerald Mosse) 9th
Paolini (GER) (Andreas Wohler, Germany; Eddie Pedroza) 10th
2005 won by Makybe Diva
Super Kid (NZ) (John Moore, Hong Kong: Nash Rawiller) 7th
Greys Inn (USA) (Mike de Kock, South Africa; Weichong Warwing) 10th
Tosen Dandy (JPN) (Hideyuki Mori, Japan; Minoru Yoshida) 11th
2010 won by So You Think
Luen Yat Forever (Pou Choi, Macau; Dwayne Dunn) 10th
2013 won by Shamus Award
Side Glance (GB) (Andrew Balding, UK; Craig Williams) 6th
Mull Of Killough (IRE) (Jane Chapple-Hyam, UK; Steven Arnold) 11th
2014 won by Adelaide
Adelaide (IRE) (Aidan O'Brien, Ireland; Ryan Moore) 1st
Side Glance (GB) (Andrew Balding, UK; Jamie Spencer) 4th
Quest Of Honour (IRE) (Marco Botti, UK; Craig Williams) DNF
2015 won by Winx
Highland Reel (IRE) (Aidan O'Brien, Ireland; Ryan Moore) 3rd
Gailo Chop (FR) (A de Watrigant, France; Brad Rawiller) 8th
Arod (IRE) (Peter Chapple-Hyam, UK; Craig Williams) 11th
2016 won by Winx
Vadamos (FR) (Andre Fabre, France; Mark Zahra) 4th
2017 won by Winx
Folkswood (GB) (Charlie Appleby, UK; Kerrin McEvoy) 3rd

Leading winning jockeys:
5 wins Darby Munro (Hydrogen 1952, Beau Vite 1941, Mosaic 1939, Young Idea 1937, Rogilla 1933).
4 wins Jack Purtell (Bay Ribbon 1956, Rising Fast 1954, Bronton 1951, Alister 1950); Brent Thomson (Dulcify 1979, So Called 1978, Family Of Man 1977, Fury's Order 1975).
3 wins Harold Badger (Carbon Copy 1948, Chanak 1947, Ajax 1938); Glen Boss (Ocean Park 2012, So You Think 2009, Makybe Diva 2005); Hugh Bowman (Winx 2017, 2016, 2015); Neville Sellwood (Tulloch 1960, Noholme 1959, Delta 1949).

Current winning jockeys:
3 wins Glen Boss (Ocean Park 2012, So You Think 2009, Makybe Diva 2005); Hugh Bowman (Winx 2017, 2016, 2015).
2 win Damien Oliver (Northerly 2001, Dane Ripper 1997); Craig Williams (Pinker Pinker 2011, Fields Of Omagh 2006).
1 win Steven Arnold (So You Think 2010); Ryan Moore (Adelaide 2014); Luke Nolen (El Segundo 2007); Chad Schofield (Shamus Award 2013); Michael Rodd (Maldivian 2008).

Leading winning trainers:
7 wins Tommy Smith (Red Anchor 1984, Kingston Town 1982, 1981, 1980, Gunsynd 1972, Tulloch 1960, Redcraze 1957).
6 wins Jack Holt (Chanak 1947, Young Idea 1937, 1936, Highland 1928, Heroic 1926, Easingwold 1923).
5 wins Bart Cummings (So You Think 2010, 2009, Dane Ripper 1997, Saintly 1996, Taj Rossi 1973).

Current winning trainers:
3 wins Chris Waller (Winx 2017, 2016, 2015).

2 wins Lee Freedman (Makybe Diva 2005, Super Impose 1992); David Hayes (Fields Of Omagh 2006, Better Loosen Up 1990); Fred Kersley (Northerly 2002, 2001).

1 win Greg Eurell (Pinker Pinker 2011); John Hawkes (Octagonal 1995); Gary Hennessy (Ocean Park 2012); Mark Kavanagh (Maldivian 2008); Colin Little (El Segundo 2007); Tony McEvoy (Fields Of Omagh 2003); Moira Murdoch (Solvit 1994); Aidan O'Brien (Adelaide 2014); Danny O'Brien (Shamus Award 2013); Frank Ritchie (Bonecrusher 1986); John Wheeler (Our Poetic Prince 1988).

Points of interest:

The Cox Plate was divided in 1946. The first division was won by champion mare Flight (11/2); the second division was won by 50/1 longshot Leonard.

Previous winners to sire a winner: Heroic (1926) sired Ajax (1938); Rubiton (1987) sired Fields Of Omagh (2006, 2003).

Widest winning margins: 8 lengths—Winx (2016); 7 lengths—Sunline (2000); Dulcify (1979).

Highest attendance: 42,456 (2001, won by Northerly).

New Zealand-trained horses: 12 have won, the most recent are: Ocean Park (trainer Gary Hennessy, 2012); Sunline (Trevor McKee, 2000, 1999); Solvit (Moira Murdoch, 1994); The Phantom Chance (Colin Jillings, 1993); Surfer's Paradise (Dave O'Sullivan, 1991); Our Poetic Prince (John Wheeler, 1988); Bonecrusher (Frank Ritchie, 1986).

No Golden Slipper winner has won a Cox Plate—Pierro (third in 2012) and Canny Lad (third in 1990) are the only Golden Slipper winners to place in the Cox Plate as a 3YO. Sky High (GS, 1960) was third in the Cox Plate in 1961 as a 4YO.

Shamus Award (2013) was a maiden when he won the Cox Plate. The only other maiden to run in the Cox Plate was Oxberry Way (a 3YO trained by Bart Cummings), who finished last at 200/1 behind Red Anchor in 1984.

The first female to train a winner was Deidre Stein (Rising Prince, 1985). The only other winning female trainer is Moira Murdoch (Solvit, 1994).

The first $1 million Cox Plate was in 1987, won by Rubiton.

No jockey has won the Caulfield Cup, Cox Plate and Melbourne Cup in the same year.

Lee Freedman is the only trainer to win the Caulfield Cup, Cox Plate and Melbourne Cup in the same year—he did it in 1992 with three different horses: Mannerism (Caulfield Cup); Super Impose (Cox Plate) and Subzero (Melbourne Cup). Freedman went on to train Bint Marscay to win the Golden Slipper in 1993, giving him a clean sweep of the "big four" in the same season.

When Winx won in 2016 it was her 13th consecutive win; when she won in 2017 it was her 22nd consecutive win. It took her career earnings to an Australian record $15,627,925.

Winx (2017, 2016, 2015) and Kingston Town (1982, 1981, 1980) are the only horses to win three Cox Plates.

VRC Coolmore Stud Stakes (1200m)—Flemington

Of $1,000,000. Group 1. Set Weights, 3YO. November 3, 2018.

2017-18 RESULT: Time: 1:09.10 (Good 3)

FP	NO	HORSE	TRAINER	JOCKEY	MARGIN	BAR.	WGT	SP
1	8	MERCHANT NAVY	Aaron Purcell	Mark Zahra		15	57kg	$19
2	19	INVINCIBLE STAR	Gai Waterhouse & Adrian Bott	Stephen Baster	0.2L	7	55kg	$6.50ef
3	18	FORMALITY	David & Ben Hayes & Tom Dabernig	Kerrin McEvoy	0.3L	2	55kg	$20
4	20	LIMESTONE	Darren Weir	Dean Yendall	2.3L	19	55kg	$61
5	5	VIRIDINE	James Cummings	Brenton Avdulla	2.8L	1	57kg	$10
6	9	DRACARYS	Peter & Paul Snowden	Regan Bayliss	2.9L	20	57kg	$41
7	12	MALAHAT	James Cummings	Oliver Peslier	3.4L	8	57kg	$201
8	13	ANDAZ	Chris Waller	Ben Melham	3.8L	14	57kg	$51
9	15	HOUTZEN	Toby Edmonds	Jeff Lloyd	4.2L	5	55kg	$10
10	17	TULIP	David & Ben Hayes & Tom Dabernig	Jamie Spencer	5.95L	13	55kg	$17
11	11	LONE EAGLE	Mick Price	Dwayne Dunn	6.25L	11	57kg	$51
12	10	EPTIMUM	Toby Edmonds	Ryan Maloney	6.45L	4	57kg	$17
13	7	GOODFELLA	Bjorn Baker	Jason Collett	6.55L	9	57kg	$31
14	6	JUKEBOX	Aaron Purcell	Craig Williams	6.75L	3	57kg	$26
15	1	TRAPEZE ARTIST	Gerald Ryan	Tye Angland	7.15L	18	57kg	$6.50ef
16	2	KEMENTARI	James Cummings	Damian Lane	7.35L	12	57kg	$10
17	14	WASSERGEIST	Trent Busuttin & Natalie Young	Glen Boss	7.45L	16	57kg	$201
18	16	CATCHY	David & Ben Hayes & Tom Dabernig	Hugh Bowman	7.65L	17	55kg	$7.50
19	4	SUMMER PASSAGE	Lance O'Sullivan & Andrew Scott	Blake Shinn	12.65L	10	57kg	$41
20	3	THE MISSION	Paul Perry	Noel Callow	13.65L	6	57kg	$201

PAST WINNERS

YEAR	WINNER	JOCKEY	TRAINER	2ND	3RD	TIME
2017	Merchant Navy	Mark Zahra	Aaron Purcell	Invincible Star	Merchant Navy	1:09.1
2016	Flying Artie	Hugh Bowman	Mick Price	Astern	Star Turn	1:08.9
2015	Japonisme	Glyn Schofield	Chris Waller	Keen Array	Counterattack	1:09.5
2014	Brazen Beau	Joao Moreira	Chris Waller	Delectation	Kuro	1:10.7
2013	Zoustar	Jim Cassidy	Chris Waller	Not Listenin' To Me	Lion Of Belfort	1:09.2
2012	Nechita	Christian Reith	John P Thompson	Jolie Bay	Shamexpress	1:08.5
2011	Sepoy	Kerrin McEvoy	Peter Snowden	Foxwedge	Satin Shoes	1:10.4
2010	Star Witness	James Winks	Danny O'Brien	Curtana	Shrapnel	1:09.9
2009	Headway	Luke Nolen	Peter Moody	King Pulse	Shellscrape	1:08.5
2008	Northern Meteor	Nash Rawiller	Gai Waterhouse	Fist of Fury	All American	1:10.5
2007	Weekend Hussler	Brad Rawiller	Ross McDonald	Bel Mer	Scenic Blast	1:08.9
2006	Gold Edition	Jim Byrne	Ron Maund	Splashing Out	Churchill Downs	1:09.6
2005	Ferocity	Steven Arnold	Danny O'Brien	Jadescent	Undoubtedly	1:08.3
2004	Alinghi	Damien Oliver	Lee Freedman	Barley A Moment	Tirade	1:10.5
2003	Scaredee Cat	Steven Arnold	Cliff Brown	Lago Delight	Dilly Dally	1:08.8
2002	Innovation Girl	Kerrin McEvoy	Brian Mayfield-Smith	Cool Trent	Titanic Jack	1:10.8
2001	North Boy	Damien Oliver	Tony Mc Evoy	Ustinov	Malagra Miss	1:09.6
2000	So Gorgeous	Nash Rawiller	Dan O'Sullivan	Show A Heart	Sort It Out	1:12.9
1999	Spargo	Stan Aitken	Robert Smerdon	Testa Rossa	Fappianos Son	1:11.0
1998	Theatre	Darren Gauci	Rick Hore-Lacy	City Kid	Major Fun	1:10.0
1997	Show No Emotion	Craig Williams	Tony Noonan	Cornwall Queen	Schubert	1:09.7
1996	Encosta De Lago	Steven King	Lee Freedman	Pimpala Prince	My Duke	1:10.3

BACKGROUND
First run: 1969 (won by Vain). Group 2 1979-2005. Group 1 from 2006. For 2YOs from 1863 to 1965, held in the autumn. Not run 1966-67-68. For 3YOs from 1969 and run in the spring. Moved from September to Derby Day in 2006. SWP 1969-2001. Registered as the Ascot Vale Stakes.
(Information dates from 1969 when held for the first time for 3YOs)
Most recent filly to win: Nechita (2012). Note: 10 fillies have won.
Fastest time (1200m): Our Maizcay (1995) 1:08.30
Notable winners: Merchant Navy (2017); Zoustar (2013); Sepoy (2011); Weekend Hussler (2007); Gold Edition (2006); Alinghi (2004); Encosta De Lago (1996); Our Maizcay (1995); Racer's Edge (1994); Brawny Spirit (1993); Tierce (1991); Courtza (1989); Zeditave (1988); Kaapstad (1986); Campaign King (1985); Rancher (1982); Rose Of Kingston (1981); Manikato (1978); Surround (1976); Toy Show (1975); Plush (1974); Taj Rossi (1973); Century (1972); Tolerance (1971); Vain (1969).
Coolmore Stud Stakes winners had previously won:
Blue Diamond Stakes: 8—Sepoy (2011); Star Witness (2010), Alinghi (2004); Courtza (1989); Zeditave (1988); Rancher (1982); Manikato (1978); Tolerance (1971).
Golden Slipper Stakes: 6—Sepoy (2011); Tierce (1991); Courtza (1989); Manikato (1978); Toy Show (1975); Vain (1969).
Blue Diamond & Golden Slipper: 3—Sepoy (2011); Courtza (1989); Manikato (1978).
Coolmore Stud Stakes winners also won the lead-up races:
MVRC Champagne Stake s: 1—Courtza (1989).
Vain Stakes: 2—Sepoy (2011); North Boy (2001).
Quezette Stakes: 3—Alinghi (2004), Innovation Girl (2002); So Gorgeous (2000).
McNeil Stakes: 3—Merchant Navy (2017); Theatre (1998); Tierce (1991).
Up and Coming Stakes: 1—Our Maizcay (1995).
San Domenico Stakes: 4—Japonisme (2015); Gold Edition (2006); Our Maizcay (1995); Tierce (1991).
Blue Sapphire Stakes: 1—Flying Artie (2016).
Golden Rose Stakes: 1—Zoustar (2013).
Roman Consul Stakes: 4—Brazen Beau (2014); Zoustar (2013); Our Maizcay (1995); Bureaucracy (1990).
Manikato Stakes: 3—Sepoy (2011); Century (1972); Vain (1969).
Caulfield Guineas: 1—Weekend Hussler (2007).
Caulfield Sprint: 2—Sepoy (2011); Campaign King (1985).
Leading winning jockeys:
3 wins Pat Hyland (Plush 1974, Eleazar 1970, Vain 1969); Damien Oliver (Alinghi 2004, North Boy 2001, Racer's Edge 1994); Harry White (Brawny Spirit 1993, Courtza 1989, Sardius 1980).
Current winning jockeys:
3 wins Damien Oliver (Alinghi 2004, North Boy 2001, Racer's Edge 1994).
2 wins Steven Arnold (Ferocity 2005, Scaredee Cat 2003); Kerrin McEvoy (Sepoy 2011, Innovation Girl 2002); Nash Rawiller (Northern Meteor 2008, So Gorgeous 2000).
1 win Hugh Bowman (Flying Artie 2016); Jim Byrne (Gold Edition 2006); Joao Moreira (Brazen Beau 2014); Luke Nolen (Headway 2009); Brad Rawiller (Weekend Hussler 2007); Christian Reith (Nechita 2012); Glyn Schofield (Japonisme 2015); Craig Williams (Show No Emotion 1997); James Winks (Star Witness 2010); Mark Zahra (Merchant Navy 2017).
Leading winning trainer:
4 wins Angus Armanasco (Zeditave 1988, Sardius 1980, Ballyred 1977, Tolerance 1971).
Current winning trainers:
3 wins Chris Waller (Japonisme 2015, Brazen Beau 2014, Zoustar 2013).
2 wins Danny O'Brien (Star Witness 2010, Ferocity 2005).
1 win Cliff Brown (Scaredee Cat 2003); Clarry Conners (Tierce 1991); Lee Freedman (Encosta De Lago 1996); John Hawkes (Tolhurst 1979); Tony McEvoy (North Boy 2001); Tony Noonan (Show No Emotion 1997); Dan O'Sullivan (So Gorgeous 2000); Mick Price (Flying Artie 2016); Aaron Purcell (Merchant Navy 2017); Gerald Ryan (Racer's Edge 1994); Grant Searle (Our Maizcay 1995); Robert Smerdon (Spargo 1999); Peter Snowden (Sepoy 2011); John Thompson (Nechita 2012); Gai Waterhouse (Northern Meteor 2008).
Points of interest:
Vain (1969) is the sire of Top Post (1983); Encosta De Lago (1996) is the sire Alinghi (2004) and Northern Meteor (2008); Northern Meteor (2008) is the sire of Zoustar (2013).
Gold Edition (2006) backed up at the Melbourne Cup Carnival to win the Red Roses Stakes on VRC Oaks day.
When the Ascot Vale Stakes was Victoria's premier autumn race for two-year-olds from 1863 to 1965 and held on Australian Cup day, it was won by trainer James Scobie 12 times and jockey Bobby Lewis nine times—all of Lewis's wins were on Scobie-trained horses.
James Scobie's winners were: Cyden 1926, Rosina 1922, Isa 1921, Midilli 1920, Thrice 1917, Deneb 1916, Two 1915, Wolawa 1912, Charles Stuart 1905, Emir 1903, Hautvilliers 1901, Malster 1900). Lewis' nine were Rosina, Isa, Thrice, Deneb, Two, Wolawa, Charles Stuart, Emir and Hautvilliers.

VRC Kennedy Mile (1600m)—Flemington

Of $1,000,000. Group 1. Quality, Minimum Weight 52.5kg. November 3, 2018.

2017-18 RESULT: Time: 1:35.01 (Good 3)

FP	NO	HORSE	TRAINER	JOCKEY	MARGIN	BAR.	WGT	SP
1	9	SHILLELAGH	Chris Waller	Michael Dee		2	52kg	$12
2	5	TOM MELBOURNE	Chris Waller	Glen Boss	0.2L	6	53.5kg	$5
3	14	WYNDSPELLE	Michael Kent	Craig Williams	2.95L	7	52kg	$41
4	12	ALL OUR ROADS	Chris Waller	Jeff Lloyd	3.05L	1	52kg	$8.50
5	13	RADIPOLE	Michael Moroney	Patrick Moloney	3.25L	11	52kg	$21
6	8	OMEI SWORD	Chris Waller	Tommy Berry	3.75L	8	52kg	$31
7	10	SOVEREIGN NATION	David & Ben Hayes & Tom Dabernig	Regan Bayliss	4.25L	3	52kg	$14
8	1	TOSEN STARDOM	Darren Weir	Damian Lane	5.25L	9	58kg	$4.80f
9	3	SENSE OF OCCASION	Kris Lees	Corey Brown	6.5L	4	56.5kg	$101
10	6	EGG TART	Chris Waller	Kerrin McEvoy	7.25L	10	52kg	$6.50
11	11	SO SI BON	Robbie Laing	Craig Newitt	7.45L	12	52kg	$26
12	7	DIBAYANI	David & Ben Hayes & Tom Dabernig	Cory Parish	7.95L	5	52kg	$21
13	2	LUCKY HUSSLER	Darren Weir	Blake Shinn	8.95L	14	56.5kg	$10
14	4	MCCREERY	Chris Waller	Brenton Avdulla	9.35L	13	53.5kg	$31

PAST WINNERS

YEAR	WINNER	JOCKEY	TRAINER	2ND	3RD	TIME
2017	Shillelagh	Michael Dee	Chris Waller	Tom Melbourne	Wyndspelle	1:35.0
2016	Le Romain	Hugh Bowman	Kris Lees	McCreery	Tivaci	1:34.9
2015	Turn Me Loose	Kerrin McEvoy	Murray Baker	Politeness	Rock Sturdy	1:36.2
2014	Hucklebuck	Domenic Tourneur	Phillip Stokes	Lucky Hussler	The Cleaner	1:34.6
2013	Boban	Glyn Schofield	Chris Waller	Smokin' Joey	Speediness	1:36.5
2012	Happy Trails	Damien Oliver	Paul Beshara	Fawkner	Secret Admirer	1:35.9
2011	Albert The Fat	Mark Zahra	Chris Waller	King's Rose	Secret Admirer	1:36.0
2010	Wall Street	Hugh Bowman	Jeff Lynds	Dao Dao	Chasm	1:36.7
2009	All American	Corey Brown	David Hayes	So You Think	Gold Salute	1:33.9
2008	All Silent	Dwayne Dunn	Grahame Begg	Sea Battle	Mimi Lebrock	1:35.8
2007	Tears I Cry	Nikita Berriman	Ciaron Maher	Bird Dancer	Shinzig	1:35.2
2006	Divine Madonna	Stephen Baster	Mark Kavanagh	Niconero	Valedictum	1:35.5
2005	Valedictum	Steven King	Danny O'Brien	Infinite Grace	Shania Dane	1:34.9
2004	Sky Cuddle	Jason Benbow	Peter Moody	Lad Of The Manor	Skewiff	1:39.1
2003	Titanic Jack	Brett Prebble	Tom Hughes Jnr	True Glo	Crawl	1:34.7
2002	Scenic Peak	Danny Nikolic	Danny J Bougoure	Crawl	Excellerator	1:33.4
2001	Desert Eagle	Kerrin McEvoy	Mathew Ellerton	Emission	La Bella Dama	1:37.3
2000	Testa Rossa	Patrick Payne	Dean Lawson	Weasel Will	Crawl	1:35.5
1999	Bonanova	Jim Cassidy	Grahame Begg	Umrum	Nina Haraka	1:38.2
1998	Bezeal Bay	Jim Cassidy	Paul Perry	Buster Jones	Pursuits	1:35.2

BACKGROUND

First run: 1881 (won by Courtenay). Group 1 since 1979. Run over 1800m 1881-94; 1600m since 1895. Previously known as the Nissan Stakes, Honda Stakes, Chrysler Stakes, Ampol Stakes, George Adams Handicap, and more recently the Emirates Stakes (1998-2015). Registered name Cantala Stakes (replaced the Coburg Stakes, 1881 to 1918). Moved from Final Day to Derby Day in 2016.
(Statistics date from 1919 when registered as the Cantala Stakes.)
Most recent mare to win: Shillelagh (2017).
Most recent 3YO to win: C&G—Silver Bounty (1980); Filly—Storm Queen (1966).
Multiple winners: 4—Seascay (1995, 1994); Heroic Stone (1967, 1965); Aquanita (1961, 1960); Amounis (1929, 1926).
Fastest time (1600m): Scenic Peak (2002) 1:33.40.

Notable winners: Le Romain (2016); Turn Me Loose (2015); Boban (2013); Testa Rossa (2000); Shaftesbury Avenue (1990); Better Loosen Up (1989); Magari (1982); Silver Bounty (1980); Family Of Man (1978); Maybe Mahal (1976); Taj Rossi (1973); All Shot (1972); Gunsynd (1971); Vain (1969); Storm Queen (1966); Wenona Girl (1963); Aquanita (1961, 1960); Matrice (1956); Prince Cortauld (1954); Royal Gem (1945); Amounis (1929, 1926); Violoncello (1922).

Cantala Stakes winners won the lead-up races:
Tesio Stakes: 1—Miss Margaret (1996).
Sir Rupert Clarke Stakes: 2—Testa Rossa (2000); Magari (1982).
Epsom Handicap: 6—Chanteclair (1986); Riverdale (1984); Gunsynd (1971); Vaals (1927); Amounis (1926); Claro (1923).
Toorak Handicap: 5—Magari (1982); All Shot (1972); Gunsynd (1971); Burberry (1943); Gold Salute (1940).
Sir Rupert Clarke Stakes & Toorak Handicap: 1—Magari (1982).
Seymour Cup: 1—Turn Me Loose (2015).
MVRC Crystal Mile: 2—Turn Me Loose (2015); Dazzling Duke (1985).
Cox Plate: 4—Taj Rossi (1973); Highland (1928); The Night Patrol (1924); Violoncello (1922).

Cantala Stakes and the Sydney "miles":
Epsom Handicap: 7—Boban (2013); Chanteclair (1986); Riverdale (1984); Gunsynd (1971); Vaals (1927); Amounis (1926); Claro (1923).
Doncaster Handicap (same season): 2—Catalan Opening (Emirates 1996); Gunsynd (1972).

Leading winning jockeys:
6 wins Roy Higgins (Skyjack 1974; Taj Rossi 1973; Gunsynd 1971; Storm Queen 1966; Brandy Lad 1964; Woambra 1962).
3 wins Jim Cassidy (Bonanova 1999, Bezeal Bay, Shaftesbury Avenue 1990); Wayne Treloar (Dazzling Duke 1985, Bit Of A Skite 1979, Galway Bay 1977).

Current winning jockeys:
2 wins Hugh Bowman (Le Romain 2016, Wall Street 2010); Kerrin McEvoy (Turn Me Loose 2015; Desert Eagle 2001).
1 win Stephen Baster (Divine Madonna 2006); Jason Benbow (Sky Cuddle 2004); Nikita Beriman (Tears I Cry 2007); Corey Brown (All American 2009); Michael Dee (Shillelagh 2017); Dwayne Dunn (All Silent 2008); Damien Oliver (Happy Trails 2012); Brett Prebble (Titanic Jack 2003); Glyn Schofield (Boban 2013); Dom Tourneur (Hucklebuck 2014); Mark Zahra (Albert The Fat 2011).

Leading winning trainers:
6 wins Bart Cummings (Catalan Opening 1997; Shaftesbury Avenue 1990; Maybe Mahal 1976; Skyjack 1974; Taj Rossi 1973; Storm Queen 1966).
4 wins David Hayes (All Americain 2009; Seascay 1994; Primacy 1993; Planet Ruler 1992).
3 wins Tommy Smith (Chanteclair 1986, Galway Bay 1977, Gunsynd 1971).

Current winning trainers:
4 wins David Hayes (All Americain 2009; Seascay 1994; Primacy 1993; Planet Ruler 1992).
3 wins Chris Waller (Shillelagh 2017, Boban 2013, Albert The Fat 2011).
2 wins Lee Freedman (Pontorma 1991, Warned 1987).
1 win Murray Baker (Turn Me Loose 2015); Paul Beshara (Happy Trails 2012); Danny Bougoure (Scenic Peak 2002); Gary Carson (Silver Bounty 1980); Mathew Ellerton (Desert Eagle 2001); Tom Hughes Jnr (Titanic Jack 2003); Mark Kavanagh (Divine Madonna 2006); Kris Lees (Le Romain 2016); Jeff Lynds (Wall Street 2010); Ciaron Maher (Tears I Cry 2007); Peter Moody (Sky Cuddle 2004); Danny O'Brien (Valedictum 2005); Paul Perry (Bezeal Bay 1998); Phillip Stokes (Hucklebuck 2014).

Points of interest:
Vain (1969) won three races during the four-day Flemington carnival. He also won the VRC Stakes (1200m, Derby day) and the Linlithgow Stakes (1400m, Oaks day). David Hayes has trained four Cantala Stakes winners—All American (2010); Seascay (1994); Primacy (1993), Planet Ruler (1992).
Nikita Beriman became the first woman to ride a Group 1 winner in Victoria when she won on Tears I Cry (2007).

VRC Myer Classic (1600m)—Flemington

Of $500,000. Group 1. Weight For Age, 3YO&Up Fillies & Mares. November 3, 2018.

2017-18 RESULT: Time: 1:35.26 (Good 3)

FP	NO	HORSE	TRAINER	JOCKEY	MARGIN	BAR.	WGT	SP
1	16	SHOALS	Anthony Freedman	Dean Yendall		10	50kg	$4.80
2	13	ECKSTEIN	Kurt Goldman	Brenton Avdulla	0.1L	12	57kg	$41
3	8	DIXIE BLOSSOMS	Ron Quinton	Corey Brown	0.2L	8	57kg	$12
4	10	PROMPT RESPONSE	Gai Waterhouse & Adrian Bott	Blake Shinn	0.3L	13	57kg	$13
5	3	FOXPLAY	Chris Waller	Kerrin McEvoy	1.05L	11	57kg	$10
6	14	NOW OR LATER	Robert Smerdon	Craig Williams	1.25L	7	57kg	$12
7	11	FRENCH EMOTION	Chris Waller	Brad Rawiller	2L	6	57kg	$41
8	6	HEAVENS ABOVE	Tim Martin	Adam Hyeronimus	2.4L	9	57kg	$16
9	2	GLOBAL GLAMOUR	Gai Waterhouse & Adrian Bott	Tim Clark	2.9L	3	57kg	$6
10	7	DANISH TWIST	Kris Lees	Glyn Schofield	3.1L	15	57kg	$71
11	1	FLYING JESS	John Moloney	Tye Angland	3.2L	14	57kg	$31
12	9	DAYSEE DOOM	Ron Quinton	Ben Melham	3.3L	16	57kg	$19
13	12	SWORD OF LIGHT	Mathew Ellerton & Simon Zahra	Damian Lane	5.8L	2	57kg	$51
14	5	SILENT SEDITION	Andrew Noblet	Katelyn Mallyon	7.3L	4	57kg	$8
15	17	ELLICAZOOM	Neville Parnham	Steven Parnham	10.05L	5	57kg	$101
16	4	I AM A STAR	Shane Nichols	Dwayne Dunn	14.8L	1	57kg	$26

PAST WINNERS

YEAR	WINNER	JOCKEY	TRAINER	2ND	3RD	TIME
2017	Shoals	Dean Yendall	Anthony Freedman	Eckstein	Dixie Blossoms	1:35.2
2016	I Am A Star	Dean Yendall	Shane Nichols	French Emotion	Denmagic	1:35.6
2015	Politeness	Dwayne Dunn	Robert Smerdon	Fenway	Azkadellia	1:37.7
2014	Bonaria	Michael Rodd	Pat Hyland	Sweet Idea	Catkins	1:36.5
2013	Red Tracer	Nash Rawiller	Chris Waller	Catkins	Fire Up Fifi	1:36.4
2012	Appearance	Michael Rodd	Guy Walter	Soft Sand	Secret Admirer	1:34.9
2011	Hurtle Myrtle	Damien Oliver	Matthew Smith	Sacred Choice	Dysphonia	1:37.5
2010	Sacred Choice	Corey Brown	Joseph Pride	Typhoon Tracy	Hot Danish	1:38.9
2009	Typhoon Tracy	Luke Nolen	Peter Moody	Lady Lynette	Zarita	1:35.3
2008	Forensics	Kerrin McEvoy	Peter Snowden	Absolutely Fabulous	Mimi Lebrock	1:35.9
2007	Divine Madonna	Michael Rodd	Mark Kavanagh	Translate	Red for Lou	1:36.1
2006	Lyrical Bid	Craig Williams	Brian Mayfield-Smith	Sea Change	Kosi Bay	1:37.6
2005	Lotteria	Larry Cassidy	Gai Waterhouse	Miss Potential	Shania Dane	1:35.4
2004	Miss Potential	Glen Boss	Bill Borrie	Alinghi	Infinite Grace	1:37.5
2003	Zanna	Corey Brown	John Hawkes	Infinite Grace	Mrs Tendulkar	1:38.4
2002	Miss Zoe	Justin Sheehan	Les Bridge	Purple Groove	Ramanos Star	1:35.8
2001	Market Price	Glen Boss	Tony Mcevoy	Pernod	Calm Smytzer	1:34.2
2000	Super Sequel	Darren Gauci	Robert Priscott	Its Platonic	Nova Claus	1:37.8
1999	Noircir	Matt Gatt	Mark Houlahan	Veil	Our Erin	1:36.4
1998	Bonanova	Damien Oliver	Grahame Begg	Lucys Way	Graceful Encounter	1:37.1
1997	Prairie	Darren Gauci	John Hawkes	On A Swing	Spectrum	1:36.8

BACKGROUND

First run: 1988 (won by Concordance). Listed race 1988-94; Group 3 1995 & 1996; Group 2 1997-2003; Group 1 from 2004. WFA from 2002. Registered as the VRC Empire Rose Stakes. Also known as the Nestle Peters Classic, Hardy Brothers Classic, Hong Kong Bank Stakes and Honda Legend.
3YOs to win: 2—Shoals (2017); I Am A Star (2016).
Fastest time (1600m): Market Price (2001) 1:34.20
Notable winners: Shoals (2017); Red Tracer (2013); Appearance (2012); Sacred Choice (2010); Typhoon Tracy (2009); Divine Madonna (2007); Lotteria (2005); Miss Potential (2004); Bonanova (1998); Excited Angel (1992); Western Chorus (1991); Natural Wonder (1990).

Myer Classic winners won the lead-up races:
How Now Stakes: 1—Politeness (2015).
Northwood Plume Stakes: 1—Politeness (2015).
Tristarc Stakes: 3—Red Tracer (2013); Typhoon Tracy (2009); Mingling Glances (1993).
Rose Of Kingston Stakes (Blazer Stakes): 1—Sedately (1994).
Let's Elope Stakes: 2—Rose Of Portland (1996); Natural Wonder (1990).
Toorak Handicap: 1—Divine Madonna (2007).
Myer Classic winners won in the following autumn:
Surround Stakes: 1—Shoals (Myer Classic 2017).
Robert Sangster Stakes: 2—Shoals (Myer Classic 2017); Western Chorus (1991)
Coolmore Classic: 1—Appearance (Myer Classic 2012).
Queen Of The Turf: 3—Appearance (Myer Classic (2012); Typhoon Tracy (2009); Excited Angel (1992).
Myer Classic winners won in the same year:
Coolmore Classic: 1—Typhoon Tracy (2009).
Queen Of The Turf: 2—Forensics (2008); Divine Madonna (2007).
Leading winning jockey:
3 wins Darren Gauci (Super Sequel 2000, Prairie 1997, Excited Angel 1992); Michael Rodd (Bonaria 2014, Appearance 2012, Divine Madonna 2007).
Current winning jockeys:
3 wins Michael Rodd (Bonaria 2014, Appearance 2012, Divine Madonna 2007).
2 wins Glen Boss (Miss Potential 2004, Market Price 2001); Corey Brown (Sacred Choice 2010, Zanna 2003); Damien Oliver (Hurtle Myrtle 2011, Bonanova 1998); Dean Yendall (Shoals 2017, I Am A Star 2016).
1 win Larry Cassidy (Lotteria 2005); Dwayne Dunn (Politeness 2015); Matthew Gatt (Noircir 1999); Kerrin McEvoy (Forensics 2008); Luke Nolen (Typhoon Tracy 2009); Nash Rawiller (Red Tracer 2013); Craig Williams (Lyrical Bid 2006).
Leading winning trainer:
2 wins John Hawkes (Zanna 2003, Prairie 1997).
Current winning trainers:
2 wins John Hawkes (Zanna 2003, Prairie 1997).
1 win Alex Aquilina (Aunty Mary 1995); Les Bridge (Miss Zoe 2002); Ricky Bruhn (Sedately 1994); Paul Cave (Mingling Glances 1993); Jim Conlan (Excited Angel 1992); Anthony Freedman (Shoals 2017); Pat Hyland (Bonaria 2014); Mark Kavanagh (Divine Madonna 2007); Tony McEvoy (Market Price 2001); Shane Nichols (I Am A Star 2016); Joe Pride (Sacred Choice 2010); Robert Priscott (Super Sequel 2000); Robert Smerdon (Politeness 2015); Matthew Smith (Hurtle Myrtle 2011); Peter Snowden (Forensics 2008); Chris Waller (Red Tracer 2013); Gai Waterhouse (Lotteria 2005); Chris Wood (Echo Lass 1989).
Point of interest:
Lotteria (2005) finished third to Makybe Diva in the 2005 Cox Plate seven days before winning the Myer Classic.

VRC AAMI Victoria Derby—Flemington
Of $2,000,000. Group 1. Set Weights, 3YO. November 3, 2018.

2017-18 RESULT: Time: 2:37.55 (Good 3)

FP	NO	HORSE	TRAINER	JOCKEY	MARGIN	BAR.	WGT	SP
1	1	ACE HIGH	David Payne	Tye Angland		3	55.5kg	$7f
2	6	SULLY	Trent Busuttin & Natalie Young	Hugh Bowman	2L	14	55.5kg	$7.50
3	3	ASTORIA	James Cummings	Damian Lane	2.2L	1	55.5kg	$8
4	9	PISSARO	Robbie Laing	Noel Callow	2.7L	9	55.5kg	$51
5	5	MAIN STAGE	Trent Busuttin & Natalie Young	Michael Walker	2.8L	13	55.5kg	$12
6	8	ABERRO	Matt Laurie	Ben Melham	3.55L	12	55.5kg	$41
7	16	WOLFE TONE	Francis Finnegan	Jye McNeil	3.75L	16	55.5kg	$201
8	7	WEATHER WITH YOU	Murray Baker & Andrew Forsman	Mark Zahra	3.95L	2	55.5kg	$7.50
9	4	ESHTIRAAK	David & Ben Hayes & Tom Dabernig	Kerrin McEvoy	4.45L	5	55.5kg	$12
10	11	OCEAN'S FOURTEEN	Aaron Purcell	Luke Nolen	4.55L	6	55.5kg	$12
11	2	TANGLED	Chris Waller	Blake Shinn	5.3L	10	55.5kg	$8
12	15	ROCKARRAL	Tony McEvoy	John Allen	5.5L	7	55.5kg	$61
13	12	GREYCLIFFE	Matt Cumani	Jordan Childs	5.7L	8	55.5kg	$11
14	14	NOTHING TOO HARD	Paul Perry	Beau Mertens	6.45L	11	55.5kg	$101
15	10	JUSTICE FAITH	David & Ben Hayes & Tom Dabernig	Craig Williams	7.95L	15	55.5kg	$61
16	13	JOHNNY VINKO	Trent Busuttin & Natalie Young	Stephen Baster	8.15L	4	55.5kg	$41

PAST WINNERS

YEAR	WINNER	JOCKEY	TRAINER	2ND	3RD	TIME
2017	Ace High	Tye Angland	David Payne	Sully	Astoria	2:37.5
2016	Prized Icon	Glyn Schofield	James Cummings	Sacred Elixir	Inference	2:36.1
2015	Tarzino	Craig Newitt	Mick Price	Etymology	Kia Ora Koutou	2:38.3
2014	Preferment	Damien Oliver	Chris Waller	Bondeiger	Nozomi	2:37.8
2013	Polanski	Hugh Bowman	Robbie Laing	Complacent	Thunder Fantasy	2:38.6
2012	Fiveandahalfstar	Damien Oliver	Anthony Cummings	Super Cool	Rawnaq	2:35.9
2011	Sangster	Hugh Bowman	Trent Busuttin	Induna	Sabrage	2:40.3
2010	Lion Tamer	Hugh Bowman	Murray & Bjorn Baker	Praecido	Retrieve	2:46.4
2009	Monaco Consul	Corey Brown	Michael Moroney	Extra Zero	Viking Legend	2:41.6
2008	Rebel Raider	Clare Lindop	Leon Macdonald	Whobegotyou	Pre Eminence	2:36.9
2007	Kibbutz	Craig Williams	David Hayes	Littorio	Marching	2:40.9
2006	Efficient	Michael Rodd	Graeme Rogerson	Gorky Park	Teranaba	2:38.3
2005	Benicio	Noel Callow	Lee Freedman	Duelled	Headturner	2:37.0
2004	Plastered	Paul Harvey	Lindsey Smith	Savabeel	Count Ricardo	2:35.4
2003	Elvstroem	Damien Oliver	Tony Vasil	Kempinsky	Our Bahare	2:38.9
2002	Helenus	Steven King	Leon Corstens	Hydrometer	Aint There	2:40.5
2001	Amalfi	Damien Oliver	Peter Moody	Zarek	Pentastic	2:34.6
2000	Hit The Roof	Glen Boss	David Hall	Universal Prince	Falls The Shadow	2:39.0
1999	Blackfriars	Greg Childs	Peter C Hayes	Shogun Lodge	Diatribe	2:36.3
1998	Arena	Larry Cassidy	John Hawkes	Sky Heights	Lawyer	2:35.1
1997	Second Coming	Greg Childs	Michael Moroney	Tie The Knot	Kalastaire	2:36.3

BACKGROUND

First run: 1855 (won by Rose Of May). Group 1 since 1979. Run over 2400m until 1973, when changed to 2500m. Australia's oldest classic.
Fastest Time (2500m): Star Of The Realm (1991) 2:33.60
Fillies To Win: 13—Frances Tressady (1923); Furious (1921); Carlita (1914); Wilari (1911); Lady Wallace (1905); Briseis (1876); Miss Jessie (1871); Florence (1870); Sea Gull (1866); Flying Colours (1860); Tricolor (1857); Flying Doe (1856); Rose Of May (1855). Note: The last filly to place in the Victoria Derby was Born To Be Queen, who finished third to Handy Proverb in 1985. But Beautiful was third to Sir Blink in 1958 and Tranquil Star finished second to Lucrative in 1940.

Victoria Derby winners have won the lead-up races:
Bill Stutt Stakes: 8—Helenus (2002); Blevic (1994); Red Anchor (1984); Taj Rossi (1973); Daryl's Joy (1969); Always There (1968); New Statesman (1961); Skipton (1941).
Caulfield Guineas: 16—Helenus (2002); Mahogany (1993); Red Anchor (1984); Grosvenor (1982); Sovereign Red (1980); Coppelius (1962); Tulloch (1957); Hydrogen (1951); Great Britain (1942); Lucrative (1940); Theo (1934); Liberal (1932); Rampion (1926); Eusebius (1918); Patrobas (1915); Lady Wallace (1905); Wallace (1895). Note: Lady Wallace (1905) is the only filly to take the double against the colts and geldings.
Stutt Stakes & Caulfield Guineas: 2—Helenus (2002); Red Anchor (1984).
Spring Champion Stakes: 4—Ace High (2017); Monaco Consul (2009); Nothin' Leica Dane (1995); Stylish Century (1989).
Caulfield Classic: 6—Polanski (2013); Amalfi (2001); Blackfriars (1999); Nothin' Leica Dane (1995); Omnicorp (1987); Unaware (1976).
The MV Vase: 5—Efficient (2006); Plastered (2004); Helenus (2002); Blevic (1994); Raveneaux (1986). Note: Since 1986, when the AAMI Vase was first run over 2040 metres, 16 Victoria Derby winners have had their final lead-up run in the Vase. They are: Prized Icon (2016); Tarzino (2015); Lion Tamer (2010); Kibbutz (2007); Efficient (2006); Benicio (2005); Plastered (2004); Elvstroem (2003); Helenus (2002); Second Coming (1997); Portland Player (1996); Blevic (1994); Mahogany (1993); Redding (1992); King's High (1988); Raveneaux (1986).
Caulfield Guineas & MV Vase: 1—Helenus (2002).
Cox Plate: 6—Red Anchor (1984); Taj Rossi (1973); Daryl's Joy (1969); Alister (1950); Delta (1949); Manfred (1925). Note: Four Victoria Derby winners have won the Cox Plate the following year as 4YOs—Dulcify (1979); Tobin Bronze (1966); Hydrogen (1952); Phar Lap (1930).
Victoria Derby winners went on to win in same campaign:
Melbourne Cup: 12—Skipton (1941); Hall Mark (1933); Trivalve (1927); Patrobas (1915); Prince Foote (1909); Poseidon (1906); Merriwee (1899); Newhaven (1896); Martini Henry (1883); Grand Flaneur (1880); Briseis (1876); Lantern (1864). Note: Briseis (1876) is the only filly to complete the Derby and Cup double. She also won the 1876 VRC Oaks.
The most recent Victoria Derby winners to run in the Melbourne Cup at three—Arena (1998, 15th to Jezabeel); Nothin' Leica Dane (1995, 2nd to Doriemus); Stylish Century (1989, Distanced behind Tawrrific). Phar Lap (1929) and Efficient (2006) are the only horses to win the Melbourne Cup as 4YOs after winning the Victoria Derby.
Longines Mile (Cantala Stakes): 1—Taj Rossi (1973)
Victoria Derby winners won the following autumn:
ATC Australian Derby (since 1979 when the ATC Derby moved from the spring to the autumn): 2—Mahogany (ATC Derby 1994); Dulcify (1979).
ATC Australian Derby (before 1979 when both run in the spring): 34—Classic Mission (1971); Silver Sharpe (1970); Tulloch (1957); Prince Morvi (1953); Alister (1950); Reading (1939); Nuffield (1938); Talking (1936); Theo (1934); Hall Mark (1933); Phar Lap (1929); Trivalve (1927); Rampion (1926); Manfred (1925); Salistros (1920); Richmond Main (1919*); Biplane (1917); Beragoon (1913); Prince Foote (1909); Mountain King (1907); Poseidon (1906); Sylvanite (1904); Abundance (1902); Hautvillers (1901); Amberite (1897); Camoola (1892); Trident (1886); Nordenfeldt (1885); Navigator (1882); Grand Flaneur (1880); Loup Garou (1872); Florence (1870); Charon (1869); Fireworks (1867). *Dead heat in the ATC Derby.
Leading winning jockeys:
8 wins Bobby Lewis (Trivalve 1927, Furious 1921, Carlita 1914, Wolawa 1912, Alawa 1908, Sylvanite 1904, Hautvilliers 1901, Maltster 1900).
7 wins Tom Hales (The Admiral 1890, Dreadnought 1889, Ensign 1888, Trident 1886, Navigator 1882, Grand Flaneur 1880, Briseis 1876).
Current winning jockeys:
5 wins Damien Oliver (Preferment 2014, Fiveandahalfstar 2012, Elvstroem 2003, Amalfi 2001, Redding 1992).
3 wins Hugh Bowman (Polanski 2013, Sangster 2011, Lion Tamer 2010).
1 win Tye Angland (Ace High 2017); Glen Boss (Hit The Roof 2000); Corey Brown (Monaco Consul 2009); Noel Callow (Benicio 2005); Larry Cassidy (Arena 1998); Clare Lindop (Rebel Raider 2008); Craig Newitt (Tarzino 2015); Michael Rodd (Efficient 2006); Glyn Schofield (Prized Icon 2016); Craig Williams (Kibbutz 2007).
Leading winning trainers:
8 wins James Scobie (Hua 1937, Trivalve 1927, Wolowa 1912, Alawa 1908, Sylvanite 1904, F.J.A. 1903, Hautvilliers 1901, Maltster 1900).
6 wins Tom Payten (Cocos 1898, Camoola 1892, Dreadnought 1889, Ensign 1888, Trident 1896, Nordenfeldt 1885).
5 wins Bart Cummings (Omnicorp 1987, Bounty Hawk 1983, Stormy Rex 1977, Taj Rossi 1973, Dayana 1972); Tommy Smith (Red Anchor 1984, Brewery Boy 1981, Silver Sharpe 1970, Travel Boy 1959, Tulloch 1957).
Current winning trainers:
3 wins Lee Freedman (Benicio 2005, Portland Player 1996, Mahogany 1993).
2 wins John Hawkes (Arena 1998, Galena Boy 1975); David Hayes (Kibbutz 2007, Blevic 1994); Mike Moroney (Monaco Consul 2009, Second Coming 1997).

1 win Murray & Bjorn Baker (Lion Tamer 2010); Trent Busuttin (Sangster 2011); Leon Corstens (Helenus 2002); Anthony Cummings (Fiveandahalfstar 2012); James Cummings (Prized Icon 2016); David Hall (Hit The Roof 2000); Robbie Laing (Polanski 2013); Leon Macdonald (Rebel Raider 2008); John Meagher (Star Of The Realm 1991); David Payne (Ace High 2017); Mick Price (Tarzino 2015); Graeme Rogerson (Efficient 2006); Lindsey Smith (Plastered 2004); Tony Vasil (Elvstroem 2003); Chris Waller (Preferment 2014); Gai Waterhouse (Nothin' Leica Dane 1995).

Breeding:
Tricolor, who won in 1857, is the dam of Oriflamme, the colt who won in 1863. Wallace (1895) is the sire of the six Victoria Derby winners F.J.A. (1903); Lady Wallace (1905); Mountain King (1907); Wilari (1911), Wolawa (1912); Patrobas (1915).

Fireworks, who won two Victoria Derbys—in 1867 and on News Years Day in 1868—is the sire of Robin Hood (1875). Prince Foote (1909) is the sire of Richmond Main (1919).

Grosvenor (1982) is the sire of Omnicorp (1987).

Points Of Interest:
Blackfriars (1999) survived a protest from Shogun Lodge. Star Of The Realm (1991) survived a protest from Naturalism. Coppelius (1962) survived a protest from Bright Blend. Browlock (1858) survived a protest from Pakenham. Malachite (2nd to The Harvester in 1894) is the only Victoria Derby winner to be first past the post but to lose the race on protest.

Trainer Colin Hayes (King's High 1988; Dulcify 1978; Unaware 1976; Haymaker 1974) is the father of David Hayes (Kibbutz 2007; Blevic 1994) and Peter Hayes (Blackfriars 1999).

Tommy Smith (Red Anchor 1984; Brewery Boy 1981; Silver Sharpe 1970; Travel Boy 1959; Tulloch 1957) is the father of Gai Waterhouse (Nothin' Leica Dane 1995). Waterhouse is the only woman to train a winner of the Victoria Derby.

Four generations of Cummings have trained winners of the Victoria Derby: Jim Cummings (Comic Court 1948) is the father of Bart Cummings (Omnicorp 1987; Bounty Hawk 1983; Stormy Rex 1977; Taj Rossi 1973; Dayana 1972); Bart Cummings is the father of Anthony Cummings (Fiveandahalfstar 2012); Anthony's son, James, trained Prized Icon to win in 2016.

Clare Lindop (Rebel Raider 2008) is the only woman jockey to win the Victoria Derby.

VRC Lexus Melbourne Cup—Flemington
Of $7,300,000. Group 1. Handicap, Minimum Weight 50kg. November 6, 2018.

2017-18 RESULT: Time: 3:21.19 (Good 3)

FP	NO	HORSE	TRAINER	JOCKEY	MARGIN	BAR.	WGT	SP
1	22	REKINDLING	Joseph O'Brien	Corey Brown		4	51.5kg	$15
2	7	JOHANNES VERMEER	Aidan O'Brien	Ben Melham	0.4L	3	54.5kg	$13
3	9	MAX DYNAMITE	William Mullins	Zac Purton	2.9L	2	54kg	$20
4	13	BIG DUKE	Darren Weir	Brenton Avdulla	5.65L	5	53.5kg	$21
5	18	NAKEETA	Iain Jardine	Glyn Schofield	6.4L	19	53kg	$41
6	21	THOMAS HOBSON	William Mullins	Ben Allen (a)	8.65L	20	52kg	$21
7	4	TIBERIAN	Alain Couetil	Oliver Peslier	9.15L	22	55.5kg	$31
8	17	LIBRAN	Chris Waller	Dwayne Dunn	9.65L	7	53kg	$61
9	5	MARMELO	Hughie Morrison	Hugh Bowman	9.75L	16	55kg	$7ef
10	12	WICKLOW BRAVE	William Mullins	Stephen Baster	10.5L	8	54kg	$71
11	6	RED CARDINAL	Andreas Wohler	Kerrin McEvoy	11.25L	23	55kg	$16
12	2	ALMANDIN	Robert Hickmott	Frankie Dettori	11.45L	14	56.5kg	$7ef
13	24	CISMONTANE	Gai Waterhouse & Adrian Bott	Beau Mertens	12.2L	17	50kg	$41
14	23	AMELIE'S STAR	Darren Weir	Dean Yendall	12.95L	10	51kg	$21
15	15	BOOM TIME	David & Ben Hayes & Tom Dabernig	Cory Parish	13.95L	9	53kg	$31
16	20	WALL OF FIRE	Hugo Palmer	Craig Williams	15.45L	15	53kg	$11
17	19	SINGLE GAZE	Nick Olive	Kathy O'Hara	15.85L	11	53kg	$31
18	14	US ARMY RANGER	Joseph O'Brien	Jamie Spencer	16.15L	21	53.5kg	$71
19	3	HUMIDOR	Darren Weir	Blake Shinn	16.65L	13	56kg	$11
20	1	HARTNELL	James Cummings	Damian Lane	28.65L	12	57.5kg	$26
21	10	VENTURA STORM	David & Ben Hayes & Tom Dabernig	Glen Boss	30.15L	6	54kg	$31
22	8	BONDI BEACH	Robert Hickmott	Michael Walker	31.4L	1	54kg	$71
23	16	GALLANTE	Robert Hickmott	Michael Dee	99.9L	18	53kg	$91

PAST WINNERS

YEAR	WINNER	JOCKEY	TRAINER	2ND	3RD	TIME
2017	Rekindling	Corey Brown	Joseph O'Brien	Johannes Vermeer	Max Dynamite	3:21.1
2016	Almandin	Kerrin McEvoy	Robert Hickmott	Heartbreak City	Hartnell	3:20.5
2015	Prince Of Penzance	Michelle Payne	Darren Weir	Max Dynamite	Criterion	3:23.1
2014	Protectionist	Ryan Moore	Andreas Wohler	Red Cadeaux	Who Shot Thebarman	3:17.7
2013	Fiorente	Damien Oliver	Gai Waterhouse	Red Cadeaux	Mount Athos	3:20.3
2012	Green Moon	Brett Prebble	Robert Hickmott	Fiorente	Jakkalberry	3:20.4
2011	Dunaden	Christoph Lemaire	Mikel Delzangles	Red Cadeaux	Lucas Cranach	3:20.8
2010	Americain	Gerald Mosse	Alain De Royer Dupre	Maluckyday	So You Think	3:26:8
2009	Shocking	Corey Brown	Mark Kavanagh	Crime Scene	Mourilyan	3:23.8
2008	Viewed	Blake Shinn	Bart Cummings	Bauer	C'est La Guerre	3:20.4
2007	Efficient	Michael Rodd	Graeme Rogerson	Purple Moon	Mahler	3.23.3
2006	Delta Blues	Yasunari Iwata	Katsuhiko Sumii	Pop Rock	Maybe Better	3.21.5
2005	Makybe Diva	Glen Boss	Lee Freedman	On A Jeune	Xcellent	3.19.1
2004	Makybe Diva	Glen Boss	Lee Freedman	Vinnie Roe	Zazzman	3.28.5
2003	Makybe Diva	Glen Boss	David Hall	She's Archie	Jardine's Lookout	3.19.9
2002	Media Puzzle	Damien Oliver	Dermot Weld	Mr Prudent	Beekeeper	3.16.9
2001	Ethereal	Scott Seamer	Sheila Laxon	Give The Slip	Persian Punch	3.21.0
2000	Brew	Kerrin McEvoy	Michael Moroney	Yippyio	Second Coming	3.18.6
1999	Rogan Josh	John Marshall	Bart Cummings	Central Park	Lahar	3.19.6
1998	Jezabeel	Chris Munce	Brian Jenkins	Champagne	Persian Punch	3.18.5
1997	Might And Power	Jim Cassidy	Jack Denham	Doriemus	Markham	3.18.3

BACKGROUND

First run: 1861 (won by Archer).
Most recent mare to win: Makybe Diva (2005). Makybe Diva also won in 2003 and 2004—13 mares (not including fillies) have won the Melbourne Cup. The others are: Ethereal (2001), Jezabeel (1998); Let's Elope (1991); Empire Rose (1988); Light Fingers (1965); Hi Jinx (1960); Evening Peal (1956); Rainbird (1945); Rivette (1939); Acrasia (1904).
3YOs to win: 23 3YOs have won the Cup, but not since Skipton in 1941. Three 3YO fillies—Sister Oliver (1921), Auraria (1895) and Briseis (1876).
Multiple winners: 5—Makybe Diva (2005, 2004, 2003); Think Big (1975, 1974); Rain Lover (1969, 1968); Peter Pan (1934, 1932); Archer (1862, 1861).
Melbourne Cup winners won the key lead-up races:
Caulfield Cup: 11—Ethereal (2001); Might And Power (1997); Doriemus (1995); Let's Elope (1991); Gurner's Lane (1982); Galilee (1966); Even Stevens (1962); Rising Fast (1954); Rivette (1939); The Trump (1937); Poseidon (1906).
Cox Plate: 5—Makybe Diva (2005); Saintly (1996); Rising Fast (1954); Phar Lap (1930); Nightmarch (1929).
Lexus Stakes (Hotham Handicap): 8—Shocking (2009); Brew (2000); Think Big (1974); Baystone (1958); Foxzami (1949); Sirius (1944); Dark Felt (1943); White Nose (1931).
Mackinnon Stakes: 16—Rogan Josh (1999); Let's Elope (1991); Empire Rose (1988); At Talaq (1986); Gold And Black (1977); Rain Lover (1968); Rising Fast (1954); Dalray (1952); Delta (1951): Comic Court (1950); The Trump (1937); Peter Pan (1934, 1932); Phar Lap (1930); Carbine (1890); Malua (1884).
Geelong Cup: 3—Dunaden (2011), Americain (2010), Media Puzzle (2002).
Turnbull Stakes 5—Green Moon (2012); Makybe Diva (2005), Let's Elope (1991), Rising Fast (1954), Comic Court (1950).
Moonee Valley Cup: 4—Kingston Rule (1990), Wodalla (1953), Blue Spec (1905), Clean Sweep (1900). Note" Prince Of Penzance (2015) won the 2014 Moonee Valley Cup and finished third in 2015.
Herbert Power Handicap: 6—Rogan Josh (1999), Arwon (1978), Van Der Hum (1976), Gala Supreme (1973), Colonus (1942), Poseidon (1906).
The Metropolitan: 5—Macdougal (1959), Straight Draw (1957), Dalray (1952), Delta (1951), Tim Whiffler (1867).
The Bart Cummings (from 2007): 1—Almandin (2016).
Harry White Classic (from 2011): 1—Almandin (2016).
Melbourne Cup winners also won in the same year:
Sydney Cup: 2—Makybe Diva (2004), Carbine (1890).
Adelaide Cup: 4—Subzero (1992), Just A Dash (1981), Rain Lover (1968), Malua (1884).
Brisbane Cup: 2—Viewed (2008, 2400m); Macdougal (1959, 3200mm).
The Derbys:
Victoria Derby: Efficient (2007) and Phar Lap (1930) are the only two Derby winners to return at four to win the Cup. Twelve 3YOs have won the Derby-Cup double at the same meeting, the most recent in Skipton in 1941. Briseis (1876) is the only filly to complete the double. She also won the VRC Oaks in the same week. The most recent Victoria Derby winners to contest the Cup are: Arena (1998, 15th behind Jezabeel), Nothin' Leica Dane (1995, 2nd Doriemus), Stylish Century (1989, distanced Tawrrific).
ATC Australian Derby: Peter Pan (1934) is the most recent ATC Derby winner to win the Melbourne Cup, he was a 5YO (Peter Pan also won the double as a 3YO in 1932). Hall Mark won the double in 1933 as a 3YO (the Derby was run in the spring until 1979). Phar Lap (1930) is the most recent ATC Derby winner to win the Cup as a 4YO.
Interesting historical pointers:
Melbourne Cup winners after a previous Cup placing: 9—Fiorente (2013, 2nd 2012); Empire Rose (1988, 2nd 1987); Hyperno (1979, 3rd 1977); Gold And Black (1977, 2nd 1976); Phar Lap (1930, 3rd 1929); Spearfelt (1926, 3rd 1924); Westcourt (1917, 2nd 1915); The Grafter (1898, 2nd 1897); Carbine (1890, 2nd 1889).
Winners by age (according to southern hemisphere time): 3YOs 23 (most recent colt Skipton 1941, filly Sister Olive 1921); 4YOs 43 (entire Rekindling 2017*, Shocking 2009, mare Ethereal 2001); 5YO 44 (mare Makybe Diva 2003*, Protectionist 2014*); 6YO 33 (gelding Prince Of Penzance 2015, mare Makybe Diva 2004*); 7YO 11 (gelding Almandin 2016*, mare Makybe Diva *2005); 8YO 2 (Catalogue 1938). *bred to northern hemisphere time.
Heaviest weight to win: Carbine 66kg (1890); Archer 64.5kg (1862); Poitrel 63.5kg (1920); Phar Lap 62.5kg (1930); Peter Pan 61.5kg (1934); Dalray 61kg (1952); Rain Lover 60.5kg (1969). Note: the two highest winning weights by a mare are Makybe Diva's 58kg (2005) and 55.5kg (2004).
Heaviest allotted weights (but did not run): The Barb 73.5kg (1869); Archer 71.5kg (1863); Carbine 69kg (1891).
Heaviest weight carried: Phar Lap (68kg, 7th 1931); Peter Pan 66kg (unplaced, 1935); Eurythmic 66kg (unplaced 1921).
Original top weights to win: 6—Comic Court 59.5kg (1950); Peter Pan 61.5kg (1934); Phar Lap 62.5kg (1930); Poitrel 63.5kg (1920); Carbine 66kg (1890); Archer 64.5kg (1862).

Most starts: Shadow King 6, Barwon 5, Musidora (mare) 5, Toryboy 5, Skybeau 5, Red Cadeaux 5
Brothers to win: Gaulus (1897) and The Grafter (1898) are the only brothers to win the Cup. The Grafter also finished second behind his brother in 1897.
Shortest-priced winners: Phar Lap 8-11, $1.72 (1930); Revenue 7-4, $2.75 (1901),;Archer 2-1, $3.00 (1862); Rising Fast 5-2 $3.50 (1954); Makybe Diva 5-2 $3.50 (2004); Tim Whiffler 5-2 $3.50 (1867). Phar Lap is the only horse to start odds-on in the Cup. He also is the second shortest-priced starter, when even money (1-1, $2.00) in 1929 (3rd).
Longest-priced winners: Prince Of Penzance 100-1 $101 (2015); Old Rowley 100-1 $101 (1940); Wotan 100-1 $101 (1936); The Pearl 100-1 $101 (1871). Post 1945—Prince Of Penzance 100-1 $101 (2015); Hi Jinx 50-1 $51 (1960); Piping Lane 40-1 $41 (1972).
Highest attendance: 2003, won by Makybe Diva (122,736); 2000 Brew (121,015); 1926 Spearfelt (118,877).
Imported winners: 16 imported winners of 18 races—Almandin (born Germany, trained Australia, 2016); Protectionist (born Germany, trained Germany, 2014); Fiorente (Ireland/Australia, 2013); Green Moon (Ireland/Australia, 2012); Dunaden (France, 2011), Americain (USA/France 2010), Delta Blues (Japan 2006), Makybe Diva (GB/Australia, 2005, 2004, 2003); Media Puzzle (Ireland 2002), Jeune (GB/Australia 1994), Vintage Crop (Ireland 1993), Kingston Rule (USA/Australia 1990), At Talaq (USA/Australia 1986), Beldale Ball (USA/Australia 1980), Backwood (GB/Australia 1924), Comedy King (GB/Australia 1910).
Leading winning jockeys:
4 wins Bobby Lewis (Trivalve 1927, Artilleryman 1919, Patrobas 1915, The Victory 1902); Harry White (Hyperno 1979, Arwon 1978, Think Big 1975 and 1974).
3 wins Glen Boss (Makybe Diva 2005, 2004, 2003); Jim Johnson (Rain Lover 1969, 1968, Gatum Gatum 1963); Bill McLachlan (Westcourt 1917, Comedy King 1919, Prince Foote 1909); Darby Munro 3 (Russia 1946, Sirius 1944, Peter Pan 1934); Damien Oliver (Fiorente 2013, Media Puzzle 2002, Doriemus 1995); Jack Purtell (Rising Fast 1954, Wodalla 1953, Hiraji 1947).
Current winning jockeys:
3 wins Glen Boss (Makybe Diva 2005, 2004, 2003); Damien Oliver (Fiorente 2013, Media Puzzle 2002, Doriemus 1995).
2 wins Corey Brown (Rekindling 2017, Shocking 2009); Kerrin McEvoy (Almandin 2016, Brew 2000).
1 win Tony Allan (Empire Rose 1988); Yasunari Iwata (Delta Blues 2006); Christophe Lemaire (Dunaden 2011); Ryan Moore (Protectionist 2014); Gerald Mosse (Americain 2010); Michelle Payne (Prince Of Penzance 2015); Brett Prebble (Green Moon 2012); Michael Rodd (Efficient 2007); Blake Shinn (Viewed 2008).
Leading winning trainers:
12 wins Bart Cummings (Viewed 2008, Rogan Josh 1999, Saintly 1996, Let's Elope 1991, Kingston Rule 1990, Hyperno 1979, Gold And Black 1977, Think Big 1975 and 1974, Red Handed 1967, Galilee 1966, Light Fingers 1965).
5 wins Lee Freedman (Makybe Diva 2005 and 2004, Doriemus 1995, Subzero 1992, Tawrrific 1989), Etienne de Mestre (Calamia 1878, Chester 1877, Tim Whiffler 1867, Archer 1862 and 1861).
4 wins Richard Bradfield (Backwood 1924, Night Watch 1918, The Victory 1902, Patron 1894); Walter Higginbotham (Blue Spec 1905, Newhaven 1896, Carbine 1890, Mentor 1888); James Scobie (Trivalve 1927, Bitalli 1923, King Ingoda 1922, Clean Sweep 1900); John Tait (The Quack 1972, The Pearl 1871, Glencoe 1868, The Barb 1866).
Current winning trainers:
5 wins Lee Freedman 5 (Makybe Diva 2005, 2004, Doriemus 1995, Subzero 1992, Tawrrific 1989).
2 wins Robert Hickmott (Almandin 2016, Green Moon 2012); Dermot Weld (Media Puzzle 2002, Vintage Crop 1993).
1 win Mikel Delzangles (Dunaden 2011); Alain de Royer Dupre (Americain 2010); David Hall (Makybe Diva 2003); David Hayes (Jeune 1994); Brian Jenkins (Jezabeel 1998); Mark Kavanagh (Shocking 2009); Laurie Laxon (Empire Rose 1988); Sheila Laxon (Ethereal 2001); John Meagher (What A Nuisance 1985); Michael Moroney (Brew 2000); Joseph O'Brien (Rekindling 2017); Graeme Rogerson (Efficient 2007); Katsuhiko Sumii (Delta Blues 2006); Gai Waterhouse (Fiorente 2013); Darren Weir (Prince Of Penzance 2015); Andreas Wohler (Protectionist 2014).
Cup trivia:
Michelle Payne (Prince Of Penzance 2015) is the first female jockey to win the Melbourne Cup. The first female to ride in the Cup was New Zealand's Maree Lyndon, who rode Argonaut Style to finish 20th behind Kensei in 1987.
The Cup has been postponed twice. In 1870 when it was delayed seven days due to heavy rain, and again in 1916 due to rain, when it was put back from Tuesday to the following Saturday. During the war years—1942-1944—the Cup was held on a Saturday, the second day of two-day meeting.
Barriers: No horse has won the Cup from barrier 18. The winningest barriers are—11 (8) and 5 (7).
Saddlecloths: The winningest saddlecloths are—No 4 (11); No 12 (11).
Rekindling (2017) and Comedy King (1910) are the only northern hemisphere-bred 3YOs to win, They raced in Australia as 4YOs with a weight allowance.

VRC Kennedy Oaks (2500m)—Flemington

Of $1,000,000. Group 1. Set Weights, 3YO Fillies. November 8, 2018.

2017-18 RESULT: Time: 2:37.25 (Good 3)

FP	NO	HORSE	TRAINER	JOCKEY	MARGIN	BAR.	WGT	SP
1	4	PINOT	Gai Waterhouse & Adrian Bott	Stephen Baster		6	55.5kg	$5.50
2	3	BRING ME ROSES	Tony McEvoy	Luke Currie	1.25L	7	55.5kg	$31
3	6	HIYAAM	Mick Price	Michael Dee	2.75L	5	55.5kg	$21
4	2	LUVALUVA	John Sargent	Blake Shinn	2.85L	10	55.5kg	$6.50
5	12	MISS ADMIRATION	Mick Price	Noel Callow	2.95L	1	55.5kg	$151
6	1	ALOISIA	Aaron Purcell	Luke Nolen	3.15L	9	55.5kg	$1.80f
7	5	RIMRAAM	David & Ben Hayes & Tom Dabernig	Kerrin McEvoy	3.25L	12	55.5kg	$16
8	8	RELIABLE DAME	Anthony Freedman	Craig Williams	7.25L	4	55.5kg	$26
9	9	SWEET MISCHIEF	Tony McEvoy	Jamie Kah	7.35L	3	55.5kg	$91
10	10	FOUR KOALAS	Brian McGrath	Hugh Bowman	12.35L	8	55.5kg	$101
11	7	LUCKY LOUIE	Anthony & Edward Cummings	Ben Melham	12.85L	11	55.5kg	$71
12	11	CIRCULEIGHT	Trent Busuttin & Natalie Young	Michael Walker	27.85L	2	55.5kg	$101

PAST WINNERS

YEAR	WINNER	JOCKEY	TRAINER	2ND	3RD	TIME
2017	Pinot	Stephen Baster	Gai Waterhouse & Adrian Bott	Bring Me Roses	Hiyaam	2:37.2
2016	Lasqueti Spirit	Brenton Avdulla	Lee Curtis	Harlow Gold	Eleonora	2:37.7
2015	Jameka	Damien Oliver	Ciaron Maher	Honesta	Ambience	2:43.3
2014	Set Square	Hugh Bowman	Ciaron Maher	Thunder Lady	Golconda	2:39.3
2013	Kirramosa	Nash Rawiller	John Sargent	Zanbagh	Solicit	2:40.6
2012	Dear Demi	Jim Cassidy	Clarry Conners	Zydeco	Summerbliss	2:35.8
2011	Mosheen	Danny Nikolic	Robert Smerdon	Dowager Queen	Roma Giaconda	2:39.3
2010	Brazilian Pulse	Craig Williams	Michael Moroney	Shamrocker	Placement	2:41.6
2009	Faint Perfume	Michael Rodd	Bart Cummings	Valdemoro	Savsbelle	2:37.2
2008	Samantha Miss	Hugh Bowman	Kris Lees	Miss Scarlatti	Allez Wonder	2:37.5
2007	Arapaho Miss	Corey Brown	Pat Carey	Serious Speed	Marjorie	2:36.8
2006	Miss Finland	Craig Williams	David Hayes	Tuesday Joy	Anamato	2:37.2
2005	Serenade Rose	Steven King	Lee Freedman	Florica Danica	Empress Lily	2:36.3
2004	Hollow Bullet	David Taggart	John Mcardle	Kylikwong	Storm Alert	2:31.2
2003	Special Harmony	Damien Oliver	Lee Freedman	Dane Belltar	Timbourina	2:39.0
2002	Bulla Borghese	Chris Munce	Ron Quinton	Lashed	Antique	2:36.3
2001	Magical Miss	Steven Arnold	Bart Cummings	Manang	Li Lo Lill	2:34.7
2000	Lovelorn	Brett Prebble	John Hawkes	Lan Kwai Fong	Lolita Star	2:35.3
1999	Tributes	Darren Gauci	John Hawkes	My Sienna	Shizu	2:34.3
1998	Grand Archway	Opie Bosson	Graeme Rogerson	Rose O'War	Zazabelle	2:37.7
1997	Kensington Palace	Damien Oliver	Lee Freedman	Only A Lady	Kilmore Quay	2:41.3

BACKGROUND

First run: 1859 (won by Birdswing). Group 1 since 1979. Run over 2400m until 1973, when changed to 2500m. First run in the same year as the first Melbourne Cup. Also known as the Crown Oaks (1995-2016)

Fastest Time (2500m): Hollow Bullet (2004) 2:31.20

Notable winners: Jameka (2015); Mosheen (2011); Faint Perfume (2009); Samantha Miss (2008); Miss Finland (2006); Serenade Rose (2005); Special Harmony (2003); Grand Archway (1998); Saleous (1995); Northwood Plume (1994); Slight Chance (1992); Research (1988); Spirit Of Kingston (1984); Rose Of Kingston (1981); Surround (1976); Denise's Joy (1975); Toltrice (1972); Light Fingers (1964); Indian Summer (1961); Evening Peal (1955); Chicquita (1949); Nizam's Ring (1947); French Gem (1938); Frances Tressady (1923); Furious (1921); Carlita (1914); Sweet Nell (1903); Auraria (1895); Briseis (1876); Sylvia (1867).

VRC Oaks winners won the lead-up races:
Edward Manifold: 17—Mosheen (2011); Serenade Rose (2005); Special Harmony (2004); Richfield Lady (1991); Spirit Of Kingston (1984); Taj Eclipse (1983); Chosen Lady (1967); Gipsy Queen (1965); Light Fingers (1964); Arctic Star (1962); Indian Summer (1961); Lady Sybil (1960); Mintaway (1959); Lady Havers (1951); Chicquita (1949); Primavera (1941); Siren (1936).
Thousand Guineas: 17—Miss Finland (2006); Special Harmony (2003); Magical Miss (2001); Northwood Plume (1994); Arborea (1993); Richfield Lady (1991); Tristanagh (1989); Toltrice (1972); Rom's Stiletto (1982); Brava Jeannie (1979); Gipsy Queen (1965); Indian Summer (1961); Lady Mogambo (1954); True Course (1950); Chicquita (1949); Nizam's Ring (1947); Sweet Chime (1946).
Edward Manifold & Thousand Guineas: 3—Richfield Lady (1991); Indian Summer (1961); Chicquita (1949).
VRC Oaks Trial (first run in 2017): 1—Pinot (2017).
Ethereal Stakes (first run in 2010): 2—Pinot (2017); Set Square (2014).
MV Vase: 1—Jameka (2015).
Wakeful Stakes: 35—Kirramosa (2013); Brazilian Pulse (2010); Faint Perfume (2009); Serenade Rose (2005); Hollow Bullet (2004); Grand Archway (1998); Kensington Palace (1997); Saleous (1995); Arborea (1993); Richfield Lady (1991); Tristanagh (1989); Research (1988); Diamond Shower (1986); November Rain (1980); Brava Jeannie (1979); Scomled (1978); Leica Show (1974); Toltrice (1972); Sanderae (1970); Light Fingers (1964); Indian Summer (1961); Chicola (1958); Evening Peal (1955); True Course (1950); Chicquita (1949); Grey Nurse (1948); Nizam's Ring (1947); Sweet Chime (1946); Three Wheeler (1943); East End (1942); Session (1940); Prairie Moon (1937); Siren (1935); Golden Hair (1933); Protea (1932).
Edward Manifold & Thousand Guineas: 3—Richfield Lady (1991); Indian Summer (1961); Chicquita (1949).
Thousand Guineas & Wakeful Stakes: 10—Arborea (1993); Richfield Lady (1991); Tristanagh (1989); Brava Jeannie (1979); Toltrice (1972); Indian Summer (1961); True Course (1950); Chicquita (1949); Nizam's Ring (1947); Sweet Chime (1946).
Edward Manifold, Thousand Guineas & Wakeful Stakes: 3—Richfield Lady (1991); Indian Summer (1961); Chicquita (1949).
The Oaks double:
VRC Oaks & AJC Oaks: 15—Serenade Rose (season 2005-06); Grand Archway (1998-99); Research (1988-89); November Rain (1980-81); Surround (1976-77); Farmer's Daughter (1966-67); Light Fingers (1964-65); Arctic Star (1962-63); Indian Summer (1961-62); Chicola (1958-59); Evening Peal (1955-56); True Course (1950-51); Sweet Chime (1946-47); Session (1940-41); Gallantic (1931-32).
The VRC Oaks and the majors:
VRC Oaks winners to win the Melbourne Cup as a 4YO: 2—Light Fingers (1964-65); Evening Peal (1955-56).
Melbourne Cup & VRC Oaks (same year): 2—Auraria (1895); Briseis (1876). Note: Sister Olive (1921) is the only other 3YO filly to win the Melbourne Cup. She finished third to Furious in the VRC Oaks. Briseis (1876) also won the Victoria Derby.
Cox Plate & VRC Oaks: 1—Surround (1976). Note: Surround is the only 3YO filly to win the Cox Plate.
Caulfield Cup & VRC Oaks: 1—Sweet Nell (1903). Note: Sweet Nell is the only 3YO filly to win the Caulfield Cup.
Golden Slipper & VRC Oaks: 1—Miss Finland (2006).
Leading winning jockeys:
7 wins Bobby Lewis (Furious 1921, Rosanna 1915, Carlita 1914, Mint Sauce 1913, Moe 1912, Sweet Nell 1903, Thunder Queen 1896).
5 wins Jim Cassidy (Dear Demi 2012, Weekend Delight 1990, Tristanagh 1989, Sandy's Pleasure 1987, Diamond Shower 1986); Tom Hales (Spice 1889, Uralla 1885, Royal Maid 1881, Pardon 1877, Briseis 1876); Roy Higgins (Rose Of Kingston 1981; Leica Show 1975, Kiss Me Cait 1971, Sanderae 1970, Light Fingers 1964).
Current winning jockeys:
4 wins Damien Oliver (Jameka 2015, Special Harmony 2003, Kensington Palace 1997, Northwood Plume 1994).
2 wins Hugh Bowman (Set Square 2014, Samantha Miss 2008); Craig Williams (Brazilian Pulse 2010, Miss Finland 2006).
1 win Steven Arnold (Magical Miss 2001); Brenton Avdulla (Lasqueti Spirit 2016); Stephen Baster (Pinot 2017); Glen Boss (My Brightia 1996); Opie Bosson (Grand Archway 1998); Corey Brown (Arapaho Miss 2007); Brett Prebble (Lovelorn 2000); Nash Rawiller (Kirramosa 2013); Michael Rodd (Faint Perfume 2009).
Leading winning trainers:
9 wins Bart Cummings (Faint Perfume 2009, Magical Miss 2001, Richfield Lady 1991, Weekend Delight 1990, Tristanagh 1989, Taj Eclipse 1983, Leica Show 1974, Sanderae 1970, Light Fingers 1964); James Wilson sen (Nitre 1899, Royal Maid 1881, Petrea 1879, Melita 1878, Pardon 1877, Briseis 1876, Maid of All Work 1875, Sunshine 1872, My Dream 1868).
4 wins Lee Freedman (Serenade Rose 2005, Special Harmony 2003, Kensington Palace 1997, Northwood Plume 1994); Walter Hickenbotham (Folly Queen 1917, Nushka 1908, Red Streak 1904, Fishery 1902); James Scobie (Rosanna 1915, Mint Sauce 1913, Moe 1912, Sweet Nell 1903); Tommy Smith (Show Ego 1977, Denise's Joy 1975, Kiss Me Cait 1971, Waterlady 1952).
Current winning trainers:
4 wins Lee Freedman (Serenade Rose 2005, Special Harmony 2003, Kensington Palace 1997, Northwood Plume 1994).

3 wins Clarry Conners (Dear Demi 2012, Arborea 1993, Research 1988); John Hawkes (Lovelorn 2000, Tributes 1999, Toltrice 1972).

2 wins Ciaron Maher (Jameka 2015, Set Square 2014).

1 win Pat Carey (Arapaho Miss 2007); Lee Curtis (Lasqueti Spirit 2016); David Hayes (Miss Finland 2006); Pat Hyland (Saleous 1995); Kris Lees (Samantha Miss 2008); John McArdle (Hollow Bullet 2004); Michael Moroney (Brazilian Pulse 2010); Ron Quinton (Bulla Borghese 2002); Graeme Rogerson (Grand Archway 1998); John Sargent (Kirramosa 2013); Robert Smerdon (Mosheen 2011); Gai Waterhouse & Adrian Bott (Pinot 2017).

Points of interest:

Sanderae (1970) is the granddam of Sandy's Pleasure (1987). Amarco (1957) is the dam of champion galloper Tobin Bronze (Cox Plate x 2, Caulfield Cup and Victoria Derby). Toltrice (1972) is the dam of Seltrice (WA Derby) and Almurtajaz (Memsie Stakes). Denise's Joy (1975) is the dam of Joie Denise (Qld Oaks), who is the dam of Sunday Joy (AJC Oaks) and Tuesday Joy (Wakeful Stakes).

True Course (1950) is the dam of Eld (Wakeful Stakes). Chicquita (1949) is the dam of Eskimo Prince (Golden Slipper). French Gem (1938) is the dam of Beau Gem (Victoria Derby) and Royal Gem (champion, Caulfield Cup etc and sire of Kentucky Derby winner Dark Star).

Pat Hyland rode Rom's Stiletto (1982) and trained Saleous (1995).

Ron Quinton rode Sandy's Pleasure (1987) and November Rain (1980), and trained Bulla Borghese (2002).

Neville Begg trained November Rain (1980) and his son Grahame trained Sandy's Pleasure (1987).

The first two Oaks—1859 (Birdswing) and 1860 (Flying Colours)—were won in walkovers.

Lasqueti Spirit (2016) was a maiden before she won the Oaks. She led most of the way.

VRC Darley Classic (1200m)—Flemington
Of $1,000,000. Group 1. Weight For Age. November 10, 2018.

2017-18 RESULT: Time: 1:08.74 (Good 3)

FP	NO	HORSE	TRAINER	JOCKEY	MARGIN	BAR.	WGT	SP
1	2	REDZEL	Peter & Paul Snowden	Kerrin McEvoy		9	58.5kg	$4
2	4	TERRAVISTA	Joseph Pride	Brenton Avdulla	0.75L	6	58.5kg	$31
3	6	IMPENDING	James Cummings	Corey Brown	1.5L	10	58.5kg	$9.50
4	1	CHAUTAUQUA	Michael, Wayne & John Hawkes	Dwayne Dunn	2.5L	12	58.5kg	$4.80
5	8	CLEARLY INNOCENT	Kris Lees	Blake Shinn	2.7L	8	58.5kg	$26
6	9	ROCK MAGIC	Chris Gangemi	Damian Lane	3.45L	1	58.5kg	$41
7	3	VEGA MAGIC	David & Ben Hayes & Tom Dabernig	Luke Nolen	4.2L	3	58.5kg	$6.50
8	14	SUPER CASH	Andrew Noblet	Katelyn Mallyon	4.3L	7	56.5kg	$61
9	13	MISSROCK	Robbie Laing	Noel Callow	4.4L	4	56.5kg	$41
10	5	MALAGUERRA	Peter Gelagotis	Ben Melham	6.65L	13	58.5kg	$12
11	7	REDKIRK WARRIOR	David & Ben Hayes & Tom Dabernig	Regan Bayliss	7.05L	2	58.5kg	$9.50
12	11	MAN FROM UNCLE	Anthony & Edward Cummings	Michael Dee	7.35L	11	58.5kg	$61
13	10	SPIETH	Bryce Heys	Brad Rawiller	17.35L	5	58.5kg	$16

PAST WINNERS

YEAR	WINNER	JOCKEY	TRAINER	2ND	3RD	TIME
2017	Redzel	Kerrin McEvoy	Peter & Paul Snowden	Terravista	Impending	1:08.7
2016	Malaguerra	Ben Melham	Peter Gelagotis	Spieth	Fell Swoop	1:10.2
2015	Delectation	James McDonald	Chris Waller	Chautauqua	Terravista	1:10.0
2014	Terravista	Hugh Bowman	Joseph Pride	Chautauqua	Lankan Rupee	1:08.7
2013	Buffering	Damian Browne	Robert Heathcote	Shamexpress	Moment Of Change	1:10.3
2012	Mental	Kerrin McEvoy	Peter Snowden	Sea Siren	Hallowell Belle	1:09.0
2011	Black Caviar	Luke Nolen	Peter Moody	Buffering	Mid Summer Music	1:08.3
2010	Black Caviar	Ben Melham	Peter Moody	Star Witness	Ortensia	1:07.9
2009	All Silent	Nicholas Hall	Grahame Begg	Wanted	Bank Robber	1:08.7
2008	Swick	Michael Rodd	Bart Cummings	Turffontein	Sunburnt Land	1:11.0
2007	Miss Andretti	Craig Newitt	Lee Freedman	Gold Edition	Stanzout	1:08.9
2006	Dance Hero	Chris Munce	Gai Waterhouse	Shadoways	Miss Andretti	1:08.6
2005	Glamour Puss	Steven King	Danny O'Brien	Barely A Moment	Cape Of Good Hope	1:08.9
2004	Takeover Target	Jay Ford	Joe Janiak	Recurring	St Basil	1:08.2
2003	Ancient Song	Scott Seamer	Peter Moody	Into The Night	Blessum	1:11.0
2002	Rubitano	Nash Rawiller	Brian Mayfield-Smith	Intelligent Star	Cosmic Strike	1:07.1
2001	Sudurka	Danny Nikolic	Brian Mayfield-Smith	Hire	Camena	1:08.4
2000	Easy Rocking	Jim Cassidy	Ron Quinton	Umrum	Tilt The Scales	1:10.0
1999	Pharein	Brett Prebble	David Hall	Toledo	Cannyanna	1:07.9
1998	Flavour	Greg Childs	John Hawkes	Scandinavia	Towkay	1:09.5
1997	Notoire	Len Beasley	Paul Perry	Rock You	Flavour	1:11.1

BACKGROUND

First run: 1960 (won by Karina). Group 1 since 1979. Handicap until 2007 when changed to weight-for-age. Renamed and moved from Saturday (Derby Day) to Final Day in 2007. Also known as the Craven A Stakes, Pure-Pak Stakes, Gadsden Stakes, Southcorp Stakes, the Salinger Stakes and Patinack Farm Classic. Registered name Victoria Racing Club Stakes.
Most recent mare to win: Black Caviar (2011). Note: Eight mares have won.
Most recent 3YO to win: Filly—Pharein (1999); C&G—Scamanda (1974). Note: Seven 3YOs have won the VRC Classic.
Multiple winners: 3—Black Caviar (2011, 2010); Planet Ruler (1990, 1989); River Rough (1984, 1983).
Fastest time (1200m): Rubitano (2002) 1:07.10
Notable winners: Redzel (2017); Buffering (2013); Black Caviar (2011, 2010); Miss Andretti (2007); Dance Hero (2006); Takeover Target (2004); Gold Ace (1996); Hareeba (1994); Special (1988); Lord Ballina (1985); River Rough (1984,1983); Always Welcome (1978); Maybe Mahal (1976); Scamanda (1974); Century (1973); Dual Choice (1970); Vain (1969); Star Of Heaven (1964); Ripa (1963); Samson (1962).

VRC Classic winners won the lead-up races:
The Shorts: 3—Redzel (2017); Terravista (2014); Welsh Prince (1971).
Manikato Stakes: 2—Dual Choice (1970); Vain (1969).
Gilgai Stakes: 2—All Silent (2009); Hareeba (1994).
Caulfield Sprint: 2—Rubitano (2002); River Rough (1984).
Schillaci Stakes: 2—Black Caviar (2011, 2010).
Moir Stakes: 3—Black Caviar (2011, 2010); Miss Andretti (2007).
The Everest (first run in 2017): 1—Redzel (2017).
Linlithgow Stakes (1200m, run on Derby Day): 6—Glamour Puss (2005); Pharein (1999); Always Welcome (1978); Scamanda (1974); Vain (1969); Star Of Heaven (1964). Note: No horse has completed the double since the races "swapped" in 2007. (The Linlithgow was run on Oaks Day until 1997, when it was moved to Final Day, and then swapped with the VRC Classic in 2007.)

VRC Classic and the autumn features:
Lightning Stakes (same year): 5—Black Caviar (2011); Miss Andretti (2007); Gold Ace (1996); Special (1988); River Rough (1984).
Lightning Stakes (same season): 7—Black Caviar (VRC Classic 2011); River Rough (1983, 1984); Maybe Mahal (1977); Century (1974); Dual Choice (1971); Marmion (1965).
Newmarket Handicap (same year): 5—Black Caviar (2011); Miss Andretti (2007); Rubitano (2002); Special (1988); Century (1973).
Newmarket Handicap (same season): 2—Black Caviar (VRC Classic 2010) Brawny Spirit (1995).

VRC Classic and Royal Ascot:
Three VRC Classic winners—Black Caviar, Miss Andretti and Takeover Target—have won at Royal Ascot. Takeover Target (2004) won the G2 King's Stand in 2006; Miss Andretti (2007) won the VRC Classic after winning the 2007 G2 King's Stand Stakes; Black Caviar (2011, 2010) won the 2012 G1 Diamond Jubilee Stakes.

Leading winning jockey:
3 wins Robert Heffernan (Zegna 1981, Watney 1980, Rooney 1979).

Current winning jockeys:
2 wins Kerrin McEvoy (Redzel 2017, Mental 2012); Ben Melham (Malaguerra 2016, Black Caviar 2010).
1 win Hugh Bowman (Terravista 2014); Damian Browne (Buffering 2013); Jay Ford (Takeover Target 2004); Nicholas Hall (All Silent 2009); James McDonald (Delectation 2015); Craig Newitt (Miss Andretti 2007); Luke Nolen (Black Caviar 2011); Brett Prebble (Pharein 1999); Nash Rawiller (Rubitano 2002); Michael Rodd (Swick 2008).

Leading winning trainers:
6 wins Bart Cummings (Swick 2008, Unspoken Word 1992, Taj Quillo 1986, Forgone Conclusion 1982, Maybe Mahal 1976, Century 1973).
3 wins Colin Hayes (Planet Ruler 1989, Special 1988, Always Welcome 1978); Bob Hoysted (River Rough 1984, 1983, Scamanda 1974); Peter Moody (Black Caviar 2011, 2010, Ancient Song 2003); Tommy Smith (Lord Ballina 1985, Galway Bay 1977, Welsh Prince 1971).

Current winning trainers:
2 wins David Hayes (Alishan 1993, Planet Ruler 1990); Peter Snowden (Redzel 2017, Mental 2012).
1 win Grahame Begg (All Silent 2009); Anthony Cummings (Final Card 1991); Peter Gelagotis (Malaguerra 2016); David Hall (Pharein 1999); John Hawkes (Flavour 1998); Robert Heathcote (Buffering 2013); Joe Janiak (Takeover Target 2004); Danny O'Brien (Glamour Puss 2005); Paul Perry (Notoire 1997); Joseph Pride (Terravista 2014); Ron Quinton (Easy Rocking 2000); Peter & Paul Snowden (Redzel 2017); Chris Waller (Delectation 2015); Gai Waterhouse (Dance Hero 2006).

Points of interest:
Vain (1969) is the sire of Zegna (1981).
Gold Ace (Dieu D'Or -Coup De Chance) won in 1996. He is a three-quarter brother to Final Card (Elounda Bay-Coup De Chance) who won in 1991.
All Silent won the 2008 G1 Cantala Stakes (1600m) on Final Day, and returned as a short-course sprinter to win the VRC Classic in 2009.
Dance Hero (2006) and Vain (1969) are the only Golden Slipper winners to also win the VRC Classic. Vain won at Flemington as a 3YO, Dance Hero was five.

VRC Seppelts Wines Stakes (2000m)—Flemington
Of $1,500,000. Group 1. Weight For Age, 3YO&Up. Novermber 10, 2018.

2017-18 RESULT: Time: 2:01.22 (Good 3)

FP	NO	HORSE	TRAINER	JOCKEY	MARGIN	BAR.	WGT	SP
1	4	TOSEN STARDOM	Darren Weir	Damian Lane		4	59kg	$6.50
2	1	HAPPY CLAPPER	Patrick Webster	Blake Shinn	1.5L	5	59kg	$8
3	2	IT'S SOMEWHAT	James Cummings	Brenton Avdulla	1.7L	10	59kg	$18
4	13	THE TAJ MAHAL	Aidan O'Brien	Ben Melham	1.8L	2	57.5kg	$16
5	7	FOLKSWOOD	Charlie Appleby	Kerrin McEvoy	1.9L	13	59kg	$3.60f
6	15	CLIFF'S EDGE	Darren Weir	Dean Yendall	2.1L	9	51kg	$6.50
7	9	HARLEM	David & Ben Hayes & Tom Dabernig	Regan Bayliss	2.3L	7	59kg	$31
8	11	ODEON	Mathew Ellerton & Simon Zahra	Chris Symons	2.5L	3	58.5kg	$14
9	5	SENSE OF OCCASION	Kris Lees	Corey Brown	2.7L	6	59kg	$51
10	12	SO SI BON	Robbie Laing	Noel Callow	3.2L	1	58.5kg	$61
11	3	GAILO CHOP	Darren Weir	John Allen	3.3L	8	59kg	$8
12	14	SAMOVARE	David & Ben Hayes & Tom Dabernig	Dwayne Dunn	4.05L	12	56.5kg	$51

PAST WINNERS

YEAR	WINNER	JOCKEY	TRAINER	2ND	3RD	TIME
2017	Tosen Stardom	Damian Lane	Darren Weir	Happy Clapper	It's Somewhat	2:01.2
2016	Awesome Rock	Stephen Baster	Leon & Troy Corstens	Hauraki	Seaburge	2:02.4
2015	Gailo Chop	Ben Melham	Antoine De Watrigant	Rising Romance	Contributer	2:03.5
2014	Happy Trails	Damien Oliver	Paul Beshara	He's Your Man	Farraaj	2:02.2
2013	Side Glance	Jamie Spencer	Andrew Balding	Dear Demi	Moriarty	2:03.5
2012	Alcopop	Craig Williams	Jake Stephens	Glass Harmonium	Ocean Park	2:01.2
2011	Glass Harmonium	Damien Oliver	Michael Moroney	Mourayan	Rekindled Interest	2:02.7
2010	So You Think	Steven Arnold	Bart Cummings	Descarado	Ginga Dude	2:04.9
2009	Scenic Shot	Shane Scriven	Daniel Morton	Miss Maren	Viewed	2:03.4
2008	Thesio	Nash Rawiller	Gai Waterhouse	Barbaricus	Sirmione	2:03.8
2007	Sirmione	Peter Mertens	Bart Cummings	Princess Coup	Zipping	2:02.3
2006	Desert War	Chris Munce	Gai Waterhouse	Growl	Aqua dAmore	2:02.3
2005	Lad of The Manor	Greg Childs	Roger Hoysted	Our Smoking Joe	Lachlan River	2:01.7
2004	Grand Armee	Damien Oliver	Gai Waterhouse	Confectioner	Vouvray	2:00.9
2003	Casual Pass	Glen Boss	Mathew Ellerton	Pentastic	Fields of Omagh	2:05.8
2002	Lonhro	Darren Beadman	John Hawkes	Royal Code	Distinctly Secret	2:02.6
2001	La Bella Dama	Scott Seamer	Graeme Rogerson	Hill of Grace	Emission	2:01.5
2000	Oliver Twist	Greg Childs	Brian Mayfield-Smith	Camarena	Slavonic	2:05.4
1999	Rogan Josh	John Marshall	Bart Cummings	Rebel	Oliver Twist	2:00.3
1998	Champagne	Greg Hall	Laurie Laxon	Northern Drake	Aerosmith	2:02.3
1997	Ebony Grosve	Shane Dye	Graeme Rogerson	Istidaad	Filante	2:02.6

BACKGROUND

First run: 1869 (won by Glencoe). Group 1 since 1979. Previously known as the Melbourne (10f) Stakes. Moved from Derby Day to Final Day in 2016. Registered as the LKS Mackinnon Stakes. Named the Emirates Stakes from 2016.
Most recent mare to win: La Bella Dama (2001).
Most recent 3YO to win: Casual Pass (2003). Note: Six 3YOs have won.
Multiple winners: 13—Belmura Lad (1981, 1980); Rising Fast (1955, 1954); Comic Court (1950, 1949); Tranquil Star (1944, 1944, 1942); Beau Vite (1941, 1940); Peter Pan (1934, 1932); Phar Lap (1931, 1930); Eurythmic (1921, 1920); Cetigne (1919, 1917); Wakeful (1903, 1902, 1901); Battalion (1898, 1897); Chester (1880, 1878); Dagworth (1874, 1873).
Fastest time (2000m): Horlicks (1989) 2:00.30
Notable winners: So You Think (2010); Grand Armee (2004); Lonhro (2002); Let's Elope (1991); Better Loosen Up (1990); Horlicks (1989); Rubiton (1987); Dulcify (1979); Leilani (1974); Rain Lover (1968); Winfreux (1967); Tobin Bronze (1966); Sir Dane (1964); Aquanita (1962); Sky High (1961); Tulloch (1960); Rising Fast (1955, 1954); Dalray (1952); Delta (1951); Comic Court (1950, 1959); Flight (1946); Tranquil Star (1945, 1944, 1942); Beau Vite (1941, 1940); Ajax (1938); Peter Pan (1934 & 1932); Phar Lap (1931, 1930); Manfred

(1926); Gloaming (1924); Eurythmic (1920 & 1921); Poseidon (1907); Wakeful (1903, 1902 & 1901); Carbine (1889); Malua (1884); Tim Whiffler (1870).

Mackinnon Stakes winners won the lead-up races:
Turnbull Stakes: 28—Let's Elope (1991); Better Loosen Up (1990); Dulcify (1979); Leilani (1974); Australasia (1973); Tobin Bronze (1966); Sir Dane (1964), Aquanita (1962); Rising Fast (1954); Comic Court (1950, 1949), Amana (1943); Ajax (1938); High Syce (1929); Manfred (1926), Eurythmic (1920); Gladsome (1904); Wakeful (1903); Mora (1899); Hova (1895); Marvel (1891); Trenton (1885); Darebin (1882); First King (1879); Robinson Crusoe (1877); Dagworth (1874); Warrior (1871); Tim Whiffler (1870).
Underwood Stakes: 8—So You Think (2010); Rubiton (1987); Bounty Hawk (1984); Tobin Bronze (1966); Aquanita (1962); Trellios (1959); Ajax (1938); Phar Lap (1931).
Caulfield Stakes: 22—So You Think (2010); Lonhro (2002); Winfreux (1967); Sky High (1961); Rising Fast (1954); Comic Court (1950); Amana (1943); Tranquil Star (1942); Ajax (1938); Gothic (1928); Manfred (1926); Eurythmic (1921, 1920); Magpie (1918); Lavendo (1916); Traquette (1915); Solution (1906); Gladsome (1904); Wakeful (1902, 1901); Marvel (1891); Isonomy (1886).
Underwood, Caulfield Stakes and Cox Plate: 2—So You Think (2010), Ajax (1938).
Cox Plate: 22—So You Think (2010); Better Loosen Up (1990); Rubiton (1987); Rising Prince (1985); Dulcify (1979); Family Of Man (1978); Tobin Bronze (1966); Sir Dane (1964); Aquanita (1962); Tulloch (1960); Rising Fast (1954); Hydrogen (1953); Flight (1946); Tranquil Star (1944, 1942); Amana (1943); Beau Vite (1941, 1940); Ajax (1938); Rogilla (1933); Phar Lap (1931, 1930).
Caulfield Cup: 10—Paris Lane (1994); Let's Elope (1991); Leilani (1974); Rising Fast (1955, 1954); Tranquil Star (1942); The Trump (1937); Manfred (1926); Poseidon (1907); Eurythmic (1920).

Mackinnon Stakes winners won in the same campaign:
Melbourne Cup: 16—Rogan Josh (1999); Let's Elope (1991); Empire Rose (1988); At Talaq (1986); Gold And Black (1977); Rain Lover (1968); Rising Fast (1954); Dalray (1952); Delta (1951); Comic Court (1950); The Trump (1937); Peter Pan (1932, 1934); Phar Lap (1930); Carbine (1890); Malua (1884). Note: the Mackinnon Stakes now run after the Melbourne Cup—moved from Derby Day to Final Day in 2016.
Caulfield Cup & Melbourne Cup: 3—Let's Elope (1991); Rising Fast (1954); The Trump (1937).
Zipping Classic: No horse has won the double since the Zipping Classic was altered from a handicap to WFA in 1999.
Japan Cup: 2—Better Loosen Up (1990); Horlicks (1989).

Leading winning jockeys:
5 wins Jim Johnson (Voleur 1970, Rain Lover 1968, Winfreux 1967, Tobin Bronze 1966, Yangtze 1965); Damien Oliver (Happy Trails 2014, Glass Harmonium 2011, Grand Armee 2004, Danewin 1995, Paris Lane 1994).
4 wins Bobby Lewis (Manfred 1926, Alawa 1909, Battalion 1898, 1897); George Moore (Roman Consul 1969, Summer Fair 1963, Sky High 1961, Hydrogen 1953); Darby Munro (Beau Vite 1941, Sylvandale 1935, Peter Pan 1934, Rogilla 1933); Jim Pike (Phar Lap 1931, 1930, Gothic 1928, Son Of The Marsh 1910).

Current winning jockeys:
5 wins Damien Oliver (Happy Trails 2014, Glass Harmonium 2011, Grand Armee 2004, Danewin 1995, Paris Lane 1994)
1 win Tony Allan (Empire Rose 1988); Steven Arnold (So You Think 2010); Stephen Baster (Awesome Rock 2016); Glen Boss (Casual Pass 2003); Damian Lane (Tosen Stardom 2017); Jamie Spencer (Side Glance 2013); Ben Melham (Gailo Chop 2015); Nash Rawiller (Theseo 2008); Craig Williams (Alcopop 2012).

Leading winning trainer:
11 wins Bart Cummings (So You Think 2010, Sirmione 2007, Rogan Josh 1999, Let's Elope 1991, Bounty Hawk 1984, Belmura Lad 1981, 1980, Gold And Black 1976, Leilani 1974, Voleur 1970, Trellios 1959).

Current winning trainers:
4 wins Gai Waterhouse (Theseo 2008, Desert War 2006, Grand Armee 2004, All Our Mob 1996).
2 wins Laurie Laxon (Champagne 1998, Empire Rose 1988); Graeme Rogerson (La Bella Dama 2001, Ebony Grosve 1997).
1 win Andrew Balding (Side Glance 2013); Paul Beshara (Happy Trails 2014); Leon & Troy Corstens (Awesome Rock 2016); Antoine de Watrigant (Gailo Chop 2015); Mathew Ellerton (Casual Pass 2003); John Hawkes (Lonhro 2002); David Hayes (Better Loosen Up 1990); Michael Moroney (Glass Harmonium 2011); Daniel Morton (Scenic Shot 2009); Jake Stephens (Alcopop 2012); Darren Weir (Tosen Stardom 2017); John Wheeler (Veandercross 1992).

Points of interest:
Isonomy (1886) won in a run-off after a dead-heat with Bookla.
Viewed (2008) is the most recent Melbourne Cup winner to start in the Mackinnon Stakes—he finished 11th behind Theseo.

WATC Railway Stakes (1600m)—Ascot
Of $1,000,000. Group 1. Quality, Min Weight 53kg, 3YO&Up. November 24, 2018.

2017-18 RESULT: Time: 1:35.81 (Good 3)

FP	NO	HORSE	TRAINER	JOCKEY	MARGIN	BAR.	WGT	SP
1	6	GREAT SHOT	Rhys Radford	Craig Staples		8	53.5kg	$31
2	1	BLACK HEART BART	Darren Weir	Brad Rawiller	0.15L	6	59kg	$8
3	3	TOM MELBOURNE	Chris Waller	Damien Oliver	0.35L	1	55kg	$5f
4	16	VARIATION	Stephen Miller	Brad Parnham	0.75L	3	53kg	$8.50
5	12	MATERIAL MAN	Justin Warwick	Lucy Warwick	0.75L	9	53kg	$16
6	14	POUNAMU	Alan Mathews	Patrick Carbery	1.75L	11	53kg	$26
7	11	GATTING	Darren Mcauliffe	Lee Newman	2L	2	54kg	$26
8	5	ULMANN	Darren Weir	Damian Lane	2.25L	4	54.5kg	$13
9	8	ALL OUR ROADS	Chris Waller	Craig Williams	2.5L	14	53kg	$16
10	9	COSMIC STORM	Grant & Alana Williams	Jarrad Noske	2.75L	13	53kg	$51
11	15	SOVEREIGN NATION	David & Ben Hayes & Tom Dabernig	Chris Parnham	3.25L	12	53kg	$21
12	2	SCALES OF JUSTICE	Lindsey Smith	Douglas Whyte	4.5L	10	57.5kg	$10
13	7	SILVERSTREAM	Adam Durrant	William Pike	4.75L	16	53.5kg	$19
14	10	DISPOSITION	Adam Durrant	Shaun Mc Gruddy	6L	7	53kg	$61
15	13	OBSERVATIONAL	John Sadler	Joseph Azzopardi	14.25L	5	53kg	$51
16	4	SUPPLY AND DEMAND	Gai Waterhouse & Adrian Bott	Joshua Parr	49.75L	15	54.5kg	$8

PAST WINNERS

YEAR	WINNER	JOCKEY	TRAINER	2ND	3RD	TIME
2017	Great Shot	Craig Staples	Rhys Radford	Black Heart Bart	Tom Melbourne	1:35.8
2016	Scales Of Justice	Douglas Whyte	Lindsey Smith	Good Project	Perfect Reflection	1:36.1
2015	Good Project	Craig Williams	Chris Waller	Messene	Balmont Girl	1:34.5
2014	Elite Belle	Willie Pike	Grant Williams	Balmont Girl	Moriarty	1:35.3
2013	Luckygray	Shaun O'Donnell	Trevor Andrews	Platinum Rocker	Fire Up Fifi	1:36.7
2012	Mr Moet	Daniel Staeck	Adam Durrant	Luckygray	Rosie Rocket	1:35.8
2011	Luckygray	Shaun O'Donnell	Gino Poletti	He's Remarkable	Westriver Kevydonn	1:34.8
2010	Gathering	Craig Williams	John P Thompson	Famous Roman	Megatic	1:35.1
2009	Snipers Bullet	Nash Rawiller	Tracey Bartley	Tarzi	Colour Correct	1:34.2
2008	Gilded Venom	Pat Carbery	Steve Wallace	Sniper's Bullet	Annenkov	1:34:5
2007	El Presidente	Troy Turner	Bruce Watkins	Hartley's Dream	Mansion House	1:34.7
2006	Belle Bizarre	Paul King	Rod Bynder	Confectioner	Niconero	1:34.4
2005	Covertly	Lucas Camilleri	Stan Bates	Early Express	Blinded	1:34.8
2004	Modem	Paul Harvey	Trevor Andrews	Mr Sandgroper	Blinded	1:35.9
2003	Hardrada	Jason Whiting	Lou Luciani	Early Express	Mapperholic	1:35.7
2002	Old Fashion	Stephen Miller	Vern Brockman	Hardrada	Corporate Bruce	1:35.6
2001	Old Comrade	Paul Harvey	Lindsey Smith	Mr Tanzania	Finito	1:37.6
2000	Northerly	Danny Miller	Fred Kersley	Old Comrade	Lizzy Long Legs	1:35.8
1999	Slavonic	Brett Prebble	Mick Price	Sister Patricia	Corporate Bruce	1:34.8
1998	(Jan) Willoughby	Paul Harvey	Michael Pateman	Bar Dreamer	Spook	1:34.5
1998	(Dec) Machine Gun To	Pat Carbery	Michael Campbell	Jacks Or Better	On a Swing	1:36.4

BACKGROUND

First run: 1887 (won by Sir Walter). Group 1 from 1980. Run over 2400m 1887-1921; 1500m 1952-1981; 1600m 1922-51, from 1982. Run at Belmont in 2003.
Fastest Time (1600m): Marwong (1988) 1:33.70
Fillies & mares to win: 35 (those listed are since 1940)—Elite Belle (2014); Belle Bizarre (2006); Covertly (2005); Miss Muffet 1987 Dec); Jungle Dawn (1987 Jan); Eastern Temple (1984); Sarsha's Choice (1978); Starglow (1973); Millefleurs (1972); La Trice (1968); Sweet Saga (1964); Maniana (1954); Tania (1949); Thorium (1946); Flame Lady (1942); Hinda (1941); Pretoria (1940). Note: Five 3YO Fillies.
3YOs To Win: 13—*Jungle Dawn (1987 Jan); Marjoleo (1977); *Millefleurs (1972); *La Trice (1968); Big Bob (1961); Aquanita (1959); On Guard (1958); *Maniana (1954); Scorcher (1905); *Florrie (1895); Carbine (1894); Will O' The Wisp (1891); Nimrod (1887); *Five 3YO Fillies.
Multiple winners: 2—Luckygray (2013, 2011); Tudor Mak (1967, 1966).

Notable winners: Luckygray (2013); Old Comrade (2001), Northerly (2000), Island Morn (1994), Better Loosen Up (1989), Marwong (1988), Getting Closer (1983), Iko (1981), Millfleurs (1972), Tudor Mak (1966-67), Aquanita (1959).

Railway Stakes winners won the lead-up races:
WATC Sires' Produce Stakes: 1—Maniana (1954).
Asian Beau Stakes: 4—Luckygray (2011); Gilded Venom (2003); El Presidente (2007); Bold Extreme (1996). Note: Old Fashion won the Asian Beau in 2001 and the Railway in 2002; Medicine Kid won the Asian Beau in 1989 and the Railway in 1990; Classy Dresser (1994) ran second to Island Morn in the 1994 Railway.
Reeves Stakes: 1—M'Lady's Jewel (1991).
Winterbottom Stakes: 4—Hardrada (2003); Jacks Or Better (1995); M'Lady's Jewel (1991); Starglow (1973). Note: The Railway Stakes and Winterbottom Stakes are now run on the same day in late November.
WA Guineas: 1—Millefleurs (1972).
Lee Steere Stakes: 7—Slavonic (1999); Willoughby (Jan. 1998); Welcome Knight (1992); M'Lady's Jewel (1991); Getting Closer (Jan. 1983); Iko (1981); Asian Beau (1979). Note: the following horses won the double when the Lee Steere was run after the Railway Stakes—Detonator (Railway 1975); Millefleurs (1972); Big Bob (1961); Aquanita (1959); Saturate (1912).
R.J. Peters Stakes: 12—Scales Of Justice (2016); El Presidente (2007); Northerly (2000); Bold Extreme (1996); Eastern Temple (1984); Starglow (1973); Royal Spring (1971); Tudor Mak (1966); Gay Gipsy (1936); Borgia (1924); Jolly Handsome (1923) Thigen Thu Peters (Dec 1909, Railway Jan 1910).
Asian Beau Stakes & Peters Stakes: 2—El Presidente (2007); Bold Extreme (1996).
Prince Of Wales Stakes: 4—Elite Belle (2014); Willoughby (Railway, Jan. 1998); M'Lady's Jewel (1991); Asian Beau (1979).

Railway Stakes winners went on to win in the same preparation:
Hyperion Stakes (same season): 3—Luckygray (Railway 2011); Old Fashion (2002); Cambana Lad (Railway 1974). Note: Jacks Or Better won the Hyperion in 1995 and the following season won the 1995 Railway Stakes. Medicine Kid (1990) and Asian Beau (1979) did the same double. Cambana Lad is the only horse to do the sequence: Hyperion-Railway-Hyperion in 1974 and 1975.
Scahill Stakes: 4—Willoughby (1998); Bold Extreme (Railway, Dec 1996, Scahill Jan 1997); Miss Muffet (Railway, Dec 1987, Scahill, Jan 1988); Eastern Temple (Railway, Dec 1984, Scahill, Jan 1985). Note: Medicine Kid won the Scahill in January 1990, and the Railway Stakes the following season in Dec 1990.
WA Oaks: 1—Sweet Saga (1964) (as a 3YO).
Kingston Town Classic: 5—Sniper's Bullet (2009); Modem (2004); Old Comrade (2001); Island Morn (1994); Better Loosen Up (1989). Note: From 2005, the Railway was moved to be run before the Kingston Town Classic.
CB Cox Stakes: 1—Elite Belle (2014).

Leading winning jockeys:
4 wins Frank Treen (Kilrickle 1970, Tudor Mak 1966, Maniana 1954, Beau Temps 1951).
3 wins Paul Harvey (Modem 2004, Old Comrade 2001, Willoughby 1998, Jan.); Jack Marshall (Royal Thrust 1962, Thorium 1946, Bobby Breen 1944); Jimmie Miller (Comprador 1931, Coette 1930, Hint 1929).

Current winning jockeys:
3 wins Paul Harvey (Modem 2004, Old Comrade 2001, Willoughby (1998, Jan.).
2 wins Patrick Carbery (Gilded Venom 2008, Machine Gun Tom 1998, Dec.); Shaun O'Donnell (Luckygray 2013, 2011); Craig Williams (Good Report 2015, Gathering 2010).
1 win Lucas Camilleri (Covertly 2005); Willie Pike (Elite Belle 2014); Brett Prebble (Slavonic 1999); Nash Rawiller (Sniper's Bullet 2009); Daniel Staeck (Mr Moet 2012); Craig Staples (Great Shot 2017); Troy Turner (El Presidente 2007); Douglas Whyte (Scales Of Justice 2016); Jason Whiting (Hardrada 2003).

Leading winning trainers:
3 wins Bob Burns (Earl Cunje 1933, Columban 1928, Cunningham 1926); Herbert Holmes (Accivity 1919, Werenda 1914, Thigen Thu 1910); F. Ted McAuliffe (Thorium 1946, Flame Lady 1942, Hinda 1941); Pat Ward (Lilyveil 1914, Artesian 1910, Man-O-War 1907).

Current winning trainers:
2 wins Trevor Andrews (Luckygray 2013, Modem 2004); Vern Brockman (Old Fashion 2002, Alpine Wind 1977); Lou Luciani (Hardrada 2003, Island Morn 1994, Dec.); Wally Mitchell (Bold Extreme 1996, Valley Of Carome (1985); Ross Price (Welcome Knight 1992, Medicine Kid 1990); Lindsey Smith (Scales Of Justice 2016, Old Comrade 2001).
1 win Tracey Bartley (Sniper's Bullet 2009); Albert Beckett (Tudor Mak 1966); Michael Campbell (Machine Gun Tom 1998, Dec.); Adam Durrant (Mr Moet 2012); Fred Kersley (Northerly 2000); Gino Poletti (Luckygray 2011); Mick Price (Slavonic 1999); Rhys Radford (Great Shot 2017); John Thompson (Gathering 2010); Chris Waller (Good Report 2015); Bruce Watkins (El Presidente 2007); Grant Williams (Elite Belle 2014).

Points of interest:
Old Comrade (2001) and Northerly (2000) won the Australian Cup (WFA 2000m) at Flemington the following autumn. Since 2005, the Railway Stakes has moved to be run before the Kingston Town Classic. La Trice, who won in 1968, was first past the post in 1970, but lost on protest to Kilrickle.

Luckygray won the 2011 Railway Stakes, 2012 Kingston Town Classic and the 2013 Railway Stakes.

WATC Winterbottom Stakes (1200m)—Ascot
Of $1,000,000. Group 1. Weight For Age, 3YO&Up. December 1, 2018.

2017-18 RESULT: Time: 1:10.06 (Good 4)

FP	NO	HORSE	TRAINER	JOCKEY	MARGIN	BAR.	WGT	SP
1	9	VIDDORA	Lloyd Kennewell	Joe Bowditch		7	56.5kg	$5
2	12	FUHRYK	David & Ben Hayes & Tom Dabernig	Damien Oliver	1.5L	9	56.5kg	$12
3	3	DURENDAL	Chris Gangemi	Shaun Mc Gruddy	2L	1	58.5kg	$26
4	7	PROFIT STREET	Peter & Matthew Giadresco	Brad Parnham	2.75L	2	58.5kg	$21
5	1	ROCK MAGIC	Chris Gangemi	Jarrad Noske	3L	6	58.5kg	$4.20
6	2	SANTA ANA LANE	Anthony Freedman	Dean Yendall	3L	11	58.5kg	$9
7	11	DAINTY TESS	Daniel Morton	Chris Parnham	3L	5	56.5kg	$18
8	8	STATE SOLICITOR	Grant & Alana Williams	William Pike	4.5L	4	58.5kg	$5
9	13	CAIPIRINHA	Simon A Miller	Joseph Azzopardi	5.5L	12	56.5kg	$20
10	10	WHISPERING BROOK	Simon A Miller	Jason Brown	5.75L	8	56.5kg	$13
11	4	DREAM LIFTER	Paul Hunter	Mitchell Pateman	6L	3	58.5kg	$61
12	5	MALIBU STYLE	Neville Parnham	Steven Parnham	12.75L	10	58.5kg	$61

PAST WINNERS

YEAR	WINNER	JOCKEY	TRAINER	2ND	3RD	TIME
2017	Viddora	Joe Bowditch	Lloyd Kennewell	Fuhryk	Durendal	1:10.0
2016	Takedown	Tim Clark	Gary Moore	Sheidel	Rock Magic	1:10.2
2015	Buffering	Damian Browne	Robert Heathcote	Watermans Bay	Fast 'N' Rocking	1:08.1
2014	Magnifisio	Jason Brown	Jim P Taylor	Watermans Bay	Shining Knight	1:10.2
2013	Buffering	Damian Browne	Robert Heathcote	Moment Of Change	Watermans Bay	1:10.3
2012	Barakey	Jason Brown	Jim P Taylor	Power Princess	Spirit of Boom	1:10.1
2011	Ortensia	Craig Williams	Paul Messara	Rarefied	Grand Nirvana	1:10.1
2010	Hadabeclorka	Willie Pike	Brent Larsson	King Kool Kat	Whitefriars	1:08.7
2009	Ortensia	Craig Williams	Tony Noonan	Idyllic Prince	Black In Time	1:08.5
2008	Takeover Target	Jay Ford	Joe Janiak	Apache Cat	Marasco	1:09.1
2007	Glory Hunter	Lucas Camilleri	Lindsey Smith	Charlie Beau	Dark Target	1:10.4
2006	Marasco	Damien Oliver	Fred Kersley	Grasspatch Girl	Electric General	1:10.0
2005	Miss Andretti	Kevin Forrester	David Mueller	Avenida Madero	Rescuer	1:09.7
2004	Ellicorsam	Willie Pike	Sharon Miller	Redwoldt	Modem	1:08.6
2003	Hardrada	Jason Whiting	Lou Luciani	Irish Pride	Golden Delicious	1:11.3
2002	Hardrada	Jason Whiting	Lou Luciani	Kaprats	Fair Alert	1:08.7
2001	Fair Alert	Alana Williams	Owen Sweetman	Old Fashion	Corporate Bruce	1:11.5
2000	Noble Sky	Peter Knuckey	John Price	Star System	Victory Trump	1:10.6
1999	Double Blue	David O'Heare	Albie Beckett	Willoughby	Rory's Ratio	1:10.5
1998	Bradson	Jason Brown	Len Morton	Century Blazer	Zedavite	1:10.5
1997	Cranky Tikit	Craig Staples	Sarah Searle	Willoughby	Cash In The Bank	1:10.2

BACKGROUND

First run: 1952 (won by Raconteur). Group 2 1979-2010. Group 1 from 2011. Run over 1400m 1952-92. 1200m since 1993. Run at Belmont in 2003.
Most recent mare to win: Viddora (2017).
Most recent 3YO to win: C&G—Hardrada (2002); Filly—Belinda's Star (1975). Note: Six 3YOs have won.
Multiple winners: 6—Buffering (2015, 2013); Ortensia (2011, 2009); Hardrada (2003, 2002); Belinda's Star (1976, 1975); La Trice (1971, 1970); Asteroid (1955, 1953).
Fastest time (1200m): Buffering (2015) 1:08.17
Notable winners: Buffering (2015, 2013); Barakey (2012); Ortensia (2011, 2009); Takeover Target (2008); Marasco (2006); Miss Andretti (2005); Ellicorsam (2004); Hardrada (2003, 2002); Jacks Or Better (2005); Barrosa Boy (1992); M'Lady's Jewel (1991); Carry A Smile (1989); Sky Filou (1988); Placid Ark (1987); Fimiston (1986); Asian Beau (1979); Romantic Dream (1977); Big Bob (1963); Nicopolis (1962); Chestnut Lady (1954); Raconteur (1952).

Winterbottom Stakes winners won the lead-up races:
Moir Stakes: 1—Buffering (2015).
Manikato Stakes: 1—Buffering (2013).
Darley Classic: 1—Buffering (2013).
Asian Beau Stakes: 2 – Fimiston (1986); Nitro Lad (1982).
Colonel Reeves Stakes: 2—Barakey (2012); M'lady's Jewel (1991).
Prince Of Wales Stakes (before 2008 was run after the Winterbottom): 7—Miss Andretti (2005); M'Lady's Jewel (1991); Carry A Smile (1989); Fimiston (1988); Belinda's Star (1976, 1975); Starglow (1973); Sherolythe (1969). Note: Belinda's Star completed the double in successive years.
Lee Steere Stakes (before 2008 was run after the Winterbottom): 10—Magnifisio (2014); Ellicorsam (2004); Hardrada (2002); M'Lady's Jewel (1991); Carry A Smile (1989); Sky Filou (1988); Asian Beau (1979); Sherolythe (Winterbottom Nov 1969; Lee Steere Jan 1970); McHarry (Winterbottom Nov 1956; Lee Steere Jan 1957); Chestnut Lady (Winterbottom Nov 1954; Lee Steere Jan 1955).

Winterbottom Stakes and other features now run on the same day:
WA Guineas: 2—Nicopolis (1962); Raconteur (1952).
Railway Stakes: 4—Hardrada (2003); Jacks Or Better (1995); M'Lady's Jewel (1991); Starglow (1973).

Leading winning jockey:
3 wins Jason Brown (Magnifisio 2014, Barakey 2012, Bradson 1998).

Current winning jockeys:
3 wins Jason Brown (Magnifisio 2014, Barakey 2012, Bradson 1998).
2 wins Damian Browne (Buffering 2015, 2013); Willie Pike (Hadabeclorka 2010, Ellicorsam 2004); Jason Whiting (Hardrada 2003, 2002); Craig Williams (Ortensia 2011, 2009).
1 win Joe Bowditch (Viddora 2017); Lucas Camilleri (Glory Hunter 2007); Tim Clark (Takedown 2016); Jay Ford (Takeover Target 2008); Kevin Forrester (Miss Andretti 2005); Paul Harvey (French Sound 1996); Peter Knuckey (Noble Sky 2000); Shaun O'Donnell (Sir Tinka 1993); Damien Oliver (Marasco 2006); Craig Staples (Cranky Tikit 1997).

Leading winning trainer:
3 wins Wally Mitchell (Placid Ark 1987, Nitro Lad 1982, Scarlet Gem 1980).

Current winning trainers:
3 wins Wally Mitchell (Placid Ark 1987, Nitro Lad 1982, Scarlet Gem 1980).
2 wins Lou Luciani (Hardrada 2003, 2002); Sharon Miller (Ellicorsam 2004, Petite Amour 1994).
1 win Albert Beckett (Double Blue 1999); Rob Heathcote (Buffering 2013); Joe Janiak (Takeover Target 2008); Lloyd Kennewell (Viddora 2017); Fred Kersley (Marasco 2006); Brent Larsson (Hadabeclorka 2010); Ted Martinovich (Carry A Smile 1989); Paul Messara (Ortensia 2011); Gary Moore (Takedown 2016); Tony Noonan (Ortensia 2009); John Price (Noble Sky 2000); Lindsey Smith (Glory Hunter 2007); Jim Taylor (Barakey 2012).

Points of interest:
Not only is M'Lady's Jewel the only horse to win a Reeves Stakes, Prince Of Wales Stakes, Winterbottom Stakes, Lee Steere Stakes and Railway Stakes, she did it in the one dominant campaign in the summer of 1991.
Miss Andretti won four Victorian Group 1 races in the 2006-07 season when trained by Lee Freedman—the Manikato Stakes, Australia Stakes and Lightning Stakes at M. Valley, and the Newmarket Hcp at Caulfield.
Placid Ark (1987) previously won the 1987 Melbourne G1 sprint treble—Lightning Stakes (Flemington), Oakleigh Plate (Caulfield) and Newmarket Handicap (Flemington)—as a 3YO, the first horse to complete the feat.
Barrosa Boy (1992) won the Winterbottom after a successful winter campaign in Brisbane, winning the 1992 G1 Doomben 10,000 at Doomben.
Ellicorsam (2004) won the 2006 G1 Robert Sangster Stakes at Morphettville for new trainer Lee Freedman.
Sky Filou (1988) previously won the 1987 G1 Salinger Stakes at Flemington.
Fimiston (1982) is the sire of Winterbottom winners Ellicorsam (2004) and Fair Alert (2001). Raconteur (1952) sired the winner Acello (1972).
Eric Treffone won the first Winterbottom riding Raconteur in 1952. He also trained Watersan to win in 1965.
Graeme Webster snr—rode Starglow (1973) and Asian Beau (1979); as a trainer he won with Sir Tinka (1993).

WATC Kingston Town Classic (1800m)—Ascot
Of $1,000,000. Group 1. Weight For Age, 3YO&Up. December 8, 2018.

2017-18 RESULT: Time: 1:49.50 (Good 4)

FP	NO	HORSE	TRAINER	JOCKEY	MARGIN	BAR.	WGT	SP
1	5	POUNAMU	Alan Mathews	Patrick Carbery		8	59kg	$21
2	6	MATERIAL MAN	Justin Warwick	Mitchell Pateman	0.5L	6	59kg	$31
3	13	ACHERNAR STAR	Simon A Miller	Chris Parnham	0.75L	4	52kg	$8.50
4	15	PERFECT JEWEL	Grant & Alana Williams	William Pike	1.5L	9	50kg	$5.50
5	2	IT'S SOMEWHAT	James Cummings	Brenton Avdulla	2L	11	59kg	$7
6	12	ROYAL STAR	Grant & Alana Williams	Jarrad Noske	2.25L	10	56.5kg	$41
7	14	MONEY MAHER	Daniel & Ben Pearce	Joseph Azzopardi	3.25L	2	52kg	$41
8	3	GREAT SHOT	Rhys Radford	Craig Staples	4.5L	12	59kg	$41
9	1	BLACK HEART BART	Darren Weir	Brad Rawiller	5.25L	1	59kg	$3.20f
10	11	COSMIC STORM	Grant & Alana Williams	Glenn Smith	5.25L	3	57kg	$41
11	4	TOM MELBOURNE	Chris Waller	Damien Oliver	5.5L	7	59kg	$9
12	8	LIFE LESS ORDINARY	Chris Waller	Douglas Whyte	7.25L	5	59kg	$14
13	7	ALL OUR ROADS	Chris Waller	Michael Walker	8L	13	59kg	$41

PAST WINNERS

YEAR	WINNER	JOCKEY	TRAINER	2ND	3RD	TIME
2017	Pounamu	Pat Carbery	Alan Mathews	Material Man	Achernar Star	1:49.5
2016	Stratum Star	Damian Lane	Darren Weir	Scales Of Justice	Perfect Reflection	1:49.4
2015	Perfect Reflection	Willie Pike	Grant Williams	Delicacy	Dark Musket	1:53.7
2014	Moriarty	Douglas Whyte	Chris Waller	Disposition	Elite Belle	1:48.7
2013	Ihtsahymn	Steven Parnham	Fred Kersley	Luckygray	Rohan	1:49.9
2012	Luckygray	Shaun O'Donnell	Gino Poletti	Mr Moet	God Has Spoken	1:50.6
2011	Playing God	Steven Parnham	Neville Parnham	Ranger	King Saul	1:49.5
2010	Playing God	Steven Parnham	Neville Parnham	Impressive Jeuney	Trusting	1:48.9
2009	Sniper's Bullet	Damien Oliver	Tracey Bartley	God Has Spoken	Scenic Shot	1:46.9
2008	Niconero	Brad Rawiller	David Hayes	Gilded Venom	Sniper's Bullet	1:46.9
2007	Megatic	Paul Harvey	Albert Beckett	Guyno	New Spice	1:48.0
2006	Niconero	Brad Rawiller	David Hayes	Scenic Shot	Daka's Gem	1:47.4
2005	Early Express	Jason Whiting	Peter Giadresco	Lock The Vault	Bon Argent	1:48.0
2004	Modem	Paul Harvey	Trevor Andrews	Free At Last	True Steel	1:50.1
2003	True Steel	Clint Harvey	Maxine Payne	Milanova	Hardrada	2:03.6
2002	Blevvo	Peter Farrell	David Harrison	Finito	Corporate Bruce	1:52.1
2001	Old Comrade	Paul Harvey	Lindsey Smith	Miss Precisely	Shot Of Thunder	1:50.0
2000	Old Comrade	Paul Harvey	Lindsey Smith	Umrum	Slideaway	1:36.2
1999	St Clemens Belle	Jim Cassidy	Russell Cameron	Iron Horse	Slavonic	1:34.9
1998	Old Nick	Peter Knuckey	Greg Harper	Pennyweight Point	Summer Beau	1:48.8
1997	Summer Beau	Danny Miller	Bob Taylor	Maximal	Brooklyn Bridge	1:48.5

BACKGROUND
First run: 1976 (won by Family Of Man). Group 1 from 1979. Run over 1600m 1999-2000; 2000m 2003. Run at Belmont in 2003. Formerly known as the Fruit 'N' Veg Stakes, Western Mail Classic, Winfield Stakes, Rothwell Stakes, Beat Diabetes Stakes and the Marlboro Stakes.
Fastest Time (1800m): Better Loosen Up (1989) & Bar Landy (1990) 1:47.20
Mares to win: 3—St. Clemens Belle (1999); Credit Account (1993); Doodlakine Lass (1987). Note: Perfect Reflection (2015) is the only 3YO filly to win.
3YOs to win: 15—Perfect Reflection* (2015); Playing God (2010); Megatic (2007); Old Comrade (2000); Old Nick (1998); Summer Beau (1996); Old Role (1991); Military Plume (1986); Rant And Rave (1985); Importune (1984); Bounty Hawk (1983); Sovereign Red (1980); Mighty Kingdom (1979); Stormy Rex (1977); Family Of Man (1976). *the only filly
Multiple winners: 5—Playing God (2011, 2010); Niconero (2008, 2006); Old Comrade (2001, 2000); Summer Beau (1997, 1996); Family Of Man (1978, 1976).
Notable winners: Stratum Star (2016); Playing God (2011, 2010); Niconero (2008, 2006); Old Comrade (2001, 2000); Summer Beau (1997, 1996); Island Morn (1994); Better Loosen Up (1989); Vo Rogue (1988); Military Plume (1986); Bounty Hawk (1983), Kingston Town (1982); Sovereign Red (1980); Mighty Kingdom (1979); Family Of Man (1978, 1976); Stormy Rex (1977).

Kingston Town Classic winners won the spring lead-up races:
Caulfield Cup: 1—Mighty Kingdom (1979).
Victoria Derby: 3—Bounty Hawk (1983); Sovereign Red (1980); Stormy Rex (1977).
Cox Plate: 1—Kingston Town (1982).
WA Champion Fillies Stakes: 1—Perfect Reflection (2015).
Belgravia Stakes: 1—Perfect Reflection (2015).
R.J. Peters Stakes: None. Note: In 2001, Old Comrade finished second in the Peters Stakes, and won the Kingston Town Classic; as did Island Morn in 1994.
Railway Stakes: 5—Sniper's Bullet (2009); Modem (2004); Old Comrade (2001); Island Morn (1994); Better Loosen Up (1989). Note: Until 2005, the Railway was run after the Kingston Town Classic.
WA Guineas: 6—Ihtsahymn (2013); Playing God (2010); Megatic (2007); Old Nick (1998); Summer Beau (1996); Importune (1984). Note: Summer Beau (1996) also won the Kingston Town Classic in 1997.

Kingston Town Classic winners went on to win in the same preparation:
C.B. Cox Stakes: 3—Pounamu (2017); Ihtsahymn (2013); Early Express (2005).
Perth Cup: None.

Kingston Town Classic and the Australian Cup:
Australian Cup (same season): 2—Niconero (Kingston Town Classic 2008); Old Comrade (2001).

Leading winning jockeys:
4 wins Paul Harvey (Megatic 2007, Modem 2004, Old Comrade 2001, 2000).
3 wins Steven Parnham (Ihtsahymn 2013, Playing God 2012, 2011).

Current winning jockeys:
4 wins Paul Harvey (Megatic 2007, Modem 2004, Old Comrade 2001, 2000).
3 wins Steven Parnham (Ihtsahymn 2013, Playing God 2012, 2011).
2 wins Brad Rawiller (Niconero 2008, 2006); Shaun O'Donnell (Luckygray 2012, Summer Beau 1996).
1 win Pat Carbery (Pounamu 2017); Peter Farrell (Blevvo 2002); Clint Harvey (True Steel 2003); Peter Knuckey (Old Nick 1998); Damian Lane (Stratum Star 2016); Damien Oliver (Sniper's Bullet 2009); Willie Pike (Perfect Reflection 2015); Jason Whiting (Early Express 2005); Douglas Whyte (Moriarty 2014).

Leading winning trainers:
3 wins David Hayes (Niconero 2008, 2006, Credit Account 1993).
2 wins Albert Beckett (Megatic 2007, Old Role 1991); Bart Cummings (Bounty Hawk 1983, Stormy Rex 1977); George Hanlon (Family Of Man 1978, 1976); Colin Hayes (Better Loosen Up 1989, Military Plume 1986); Lindsey Smith (Old Comrade 2001, 2000); Tommy Smith (Kingston Town 1982, Mighty Kingdom 1979); Bob Taylor (Summer Beau 1997, 1996).

Current winning trainers:
3 wins David Hayes (Niconero 2008, 2006, Credit Account 1993).
2 wins Albert Beckett (Megatic 2007, Old Role 1991); Lindsey Smith (Old Comrade 2001, 2000).
1 win Trevor Andrews (Modem 2004); Tracey Bartley (Sniper's Bullet 2009); Russell Cameron (St. Clements Belle 1999); Peter Giadresco (Early Express 2005); David Harrison (Blevvo 2002); Lou Luciani (Island Morn 1994); Alan Mathews (Pounamu 2017); Maxine Payne (True Steel 2003); Chris Waller (Moriarty 2014); Darren Weir (Stratum Star 2016); Grant Williams (Perfect Reflection 2015).

Point of interest:
The mares, Alcove and Circles Of Gold, dead-heated for second behind Summer Beau in 1996.

MRC Ladbrokes Orr Stakes (1400m)—Caulfield
Of $500,000. Group 1. Weight For Age, 3YO&Up. February 9, 2019.

2017-18 RESULT: Time: 1:24.79 (Good 3)

FP	NO	HORSE	TRAINER	JOCKEY	MARGIN	BAR.	WGT	SP
1	1	HARTNELL	James Cummings	Craig Williams		11	59kg	$6
2	10	SINGLE GAZE	Nick Olive	Kathy O'Hara	0.1L	1	57kg	$19
3	4	BRAVE SMASH	Darren Weir	John Allen	0.2L	5	59kg	$9.50
4	8	THRONUM	David & Ben Hayes & Tom Dabernig	Mark Zahra	0.3L	7	59kg	$10
5	5	LORD OF THE SKY	Robbie Laing	Damien Oliver	0.7L	9	59kg	$51
6	12	ABBEY MARIE	Michael Kent	Luke Nolen	0.8L	3	57kg	$31
7	14	MIGHTY BOSS	Mick Price	Michael Walker	0.9L	4	55.5kg	$11
8	7	MR SNEAKY	Anthony Freedman	Kerrin McEvoy	1.2L	12	59kg	$9
9	9	DOLLAR FOR DOLLAR	Tony McEvoy	Jamie Kah	1.3L	6	59kg	$16
10	11	SHILLELAGH	Chris Waller	Michael Dee	2.3L	2	57kg	$10
11	3	TOSEN STARDOM	Darren Weir	Damian Lane	2.4L	13	59kg	$4f
12	13	JESTER HALO	Darren Kolpin	Christine Puls	3.15L	8	57kg	$101
13	6	TSHAHITSI	Chris Crook & Imogen Miller	Brendon McCoull	3.45L	10	59kg	$16

PAST WINNERS

YEAR	WINNER	JOCKEY	TRAINER	2ND	3RD	TIME
2018	Hartnell	Craig Williams	James Cummings	Single Gaze	Brave Smash	1:24.7
2017	Black Heart Bart	Brad Rawiller	Darren Weir	Turn Me Loose	Ecuador	1:22.5
2016	Suavito	Luke Currie	Nigel Blackiston	Lucky Hussler	Hucklebuck	1:23.4
2015	Dissident	Ben Melham	Peter Moody	Entirely Platinum	Mourinho	1:23.3
2014	Moment Of Change	Luke Nolen	Peter Moody	Eurozone	Shamus Award	1:23.0
2013	All Too Hard	Dwayne Dunn	Michael, Wayne & John Hawkes	Mawingo	Mr Moet	1:22.8
2012	Black Caviar	Luke Nolen	Peter Moody	Southern Speed	Playing God	1:25.1
2011	Typhoon Tracy	Luke Nolen	Peter Moody	Heart Of Dreams	Ortensia	1:22.7
2010	Typhoon Tracy	Luke Nolen	Peter Moody	Heart Of Dreams	Sirmione	1:23.4
2009	Maldivian	Michael Rodd	Mark Kavanagh	Alamosa	Theseo	1:24.0
2008	Shinzig	Stephen Baster	Mick Price	Niconero	Rubiscent	1:23.8
2007	El Segundo	Damien Oliver	Colin Little	Marasco	Aqua Damore	1:23.2
2006	Perfect Promise	Craig Newitt	Lee Freedman	Lad Of The Manor	Fields Of Omagh	1:22.3
2005	Elvstroem	Nash Rawiller	Tony Vasil	Savabeel	Lad Of The Manor	1:22.8
2004	Lonhro	Darren Beadman	John Hawkes	Vocabulary	Sound Action	1:21.9
2003	Yell	Darren Gauci	John Hawkes	Fields Of Omagh	Innovation Girl	1:22.5
2002	Barkada	Scott Seamer	Lee Freedman	Northerly	Cent Home	1:24.6
2001	Desert Sky	Darren Gauci	Mathew Ellerton	Skoozi Please	Hit The Roof	1:21.6
2000	Redoutes Choice	Darren Beadman	Rick Hore-Lacy	Miss Pennymoney	Intergaze	1:24.1
1999	Grand Archway	Shane Dye	Graeme Rogerson	Bezeal Bay	Istidaad	1:24.0
1998	Special Dane	Greg Childs	Brian Mayfield-Smith	Al Mansour	Might And Power	1:22.5

BACKGROUND

First run: 1925 (won by The Night Patrol). Group 2 1980-92. Group 1 from 1993. WFA with penalties: 1925-42. Handicap: 1943-45. WFA since 1946. Run over 1600m 1925-42, 1944-56, 1961-63, 2006-2010; 2400m 1943. Run at Williamstown until 1940. Moonee Valley 1941-42, 1944, 1946-48, 1950-54, 1956-57. Flemington 1943, 1945. Sandown 1966-96. Caulfield 1949, 1955, 1958-65, from 1997.
Most recent mare to win: Suavito (2016).
3YOs to win: 19—All Too Hard (2013); Yell (2003); Barkada (2002); Desert Sky (2001); Redoute's Choice (2000); Grand Archway* (1999); Special Dane (1998); Manikato (1979); Surround* (1977); Longfella (1973); Highfire (1958); Ungar (1949); Lawrence (1944); High Caste (1940); Hua (1938); Iva* (1937); Cardinal (1936); Liberal (1933); Gallopade (1930). *fillies
Multiple winners: 4—Typhoon Tracy (2011, 2010); Vo Rogue (1990, 1989, 1988); Manikato (1981, 1980, 1979); Lord (1960, 1959).
Fastest time (Caulfield 1400m): Desert Sky (2001) 1:21.60
Notable winners: Hartnell (2018); Black Heart Bart (2017); All Too Hard (2013); Black Caviar (2012), Typhoon Tracy (2011, 2010); Elvstroem (2005); Lonhro (2004); Redoute's Choice (2000); Grand Archway (1999); Saintly

(1997); Jeune (1995); Durbridge (1993); Let's Elope (1992); Vo Rogue (1990, 1989, 1988); At Talaq (1987); Manikato (1981, 1980, 1979); Hyperno (1978); Surround (1977); Leilani (1975); All Shot (1974); Winfreux (1968); Tobin Bronze (1967); Aquanita (1963); Wenona Girl (1962); Lord (1960, 1959); Rising Fast (1956); Comic Court (1951); Attley (1947); Flight (1946); High Caste (1940); Gaine Carrington (1934); Gothic (1929); Heroic (1927); Whittier (1926).

Orr Stakes winners won the lead-up races:
Australia Stakes: 3—Black Caviar (2012); El Segundo (2007); Yell (2003).
Carlyon Stakes: 2—El Segundo (2007); Yell (2003).

Orr Stakes winners to go on to win feature races in same preparation:
Futurity Stakes: 18—Black Heart Bart (2017); Moment Of Change (2014); All Too Hard (2013); Typhoon Tracy (2010); Yell (2003); Desert Sky (2001); Primacy (1994); Vo Rogue (1988); Manikato (1981, 1980, 1979); Crewman (1970); Lord (1959); Prince Cortauld (1955); St Razzle (1950); Attley (1947); Drum Net (1945); Burrabil (1942). Note: the Futurity distance was increased from 1400m to 1600m from 2006-2010.
Peter Young Stakes: 17—Elvstroem (2005); Lonhro (2004); Let's Elope (1992); Vo Rogue (1989, 1988); Lawman (1982); Leilani (1975); Winfreux (1968); Tobin Bronze (1967); Aquanita (1963); Lord (1960, 1959); Comic Court (1951); Attley (1947); Flight (1946); High Caste (1940); Whittier (1926).
Australian Cup: 6—Lonhro (2004); Let's Elope (1992); Vo Rogue (1990, 1989); Leilani (1975); Crewman (1970).
Peter Young & Australian Cup: 4—Lonhro (2004); Let's Elope (1992); Vo Rogue (1989); Leilani (1975).
George Ryder Stakes: 3—Lonhro (2004); Manikato (1980, 1979).
All Aged Stakes: 4—Dissident (2015); All Too Hard (2013); Tobin Bronze (1967); Lord (1959).

The Orr Stakes and the spring majors:
Cox Plate (spring) & Orr Stakes (autumn): 8—Maldivian (Orr 2009); Saintly (1997); Surround (1977); Tobin Bronze (1967); Aquanita (1963); Flight (1946); Heroic (1927); The Night Patrol (1925).
Melbourne Cup (spring) & Orr Stakes (autumn): 5—Saintly (Orr 1997); Jeune (1995); Let's Elope (1992); At Talaq (1987); Comic Court (1951).

Leading winning jockeys:
5 wins Michael Clarke (Planet Ruler 1991, At Talaq 1987, Delightful Belle 1986, Fine Offer 1985, Qubeau 1984).
4 wins Roy Higgins (Lawman 1982, Leilani 1975, Abdul 1972, Black Onyx 1971); Geoff Lane (Anonyme 1961, Lord 1960, 1959, Golden Doubles 1957); Luke Nolen (Moment Of Change 2014, Black Caviar 2012, Typhoon Tracy 2011, 2010).

Current winning jockeys:
4 wins Luke Nolen (Moment Of Change 2014, Black Caviar 2012, Typhoon Tracy 2011, 2010).
3 wins Cyril Small (Vo Rogue 1990, 1989, 1988).
2 wins Damien Oliver (El Segundo 2007, Durbridge 1993).
1 win Stephen Baster (Shinzig 2008); Luke Currie (Suavito 2016); Dwayne Dunn (All Too Hard 2013); Ben Melham (Dissident 2015); Craig Newitt (Perfect Promise 2006); Brad Rawiller (Black Heart Bart 2017); Nash Rawiller (Elvstroem 2005); Michael Rodd (Maldivian 2009); Craig Williams (Hartnell 2018).

Leading winning trainers:
5 wins Ken Hilton (Future 1965, Havelock 1964, Lord 1960, 1959, Ellerslie 1953); Peter Moody (Dissident 2015; Moment Of Change 2014, Black Caviar 2012, Typhoon Tracy 2011, 2010);
4 wins Geoff Murphy (Hyperno 1978, Surround 1977, Plush 1976, Abdul 1972).

Current winning trainers:
3 wins John Hawkes (All Too Hard 2012, Lonhro 2004, Yell 2003); David Hayes (Jeune 1995, Primacy 1994, Planet Ruler 1991).
1 win Nigel Blackiston (Suavito 2016); James Cummings (Hartnell 2018); Mathew Ellerton (Desert Sky 2001); Michael, Wayne & John Hawkes (All Too Hard 2013); Mark Kavanagh (Maldivian 2009); Colin Little (El Segundo 2007); Mick Price (Shinzig 2008); Graeme Rogerson (Grand Archway 1999); Gerald Ryan (Racer's Edge 1996); Tony Vasil (Elvstroem 2005); Darren Weir (Black Heart Bart 2017).

Point of interest:
Since 2002, three Cox Plate winners have finished second in the Orr the following autumn—Savabeel (2005), Fields Of Omagh (2003), Northerly (2002).

VRC Black Caviar Lightning Stakes (1000m)—Flemington
Of $750,000. Group 1. Weight For Age. February 16, 2019.

2017-18 RESULT: Time: 56.33 (Good 3)

FP	NO	HORSE	TRAINER	JOCKEY	MARGIN	BAR.	WGT	SP
1	4	REDKIRK WARRIOR	David & Ben Hayes & Tom Dabernig	Regan Bayliss		7	58.5kg	$10
2	1	REDZEL	Peter & Paul Snowden	Kerrin McEvoy	0.1L	9	58.5kg	$1.80f
3	8	MISSROCK	Robbie Laing	Damien Oliver	1.35L	6	56.5kg	$21
4	7	SUPIDO	Michael Kent	Beau Mertens	1.55L	10	58.5kg	$26
5	5	ROCK MAGIC	Chris Gangemi	Michael Dee	1.75L	1	58.5kg	$51
6	6	BALL OF MUSCLE	Joseph Pride	Craig Williams	3.75L	2	58.5kg	$26
7	3	HEY DOC	Tony McEvoy	Luke Currie	5.75L	3	58.5kg	$9.50
8	2	TERRAVISTA	Joseph Pride	Mark Zahra	5.85L	4	58.5kg	$13
9	9	SUPER TOO	Marc Conners	Stephen Baster	5.95L	5	56.5kg	$21
10	10	FORMALITY	David & Ben Hayes & Tom Dabernig	Dwayne Dunn	11.95L	8	53.5kg	$9

PAST WINNERS

YEAR	WINNER	JOCKEY	TRAINER	2ND	3RD	TIME
2018	Redkirk Warrior	Regan Bayliss	David & Ben Hayes & Tom Dabernig	Redzel	Missrock	0:56.3
2017	Terravista	Corey Brown	Joe Pride	Spieth	Star Turn	0:57.2
2016	Chautauqua	Dwayne Dunn	Michael, Wayne & John Hawkes	Terravista	Japonisme	0:57.0
2015	Lankan Rupee	Craig Newitt	Mick Price	Brazen Beau	Deep Field	0:56.2
2014	Snitzerland	Brenton Avdulla	Gerald Ryan	Shamexpress	Samaready	0:57.1
2013	Black Caviar	Luke Nolen	Peter Moody	Moment Of Change	Golden Archer	0:55.4
2012	Black Caviar	Luke Nolen	Peter Moody	Hay List	Buffering	0:55.5
2011	Black Caviar	Luke Nolen	Peter Moody	Hay List	Warm Love	0:57.2
2010	Nicconi	Damien Oliver	David Hayes	Wanted	Shellscrape	0:57.1
2009	Scenic Blast	Steven Arnold	Daniel Morton	Typhoon Zed	Grand Duels	0:56.9
2008	Apache Cat	Corey Brown	Greg Eurell	Swick	Stanzout	0:57.3
2007	Miss Andretti	Craig Newitt	Lee Freedman	Magnus	Ticklish	0:57.2
2006	Takeover Target	Jay Ford	Joe Janiak	Gods Own	Cape Of Good Hope	0:56.8
2005	Fastnet Rock	Glen Boss	Paul Perry	Alinghi	Cape Of Good Hope	0:57.3
2004	Regimental Gal	Steven King	Shaun Dwyer	Our Egyptian Raine	Mistegic	0:57.0
2003	Choisir	Glen Boss	Paul Perry	Spinning Hill	Azevedo	0:56.9
2002	Spinning Hill	Steven Arnold	Guy Walter	Mistegic	Chong Tong	0:57.1
2001	Sports	Darren Gauci	John Hawkes	Black Bean	Easy Rocking	0:57.0
2000	Testa Rossa	Damien Oliver	Dean Lawson	Falvelon	Magic Music	0:56.0
1999	Isca	Greg Childs	Peter C Hayes	Toledo	Scandinavia	0:57.6
1998	General Nediym	Brian York	Bill Mitchell	Notoire	Show No Emotion	0:57.9

BACKGROUND

First run: 1955 (won by Gay Vista). Group 2 1980-86. Group 1 from 1987. Run at Moonee Valley in 2007. Renamed the Black Caviar Lightning in 2013.
Most recent mare to win: Snitzerland (2014).
Most recent 3YO to win: C&G—Fastnet Rock (2005); Filly—Regimental Gal (2004). Note: 22 3YOs (eight fillies) have won.
2YOs to win: 3—Desirable (filly, 1976); Ritmar (filly, 1959); Misting (colt, 1958). Note: 27 2YOs have contested the Lightning Stakes—most recent Clever Zoe (1993) second behind Schillaci.
Multiple winners: 7—Black Caviar (2013, 2012, 2011); Mahogany (1997, 1995); Schillaci (1993, 1992); River Rough (1985, 1984); Maybe Mahal (1978, 1979); Wenona Girl (1964, 1983); Sky High (1962, 1961).
Fastest time (Flemington 1000m): Black Caviar (2013) 55.42 secs
Notable winners: Redkirk Warrior (2018); Chautauqua (2016); Lankan Rupee (2015); Black Caviar (2013, 2012, 2011); Scenic Blast (2009); Apache Cat (2008); Miss Andretti (2007); Takeover Target (2006); Choisir (2003); Spinning Hill (2002); Testa Rossa (2000); General Nediym (1998); Mahogany (1997, 1995); Schillaci (1993, 1992); Shaftesbury Avenue (1991); Redelva (1990); Zeditave (1989); Special (1988); The Judge (1979); Maybe Mahal (1978, 1977); Century (1974); Dual Choice (1971); Storm Queen (1967); Citius (1966); Wenona Girl (1964, 1963); Sky High (1962, 1961); Todman (1960).The lead-up races won by Lightning Stakes winners: Rubiton Stakes: 2—Schillaci (1993); Zeditave (1989).

Lightning winners went on to win in the same preparation:
Oakleigh Plate: 5—Fastnet Rock (2005); Schillaci (1992); Placid Ark (1987); Dual Choice (1971); Citius (1966).
Newmarket Handicap: 13—Redkirk Warrior (2018); Black Caviar (2011); Scenic Blast (2009); Miss Andretti (2007); Takeover Target (2006); Isca (1999); General Nediym (1998); Shaftesbury Avenue (1991); Special (1988); Placid Ark (1987); Maybe Mahal (1978); Cap d'Antibes (1975); Black Onyx (1970).
Sprint treble: Lightning, Oakleigh & Newmarket: 2—Schillaci (1992); Placid Ark (1987).
Futurity Stakes: 6—Testa Rossa (2000); Schillaci (1993); Zeditave (1989); Wenona Girl (1963); Todman (1960).
Oakleigh Plate & Newmarket Hcp & Futurity Stakes: 1—Schillaci (1992).
William Reid Stakes: 7—Black Caviar (2013, 2011); Miss Andretti (2007); Regimental Gal (2004); Zeditave (1989); River Rough (1985); Apache Cat (2008). Note: The William Reid Stakes was run before the Lightning to 2012.
The Galaxy: 2—Gold Ace (1996); Schillaci (1992).
T.J. Smith Stakes: 4—Black Caviar (2013, 2011); Mahogany (1997); Apache Cat (2008).
Doncaster Handicap: 3—Hula Chief (1986); Maybe Mahal (1978); Citius (1966).
Lightning Stakes and Royal Ascot:
King's Stand Stakes (1000m, Royal Ascot): 4—Scenic Blast (2009); Miss Andretti (2007); Takeover Target (2006); Choisir (2003).
Diamond (Golden) Jubilee Stakes (1200m, Royal Ascot): 2—Black Caviar (2012); Choisir (2003).
Leading winning jockeys:
5 wins Damien Oliver (Nicconi 2010, Testa Rossa 2000, Gold Ace 1996, Schillaci 1993, 1992).
4 wins Harry White (The Judge 1979, Cap d'Antibes 1975, Zambari 1972, Black Onyx 1970).
Current winning jockeys:
5 wins Damien Oliver (Nicconi 2010, Testa Rossa 2000, Gold Ace 1996, Schillaci 1993, 1992).
3 wins Luke Nolen (Black Caviar 2013, 2012, 2011).
2 wins Steven Arnold (Scenic Blast 2009, Spinning Hill 2002); Glen Boss (Fastnet Rock 2005, Choisir 2003); Corey Brown (Terravista 2017, Apache Cat 2008); Craig Newitt (Lankan Rupee 215, Miss Andretti 2007).
1 win Brenton Avdulla (Snitzerland 2014); Regan Bayliss (Redkirk Warrior 2018); Dwayne Dunn (Chautauqua 2016); Jay Ford (Takeover Target 2006).
Leading winning trainers:
7 wins Bart Cummings (Shaftesbury Avenue 1991, Hula Chief 1986, Maybe Mahal 1978, 1977, Cap d'Antibes 1975, Century 1974, Storm Queen 1967).
6 wins Lee Freedman (Miss Andretti 2007, Mahogany 1997, Gold Ace 1996, Mahogany 1995, Schillaci 1993, 1992).
4 wins Bob Hoysted (River Rough 1985, 1984, Demus 1983, Make Mine Roses 1973).
Current winning trainers:
6 wins Lee Freedman (Miss Andretti 2007, Mahogany 1997, Gold Ace 1996, Mahogany 1995, Schillaci 1993, 1992).
2 wins John Hawkes (Chautauqua 2016, Sports 2001); David Hayes (Redkirk Warrior 2018, Nicconi 2010); Paul Perry (Fastnet Rock 2005, Choisir 2003);
1 win Shaun Dwyer (Regimental Gal 2004); Greg Eurell (Apache Cat 2008); Ian Harrison (Keltrice 1994); Michael, Wayne & John Hawkes (Chautauqua 2016); David & Ben Hayes & Tom Dabernig (Redkirk Warrior 2018); Joe Janiak (Takeover Target 2006); Wally Mitchell (Placid Ark 1987); Daniel Morton (Scenic Blast 2009); Mick Price (Lankan Rupee 2015); Joe Pride (Terravista 2017); Gerald Ryan (Snitzerland 2014).
Point of interest:
Winners to sire winners—General Nediym 1998 (sire of Regimental Gal 2004); Zeditave 1989 (Sports 2001); The Judge 1979 (Zeditave 1989).
Redkirk Warrior (GB) (2018) is the first northern hemisphere-bred winner of the Lightning Stakes.

MRC Ladbrokes Blue Diamond Stakes (1200m)—Caulfield
Of $1,500,000. Group 1. Set Weights, 2YO. February 23, 2019.

2017-18 RESULT: Time: 1:09.86 (Good 3)

FP	NO	HORSE	TRAINER	JOCKEY	MARGIN	BAR.	WGT	SP
1	2	WRITTEN BY	Grahame Begg	Jordan Childs		15	56.5kg	$5.50F
2	10	ENBIHAAR	David & Ben Hayes & Tom Dabernig	Cory Parish	2.5L	16	54.5kg	$21
3	16	OOHOOD	Tony McEvoy	Luke Currie	2.7L	9	54.5kg	$9
4	4	PRAIRIE FIRE	Mick Price	Mark Zahra	3.95L	1	56.5kg	$8.50
5	6	ENCRYPTION	James Cummings	Damian Lane	4.05L	12	56.5kg	$13
6	17	ARISTOCRATIC MISS	Tony McEvoy	Jamie Kah	4.55L	14	54.5kg	$101
7	15	QAFILA	David & Ben Hayes & Tom Dabernig	Dwayne Dunn	5.3L	13	54.5kg	$20
8	12	LADY HORSEOWNER	Greg Eurell	Nikita Beriman	8.05L	10	54.5kg	$51
9	13	ENNIS HILL	David & Ben Hayes & Tom Dabernig	Stephen Baster	8.8L	3	54.5kg	$7.50
10	18	MORE THAN EXCEED	Phillip Stokes	Dom Tourneur	8.9L	7	56.5kg	$61
11	11	KINKY BOOM	Tony McEvoy	Craig Williams	9.65L	11	54.5kg	$9
12	1	LONG LEAF	David & Ben Hayes & Tom Dabernig	Kerrin McEvoy	11.15L	6	56.5kg	$8.50
13	9	GRAND SYMPHONY	Robbie Griffiths	Jye McNeil	12.9L	4	56.5kg	$101
14	8	PLAGUE STONE	James Cummings	Ben Melham	13L	5	56.5kg	$8.50
15	3	RUN NAAN	Tony McEvoy	Andrew Mallyon	13.1L	2	56.5kg	$31
16	14	CROSSING THE ABBEY	Tim Hughes	Luke Nolen	16.6L	8	54.5kg	$101

PAST WINNERS

YEAR	WINNER	JOCKEY	TRAINER	2ND	3RD	TIME
2018	Written By	Jordan Childs	Grahame Begg	Enbihaar	Oohood	1:09.8
2017	Catchy	Craig Williams	David & Ben Hayes & Tom Dabernig	Pariah	Formality	1:09.3
2016	Extreme Choice	Craig Newitt	Mick Price	Flying Artie	Zamzam	1:08.9
2015	Pride Of Dubai	Damian Browne	Peter & Paul Snowden	Reemah	Lake Geneva	1:10.5
2014	Earthquake	Damian Browne	Peter Snowden	Jabali	Cornrow	1:09.8
2013	Miracles Of Life	Lauren Stojakovic	Daniel Clarken	Fast 'N' Rocking	Godiva Rock	1:09.7
2012	Samaready	Craig Newitt	Mick Price	No Looking Back	Armed For Action	1:10.4
2011	Sepoy	Kerrin McEvoy	Peter Snowden	Hallowell Belle	Masthead	1:08.5
2010	Star Witness	Nicholas Hall	Danny O'Brien	Shaaheq	Beneteau	1:10.4
2009	Reward For Effort	Luke Nolen	Peter Moody	Real Saga	Maka Ena	1:09.8
2008	Reaan	Dwayne Dunn	David Hayes	All American	Burgeis	1.11.4
2007	Sleek Chassis	Dwayne Dunn	David Hayes	Zizou	Shrewd Rhythm	1:09.8
2006	Nadeem	Dwayne Dunn	David Hayes	Miss Finland	Wonderful World	1:12.0
2005	Undoubtedly	Dwayne Dunn	Mark Kavanagh	Seidnazar	Perectly Ready	1:08.9
2004	Alinghi	Damien Oliver	Lee Freedman	Wager	World Peace	1:09.8
2003	Kusi	Corey Brown	John Hawkes	Halibery	Divine Secret	1:11.0
2002	Bel Esprit	Wayne Treloar	John Symons	Brief Embrace	Pillaging	1:09.2
2001	True Jewels	Kerrin McEvoy	Michael Moroney	La Lagune	Spectatorial	1:09.0
2000	Road To Success	Jim Cassidy	John Salanitri	Ponton Flyer	Mannington	1:09.8
1999	Redoutes Choice	Danny Nikolic	Rick Hore-Lacy	Testa Rossa	Dangerous	1:08.7
1998	Danelagh	Greg Hall	Lee Freedman	Danari	Piccadilly Circus	1:10.1

BACKGROUND

First run: 1971 (won by Tolerance). Group 1 from 1980. Run at Flemington in 1996 (won by Paint).
Fastest time (1200m Caulfield): Hurricane Sky (1994): 1:08.1.
Most recent filly to win: Catchy (2017): 19 fillies have won (the first was Forina in 1974).
Most recent colt/gelding to win: Written By (2018); gelding: Kusi (2003).
Notable winners: Written By (2018); Catchy (2017); Extreme Choice (2016); Pride Of Dubai (2015); Miracles Of Life (2013); Sepoy (2011); Star Witness (2010); Alinghi (2004); Bel Esprit (2002); Redoute's Choice (1999); Hurricane Sky (1994); Courtza (1989); Zeditave (1988); Midnight Fever (1987); Bounding Away (1986); Rancher (1982); Star Shower (1979); Manikato (1978); Blazing Saddles (1977); Lord Dudley (1975); New Gleam (1973); John's Hope (1972); Tolerance (1971).

Blue Diamond winners and the spring 2YO races:
Maribyrnong Trial Stakes: 2—Sepoy (Blue Diamond 2011); Star Shower (1979).
Maribyrnong Plate: 6—Nadeem (Blue Diamond 2005) Bel Esprit (2002); Rancher (1982); Star Shower (1979); Blazing Saddles (1977); New Gleam (1973).
Merson Cooper Stakes: 4—Canonise (Blue Diamond 1991); Rancher (1982); Star Shower (1979); Blazing Saddles (1977).

Blue Diamond winners won the lead-up races:
Magic Millions Gold Coast: (None) Note: Testa Rossa won the 1999 Magic Millions before finishing second to Redoute's Choice in the Blue Diamond Stakes.
Chairman's Stakes: 2—Extreme Choice (2016); Redoute's Choice (1999). The Chairman's was run after the Blue Diamond 2002-2010.
Talindert Stakes: 3—Star Witness (2010); Sleek Chassis (2007); Riva Diva (1992).
Blue Diamond Preview (1000m C&G): 7—Sepoy (2011); Reward For Effort (2009); Reaan (2008); Bel Esprit (2002); Knowledge (1997); Zeditave (1988); Rancher (1982).
Blue Diamond Preview (1000m, Fillies): 3—Miracles Of Life (2013); Midnight Fever (1987), Bounding Away (1986).
Blue Diamond Prelude (1100m, C&G): 5—Written By (2018); Sepoy (2011); Bel Esprit (2002); Let's Get Physical (1985); Rancher (1982).
Blue Diamond Prelude (1100m, Fillies): 8—Catchy (2017); Earthquake (2014); Samaready (2012); Alinghi (2004); Lady Jakeo (1993); Courtza (1989); Midnight Fever (1987); Love A Show (1983).
Preview & Prelude & Blue Diamond: 4—Sepoy (2011); Bel Esprit (2002); Midnight Fever (1987); Rancher (1982). Note: Midnight Fever is the only filly to complete the treble.

Blue Diamond winners went on to win in the same preparation:
VRC Sires' Produce Stakes: 3—Street Cafe (1984); Lord Dudley (1975); Tolerance (1971).
Golden Slipper: 5—Sepoy (2011); Courtza (1989); Bounding Away (1986); Manikato (1978); John's Hope (1972).
ATC Sires' Produce: 2—Pride Of Dubai (2015); Bounding Away (1986).
ATC Champagne Stakes: 1—Bounding Away (1986).
Golden Slipper, ATC Sires' & ATC Champagne Stakes: 1—Bounding Away (1986).
Blue Diamond placegetters to win Golden Slipper: 4—Miss Finland (2006, 2nd Blue Diamond to Nadeem); Flying Spur (1995, 2nd, Principality); Canny Lad (1990, 2nd, Mahaasin); Fairy Walk (1971, 3rd, Tolerance).

Blue Diamond winners to win as spring 3YOs:
Caulfield Guineas: 2—Redoute's Choice (1999); Manikato (1978).
Thousand Guineas: 1—Alinghi (2004).
Coolmore Stud Stakes: 8— Sepoy (2011); Star Witness (2010); Alinghi (2004); Courtza (1989); Zeditave (1988); Rancher (1982); Manikato (1978); Tolerance (1971).

Breeding facts:
Winner to sire a winner: Redoute's Choice (Nadeem 2006, Undoubtedly 2005). Redoute's Choice is the sire of Not A Single Doubt, who sired Miracles Of Life (2013) and Extreme Choice (2016).
No past winner is the dam of a winner. However, Bel Esprit, who won in 2002, is out of Bespoken, a half-sister to Mahaasin (1990).

Leading winning jockeys:
4 wins Dwayne Dunn (Reaan 2008, Sleek Chassis 2007, Nadeem 2006, Undoubtedly 2005); Roy Higgins (Star Shower 1979, Blazing Saddles 1977, Lord Dudley 1975, Tolerance 1971).
3 wins Greg Hall (Danelagh 1998, Lady Jakeo 1993, Zeditave 1988)

Current winning jockeys:
4 wins Dwayne Dunn (Reaan 2008, Sleek Chassis 2007, Nadeem 2006, Undoubtedly 2005).
2 wins Damian Browne (Pride Of Dubai 2015, Earthquake 2014); Kerrin McEvoy (Sepoy 2011, True Jewels 2001); Craig Newitt (Extreme Choice 2016; Samaready 2012).
1 win Corey Brown (Kusi 2003*); Jordan Childs (Written By 2018); Nicholas Hall (Star Witness 2010); Luke Nolen (Reward For Effort 2009); Damien Oliver (Alinghi 2004); Lauren Stojakovic (Miracles Of Life 2013); Craig Williams (Catchy 2017).

Leading winning trainers:
6 wins David Hayes (Catchy 2017, Reaan 2008, Sleek Chassis 2007, Nadeem 2006, Principality 1995, Canonise 1991).
3 wins Angus Armanasco (Zeditave 1988, Forina 1974, Tolerance 1971); Lee Freedman (Alinghi 2004, Danelagh 1998, Knowledge 1997); Colin Hayes (Mahaasin 1990, Midnight Fever 1987, Out Of Danger 1976); Tommy Smith (Bounding Away 1986, Blazing Saddles 1977, John's Hope 1972); Peter Snowden (Pride Of Dubai 2015, Earthquake 2014, Sepoy 2011).

Current winning trainers
6 wins David Hayes (Catchy 2017, Reaan 2008, Sleek Chassis 2007, Nadeem 2006, Principality 1995, Canonise 1991).
3 wins Lee Freedman (Alinghi 2004, Danelagh 1998, Knowledge 1997); Peter Snowden (Pride Of Dubai 2015, Earthquake 2014, Sepoy 2011).

2 wins Mick Price (Extreme Choice 2016, Samaready 2012); Gerald Ryan (Paint 1996, Hurricane Sky 1994).
1 win Grahame Begg (Written Tycoon 2018); Daniel Clarken (Miracles Of Life 2013); John Hawkes (Kusi 2003*); David & Ben Hayes & Tom Dabernig (Catchy 2017); Mark Kavanagh (Undoubtedly 2005); Michael Moroney (True Jewels 2001); Danny O'Brien (Star Witness 2010); John Sadler (Lady Jakeo 1994); John Salanitri (Road To Success 2000); Peter & Paul Snowden (Pride Of Dubai 2015); Robert Smerdon (Let's Get Physical 1985); John Symons (Bel Esprit 2002).
*First past the post Roedean was disqualified after a positive swab.

Winning barriers (48 winners)

BARRIER	WINS	MOST RECENT WINNER
1	3	Miracles Of Life (2013)
2	4	True Jewels (2001)
3	4	Bel Esprit (2002)
4	5	Pride Of Dubai (2015)
5	5	Sepoy (2011)
6	1	Black Shoes (1981)
7	5	Samaready (2012)
8	2	Mahaasin (1990)
9	3	Reaan (2008)
10	3	Danelagh (1998)
11	2	Extreme Choice (2016)
12	2	Nadeem (2006)
13	3	Catchy (2017)
14	1	Star Witness (2010)
15	4	Written By (2018)
16	-	
17	1	Street Café (1984)
18	-	

Note: Roedean (2003), later disqualified, started from barrier 4.

History of Blue Diamond winners in the Golden Slipper:

YEAR	HORSE	PLACING (GOLDEN SLIPPER WINNER)
2018	Written By	4th (won by Estijaab)
2017	Catchy	16th (She Will Reign)
2016	Extreme Choice	8th (Capitalist)
2014	Earthquake	2nd (Mossfun)
2012	Samaready	3rd (Pierro)
2011	Sepoy	WON
2009	Reward For Effort	7th (Phelan Ready)
2008	Reaan	16th (Sebring)
2007	Sleek Chassis	14th (Forensics)
2005	Undoubtedly	15th (Stratum)
2004	Alinghi	3rd (Dance Hero)
2003	Kusi	12th (Polar Success)
2002	Bel Esprit	5th (Calaway Gal)
2001	True Jewels	5th (Ha Ha)
2000	Road To Success	15th (Belle Du Jour)
1998	Danelagh	8th (Prowl)
1997	Knowledge	7th (Guineas)
1996	Paint	2nd (Merlene)
1995	Principality	8th (Flying Spur)
1994	Hurricane Sky	5th (Danzero)
1991	Canonise	2nd (Tierce)
1990	Mahaasin	11th (Canny Lad)
1989	Courtza	WON
1988	Zeditave	6th (Star Watch)
1987	Midnight Fever	11th (Marauding)
1986	Bounding Away	WON
1984	Street Café	8th (Inspired)
1983	Love A Show	3rd (Sir Dapper)
1981	Black Shoes	12th (Full On Aces)
1980	Aare	6th (Dark Eclipse)
1978	Manikato	WON
1977	Blazing Saddles	3rd (Luskin Star)
1974	Forina	9th (Hartshill)
1972	John's Hope	WON
1971	Tolerance	11th (Fairy Walk)

MRC Futurity Stakes (1400m)—Caulfield

Of $500,000. Group 1. Weight For Age, 3YO&Up. February 23, 2019.

2017-18 RESULT: Time: 1:23.16 (Good 3)

FP	NO	HORSE	TRAINER	JOCKEY	MARGIN	BAR.	WGT	SP
1	3	BRAVE SMASH	Darren Weir	Craig Williams		9	59kg	$4.80F
2	1	TOSEN STARDOM	Darren Weir	Ben Allen (a)	0.75L	5	59kg	$6
3	11	SHOWTIME	Michael, Wayne & John Hawkes	Dwayne Dunn	0.95L	10	55.5kg	$7
4	2	HUMIDOR	Darren Weir	Damian Lane	2.95L	2	59kg	$10
5	8	SNITZSON	David & Ben Hayes & Tom Dabernig	Kerrin McEvoy	3.7L	1	59kg	$41
6	6	MR SNEAKY	Anthony Freedman	Mark Zahra	3.8L	8	59kg	$10
7	9	SHILLELAGH	Chris Waller	Michael Dee	6.05L	11	57kg	$15
8	10	MIGHTY BOSS	Mick Price	Michael Walker	6.25L	3	55.5kg	$5
9	7	WYNDSPELLE	Michael Kent	Beau Mertens	7.5L	6	59kg	$71
10	5	SOVEREIGN NATION	David & Ben Hayes & Tom Dabernig	Regan Bayliss	9L	4	59kg	$31
11	4	LORD OF THE SKY	Robbie Laing	Damien Oliver	10L	7	59kg	$11

PAST WINNERS

YEAR	WINNER	JOCKEY	TRAINER	2ND	3RD	TIME
2018	Brave Smash	Craig Williams	Darren Weir	Tosen Stardom	Showtime	1:23.1
2017	Black Heart Bart	Brad Rawiller	Darren Weir	Tosen Stardom	Ecuador	1:22.9
2016	Turn Me Loose	Opie Bosson	Murray Baker	Stratum Star	Suavito	1:22.2
2015	Suavito	Damien Oliver	Nigel Blackiston	Smokin' Joey	Dissident	1:23.0
2014	Moment Of Change	Luke Nolen	Peter Moody	Sertorius	Pinwheel	1:23.4
2013	All Too Hard	Dwayne Dunn	Michael, Wayne & John Hawkes	Glass Harmonium	King Mufhasa	1:23.0
2012	King Mufhasa	Nash Rawiller	Stephen Mckee	Pinker Pinker	Adamantium	1:23.8
2011	More Joyous	Nash Rawiller	Gai Waterhouse	Whobegotyou	Dao Dao	1:21.7
2010	Typhoon Tracy	Luke Nolen	Peter Moody	Dao Dao	Sniper's Bullet	1:34.4
2009	Niconero	Craig Williams	David Hayes	Light Fantastic	Alamosa	1:36.4
2008	Niconero	Craig Williams	David Hayes	Cargo Cult	Miss Finland	1:34.8
2007	Aqua Damore	Stephen Baster	Gai Waterhouse	Seachange	El Segundo	1:35.7
2006	Fields Of Omagh	Steven King	David Hayes	Red Dazzler	Rosden	1:34.2
2005	Regal Roller	Mark Flaherty	Clinton McDonald	Super Elegant	Modem	1:24.6
2004	Reset	Danny Nikolic	Graeme Rogerson	Vocabulary	Yell	1:23.7
2003	Yell	Darren Gauci	John Hawkes	Innovation Girl	Roman Arch	1:21.9
2002	Dash For Cash	Kerrin McEvoy	Rick Hore-Lacy	Chattanooga	Aquiver	1:23.0
2001	Desert Sky/Mr. Murphy	Darren Gauci/Damien Oliver	Mathew Ellerton/Lee Freedman		Porto Roca	1:22.8
2000	Testa Rossa	Damien Oliver	Dean Lawson	Miss Pennymoney	Redoute's Choice	1:23.7
1999	Rustic Dream	Peter Mertens	Mick Price	Al Mansour	Helm	1:22.1
1998	Encounter	Shane Dye	Clarry Conners	Al Mansour	Rebel	1:23.5

BACKGROUND

First run: 1898 (won by Resolute). Group 1 since 1980. Run over 1400m until 1979 when run over 1800m; 1980-2005 1400m and from 2013. 2006-2012 1600m. Weight-for-age since 1979. Run at Flemington in 1996.

Fillies and mares to win: 13—Suavito (2015); More Joyous (2011); Typhoon Tracy (2010); Aqua D'Amore (2007); Mannerism (1992); *Cendrillon (1967); Wenona Girl (1963); Waltzing Lily (1934); *Brattle (1914); Gladsome (1906, 1905); *Playaway (1904); *Aurous (1901). * 3YO filly

Three-year-olds to win (since WFA, 1979): 14—All Too Hard (2013); Reset (2004); Yell (2003); Dash For Cash (2002); Desert Sky (2001 (dead-heat)); Mr. Murphy (2001 (dead-heat)); Encounter (1998); Mouawad (1997); Ark Regal (1990); Zeditave (1989); Rubiton (1987); Campaign King (1986); Galleon (1982); Manikato (1979). *2001 dead-heat between 3YOs

Multiple winners: 7—Niconero (2009, 2008); Schillaci (1995, 1993); Manikato (1983, 1981, 1980, 1979); Idolou (1974, 1973); St. Razzle (1950, 1949); Ajax (1940, 1938, 1939); *Gladsome (1906, 1905). *Mare

Fastest time (1400m): More Joyous (2011) 1:21.79.

Futurity Stakes winners won the lead-up races:
Rubiton Stakes: 3—Schillaci (1993, 1995); Redelva (1991); Zeditave (1989).

Lightning Stakes: 5—Testa Rossa (2000); Schillaci (1993); Zeditave (1989); Wenona Girl (1963); Todman (1960).
Orr Stakes: 18—Black Heart Bart (2017); Moment Of Change (2014); All Too Hard (2013); Typhoon Tracy (2010); Yell (2003); Desert Sky (2001); Primacy (1994); Vo Rogue (1988); Manikato (1981, 1980, 1979); Crewman (1970); Lord (1959); Prince Cortauld (1955); St Razzle (1950); Attley (1947); Drum Net (1945); Burrabil (1942). Note: the Futurity distance was increased from 1400m to 1600m 2006-2012.
Futurity Stakes winners went on to win in the same preparation:
Peter Young Stakes: 9—Vo Rogue (1988); Lord (1959); Attley (1947); Ajax (1939); Ammon Ra (1932); Amounis (1930); The Hawk (1924): Eurythmic (1922); Soultline (1909). Note: The Peter Young Stakes (ex-St George Stakes) is now run on the same day as the Futurity Stakes.
Australian Guineas: 4—Reset (2004); Dash For Cash (2002); Mr. Murphy (2001); Mouawad (1997).
Newmarket Handicap: 7—Royal Gem (1948); Bernborough (1946); Ajax (1938); Regular Bachelor (1936); Gothic (1928); Soultline (1909); Sir Foote (1902).
William Reid Stakes: 13—Yell (2003); Redelva (1991); Zeditave (1989); Vo Rogue (1988); Campaign King (1986); Manikato (1983, 1981, 1980, 1979); Crewman (1970); Magic Ruler (1969); Star Affair (1966); Heros (1935). Note: William Reid Stakes was run before the Futurity until 2012.
Ranvet Stakes: 3—Bernborough (1946); Ammon Ra (1932); The Hawk (1925).
George Ryder Stakes: 4—Mouawad (1997); Schillaci (1993); Manikato (1980, 1979).
All Aged Stakes: 13—All Too Hard (2013); Vite Cheval (1985); Always Welcome (1978); Sky High (1961); Lord (1959); San Domenico (1952); Bernborough (1946); Ajax (1940, 1939, 1938); Winooka (1933); Amounis (1930); Gladsome (1905).
Futurity Stakes winners also won:
Golden Slipper Stakes: 3—Manikato (GS 1978, Futurity 1979-80-81, 1983); Sky High (GS 1960, Futurity 1961), Todman (GS 1957, Futurity 1960).
Blue Diamond Stakes: 1—Zeditave (BD 1988, Futurity 1989).
Cox Plate (same year): 5—Fields Of Omagh (2006); Rubiton (1987); Gunsynd (1972); Ajax (1938); Phar Lap (1931).
Cox Plate (same season): 1—Star Affair (1966).
Cantala Stakes (same season): 6—Turn Me Loose (Futurity 2016); Primacy (1994); Prince Cortauld (1955); Royal Gem (1946); Burrabil (1942); Amounis (1930).
Leading winning jockeys:
8 wins Roy Higgins (Manikato 1980, Martindale 1975, Gunsynd 1972, Silver Spade 1971, Magic Ruler 1969, Star Affair 1966, Sir Dane 1965, Aquanita 1962).
4 wins Damien Oliver (Suavito 2015, Mr. Murphy 2001, Testa Rossa 2000, Mannerism 1992); Bill Williamson (The Orb 1956, Bob Cherry 1953, San Domenico 1952, St. Razzle 1949).
3 wins Harold Badger (Ajax 1940, 1939, 1938); Bobby Lewis (Salatis 1923, Eudorus 1913, Sir Leonard 1903); Bill McLachlan (Brattle 1914, Popinjay 1912, Soultline 1909); Jim Pike (Phar Lap 1931, Gothic 1928, The Hawk 1924); Jack Purtell (Attley 1947, Drum Net 1945, Zonda 1943).
Current winning jockeys:
4 wins Damien Oliver (Suavito 2015, Mr. Murphy 2001, Testa Rossa 2000, Mannerism 1992).
3 wins Craig Williams (Brave Smash 2018, Niconero 2009, 2008).
2 wins Luke Nolen (Moment Of Change 2014, Tyohoon Tracy 2010); Nash Rawiller (King Mufhasa 2012, More Joyous 2011).
1 win Stephen Baster (Aqua D'Amore 2007); Opie Bosson (Turn Me Loose 2016); Grant Cooksley (Mouawad 1996); Dwayne Dunn (All Too Hard 2013); Kerrin McEvoy (Dash For Cash 2002); Brad Rawiller (Black Heart Bart 2017); Cyril Small (Vo Rogue 1988).
Leading winning trainers:
5 wins Angus Armanasco (Zeditave 1989, Crewman 1970, Magic Ruler 1969, Star Affair 1966, Zariba 1958); Lou Robertson (Iron Duke 1951, Counsel 1944, Zonda 1943, Gothic 1928, Top Gallant 1926).
4 wins Lee Freedman (Mr. Murphy 2001, Schillaci 1995, 1993, Mannerism 1992); David Hayes (Niconero 2009, 2008, Fields Of Omagh 2006, Primacy 1994); Bob Hoysted (Manikato 1983, 1981, 1980, 1979); Maurice McCarten (Wenona Girl 1963, Todman 1960, Prince Cortauld 1955, Bob Cherry 1953).
Current winning trainers:
4 wins Lee Freedman (Mr. Murphy 2001, Schillaci 1995, 1993, Mannerism 1992); David Hayes (Niconero 2009, 2008, Fields Of Omagh 2006, Primacy 1994).
3 wins John Hawkes (All Too Hard 2013, Yell 2003, King's Helmet 1976).
2 wins Clarry Conners (Encounter 1998, Mouawad 1997); Gai Waterhouse (More Joyous 2011, Aqua D'Amore 2007); Darren Weir (Brave Smash 2018, Black Heart Bart 2017).
1 win Murray Baker (Turn Me Loose 2016); Nigel Blackiston (Suavito 2015); Mathew Ellerton (Desert Sky 2001); Michael, Wayne & John Hawkes (All Too Hard 2013); Clinton McDonald (Regal Roller 2005); Steve McKee (King Mufhasa 2012); Mick Price (Rustic Dream 1999); Steve Richards (Ark Regal 1990); Graeme Rogerson (Reset 2004); Bruce Wallace (Star Dancer 1996).

Points of interest:

Dead-heats (first): 2—*Desert Sky/Mr. Murphy (2001); Heros/Synagogue (1935); *at WFA.

In 1960, the brothers Todman and Noholme (Star Kingdom-Oceana) won the Futurity Stakes (Todman) and the All Aged Stakes (Noholme, at Randwick).

Phar Lap is the only horse to win the Melbourne Cup (1930) and return in the autumn the same season to win the Futurity Stakes (1931). Jockey Jim Pike rates Phar Lap's Futurity win the "only time Phar Lap was fully extended and probably his best win".

Mannerism (1992) is the most recent horse to win the Futurity Stakes and Caulfield Cup in the same year.

Manikato won four Futurity Stakes between 1979 to 1983—he finished second behind Galleon in 1982. His win in 1979 (as a 3YO) was over 1800m, the only time the Futurity was run at that distance.

In 1967, star filly Cendrillon won the Futurity under handicap conditions carrying 9st 4lbs (59kg). The 3YO colt, Star Affair, won in 1966 under 9st 12lbs (62.5kg).

Ajax won three Futurity Stakes—1938-40—and in his last two wins he carried 66kg. Aquanita's 66.5kg in 1962 is the heaviest weight carried to win the Futurity.

Reset (2004) retired unbeaten in five starts after winning the Futurity.

Maurice McCarten rode two winners of the Futurity (Ammon Ra 1932, Gold Rod 1937) and trained four winners (Bob Cherry 1953, Prince Cortauld 1955, Todman 1960, Wenona Girl 1963).

Brave Smash (JPN) (2018) is the first northern hemisphere-bred horse to win the Futurity since Bob Cherry in 1953—11 imported horses have won the race; the first was Sir Foote (GB) in 1902.

MRC Oakleigh Plate (1100m)—Caulfield

Of $500,000. Group 1. Handicap, Minimum Weight 50kg. February 23, 2019.

2017-18 RESULT: Time: 1:03.00 (Good 3)

FP	NO	HORSE	TRAINER	JOCKEY	MARGIN	BAR.	WGT	SP
1	2	RUSSIAN REVOLUTION	Peter & Paul Snowden	Mark Zahra		10	56.5kg	$4.60F
2	8	SNITTY KITTY	Henry Dwyer	Beau Mertens	0.2L	17	53.5kg	$9
3	4	HELLBENT	Darren Weir	Ben Allen (a)	0.3L	9	54.5kg	$16
4	18	BOOKER	Mathew Ellerton & Simon Zahra	Ben Thompson	0.4L	15	51.5kg	$7
5	11	BONS AWAY	Aaron Purcell	Linda Meech	0.6L	14	53.5kg	$15
6	17	CATCHY	David & Ben Hayes & Tom Dabernig	Craig Williams	1.85L	8	51.5kg	$9
7	12	LADY ESPRIT	Aaron Purcell	Regan Bayliss	2.05L	18	53.5kg	$71
8	19	QUILISTA	Darren Weir	Harry Coffey	2.35L	3	53.5kg	$61
9	13	ROCK 'N' GOLD	Mathew Ellerton & Simon Zahra	Damien Thornton	2.45L	13	53.5kg	$151
10	16	SHE WILL REIGN	Gary Portelli	Ben Melham	2.55L	16	53kg	$9
11	6	FUHRYK	David & Ben Hayes & Tom Dabernig	Stephen Baster	3.05L	5	53.5kg	$16
11	10	SWORD OF LIGHT	Mathew Ellerton & Simon Zahra	Katelyn Mallyon	3.05L	6	53.5kg	$151
13	1	FLAMBERGE	Mathew Ellerton & Simon Zahra	Damian Lane	3.25L	7	57kg	$21
14	15	GLENALL	Michael, Wayne & John Hawkes	Dwayne Dunn	3.35L	4	53.5kg	$16
15	14	PALAZZO PUBBLICO	Matthew Smith	Michael Dee	4.85L	1	53.5kg	$101
16	3	SHEIDEL	David & Ben Hayes & Tom Dabernig	Damien Oliver	7.35L	11	55kg	$21
17	5	ILLUSTRIOUS LAD	Peter Gelagotis	Anthony Darmanin	9.1L	2	54kg	$26
18	9	PRUSSIAN VIXEN	Michael Mehegan	Dean Yendall	9.85L	12	53.5kg	$81

PAST WINNERS

YEAR	WINNER	JOCKEY	TRAINER	2ND	3RD	TIME
2018	Russian Revolution	Mark Zahra	Peter & Paul Snowden	Snitty Kitty	Hellbent	1:03.0
2017	Sheidel	Joao Moreira	David & Ben Hayes & Tom Dabernig	Faatinah	Extreme Choice	1:02.1
2016	Flamberge	Damian Lane	Peter Moody	Fell Swoop	Heatherly	1:02.5
2015	Shamal Wind	Dwayne Dunn	Robert Smerdon	Under The Louvre	Fast 'n' Rocking	1:02.2
2014	Lankan Rupee	Craig Newitt	Mick Price	Spirit Of Boom	Knoydart	1:02.7
2013	Mrs Onassis	Kerrin McEvoy	Gerald Ryan	Facile Tigre	Spirit Of Boom	1:03.1
2012	Woorim	Damian Browne	Robert Heathcote	Elite Falls	Facile Tigre	1:03.4
2011	Eagle Falls	Damien Oliver	David Hayes	Avenue	Hinchinbrook	1:02.2
2010	Starspangledbanner	Danny Nikolic	Leon Corstens	(DH) Here De Angels/Arinos		1:03.1
2009	Swiss Ace	Ken Pope	Mick Mair	Lucky Secret	Typhoon Zed	1:02.8
2008	Weekend Hussler	Brad Rawiller	Ross McDonald	Magnus	Tramuntana	1:03.2
2007	Undue	Steven Arnold	Shane Clarke	Poets Voice	Magnus	1:02.7
2006	Snitzel	Craig Newitt	Gerald Ryan	Virage De Fortune	Takeover Target	1:04.4
2005	Fastnet Rock	Glen Boss	Paul Perry	Segments	Legally Bay	1:02.5
2004	Reactive	Matt Pumpa	Brian Mayfield-Smith	Ancient Song	Suit	1:03.4
2003	River Dove	Stephen Baster	Mathew Ellerton	North Boy	Choisir	1:04.5
2002	Sudurka	Nash Rawiller	Brian Mayfield-Smith	Mistegic	Straight Ace	1:02.5
2001	Miss Kournikova	Brett Prebble	Mathew Ellerton	Miss Pennymoney	Show A Heart	1:02.0
2000	Sports	Danny Nikolic	John Hawkes	Falvelon	Rancho Spark	1:04.5
1999	Dantelah	Jim Cassidy	Paul Perry	Paint	Magic Music	1:02.8
1998	Singing The Blues	Chad Davies	Jon Inglis	Rock You	Jugulator	1:03.2

BACKGROUND

First run: 1884 (won by Malua). Group 1 since 1980. Run over 1200m 1884-1972. Run at Flemington 1941-44. Run at Sandown in 1996. Race abandoned in 1921.

Mares and fillies to win: 37—Sheidel (2017); Shamal Wind (2015); Mrs Onassis (2013); Reactive (2004); River Dove (2003); *Miss Kournikova (2001); Dantelah (1999); *With Me (1991); Scarlet Bisque (1990); Mistress Anne (1979); Dual Choice (1972, *1971); *Citius (1962); Adelina (1957); Kind Link (1947); Delina (1946); Ava (1945); Zonda (1941); Belle Stilhouette (1936); Arachne (1935); Figure (1930); Day Dreamer (1929); *Baringhup (1927); Perspective (1926); Wish Wind (1922); Molly's Robe (1920); Poitrina (1918); Tullia (1916); Brattle (1915); Queen Of Scots (1912); Celerity (1910); Beresina (1907); Pendant (1903); Wakeful (1901); *Wild Rose (1891); Nectarine (1889); *Marie Louise (1885). *3YO fillies.

Most recent 3YO to win: C&G—Starspangledbanner (2010); Filly—Miss Kournikova (2001).

Multiple winners: 2—Dual Choice (1971, 1972); Aurie's Star (1939, 1937).

Fastest time (1100m): Miss Kournikova (2001) 1:02.00

Notable winners: Lankan Rupee (2014); Starspangledbanner (2010); Weekend Hussler (2008); Fastnet Rock (2005); Spartacus (1997); Schillaci (1992); Snippets (1988); Placid Ark (1987); Turf Ruler (1980); Zephyr Bay (1975); Tontonan (1974); Dual Choice (1972-71); Citius (1966); Time And Tide (1965); San Domenico (1949); Aurie's Star (1939, 1937); Wakeful (1901); Malua (1884).

Oakleigh Plate winners won the lead-up races:
Rubiton Stakes: 2—Lankan Rupee (2014); Spartacus (1997).
Lightning Stakes: 5—Fastnet Rock (2005); Schillaci (1992); Placid Ark (1987); Dual Choice (1971); Citius (1966).

Oakleigh Plate winners went on to win in the same preparation:
Newmarket Handicap: 11—Lankan Rupee (2014); Weekend Hussler (2008); Schillaci (1992); Placid Ark (1987); Gold Stakes (1959); Birdwood (1954); Cromwell (1952); Aurie's Star (1937); Wakeful (1901); William Tell (1886); Malua (1884).
Lightning & Newmarket: 2—Schillaci (1992); Placid Ark (1987).
William Reid Stakes: 6—Flamberge (2016); Spartacus (1997); Dual Choice (1971); Marmion (1967); New Statesman (1962); Figure (1930). Note since 2013 the William Reid Stakes has moved from January/February to March (after the Oakleigh Plate).
The Galaxy: 3—Schillaci (1992); Snippets (1998); Mistress Anne (1975).
TJ Smith Stakes: 1—Lankan Rupee (2014).

Leading winning jockeys:
3 wins Bill Duncan (Blematic 1932-2nd Div, Umbertana 1932-1st Div, Cielo 1919); Roy Higgins (Zephyr Bay 1975, Alrello 1970, Marmion 1967); Noel McGrowdie (Lucky Strike 1956, Birdwood 1954, Tahnoor 1948); Harry White (Coal Pak 1986, Tontonan 1974, Zambari 1973)

Current winning jockeys:
2 wins Stephen Baster (River Dove 2003, Mookta 1993); Craig Newitt (Lankan Rupee 2014, Snitzel 2006); Damien Oliver (Eagle Falls 2011, Schillaci 1992).
1 win Steven Arnold (Undue 2007); Glen Boss (Fastnet Rock 2005); Damian Browne (Woorim 2012); Dwayne Dunn (Shamal Wind 2015); Damian Lane (Flamberge 2016); Kerrin McEvoy (Mrs Onassis 2013); Ken Pope (Swiss Ace 2009); Joao Moreira (Sheidel 2017); Brett Prebble (Miss Kournikova 2001); Brad Rawiller (Weekend Hussler 2008); Nash Rawiller (Sudurka 2002); Mark Zahra (Russian Revolution 2018).

Leading winning trainers:
4 wins Tom Payten (Popinjay 1914, Coil 1896, Camoola 1882, Titan 1890); Tommy Smith (Zambari 1973, Kilshery 1963, Dubbo 1958, Adeline 1957).
3 wins Hugh Munro (Blairgour 1911, Wandin 1906, Wakeful 1901); Lou Robertson (Delina 1946, Zonda 1941, First Arrow 1931).

Current winning trainers:
2 wins John Hawkes (Sports 2000, Harpagus 1982); David Hayes (Sheidel 2017, Eagle Falls 2011); Paul Perry (Fastnet Rock 2005, Dantelah 1999); Gerald Ryan (Mrs Onassis 2013, Snitzel 2006).
1 win Shane Clarke (Undue 2007); Leon Corstens (Starspangledbanner 2010); Mathew Ellerton (Miss Kournikova 2001); David Hall (Khaptingly 1995); David & Ben Hayes & Tom Dabernig (Sheidel 2017); Rob Heathcote (Woorim 2012); Mick Mair (Swiss Ace 2009); Peter McKenzie (Mr. Illusion 1985); Wally Mitchell (Placid Ark 1987); Mick Price (Lankan Rupee 2014); Mark Riley (Mookta 1993); John Sadler (Kenvain 1994); Robert Smerdon (Shamal Wind 2015); Peter & Paul Snowden (Russian Revolution 2018).

Points of interest:
Snippets (1988) is the sire of Spartacus (1997). Malua (1884) won the 1884 Melbourne Cup. Tontonan (1974) is the only Golden Slipper winner (1973) to win the Oakleigh Plate. Starspangledbanner (2010), Weekend Hussler (2008) and Dual Choice (1971) are the only 3YOs to also win the Caulfield Guineas.
Malua (1884) won the 1889 Grand National Hurdle.
Champion mare Wakeful won the Oakleigh Plate in 1901—10 years later in 1911, her son Blairgour also won. Both were trained by Hugh Munro.
Jockey Bill Duncan won both divisions in 1932 on Umbertana (1st Div) and Blematic (2nd Div).

ATC Chipping Norton Stakes (1600m)—Warwick Farm
Of $600,000. Group 1. Weight For Age, 3YO&Up. March 2, 2019.

2017-18 RESULT: Time: 1:34.92 (Soft 5)

FP	NO	HORSE	TRAINER	JOCKEY	MARGIN	BAR.	WGT	SP
1	7	WINX	Chris Waller	Hugh Bowman		6	57kg	$1.09F
2	4	PRIZED ICON	Kris Lees	Glyn Schofield	7L	4	59kg	$16
3	1	CLASSIC UNIFORM	Gary Moore	Andrew Adkins	7.5L	2	59kg	$51
4	3	LIBRAN	Chris Waller	Brenton Avdulla	8.5L	1	59kg	$71
5	5	STAMPEDE	Gai Waterhouse & Adrian Bott	Tim Clark	10.9L	5	59kg	$21
6	2	WHO SHOT THEBARMAN	Chris Waller	Tye Angland	11.1L	3	59kg	$91
7	8	LASQUETI SPIRIT	Lee Curtis	Jay Ford	14.2L	7	57kg	$101
8	9	VINLAND	Tony McEvoy	Kerrin McEvoy	23.1L	8	56kg	$71
9	6	JEMADAR	David Pfieffer	Adam Hyeronimus	32.8L	9	59kg	$101

PAST WINNERS

YEAR	WINNER	JOCKEY	TRAINER	2ND	3RD	TIME
2018	Winx	Hugh Bowman	Chris Waller	Prized Icon	Classic Uniform	1:34.9
2017	Winx	Hugh Bowman	Chris Waller	Lasqueti Spirit	Who Shot Thebarman	1:40.3
2016	Winx	Hugh Bowman	Chris Waller	Dibayani	Hauraki	1:33.9
2015	Contributer	James McDonald	John O'Shea	Hartnell	He's Your Man	1:36.5
2014	Boban	Glyn Schofield	Chris Waller	It's A Dundeel	Hawkspur	1:38.1
2013	Shoot Out	Hugh Bowman	Chris Waller	Monton	Danleigh	1:35.8
2012	Shoot Out	Hugh Bowman	Chris Waller	Danleigh	Trusting	1:37.4
2011	Danleigh	Hugh Bowman	Chris Waller	Centennial Park	Sacred Choice	1:35.7
2010	Theseo	Nash Rawiller	Gai Waterhouse	Rangirangdoo	Danleigh	1:37.4
2009	Tuesday Joy	Corey Brown	Gai Waterhouse	Vision And Power	Gallant Tess	1:34.8
2008	Casino Prince	Damien Oliver	Anthony Cummings	Tuesday Joy	Sniper's Bullet	1:36.4
2007	He's No Pie Eater	Zac Purton	Graeme Rogerson	Desert War	Mentality	1:37.6
2006	Desert War	Larry Cassidy	Gai Waterhouse	Eremein	Ike's Dream	1:36.3
2005	Grand Armee	Danny Beasley	Gai Waterhouse	Court's In Session	Winning Belle	1:35.4
2004	Starcraft	Glen Boss	Garry Newham	Ambulance	Gentle Genius	1:40.8
2003	Lonhro	Darren Beadman	John Hawkes	Shogun Lodge	Dress Circle	1:37.9
2002	Tie The Knot	Patrick Payne	Guy Walter	Freemason	Universal Prince	1:37.3
2001	Tie The Knot	Patrick Payne	Guy Walter	Dottoressa	Referral	1:35.8
2000	Tie The Knot	Shane Dye	Guy Walter	Adam	Staging	1:37.7
1999	Tie The Knot	Shane Dye	Guy Walter	Forgotten Hero	Darazari	1:37.6
1998	Encounter	Shane Dye	Clarry Conners	Our Air	Filante	1:36.7
1997	Octagonal	Shane Dye	John Hawkes	Juggler	Dupain	1:36.3

BACKGROUND

First run: 1925 (won by Wallace Mortlake). Group 2 1980-85. Group 1 from 1986. Run over 2000m 1925-72; 2100m 1973-79; 1600m from 1980. Run at Warwick Farm 1979-91, 1992-2000, 2002-07, 2010-15, from 2018. Run at Randwick all other times. Not held in 1942. Registered name is Chipping Norton Stakes.
Most recent mare to win: Winx (2018). Note 1: before Winx (2018, 2017, 2016) it was Emancipation (1984). Note 2: the 3YO filly Heat Of The Moment won in 1986.
Most recent 3YO to win: C&G—He's No Pie Eater (2007); Filly—Heat Of The Moment (1986).
Multiple winners: 10—Winx (2018, 2017, 2016); Shoot Out (2013, 2012); Tie The Knot (2002, 2001, 2000, 1999); Super Impose (1992, 1991); Apollo Eleven (1975, 1973); Tulloch (1960, 1958); Carioca (1955, 1953); Carbon Copy (1950, 1949); Katanga (1945, 1944); Lough Neagh (1937, 1936, 1933).
Fastest time (1600m): Embasadora (1980) 1:34.30
Notable winners: Winx (2018, 2017, 2016); Shoot Out (2013, 2012), Tuesday Joy (2009); Desert War (2006); Grand Armee (2005); Starcraft (2004); Tie The Knot (2002, 2001, 2000, 1999); Octagonal (1997); Juggler (1996); Super Impose (1991-92); Emancipation (1984); Taras Bulba (1976); Apollo Eleven (1975, 1973); Gay Icarus (1971); Rain Lover (1969); Sky High (1962); Tulloch (1960, 1958); Carioca (1955, 1953); Delta (1952); Comic Court (1951); Carbon Copy (1950, 1949); Bernborough (1946); Katanga (1945, 1944); Tranquil Star (1941); Lough Neagh (1937, 1936, 1933); Phar Lap (1930); Limerick (1928); Amounis (1927); Windbag (1926).
Chipping Norton winners won the lead-up races:
Expressway Stakes: 2—Lonhro (2003); Tie The Knot (2001).

Apollo Stakes: 11—Winx (2017, 2016); Contributer (2015); Tuesday Joy (2009); Grand Armee (2005); Lonhro (2003); Juggler (1996); Pharaoh (1995); Emancipation (1984); Dalmacia (1983); Embasadora (1980).

Chipping Norton winners also won in the same preparation:
Australian Cup: 1—Octagonal (1987).
Ranvet Stakes: 13—Contributer (2015); Theseo (2010); Tie The Knot (2001, 2000); Super Impose (1991); Sky High (1962); Tulloch (1958); Gallant Archer (1954); Bernborough (1946); Lough Neagh (1937, 1936, 1933); Limerick (1928).
George Ryder Stakes: 7—Winx (2018, 2017, 2016) Lonhro (2003); Heat Of The Moment (1986); Emancipation (1984); Prince Ruling (1981).
Tancred Stakes: 4—Tie The Knot (2000, 1999); Octagonal (1987); Apollo Eleven (1983).
Doncaster Handicap: 3—Winx (2016); Pharoah (1995); Super Impose (1991).
Australian Derby: 5—Starcraft (2004); Dr. Grace (1990); Tulloch* (Derby 1957, Chipping Norton 1958); Carbon Copy* (Derby 1957; Chipping Norton 1958; Phar Lap* (Derby 1929, Chipping Norton 1930). *Note: Derby run in the spring to 1977.
AJC Queen Elizabeth Stakes: 13—Winx (2018, 2017); Grand Armee (2005); Lonhro (2003); Rising Prince (1985); Taras Bulba (1976); Apollo Eleven (1973); Gay Icarus (1971); General Command (1968); Prince Grant (1966); Tulloch (1960, 1958); Caesar (1959).
Sydney Cup: 6—Tie The Knot (1999); Apollo Eleven (1983); General Command (1968); Prince Grant (1966); Carioca (1953); Carbon Copy (1949).

Chipping Norton winners to win spring features same season:
George Main Stakes: 5—Winx (Chipping Norton 2018, 2017); Shoot Out (2013); Grand Armee (2005); Encounter (1998).
Cox Plate: 5—Winx (Chipping Norton 2018, 2017, 2016); Carbon Copy (1949); Tranquil Star (1942): Note: Winx (2016); Super Impose (1992); Rising Prince (1985); Tulloch (1960); Phar Lap (1930); Amounis (1927) won the Chipping Norton and Cox Plate in the same year.
Melbourne Cup: 4—Rain Lover (Chipping Norton 1969); Delta (1952); Comic Court (1951); Windbag (1926).

Leading winning jockeys:
6 wins Hugh Bowman (Winx 2018, 2017, 2016, Shoot Out 2013, 2012, Danleigh 2011).
4 wins Darren Beadman (Starcraft 2004, Super Impose 1992, 1991, Heat Of The Moment 1986); Billy Cook (Carioca 1955, 1953, Fresh Boy 1948, Chide 1931); Shane Dye (Tie The Knot 2000, 1999, Encounter 1998, Octagonal 1997); Kevin Langby (Rising Prince 1985, Taras Bulba 1976, Igloo 1974, Striking Force 1967); George Moore (Great Exploits 1970, General Command 1968, Prince Grant 1966, Tulloch 1958); Darby Munro (Grand Archer 1954, Katanga 1945, 1944, Reading 1940); Frank Shean (Veiled Threat 1943, Tranquil Star 1941, Lough Neagh 1937, 1936)

Current winning jockeys:
6 wins Hugh Bowman (Winx 2018, 2017, 2016, Shoot Out 2013, 2012, Danleigh 2011).
2 wins Glen Boss (Starcraft 2004, Telesto 1994); Larry Cassidy (Desert War 2006, Juggler 1996).
1 win Corey Brown (Tuesday Joy 2009); Damien Oliver (Casino Prince 2008), James McDonald (Contributer 2015); Zac Purton (He's No Pie Eater 2007); Glyn Schofield (Boban 2014), Nash Rawiller (Theseo 2010).

Leading winning trainers:
10 wins Tommy Smith (Vivacite 1982, Embasadora 1980, Taras Bulba 1976, Igloo 1974, Great Exploits 1970, Prince Grant 1966, Tulloch 1960, 1958, Caesar 1959, Sumerset Fair 1956).
7 wins Chris Waller (Winx 2018, 2017, 2016, Boban 2014, Shoot Out 2013, 2012, Danleigh 2011).
6 wins Gai Waterhouse (Theseo 2010, Tuesday Joy 2009, Desert War 2006, Grand Armee 2005, Juggler 1996, Pharoah 1995).
4 wins Guy Walter (Tie The Knot 2002, 2001, 2000, 1999).

Current winning trainers:
7 wins Chris Waller (Winx 2018, 2017, 2016, Boban 2014, Shoot Out 2013, 2012, Danleigh 2011).
6 wins Gai Waterhouse (Theseo 2010, Tuesday Joy 2009, Desert War 2006, Grand Armee 2005, Juggler 1996, Pharoah 1995).
2 wins John Hawkes (Lonhro 2003, Octagonal 1997);
1 win Anthony Cummings (Casino Prince 2008); John O'Shea (Contributer 2015); Graeme Rogerson (He's No Pie Eater 2007); Bruce Wallace (Kingston Bay 1993).

Point of interest:
In 1946, the great Bernborough beat the champion mare Flight in one of the most publicised clashes of the time.
In 2017, it was Winx's 15th consecutive win.
In 2018, it was Winx's 23rd consecutive win.

ATC Surround Stakes (1400m)—Warwick Farm
Of $500,000. Group 1. Set Weights, 3YO Fillies. March 2, 2019.

2017-18 RESULT: Time: 1:23.46 (Soft 5)

FP	NO	HORSE	TRAINER	JOCKEY	MARGIN	BAR.	WGT	SP
1	1	SHOALS	Anthony Freedman	Joshua Parr		4	56kg	$13
2	7	TORVILL	Clarry Conners	Christian Reith	0.5L	11	56kg	$18
3	5	RIMRAAM	David & Ben Hayes & Tom Dabernig	Kerrin McEvoy	0.7L	3	56kg	$26
3	6	SHUMOOKH	Gai Waterhouse & Adrian Bott	Tim Clark	0.7L	1	56kg	$4
5	10	MOSS TRIP	Peter & Paul Snowden	Brenton Avdulla	1.5L	2	56kg	$20
6	2	ALIZEE	James Cummings	Glyn Schofield	1.8L	10	56kg	$2.70f
7	11	TOUCH OF MINK	Matthew Smith	Rachel King (a)	2.5L	8	56kg	$101
8	9	YULONG XINGSHENG	Kris Lees	Jeff Lloyd	3.7L	6	56kg	$51
9	3	MELODY BELLE	Stephen Autridge & Jamie Richards	Hugh Bowman	3.8L	9	56kg	$9.50
10	4	FROLIC	Edward O'Rourke	Jason Collett	4.7L	5	56kg	$9
11	8	UNFORGOTTEN	Chris Waller	Jay Ford	7.6L	7	56kg	$12

YEAR	WINNER	JOCKEY	TRAINER	2ND	3RD	TIME
2018	Shoals	Josh Parr	Anthony Freedman	Torvill	Rimraam	1:23.4
2017	La Bella Diosa	Jason Collett	Mandy & Matt Brown	Omei Sword	Global Glamour	1:25.6
2016	Ghisoni	James McDonald	John O'Shea	Single Gaze	Stay With Me	1:21.3
2015	First Seal	Blake Shinn	John P Thompson	Supara	Slightly Sweet	1:22.9
2014	Thump	Jim Cassidy	Kris Lees	Real Surreal	Lucia Valentina	1:23.5
2013	Dear Demi	Jim Cassidy	Clarry Conners	Driefontein	Longport	1:22.2
2012	Streama	Hugh Bowman	Guy Walter	Sea Siren	Hallowell Belle	1:24.7
2011	Parables	Rod Quinn	Peter Snowden	Red Tracer	Rose Of Peace	1:22.3
2010	More Joyous	Nash Rawiller	Gai Waterhouse	Hurtle Myrtle	So Anyway	1:23.6
2009	Portillo	Corey Brown	Peter Snowden	Romneya	Rocha	1:21.8
2008	Chinchilla Rose	Stephen Baster	Steele Ryan	Occurrence	Mimi Lebrock	1:24.2
2007	Gold Edition	Jim Cassidy	Ron Maund	Tuesday Joy	Just Dancing	1:22.3
2006	Regal Cheer	Glen Boss	Joseph Pride	Mnemosyne	Star Mystic	1:22.8
2005	Lotteria	Chris Munce	Gai Waterhouse	Shania Dane	Johan's Toy	1:22.8
2004	Only Words	Rod Quinn	John Hawkes	Ike's Dream	Shamekha	1:25.9
2003	Bollinger	Damien Oliver	Gai Waterhouse	Bumptious	Sunday Joy	1:23.1
2002	Hosannah	Darren Beadman	John Hawkes	Heritiere	Quays	1:22.8
2001	On Type	Brian York	Gai Waterhouse	Maitland Gold	Miss Kournikova	1:22.7
2000	Ad Alta	Darren Beadman	Tony Gillies	Spinning Hill	Camena	1:24.0
1999	Savannah Success	Brian York	Graeme Rogerson	Confer	Rubicall	1:24.0
1998	Staging	John Powell	Clarry Conners	Dantelah	Stella Cadente	1:23.7
1997	Dashing Eagle	John Marshall	Bart Cummings	Assertive Lass	Priceless Joy	1:21.8

BACKGROUND
First run: 1979 (won by Impede). Group 3 1979-85. Group 2 from 1986 except 1990 when run as a Group 3. Group 1 from 2018. Run at Warwick Farm 1979; 1982-2007; 2010-15, from 2018. Randwick 1980-81, 2008-09, 2016-18.
Fastest time (1400m): Glenview (1989) 1:21.60
Notable winners: Shoals (2018): First Seal (2015); Dear Demi (2013); Streama (2012); More Joyous (2010); Gold Edition (2007); Lotteria (2005); Bollinger (2003); Savannah Success (1999); Staging (1998); Dashing Eagle (1997); Shame (1996); Skating (1993).
Surround Stakes winners won the lead-up races:
Light Fingers Stakes: 4—More Joyous (2010); Staging (1998); Skating (1993); Office (1992). Note: From 2010 to 2015, the six winners of the Surround Stakes ran in the Light Fingers Stakes as their final lead-up race.
Surround Stakes winners went on to win in the same preparation:
Storm Queen Stakes: 2—Savannah Success (1999); Impede (1979).
Coolmore Classic: 4—Regal Cheer (2006); Bollinger (2003); Skating (1993); Avon Angel (1985).
Australian Oaks: 1—Streama (2012).
Queen Of The Turf Stakes: 1—Shame (1996).
Phar Lap Stakes: 1—Only Words (2004).
Robert Sangster Stakes: 1—Shoals (2018).
Leading winning jockeys: 3 wins Darren Beadman (Hosannah 2002, Ad Alta 2000, Ochiltree 1990);

Jim Cassidy (Thump 2014, Dear Demi 2013, Gold Edition 2007).

2 wins Peter Cook (Ma Chiquita 1986, Brava Jeannie 1980); Shane Dye (Office 1992, Let's Hurry 1991); John Marshall (Dashing Eagle 1997, Glenview 1989); Larry Olsen (Royal Regatta 1983, Hanalei 1981); Rod Quinn (Parables 2011, Only Words 2004); Ron Quinton (La Caissiere 1984, Lost World 1982); Brian York (On Type 2001, Savannah Success 1999).

Current winning jockeys: 1 win Stephen Baster (Chinchilla Rose 2008); Glen Boss (Regal Cheer 2006); Hugh Bowman (Streama 2012); Corey Brown (Portillo 2009); Larry Cassidy (Shame 1996); Jason Collett (La Bella Diosa 2017); Grant Cooksley (Skating 1993); James McDonald (Ghisoni 2016); Damien Oliver (Bollinger 2003); Josh Parr (Shoals 2018); Nash Rawiller (More Joyous 2010); Blake Shinn (First Seal 2015).

Leading winning trainers: 4 wins Gai Waterhouse (More Joyous 2010, Lotteria 2005, Bollinger 2003, On Type 2001).

3 wins Neville Begg (Judyann 1988, La Caissiere 1984, Hanalei 1981); Bart Cummings (Dashing Eagle 1997, Glenview 1989, Royal Regatta 1983); John Hawkes (Only Words 2004, Hosannah 2002, Shame 1996); Graeme Rogerson (Savannah Success 1999, So Keen 1994, Skating 1993).

Current winning trainers: 3 wins John Hawkes (Only Words 2004, Hosannah 2002, Shame 1996); Graeme Rogerson (Savannah Success 1999, So Keen 1994, Skating 1993).

2 wins Clarry Conners (Dear Demi 2013, Staging 1998); Peter Snowden (Parables 2011, Portillo 2009); John Thompson (First Seal 2015, Thump 2014).

1 win Mandy & Matt Brown (La Bella Diosa 2017); Greg Eurell (Princess D'Or 1995); Anthony Freedman (Shoals 2018); Tony Gillies (Ad Alta 2000); John O'Shea (Ghisoni 2016); Joe Pride (Regal Cheer 2006); Steele Ryan (Chinchilla Rose 2008).

Points of interest: La Caissiere (1984) is the dam of Dashing Eagle (1997).

Gai Waterhouse has trained four winners (see above). Her father Tommy Smith trained the first Surround Stakes winner, Impede (1976). John Thompson, who trained Thump to win in 2014, is the son of Vic Thompson, trainer of Ochiltree (1990).

Khaptivaan (1987) was ridden by New Zealand jockey Maree Lyndon.

VRC Australian Guineas (1600m)—Flemington
Of $1,000,000. Group 1. Set Weights, 3YO. March 2, 2019.

2017-18 RESULT: Time: 1:34.99 (Good 3)

FP	NO	HORSE	TRAINER	JOCKEY	MARGIN	BAR.	WGT	SP
1	11	GRUNT	Mick Price	Damien Oliver		16	56.5kg	$5.50
2	13	PEACEFUL STATE	Darren Weir	Brad Rawiller	0.5L	10	56.5kg	$8.50
3	16	BRING ME ROSES	Tony McEvoy	Luke Currie	2L	1	54.5kg	$21
4	6	VILLERMONT	Aaron Purcell	Luke Nolen	3.5L	6	56.5kg	$26
5	9	HOLY SNOW	Mick Price	Michael Dee	4.5L	13	56.5kg	$19
6	5	MURAAQEB	David & Ben Hayes & Tom Dabernig	Damian Lane	4.6L	14	56.5kg	$17
7	2	CLIFF'S EDGE	Darren Weir	John Allen	4.7L	15	56.5kg	$4.60f
8	3	EMBELLISH	Stephen Autridge & Jamie Richards	Opie Bosson	5.45L	8	56.5kg	$16
9	10	SALSAMOR	Trent Busuttin & Natalie Young	Jordan Childs	5.65L	11	56.5kg	$61
10	7	MAIN STAGE	Trent Busuttin & Natalie Young	Regan Bayliss	6.05L	4	56.5kg	$12
11	8	ADDICTIVE NATURE	Bjorn Baker	Craig Williams	7.3L	7	56.5kg	$16
12	12	BLACK SAIL	Aaron Purcell	Ben Thompson	8.05L	3	56.5kg	$101
13	15	ALOISIA	Aaron Purcell	Mark Zahra	8.45L	12	55kg	$11
14	1	MIGHTY BOSS	Mick Price	Michael Walker	9.95L	2	56.5kg	$17
15	14	MR SO AND SO	Anthony Freedman	Beau Mertens	10.15L	5	56.5kg	$41
16	4	LEVENDI	Peter Gelagotis	Ben Melham	25.15L	9	56.5kg	$31

PAST WINNERS

YEAR	WINNER	JOCKEY	TRAINER	2ND	3RD	TIME
2018	Grunt	Damien Oliver	Mick Price	Peaceful State	Bring Me Roses	1:34.9
2017	Hey Doc	Luke Currie	Tony McEvoy	Prized Icon	Snitzson	1:34.0
2016	Palentino	Mark Zahra	Darren Weir	Tarzino	Risque	1:35.2
2015	Wandjina	Brett Prebble	Gai Waterhouse	Alpine Eagle	Stratum Star	1:35.1
2014	Shamus Award	Craig Williams	Danny O'Brien	Criterion	Thunder Fantasy	1:36.4
2013	Ferlax	Stephen Baster	Jim Conlan	You're So Good	Sheer Talent	1:35.0
2012	Mosheen	Danny Nikolic	Robert Smerdon	Strike The Stars	Mister Milton	1:37.0
2011	Shamrocker	Glen Boss	Danny O'Brien	Bullbars	Playing God	1:35.3
2010	Rock Classic	Michael Rodd	Bart Cummings	Set For Fame	Linton	1:36.8
2009	Heart Of Dreams	Craig Newitt	Mick Price	Von Costa De Hero	Lucky Thunder	1:35.8
2008	Light Fantastic	Craig Newitt	Mick Price	Marching	Playwright	1:36.4
2007	Miss Finland	Craig Williams	David Hayes	Casino Prince	Jokers Wild	1:36.0
2006	Apache Cat	Noel Callow	Greg Eurell	Darcy Brahma	Thin And Crispy	1:34.0
2005	Al Maher	Noel Callow	Gai Waterhouse	Danehill Express	Econsul	1:34.4
2004	Reset	Danny Nikolic	Graeme Rogerson	Starcraft	Under The Bridge	1:34.5
2003	Delago Brom	Patrick Payne	Tommy Hughes Jnr	Tycoon Ruler	Thorn Park	1:35.9
2002	Dash For Cash	Scott Seamer	Rick Hore-Lacy	Royal Code	Ustinov	1:35.3
2001	Mr Murphy	Damien Oliver	Lee Freedman	Neptunes Journey	Outgate	1:34.4
2000	Pins	Shane Dye	Clarry Conners	Freemason	Hades	2:02.3
1999	Dignity Dancer	Jim Cassidy	Bill Mitchell	Mossman	Lease	1:59.0
1998	Gold Guru	Greg Childs	Leon Macdonald	Zonda	Il Don	2:00.5
1997	Mouawad	Grant Cooksley	Clarry Conners	O'Reilly	Tarnpir Lane	1:36.5

BACKGROUND

First run: 1986 (won by True Version). Group 3 1986. Group 1 from 1987. Run over 2000 1998-2000. Run at Caulfield in 2007.
Most recent filly to win: Mosheen (2012). Note: Shamrocker (2010), Miss Finland (2007) and Triscay (1991) are the only other fillies to win.
Fastest time (1600m Flemington): Apache Cat (2006) & Jolly Old Mac (1992) 1:34.00
Notable winners: Shamus Award (2014); Mosheen (2012); Miss Finland (2007); Apache Cat (2006); Reset (2004); Delago Brom (2003); Dash For Cash (2002); Pins (2000); Dignity Dancer (1999); Gold Guru (1998); Flying Spur (1996); Mahogany (1994); Triscay (1991); Zabeel (1990); King's High (1989); Military Plume (1987).

Australian Guineas winners won the lead-up races:
C S Hayes Stakes: 6—Grunt (2018); Hey Doc (2017); Dash For Cash (2002); Mouawad (1997); Mahogany (1994); Zabeel (1990).
Alister Clark Stakes: 5—Mr. Murphy (2001); Pins (2000); Dignity Dancer (1999); Zabeel (1990); Flotilla (1988). Note: Zabeel (1990) and Flotilla (1988) won the double when the Alister Clark (2040m) was run after the Guineas.
Autumn Stakes: 4—Light Fantastic (2008); Apache Cat (2006); Dignity Dancer (1999); King's High (1989).
Autumn Classic: 4—Pins (2000); Dignity Dancer (1999); Gold Guru (1998); King's High (1989).
Futurity Stakes: 4—Reset* (2004); Dash For Cash (2002); Mr. Murphy (2001); Mouawad (1997).
*The Futurity was run after the Guineas in 2004.

Australian Guineas winners went on to win in the same preparation:
Randwick Guineas: 1—Mosheen (2012).
Rosehill Guineas: None.
Australian Derby: 3—Shamrocker (2011); Gold Guru (1998); Mahogany (1994).
Storm Queen Stakes: 2—Mosheen (2012); Miss Finland (2007)
Australian Oaks: 1—Triscay (1991).
All Aged Stakes: 1—Flying Spur (1996).

Australian Guineas winners also won:
Golden Slipper (2YO): 2—Miss Finland (Guineas 2007); Flying Spur (1996).
Caulfield Guineas (spring): 1—Mahogany (Guineas 1994).
Thousand Guineas (spring): 1—Miss Finland (Guineas 2007).
Victoria Derby (spring): 2—Mahogany (Guineas 1994); King's High (1989).
VRC Oaks (spring): 2—Mosheen (Guineas 2012); Miss Finland (2007).
Cox Plate (spring): 1—Shamus Award (Cox Plate 2013, Guineas 2014)

Leading winning jockeys:
3 wins Damien Oliver (Grunt 2018, Mr. Murphy 2001, Flying Spur 1996).
2 wins Noel Callow (Apache Cat 2006, Al Maher 2005); Jim Cassidy (Dignity Dancer 1999, Baryshnikov 1995); Greg Childs (Gold Guru 1998, Kenny's Best Pal 1993); Michael Clarke (Zabeel 1990, Military Plume 1987); Darren Gauci (Jolly Old Mac 1992, True Version 1986); Greg Hall (Mahogany 1994, Flotilla 1988); Craig Newitt (Heart Of Dreams 2009, Light Fantastic 2008); Danny Nikolic (Mosheen 2012, Reset 2004); Craig Williams (Shamus Award 2014, Miss Finland 2007).

Current winning jockeys:
3 wins Damien Oliver (Grunt 2018, Mr. Murphy 2001, Flying Spur 1996).
2 wins Noel Callow (Apache Cat 2006, Al Maher 2005); Craig Newitt (Heart Of Dreams 2009, Light Fantastic 2008); Craig Williams (Shamus Award 2014, Miss Finland 2007).
1 win Stephen Baster (Ferlax 2013); Glen Boss (Shamrocker 2011); Grant Cooksley (Mouawad 1997); Luke Currie (Hey Doc 2017); Brett Prebble (Wandjina 2015); Michael Rodd (Rock Classic 2010); Mark Zahra (Palentino 2016).

Leading winning trainers:
3 wins Lee Freedman (Mr. Murphy 2001, Flying Spur 1996, Mahogany 1994); Colin Hayes (Zabeel 1990, King's High 1989, Military Plume 1987).

Current winning trainers:
3 wins Lee Freedman (Mr. Murphy 2001, Flying Spur 1996, Mahogany 1994); Mick Price (Grunt 2018, Heart Of Dreams 2009, Light Fantastic 2008).
2 wins Clarry Conners (Pins 2000, Mouawad 1997); Danny O'Brien (Shamus Award 2014, Shamrocker 2011); Gai Waterhouse (Wandjina 2015, Al Maher 2005).
1 win Jim Conlan (Ferlax 2013); Greg Eurell (Apache Cat 2006); David Hayes (Miss Finland 2007); Tom Hughes jnr (Delago Brom 2003); Tony McEvoy (Hey Doc 2017); Graeme Rogerson (Reset 2004); John Sadler (Jolly Old Mac 1992); Robert Smerdon (Mosheen 2012); Darren Weir (Palentino 2016).

Points of interest:
Zabeel (1990) is the sire of Reset (2004). Zabeel (Sir Tristram-Lady Giselle) won in 1990. Zabeel's half-brother Baryshnikov (Kenmare-Lady Giselle) won in 1995. Reset is the only horse to win the Australian Guineas and the Futurity Stakes in the same preparation.
No New Zealand-trained horse has won the Australian Guineas.
Palentino (2016) survived a protest from runner-up Tivaci (Nick Hall)—two weeks earlier, the rider of Tivaci (Craig Williams) successfully protested against Palentino to win the G3 C S Hayes Stakes at Flemington.

ATC Randwick Guineas (1600m)—Randwick

Of $1,000,000. Group 1. Set Weights, 3YO. March 9, 2019.

2017-18 RESULT: Time: 1:33.72 (Good 4)

FP	NO	HORSE	TRAINER	JOCKEY	MARGIN	BAR.	WGT	SP
1	3	KEMENTARI	James Cummings	Glyn Schofield		4	56.5kg	$2.35F
2	5	PIERATA	Gregory Hickman	Corey Brown	1.5L	1	56.5kg	$5.50
3	2	TRAPEZE ARTIST	Gerald Ryan	Tim Clark	1.8L	10	56.5kg	$10
4	1	ACE HIGH	David Payne	Tye Angland	2.3L	2	56.5kg	$19
5	11	SIEGE OF QUEBEC	Gai Waterhouse & Adrian Bott	Christian Reith	2.5L	8	56.5kg	$41
6	12	KAONIC	Chris Waller	Brenton Avdulla	3L	5	56.5kg	$21
7	10	D'ARGENTO	Chris Waller	Andrew Adkins	3.4L	14	56.5kg	$6
8	13	CONDOR	Paul Perry	Joshua Parr	3.5L	7	56.5kg	$151
9	9	CAPITAL GAIN	Paul Butterworth	Adam Hyeronimus	5.4L	3	56.5kg	$201
10	6	SULLY	Trent Busuttin & Natalie Young	Blake Shinn	5.5L	11	56.5kg	$61
11	4	AGE OF FIRE	Stephen Autridge & Jamie Richards	Jason Collett	5.9L	13	56.5kg	$51
12	14	TANGMERE	Chris Waller	Kerrin McEvoy	6.5L	12	56.5kg	$101
13	7	PEACEFUL STATE	Darren Weir	Brad Rawiller	7.4L	9	56.5kg	$9.50
14	8	TANGLED	Chris Waller	Jay Ford	8.2L	6	56.5kg	$101

PAST WINNERS

YEAR	WINNER	JOCKEY	TRAINER	2ND	3RD	TIME
2018	Kementari	Glyn Schofield	James Cummings	Pierata	Trapeze Artist	1:33.7
2017	Inference	Tommy Berry	Michael, Wayne & John Hawkes	Invincible Gem	Comin' Through	1:40.9
2016	Le Romain	Christian Reith	Kris Lees	Press Statement	Gold Ambition	1:33.8
2015	Hallowed Crown	Hugh Bowman	Bart & James Cummings	Sweynesse	Shooting To Win	1:35.0
2014	Dissident	Jim Cassidy	Peter Moody	El Roca	Eurozone	1:36.3
2013	It's A Dundeel	James McDonald	Murray Baker	Proisir	Tatra	1:35.1
2012	Mosheen	Danny Nikolic	Robert Smerdon	Said Com	Laser Hawk	1:37.6
2011	Ilovethiscity	Brenton Avdulla	Grahame Begg	Skilled	Light Brigade	1:35.3
2010	Shoot Out	Stathi Katsidis	John Wallace	Viking Legend	Captain Sonador	1:34.9
2009	Metal Bender	Danny Nikolic	Jack Denham	Rock Kingdom	Caymans	1:36.5
2008	Weekend Hussler	Brad Rawiller	Ross McDonald	Triple Honour	Arlington	1:36.3
2007	Mentality	Darren Beadman	John Hawkes	Teranaba	Sniper's Bullet	1:35.7
2006	Hotel Grand	Jay Ford	Anthony Cummings	Flying Pegasus	Primus	1:35.8
2005	Jymcarew	Glen Boss	Bob Thomsen	Eremein	Cheval De Troy	1:57.4
2004	Niello	Darren Beadman	John Hawkes	Timbourina	Dancing Daggers	1:57.2
2003	Fine Society	Corey Brown	John Hawkes	Beaver	Hydrometer	1:57.0
2002	Carnegie Express	Jim Cassidy	Gai Waterhouse	Pentastic	Another Warrior	1:56.2
2001	Universal Prince	Justin Sheehan	Bede Murray	Danamite	Scenic Warrior	1:57.4
2000	Fairway	Brian York	Jack Denham	Oval Office	Cloth Of God	1:58.7
1999	Arena	Larry Cassidy	John Hawkes	Lawyer	El Duce	1:49.6
1998	Tycoon Lil	Grant Cooksley	Colin Jillings	Tricove	Brave Prince	1:49.0
1997	Intergaze	Craig Carmody	Rod Craig	Might And Power	Great Command	1:47.9

BACKGROUND

First run: 1935 (won by Hadrian). Group 1 since 1980. Run over 1800m 1935-56; 1958-72; 2000m 1957; 1850m 1973-75; 1900m 1976-2005. Run in the spring until 1979. Until 2006 run at Canterbury, named the Canterbury Guineas. Switched to Randwick in 2006, reduced to 1600m. Run at Warwick Farm 2012.
Most recent filly to win: Mosheen (2012).
Fastest time (Randwick 1600m): 1:33.72 (Kementari 2018).
Notable winners: Kementari (2018); Le Romain (2016); Dissident (2014); It's A Dundeel (2013); Mosheen (2012); Shoot Out (2010); Weekend Hussler (2008); Niello (2004); Universal Prince (2001); Fairway (2000); Arena (1999); Intergaze (1997); Octagonal (1996); Veandercross (1992); Spirit Of Kingston (1985); Mr. McGinty (1983); Belmura Lad (1977); Imagele (1973); Royal Show (1970); Broker's Tip (1968); Martello Towers (1959); Todman (1957); Delta (1949).

Randwick Guineas winners won the lead-up races.
Australian Guineas: 1—Mosheen (2012).
Eskimo Prince: 1—Kementari (2018).
Hobartville Stakes: 3—Kementari (2018); Ilovethiscity (2011); Arena (1999).Randwick Guineas winners went on to win in the same preparation:
Rosehill Guineas: 14—It's A Dundeel (2013); Metal Bender (2009); Niello (2004); Carnegie Express (2002); Octagonal (1996); Riverina Charm (1989); Spirit Of Kingston (1985); Imagele (1973); Royal Show (1970); Fair Summer (1965); Martello Towers (1959); Pride Of Egypt (1954); Moorland (1943); Hadrian (1935).
George Ryder Stakes: 1—Weekend Hussler (2009).
Storm Queen Stakes: 1—Mosheen (2012).
Australian Derby: 13—It's A Dundeel (2013); Shoot Out (2010); Universal Prince (2001); Fairway (2000); Octagonal (1996); Belmura Lad (1977); Imagele (1973); Summer Fiesta (1963); Summer Prince (1962); Persian Lyric (1960); Martello Towers (1959); Prince Morvi (1953); Moorland (1943).
Rosehill Guineas, Australian Derby (Triple Crown, from 2006): 1—It's A Dundeel (2013).
Randwick Guineas and the spring 3YO features (same season, since 2006):
Golden Rose: None.
Caulfield Guineas: 1—Weekend Hussler (Randwick Guineas 2008).
Leading winning jockey:
6 wins George Moore (Garcon 1966, Summer Fiesta 1963, Summer Prince 1962, Kilshery 1961, Movie Boy 1956, Forest Beau 1951).
Current winning jockeys:
2 wins Grant Cooksley (Tycoon Lil 1998, Kingston Bay 1993).
1 win Brenton Avdulla (Ilovethiscity 2011); Tommy Berry (Inference 2017); Glen Boss (2005); Corey Brown (Fine Society 2003); Larry Cassidy (Arena 1999); Jay Ford (Hotel Grand 2006); James McDonald (It's A Dundeel 2013); Brad Rawiller (Weekend Hussler 2008); Christian Reith (Le Romain 2016); Glyn Schofield (Kementari 2018); Robert Thompson (Sharscay 1995).
Leading winning trainers:
11 wins Tommy Smith (Rocky Top 1980, Chasta Bellota 1976, Imagele 1973, Lord Ben 1972, Royal Show 1970, Garcon 1966, Summer Fiesta 1963, Summer Prince 1962, Kilshery 1961, Movie Boy 1956, Forest Beau 1951).
6 wins John Hawkes (Inference 2017, Mentality 2007, Niello 2004, Fine Society 2003, Arena 1999. Octagonal 1996).
5 wins Jack Denham (Metal Bender 2009, Fairway 2000, Sydney Cove 1974, Egyptian 1971, Fair Summer 1965).
Current winning trainers:
6 wins John Hawkes (Inference 2017, Mentality 2007, Niello 2004, Fine Society 2003, Arena 1999. Octagonal 1996).
2 wins Michael, Wayne & John Hawkes (Inference 2017, Mentality 2007).
1 win Murray Baker (It's A Dundeel 2013); Rod Craig (Intergaze 1997); Anthony Cummings (Hotel Grand 2006); James Cummings (Kementari 2018); David Hayes (Western Red 1994); Kris Lees (Le Romain 2016); Robert Smerdon (Mosheen 2012); John Wallace (Shoot Out 2010); Bruce Wallace (Kingston Bay 1993); Gai Waterhouse (Carnegie Express 2002); John Wheeler (Veandercross 1992).
Points of interest:
This race has changed in emphasis now that it is run over 1600m. It become a crucial lead-up to races like the George Ryder Stakes (1500m) at Rosehill, and the Doncaster Handicap. Mentality (2007) was runner-up to Haradasun in those races after winning the Randwick Guineas.

ATC Canterbury Stakes (1300m)—Randwick

Of $500,000. Group 1. Weight For Age, 3YO&Up. March 9, 2019.

2017-18 RESULT: Time: 1:14.25 (Good 4)

FP	NO	HORSE	TRAINER	JOCKEY	MARGIN	BAR.	WGT	SP
1	1	HAPPY CLAPPER	Patrick Webster	Blake Shinn		1	59kg	$4.60F
2	7	GLOBAL GLAMOUR	Gai Waterhouse & Adrian Bott	Tim Clark	1.3L	8	57kg	$5.50
3	6	INVINCIBLE GEM	Kris Lees	Corey Brown	2.8L	6	57kg	$7.50
4	3	ENDLESS DRAMA	Chris Waller	Tye Angland	3.6L	4	59kg	$9
5	9	TULIP	David & Ben Hayes & Tom Dabernig	Jason Collett	4.1L	2	54kg	$8
6	2	CLEARLY INNOCENT	Kris Lees	Glyn Schofield	4.7L	3	59kg	$7.50
7	8	SHOWTIME	Michael, Wayne & John Hawkes	Brenton Avdulla	5L	5	56kg	$6
8	5	FOXPLAY	Chris Waller	Kerrin McEvoy	5.8L	9	57kg	$12
9	4	DERRYN	David & Ben Hayes & Tom Dabernig	Joshua Parr	8.2L	7	59kg	$61

PAST WINNERS

YEAR	WINNER	JOCKEY	TRAINER	2ND	3RD	TIME
2018	Happy Clapper	Blake Shinn	Pat Webster	Global Glamour	Invincible Gem	1:14.2
2017	Le Romain	Glyn Schofield	Kris Lees	Chautauqua	Hauraki	1:20.0
2016	Holler	James McDonald	John O'Shea	First Seal	Kermadec	1:15.4
2015	Cosmic Endeavour	James McDonald	Gai Waterhouse	Catkins	Criterion	1:15.7
2014	Appearance	Kerrin McEvoy	Guy Walter	Not Listenin'Tome	Red Tracer	1:17.2
2013	Pierro	Jim Cassidy	Gai Waterhouse	More Joyous	Solzhenitsyn	1:15.9
2012	More Joyous	Nash Rawiller	Gai Waterhouse	Monton	Metal Bender	1:18.4
2011	More Joyous	Nash Rawiller	Gai Waterhouse	Love Conquers All	Demerit	1:17.8
2010	Hot Danish	Tim Clark	Les Bridge	Black Piranha	Mr Baritone	1:16.4
2009	All Silent	Damien Oliver	Grahame Begg	Forensics	Royal Discretion	1:16.5
2008	Mentality	Darren Beadman	John Hawkes	Racing To Win	Sniper's Bullet	1:32.3
2007	Malcolm	Darren Beadman	John Hawkes	Cheeky Choice	Kosi Bay	1:16.5
2006	Paratroopers	Darren Beadman	John Hawkes	Patezza	Dance Hero	1:16.2
2005	Dance Hero	Chris Munce	Gai Waterhouse	Falkirk	Ike's Dream	1:17.0
2004	Yell	Darren Beadman	John Hawkes	Grand Armee	True Glo	1:16.0
2003	Defier	Chris Munce	Guy Walter	Cosmic Rays	Gordo	1:09.1
2002	Empire	Jim Cassidy	Max Lees	Diamond Dane	Shogun Lodge	1:10.3
2001	Shogun Lodge	Glen Boss	Bob Thomsen	Assertive Lad	El Mirada	1:10.0
2000	Easy Rocking	Darren Beadman	Ron Quinton	Referral	Guineas	1:11.5
1999	Kidman's Cove	Len Beasley	John Size	Prowl	Shinkansea	1:09.7
1998	Quick Flick	Mark De Montfort	Tim Donnelly	Guineas	Masked Party	1:09.8
1997	All Our Mob	Chris Munce	Gai Waterhouse	Quick Flick	Sovereign State	1:08.4

BACKGROUND

First run: 1929 (won by Amounis). Group 2 1979-2012. Group 1 from 2013. Run at Canterbury 1929-1972, 2008, Rosehill 1973-75, 1980, 1981, 1997, 1998, 2004-07, 2009-13, Randwick from 2014. Run over 1200m before 2004; 1300m from 2004 to 2007. Not held 1958 & 1978. Switched from spring to autumn in 1979.
Most recent mare to win: Cosmic Endeavour (2015).
Most recent 3YO to win: C&G—Holler (2016); Filly—Emancipation (1983).
Multiple winners: 5—More Joyous (2012, 2011); At Sea (1989, 1988); Sky High (1962, 1961); San Domenico (1951, 1950); Holdfast (1932, 1931, 1930).
Fastest time (1300m, Randwick): Happy Clapper (2018) 1:14.25
Notable winners: Happy Clapper (2018); Le Romain (2017); Appearance (2014); Pierro (2013); More Joyous (2012, 2011); Mentality (2008); Dance Hero (2005); Shogun Lodge (2000); All Our Mob (1997); Placid Ark (1987); Sir Dapper (1984); Emancipation (1983); Manikato (1982); Hartshill (1976); Baguette (1971); Sky High (1962, 1961); San Domenico (1951, 1950); Tea Rose (1944); Beau Vite (1939); Lough Neagh (1934); Chatham (1933); Amounis (1929).

Canterbury Stakes winners won the lead-up races (since 1978 when moved from spring to autumn):
Australia Stakes: 1—Holler (2016).
Liverpool City Cup: None.
Expressway Stakes: 5—Appearance (2014); Kidman's Cove (1999); At Sea (1988); Avon Angel (1986); Sir Dapper (1984).
Apollo Stakes: 4—Appearance (2014); Kidman's Cove (1999); Quick Flick (1998); At Sea (1988).
Southern Cross Stakes: 3—Le Romain (2017); Big Dreams (1993); Avon Angel (1986).

Canterbury Stakes winners went on to win in the same preparation:
George Ryder Stakes: 4—Pierro (2012); Quick Flick (1998); Straussbrook (1990); Emancipation (1983). Note: Baguette (1971) and Regoli (1953) won when the Canterbury Stakes was run in the spring.
Ajax Stakes: None.
Doncaster Handicap: 3—Happy Clapper (2018); Sprint By (1996); Emancipation (1983). Note: Broker's Tip (1970) and Bernbrook (1949) won both when the Canterbury Stakes was run in the spring.
Queen Elizabeth Stakes: 1—More Joyous (2012).
Queen Of The Turf Stakes: 2—More Joyous (2012, 2011). Note 1: Favoured (1974) won when the Canterbury Stakes was run in the spring. Note 2: since 2012, the Queen Of The Turf has moved to later in April, after the Canterbury Stakes.
All Aged Stakes: 2—Hot Danish (2010); Paratroopers (2006). Note: Broker's Tip (1970), Sky High (1961) and Yaralla (1942) won when Canterbury Stakes was run in the spring.
Doomben 10,000: 1—Hot Danish (2010).

Leading winning jockeys:
7 wins Darren Beadman (Mentality 2008, Malcolm 2007, Paratroopers 2006, Yell 2004, Easy Rocking 2000, At Sea 1989, 1988).
6 wins Darby Munro (Shannon 1947, Katanga 1943, Reading 1941, Beaulivre 1940, Lough Neagh 1934).
5 wins Jim Cassidy (Pierro 2013, Empire 2002, Big Dreams 1993, Chimes Square 1985); Billy Cook (Gay Monarch 1948, Beau Vite 1939, Arachne 1936, Holdfast 1932, 1930).

Current winning jockeys:
2 wins Glen Boss (Shogun Lodge 2001, Sprint By 1995); James McDonald (Holler 2016, Cosmic Endeavour 2015); Nash Rawiller (More Joyous 2012, 2011);
1 win Larry Cassidy (Al Akbar 1994); Tim Clark (Hot Danish 2010), Grant Cooksley (Miss Kariba 1995); Kerrin McEvoy (Appearance 2014); Damien Oliver (All Silent 2009); Glyn Schofield (Le Romain 2017); Blake Shinn (Happy Clapper 2018).

Leading winning trainers:
7 wins Gai Waterhouse (Cosmic Endeavour 2015, Pierro 2013, More Joyous 2012, 2011, Dance Hero 2005, All Our Mob 1997, Sprint By 1996).
4 wins John Hawkes (Mentality 2008, Malcolm 2007, Paratroopers 2006, Yell 2004).

Current winning trainers:
7 wins Gai Waterhouse (Cosmic Endeavour 2015, Pierro 2013, More Joyous 2012, 2011, Dance Hero 2005, All Our Mob 1997, Sprint By 1996).
4 wins John Hawkes (Mentality 2008, Malcolm 2007, Paratroopers 2006, Yell 2004).
2 wins Michael, Wayne & John Hawkes (Mentality 2008, Malcolm 2007); Pat Webster (Happy Clapper 2018, At Sea 1989).
1 win Les Bridge (Sir Dapper 1984); Tom Donnelly (Quick Flick 1998); David Hayes (Alishan 1992); Kris Lees (Le Romain 20017); John O'Shea (Holler 2016); Ron Quinton (Easy Rocking 2000); John Size (Kidman's Cove 1999).

Point of interest:
Dance Hero (2005) is the only horse to win the Royal Sovereign Stakes and Canterbury Stakes in the same year.

VRC TAB Australian Cup (2000m)—Flemington
Of $1,500,000. Group 1. Weight For Age. March 9, 2019.

2017-18 RESULT: Time: 2:00.46 (Good 3)

FP	NO	HORSE	TRAINER	JOCKEY	MARGIN	BAR.	WGT	SP
1	7	HARLEM	David & Ben Hayes & Tom Dabernig	Michael Walker		4	59kg	$61
2	4	GAILO CHOP	Darren Weir	Mark Zahra	0.5L	10	59kg	$2.60f
3	5	VENTURA STORM	David & Ben Hayes & Tom Dabernig	Regan Bayliss	1.25L	2	59kg	$31
4	2	ALMANDIN	Liam Howley	Damien Oliver	1.45L	11	59kg	$4.40
5	11	SINGLE GAZE	Nick Olive	Kathy O'Hara	1.85L	5	57kg	$9
6	10	HOMESMAN	Liam Howley	Michael Dee	2.25L	3	58.5kg	$21
7	8	LORD FANDANGO	Archie Alexander	Jordan Childs	2.35L	1	59kg	$71
8	9	THE TAJ MAHAL	Liam Howley	Ben Melham	2.85L	7	58.5kg	$9
9	3	AMBITIOUS	Anthony Freedman	Damian Lane	4.1L	12	59kg	$21
10	1	HARTNELL	James Cummings	Craig Williams	4.85L	6	59kg	$9.50
11	6	SUPPLY AND DEMAND	Gai Waterhouse & Adrian Bott	Stephen Baster	11.85L	9	59kg	$41
12	12	DEVISE	Shaune Ritchie	Chad Schofield	21.85L	8	57kg	$31

PAST WINNERS

YEAR	WINNER	JOCKEY	TRAINER	2ND	3RD	TIME
2018	Harlem	Michael Walker	David & Ben Hayes & Tom Dabernig	Gailo Chop	Ventura Storm	2:00.4
2017	Humidor	Damian Lane	Darren Weir	Jameka	Exospheric	2:01.0
2016	Preferment	Hugh Bowman	Chris Waller	Awesome Rock	Rising Romance	2:03.9
2015	Spillway	Michael Walker	David Hayes & Tom Dabernig	Extra Zero	Happy Trails	2:00.0
2014	Fiorente	Damien Oliver	Gai Waterhouse	Green Moon	Foreteller	2:03.6
2013	Super Cool	Michael Rodd	Mark Kavanagh	Fiveandahalfstar	Tanby	2:00.9
2012	Manighar	Luke Nolen	Peter Moody	Southern Speed	Americain	2:01.2
2011	Shocking	Corey Brown	Mark Kavanagh	Linton	Playing God	2:00.9
2010	Zipping	Nicholas Hall	Robert Hickmott	Sirmione	Moatize	2:03.6
2009	Niconero	Craig Williams	David Hayes	Theseo	Zagreb	2:03.1
2008	Sirmione	Peter Mertens	Bart Cummings	Princess Coup	Casino Prince	2:00.8
2007	Pompeii Ruler	Craig Newitt	Mick Price	Marasco	Tawqeet	2:01.5
2006	Roman Arch	Craig Newitt	Robbie Laing	Candy Vale	Our Smoking Joe	2:02.8
2005	Makybe Diva	Glen Boss	Lee Freedman	Winning Belle	Lad Of The Manor	1:58.7
2004	Lonhro	Darren Beadman	John Hawkes	Delzao	Elvstroem	2:01.6
2003	Northerly	Patrick Payne	Fred Kersley	Natural Blitz	Don Eduardo	2:01.4
2002	Old Comrade	Paul Harvey	Lindsey Smith	Northerly	Rain Gauge	1:59.8
2001	Northerly	Greg Childs	Fred Kersley	Hit The Roof	Kaapstad Way	1:59.4
2000	Intergaze	Craig Carmody	Rod Craig	Arena	Streak	2:00.9
1999	Istidaad	Greg Childs	Peter C Hayes	Intergaze	Thackeray	1:59.4
1998	Dane Ripper	Steven King	Bart Cummings	Delinquent	Marble Halls	2:02.4
1997	Octagonal	Shane Dye	John Hawkes	Gold City	Juggler	2:01.0

BACKGROUND

First run: 1863 (won by Barwon). Group 1 since 1980. WFA since 1979, except for 1982-86 when a handicap. Run over 3600m 1863-1942; 3400m 1943-62; 2800m 1963; 2000m since 1964. Run at Caulfield in 2007.
Mares to win (since run over 2000m in 1964): 6—Makybe Diva (2005); Dane Ripper (1998); Starstruck (1995); Let's Elope (1992); Playful Princess (1986); Leilani (1975). Note: 27 mares have won the Australian Cup since 1863.
Three-year-olds to win: 8—Super Cool (2013); Saintly (1996); Noble Peer (1985); Dulcify (1979); Lord Dudley (1976); Bush Win (1974); Gladman (1973); Gay Icarus (1971). Note: No 3YO filly has won the Australian Cup since it was run over 2000m.
Multiple winners (since 1863): 6—Northerly (2003, 2001); Vo Rogue (1990, 1989); Ming Dynasty (1980, 1978); Craftsman (1966, 1965); Welkin Prince (1963, 1962); Woodman (1866, 1865).
Fastest time (Flemington 2000m): Makybe Diva (2005) 1:58.70
Australian Cup winners won the lead-up races: (since 1964, when Australian Cup was reduced from 2800m to 2000m): Peter Young Stakes: 12—Fiorente (2014); Pompeii Ruler (2007); Lonhro (2004); Northerly (2003); Istidaad (1999); Dane Ripper (1998); Durbridge (1994); Let's Elope (1992); Vo Rogue (1989); Hyperno (1981); Leilani (1975); Gay Icarus (1971).

Blamey Stakes: 7—Durbridge (1994); Better Loosen Up (1991); Vo Rogue (1989); Kip (1982); Hyperno (1981); Lord Dudley (1976); Gay Icarus (1971). Note: the Blamey Stakes has since moved from February, before the Australian Cup, to after the cup in mid-March.
Blamey Stakes & Peter Young Stakes: 3—Vo Rogue (1989); Hyperno (1981); Gay Icarus (1971).
Futurity Stakes: 2—Niconero (2009-Futurity 1600m); Crewman (1970-Futurity 1400m).
C.F. Orr Stakes: 6—Lonhro (2004); Let's Elope (1992); Vo Rogue (1990, 1989); Leilani (1974); Crewman (1970).
C.F. Orr Stakes & Futurity Stakes: 1—Crewman (1970).
C.F. Orr Stakes & Blamey Stakes & Peter Young Stakes: 1—Vo Rogue (1989).

Australian Cup winners went on to win in the same preparation: (since 1964, when Australian Cup was reduced from 2800m to 2000m):
Ranvet Stakes: 2—Manighar (2012); Veandercross (1993).
The BMW: 3—Manighar (2012); Makybe Diva (2005); Octagonal (1997).
Ranvet Stakes & The BMW: 1—Manighar (2012).
ATC Australian Derby: 1—Dulcify (1979).
ATC Queen Elizabeth Stakes: 5—Durbridge (1994); Veandercross (1993); Ming Dynasty (1978); Ngawyni (1977); Gay Icarus (1970).

Australian Cup and spring majors: (since 1964, when Australian Cup was reduced from 2800m to 2000m):
Melbourne Cup (same year): 2—Makybe Diva (2005); Saintly (1996).
Melbourne Cup (same season): 3—Fiorente (Australian Cup 2014); Makybe Diva (2005); Let's Elope (1992).
Caulfield Cup (same year): 1—Ming Dynasty (1980).
Cox Plate (same year): 3—Makybe Diva (2005); Northerly (2001); Saintly (1986).
Cox Plate (same season): 5—Northerly (Australian Cup 2003); Dane Ripper (1998); Better Loosen Up (1991); Bonecrusher (1987); Family Of Man (1978).
Victoria Derby (same season): 1—Dulcify (Australian Cup 1979). Note: Craftsman is the only other horse to win both races since 1964. He won the Derby in 1963 and the Australian Cup in 1965 and 1966. No horse has won a VRC Oaks and Australian Cup.

Leading winning jockeys (all time):
8 wins Tom Hales (Dreadnought 1890, Carlyon 1888, Trident 1887, Morpeth 1884, Navigator 1883, Savanaka 1879, Richmond 1876, Lurline 1875).
5 wins Harry White (Noble Peer 1985, Ming Dynasty 1981, Crewman 1970, Bore Head 1967).
4 wins Ron Hutchinson (Pushover 1956, Arbroath 1953, Bold John 1950, Spectre 1945).

Current winning jockeys:
2 wins Craig Newitt (Pompeii Ruler 2007, Roman Arch 2006); Cyril Small (Vo Rogue 1990, 1989); Michael Walker (Harlem 2018, Spillway 2014).
1 win Glen Boss (Makybe Diva 2005); Hugh Bowman (Preferment 2016); Corey Brown (Shocking 2011); Kevin Forrester (Admiral Lincoln 1984); Nicholas Hall (Zipping 2010); Paul Harvey (Old Comrade 2002); Damian Lane (Humidor 2017); Luke Nolen (Manighar 2012); Damien Oliver (Fiorente 2014); Michael Rodd (Super Cool 2013); Craig Williams (Niconero 2009).

Leading winning trainers (all time):
13 wins Bart Cummings (Sirmione 2008, Dane Ripper 1998, Saintly 1996, Let's Elope 1992, Noble Peer 1985, Hyperno 1981, Ming Dynasty 1980, 1978, Ngawyni 1977, Lord Dudley 1976, Leilani 1975, Gladman 1973, Arctic Coast 1968).
4 wins David Hayes (Harlem 2018, Spillway 2015; Niconero 2008, Better Loosen Up 1991); James Scobie (Pilliewinkle 1926, Macadam 1920, Dreamland 1901, Ringwood 1885).
3 wins Colin Hayes (Spectrum 1983, Dulcify 1979, Bush Win 1974); Geoff Murphy (Admiral Lincoln 1984, Welkin Prince 1963, 1962).

Current winning trainers:
4 wins David Hayes (Harlem 2018, Spillway 2015; Niconero 2008, Better Loosen Up 1991).
2 wins Lee Freedman (Makybe Diva 2005, Durbridge 1994); John Hawkes (Lonhro 2004, Octagonal 1997); David Hayes & Tom Dabernig (Harlem 2018, Spillway 2015); Mark Kavanagh (Super Cool 2013, Shocking 2011); Fred Kersley (Northerly 2003, 2001).
1 win Rod Craig (Intergaze 2000); David & Ben Hayes & Tom Dabernig (Harlem 2018); Robert Hickmott (Zipping 2010); Robbie Laing (Roman Arch 2006); Mick Price (Pompeii Ruler 2007); Frank Ritchie (Bonecrusher 1987); Lindsey Smith (Old Comrade 2002); Chris Waller (Preferment 2016); Gai Waterhouse (Fiorente 2014); John Wheeler (Veandercross 1993); Darren Weir (Humidor 2017).

Points of interest:
Youtha and Cyron dead-heated for first in 1969; Prizefighter and Saxonite dead-heated for first in 1912.
Tim Whiffler—two top-class horses raced with this name at the same time in 1867. "Sydney" Tim won the Melbourne Cup, while "Melbourne" Tim won the Australian Cup. To add further confusion, another Tim Whiffler was imported around the same time from England to stand at stud. He sired Melbourne Cup winners Briseis (1876) and Darriwell (1879) and the Australian Cup winners Sybil (1877) and Pollio (1882).
Winner to sire a winner: 6—Octagonal (1997) sire of Lonhro (2004); Spearfelt (1927) sire of New Cashmere (1942); Havoc (1895) sire of Prizefighter (1912); Bobadil (1899) sire of Pendil (1909) and The Parisian (1911); Lochiel (1889) sire of Great Scot (1903), Lord Ullin's Daughter (1905) and Tartan (1906); Richmond (1876) sire of Broken Hill (1894).
Winning mare to produce a winner: 1—Norma (1870), dam of Pollio (1882).
Oldest winners: Zipping (2010) and Yootha (1969) aged 8; Roman Arch (2006) and Hyperno (1981) aged 7.
Preferment (2016) won on protest from Awesome Rock.

VRC Newmarket Handicap (1200m)—Flemington
Of $1,250,000. Group 1. Handicap, Minimum Weight 50kg. March 9, 2019.

2017-18 RESULT: Time: 1:08.33 (Good 3)

FP	NO	HORSE	TRAINER	JOCKEY	MARGIN	BAR.	WGT	SP
1	1	REDKIRK WARRIOR	David & Ben Hayes & Tom Dabernig	Regan Bayliss		15	57.5kg	$7
2	2	BRAVE SMASH	Darren Weir	Craig Williams	0.1L	2	56.5kg	$9
3	11	MERCHANT NAVY	Aaron Purcell	Chad Schofield	0.3L	4	52kg	$6.50f
4	5	ROCK MAGIC	Chris Gangemi	Damian Lane	0.8L	6	53kg	$13
5	6	SUPIDO	Michael Kent	Beau Mertens	1.1L	14	52.5kg	$15
6	4	RICH CHARM	Udyta Clarke	Patrick Moloney	2.85L	5	52.5kg	$8
7	14	BOOKER	Mathew Ellerton & Simon Zahra	Ben Thompson	2.95L	3	50kg	$7
7	12	MISSROCK	Robbie Laing	Craig Newitt	2.95L	11	52kg	$21
9	9	KEN'S DREAM	Darren Weir	Dean Yendall	3.15L	8	52kg	$19
10	10	LUCKY LIBERTY	Henry Dwyer	Chris Parnham	4.15L	13	52kg	$61
11	15	CATCHY	David & Ben Hayes & Tom Dabernig	Cory Parish	4.55L	9	50kg	$14
12	7	THRONUM	David & Ben Hayes & Tom Dabernig	Michael Dee	5.55L	7	52.5kg	$12
13	13	SO SI BON	David & Ben Hayes & Tom Dabernig	Michael Walker	7.3L	12	52.5kg	$26
14	3	LORD OF THE SKY	Robbie Laing	Kathy O'Hara	8.05L	1	52.5kg	$81
15	8	FASTNET TEMPEST	David & Ben Hayes & Tom Dabernig	Ben Allen (a)	12.05L	10	52kg	$41

PAST WINNERS

YEAR	WINNER	JOCKEY	TRAINER	2ND	3RD	TIME
2018	Redkirk Warrior	Regan Bayliss	David & Ben Hayes & Tom Dabernig	Brave Smash	Merchant Navy	1:08.3
2017	Redkirk Warrior	Regan Bayliss	David & Ben Hayes & Tom Dabernig	Voodoo Lad	Star Turn	1:09.0
2016	The Quarterback	Craig Newitt	Robbie Griffiths	Black Heart Bart	Chautauqua	1:09.2
2015	Brazen Beau	Joao Moreira	Chris Waller	Chautauqua	Terravista	1:09.2
2014	Lankan Rupee	Chad Schofield	Mick Price	Spirit Of Boom	Knoydart	1:09.2
2013	Shamexpress	Craig Newitt	Danny O'Brien	Moment Of Change	Aeronautical	1:08.1
2012	Hay List	Glyn Schofield	John McNair	Buffering	Foxwedge	1:08.7
2011	Black Caviar	Luke Nolen	Peter Moody	Crystal Lily	Beaded	1:07.3
2010	Wanted	Luke Nolen	Peter Moody	Eagle Falls	Starspangledbanner	1:10.1
2009	Scenic Blast	Steven Arnold	Daniel Morton	Swiss Ace	Aichi	1:08.7
2008	Weekend Hustler	Brad Rawiller	Ross McDonald	Magnus	Grand Duels	1:09.0
2007	Miss Andretti	Craig Newitt	Lee Freedman	Gold Edition	Undue	1:07.7
2006	Takeover Target	Jay Ford	Joe Janiak	Snitzel	Stratum	1:08.3
2005	Alinghi	Damien Oliver	Lee Freedman	Fastnet Rock	Foreplay	1:08.1
2004	Exceed And Excel	Corey Brown	Tim Martin	Titanic Jack	Regimental Gal	1:08.7
2003	Belle Du Jour	Danny Nikolic	Clarry Conners	Bel Esprit	Super Impressive	1:08.6
2002	Rubitano	Stephen Baster	Brian Mayfield-Smith	North Boy	Mistegic	1:09.0
2001	Toledo	Damien Oliver	Russell Cameron	Show A Heart	Mannington	1:08.6
2000	Miss Pennymoney	Danny Beasley	Jim Conlan	Black Bean	Falvelon	1:07.6
1999	Isca	Greg Childs	Peter C Hayes	Dantelah	Normal Practice	1:07.8
1998	General Nediym	Brian York	Bill Mitchell	Toledo	Scandinavia	1:09.2
1997	Ruffles	Shane Dye	Max Lees	Catalan Opening	All Our Mob	1:08.9
1996	Brawny Spirit	Michael Clarke	Mick Winks	Sequalo	Royal Discard	1:07.7

BACKGROUND

First run: 1874 (won by Maid Of Avenel).
Multiple winners: 5—Redkirk Warrior (2018, 2017); Razor Sharp (1983, 1982); Correct (1961, 1960); Gothic (1928, 1927); *Aspen (1881, 1880); *mare.
Mares to win: 24 (25 wins)—Black Caviar (2011); Miss Andretti (2007); Belle Du Jour (2003); Ruffles (1997); Special (1988); Maybe Mahal (1978); Begonia Belle (1969); Ripa (1965); Three Wheeler (1945); Orteli (1944);

Lady Linden (1932); Red Dome (1920); Amata (1916); Queen Of Scots (1911); Pendant (1906); Playaway (1905); Wakeful (1901); Amiable (1898); Laundress (1895); Wild Rose (1892); Sedition (1889); Aspen (1881, 1880); Lady Ellen (1878); Calumny (1875).

3YO fillies to win: 15—Alinghi (2005); Miss Pennymoney (2000); Isca (1999); Desirable (1977); Toy Show (1976); Cap d'Antibes (1975); Cultured (1953); Gay Queen (1947); Kelos (1942); Waltzing Lily (1933); Molly's Robe (1919); Chantress (1903); Maluma (1896); Tyropean (1883); Maid Of Avenel (1874).

3YO colts and geldings to win: 30—Shamexpress (2013); Wanted (2010); Weekend Hussler (2008); Exceed And Excel (2004); General Nediym (1998); Primacy (1993); Schillaci (1992); Placid Ark (1987); Elounda Bay (1981); Century (1973); Baguette (1971); Manihi (1968); Nebo Road (1967); Correct (1960); Kingster (1956); High Jip (1950); All Veil (1941); Ajax (1938); St. Ardent (1929); Gothic (1927); Valiard (1925); Quintus (1924); Blague (1915); Relievo (1913); Desire (1912); Mala (1910); Ebullition (1907); Sir Foote (1902); Hova (1894); Cranbrook (1888).

Fastest time (Flemington 1200m): Black Caviar (2011) 1:07.36

Newmarket Handicap winners also won in the same preparation in Melbourne:
Lightning Stakes: 14—Redkirk Warrior (2018); Black Caviar (2011); Scenic Blast (2009); Miss Andretti (2007); Takeover Target (2006); Isca (1999); General Nediym (1998); Schillaci (1992); Shaftesbury Avenue (1991); Special (1998); Placid Ark (1987); Maybe Mahal (1978); Cap d'Antibes (1975); Black Onyx (1970).
Oakleigh Plate: 11—Lankan Rupee (2014); Weekend Hussler (2008); Schillaci (1992); Placid Ark (1987); Gold Stakes (1959); Birdwood (1954); Cromwell (1952); Aurie's Star (1937); Wakeful (1901); William Tell (1886); Malua (1884).
Lightning Stakes & Oakleigh Plate: 2—Schillaci (1992); Placid Ark (1987). Note: Both Schillaci and Placid Ark were 3YOs when they completed the Melbourne autumn sprint treble.
Futurity Stakes: 6—Royal Gem (1948); Bernborough (1946); Ajax (1938); Gothic (1928); Soultime (1909); Sir Foote (1902). Note: Futurity 1400m to 1600m 2006-2012.
William Reid Stakes: 5—Black Caviar (2011); Miss Andretti (2007); Miss Pennymoney (2000); All Veil (1941); Waltzing Lily (1933). Note: run before the Newmarket to 2012.
William Reid Stakes & Lightning Stakes (when run in that order to 2012) : 2—Black Caviar (2011); Miss Andretti (2007).

Newmarket winners to win in Sydney autumn:
The Galaxy: 1—Schillaci (1992).
T J Smith Stakes: 2—Lankan Rupee (2014); Black Caviar (2011): Note: Takeover Target won the Newmarket 2006 and TJ Smith 2009. Black Caviar also won the TJ Smith in 2013.
Doncaster Hcp: 4—Maybe Mahal (1978); Mildura (1941); Sir Foote (1902), Wakeful (1901).
George Ryder Stakes: 3—Weekend Hussler (2008); Baguette (1971); Greenline (1930). Note: Schillaci won the Newmarket in 1992 and the Ryder in 1993.
Doomben Cup: 1—Bernborough (1946). Note: Bernborough also won 1946 Doomben 10,000.

Spring features and the Newmarket:
Manikato Stakes (same season): 2—Miss Andretti (2007); Century (1973).
Caulfield Guineas (as 3YOs): 3—Weekend Hussler (2008); Ajax (1938); Brague (1915),
Coolmore Stud Stakes (same season): 4—Weekend Hussler (2008); Alinghi (2005); Toy Show (1976); Century (1973). Note: Brawny Spirit (Coolmore 1993, Newmarket 1996).
VRC Classic (from 2007 when 1200m WFA)—same season: 2—Black Caviar (2011); Miss Andretti (2007).
VRC Classic (from 2007 when 1200m WFA)—same year: 2—Black Caviar (2011); Miss Andretti (2007).

Newmarket winners and the 2YO majors:
Golden Slipper Stakes: 3—Belle Du Jour (Slipper 2000, Newmarket 2003); Toy Show (Slipper 1975, Newmarket 1976); Baguette (Slipper 1970, Newmarket 1971).
Blue Diamond Stakes: 1—Alinghi (Blue Diamond 2004, Newmarket 2005).

Leading winning jockeys:
3 wins Harold Badger (Gay Queen 1947, All Veil 1941, Ajax 1938); Craig Newitt (The Quarterback 2016, Shamexpress 2013, Miss Andretti 2007); Damien Oliver (Alinghi 2005, Toledo 2001, Schillaci 1992); Athol Mulley (Nebo Road 1967, Kingster 1956; Bernborough 1946); Harry White (Gold Trump 1990, Cap d"Antibes 1975, Manihi 1968).

Current winning jockeys:
3 wins Craig Newitt (The Quarterback 2016, Shamexpress 2013, Miss Andretti 2007); Damien Oliver (Alinghi 2005, Toledo 2001, Schillaci 1992).
2 wins Stephen Baster (Rubitano 2002, Mookta 1994); Regan Bayliss (Redkirk Warrior 2018, 2017); Luke Nolen (Black Caviar 2011, Wanted 2010).
1 win Steven Arnold (Scenic Blast 2009); Corey Brown (Exceed And Excel 2004); Jay Ford (Takeover Target 2006); Brad Rawiller (Weekend Hussler 2008); Chad Schofield (Lankan Rupee 2014); Glyn Schofield (Hay List 2012).

Leading winning trainers:
8 wins Bart Cummings (Shaftesbury Avenue 1991, Gold Trump 1990, Elounda Bay 1981, Better Beyond 1979, Maybe Mahal 1978, Cap d'Antibes 1975, Century 1973, Crown 1972).
4 wins Colin Hayes (Grandiose 1989, Special 1988, Red Tempo 1985, Desirable 1977).
3 wins Lee Freedman (Miss Andretti 2007, Alinghi 2005, Schillaci 1992); David Hayes (Redkirk Warrior 2018, 2017, Primacy 1993); Frank Musgrave (Ajax 1938, Parkwood 1930, Amata 1916); Lou Robertson (Three Wheeler 1945, Gothic 1928, 1927).

Current winning trainers:
3 wins Lee Freedman (Miss Andretti 2007, Alinghi 2005, Schillaci 1992); David Hayes (Redkirk Warrior 2018, 2017, Primacy 1993).
2 wins David & Ben Hayes & Tom Dabernig (Redkirk Warrior 2018, 2017).
1 win Russell Cameron (Toledo 2001); Jim Conlan (Miss Pennymoney 2000); Clarry Conners (Belle Du Jour 2003); Robbie Griffiths (The Quarterback 2016); Joe Janiak (Takeover Target 2006); Tim Martin (Exceed And Excel 2004); John McNair (Hay List 2012); Wally Mitchell (Placid Ark 1987); Daniel Morton (Scenic Blast 2009); Danny O'Brien (Shamexpress 2013); Mick Price (Lankan Rupee 2014); Mark Riley (Mookta 1994); Gai Waterhouse (All Our Mob 1994).

Point of interest:
The incomparable Malua (1884) also won the 1884 Melbourne Cup (3200m) and 1888 GN Hurdle (4800m).
Redkirk Warrior (GB) (2017) is the first horse to win the Newmarket first-up since Polycrates (GB) in 1917.
Redkirk Warrior (2018, 2017) is the first imported horse to win since Gothic (GB) (1928, 1927).

ATC Coolmore Classic (1500m)—Rosehill

Of $600,000. Group 1. Quality, Min Weight 50kg, 3YO&Up Fillies & Mares. March 16, 2019.

2017-18 RESULT: Time: 1:28.28 (Good 4)

FP	NO	HORSE	TRAINER	JOCKEY	MARGIN	BAR.	WGT	SP
1	3	DAYSEE DOOM	Ron Quinton	Andrew Adkins		14	57kg	$21
2	18	OREGON'S DAY	Mick Price	Michael Dee	0.2L	6	51kg	$11
3	2	SILENT SEDITION	Andrew Noblet	Craig Williams	0.3L	7	57.5kg	$10
4	11	ECKSTEIN	Kurt Goldman	Brenton Avdulla	0.6L	12	53kg	$21
5	5	PROMPT RESPONSE	Gai Waterhouse & Adrian Bott	Blake Shinn	0.7L	10	56.5kg	$19
6	1	DIXIE BLOSSOMS	Ron Quinton	Corey Brown	0.9L	4	57.5kg	$9.50
7	17	JUST DREAMING	Kris Lees	Rachel King (a)	1L	13	51kg	$19
8	9	AIDE MEMOIRE	Kris Lees	Jason Collett	1.2L	5	54kg	$17
9	4	HEAVENS ABOVE	Tim Martin	Tye Angland	1.3L	9	56.5kg	$26
10	10	DANISH TWIST	Kris Lees	Tim Clark	1.8L	11	53kg	$61
11	15	BRING ME ROSES	Tony McEvoy	Dean Yendall	2.1L	8	51kg	$13
12	12	FLIPPANT	Peter & Paul Snowden	Jay Ford	2.2L	16	53kg	$61
13	8	ALIZEE	James Cummings	Glyn Schofield	2.3L	15	54kg	$12
14	7	EGG TART	Chris Waller	Kerrin McEvoy	3.9L	3	55.5kg	$4.80f
15	14	FRANCALETTA	Murray Baker & Andrew Forsman	Stephen Baster	5.4L	2	52kg	$13
16	13	RAIMENT	James Cummings	Michael Walker	5.8L	1	52.5kg	$9
17	6	ZANBAGH	John P Thompson	Christian Reith	6.9L	17	56kg	$151

PAST WINNERS

YEAR	WINNER	JOCKEY	TRAINER	2ND	3RD	TIME
2018	Daysee Doom	Andrew Adkins	Ron Quinton	Oregon's Day	Silent Sedition	1:28.2
2017	Heavens Above	Tye Angland	Tim Martin	Silent Sedition	Danish Twist	1:29.6
2016	Peeping	Sam Clipperton	Ron Quinton	Azkadellia	Solicit	1:27.5
2015	Plucky Belle	Linda Meech	Peter Moody	First Seal	Diamond Drille	1:29.3
2014	Steps In Time	Jim Cassidy	Joseph Pride	Sweet Idea	Catkins	1:28.7
2013	Appearance	Blake Shinn	Guy Walter	Red Tracer	Norzita	1:28.3
2012	Ofcourseican	Kathy O'Hara	Ron Quinton	Secret Admirer	King's Rose	1:30.3
2011	Aloha	Glen Boss	Mick Price	Jersey Lily	Melito	1:30.5
2010	Alverta	Tye Angland	Paul Messara	Gold Water	Palacio De Cristal	1:28.5
2009	Typhoon Tracy	Glen Boss	Peter Moody	Culminate	Gallant Tess	1:29.9
2008	Eskimo Queen	Mark Zahra	Michael Moroney	Hot Danish	Deloraine	1:33.5
2007	Tuesday Joy	Darren Beadman	Gai Waterhouse	Doubting	Divine Madonna	1:30.7
2006	Regal Cheer	Michael Rodd	Joseph Pride	Star Shiraz	Mnemosyne	1:30.2
2005	Danni Martine	Darren Beadman	Guy Walter	Forum Floozie	Johan's Toy	1:29.5
2004	Shamekha	Jim Cassidy	Gai Waterhouse	Private Steer	Forum Floozie	1:28.3
2003	Bollinger	Chris Munce	Gai Waterhouse	Lovely Jubly	Galapagos Girl	1:29.5
2002	Sunline	Greg Childs	Trevor Mckee	Gentle Genius	Nanny Maroon	1:30.0
2001	Porto Roca	Damien Oliver	Danny O'Brien	Lady Mulan	Belle Du Jour	1:28.1
2000	Sunline	Greg Childs	Trevor Mckee	Beat The Fade	Noircir	1:28.8
1999	Camino Rose	Corey Brown	Marc Conners	Bonanova	Rainbow Bubbles	1:29.5
1998	Shindig	Len Beasley	Max Lees	Camino Rose	Stella Cadente	1:27.2
1997	Assertive Lass	Shane Dye	Gai Waterhouse	Hello Darl	Misty Dawn	1:28.9

BACKGROUND

First run: 1973 (won by Miss Personality). Group 2 1980-83. Group 1 from 1984. Previously known as the Rosemount Classic, Orlando Wines Classic, Winfield Classic, Thoroughbred Breeders Stakes and STC Fillies And Mares Classic. Registered name ATC T.A.D. Kennedy Stakes.
Most recent 3YO filly to win: Tuesday Joy (2007). Note: 17 fillies have won.
Multiple winners: 1—Sunline (2000, 2002).
Fastest time (1500m): Shindig (1998) 1:27.20
Notable winners: Appearance (2013); Alverta (2010); Typhoon Tracy (2009); Shamekha (2004); Sunline (2000, 2002); Assertive Lass (1997); Skating (1993); Bounding Away (1987); Emancipation (1984); Sheraco (1982); Stage Hit (1980); Princess Talaria (1978).

Coolmore Classic winners won the lead-up races:
Breeders' Classic: 1—Alverta (2010).
Millie Fox Stakes: 1—Daysee Doom (2018).
Liverpool City Cup: 2—Ofcourseican (2012); Chlorophyll (1996).
Frances Tressady Stakes: 3—Aloha (2011); Typhoon Tracy (2009); Acushla Marie (1992).
Sunline Stakes: 1—Acushla Marie (1992).
Surround Stakes: 4—Regal Cheer (2006); Bollinger (2003); Skating (1993); Avon Angel (1985).
Chipping Norton Stakes 1—Emancipation (2004).
Coolmore Classic winners went on to win in the same preparation:
Queen Of The Turf Stakes: 3—Appearance (2013); Camino Rose (1999); Favoured (1974).
South Pacific Classic: 1—Bollinger (2003).
Doncaster Handicap: 2—Sunline (2002); Skating (1993).
All Aged Stakes: 3—Sunline (2000, 2002); Emancipation (1984).
Coolmore Classic and the spring fillies' and mares' 1600m features:
Flight Stakes & Coolmore Classic (same season): 1—Bounding Away (Coolmore 1987).
Thousand Guineas (same season): 1—Princess Talaria (Coolmore 1978).
Myer Classic (same year): 1—Typhoon Tracy (2009).
Myer Classic (same season): 1—Appearance (Coolmore 2013).
Leading winning jockey:
4 wins Jim Cassidy (Steps In Time 2014, Shamekha 2004, Flitter 1995, Satin Sand 1986).
Current winning jockeys:
2 wins Tye Angland (Heavens Above 2017, Alverta 2010); Glen Boss (Aloha 2011, Typhoon Tracy 2009).
1 win Andrew Adkins (Daysee Doom 2018); Corey Brown (Camino Rose 1999); Larry Cassidy (Kapchat 1994); Sam Clipperton (Peeping 2016); Wayne Davis (Acushla Marie 1992); Linda Meech (Plucky Belle 2015); Kathy O'Hara (Ofcourseican 2012); Damien Oliver (Porto Roco 2001); Michael Rodd (Regal Cheer 2006); Blake Shinn (Appearance 2013); Mark Zahra (Eskimo Queen 2008).
Leading winning trainers:
5 wins Max Lees (Shindig 1998, Chlorophyll 1996, Flitter 1995, Quicksilver Cindy 1991, Satin Sand 1986).
4 wins Bart Cummings (Red Express 1989, Sheraco 1982, Cordon Rose 1981, Stage Hit); Gai Waterhouse (Tuesday Joy 2009, Shemakha 2004, Bollinger 2003, Assertive Lass 1997)
Current winning trainers:
4 wins Gai Waterhouse (Tuesday Joy 2009, Shemakha 2004, Bollinger 2003, Assertive Lass 1997).
3 wins Ron Quinton (Daysee Doom 2018, Peeping 2016, Ofcourseican 2012); Joe Pride (Steps In Time 2014, Regal Cheer 2006).
1 win Marc Conners (Camino Rose 1999); Tim Martin (Heavens Above 2017); John Meagher (Kapchat 1994); Paul Messara (Alverta 2010); Michael Moroney (Eskimo Queen 2008); Danny O'Brien (Porto Roca 2001); Mick Price (Aloha 2011); Graeme Rogerson (Skating 1993).
Points of interest:
Bounding Away (1987) is the only Golden Slipper winner to win the Coolmore Classic. She won the Slipper in 1986.
Typhoon Tracy (2009) was named Australian Horse of the Year in the 2009/2010 season.
Ron Quinton has trained three winners of the Coolmore Classic—Daysee Doom (2018), Peeping (2016), Ofcourseican (2012)—and rode two winners—Emancipation (1984) and Miss Personality (1973).

MVRC William Reid Stakes (1200m)—Moonee Valley
Of $500,000. Group 1. Weight For Age, 3YO&Up. March 22, 2019.

2017-18 RESULT: Time: 1:09.36   (Good 3)

FP	NO	HORSE	TRAINER	JOCKEY	MARGIN	BAR.	WGT	SP
1	2	HELLBENT	Darren Weir	Craig Williams		10	58.5kg	$10
2	4	THRONUM	David & Ben Hayes & Tom Dabernig	Mark Zahra	0.5L	3	58.5kg	$8
3	10	CATCHY	David & Ben Hayes & Tom Dabernig	Dwayne Dunn	1.5L	4	54kg	$15
4	3	SUPIDO	Michael Kent	Beau Mertens	2.25L	6	58.5kg	$9
5	1	ROCK MAGIC	Chris Gangemi	Damian Lane	3.5L	5	58.5kg	$7
6	5	BONS AWAY	Aaron Purcell	Linda Meech	4L	2	58.5kg	$17
7	8	PARIAH	Peter & Paul Snowden	Blake Shinn	4.3L	7	56kg	$6
8	9	SHE WILL REIGN	Gary Portelli	Ben Melham	6.55L	1	54kg	$7
9	6	SECRET AGENDA	Mick Price	Damien Oliver	6.85L	8	56.5kg	$5.50f
10	7	FUHRYK	David & Ben Hayes & Tom Dabernig	Stephen Baster	51.85L	9	56.5kg	$31

PAST WINNERS

YEAR	WINNER	JOCKEY	TRAINER	2ND	3RD	TIME
2018	Hellbent	Craig Williams	Darren Weir	Thronum	Catchy	1:09.3
2017	Silent Sedition	Katelyn Mallyon	Andrew Noblet	Hellbent	Star Turn	1:10.1
2016	Flamberge	Brad Rawiller	Peter Moody	Holler	Japonisme	1:09.8
2015	Lucky Hussler	Glen Boss	Darren Weir	Vain Queen	Griante	1:10.3
2014	Spirit Of Boom	Michael Rodd	Tony Gollan	Fontelina	Unpretentious	1:11.1
2013	Black Caviar	Luke Nolen	Peter Moody	Karuta Queen	Fawkner	1:11.0
2012	Foxwedge	Nash Rawiller	John O'shea	Hay List	Buffering	1:10.2
2011	Black Caviar	Luke Nolen	Peter Moody	Crystal Lily	Hinchinbrook	1:10.0
2010	Turffontein	Glen Boss	Anthony Cummings	Wanted	Sniper's Bullet	1:11.6
2009	Apache Cat	Damien Oliver	Greg Eurell	Vormista	Time Thief	1:09.6
2008	Apache Cat	Corey Brown	Greg Eurell	Stanzout	Monet Rules	1:09.6
2007	Miss Andretti	Craig Newitt	Lee Freedman	Any Suggestion	Rewaaya	1:10.2
2006	Virage De Fortune	Greg Childs	Bruce Mclachlan	Rewaaya	Undue	1:10.0
2005	Cape Of Good Hope	Brett Prebble	David Oughton	Super Elegant	Spark Of Life	1:10.3
2004	Regimental Gal	Steven King	Shaun Dwyer	Our Egyptian Raine	Legally Bay	1:10.3
2003	Yell	Darren Gauci	John Hawkes	Dash For Cash	Spinning Hill	1:10.5
2002	Toledo	Steven Arnold	Russell Cameron	Show A Heart	North Boy	1:11.8
2001	Bomber Bill	Steven Arnold	Russell Cameron	Scenic Warrior	Nina Haraka	1:11.4
2000	Miss Pennymoney	Brett Prebble	Jim Conlan	Redoutes Choice	St Chrisoph	1:10.7
1999	Grand Archway	Shane Dye	Graeme Rogerson	Theatre	Flavour	1:10.9
1998	Stella Cadente	Shane Dye	John Morish	Al Mansour	Spartacus	1:11.7
1997	Spartacus	Greg Childs	Rick Hore-Lacy	Mahogany	Khaptingly	1:10.3

BACKGROUND
First run: 1925 (won by The Night Patrol), Group 2 1980-86. Group 1 from 1987. Run over 1000m in 1971. Run at Flemington in 1995. Raced as Australia Made Stakes 1994, 1995. Australia Stakes 1996-2009. Has been run as early as January (up to 2012), and is since then has been run in March. Registered name is the William Reid Stakes.
Most recent mare to win: Silent Sedition (2017). Note: 13 mares have won.
Most recent 3YO to win: C&G: Foxwedge (2012); Filly: Virage de Fortune (2006). Note: 25 3YOs (10 fillies) have won.
Multiple winners: 8—Black Caviar (2013, 2011); Apache Cat (2009, 2008); Manikato (1983, 1982, 1981, 1980, 1979); All Shot (1974, 1973); Golden Doubles (1958, 1957); Flying Halo (1955, 1953, 1952); Heros (1935, 1934); The Night Patrol (1926, 1925).
Fastest time (1200m, Moonee Valley): Spanish Mix (1993) 1:08.80
Notable winners: Black Caviar (2013, 2011); Apache Cat (2009, 2008); Miss Andretti (2007); Cape Of Good Hope (2005); Bomber Bill (2001); Grand Archway (1999); Spartacus (1997); Hareeba (1995); Redelva (1991); Zeditave (1989); Vo Rogue (1988); Canny Lass (1987); Campaign King (1986); Manikato (1983, 1982, 1981, 1980, 1979); Family Of Man (1978); Toy Show (1977); Lord Dudley (1976); Dual Choice (1972); Crewman (1970); Winfreux (1968); Star Affair (1966); Flying Halo (1955, 1953, 1952); St. Joel (1954); Comic Court

(1951); Tranquil Star (1946); Waltzing Lily (1933); Gothic (1929); Heroic (1927); The Night Patrol (1926, 1925).
William Reid Stakes winners also won in Melbourne in the same preparation: (note: the William Reid was moved from January to March in 2013).
Lightning Stakes: 6—Black Caviar (2011); Apache Cat (2008); Miss Andretti (2007); Regimental Gal (2004); Zeditave (1989); River Rough (1985). Note: Miss Andretti won the 2007 Lightning Stakes at Moonee Valley.
Orr Stakes: 15—Yell (2003); Grand Archway (1999); Vo Rogue (1988); Qubeau (1984); Manikato (1981, 1980, 1979); All Shot (1974); Crewman (1970); Golden Doubles (1957); Comic Court (1951); Hua (1938); Gothic (1929); Heroic (1927); The Night Patrol (1925). Note: Flying Halo (1954) won the William Reid Stakes in 1952-53 and 1955.
Futurity Stakes: 13—Yell (2003); Redelva (1991); Zeditave (1989); Vo Rogue (1988); Campaign King (1986); Manikato (1983, 1981, 1980, 1979); Crewman (1970); Magic Ruler (1969); Star Affair (1966); Heros (1935).
Orr & Futurity: 4—Yell (2003); Vo Rogue (1988); Manikato (1981); Crewman (1970).
Orr & Futurity & Australian Cup: 1—Crewman (1970).
Oakleigh Plate: 6—Flamberge (2016); Spartacus (1997); Dual Choice (1971); Marmion (1967); New Statesman (1962); Figure (1930).
William Reid Stakes went on to win in the same preparation in Sydney and Brisbane:
TJ Smith Stakes: 3—Black Caviar (2013, 2011); Apache Cat (2008).
BRC Cup: 2—Black Caviar (2011); Apache Cat (2008).
Doomben 10,000: 4—Spirit Of Boom (2014); Apache Cat (2009, 2008); Manikato (1979).
The Moonee Valley spring/autumn sprint double:
Manikato Stakes (spring) & William Reid Stakes (autumn): 4—Miss Andretti (Australia Stakes 2007); Manikato (1980, 1983); Dual Choice (1972).
Carlyon Stakes: 2—Yell (2003); Hareeba (1995).
William Reid Stakes and Royal Ascot:
Royal Ascot (UK in June): 2—Miss Andretti (2007 King's Stand Stakes); Cape Of Good Hope (2005 Golden Jubilee Stakes). Note: Black Caviar (2013, 2011) won the Diamond (Golden) Jubilee Stakes at Royal Ascot in 2012.
Leading winning jockeys:
5 wins Roy Higgins (All Shot 1973, Magic Ruler 1969, Winfreux 1968, Star Affair 1966, Comtempler 1965); Jack Purtell (New Statesman 1962, Lady Major 1961, Flying Halo 1955, Comic Court 1951, Chatasan 1952).
Current winning jockeys:
2 wins Steven Arnold (Toledo 2002, Bomber Bill 2001); Glen Boss (Lucky Hussler 2015, Turffontein 2010); Luke Nolen (Black Caviar 2013, 2011); Brett Prebble (Cape Of Good Hope 2005, Miss Pennymoney 2000); 1 win Corey Brown (Apache Cat 2008); Kevin Forrester (Wrap Around 1992); Katelyn Mallyon (Silent Sedition 2017); Craig Newitt (Miss Andretti 2007); Damien Oliver (Apache Cat 2009); Brad Rawiller (Flamberge 2016); Nash Rawiller (Foxwedge 2012); Michael Rodd (Spirit Of Boom 2014); Cyril Small (Vo Rogue 1988); Craig Williams (Hellbent 2018).
Leading winning trainer:
6 wins Bob Hoysted (River Rough 1985, Manikato 1983, 1982, 1981, 1980, 1979).
Current winning trainers:
3 wins John Hawkes (Yell 2003, Strategic 1996, Spanish Mix 1993).
2 wins Russell Cameron (Toledo 2002, Bomber Bill 2001); Greg Eurell (Apache Cat 2009, 2008); Darren Weir (Hellbent 2018, Lucky Hussler 2015).
1 win Anthony Cummings (Turffontein 2010); Shaun Dwyer (Regimental Gal 2004); Tony Gollan (Spirit Of Boom 2014); David Hayes (Wrap Around 1992); Andrew Noblet (Silent Sedition 2017); John O'Shea (Foxwedge 2012); John Sadler (Lady Jakeo 1994).
Points of interest:
Comic Court (1951) won the William Reid Stakes first-up in the autumn after winning the 1950 Melbourne Cup.
Star Affair (1966), Chanak (1948), Heroic (1927) and The Night Patrol (1925) won the William Reid Stakes first-up after winning the Cox Plate in the spring.
Zeditave (1989) is the sire of Strategic (1996); Heroic (1927) is the sire of Heros (1934-35) and Hua (1938); The Night Patrol (1925-26) is the sire of Middle Watch (1932). Star Affair (Star Kingdom-Royal Lark) won in 1966. His three-quarter brother Crewman (Todman-Royal Lark) won in 1970.
Three generations of the Cummings family have trained William Reid Stakes winners—James Cummings won with Comic Court (1951); James's son Bart Cummings has won the race three times (Campaign King 1986, Lord Dudley 1976, Leica Show 1975); and Bart's son Anthony won with Turffontein in 2010.
Silent Sedition (2017) provided jockey Katelyn Mallyon and trainer Andrew Noblet with their first Group 1 win.

ATC Golden Slipper Stakes (1200m)—Rosehill
Of $3,500,000. Group 1. Set Weights, 2YO. March 23, 2019.

2017-18 RESULT: Time: 1:12.01 (Soft 6)

FP	NO	HORSE	TRAINER	JOCKEY	MARGIN	BAR.	WGT	SP
1	11	ESTIJAAB	Michael, Wayne & John Hawkes	Brenton Avdulla		14	54.5kg	$8.50
2	12	OOHOOD	Tony McEvoy	Zac Purton	0.2L	10	54.5kg	$17
3	10	SUNLIGHT	Tony McEvoy	Luke Currie	1.5L	5	54.5kg	$5
4	1	WRITTEN BY	Grahame Begg	Jordan Childs	1.8L	4	56.5kg	$4.80f
5	15	SEABROOK	Mick Price	Damien Oliver	2.1L	11	54.5kg	$13
6	4	LONG LEAF	David & Ben Hayes & Tom Dabernig	Blake Shinn	3.1L	15	56.5kg	$41
7	13	FIESTA	Chris Waller	Kerrin McEvoy	3.3L	16	54.5kg	$26
8	8	SANDBAR	Brad Widdup	Christian Reith	4L	3	56.5kg	$14
9	14	SIZZLING BELLE	Nick Olive	Kathy O'Hara	4.2L	1	54.5kg	$91
10	3	AYLMERTON	Jean Dubois	Tommy Berry	4.4L	8	56.5kg	$17
11	16	SECRET LADY	Gary Portelli	Ben Melham	4.9L	12	54.5kg	$201
12	6	EF TROOP	Tony Gollan	Jason Collett	5L	2	56.5kg	$21
13	2	SANTOS	Gai Waterhouse & Adrian Bott	Tim Clark	5.1L	7	56.5kg	$16
14	5	PERFORMER	Chris Waller	Hugh Bowman	5.3L	13	56.5kg	$7.50
15	17	QAFILA	David & Ben Hayes & Tom Dabernig	Craig Williams	8.3L	9	54.5kg	$41
16	7	PRAIRIE FIRE	Mick Price	Mark Zahra	11.7L	6	56.5kg	$31

PAST WINNERS

YEAR	WINNER	JOCKEY	TRAINER	2ND	3RD	TIME
2018	Estijaab	Brenton Avdulla	Michael, Wayne & John Hawkes	Oohood	Sunlight	1:12.0
2017	She Will Reign	Ben Melham	Gary Portelli	Frolic	Tulip	1:15.0
2016	Capitalist	Blake Shinn	Peter & Paul Snowden	Yankee Rose	Flying Artie	1:10.5
2015	Vancouver	Tommy Berry	Gai Waterhouse	English	Lake Geneva	1:09.7
2014	Mossfun	James McDonald	Michael, Wayne & John Hawkes	Earthquake	Bring Me The Maid	1:12.1
2013	Overreach	Tommy Berry	Gai Waterhouse	Sidestep	Sweet Idea	1:11.0
2012	Pierro	Nash Rawiller	Gai Waterhouse	Snitzerland	Samaready	1:09.7
2011	Sepoy	Kerrin McEvoy	Peter Snowden	Mosheen	Elite Falls	1:10.0
2010	Crystal Lily	Brett Prebble	Mathew Ellerton & Simon Zahra	Decision Time	More Strawberries	1:10.7
2009	Phelan Ready	Brad Rawiller	Bruce & Jason Mclachlan	Headway	Manhattan Rain	1:11.7
2008	Sebring	Glen Boss	Gai Waterhouse	Von Costa De Hero	Portillo	1:12.9
2007	Forensics	Damien Oliver	John Hawkes	Zizou	Meurice	1:09.3
2006	Miss Finland	Craig Williams	David Hayes	Pure Energy	Churchill Downs	1:09.5
2005	Stratum	Len Beasley	Paul Perry	Fashions Afield	Media	1:09.6
2004	Dance Hero	Chris Munce	Gai Waterhouse	Charge Forward	Alinghi	1:08.6
2003	Polar Success	Danny Beasley	Graeme Rogerson	How Funny	Hasna	1:09.0
2002	Calaway Gal	Scott Seamer	Bruce Brown	Victory Vein	Choisir	1:08.8
2001	Ha Ha	Jim Cassidy	Gai Waterhouse	Excellerator	Red Hannigan	1:08.9
2000	Belle Du Jour	Len Beasley	Clarry Conners	Crowned Glory	Assertive Lad	1:09.5
1999	Catbird	Mark De Montfort	Frank Cleary	Align	Shogun Lodge	1:09.9
1998	Prowl	Chris Munce	Clarry Conners	Shovhog	Glammis	1:09.5
1997	Guineas	Darren Beadman	John Hawkes	Encounter	Regal Chamber	1:08.9

BACKGROUND

First run: 1957 (won by Todman). Group 1 from 1979.
Fillies to win: 27—Estijaab (2018); She Will Reign (2017); Mossfun (2014); Overreach (2013); Crystal Lily (2010), Forensics (2007), Miss Finland (2006), Polar Success (2003), Calaway Gal (2002), Ha Ha (2001), Belle Du Jour (2000), Merlene (1996), Bint Marscay (1993), Burst (1992), Courtza (1989), Bounding Away (1986), Dark Eclipse (1980), Century Miss (1979), Vivarchi (1976), Toy Show (1975), Hartshill (1974), Fairy Walk (1971), Sweet Embrace (1967), Storm Queen (1966), Reisling (1965), Birthday Card (1962), Magic Night (1961).

Geldings to win: 6—Phelan Ready (2009); Dance Hero (2004), Prowl (1998), Inspired (1984), Manikato (1978), Tontonan (1973).
Fastest time (1200m): Dance Hero (2004): 1.08.60.
Golden Slipper winners on the lead-up races:
Blue Diamond Stakes: 5—Sepoy (2011), Courtza (1989), Bounding Away (1986), Manikato (1978); John's Hope (1972).
Blue Diamond placegetters: 4—Miss Finland (2nd 2006), Flying Spur (2nd 1995), Canny Lad (2nd 1990), Fairy Walk (3rd 1971).
VRC Sires' Produce Stakes: 5—Canny Lad (1990), Full On Aces (1981), Vain (1969), Storm Queen (1966), Pago Pago (1963).
Magic Millions: 3—Capitalist (2016); Phelan Ready (2009), Dance Hero (2004).
Inglis Nursery: 1—She Will Reign (2017).
Breeders' Plate: 7—Capitalist (2016); Pierro (2012), Sebring (2008), Luskin Star (1977), Baguette (1970), Eskimo Prince (1964), Sky High (1960). Note: Held in the spring until 2007.
Widden Stakes: 2—Mossfun (2014); Overreach (2013);
Silver Slipper Stakes: 6—She Will Reign (2017); Mossfun (2014); Pierro (2012), Luskin Star (1977), Baguette (1970), Eskimo Prince (1964). Note: Held in the spring until 1997.
Todman Stakes: 4—Pierro (2012), Tierce (1991), Marauding (1987), Luskin Star (1977).
Todman Stakes placegetters: 6—Capitalist (2nd 2016); Sepoy (2nd 2011), Phelan Ready (2nd 2009), Danzero (3rd 1994), Sir Dapper (2nd 1983), Marscay (2nd, 1982), Tontonan (3rd 1973).
Reisling Stakes: 7—Estijaab (2018); Overreach (2013); Polar Success (2003), Belle Du Jour (2000), Merlene (1996), Burst (1992), Hartshill (1974).
Reisling Stakes placegetters: 2—She Will Reign (2017—second behind Frolic); Mossfun (2014—second behind Earthquake in the Reisling).
Pago Pago Stakes: 3—Stratum (2005), Rory's Jester (1985), Inspired (1984).
Magic Night Stakes: 4—Bint Marscay (1993), Bounding Away (1986), Dark Eclipse (1980), Toy Show (1975).
Golden Slipper winners went on to win in the same preparation:
ATC Sires' Produce Stakes: 13—Pierro (2012), Sebring (2008), Dance Hero (2004), Merlene (1996), Burst (1992), Tierce (1991), Full On Aces (1981), Luskin Star (1977), Toy Show (1975), Tontonan (1973), Baguette (1970), Eskimo Prince (1964), Fine And Dandy (1959).
ATC Champagne Stakes: 12—Pierro (2012), Dance Hero (2004), Burst (1992), Tierce (1991), Bounding Away (1986), Luskin Star (1977), Vivarchi (1976), Baguette (1970), Vain (1969), Storm Queen (1966), Sky High (1960), Todman (1957). Note: run over 1200m until 1972 when changed to 1600m.
ATC Sires' Produce & Champagne Stakes: 6—Pierro (2012), Dance Hero (2004), Burst (1992), Tierce (1991), Luskin Star (1977), Baguette (1970).
Magic Millions, Sires' Produce & Champagne Stakes: 1—Dance Hero (2004).
Golden Slipper winners and the following season:
San Domenico Stakes: 2—Tierce (1991); Sir Dapper (1983).
Flight Stakes: 2—Ha Ha (2001); Bounding Away (1986).
Manikato Stakes: 2—Sepoy (2011); Vain (1969).
Thousand Guineas: 2—Miss Finland (2006); Toy Show (1975).
Caulfield Guineas: 4—Manikato (1978); Luskin Star (1977); Vain (1969); *Storm Queen (1966). *filly.
Coolmore Stud Stakes: 5—Sepoy (2011); Tierce (1991); Courtza (1989); Manikato (1978); Toy Show (1975); Vain (1969).
Victoria Derby: 1—Sky High (1960).
VRC Oaks: 1—Miss Finland (2006).
Lightning Stakes: 2—Storm Queen (GS 1966, Lightning 1977); Sky High (GS 1960, Lightning 1961).
Oakleigh Plate: 1—Tontonan (GS 1973, Oakleigh 1974).
Newmarket Handicap: 2—Toy Show (GS 1975, Newmarket 1976); Baguette (GS 1970, Newmarket 1971).
Canterbury Stakes: 5—Pierro (GS 2012, CS 2013); Dance Hero (GS 2004, CS 2005); Sir Dapper (GS 1983, CS 1984); Baguette (GS 1970, CS 1971); Sky High (GS 1960, CS 1961).
Doncaster Handicap: 1—Tontonan (GS 1973, Doncaster 1974.)
Australian Derby: 1—Skyline (1958): Note: before 1979 the Derby was run in the spring.
Australian Oaks: 1—Bounding Away (GS 1986, Oaks 1987).
No horse has won the Golden Slipper and also a:
Melbourne Cup, Caulfield Cup, Cox Plate, The BMW, Australian Cup, ATC Queen Elizabeth Stakes, Stradbroke Handicap, Toorak Handicap, Queensland Derby, Queensland Oaks, Doomben Cup.
Leading winning jockeys:
4 wins Shane Dye (Burst 1992, Tierce 1991, Canny Lad 1990 Courtza 1989); Ron Quinton (Marauding 1987, Rory's Jester 1985, Sir Dapper 1983, Marscay 1982).
3 wins Mick Dittman (Bint Marscay 1993, Bounding Away 1986, Full On Aces 1981); Athol Mulley (Eskimo Prince 1964, Sky High 1960, Skyline 1958); Kevin Langby (Toy Show 1975, Hartshill 1974, John's Hope 1972).

Current winning jockeys:
2 wins Tommy Berry (Vancouver 2015, Overreach 2013); Glen Boss (Sebring 2008, Flying Spur 1995).
1 win Brenton Avdulla (Estijaab 2018); James McDonald (2014); Kerrin McEvoy (Sepoy 2011); Ben Melham (She Will Reign 2017); Damien Oliver (Forensics 2007); Brett Prebble (Crystal Lily 2010); Brad Rawiller (Phelan Ready 2009); Nash Rawiller (Pierro 2012); Blake Shinn (Capitalist 2016); Craig Williams (Miss Finland 2006).

Leading winning trainers:
6 wins Tommy Smith (Star Watch 1988, Bounding Away 1986, Toy Show 1975, Hartshill 1974, John's Hope 1972, Fairy Walk 1971); Gai Waterhouse (Vancouver 2015, Overreach 2013, Pierro 2012, Sebring 2008, Dance Hero 2004, Ha Ha 2001).
4 wins Clarry Conners (Belle Du Jour 2000, Prowl 1998, Burst 1992, Tierce 1991); Bart Cummings (Century Miss 1979, Vivarchi 1976, Tontonan 1973, Storm Queen 1966); Lee Freedman (Merlene 1996, Flying Spur 1995, Danzero 1994, Bint Marscay 1993).

Current winning trainers:
6 wins Gai Waterhouse (Vancouver 2015, Overreach 2013, Pierro 2012, Sebring 2008, Dance Hero 2004, Ha Ha 2001).
4 wins Clarry Conners (Belle Du Jour 2000, Prowl 1998, Burst 1992, Tierce 1991); Lee Freedman (Merlene 1996, Flying Spur 1995, Danzero 1994, Bint Marscay 1993); John Hawkes (Estijaab 2018, Mossfun 2014, Forensics 2007, Guineas 1997).
2 wins Michael, Wayne & John Hawkes (Estijaab 2018, Mossfun 2014); Peter Snowden (Capitalist 2016, Sepoy 2011).
1 win Les Bridge (Sir Dapper 1983); Bruce Brown (Calaway Gal 2002); Mathew Ellerton & Mark Zahra (Crystal Lily 2010); David Hayes (Miss Finland 2006); Jason McLachlan (Phelan Ready 2009, in partnership with his father Bruce); Paul Perry (Stratum 2005); Gary Portelli (She Will Reign 2017); Graeme Rogerson (Polar Success 2003); Peter & Paul Snowden (Capitalist 2016).

Leading winning owners or part-owners:
7 wins Jack Ingham (Prowl 1988, Guineas 1997, Burst 1992, Star Watch 1988, Marauding 1987, John's Hope 1972, Sweet Embrace 1967).
5 wins Bob Ingham (Forensics 2007, Guineas 1997, Star Watch 1988, John's Hope 1972, Sweet Embrace 1967).
3 wins Newhaven Park (Kelly family) (Prowl 1998, Burst 1992, Marauding 1987).

Winner to sire a winner:

WINNER	YEAR	PROGENY (YEAR)
Stratum	2005	Crystal Lily (2010)
Flying Spur	1995	Forensics (2007)
Danzero	1994	Dance Hero (2004).
Marauding	1987	Burst (1992), Prowl (1998).
Marscay	1982	Bint Marscay (1993).
Baguette	1970	Dark Eclipse (1980).
Vain	1969	Inspired (1984), Sir Dapper (1983).
Todman	1957	Sweet Embrace (1967), Eskimo Prince (1964).

Leading sires:

SIRE	WINS	WINNERS
Danehill	5	Ha Ha (2001), Catbird (1999), Merlene (1996), Flying Spur (1995), Danzero (1994).
*Star Kingdom	5	Magic Night (1961), Sky High (1960), Fine And Dandy (1959), Skyline (1958), Todman (1957).

*sired the first five Golden Slipper winners.

Brothers to win: Sky High (1960), Skyline (1958). Colts by Star Kingdom from Flight's Daughter.

ATC George Ryder Stakes (1500m)—Rosehill
Of $1,000,000. Group 1. Weight For Age, 3YO&Up. March 23, 2019.

2017-18 RESULT: Time: 1:31.48   (Soft 7)

FP	NO	HORSE	TRAINER	JOCKEY	MARGIN	BAR.	WGT	SP
1	8	WINX	Chris Waller	Hugh Bowman		6	57kg	$1.16F
2	1	HAPPY CLAPPER	Pat Webster	Blake Shinn	0.8L	4	59kg	$21
3	6	KEMENTARI	James Cummings	Brenton Avdulla	1.6L	5	56kg	$8.50
4	3	CRACK ME UP	Bjorn Baker	Jason Collett	4.5L	2	59kg	$71
5	5	INVINCIBLE GEM	Kris Lees	Zac Purton	4.6L	1	57kg	$41
6	2	CLEARLY INNOCENT	Kris Lees	Tommy Berry	5.4L	3	59kg	$81

PAST WINNERS

YEAR	WINNER	JOCKEY	TRAINER	2ND	3RD	TIME
2018	Winx	Hugh Bowman	Chris Waller	Happy Clapper	Kementari	1:31.4
2017	Winx	Hugh Bowman	Chris Waller	Le Romain	Chautauqua	1:34.8
2016	Winx	Hugh Bowman	Chris Waller	Kermadec	Press Statement	1:28.7
2015	Real Impact	James McDonald	Noriyuki Hori	Criterion	Kermadec	1:28.2
2014	Gordon Lord Byron	Craig Williams	Tom Hogan	Speediness	El Roca	1:30.9
2013	Pierro	Nash Rawiller	Gai Waterhouse	King Mufhasa	Shoot Out	1:31.0
2012	Metal Bender	Michael Rodd	Chris Waller	Rekindled Interest	Secret Admirer	1:28.8
2011	Rangirangdoo	Corey Brown	Chris Waller	Love Conquers All	Triple Elegance	1:29.4
2010	Danleigh	Hugh Bowman	Chris Waller	Dao Dao	King Mufhasa	1:30.2
2009	Vision And Power	Jim Cassidy	Joseph Pride	Black Piranha	King Mustafa	1:31:5
2008	Weekend Hussler	Brad Rawiller	Ross McDonald	Racing To Win	Casino Prince	1:31.7
2007	Haradasun	Glen Boss	Tony Vasil	Mentality	Apache Cat	1:29.2
2006	Racing To Win	Glen Boss	John O'Shea	Paratroopers	Lad Of The Manor	1:27.8
2005	Court's In Session	Hugh Bowman	Guy Walter	Patezza	Sky Cuddle	1:28.5
2004	Lonhro	Darren Beadman	John Hawkes	Grand Armee	Private Steer	1:27.2
2003	Lonhro	Darren Beadman	John Hawkes	Dash For Cash	Defier	1:30.7
2002	Lord Essex	Rod Quinn	John Hawkes	Shogun Lodge	Crawl	1:29.5
2001	Landsighting	Corey Brown	Noel Mayfield-Smith	Shogun Lodge	Crawl	1:27.6
2000	Al Mansour	Len Beasley	John Size	Bonanova	Hire	1:30.5
1999	Referral	Corey Brown	Steve Englebrecht	Juggler	Mossman	1:28.2
1998	Quick Flick	Mark De Montfort	Tim Donnelly	Encounter	Blazing Steel	1:28.9
1997	Mouawad	Grant Cooksley	Clarry Conners	Shame	Secret Savings	1:27.7

BACKGROUND

First run: 1903 (won by Cressy). Group 1 from 1980. Run over 1300m 1903-08. 1200m 1909-14; 1400m 1929-84; 1450m 1985; 1500m from 1986. Previously known as the Railway Handicap, Railway Quality Handicap, Elizabeth Farm Stakes and CP Air Quality Handicap.

Fillies & mares to win (since 1930): 12—Winx (2018, 2017, 2016); *Heat Of The Moment (1986); *Emancipation (1984, 1983); Pure Of Heart (1982); Cigarette (1940); Cereza (1937); Gay Blonde (1936); Sarcherie (1935); *Leila Vale (1933). *3YO Fillies

3YOs to win: 29—Pierro (2013); Weekend Hussler (2008); Haradasun (2007); Racing To Win (2006); Mouawad (1997); Ravarda (1996); Bureaucracy (1991); Straussbrook (1990); *Heat Of The Moment (1986); Hula Drum (1985); *Emancipation (1983); Manikato (1979); Command Module (1978); Pacific Ruler (1977); Itchy Feet (1974); Baguette (1971); Time And Tide (1964); Prince Regoli (1962); New Spec (1957); Heroic Sovereign (1948); Melhoro (1945); Warlock (1944); Evergreen (1941); *Leila Vale (1934); *Ascalon (1928); Braehead (1922); *Eugeny (1915); *Vauntie (1910); Marvel Loch (1904). *Six 3YO fillies—only Heat Of The Moment (1986) and Emancipation (1983) since 1934.

Multiple Winners: 8—Winx (2018, 2017, 2016); Lonhro (2004, 2003); Campaign King (1988, 1987); Emancipation (1984, 1983); Manikato (1980, 1979); Foresight (1969, 1968); Time And Tide (1967, 1964); Prince Regoli (1963, 1962).

Notable winners: Winx (2018, 2017, 2016); Gordon Lord Byron (2014); Pierro (2013); Metal Bender (2011); Weekend Hussler (2008); Haradasun (2007); Racing To Win (2006); Lonhro (2004, 2003); Mouawad (1997); Schillaci (1993); Campaign King (1988, 1987); Emancipation (1984, 1983); Manikato (1980, 1979); Baguette (1971); Time And Tide (1967, 1964); Carioca (1954); Bragger (1946); Marvel Loch (1904).

Fastest Time (1500m): Lonhro (2004) 1:27.20.

George Ryder Stakes winners won the lead-up races:
Newmarket Handicap: 3—Weekend Hussler (2008); Baguette (1971); Greenline (1930).
Hobartville Stakes: 2—Pierro (2013); Racing To Win (2006).

Expressway Stakes: 1—Lonhro (2003).
Apollo Stakes: 6—Winx (2017, 2016); Danleigh (2010); Lonhro (2003); Quick Flick (1998); Emancipation (1984).
Chipping Norton Stakes: 7—Winx (2018, 2017, 2016); Lonhro (2003); Heat Of The Moment (1986); Emancipation (1984); Prince Ruling (1981).
Canterbury Stakes: 6—Pierro (2013); Quick Flick (1998); Straussbrook (1990); Emancipation (1983); Baguette (1971); Regoli (1953).
Randwick Guineas (from 2007): 1—Weekend Hussler (2008).

George Ryder Stakes winners went on to win in the same preparation:
Doncaster Handicap: 7—Winx (2016); Vision And Power (2009); Haradasun (2007); Racing To Win (2006); Emancipation (1983); Dalrello (1975); Dame Acre (1918).
All Aged Stakes: 7—Campaign King (1987); Emancipation (1984); All Shot (1973); Triton (1972); Foresight (1969); Fuji San (1927); Claro (1924).
ATC Queen Elizabeth Stakes: 3—Winx (2018, 2017); Lonhro (2003).
BRC Cup: 1—Lord Essex (2002).
Doomben 10,000: 3—Campaign King (1988); Manikato (1979); Baguette (1971).
Stradbroke Handicap: 2—Campaign King (1988); Triton (1972).

Leading winning jockeys:
5 wins Hugh Bowman (Winx 2018, 2017, 2016, Danleigh 2010, Court's In Session 2005).
4 wins Billy Cook (Carioca 1954, Warlock 1944, Evergreen 1941, High 1935).
3 wins Darren Beadman (Lonhro 2004, 2003, March Hare 1995); Corey Brown (Rangirangdoo 2011, Landsighting 2001, Referral 1999); George Moore (Baguette 1971, Rush Bye 1965, Bragger 1946); Ron Quinton (Hula Drum 1985, Emancipation 1984, 1983).

Current winning jockeys:
5 wins Hugh Bowman (Winx 2018, 2017, 2016, Danleigh 2010, Court's In Session 2005).
3 wins Corey Brown (Rangirangdoo 2011, Landsighting 2001, Referral 1999).
2 wins Glen Boss (Haradasun 2007, Racing To Win 2006).
1 win Grant Cooksley (Mouawad 1997); James McDonald (Real Impact 2015); Damien Oliver (Schillaci 1993); Brad Rawiller (Weekend Hussler 2008); Nash Rawiller (Pierro 2013); Michael Rodd (Metal Bender 2012); Craig Williams (Gordon Lord Byron 2014).

Leading winning trainers:
6 wins Chris Waller (Winx 2018, 2017, 2016, Metal Bender 2012, Rangirangdoo 2011, Danleigh 2010).
4 wins William Booth (Volpi 1933, Meenah 1924, Chrysolaus 1920, Dame Acre 1918); Harry Plant (Time And Tide 1967, 1964, Coniston 1952, Buzmark 1950).
3 win Neville Begg (Emancipation 1984, 1983, Heat Of The Moment 1986); Bart Cummings (Campaign King 1988, 1987, Hula Drum 1985); Harry England (High 1935, Eugeny 1915, Miocene 1912); John Hawkes (Lonhro 2004, 2003, Lord Essex 2002).

Current winning trainers:
6 wins Chris Waller (Winx 2018, 2017, 2016, Metal Bender 2012, Rangirangdoo 2011, Danleigh 2010).
3 win John Hawkes (Lonhro 2004, 2003, Lord Essex 2002).
1 win Grahame Begg (Telesto 1994); Clarry Conners (Mouawad 1997); Tim Donnelly (Quick Flick 1998); Steve Englebrecht (Referral 1999); Bryan Guy (Ravarda 1996); Tom Hogan (Gordon Lord Byron 2014); Noriyuki Hori (Real Impact 2015); Noel Mayfield-Smith (Landsighting 2001); John O'Shea (Racing To Win 2006); Joe Pride (Vision And Power 2009); John Size (Al Mansour 2000); Tony Vasil (Haradasun 2007); Gai Waterhouse (Pierro 2013).

Points of interest:
Only Lonhro has won an Expressway Stakes, Apollo Stakes and George Ryder Stakes in the same preparation. He also trained on to win the ATC Queen Elizabeth Stakes (2000m) at Randwick, the only horse to complete the double.
Maurice McCarten and James Barden rode and trained winners of the George Ryder. McCarten trained Regoli (1953) and rode Mohican (1938) and Cereza (1937). Barden trained Greenline (1930) and Sunlike (1914), and rode Lord Merv (1908).
Ireland's Gordon Lord Byron (2014), trained by Tom Hogan, is the first NH-trained winner of the George Ryder.
Real Impact (2015) was trained in Japan by Noriyuki Hori.
Winx (2017) completed her 16th consecutive win.
Winx (2018) broke the world record for Group 1 wins on the flat—17, beating USA star John Henry (16). It was her 24th consecutive win.

ATC Ranvet Stakes (2000m)—Rosehill
Of $700,000. Group 1. Weight For Age, 3YO&Up. March 23, 2019.

2017-18 RESULT: Time: 2:04.78 (Soft 7)

FP	NO	HORSE	TRAINER	JOCKEY	MARGIN	BAR.	WGT	SP
1	1	GAILO CHOP	Darren Weir	Mark Zahra		4	59kg	$2.05F
2	8	SINGLE GAZE	Nick Olive	Kathy O'Hara	3L	1	57kg	$5
3	4	PRIZED ICON	Kris Lees	Hugh Bowman	3.2L	2	59kg	$11
4	9	CONSENSUS	Stephen McKee	Jason Collett	6.5L	7	57kg	$26
5	6	SARRASIN	Richard Freedman	Zac Purton	6.6L	6	59kg	$19
6	3	HARLEM	David & Ben Hayes & Tom Dabernig	Michael Walker	6.8L	5	59kg	$13
7	5	VENTURA STORM	David & Ben Hayes & Tom Dabernig	Damien Oliver	10.6L	8	59kg	$8.50
8	2	CLASSIC UNIFORM	Gary Moore	Tim Clark	16.6L	3	59kg	$13

PAST WINNERS

YEAR	WINNER	JOCKEY	TRAINER	2ND	3RD	TIME
2018	Gailo Chop	Mark Zahra	Darren Weir	Single Gaze	Prized Icon	2:04.7
2017	Our Ivanhowe	Kerrin McEvoy	Lee & Anthony Freedman	Hartnell	The United States	2:10.6
2016	The United States	Kerrin McEvoy	Robert Hickmott	Hauraki	Criterion	2:03.1
2015	Contributer	James McDonald	John O'Shea	Tosen Stardom	Lucia Valentina	2:03.1
2014	Silent Achiever	Nash Rawiller	Roger James	Carlton House	It's A Dundeel	2:02.3
2013	Foreteller	Jim Cassidy	Chris Waller	Fiveandahalfstar	Makuckyday	2:01.5
2012	Manighar	Luke Nolen	Peter Moody	Rangirangdoo	Shoot Out	2:04.7
2011	Zavite	Glen Boss	Anthony Cummings	Descarado	Hawk Island	2:05.5
2010	Theseo	Nash Rawiller	Gai Waterhouse	Rangirangdoo	Speed Gifted	2:02.3
2009	Thesio	Nash Rawiller	Gai Waterhouse	Viewed	Moatize	2:04.4
2008	Tuesday Joy	Darren Beadman	Gai Waterhouse	Princess Coup	Desert War	1:55.4
2007	Desert War	Hugh Bowman	Gai Waterhouse	Confectioner	Rallings	2:01.9
2006	Eremein	Glen Boss	Allan Denham	Our Smoking Joe	Desert War	2:05.9
2005	Grand Armee	Danny Beasley	Gai Waterhouse	Vouvray	Hugs Dancer	2:00.9
2004	Sound Action	Wayne Hokai	Roberta Maguire	Ambulance	Makybe Diva	2:03.2
2003	Republic Lass	Glen Boss	Guy Walter	Northerly	Freemason	2:01.0
2002	Universal Prince	Justin Sheehan	Bede Murray	Dress Circle	Freemason	2:05.0
2001	Tie The Knot	Patrick Payne	Guy Walter	Hill Of Grace	Giovana	2:02.9
2000	Tie The Knot	Shane Dye	Guy Walter	Arena	Showella	2:05.9
1999	Darazari	Glen Boss	Bruce Wallace	Tie The Knot	Nahayan	2:01.9
1998	Gold Guru	Shane Dye	Leon Macdonald	Might And Power	Vitrinite	2:00.2
1997	Arkady	John Marshall	John Morish	Hula Flight	The Bandette	2:01.8

BACKGROUND

First run: 1902 (Lady Grafton). Group 1 since 1980. Run over 1800m 1903-62; 1500m 1963-72; 1750m 1973-78; 2000m from 1979. Registered as the Rawson Stakes. Also known as the Segenhoe Stakes. Held at Canterbury in 2008 (1900m). Not held in 1942 and 1913.
Fillies & Mares to win: 14—Silent Achiever (2014); Tuesday Joy (2008); Sound Action (2004); Republic Lass (2003); Electronic (1996); Minuetto (1980); Wenona Girl (1964, 1961); Tarien (1953); Sarcherie (1930); Valicare (1926); Furious (1923); Maltine (1909); Air Motor (1904). Note: Wenona Girl (1961) and Valicare (1926) are the only 3YO fillies to win the Ranvet.
3YOs to win: 23—Gold Guru (1998); Stony Bay (1995); Beau Zam (1988); Myocard (1987); Marceau (1978); Balmerino (1976); Bankrupt (1974); Gunsynd (1971); Regal Rhythm (1968); *Wenona Girl (1961); Bold Pilot (1959); Tulloch (1958); Arlunya (1956); Forest Beau (1952); Dickens (1950); Vagabond (1949); Falcon Knight (1944); Dashing Cavalier (1940); Ammon Ra (1932); Limerick (1927); *Valicare (1926); Cetigne (1916); Great Scot (1903). *3YO fillies.
Multiple winners: 12—Theseo (2010, 2009); Tie The Knot (2001, 2000); Beau Zam (1989, 1988); Marceau (1979, 1978); Gunsynd (1973, 1971); Regal Rhythm (1972, 1968); Wenona Girl (1964, 1961); Sky High (1963, 1962); Columnist (1948, 1947); Lough Neagh (1937, 1936, 1933); Limerick (1928, 1927); Malt King (1912, 1911). Note: Tie The Knot was first past the post in 1999, but lost on protest to Darazari.
Fastest Time (2000m): Gold Guru (1998) 2:00.20
Ranvet Stakes winners won the lead-up races:
Peter Young Stakes: 8—Gailo Chop (2018); Foreteller (2013); Theseo (2009); Hyperno (1981): Minuetto (1980); Redcraze (1957); The Hawk (1925); Artilleryman (1920).

Australian Cup: 3—Manighar (2012); Veandercross (1993); Great Scot (1903).
Apollo Stakes: 4—Desert War (2007); Grand Armee (2005); Beau Zam (1989); Dalmacia (1983).
Chipping Norton Stakes: 12—Theseo (2010); Tie The Knot (2001, 2000); Super Impose (1991); Sky High (1962); Tulloch (1958); Gallant Archer (1954); Bernborough (1946); Lough Neagh (1937, 1936, 1933); Limerick (1928).

Ranvet Stakes winners went on to win in the same preparation:
Tancred Stakes: 9—Silent Achiever (2014); Manighar (2012); Tuesday Joy (2008); Eremein (2006); Tie The Knot (2000); Stony Bay (1995); Beau Zam (1988); Myocard (1987); Alibhai (1985).
Australian Derby (since 1979 when Ranvet increased to 2000m): 2—Gold Guru (1998); Beau Zam (1988).
Doncaster Handicap: 3—Super Impose (1991); Time And Tide (1965); Whittier (1924).
All Aged Stakes: 15—Broker's Tip (1970); Foresight (1969); Even Better (1966); Wenona Girl (1964); Tulloch (1958); Prince Morvi (1955); Bernborough (1946); Peter Pan (1935); Valicare (1926); The Hawk (1925); Beauford (1922); Malt King (1912, 1911); Bobrikoff (1910).
ATC Queen Elizabeth Stakes: 4—Eremein (2006); Grand Armee (2005); Veandercross (1993); Tulloch (1958).
Sydney Cup: 1—My Eagle Eye (1992).
Doomben Cup: 2—Marceau (1978); Bernborough (1946).

Ranvet Stakes winners also won:
Golden Slipper: 1—Sky High (Golden Slipper 1960; Ranvet 1963, 1962).
Melbourne Cup (same season): 5—Peter Pan (Ranvet 1935); Nightmarch (1930); Poitrel (1921); Artilleryman (1920); Westcourt (1918). Note: Hyperno (1981) won the Melbourne Cup in 1979; Poseidon (1908) won the Melbourne Cup in 1906.
Cox Plate (same year): 2—Better Loosen Up (1990); Beau Vite (1941).
Cox Plate (same season): 4—Gunsynd (Ranvet 1973); Beau Vite (1941); Rogilla (1934); Nightmarch (1930). Note: Super Impose (1991) won the Cox Plate in 1992; Tulloch (1958) won the Cox Plate in 1960.

Leading winning jockeys:
6 wins George Moore (Wenona Girl 1964, Sky High 1963, 1962, Tulloch 1958, Tarien 1953, Forest Beau 1952).
4 wins Glen Boss (Zavite 2011, Eremein 2006, Republic Lass 2003, Darazari 1999); Kevin Langby (Passetreul 1975, Gunsynd 1973, Foresight 1969, Striking Force 1967); Maurice McCarten (Spear Chief 1939, Ammon Ra 1932, Limerick 1928, 1927)

Current winning jockeys:
4 wins Glen Boss (Zavite 2011, Eremein 2006, Republic Lass 2003, Darazari 1999).
3 wins Nash Rawiller (Silent Achiever 2014, Theseo 2010, 2009).
2 wins Kerrin McEvoy (Our Ivanhowe 2017, The United States 2016).
1 win Hugh Bowman (Desert War 2007); Larry Cassidy (Stony Bay 1995); Grant Cooksley (My Eagle Eye 1992); Luke Nolen (Manighar 2012); Mark Zahra (2018).

Leading winning trainers:
12 wins Tommy Smith (Alibhai 1985, Marceau 1979, 1978, Passetreul 1975, Gunsynd 1973, 1971, Regal Rhythm 1972, 1968, Tulloch 1958, Redcraze 1957, Tarien 1953, Forest Beau 1952).
7 wins Gai Waterhouse (Theseo 2010, 2009, Tuesday Joy 2008, Desert War 2007, Grand Armee 2005, Electronic 1996, Stony Bay 1995).
4 wins Maurice McCarten (Wenona Girl 1964, 1961, Prince Morvi 1955, Dickens 1950).

Current winning trainers:
7 wins Gai Waterhouse (Theseo 2010, 2009, Tuesday Joy 2008, Desert War 2007, Grand Armee 2005, Electronic 1996, Stony Bay 1995).
1 win Murray Baker (My Eagle Eye 1992); Anthony Cummings (Zavite 2011); Allan Denham (Eremein 2006); Lee & Anthony Freedman (Our Ivanhowe 2017); David Hayes (Dark Ksar 1994); Robert Hickmott (The United States 2016); Roger James (Silent Achiever 2014); Leon Macdonald (Gold Guru 1998); Roberta Maguire (Sound Action 2004); Brian Smith (Balmerino 1976); Bruce Wallace (Darazari 1999); Chris Waller (Foreteller 2013); Darren Weir (Gailo Chop 2018); John Wheeler (Veandercross 1993).

Points of interest:
Tie The Knot, who won in 2001 and 2000 was first past the post in 1999, but lost on protest to Darazari.
Head-heat: Poitrel and Richmond Main dead-heated for first in 1921.
Maurice McCarten rode four winners of the Ranvet—Spear Chief 1939, Ammon Ra 1932, Limerick 1928, 1927—and also trained four winners—Wenona Girl 1964, 1961, Prince Morvi 1955, Dickens 1950. Arthur Ward rode three winners—Redcraze in 1957, Vagabond 1949, Columnist 1948) and trained Even Better (1965) and Foresight (1969). Jack Denham trainer Purple Patch to win in 1977, ridden by his son Allan, who later trained Eremein to win (2006).
Maurice McCarten rode Spear Chief to win the 1939 Rawson Stakes (three starters) when the 33/1 chance upset the favourite Ajax (1/40), who was going for his 19th consecutive win.

ATC The Galaxy (1100m)—Rosehill
Of $700,000. Group 1. Handicap, Min Weight 50kg, 3YO&Up. March 23, 2019.

2017-18 RESULT: Time: 1:04.30 (Soft 6)

FP	NO	HORSE	TRAINER	JOCKEY	MARGIN	BAR.	WGT	SP
1	3	IN HER TIME	Benjamin Smith	Zac Purton		10	55kg	$4F
2	5	ENGLISH	Gai Waterhouse & Adrian Bott	Sam Clipperton	0.8L	3	54.5kg	$16
3	13	VIRIDINE	James Cummings	Brenton Avdulla	1.6L	8	51kg	$4.20
4	10	SNITTY KITTY	Henry Dwyer	Tim Clark	2.8L	5	52kg	$4.80
5	15	THE MISSION	Paul Perry	Rachel King (a)	3L	7	50kg	$101
6	7	BALL OF MUSCLE	Joseph Pride	Jason Collett	3.6L	1	53kg	$11
7	1	LE ROMAIN	Kris Lees	Hugh Bowman	3.9L	9	58kg	$16
8	6	TAKEDOWN	Gary Moore	Tommy Berry	6.4L	11	54.5kg	$71
9	12	LADY ESPRIT	Aaron Purcell	Kathy O'Hara	7.3L	4	51kg	$31
10	2	JUNGLE EDGE	Mick Bell	Kevin Forrester	7.7L	6	55.5kg	$7
11	11	DERRYN	David & Ben Hayes & Tom Dabernig	Andrew Adkins	14.7L	2	52kg	$31

PAST WINNERS

YEAR	WINNER	JOCKEY	TRAINER	2ND	3RD	TIME
2018	In Her Time	Zac Purton	Benjamin Smith	English	Viridine	1:04.3
2017	Russian Revolution	Kerrin McEvoy	Peter & Paul Snowden	Redzel	Jungle Edge	1:07.6
2016	Griante	Craig Williams	David Brideoake	Shiraz	Dothraki	1:03.7
2015	Sweet Idea	Blake Shinn	Gai Waterhouse	Kuro	Miracles Of Life	1:02.6
2014	Tiger Tees	Nash Rawiller	Joseph Pride	Anatina	Villa Verde	1:05.0
2013	Bel Sprinter	Kerrin McEvoy	Jason Warren	Snitzerland	Decision Time	1:02.8
2012	Temple Of Boom	James McDonald	Tony Gollan	Nobby Snip	Ladys Angel	1:03.4
2011	Atomic Force	Tim Clark	Darren Smith	Thankgodyou'rehere	Cardinal Virtue	1:05.3
2010	Shellscrape	Dwayne Dunn	Chris Waller	Swift Alliance	Stryker	1:03.2
2009	Nicconi	Craig Williams	David Hayes	Danleigh	Gold Trail	1:03.5
2008	Typhoon Zed	Tim Clark	Tim Martin	Keen Commander	Fritzs Princess	1:04.1
2007	Magnus	Damien Oliver	Peter Moody	Fast n Famous	Macs Tune	1:03.2
2006	Proprietor	Stephen Baster	Paul Perry	Media	Black Ink	1:03.1
2005	Charge Forward	Darren Beadman	John O'Shea	Spark Of Life	Red Oog	1:04.7
2004	Spark Of Life	Chris Munce	Allan Denham	Taikun	Blessum	1:03.7
2003	Snowland	Chris Munce	Gai Waterhouse	Star Of Florida	Bradshaw	1:04.5
2002	Mistegic	Glen Boss	Lee Curtis	Century Kid	Excellerator	1:02.7
2001	Padstow	Darren Beadman	John Size	Camena	Catatonic	1:04.0
2000	Black Bean	Brett Prebble	Mathew Ellerton	Commands	Padstow	1:02.9
1999	Masked Party	Len Beasley	Graeme Rogerson	Notoire	Rebel Rock	1:06.4
1998	La Baraka	Kevin Moses	Peter C Hayes	Masked Party	Coogee Walk	1:03.7
1997	Accomplice	Larry Cassidy	John Hawkes	Lion Hunter	Unison	1:02.3

BACKGROUND

First run: 1972 (won by Playbill). Group 2 1980-83. Group 1 from 1984. Run at Randwick to 2006, 2008-2011. Warwick Farm 2007. Rosehill from 2011.
Most recent mare to win: In Her Time (2018). Note: 3YO filly La Baraka won in 1998.
Most recent 3YO to win: C&G—Russian Revolution (2017); Filly—La Baraka (1998).
Multiple winners: 1—Grey Receiver (1982, 1981).
Fastest time (Rosehill 1100m): Sweet Idea (2015) 1:02.69
Notable winners: Charge Forward (2005); Spark Of Life (2004); Gold Ace (1996); Schillaci (1992); Mr. Tiz (1991); Snippets (1988); Grey Receiver (1981 & 1982); Hit It Benny (1980); Mistress Anne (1979); Luskin Star (1978); Bletchingly (1975).
The Galaxy winners won the lead-up races:
William Reid Stakes: None. Note: The only Australia Stakes winner placed in a The Galaxy was Toy Show (1977), who ran third to Salaam.
Lightning Stakes: 2—Gold Ace (1996); Schillaci (1992).
Oakleigh Plate: 3—Schillaci (1992); Snippets (1998); Mistress Anne (1975).
Newmarket Handicap: 1—Schillaci (1992).

Lightning, Oakleigh & Newmarket: 1—Schillaci (1992).
Liverpool City Cup: None.
Challenge Stakes: 2—Snippets (1988); Playbill (1972).
Star Kingdom Stakes: 2—Jetball (1994); Bronze Spirit (1983).
The Galaxy winners went on to win in the same preparation:
T.J. Smith Stakes: 1—La Baraka (1998).
Kingsford Smith (BTC) Cup: 2—Accomplice (1997); Mr. Illusion (1984).
Doomben 10,000: 2—Accomplice (1997); Hit It Benny (1980).
Stradbroke Handicap: 1—Grey Receiver (1982).
Leading winning jockey:
3 wins Peter Cook (Snippets 1988, Salaam 1977, Kista 1973).
Current winning jockeys:
2 wins Tim Clark (Atomic Force 2011, Typhoon Zed 2008); Kerrin McEvoy (Russian Revolution 2017, Bel Sprinter 2013); Damien Oliver (Magnus 2007, Schillaci 1992); Craig Williams (Griante 2016, Nicconi 2009).
1 win Stephen Baster (Proprietor 2006); Glen Boss (Mistegic 2002); Larry Cassidy (Accomplice 1997); Dwayne Dunn (Shellscrape 2010); James McDonald (Temple Of Boom 2012); Brett Prebble (Black Bean 2000); Zac Purton (In Her Time 2018); Nash Rawiller (Tiger Tees 2014).
Leading winning trainers:
2 wins Bart Cummings (Luskin Star 1978, Starglow 1974); Lee Freedman (Gold Ace 1996, Schillaci 1992); Bob Thomsen (Grey Receiver 1982, 1981).
Current winning trainers:
2 wins Lee Freedman (Gold Ace 1996, Schillaci 1992).
1 win David Brideoake (2016); Lee Curtis (Mistegic 2002); Allan Denham (Spark Of Life 2004); Mathew Ellerton (Black Bean 2000); John Hawkes (Accomplice 1997); David Hayes (Nicconi 2009); Tony Gollan (Temple Of Boom 2012); Bruce Marsh (Mr. Illusion 1984); Tim Martin (Typhoon Zed 2008); John O'Shea (Charge Forward 2005); Paul Perry (Proprietor 2006); Joseph Pride (Tiger Tees 2014); Graeme Rogerson (Masked Party 1999); John Size (Padstow 2001); Benjamin Smith (In Her Time 2018); Peter & Paul Snowden (Russian Revolution 2017); Chris Waller (Shellscrape 2010); Jason Warren (Bel Sprinter 2013); Gai Waterhouse (Snowland 2003).
Points of interest:
Bletchingly (1975) is the sire of Mr. Tiz (1991). He also is the grandsire of Accomplice (1997), a son of Bletchingly's best sire son, Canny Lad; Snippets (1988) is the sire of Snowland (2003). With Me, third to Mr. Tiz in 1991, is the dam of Accomplice (1997).

ATC Rosehill Guineas (2000m)—Rosehill
Of $600,000. Group 1. Set Weights, 3YO. March 23, 2019.

2017-18 RESULT: Time: 2:06.10 (Soft 7)

FP	NO	HORSE	TRAINER	JOCKEY	MARGIN	BAR.	WGT	SP
1	8	D'ARGENTO	Chris Waller	Hugh Bowman		8	56.5kg	$3.80F
2	6	TANGLED	Chris Waller	Michael Walker	1.3L	17	56.5kg	$81
3	15	FURORE	Kris Lees	Brenton Avdulla	2.3L	5	56.5kg	$12
4	2	VIN DE DANCE	Murray Baker & Andrew Forsman	Jason Waddell	2.4L	2	56.5kg	$15
5	4	CLIFF'S EDGE	Darren Weir	John Allen	2.9L	1	56.5kg	$8.50
6	1	ACE HIGH	David Payne	Tye Angland	3L	10	56.5kg	$7
7	13	MISSION HILL	Murray Baker & Andrew Forsman	Damian Lane	3.1L	7	56.5kg	$18
8	5	MONGOLIAN CONQUEROR	Stephen Autridge & Jamie Richards	Opie Bosson	3.2L	18	56.5kg	$31
9	9	VILLERMONT	Aaron Purcell	Blake Shinn	3.3L	3	56.5kg	$11
10	7	CAPITAL GAIN	Paul Butterworth	Ben Melham	4.5L	9	56.5kg	$61
11	11	THE LORD MAYOR	Chris Waller	Kerrin McEvoy	5L	11	56.5kg	$18
12	14	MAIN STAGE	Trent Busuttin & Natalie Young	Mark Zahra	5.8L	12	56.5kg	$20
13	17	CONDOR	Paul Perry	Luke Currie	6L	14	56.5kg	$101
14	10	KAONIC	Chris Waller	Zac Purton	7.5L	15	56.5kg	$11
15	16	SO YOU WIN	Chris Waller	Craig Williams	7.7L	6	56.5kg	$41
16	12	ENDOWMENT	Chris Gibbs	Damien Oliver	8.3L	16	56.5kg	$31
17	3	AGE OF FIRE	Stephen Autridge & Jamie Richards	Jason Collett	9L	13	56.5kg	$51
18	18	TERWILLIKER	Anthony & Edward Cummings	Andrew Adkins	14.6L	4	56.5kg	$101

PAST WINNERS

YEAR	WINNER	JOCKEY	TRAINER	2ND	3RD	TIME
2018	D'Argento	Hugh Bowman	Chris Waller	Tangled	Furore	2:06.1
2017	Gingernuts	Opie Bosson	Stephen Autridge & Jamie Richards	Inference	So Si Bon	2:11.4
2016	Tarzino	Craig Newitt	Mick Price	Montaigne	Jameka	2:03.5
2015	Volkstok'n'Barrell	Craig Williams	Donna Logan	Preferment	Hallowed Crown	2:03.4
2014	Criterion	Hugh Bowman	David Payne	Thunder Fantasy	Teronado	2:05.9
2013	It's A Dundeel	James McDonald	Murray Baker	Sacred Falls	Tatra	2:02.2
2012	Laser Hawk	Nash Rawiller	Gai Waterhouse	Ocean Park	Silent Achiever	2:02.1
2011	Jimmy Choux	Jonathan Riddell	John Bary	Retrieve	Shamrocker	2:05.3
2010	Zabrasive	Nash Rawiller	John O'Shea	Rock Classic	Run For Naara	2:04.5
2009	Metal Bender	Danny Nikolic	Jack Denham	Sousa	Rock Kingdom	2:03.2
2008	Dealer Principal	Peter Robl	Anthony Cummings	Kingda Ka	Littorio	2:04.5
2007	He's No Pie Eater	Hugh Bowman	Graeme Rogerson	Ambitious General	Flumicino	2:02.7
2006	De Beers	Craig Williams	David Hayes	Oh Oklahoma	Primus	2:03.5
2005	Eremein	Corey Brown	Allan Denham	Nevis	Outback Prince	2:01.3
2004	Niello	Darren Beadman	John Hawkes	Grand Zulu	Elvstroem	2:01.1
2003	Helenus	Steven King	Leon Corstens	Mummify	Sunday Joy	2:02.7
2002	Carnegie Express	Larry Cassidy	Gai Waterhouse	Don Eduardo	Pentastic	2:00.8
2001	Sale Of Century	Larry Cassidy	John Hawkes	Danamite	Scenic Warrior	2:01.0
2000	Diatribe	Jim Cassidy	George Hanlon	Freemason	Crawl	2:04.3
1999	Sky Heights	Glen Boss	Colin Alderson	Dignity Dancer	Arena	2:00.1
1998	Tie The Knot	Shane Dye	Guy Walter	Tycoon Lil	Pursuits	2:01.3
1997	Tarnpir Lane	Darren Beadman	Cliff Brown	Intergaze	Ebony Grosve	2:00.5

BACKGROUND

First run: 1910 (won by Electric Wire). Group 1 since 1980. Run over 1400m 1910-1914; 1800m 1915-47. Not run in 1978 when moved from the spring to the autumn. Run at Randwick in 1917 (1800m), 1940 (1820m) and 1960 (2000m).

Most recent filly to win: Riverina Charm (1989). Note: Eight fillies have won the Guineas. The others are—Spirit Of Kingston (1985); Deck The Halls (1981); Wenona Girl (1960); Questing (1945); Tea Rose (1939); Furious (1921) and Carlita (1914).
Fastest time (2000m): Octagonal (1996) & Danewin (1995) 1:59.90
Notable winners: Gingernuts (2017); Tarzino (2016); Criterion (2014); It's A Dundeel (2013); Jimmy Choux (2011); Metal Bender (2009); Eremein (2005); Helenus (2003); Sky Heights (1999); Tie The Knot (1998); Octagonal (1996); Naturalism (1992); Surfers Paradise (1991); Strawberry Road (1983); Kingston Town (1980); Dulcify (1979); Imagele (1973); Eskimo Prince (1964); Wenona Girl (1960); Tulloch (1957); High Caste (1939); Ajax (1937); Phar Lap (1939); Mollison (1928); Amounis (1925); Furious (1921); Wolaroi (1918).
Rosehill Guineas winners on the lead-up races:
Chipping Norton Stakes (since 1977 after which the Guineas was moved from the spring to the autumn):
1—He's No Pie Eater (2007).
Gosford Guineas: 1—Carnegie Express (2002).
Hobartville Stakes: 17—Danewin (1995); Imagele (1973); Fair Summer (1965); Wenona Girl (1960); Martello Towers (1959); Pride Of Egypt (1954); Hydrogen (1951); Careless (1950); Prince Standard (1946); Hall Stand (1942); High Caste (1939); Aeolus (1938); Hadrian (1935); Silver King (1934); Bronze Hawk (1932); Mollison (1928); Amounis (1925).
New Zealand Derby: 4—Gingernuts (2017); Jimmy Choux (2011); Surfers Paradise (1991); Isle Of Man (1982).
Australian Guineas: None
Randwick Guineas (since 2006 when the Randwick Guineas, 1600m, took over from the Canterbury Guineas):
2—It's A Dundeel (2013); Metal Bender (2009).
Canterbury Guineas (before 2006: Canterbury Guineas, 1900m, replaced by the Randwick Guineas, 1600m):
13—Niello (2004); Carnegie Express (2002); Octagonal (1996); Riverina Charm (1989); Spirit Of Kingston (1985); Belmura Lad (1977); Imagele (1973); Royal Show (1970); Fair Summer (1965); Martello Towers (1959); Pride Of Egypt (1954); Moorland (1943); Hadrian (1935).
Rosehill Guineas winners went on to win in the same preparation:
Royal Sovereign Stakes: 1—Danewin (1995). Note: the Royal Sovereign Stakes, run in April from 2014, was previously run before the Rosehill Guineas.
Australian Derby: 20—Criterion (2014); It's A Dundeel (2013); Eremein (2005); Sky Heights (1999); Octagonal (1996); Naturalism (1992); Strawberry Road (1983); Kingston Town (1980); Dulcify (1979); Battle Sign (1975); Taras Bulba (1974); Imagele (1973); Martello Towers (1959); Tulloch (1957); Caranna (1955); Tea Rose (1944); Moorland (1943); Laureate (1941); Phar Lap (1929); Biplane (1917).
Australian Oaks: None. Note: Deck The Halls (1981) finished second to November Rain in the 1981 AJC Oaks; Questing (1945) finished second to Rose Bay in the 1946 AJC Oaks; Tea Rose (1944) finished second to Ribbon in the 1945 AJC Oaks.
Tancred Stakes: 2—Octagonal (1996); Kingston Town (1980).
Tancred Stakes & Australian Derby: 2—Octagonal (1996); Kingston Town (1980).
Queen Elizabeth Stakes (since 1977): None. Note: Tulloch (1957) completed the double in the same season when the Guineas was run in the spring and the Queen Elizabeth was run in the autumn of 1958.
Doomben Cup: 1—Danewin (1995).
Rosehill Guineas and the spring features:
Spring Champion Stakes (since 1977): 5—It's A Dundeel (Guineas 2013); Niello (2004); Tie The Knot (1998); Danewin (1995); Kingston Town (1980).
Caulfield Cup (same year, since 1977): 2—Diatribe (2000); Sky Heights (1999). Note: Tulloch (1957) was the only horse to complete the double when both races were run in the spring.
Cox Plate (same year, since 1977): 4—Surfers Paradise (1991); Strawberry Road (1983); Kingston Town (1980); Ducify (1979). Note: Octagonal (1985) is the only 3YO to win the Cox Plate in the spring, and the Rosehill Guineas (1986) in the autumn.
Victoria Derby: 13—Tarzino (2016); Helenus (2003); Dulcify (1979); Tulloch (1957); Pride Of Egypt (1954); Hydrogen (1951); Prince Standard (1946); Balloon King (1930); Phar Lap (1929); Furious (1921); Biplane (1917); Wolaroi (1916); Carlita (1914). Note: Before 1979, the Guineas was run in the early spring.
Melbourne Cup (same year, since 1977): None. Note: Phar Lap (1929) is the only horse to win the Rosehill Guineas and a Melbourne Cup (1930).
Leading winning jockeys:
4 wins Billy Cook (Pride Of Egypt 1954, Questing 1945, Hall Stand 1942, Aeolus 1938); Mick Dittman (Naturalism 1992, Alibhai 1984, Strawberry Road 1983, Deck The Halls 1981); Ed Bartle (Moorland 1943, Tidal Wave 1940, High Caste 1939, Bronze Hawk 1932); John Marshall (Solar Circle 1990, Sky Chase 1988, Ring Joe 1987, Spirit Of Kingston 1985); Athol Mulley (Eskimo Prince 1964, Bogan Road 1962, Caranna 1955, Royal Andrew 1948).
Current winning jockeys:
3 wins Hugh Bowman (D'Argento 2018, Criterion 2014, He's No Pie Eater 2007);
2 wins Larry Cassidy (Carnegie Express 2002, Sale Of Century 2001); Nash Rawiller (Laser Hawk 2012, Zabrasive 2010).

1 win Glen Boss (Sky Heights 1999); Opie Bosson (Gingernuts 2017); Corey Brown (Eremein 2005); James McDonald (It's A Dundeel 2013); Craig Newitt (Tarzino 2016); Jonathan Riddell (Jimmy Choux 2011); Craig Williams (De Beers 2006).

Leading winning trainers:
9 wins Tommy Smith (Alibhai 1984, Kingston Town 1980, Imagele 1983, Royal Show 1970, Portable 1969, Dark Briar 1966, Bold Pirate 1958, Tulloch 1957, Idlewild 1952).
4 wins Ted Hush (Gay Lover 1956, Caranna 1955, Pride Of Egypt 1954, Hydrogen 1951).

Current winning trainers:
3 wins John Hawkes (Niello 2004, Sale Of Century 2001, Octagonal 1996).
2 wins David Hayes (De Beers 2006, Star Of Maple 1994); Gai Waterhouse (Laser Hawk 2012, Carnegie Express 2002).
1 win Stephen Autridge & Jamie Richards (Gingernuts 2017); Murray Baker (It's A Dundeel 2013); John Bary (Jimmy Choux 2011); Les Bridge (Drawn 1986); Cliff Brown (Tarnpir Lane 1997); Leon Corstens (Helenus 2003); Anthony Cummings (Dealer Principal 2008); Allan Denham (Eremein 2006); John O'Shea (Zabrasive 2010); David Payne (Criterion 2014); Mick Price (Tarzino 2016); Graeme Rogerson (He's No Pie Eater 2007); Chris Waller (D'Argento 2018).

Point of interest:
Eskimo Prince (1964) is the only Golden Slipper winner to win the Rosehill Guineas.
Vin De Dance was second past the post in 2018 and relegated to fourth after a successful protest by the rider of Furore.

ATC Tancred Stakes (2400m)—Rosehill

Of $1,500,000. Group 1. Weight For Age, 3YO&Up. March 30, 2019.

2017-18 RESULT: Time: 2:30.11 (Good 4)

FP	NO	HORSE	TRAINER	JOCKEY	MARGIN	BAR.	WGT	SP
1	2	ALMANDIN	Liam Howley	Kerrin McEvoy		9	59kg	$3
2	3	AMBITIOUS	Anthony Freedman	Craig Williams	1.3L	3	59kg	$21
3	5	WHO SHOT THEBARMAN	Chris Waller	Tye Angland	1.4L	8	59kg	$61
4	1	GAILO CHOP	Darren Weir	Mark Zahra	1.6L	7	59kg	$2.30f
5	9	SINGLE GAZE	Nick Olive	Kathy O'Hara	2L	1	57kg	$7
6	6	AUVRAY	Richard Freedman	Jason Collett	2.3L	2	59kg	$21
7	4	HARLEM	David & Ben Hayes & Tom Dabernig	Michael Walker	3.2L	6	59kg	$21
8	8	VENTURA STORM	David & Ben Hayes & Tom Dabernig	Damien Oliver	5.4L	4	59kg	$21
9	10	LASQUETI SPIRIT	Lee Curtis	Jay Ford	6.7L	5	56.5kg	$151

PAST WINNERS

YEAR	WINNER	JOCKEY	TRAINER	2ND	3RD	TIME
2018	Almandin	Kerrin McEvoy	Liam Howley	Ambitious	Who Shot Thebarman	2:30.1
2017	Jameka	Hugh Bowman	Ciaron Maher	Humidor	Exospheric	2:35.6
2016	Preferment	Hugh Bowman	Chris Waller	Who Shot Thebarman	Grand Marshal	2:28.6
2015	Hartnell	James McDonald	John O'Shea	To The World	Beaten Up	2:29.5
2014	Silent Achiever	Nash Rawiller	Roger James	It's A Dundeel	Fiorente	2:34.2
2013	Fiveandahalfstar	Hugh Bowman	Anthony Cummings	Silent Achiever	Sangster	2:33.7
2012	Manighar	Luke Nolen	Peter Moody	Americain	Drunken Sailor	2:28.3
2011	Cedarberg	Damien Oliver	Pat Carey	Mourayan	Linton	2:29.7
2010	Littorio	Craig Williams	Nigel Blackiston	Zavite	No Wine No Song	2:29.3
2009	Fiumicino	Darren Beadman	Michael, Wayne & John Hawkes	Thesio	Viewed	2:34.2
2008	Tuesday Joy	Darren Beadman	Gai Waterhouse	Princess Coup	Sirmoine	2:35.8
2007	Blutigeroo	Damien Oliver	Colin Little	Railings	Gorky Park	2:26.5
2006	Eremein	Glen Boss	Allan Denham	Railings	Our Smoking Joe	2:27.0
2005	Makybe Diva	Glen Boss	Lee Freedman	Grand Armee	Vouvray	2:26.9
2004	Grand Zulu	Rod Quinn	Gwenda Markwell	Mummify	Makybe Diva	2:25.7
2003	Freemason	Darren Beadman	John Hawkes	Northerly	Republic Lass	2:26.8
2002	Ethereal	Scott Seamer	Sheila Laxon	Universal Prince	Rain Gauge	2:29.3
2001	Curata Storm	Rod Quinn	John Hawkes	Kaapstad Way	Giovana	2:27.7
2000	Tie The Knot	Shane Dye	Guy Walter	Arena	Showella	2:30.8
1999	Tie The Knot	Shane Dye	Guy Walter	Intergaze	Arena	2:29.0
1998	Might And Power	Brian York	Jack Denham	Gold Guru	Doriemus	2:27.2
1997	Octagonal	Shane Dye	John Hawkes	Arkady	Istidaad	2:27.4

BACKGROUND

First run: 1963 (won by Maidenhead). Group 1 since 1980. Run over 2000m in 1964. Quality handicap 1963-76. WFA since 1977. Registered name is the H.E. Tancred Stakes. Known as The BMW 1990-94, 2002-2017; The Mercedes Classic 1995-2001.

3YOs to win: 11—Fiveandahalfstar (2013); Grand Zulu (2004); Curata Storm (2001); Octagonal (1996); Stony Bay (1995); Kaaptive Edition (1993); Heroicity (1992); Beau Zam (1988); Myocard (1987); Bonecrusher (1986); Kingston Town (1980). Note: No 3YO filly has won The BMW. All the 3YOs have won under WFA conditions.

Mares to win: 9—Jameka (2017); Silent Achiever (2014); Tuesday Joy (2008); Makybe Diva (2005); Ethereal (2002); Miltak (1994); My Blue Denim (1981); Bright Shadow (1970*); Maidenhead (1963*). *Run as a handicap.

Multiple winners: 2—Tie The Knot (2000 & 1999); Octagonal (1997 & 1996).

Fastest Time (2400m): Grand Zulu (2004) 2:25.70

Notable winners: Almandin (2018); Jameka (2017); Preferment (2016); Silent Achiever (2014); Tuesday Joy (2008); Eremein (2006); Makybe Diva (2005); Ethereal (2002); Tie The Knot (2000, 1999); Might And Power (1998); Octagonal (1997, 1996); Sydeston (1990); Our Poetic Prince (1989); Beau Zam (1988); Bonecrusher (1986); Kingston Town (1980); Hyperno (1978); Apollo Eleven (1973); Tails (1972); Prince Grant (1969).

Tancred Stakes winners won the key lead-up races:

New Zealand Derby: 1—Bonecrusher (1986). Note: The NZ Derby was then run in December, now in March.
Australian Cup: 4—Preferment (2016); Manighar (2012); Makybe Diva (2005); Octagonal (1997).
Chipping Norton Stakes: 4—Tie The Knot (2000, 1999); Octagonal (1997); Apollo Eleven (1973).
Ranvet Stakes: 9—Silent Achiever (2014); Manighar (2012); Tuesday Joy (2008); Eremein (2006); Tie The Knot (2000); Stony Bay (1995); Beau Zam (1988); Myocard (1987); Alibhai (1985).
Rosehill Guineas: 2—Octagonal (1996); Kingston Town (1980).
Tancred Stakes winners went on to win in the same preparation:
Australian Derby: 5—Octagonal (1996); Beau Zam (1988); Myocard (1987); Bonecrusher (1986); Kingston Town (1980).
ATC Queen Elizabeth Stakes: 10—Eremein (2006); Might And Power (1998); Intergaze (1997); Sydeston (1990); Our Poetic Prince (1989); Prince Majestic (1982); My Blue Denim (1981); Shivaree (1979); Apollo Eleven (1973); Tails (1972).
Sydney Cup: 4—Tie The Knot (1999); Kingston Town* (1980); Apollo Eleven (1983); Maidenhead** (1963). *3YO. ** Tancred Stakes was a handicap.
Doomben Cup: 1—Might And Power (1998).
P.J. O'Shea Stakes: 2—Tails (1972); Striking Force (1966). Note: The double hasn't been completed since the Tancred became WFA in 1977.
Tancred Stakes winners also won in the previous spring:
Spring Champion Stakes: 2—Beau Zam (Tancred 1988); Kingston Town (1980).
Caulfield Cup: 3—Jameka (Tancred 2017); Might And Power (1998); Hayai (1984).
Cox Plate: 2—Octagonal (Tancred 1996); Our Poetic Prince (1989).
Victoria Derby: 1—Fiveandahalfstar (Tancred 2013).
Melbourne Cup: 4—Makybe Diva (Tancred 2005); Ethereal (2002); Might And Power (1998); Hyperno (1979).
Tancred Stakes winners won in the following spring:
Cox Plate: 4—Makybe Diva (2005); Might And Power (1998); Bonecrusher (1986); Kingston Town (1980).
Melbourne Cup: 1—Makybe Diva (2005).
Leading winning jockeys:
5 wins Shane Dye (Tie The Knot 2000 & 1999, Octagonal 1997, Stony Bay 1995, Dr. Grace 1991).
4 wins Darren Beadman (Fiumicino 2009, Tuesday Joy 2008, Freemason 2003, Octagonal 1996); Mick Dittman (Kaaptive Edition 1993, Sydeston 1990, Alibhai 1985, Our Cavalier 1977).
3 wins Hugh Bowman (Jameka 2017, Preferment 2016, Fiveandahalfstar 2013); Peter Cook (My Blue Denim 1981, Major Battle 1976, Sovereign Yacht 1975).
Current winning jockeys:
3 wins Hugh Bowman (Jameka 2017, Preferment 2016, Fiveandahalfstar 2013).
2 wins Glen Boss (Eremein 2006; Makybe Diva 2005); Damien Oliver (Cedarberg 2011; Blutigeroo 2007).
1 win Kerrin McEvoy (Almandin 2018); Luke Nolen (Manighar 2012); Nash Rawiller (Silent Achiever 2014); Craig Williams (Littorio 2010).
Leading winning trainer:
5 wins John Hawkes (Fiumicino 2009, Freemason 2003, Curata Storm 2001, Octagonal 1997, 1996).
Current winning trainers:
5 wins John Hawkes (Fiumicino 2009, Freemason 2003, Curata Storm 2001, Octagonal 1997, 1996).
2 wins Gai Waterhouse (Tuesday Joy 2008, Stony Bay 1995).
1 win Trevor Andrews (Heroicity 1992); Nigel Blackiston (Littorio 2010); Les Bridge (Major Battle 1976); Pat Carey (Cedarberg 2011); Anthony Cummings (Fiveandahalfstar); Allan Denham (Eremein 2006); Liam Howley (Almandin 2018); Roger James (Silent Achiever 2014); Sheila Laxon (Ethereal 2002); Jim Lee (Hayai 1984); Colin Little (Blutigeroo 2007); Ciaron Maher (Jameka 2017); Frank Ritchie (Bonecrusher 1986); Graeme Rogerson (Kaaptive Edition 1993); Chris Waller (Preferment 2016); John Wheeler (Our Poetic Prince 1989).
Internationals in the Tancred Stakes:
Seven northern hemisphere-trained horses have competed in the Tancred Stakes:
- 1988 (won by Beau Zam): Highland Chieftain GB (trainer John Dunlop 2nd), Vaguely Pleasant FR (Patrick Biancone, 3rd), Le Glorieux GB (Robert Collett, 5th).
- 1989 (won by Our Poetic Prince): Top Class GB (Clive Brittain, 2nd).
- 1990 (won by Sydeston): Mountain Kingdom USA (Clive Brittain, 4th), Highland Chieftain GB (John Dunlop 9th).
- 2015 (won by Hartnell): To The World JPN (Yasutoshi Ikee, 3rd).
Points of interest:
In 2000, same horses ran the trifecta in the Ranvet Stakes and the Tancred Stakes—Tie The Knot, Arena and Showella.
In 2003, the same three horses fought out the Ranvet Stakes and the Tancred Stakes. Republic Lass beat Northerly and Freemason in the Ranvet. Freemason beat Northerly and Republic Lass in the Tancred.

ATC Vinery Stud Stakes (2000m)—Rosehill

Of $500,000. Group . Set Weights, 3YO Fillies. March 30, 2019.

2017-18 RESULT: Time: 2:03.52 (Good 4)

FP	NO	HORSE	TRAINER	JOCKEY	MARGIN	BAR.	WGT	SP
1	9	HIYAAM	Mick Price	Michael Dee		1	56kg	$12
2	7	UNFORGOTTEN	Chris Waller	Kerrin McEvoy	1.8L	8	56kg	$3.70f
3	1	ALOISIA	Aaron Purcell	Mark Zahra	4.1L	13	56kg	$5
4	2	ALIZEE	James Cummings	Brenton Avdulla	5.3L	9	56kg	$7
5	8	DANZDANZDANCE	Chris Gibbs	Michael Walker	6.8L	5	56kg	$12
6	5	TORVILL	Clarry Conners	Christian Reith	7.9L	11	56kg	$21
7	14	MADAME MARKIEVICZ	Anthony & Edward Cummings	Corey Brown	8.2L	6	56kg	$201
8	12	SEMARI	Trent Busuttin & Natalie Young	Craig Williams	9.4L	7	56kg	$10
9	13	MISS ADMIRATION	Mick Price	Tim Clark	10L	4	56kg	$101
10	3	BRING ME ROSES	Tony McEvoy	Luke Currie	11L	10	56kg	$9.50
11	6	RIMRAAM	David & Ben Hayes & Tom Dabernig	Damien Oliver	15L	3	56kg	$16
12	11	DANCERS	Brad Widdup	Jason Collett	26.8L	2	56kg	$26
13	10	ALL TOO SOON	David Payne	Tye Angland	31.6L	12	56kg	$21

PAST WINNERS

YEAR	WINNER	JOCKEY	TRAINER	2ND	3RD	TIME
2018	Hiyaam	Michael Dee	Mick Price	Unforgotten	Aloisia	2:03.5
2017	Montoya's Secret	Noel Callow	Leon & Troy Corstens	Nurse Kitchen	Harlow Gold	2:09.7
2016	Single Gaze	Kathy O'Hara	Nick Olive	Valley Girl	Happy Hannah	2:03.0
2015	Fenway	Blake Shinn	Lee & Shannon Hope	First Seal	Thunder Lady	2:03.2
2014	Lucia Valentina	Hugh Bowman	Kris Lees	Solicit	Forever Loved	2:07.0
2013	Norzita	Hugh Bowman	Bart Cummings	Longport	Habibi	2:06.1
2012	Mosheen	Danny Nikolic	Robert Smerdon	Streama	Aliyana Tilde	2:02.3
2011	Mirjulisa Lass	Corey Brown	Gregory Hickman	Fibrillation	Brazilian Pulse	2:03.4
2010	Faint Perfume	Michael Rodd	Bart Cummings	Valdemoro	Absolute Faith	2:02.5
2009	Purple	Kerrin McEvoy	Peter Snowden	Gold Water	Gallica	2:07.0
2008	Heavenly Glow	Robert Thompson	Allan Denham	Galileo's Daughter	Pentura	2:09.2
2007	Miss Finland	Craig Williams	David Hayes	Banc De Fortune	Just Dancing	2:03.8
2006	Serenade Rose	Steven King	Lee Freedman	Beauty Watch	Flora Danica	2:01.3
2005	Hollow Bullet	Glen Boss	John Mcardle	Lotteria	She's Justa Tad	2:00.5
2004	Special Harmony	Damien Oliver	Lee Freedman	Shamekha	Ike's Dream	2:01.8
2003	Shower Of Roses	Chris Munce	Gai Waterhouse	Bramble Rose	Rasberry Ripple	2:04.4
2002	Sixty Seconds	Brian York	Roger James	Hosannah	Quays	2:00.1
2001	Tempest Mom	Danny Beasley	Gai Waterhouse	Rose Archway	Calm Smytzer	2:02.9
2000	Hill Of Grace	Brett Prebble	Robert Priscott	Kirkstall Lane	Miss Zoe	2:02.4
1999	Savannah Success	Brian York	Graeme Rogerson	Light Work	Camarena	2:02.4
1998	Champagne	Greg Childs	Laurie Laxon	On Air	For The Moment	2:02.4
1997	Danendri	Darren Beadman	Bart Cummings	Ellakapella	Assertive Lass	2:01.4

BACKGROUND

First run: 1979 (won by Impede). Group 2 1980-91. Group 1 from 1992. Run over 1900m in 1979. Also known as the Vinery Stud Stakes. Resgistered as the Storm Queen Stakes. Run at Canterbury in 1979.
Fastest time (2000m): Tempest Morn (2001) 2:00.17.
Notable winners: Single Gaze (2016); Lucia Valentina (2013); Norzita (2013); Mosheen (2012); Faint Perfume (2010); Miss Finland (2007); Serenade Rose (2006); Special Harmony (2004); Savannah Success (1999); Champagne (1998); Saleous (1996); Northwood Plume (1995); Slight Chance (1993); Research (1989); Centaurea (1985).

Storm Queen Stakes winners won the lead-up races:
Typhoon Tracy Stakes: 1—Norzita (2013).
Armanasco Stakes: 5—Miss Finland (2007); Serenade Rose (2006); Special Harmony (2004); Champagne (1998); Northwood Plume (1995).
Kewney Stakes: 4—Faint Perfume (2010); Special Harmony (2004); Northwood Plume (1995); Tennessee Vain (1988).

Surround Stakes: 2—Savannah Success (1999); Impede (1979).
Coolmore Classic: 1—Sheraco (1982).
Randwick Guineas: 1—Mosheen (2012).
Australian Guineas: 2—Mosheen (2012); Miss Finland (2007).
Keith Nolan Stakes: 1—Single Gaze (2016).
Storm Queen Stakes winners went on to win in the same preparation:
ATC Australian Oaks: 6—Heavenly Glow (2008); Serenade Rose (2006); Danendri (1997); Alcove (1994); Research (1989); Sheraco (1982).
Coolmore Classic & AJC Australian Oaks: 1—Sheraco (1982).
ATC Australian Derby: 1—Research (1989).
AJC Australian Derby & ATC Australian Oaks: 1—Research (1989).
Schweppes Oaks: 2—Tempest Morn (2001); Centaurea (1985).
Queensland Oaks: 3—Purple (2009); Slight Chance (1993); A Little Kiss (1990).
Storm Queen Stakes and the previous spring 3YO fillies' features:
Flight Stakes: 5—Norzita (Storm Queen 2013); Slight Chance (1993); Electrique (1992); A Little Kiss (1990; Research (1989).
Thousand Guineas: 3—Miss Finland (Storm Queen 2007); Special Harmony (2004); Northwood Plume (1995).
VRC Oaks: 10—Mosheen (Storm Queen 2012); Faint Perfume (2010); Miss Finland (2007); Serenade Rose (2006); Hollow Bullet (2005); Special Harmony (2004); Saleous (1996), Northwood Plume (1995); Slight Chance (1993); Research (1989).
Leading winning jockey:
3 wins Mick Dittman (A Little Kiss 1990, Research 1989, Centaurea 1985).
Current winning jockeys:
2 wins Hugh Bowman (Lucia Valentina 2014, Norzita 2013); Damien Oliver (Special Harmony 2004, Northwood Plume 1995).
1 win Glen Boss (Hollow Bullet 2005); Corey Brown (Mirjulisa Lass 2011); Noel Callow (Montoya's Secret 2017); Michael Dee (Hiyaam 2018); Kerrin McEvoy (Purple 2009); Kathy O'Hara (Single Gaze 2016); Brett Prebble (Hill Of Grace 2000); Robert Thompson (Heavenly Glow 2008); Craig Williams (Miss Finland 2007).
Leading winning trainers:
4 wins Bart Cummings (Norzita 2013, Faint Perfume 2010, Danendri 1997, Sheraco 1982).
3 wins Lee Freedman (Serenade Rose 2006, Special Harmony 2004, Northwood Plume 1995).
Current winning trainers:
3 wins Lee Freedman (Serenade Rose 2006, Special Harmony 2004, Northwood Plume 1995).
2 wins Gai Waterhouse (Shower Of Roses 2003, Tempest Morn 2001).
1 win Clarry Conners (Research 1989); Leon & Troy Corstens (Montoya's Secret 2017); Allan Denham (Heavenly Glow 2008); John Hawkes (English Wonder 1983); David Hayes (Miss Finland 2007); Greg Hickman (Mirjulisa Lass 2011); Tom Hughes jnr (Alcove 1994); Pat Hyland (Saleous 18996); Roger James (Sixty Seconds 2002); Laurie Laxon (Champagne 1998); Kris Lees (Lucia Valentina 2014); John McArdle (Hollow Bullet 2005); Nick Olive (Single Gaze 2016); Mick Price (Hiyaam 2018); Robert Priscott (Hill Of Grace 2000); Graeme Rogerson (Savannah Success 1999); Robert Smerdon (Mosheen 2012); Peter Snowden (Purple 2009).
Points of interest:
Tempest Morn (2001) survived a protest from Rose Archway.
Miss Finland (2007) is the only Golden Slipper winner to also win the Storm Queen Stakes.

ATC Doncaster Handicap (1600m)—Randwick

Of $3,000,000. Group 1. Handicap, Minimum Weight 49kg, 3YO&Up. April 6, 2019.

2017-18 RESULT: Time: 1:33.17 (Good 4)

FP	NO	HORSE	TRAINER	JOCKEY	MARGIN	BAR.	WGT	SP
1	3	HAPPY CLAPPER	Patrick Webster	Blake Shinn		1	57kg	$5
2	10	COMIN' THROUGH	Chris Waller	Tim Clark	2L	7	51.5kg	$19
3	13	ARBEITSAM	Gai Waterhouse & Adrian Bott	Michael Dee	2.2L	10	51kg	$26
4	16	D'ARGENTO	Chris Waller	Andrew Adkins	2.5L	15	51kg	$8.50
5	8	TOM MELBOURNE	Chris Waller	Kerrin McEvoy	2.6L	14	52kg	$15
6	15	COOL CHAP	David & Ben Hayes & Tom Dabernig	Cory Parish	3.1L	6	50kg	$41
7	11	LANCIATO	Mark Newnham	Rachel King (a)	3.6L	13	51kg	$19
8	1	HUMIDOR	Darren Weir	Mark Zahra	3.7L	4	58kg	$13
9	4	ENDLESS DRAMA	Chris Waller	Glyn Schofield	4L	3	53.5kg	$51
10	9	KEMENTARI	James Cummings	Brenton Avdulla	4.1L	2	51.5kg	$3.20f
11	12	EGG TART	Chris Waller	Craig Newitt	4.5L	9	50.5kg	$31
12	6	CRACK ME UP	Bjorn Baker	Jason Collett	4.7L	11	53kg	$21
13	5	PRIZED ICON	Kris Lees	Ben Melham	6.1L	5	53.5kg	$31
14	7	INVINCIBLE GEM	Kris Lees	Michael Walker	6.8L	12	52.5kg	$31
15	2	TOSEN STARDOM	Darren Weir	Craig Williams	7.4L	8	57.5kg	$26
16	14	MISTER SEA WOLF	Chris Waller	Jay Ford	10.2L	16	50kg	$81

PAST WINNERS

YEAR	WINNER	JOCKEY	TRAINER	2ND	3RD	TIME
2018	Happy Clapper	Blake Shinn	Pat Webster	Comin' Through	Arbeitsam	1:33.1
2017	It's Somewhat	Zac Purton	John O'Shea	Happy Clapper	Sense Of Occasion	1:39.1
2016	Winx	Hugh Bowman	Chris Waller	Happy Clapper	Azkadellia	1:35.2
2015	Kermadec	Glen Boss	Chris Waller	Real Impact	Royal Descent	1:37.6
2014	Sacred Falls	Zac Purton	Chris Waller	Royal Descent	Weary	1:39.5
2013	Sacred Falls	Tommy Berry	Chris Waller	Pierro	Norzita	1:37.9
2012	More Joyous	Nash Rawiller	Gai Waterhouse	Shoot Out	Yosei	1:35.5
2011	Sacred Choice	Tim Clark	Joseph Pride	Love Conquers All	Bold Glance	1:39.4
2010	Rangirangdoo	Nash Rawiller	Chris Waller	Road To Rock	Brilliant Light	1:34.2
2009	Vision And Power	Jim Cassidy	Joseph Pride	Black Piranha	Whobegotyou	1:36.6
2008	Triple Honour	Glen Boss	Chris Waller	Casino Prince	Pinnacles	1:38.6
2007	Haradasun	Glen Boss	Tony Vasil	Mentality	Divine Madonna	1:38.0
2006	Racing To Win	Glen Boss	John O'Shea	Johan's Toy	Bentley Biscuit	1:34.1
2005	Patezza	Danny Nikolic	Guy Walter	Court's In Session	Danni Martine	1:35.9
2004	Private Steer	Glen Boss	John O'Shea	Grand Armee	Ambulance	1:35.5
2003	Grand Armee	Danny Beasley	Gai Waterhouse	Dash For Cash	Boreale	1:36.8
2002	Sunline	Greg Childs	Trevor Mckee	Shogun Lodge	Defier	1:35.2
2001	Assertive Lad	Chris Munce	Gai Waterhouse	Shogun Lodge	Weasel Will	1:35.9
2000	Over	Darren Gauci	John Hawkes	Sunline	Zastov	1:35.0
1999	Sunline	Larry Cassidy	Trevor Mckee	Lease	Juggler	1:36.4
1998	Catalan Opening	Len Beasley	Bart Cummings	Juggler	Iron Horse	1:38.0
1997	Secret Savings	Larry Cassidy	Gai Waterhouse	All Our Mob	Ravarda	1:35.5

BACKGROUND

First run: 1866 (won by Dundee). Group 1 since 1980. Run over 1800m 1879-83. Run at Rosehill in 1942 (1700m).
Multiple winners: 9—Sacred Falls (2014, 2013); Sunline (2002, 1999); Pharaoh (1995, 1994); Super Impose (1991, 1990); Fine And Dandy (1963, 1961); Tudor Hill (1960, 1959); Slogan II (1957, 1956); Blue Legend (1947, 1946); Mildura (1941, 1940).
Fillies & Mares to win: 34—Winx (2016); More Joyous (2012); Private Steer (2004); Sunline (2002, 1999); Skating (1993); Magic Flute (1987); Emancipation (1983); My Gold Hope (1982); Maybe Mahal (1978); Analie (1973); Citius (1966); Hamurah (1938); Sarcherie (1937); Cuddle (1936); Venetian Lady (1930); Valicare (1926); Julia Grey (1922); Sydney Damsel (1920); Hem (1919); Dame Acre (1918); Wedding Day (1917); Lochano (1912); Istria (1907); Rose Petal (1903); Wakeful (1901); Parapet (1900); Crossfire (1886); Stella (1882); Briseis (1876); Myrtle (1874); Vixen (1872); Barbelle (1870); Casino (1868).

3YOs to win: 31—Kermadec (2015); Sacred Falls (2013); Haradasun (2007); Racing To Win (2006); Assertive Lad (2001); Over (2000); *Sunline (1999); *Skating (1993); Merimbula Bay (1989); Lygon Arms (1988); *Magic Flute (1987); Hula Chief (1986); Vite Cheval (1984); *Emancipation (1983); Tontonan (1974); *Analie (1973); *Citius (1966); Bernbrook (1949); Blue Legend (1946); Jacko (1932); *Valicare (1926); Garlin (1915); Hyman (1909); Chere Amie (1904); *Rose Petal (1903); Sir Foote (1902); Paris (1891); Sir William (1890); Queensland (1880); Wanderer (1873); *Vixen (1872). *3YO fillies

2YOs to win: 2—Crossfire (1886); Briseis (1876). Note: Both 2YO winners are fillies.

Fastest time (1600m, Randwick): Happy Clapper (2018) 1:33:17.

Doncaster winners also won the lead-up races:
Expressway Stakes: 1—Rangirangdoo (2010).
Southern Cross Stakes: 2—Secret Savings (1992); Gunsynd (1972).
NJC Newmarket Handicap: 1—Secret Savings (1997).
Chipping Norton Stakes: 3—Winx (2016); Pharaoh (1995); Super Impose (1991).
Canterbury Stakes: 3—Happy Clapper (2018); Sprint By (1996); Emancipation (1983).
Ajax Stakes: 4—It's Somewhat (2017); Grand Armee (2003); Vite Cheval (1984); Tontonan (1974).
VRC Newmarket Handicap: 4—Maybe Mahal (1978); Mildura (1941); Sir Foote (1902); Wakeful (1901).
Ranvet Stakes: 3—Super Impose (1991); Time And Tide (1965); Whittier (1924).
Coolmore Classic: 2—Sunline (2002); Skating (1993).
George Ryder Stakes: 7—Winx (2016); Vision And Power (2009); Haradasun (2007); Racing To Win (2006); Emancipation (1983); Dalrello (1975); Dame Acre (1918).
Queen Of The Turf Stakes: 1—More Joyous (2012).

Doncaster winners went on to win in same preparation:
All Aged Stakes: 14—Private Steer (2004); Sunline (2002); My Gold Hope (1982); Belmura Lad (1979); Tontonan (1974); Broker's Tip (1970); Unpainted (1968); Cuddle (1936); Chatham (1934); Winooka (1933); Sir Christopher (1931); Valicare (1926); Speciality (1921); Cremorne (1893).
Queen Elizabeth Stakes: 1—More Joyous (2012). Note: Sacred Falls (2014), Sacred Choice (2011), Haradasun (2007) and Gunsynd (1972) won the Doncaster Handicap and finished second in the Queen Elizabeth Stakes.
Doomben 10,000: 1—Hamurah (1938).
Stradbroke Hcp: 1—Karendi (1954).

The "big mile" double:
Epsom Handicap & Doncaster Handicap: 7—Happy Clapper (Doncaster 2018); Winx (2016); Super Impose (1991); Gunsynd (1972); Chatham (1934); Marvel (1882); Dundee (1866).
Doncaster & Epsom Handicap (same year): 4—Racing To Win (2006); Super Impose (1990, 1991); Hyman (1909).

Melbourne spring feature mile winners to win Doncaster same season:
Cantala Stakes: 2—Catalan Opening (Doncaster 1997); Gunsynd (1972).
Myer Classic: 1—Sacred Choice (Doncaster 2011).
Toorak Handicap: 1—Gunsynd (Doncaster 1972).

Leading winning jockeys:
6 wins Glen Boss (Kermadec 2015, Triple Honour 2008, Haradasun 2007, Racing To Win 2006, Private Steer 2004, Sprint By 1996).
4 wins Jack Thompson (Te Poi 1962, Slogan II 1957, 1956, Oversight 1951); Jack Toohey (Karuma 1929, The Epicure 1923, Julia Grey 1922, Specialty 1921).

Current winning jockeys:
6 wins Glen Boss (Kermadec 2015, Triple Honour 2008, Haradasun 2007, Racing To Win 2006, Private Steer 2004, Sprint By 1996).
2 wins Larry Cassidy (Sunline 1999, Secret Savings 1997); Zac Purton (It's Somewhat 2017, Sacred Falls 2014); Nash Rawiller (More Joyous 2012, Rangirangdoo 2010).
1 win Tommy Berry (Sacred Falls 2013); Hugh Bowman (Winx 2016); Tim Clark (Sacred Choice 2011); Grant Cooksley (Skating 1993); Blake Shinn (Happy Clapper 2018).

Leading winning trainers:
7 wins Tommy Smith (Lygon Arms 1988, Iko 1980, Authentic Heir 1976, Analie 1973, Gunsynd 1972, Bye Bye 1969, Unpainted 1968); Gai Waterhouse (More Joyous 2012, Grand Armee 2003, Assertive Lad 2001, Secret Savings 1997, Sprint By 1996, Pharaoh 1995, 1994).
6 wins Chris Waller (Winx 2016, Kermadec 2015, Sacred Falls 2014, 2013, Rangirangdoo 2010, Triple Honour 2008).
5 wins Bart Cummings (Catalan Opening 1998, Hula Chief 1986, Maybe Mahal 1978, Just Ideal 1977, Tontonan 1974).
4 wins Harry Plant (Time And Tide 1965, Fine And Dandy 1963, 1961, Bernbrook 1949); George Price (Mildura 1941, 1940, Gold Rod 1939, Cuddle 1936).

Current winning trainers:
7 wins Gai Waterhouse (More Joyous 2012, Grand Armee 2003, Assertive Lad 2001, Secret Savings 1997, Sprint By 1996, Pharaoh 1995, 1994).
6 wins Chris Waller (Winx 2016; Kermadec 2015, Sacred Falls 2014, 2013, Rangirangdoo 2010, Triple Honour 2008).
3 wins John O'Shea (It's Somewhat 2017, Racing To Win 2006, Private Steer 2004).
2 wins Lee Freedman (Super Impose 1991, 1990); Joe Pride (Sacred Choice 2011, Vision And Power 2009).
1 win Les Bridge (Row Of Waves 1985); John Hawkes (Over 2000); Barbara Joseph (Merimbula Bay 1989); Graeme Rogerson (Skating 1993); Pat Webster (Happy Clapper 2018); Tony Vasil (Haradasun 2007).

Points of interest:
The late Tommy Smith and his daughter Gai Waterhouse have each won the Doncaster a record seven times.
Before Super Impose (as a 5YO gelding) won his first Doncaster Handicap in 1990, 3YOs won the famous handicap in eight consecutive years.
In 1869, Falcon (Charley Stanley) finished first and Circassian (Brickwood "Brickie" Colley) finished third, but both horses were disqualified after it was found their jockeys were fighting during the race. The race was awarded to runner-up Tippler.
The heaviest weight carried to win: Chatham (1934) and Marvel (1892) 65.5kg. Since 1940—Gunsynd (1972) 60.5kg; Tobin Bronze (1967) and Super Impose (1991) 59.5kg.
Cuddle's 59kg in 1936 is the heaviest weight carried by a mare, followed by Sunline (58kg in 2002) and Maybe Mahal (57kg 1978).
Dead-heat: Only one, between Sir William and Lottery in 1877.
Imported mare Tarien, 7/4 favourite, trained by Tommy Smith and ridden by George Moore, won in 1953, but was later disqualified due to a positive swab. The race was awarded to Triclinium.
Belmura Lad (1979) held the race record of 1:33:70 until broken by Happy Clapper (2018), who ran 1:33.17.

ATC TJ Smith Stakes (1200m)—Randwick

Of $2,500,000. Group 1. Weight For Age. April 6, 2019.

2017-18 RESULT: Time: 1:08.29 (Good 4)

FP	NO	HORSE	TRAINER	JOCKEY	MARGIN	BAR.	WGT	SP
1	12	TRAPEZE ARTIST	Gerald Ryan	Tye Angland		8	56.5KG	$8
2	1	REDZEL	Peter & Paul Snowden	Kerrin McEvoy	2L	6	58.5kg	$2.30f
3	8	IN HER TIME	Benjamin Smith	Damian Lane	4L	3	56.5kg	$4.40
4	2	LE ROMAIN	Kris Lees	Glyn Schofield	4.7L	10	58.5kg	$41
5	14	THE MISSION	Paul Perry	Zac Purton	5.2L	5	56.5kg	$151
6	9	ENGLISH	Gai Waterhouse & Adrian Bott	Sam Clipperton	5.7L	11	56.5kg	$15
7	3	BRAVE SMASH	Darren Weir	Craig Williams	6.7L	2	58.5kg	$6.50
8	7	FELL SWOOP	Matthew Dale	Jay Ford	8.4L	4	58.5kg	$101
9	10	GLOBAL GLAMOUR	Gai Waterhouse & Adrian Bott	Tim Clark	9.1L	9	56.5kg	$15
10	5	TAKEDOWN	Gary Moore	Blake Shinn	9.8L	1	58.5kg	$101
11	4	JUNGLE EDGE	Mick Bell	Kevin Forrester	10.7L	7	58.5kg	$91

PAST WINNERS

YEAR	WINNER	JOCKEY	TRAINER	2ND	3RD	TIME
2018	Trapeze Artist	Tye Angland	Gerald Shinn	Redzel	In Her Time	1:08.2
2017	Chautauqua	Tommy Berry	Michael, Wayne & John Hawkes	English	Fell Swoop	1:12.4
2016	Chautauqua	Tommy Berry	Michael, Wayne & John Hawkes	Fell Swoop	English	1:10.1
2015	Chautauqua	Tommy Berry	Michael, Wayne & John Hawkes	Lord Of The Sky	Terravista	1:11.0
2014	Lankan Rupee	Craig Newitt	Mick Price	Rebel Dane	Buffering	1:12.1
2013	Black Caviar	Luke Nolen	Peter Moody	Epaulette	Bel Sprinter	1:09.6
2012	Master Of Design	Craig Williams	David Payne	Rain Affair	Hallowed Belle	1:08.8
2011	Black Caviar	Luke Nolen	Peter Moody	Hay List	Triple Honour	1:08.7
2010	Melito	Blake Shinn	Gerald Ryan	Hot Danish	Mic Mac	1:09.2
2009	Takeover Target	Nash Rawiller	Joe Janiak	Northern Meteor	Apache Cat	1:09.0
2008	Apache Cat	Corey Brown	Greg Eurell	Reigning To Win	Takeover Target	1:11.8
2007	Bentley Biscuit	Nash Rawiller	Gai Waterhouse	Black Ink	Virage De Fortune	1:10.6
2006	Red Oog	Hugh Bowman	Joseph Pride	Glamour Puss	Snitzel	1:09.8
2005	Shamekha	Darren Beadman	Gai Waterhouse	Fastnet Rock	Only Words	1:12.1
2004	Dilly Dally	Kerrin McEvoy	Leon Macdonald	Legally Bay	Mistegic	1:09.9
2003	Spinning Hill	Danny Beasley	Guy Walter	Yell	Bel Esprit	1:10.7
2002	Phoenix Park	Brian York	Gai Waterhouse	Fair Embrace	Spinning Hill	1:10.3
2001	Century Kid	Len Beasley	Graeme Rogerson	Spinning Hill	Falvelon	1:09.8
2000	Shy Hero	Jackson Morris	Patrick Webster	Easy Rocking	High Rolling	1:39.3
1999	Ab Initio	Larry Cassidy	Patrick Webster	Padstow	Life Of Riley	1:10.7
1998	La Baraka	Kevin Moses	Peter C Hayes	Masked Party	Coogee Walk	1:11.6
1997	Mahogany	Greg Hall	Lee Freedman	Ruffles	Clang	1:09.1

BACKGROUND

First run: 1997 (won by Mahogany). Listed in 1997; Group 3 1998-2001; Group 2 2002-04; Group 1 from 2005. Previously known as the Endeavour Stakes in 1997 and 1998.
Mares to win: 4—Black Caviar (2013, 2011); Shamekha (2005); Spinning Hill (2003).
Most recent 3YO to win: C&G—Trapeze Artist (2018); Filly—Melito (2010). Note: Dilly Dally (filly 2004), Century Kid (2001, gelding), Shy Hero (2000, gelding) and La Baraka (filly 1998) are the only other 3YOs to win.
Multiple winners: 2—Chautauqua (2017, 2016, 2015); Black Caviar (2013, 2011).
Fastest time (1200m): Trapeze Artist (2018) 1:08.29.
Notable winners: Trapeze Artist (2018); Chautauqua (2017, 2016, 2015); Lankan Rupee (2014); Black Caviar (2013, 2011); Takeover Target (2009); Apache Cat (2008); Mahogany (1997); Bentley Biscuit (2007); Spinning Hill (2003); Shamekha (2005).

T J Smith Stakes winners won the key lead-up races:
Expressway Stakes: 1—Trapeze Artist (2018).
Challenge Stakes: None.
Canterbury Stakes: None.
Lightning Stakes: 5—Chautauqua (2016); Black Caviar (2013, 2011); Apache Cat (2008); Mahogany (1997).
William Reid Stakes: 3—Black Caviar (2013, 2011); Apache Cat (2008).
Oakleigh Plate: 1—Lankan Rupee (2014).
Newmarket Handicap: 2—Lankan Rupee (2014); Black Caviar (2011).
The Galaxy: 1—La Baraka (1998).

T J Smith winners went on to win in the same preparation.
All Aged Stakes: 3—Trapeze Artist (2018); Bentley Biscuit (2007); Shamekha (2005).
BTC Cup: 3—Black Caviar (2011); Apache Cat (2008); Bentley Biscuit (2007).
Doomben 10,000: 1—Apache Cat (2008). Note: Red Oog (2006) won the Doomben 10,000 in 2005.

Leading winning jockeys:
3 wins Tommy Berry (Chautauqua 2017, 2016, 2015).
2 wins Luke Nolen (Black Caviar 2013, 2011); Nash Rawiller (Takeover Target 2009, Bentley Biscuit 2007).

Current winning jockeys:
3 wins Tommy Berry (Chautauqua 2017, 2016, 2015).
2 wins Luke Nolen (Black Caviar 2013, 2011); Nash Rawiller (Takeover Target 2009, Bentley Biscuit 2007).
1 win Tye Angland (Trapeze Artist 2018); Hugh Bowman (Red Oog 2006); Corey Brown (Apache Cat 2008); Larry Cassidy (Ab Initio 1999); Jackson Morris (Shy Hero 2000); Kerrin McEvoy (Dilly Dally 2004); Craig Newitt (Lankan Rupee 2014); Blake Shinn (Melito 2010); Craig Williams (Master Of Design 2012).

Leading winning trainer:
3 wins Michael, Wayne & John Hawkes (Chautauqua 2017, 2016, 2015); Gai Waterhouse (Bentley Biscuit 2007, Shamekha 2005, Phoenix Park 2002).

Current leading trainers:
3 wins Michael, Wayne & John Hawkes (Chautauqua 2017, 2016, 2015); Gai Waterhouse (Bentley Biscuit 2007, Shamekha 2005, Phoenix Park 2002).
2 wins Peter Moody (Black Caviar 2013, 2011); Gerald Ryan (Trapeze Artist 2018, Melito 2010); Pat Webster (Shy Hero 2000, Ab Initio 1999).
1 win Greg Eurell (Apache Cat 2008); Lee Freedman (Mahogany 1997); Joe Janiak (Takeover Target 2009); Leon Macdonald (Dilly Dally 2004); David Payne (Master Of Design 2012); Mick Price (Lankan Rupee 2014); Joe Pride (Red Oog 2006); Graeme Rogerson (Century Kid 2001).

Point of interest:
The race is named after the legendary trainer Tommy Smith, who trained at Randwick. His daughter, Gai Waterhouse, has trained three winners of the T.J. Smith Stakes.

ATC Australian Derby (2400m)—Randwick
Of $2,000,000. Group 1. Set Weights, 3YO. April 6, 2019.

2017-18 RESULT: Time: 2:28.73   (Good 4)

FP	NO	HORSE	TRAINER	JOCKEY	MARGIN	BAR.	WGT	SP
1	6	LEVENDI	Peter Gelagotis	Mark Zahra		3	56.5kg	$6
2	1	ACE HIGH	David Payne	Tye Angland	0.1L	2	56.5kg	$5ef
3	3	TANGLED	Chris Waller	Michael Walker	5.9L	9	56.5kg	$26
4	2	VIN DE DANCE	Murray Baker & Andrew Forsman	Jason Waddell	6.5L	4	56.5kg	$9
5	16	MAIN STAGE	Trent Busuttin & Natalie Young	Blake Shinn	6.8L	10	56.5kg	$26
6	8	FURORE	Kris Lees	Brenton Avdulla	8.3L	7	56.5kg	$5ef
7	4	MONGOLIAN CONQUEROR	Stephen Autridge & Jamie Richards	Opie Bosson	8.7L	6	56.5kg	$12
8	15	MONGOLIAN MARSHAL	Murray Baker & Andrew Forsman	Craig Williams	9.6L	18	56.5kg	$51
9	10	WEATHER WITH YOU	Murray Baker & Andrew Forsman	Jason Collett	10.3L	1	56.5kg	$21
10	17	CONDOR	Paul Perry	Craig Newitt	10.6L	13	56.5kg	$151
11	13	ENDOWMENT	Chris Gibbs	Damien Oliver	14.4L	14	56.5kg	$71
12	14	BELFAST	Trent Busuttin & Natalie Young	Kerrin McEvoy	15.3L	15	56.5kg	$14
13	12	MISSION HILL	Murray Baker & Andrew Forsman	Damian Lane	15.6L	8	56.5kg	$12
14	5	CAPITAL GAIN	Paul Butterworth	Ben Melham	22.3L	12	56.5kg	$101
15	9	SALSAMOR	Trent Busuttin & Natalie Young	Zac Purton	23.3L	17	56.5kg	$21
16	18	PISSARO	Robbie Laing	Sam Clipperton	30.3L	11	56.5kg	$301
17	7	ASTORIA	James Cummings	Glyn Schofield	35.8L	5	56.5kg	$21
18	11	THE LORD MAYOR	Chris Waller	Corey Brown	99L	16	56.5kg	$101

PAST WINNERS

YEAR	WINNER	JOCKEY	TRAINER	2ND	3RD	TIME
2018	Levendi	Mark Zahra	Peter Gelagotis	Ace High	Tangled	2:28.7
2017	Jon Snow	Damian Lane	Murray Baker & Andrew Forsman	Harper's Choice	Hardham	2:38.1
2016	Tavago	Tommy Berry	Trent Busuttin & Natalie Young	Jameka	Tally	2:33.6
2015	Mongolian Khan	Opie Bosson	Murray Baker	Hauraki	Volkstok'n'barrell	2:37.1
2014	Criterion	Hugh Bowman	David Payne	Tupac Amaru	Hooked	2:38.4
2013	It's A Dundeel	James McDonald	Murray Baker	Philippi	Kingdoms	2:33.4
2012	Ethiopia	Rhys McLeod	Pat Carey	Polish Knight	Laser Hawk	2:28.7
2011	Shamrocker	Glen Boss	Danny O'Brien	Retrieve	Anacheeva	2:29.4
2010	Shoot Out	Stathi Katsidis	John Wallace	Descarado	Monaco Consul	2:32.6
2009	Roman Emperor	Jim Cassidy	Bart Cummings	Harris Tweed	Predatory Pricer	2:31.0
2008	Nom De Jeu	Jeff Lloyd	Murray Baker	Red Ruler	Littorio	2:36.2
2007	Flumicino	Darren Beadman	John Hawkes	Ambitious General	Tuesday Joy	2:36.4
2006	Headturner	Darren Beadman	John Hawkes	De Beers	Testafiable	2:29.9
2005	Eremein	Corey Brown	Allan Denham	Stella Grande	Railings	2:35.8
2004	Starcraft	Glen Boss	Garry Newham	Braeloch	Delzao	2:34.8
2003	Clangalang	Scott Seamer	Gerald Ryan	Strasbourg	Mummify	2:32.3
2002	Don Eduardo	Damien Oliver	Lee Freedman	Carnegie Express	Pentastic	2:32.7
2001	Universal Prince	Justin Sheehan	Bede Murray	Sir Clive	Danamite	2:30.8
2000	Fairway	Brian York	Jack Denham	Shogun Lodge	Now Voyager	2:34.0
1999	Sky Heights	Glen Boss	Colin Alderson	Arena	Grand Archway	2:32.6
1998	Gold Guru	Greg Childs	Leon Macdonald	Tie The Knot	Northern Drake	2:38.4
1997	Ebony Grosve	Shane Dye	Graeme Rogerson	Danendri	Intergaze	2:28.8

BACKGROUND

First run: 1861 (won by Kyogle). Group 1 since 1979. Not run in 1978, when moved from the spring to the autumn of 1979 and won by Dulcify.

Fastest Time (2400m): Octagonal (1996) 2:28.41
Fillies To Win: 9—Shamrocker (2011); Research (1989); Tristarc (1985); Rose Of Kingston (1982); Tea Rose (1944); Picture (1898); Nellie (1879); Florence (1870); Clove (1865).
Australian Derby winners won in the previous spring during same season (since Derby moved to autumn in 1979):
Spring Champion Stakes: 5—It's A Dundeel (Derby 2013) Universal Prince (2001); Fairway (2000); Beau Zam (1988); Kingston Town (1979).
Victoria Derby: 2—Mahogany (Australian Derby 1994); Dulcify (1979). Note: 34 3YOs won the AJC Derby & Victoria Derby double before 1979, when the both Derbys were held in the spring.
Cox Plate: 1—Octagonal (1995-96 season).
Australian Derby winners won the lead-up races:
Autumn Classic: 4—Don Eduardo (2002); Gold Guru (1998); Myocard (1987); Double Century (1979).
Alister Clark Stakes: 2—Naturalism (1992); Durbridge (1991).
Manfred Stakes: 1—Don Eduardo (2002).
Australian Guineas: 3—Shamrocker (2011); Gold Guru (1998); Mahogany (1994).
Storm Queen Stakes: 1—Research (1989).
Chipping Norton Stakes: 5—Starcraft (2004); Dr. Grace (1990); Tulloch* (Derby 1957, Norton 1958); Carbon Copy* (Derby 1957; Norton 1958); Phar Lap* (Derby 1929, Norton 1930). *Derby run in the spring.
Randwick Guineas: 13—It's A Dundeel (2013); Shoot Out (2010); Universal Prince (2001); Fairway (2000); Octagonal (1996); Belmura Lad (1977); Imagele (1973); Summer Fiesta (1963); Summer Prince (1962); Persian Lyric (1960); Martello Towers (1959); Prince Morvi (1953); Moorland (1943). Note: 1600m from 2006, and previously raced as the Canterbury Guineas (1900m).
Rosehill Guineas: 20—Criterion (2014); It's A Dundeel (2013); Eremein (2005); Sky Heights (1999); Octagonal (1996); Naturalism (1992); Strawberry Road (1983); Kingston Town (1980); Dulcify (1979); Battle Sign (1975); Taras Bulba (1974); Imagele (1973); Martello Towers (1959); Tulloch (1957); Caranna (1955); Tea Rose (1944); Moorland (1943); Laureate (1941); Phar Lap (1929); Biplane (1917).
Tulloch Stakes: 7—Levendi (2018); Jon Snow (2017); Starcraft (2004); Ivory's Irish (1995); Mahogany (1994); Durbridge (1991); Prolific (1984).
Ranvet Stakes (since 1979): 2—Gold Guru (1998); Beau Zam (1988).
The BMW: 5—Octagonal (1996); Beau Zam (1988); Myocard (1987); Bonecrusher (1986); Kingston Town (1980).
New Zealand Derby: 4—Mongolian Khan (2015); Bonecrusher (1986); Ballymena (1923); Gloaming (1918).
"Autumn Triple Crown" Randwick Guineas, Rosehill Guineas & Australian Derby: 5—It's A Dundeel (2013); Octagonal (1996); Imagele (1973); Martello Towers (1959); Moorland (1943). Note: It's A Dundeel (2013) is the only winner of the three races since the Randwick Guineas (1600m) replaced the Canterbury Guineas (1900m) in 2006.
Australian Derby winners went on to win that season:
Australian Oaks: 1—Research (1989).
Sydney Cup (since 1979): 2—Our Paddy Boy (1981); Kingston Town (1980).
The BMW & Sydney Cup: 1—Kingston Town (1980).
BRC Grand Prix: 1—Kingston Town (1980).
Queensland Derby: 5—Strawberry Road (1983); Kingston Town (1980); Silver Sharpe (1970); Persian Lyric (1960); Tulloch (1957).
Australian Derby winners won as spring 4YOs:
Cox Plate: 5—Bonecrusher (1986); Strawberry Road (1983); Kingston Town (1980); Dulcify (1979); Phar Lap (1930).
Caulfield Cup: 4—Mongolian Khan (2015); Sky Heights (1999); Manfred (1925); Poseidon (1907).
The most recent Australian Derby winner to win the Melbourne Cup as a 4YO: Phar Lap (1930)
The most recent Australian Derby winner to win a Melbourne Cup as a 3YO: Hall Mark (1933).
Leading winning jockeys:
6 wins Tom Hales (Abercorn 1887, Trident 1886, Bargo 1884, Navigator 1882, Grand Flaneur 1880, Richmond 1875).
5 wins George Moore (Classic Mission 1971, Summer Fiesta 1963, Summer Prince 1962, Tulloch 1957, Playboy 1949); Darby Munro (Main Topic 1942, Reading 1939, Nuffield 1938, Allunga 1934, Hall Mark 1933).
4 wins Ernest Huxley (Bob Ray 1895, Camoola 1892, Stromboli 1891, Singapore 1889); Bobby Lewis (Trivalve 1927, Sylvanite 1904, Hautvilliers 1901, Malster 1900); Maurice McCarten (Laureate 1941, Theo 1934, Ammon Ra 1931, Ballymena 1923).
Current winning jockeys:
3 wins Glen Boss (Shamrocker 2011, Starcraft 2004, Sky Heights 1999).
1 win Tommy Berry (Tavago 2016); Opie Bosson (Mongolian Khan 2015); Hugh Bowman (Criterion 2014); Corey Brown (Eremein 2005); Larry Cassidy (Ivory's Irish 1995); Damian Lane (Jon Snow 2017); Jeff Lloyd (Nom Du Jeu 2008); James McDonald (It's A Dundeel 2013); Rhys McLeod (Ethiopia 2012); Damien Oliver (Don Eduardo 2002); Mark Zahra (Levendi 2018).

Leading winning trainers:
9 wins Tommy Smith (Kingston Town 1980, Great Lover 1976, Imagele 1973, Silver Sharpe 1970, Prince Grant 1965, Summer Fiesta 1963, Summer Prince 1962, Tulloch 1957, Playboy 1949).
5 wins Bart Cummings (Roman Emperor 2009, Ivory's Irish 1995, Beau Zam 1988, Prolific 1984, Belmura Lad 1977); Tom Payten (Cider 1912, Camoola 1892, Stromboli 1891, Singapore 1889, Abercorn 1887)
4 wins Murray Baker (Jon Snow 2017, Mongolian Khan 2015, It's A Dundeel 2013, Nom Du Jeu 2008); Tom Lamond (Charge 1896, Wheatear 1881, Nellie 1879, Kingsborough 1874); Dick Mason (Cupidon 1921, Gloaming 1918, Biplane 1917, Noctuiform 1905); Frank McGrath (Pandect 1940, Peter Pan 1932, Tanami 1910, Prince Foote 1909); James Scobie (Trivalve 1927, Sylvanite 1904, Hautvilliers 1901, Maltster 1900); John Tait (Florence 1870, Fireworks 1867, The Bart 1866, Clove 1865).

Current winning trainers:
4 wins Murray Baker (Jon Snow 2017, Mongolian Khan 2015, It's A Dundeel 2013, Nom Du Jeu 2008).
3 wins Lee Freedman (Don Eduardo 2000, Mahogany 1994, Naturalism 1992); John Hawkes (Fiumicino 2007, Headturner 2006, Octagonal 1996).
1 win Murray Baker & Andrew Forsman (Jon Snow 2017); Trent Busuttin & Natalie Young (Tavago 2016); Pat Carey (Ethiopia 2012); Clarry Conners (Research 1989); Allan Denham (Eremein 2005); Peter Gelagotis (Levendi 2018); Leon Macdonald (Gold Guru 1998); Danny O'Brien (Shamrocker 2011); David Payne (Criterion 2014); Frank Ritchie (Bonecrusher 1986); Graeme Rogerson (Ebony Grosve 1997); Gerald Ryan (Clangalang 2003); John Wallace (Shoot Out 2010).

Points of interest:
Australia's and New Zealand's highest-priced yearling at the time, Don Eduardo ($NZ3.6 million, Karaka 2000), won the Australian Derby in 2002. His dam, Diamond Lover, is a half-sister to Octagonal, who won the Derby in 1996.
In 1979, Dulcify won the race on protest from Double Century.
In 1961, Blue Era (Mel Schumacher) was first past the post, but lost on protest to Summer Fair (Tom Hill) after it was discovered Schumacher pulled Hills' leg near the finish.
Maurice McCarten rode four Derby winners (Laureate 1941, Theo 1934, Ammon Ra 1931, Ballymena 1923) and trained Deep River to win in 1952. Tom Brown rode two winners (Loup Garou 1872 and Benvolio 1873) and trained Grand Flaneur to win in 1880.
When the filly Clove won in 1865 there were only 38 nominations for the Derby, 10 horses contested the race. By 1928, 614 horses nominated for the race won by Prince Humphrey.
Murray Baker (Jon Snow 2017 in partnership with Andrew Forsman) trained his 20th Group 1 winner in Australia, breaking the record of 19 for a New Zealand-based trainer in Australia, held by John Wheeler.

ATC Sires' Produce Stakes (1400m)—Randwick

Of $1,000,000. Group 1. Set Weights, 2YO. April 6, 2019.

2017-18 RESULT: Time: 1:22.10 (Good 4)

FP	NO	HORSE	TRAINER	JOCKEY	MARGIN	BAR.	WGT	SP
1	15	EL DORADO DREAMING	Benjamin Smith	Damian Lane		12	54.5kg	$81
2	13	OOHOOD	Tony McEvoy	Zac Purton	0.1L	8	54.5kg	$3.20f
3	8	OUTRAGEOUS	Michael, Wayne & John Hawkes	Brenton Avdulla	1.1L	10	56.5kg	$61
4	2	LONG LEAF	David & Ben Hayes & Tom Dabernig	Kerrin McEvoy	1.4L	2	56.5kg	$10
5	4	SPIN	Peter & Paul Snowden	Tim Clark	1.7L	7	56.5kg	$19
6	1	ENCRYPTION	James Cummings	Glyn Schofield	1.8L	13	56.5kg	$21
7	5	BONDI	Peter & Paul Snowden	Mark Zahra	1.9L	14	56.5kg	$9
8	9	RAGGED RASCAL	Paul Perry	Joshua Parr	2.9L	6	56.5kg	$101
9	14	SEABROOK	Mick Price	Damien Oliver	3L	1	54.5kg	$5
10	3	NOT A SINGLE CENT	Ciaron Maher	Blake Shinn	3.1L	15	56.5kg	$16
11	6	SEBERATE	David & Ben Hayes & Tom Dabernig	Jason Collett	3.4L	3	56.5kg	$20
12	7	TCHAIKOVSKY	Peter & Paul Snowden	Sam Clipperton	5.3L	5	56.5kg	$6.50
13	10	RINGERDINGDING	Edward O'Rourke	Ben Melham	6L	9	56.5kg	$51
14	11	ADANA	Chris Waller	Michael Walker	6.9L	4	56.5kg	$31
15	12	AFFOGATO	Wendy Roche	Craig Newitt	7.1L	11	56.5kg	$301

PAST WINNERS

YEAR	WINNER	JOCKEY	TRAINER	2ND	3RD	TIME
2018	El Dorado Dreaming	Damian Lane	Benjamin Smith	Oohood	Outrageous	1:22.1
2017	Invader	Hugh Bowman	Peter & Paul Snowden	Summer Passage	Whispered Secret	1:26.1
2016	Yankee Rose	Zac Purton	David Vandyke	Telperion	Faraway Town	1:24.3
2015	Pride Of Dubai	Hugh Bowman	Peter & Paul Snowden	DH Odyssey Moon/Rageese		1:25.7
2014	Peggy Jean	Nash Rawiller	Gerald Ryan	Scratch Me Lucky	Cornrow	1:27.6
2013	Guelph	Kerrin McEvoy	Peter Snowden	Scandiva	Overreach	1:23.2
2012	Pierro	Nash Rawiller	Gai Waterhouse	All Too Hard	Limes	1:21.4
2011	Helmet	Kerrin McEvoy	Peter Snowden	Uate	Pane In The Glass	1:24.0
2010	Yosei	Michelle Payne	Stuart Webb	Skilled	Hinchinbrook	1:23.5
2009	Manhattan Rain	Nash Rawiller	Gai Waterhouse	Tickets	Rostova	1:23.5
2008	Sebring	Blake Shinn	Gai Waterhouse	Samantha Miss	Love And Kisses	1:25.9
2007	Camarilla	Darren Beadman	John Hawkes	Meurice	Sashenka	1:25.1
2006	Excites	Zac Purton	Guy Walter	Down The Wicket	My Middi	1:23.9
2005	Fashions Afield	Danny Beasley	Gai Waterhouse	Mnemosyne	Johnny	1:26.1
2004	Dance Hero	Glen Boss	Gai Waterhouse	Wager	Fastnet Rock	1:23.1
2003	Hasna	Len Beasley	Gai Waterhouse	Bushland	Al Jameel	1:24.7
2002	Victory Vein	Danny Beasley	Bede Murray	Choisir	Planchet	1:23.5
2001	Viscount	Rod Quinn	John Hawkes	Royal Courtship	Ha Ha	1:27.3
2000	Assertive Lad	Shane Dye	Gai Waterhouse	Reenact	Surfboard	1:25.6
1999	Align	Rod Quinn	John Hawkes	Quick Star	Dangerous	1:28.5
1998	Alf	Greg Childs	David O'Sullivan	Mossman	Shovhog	1:24.5
1997	Encounter	Shane Dye	Clarry Conners	Guineas	Adeewin	1:22.4

BACKGROUND

First run: 1867 (won by Glencoe). Group 1 since 1980. Run over 1600m 1867-69; 1200m 1905-08. Held at Rosehill in 1942. Not held 1894-1904.
Most recent filly to win: El Dorado Dreaming (2018). Note: 38 fillies have won the ATC Sires' Produce Stakes.
Fastest time (1400m): Pierro (2012) 1:21.47
Notable winners: Guelph (2013); Pierro (2012); Helmet (2011); Sebring (2008); Dance Hero (2004); Merlene (1996); Burst (1992); Snippets (1987); Luskin Star (1977); Tontonan (1973); Baguette (1970); Eskimo Prince (1964); Wenona Girl (1960); Tulloch (1957); True Course (1950); Shannon (1944); Ajax (1937); Hall Mark (1933); Ammon Ra (1931); Mollison (1928); Furious (1921); Cetigne (1915), Abercorn (1887), Chester (1877), Prince Foote (1909); Malt Queen (1908); Stromboli (1891); Robinson Crusoe (1876), Glencoe (1867).
ATC Sires' Produce winners won the lead-up races:
Magic Millions Gold Coast Classic: 1—Dance Hero (2004).

Silver Slipper Stakes: 7—Pierro (2012); Victory Vein (2002); Sovereign Slipper (1972); Luskin Star (1977); Baguette (1970); Peace Council (1965); Eskimo Prince (1964). Note: the Silver Slipper was switched from the spring to the autumn in 1998.
Breeders' Plate: 14—Pierro (2012); Sebring (2008); Encounter (1996); Luskin Star (1976); Baguette (1970); Peace Council (1965); Eskimo Prince (1964); Young Brolga (1961); Kingster (1955); Lindbergh (1954); Temeraire (1947); Magnificent (1945); Yaralla (1941); Gold Rod (1936).
Blue Diamond Stakes: 1—Pride Of Dubai (2015).
VRC Sires' Produce Stakes: 20—Full On Aces (1981); Desirable (1976); Wenona Girl (1960); Tulloch (1957); Pure Fire (1952); True Course (1950); Nuffield (1938); Gold Rod (1936); Young Idea (1935); Kuvera (1932); Mollison (1928); Royal Feast (1927); Thrice (1917); Beverage (1910); Autonomy (1892); Stromboli (1891); Titan (1890); Abercorn (1887); Warwick (1883); His Lordship (1878).
Skyline Stakes: 3—Manhattan Rain (2009); Dance Hero (2004); Viscount (2001).
Sweet Embrace Stakes: 1—Victory Vein (2002).
Black Opal Stakes: 1—St. Covet (1994).
Todman Stakes: 3—Pierro (2012); Tierce (1991); Luskin Star (1977).
Reisling Stakes: 3—Fashions Afield (2005); Merlene (1996); Burst (1992).
Golden Slipper: 14—Pierro (2012); Sebring (2008); Dance Hero (2004); Merlene (1996); Burst (1992); Tierce (1991); Bounding Away (1986); Full On Aces (1981); Luskin Star (1977); Toy Show (1975); Tontonan (1973); Baguette (1970); Eskimo Prince (1964); Fine And Dandy (1959).

ATC Sires' Produce winners went on to win in same campaign:
Champagne Stakes: 40—Guelph (2013); Pierro (2012); Helmet (2011); Dance Hero (2004); Hasna (2003); Victory Vein (2002); Viscount (2001); Assertive Lad (2000); Encounter (1997); Burst (1992); Tierce (1991); Luskin Star (1977); Baguette (1970); Time And Tide (1963); Bogan Road (1962); Lindbergh (1954); Ocean Bound (1951); True Course (1950); Temeraire (1947); Magnificent (1945); Ajax (1937); Young Idea (1935); Hall Mark (1933); Kuvera (1932); Mollison (1928); Furious (1921); Outlook (1918); Thrice (1917); Malt Queen (1908); Collarit (1906); Uralla (1885); Warwick (1883); Spinningdale (1881); His Lordship (1878); Chester (1877); Robinson Crusoe (1876); Kingsborough (1874); Rose d'Amour (1873); Lecturer (1872); Hamlet (1871).
"2YO Triple Crown" Golden Slipper & ATC Sires' Produce & Champagne Stakes: 6—Pierro (2012); Dance Hero (2005); Burst (1992); Tierce (1991); Luskin Star (1977); Baguette (1970).
BRC Sires' Produce: 4—Luskin Star (1977); Fine And Dandy (1959); Man Of Iron (1958); Tulloch (1957).
BRC T.J. Smith Classic: 2—Zephyr Zip (1979); Luskin Star (1977).

ATC Sires' Produce winners went on to win as 3YOs:
Spring Champion Stakes: 2—Yankee Rose (2016); and Latin Knight (Sires' 1971, Champion 1972) when this race was known as the Australasian Champion Stakes and run in the autumn.
Caulfield Guineas: 14—Helmet (2011); Encounter (1997); St Covet (1994); Luskin Star (1977); Tulloch (1957); Lucrative (1940); Nuffield (1938); Ajax (1937); Young Idea (1935); Ammon Ra (1931); Soorak (1922); Thrice (1917); Autonomy (1892); Rudolph (1889).
Victoria Derby: 12—Tulloch (1957); Magnificent (1945); Lucrative (1940); Reading (1939); Nuffield (1938); Hall Mark (1933); Furious (1921); Wolawa (1912); Beverage (1910); Prince Foote (1909); Trident (1886); Chester (1877).
Australian Derby: 16—Octagonal (1995, Derby 1996); Tulloch (1957); Magnificent (1945); Reading (1939); Nuffield (1938); Hall Mark (1933); Ammon Ra (1931); Cetigne (1915); Prince Foote (1909); Stromboli (1891); Abercorn (1887); Trident (1886); Nellie (1879); His Lordship (1878); Robinson Crusoe (1876); Kingsborough (1874). Note: Octagonal is the only horse to win the Sires' Produce and Derby since the Derby was moved from the spring to the autumn in 1979.

ATC Sires' Produce and the Melbourne Cup:
Melbourne Cup: 4—Hall Mark (1933, Cup 1933); Prince Foote (1909, Cup 1909); Chester (1877, Cup 1877); Glencoe (1867, Cup 1868).

Leading winning jockeys:
6 wins Shane Dye (Assertive Lad 2000, Encounter 1997, Merlene 1996, Burst 1992, Tierce 1991, Rhythmic Charm 1990); George Moore (Baguette 1970, Peace Council 1965, Time And Tide 1963, Man Of Iron 1958, Tulloch 1957, Riptide 1948).

Current winning jockeys:
3 wins Nash Rawiller (Peggy Jean 2014, Pierro 2012, Manhattan Rain 2009).
2 wins Hugh Bowman (Invader 2017, Pride Of Dubai 2015); Grant Cooksley (Octagonal 1995, Tristalove 1993); Kerrin McEvoy (Guelph 2013, Helmet 2011); Zac Purton (Yankee Rose 2016, Excites 2006).
1 win Glen Boss (Dance Hero 2004); Damian Lane (El Dorado Dreaming 2018); Michelle Payne (Yosei 2010); Blake Shinn (Sebring 2008).

Leading winning trainers:
7 wins Gai Waterhouse (Pierro 2012, Manhattan Rain 2009, Sebring 2008, Fashions Afield 2005, Dance Hero 2004, Hasna 2003, Assertive Lad 2000).
6 wins Tommy Smith (Rhythmic Charm 1990; Comely Girl 1988, Toy Show 1975; Black Onyx 1968, Peace Council 1965, Tulloch 1957).

Current winning trainers:
7 wins Gai Waterhouse (Pierro 2012, Manhattan Rain 2009, Sebring 2008, Fashions Afield 2005, Dance Hero 2004, Hasna 2003, Assertive Lad 2000).
4 wins Clarry Conners (Encounter 1997, Burst 1992, Tierce 1991, Victory Prince 1984); John Hawkes (Camarilla 2007, Viscount 2001, Align 1999, Octagonal 1995); Peter Snowden (Invader 2017, Pride Of Dubai 2015, Guelph 2013, Helmet 2011).
2 wins Peter & Paul Snowden (Invader 2017, Pride Of Dubai 2015).
1 win Lee Freedman (Merlene 1996); David Hayes (St. Covet 1994); Gerald Ryan (Peggy Jean 2014); Benjamin Smith (El Dorado Dreaming 2018); David Vandyke (Yankee Rose 2016); Stuart Webb (Yosei 2010).

Points of interest:
Cromis was first past the post in 1953, but was disqualified due to a positive swab, and the race was awarded to Royal Stream.

Kamilaroi and Geraldine dead-heated in 1880.

Owner James White won eight Sires' Produce Stakes, starting with Chester (1877) through to Autonomy (1892). He collected the trophy seven times in eight years between 1885 and 1892. His trainers were Tom Payten (5 wins), Mick Fennelly (2 wins) and Etienne de Mestre (1 win).

The breeding angle:
Guelph (2013) is a daughter of 2007 winner Camarilla.

Octagonal (1995) is the sire of Lonhro, who is the sire of Pierro (2012).

Chester (1877) sired five winners—Uralla (1885), Abercorn (1887), Titan (1890), Stromboli (1891) and Autonomy (1892).

Robinson Crusoe (1876) sired Trident (1886); Hall Mark (1933) sired Hall Stand (1942); Ajax (1937) sired Magnificent (1945); Nuffield (1938) sired Field Boy (1949); Zephyr Zip (1979) sired Diamond Shower (1986); Victory Prince (1984) sired Tierce (1991), who in turn is the sire of Encounter (1997). Snippets (1987) is the sire of Hasna (2003).

The broodmare Sappho produced four winners of the Sires' Produce—Spinningdale (1881), Nellie (1879), Kingsborough (1874) and Lecturer (1872), as well as the brilliant filly Emily, who was runner-up behind His Lordship in 1878.

ATC Queen Elizabeth Stakes (2000m)—Randwick
Of $4,000,000. Group 1. Weight For Age, 3YO&Up. April 13, 2019.

2017-18 RESULT: Time: 2:01.65   (Good 4)

FP	NO	HORSE	TRAINER	JOCKEY	MARGIN	BAR.	WGT	SP
1	9	WINX	Chris Waller	Hugh Bowman		10	57kg	$1.24F
2	2	GAILO CHOP	Darren Weir	Mark Zahra	3.8L	5	59kg	$26
3	1	HAPPY CLAPPER	Patrick Webster	Kerrin McEvoy	4.1L	9	59kg	$11
4	3	HUMIDOR	Darren Weir	Blake Shinn	4.9L	1	59kg	$14
5	7	COMIN' THROUGH	Chris Waller	Michael Walker	5.4L	2	59kg	$51
6	10	CONSENSUS	Stephen McKee	Jason Collett	8L	3	57kg	$201
7	8	ODEON	Mathew Ellerton & Simon Zahra	Damian Lane	10.4L	6	59kg	$101
8	4	AMBITIOUS	Anthony Freedman	Craig Williams	12.2L	7	59kg	$31
9	6	CLASSIC UNIFORM	Gary Moore	Andrew Adkins	16.1L	4	59kg	$151
10	5	SUCCESS DAYS	Ken Condon	Joao Moreira	18.1L	8	59kg	$61

PAST WINNERS

YEAR	WINNER	JOCKEY	TRAINER	2ND	3RD	TIME
2018	Winx	Hugh Bowman	Chris Waller	Gailo Chop	Happy Clapper	2:01.6
2017	Winx	Hugh Bowman	Chris Waller	Hartnell	Sense Of Occasion	2:07.2
2016	Lucia Valentina	Damien Oliver	Kris Lees	The United States	Happy Clapper	2:04.8
2015	Criterion	Craig Williams	David Hayes & Tom Dabernig	Red Cadeaux	Royal Descent	2:05.3
2014	It's A Dundeel	James McDonald	Murray Baker	Sacred Falls	Carlton House	2:03.7
2013	Reliable Man	Hugh Bowman	Chris Waller	It's A Dundeel	Happy Trails	2:01.8
2012	More Joyous	Nash Rawiller	Gai Waterhouse	Manighar	Secret Admirer	2:05.3
2011	My Kingdom Of Fife	Nash Rawiller	Chris Waller	Sacred Choice	Syreon	2:07.7
2010	Road To Rock	Damien Oliver	Anthony Cummings	Triple Honour	Monaco Consul	2:03.8
2009	Pompeii Ruler	Craig Newitt	Mick Price	DH Sarrera/Metal Bender		2:07.1
2008	Sarrera	Damien Oliver	Michael Moroney	Nom Du Jeu	Tuesday Joy	2:03.5
2007	Desert War	Damien Oliver	Gai Waterhouse	Haradasun	Spirit of Tara	2:04.2
2006	Eremein	Glen Boss	Allan Denham	Aqua d' Amore	Ike's Dream	2:02.4
2005	Grand Armee	Danny Beasley	Gai Waterhouse	Delzao	Mummify	2:02.6
2004	Grand Armee	Danny Beasley	Gai Waterhouse	Lonhro	Pentastic	2:03.2
2003	Lonhro	Darren Beadman	John Hawkes	Pentastic	Republic Lass	2:04.8
2002	Defier	Damien Oliver	Guy Walter	Freemason	Emission	2:04.3
2001	Shogun Lodge	Glen Boss	Bob Thomsen	Go Flash Go	El Mirada	2:05.5
2000	Georgie Boy	Len Beasley	John Size	Cronus	Referral	2:07.7
1999	Intergaze	Craig Carmody	Rod Craig	Istidaad	Sky Heights	2:03.8
1998	Might And Power	Brian York	Jack Denham	Champagne	Catalan Opening	2:05.1
1997	Intergaze	Craig Carmody	Rod Craig	Octagonal	All Our Mob	2:01.2

BACKGROUND

First run: 1954 (won by Blue Ocean). Replaced the AJC Plate (first run 1873, last run 1954 in addition to the QE Stakes that year), which also was named the Queen's Plate (1851-1857, 1862-1872), AJC Handicap (1858-1861), King's Cup (1928 and 1934). Group 1 since 1980. Run as a Quality Handicap in 1970. Run over 2400m 1954, 1970-71, 1973-78; 2800m 1955-69, 1972.

Mares to win: 8—Winx (2018, 2017); Lucia Valentina (2016); More Joyous (2012); Dinky Flyer (1987); Tristarc (1986); My Blue Denim (1981); Jandell (1975).

3YOs to win: 5—Intergaze (1997); Gay Icarus (1971); Garcon (1967); Prince Grant (1966); Tulloch (1958). No 3YO filly has won the Queen Elizabeth Stakes.

Multiple winners: 4—Winx (20189, 2017); Grand Armee (2005, 2004); Intergaze (1999. 1997); Tulloch (1961, 1960, 1958).

Fastest time (2000m): Intergaze (1997) 2:01.22.

Notable winners: Winx (2018, 2017); Criterion (2015); It's A Dundeel (2014); Reliable Man (2013); More Joyous (2012); Desert War (2007); Eremein (2006); Grand Armee (2005, 2004); Lonhro (2003); Might And Power (1998); Doriemus (1996); Jeune (1995); Rough Habit (1992); Our Poetic Prince (1989); Tristarc (1986); Ngawyni (1977); Tails (1972); Gay Icarus (1971); General Command (1968); Tulloch (1961, 1960, 1958); Prince Cortauld (1955).

Queen Elizabeth Stakes winners won feature races the previous spring:
George Main Stakes: 4—Winx (QE 2018, 2017); Road To Rock (2010); Grand Armee (2005).
Cox Plate: 4—Winx (QE 2018, 2017); Our Poetic Prince (1989); Tulloch (1961).
Melbourne Cup: 3—Might And Power (QE 1998); Doriemus (1996); Jeune (1995).
Queen Elizabeth Stakes winners won the lead-up races:
Peter Young Stakes: 2—Durbridge (1994); Gay Icarus (1971).
Australian Cup (since 1964 when Australian Cup became 2000m WFA): 5—Durbridge (1994); Veandercross (1993); Ming Dynasty (1978); Ngawyni (1977); Gay Icarus (1970).
Chipping Norton Stakes: 13—Winx (2018, 2017); Grand Armee (2005); Lonhro (2003); Rising Prince (1985); Taras Bulba (1976); Apollo Eleven (1973); Gay Icarus (1971); General Command (1968); Prince Grant (1966); Tulloch (1960, 1958); Caesar (1959).
Ranvet Stakes: 5—Desert War (2007); Eremein (2006); Grand Armee (2005); Veandercross (1993); Tulloch (1958).
George Ryder Stakes: 3—Winx (2018, 2017); Lonhro (2003).
Tancred Stakes: 10—Eremein (2006); Might And Power (1998); Intergaze (1997); Sydeston (1990); Our Poetic Prince (1989); Prince Majestic (1982); My Blue Denim (1981); Shivaree (1979); Apollo Eleven (1973); Tails (1972). Note: Prince Grant, who won QE Stakes in 1966 and The BMW in 1969, is the only horse to win both races in different years.
Doncaster Handicap: 2—More Joyous (2012); Iko (1980) Note: Haradasun (2007) and Gunsynd (1972) won the Doncaster Mile and finished second in the Queen Elizabeth Stakes. Grand Armee won the Doncaster in 2003 and the QE in 2004 and 2005.
All Aged Stakes: 3—Intergaze (1999); Rough Habit (1992); Tulloch (1958).
The Sydney autumn feature WFA treble:
Ranvet Stakes, Tancred Stakes and QE Stakes: 1—Eremein (2006).
Queen Elizabeth Stakes winners went on to win (same year):
Doomben Cup: 5—Sarrera (2008); Intergaze (1999); Might And Power (1998); Durbridge (1994); Rough Habit (1992).
Cox Plate: 5—Winx (2017); Might And Power (1998); Rising Prince (1985); Battle Heights (1974); Tulloch (1960).
Melbourne Cup: None
Imported winners:
4—Reliable Man (GB) 2013, trained by Chris Waller; My Kingdom Of Fyfe (GB) 2011, Chris Waller; Jeune (GB) 1995, David Hayes; Authaal (USA) 1988, Colin Hayes.
Winner to be placed 2nd or 3rd the previous year:
2—It's A Dundeel (2014, 2nd behind Reliable Man in 2013); Durbridge (1994, 2nd behind Veandercross 1993); Nilarco (1962, 2nd behind Tulloch 1961).
Queen Elizabeth Stakes and the Australian Derby:
Australian Derby winners to win Queen Elizabeth Stakes as 4YO (since 1979 when Derby moved spring to autumn): 3—It's A Dundeel (2014); Eremein (2006); Tristarc (1986).
Australian Derby winners to win Queen Elizabeth Stakes as 4YO (before 1979 when Derby run in spring): 1—Taras Bulba (QE 1976).
Australian Derby winners to win Queen Elizabeth Stakes as 3YO: 2—Prince Grant (QE 1966); Tulloch (1958).
Leading winning jockeys:
6 wins George Moore (General Command 1968, Prince Grant 1966, Fair Patton 1965, Burgos 1963, Tulloch 1961 & 1958).
5 wins Damien Oliver (Lucia Valentina 2016, Road To Rock 2010, Sarrera 2008, Desert War 2007, Defier 2002).
4 wins Peter Cook (Dinky Flyer 1987, Chiamare 1984, My Blue Denim 1981, Panvale 1970); Neville Sellwood (Tulloch 1960, Caesar 1959, Empire Link 1957, Prince Cortauld 1955).
Current winning jockeys:
5 wins Damien Oliver (Lucia Valentina 2016, Road To Rock 2010, Sarrera 2008, Desert War 2007, Defier 2002).
3 wins Hugh Bowman (Winx 2018, 2017, Reliable Man 2013).
2 wins Glen Boss (Eremein 2006, Shogun Lodge 2001); Nash Rawiller (More Joyous 2012, My Kingdom Of Fyfe 2011).
1 win James McDonald (It's A Dundeel 2014); Craig Newitt (Pompeii Ruler 2009); Craig Williams (Criterion 2015).
Leading winning trainer:
11 wins Tommy Smith (Chiamare 1984, Iko 1980, Taras Bulba 1976, General Command 1968, Garcon 1967, Prince Grant 1966, Fair Patton 1965, Burgos 1963, Tulloch 1961, 1960, 1958).

Current winning trainers:
4 wins Gai Waterhouse (More Joyous 2012, Desert War 2007, Grand Armee 2005 & 2004).
4 wins Chris Waller (Winx 2018, 2017, Reliable Man 2013, My Kingdom Of Fyfe 2011).
3 wins John Wheeler (Veandercross 1993, Rough Habit 1992, Our Poetic Prince 1989).
2 wins Rod Craig (Intergaze 1999, 1997); Lee Freedman (Doriemus 1996, Durbridge 1994); David Hayes (Criterion 2015, Jeune 1995).
1 win Murray Baker (It's A Dundeel 2014); Anthony Cummings (Road To Rock 2010); Allan Denham (Eremein 2006); John Hawkes (Lonhro 2003); David Hayes & Tom Dabernig (Criterion 2015); Kris Lees (Lucia Valentina 2016); Michael Moroney (Sarrera 2008); Mick Price (Pompeii Ruler 2009); John Size (Georgie Boy 2000); Kerry Walker (Dinky Flyer 1987).

Points of interest:
Shogun Lodge (2001) survived a protest from Go Flash Go.
Reliable Man (2013) won the 2011 G1 Prix du Jockey Club (French Derby).
It's A Dundeel (2013) and Nom Du Jeu (2008) were runners-up in the QE Stakes after winning the Australian Derby—both trained by Murray Baker.
Queen Elizabeth II has attended the running of the race named in her honour three times—1954 (inaugural race won by Blue Ocean), 1970 (won by Panvale at 100/1) and 1992 (won by Rough Habit).
Winx (2017) completed her 17th consecutive win.
Winx (2018) won her 25th consecutive race, equalling the winning streak of Black Caviar. Winx also recorded her 18th Group 1 win, which is a world record for a flat horse.

ATC Sydney Cup (3200m)—Randwick

Of $2,000,000. Group 1. Handicap, Minimum Weight 49kg, 3YO&Up. April 13, 2019.

2017-18 RESULT: Time: 3:20.04   (Good 4)

FP	NO	HORSE	TRAINER	JOCKEY	MARGIN	BAR.	WGT	SP
1	2	WHO SHOT THEBARMAN	Chris Waller	Blake Shinn		10	55kg	$18
2	12	ZACADA	Murray Baker & Andrew Forsman	Dean Holland	0.1L	11	50.5kg	$91
3	13	SIR CHARLES ROAD	Lance O'Sullivan & Andrew Scott	Andrew Adkins	1.1L	4	50kg	$7
4	8	AUVRAY	Richard Freedman	Glyn Schofield	1.2L	1	53kg	$13
5	15	LASQUETI SPIRIT	Lee Curtis	Jay Ford	2.4L	16	51kg	$151
6	17	PATRICK ERIN	Chris Waller	Craig Newitt	3L	15	51kg	$41
7	21	DOUKHAN	Kris Lees	Yusuke Ichikawa	4.4L	13	50kg	$101
8	1	ALMANDIN	Liam Howley	Damien Oliver	5.4L	5	57kg	$3.70f
9	4	VENTURA STORM	David & Ben Hayes & Tom Dabernig	Glen Boss	8L	8	53.5kg	$9.50
10	7	FIVE TO MIDNIGHT	Lisa Latta	Michael Dee	8.8L	9	52.5kg	$41
11	19	ADMIRAL JELLO	Kris Lees	Grant Buckley	10.9L	14	50kg	$151
12	3	LIBRAN	Chris Waller	Brenton Avdulla	11.1L	17	54kg	$61
13	9	LORD FANDANGO	Archie Alexander	Craig Williams	16.7L	2	51.5kg	$10
14	18	PERIBSEN	John O'Shea	Corey Brown	23.5L	6	50kg	$31
15	16	CISMONTANE	Gai Waterhouse & Adrian Bott	James Innes Jnr	27.4L	3	50kg	$51
16	20	ORMITO	Darren Weir	Dean Yendall	28.3L	7	50kg	$21
FF	10	ALOFT	Liam Howley	Kerrin McEvoy	0L	12	51kg	$6

PAST WINNERS

YEAR	WINNER	JOCKEY	TRAINER	2ND	3RD	TIME
2018	Who Shot Thebarman	Blake Shinn	Chris Waller	Zacada	Sir Charles Road	3:20.0
2017	Polarisation	Corey Brown	Charlie Appleby	Who Shot Thebarman	Big Duke	3:29.1
2016	Gallante	Kerrin McEvoy	Robert Hickmott	Libran	Grand Marshal	3:24.5
2015	Grand Marshal	Jim Cassidy	Chris Waller	Who Shot Thebarman	Like A Carousel	3:24.7
2014	The Offer	Tommy Berry	Gai Waterhouse	Opinion	Sertorius	3:23.8
2013	Mourayan	Hugh Bowman	Robert Hickmott	Norsqui	Aliyana Tilde	3:24.2
2012	Niwot	Dwayne Dunn	Michael, Wayne & John Hawkes	Efficient	Once Were Wild	3:20.4
2011	Stand To Gain	Rod Quinn	Chris Waller	Older Than Time	Solid Billing	3:29.1
2010	Jessicabeel	Craig Newitt	John O'Shea	Divine Rebel	Harris Tweed	3:21.8
2009	Ista Kareem	Craig Williams	Colin Little	Divine Rebel	Mr Tipsy	3:27.4
2008	No Wine No Song	Damien Oliver	Kevin Moses	Pentathon	Lang	3:25.5
2007	Gallic	Steven Arnold	Graeme Rogerson	Irazu	No Wine No Song	3:27.3
2006	County Tyrone	Jim Cassidy	Kris Lees	Zabeat	Three Chimneys	3:22.6
2005	Mahtoum	Darren Beadman	Kim Moore	County Tyrone	Philosophe	3:27.6
2004	Makybe Diva	Glen Boss	David Hall	Manawa King	Mummify	3:21.2
2003	Honor Babe	Kerrin McEvoy	Katrina Alexander	County Tyrone	Grey Song	3:30.5
2002	Henderson Bay	Darryl McLellan	Neville Mcburney	Mr. Prudent	Spirit of Westbury	3:26.7
2001	Mr. Prudent	Corey Brown	George Hanlon	Prophet's Kiss	Starina	3:26.9
2000	Streak	Steven King	Robert Smerdon	Sharscay	Ears' Ronny	3:30.3
1999	Tie The Knot	Shane Dye	Guy Walter	Praise Indeed	Lahar	3:22.8
1998	Tie The Knot	Shane Dye	Guy Walter	Doriemus	Praise Indeed	3:25.7
1997	Linesman	Larry Cassidy	Gai Waterhouse	Nothin' Leica Dane	Ebony Grosve	3:20.5

BACKGROUND

First run: 1866 (won by Yattendon). Group 1 since 1980. Run at Rosehill in 1942.

Most recent mare to win: Jessicabeel (2010). Note: Since 1960, the only other mares to win the Sydney Cup are Makybe Diva (2004), Honor Babe (2003), Palace Revolt (1989), Lowland (1969) and Maidenhead (1963).

Most recent 3YO to win: Tie The Knot (1998). Note: 30 3YOs have won the Sydney Cup.

Multiple winners: 5—Tie The Knot (1999, 1998); Veiled Threat (1944, 1942); Mosaic (1940, 1939); Carbine (1890, 1889); The Barb (1869, 1868).

Fastest time (3200m): Just A Dancer (1991) & Apollo Eleven (1973) 3:19.00.

Notable winners: Who Shot Thebarman (2018); Polarisation (2017); Makybe Diva (2004); Tie The Knot (1999, 1998); Kingston Town (1980); Battle Heights (1974); Apollo Eleven (1973); Galilee (1967); Straight Draw (1958); Sailor's Guide (1956); Carioca (1953); Carbon Copy (1949); Dark Marne (1948); Veiled Threat (1944, 1942); Mosaic (1940, 1939); Rogilla (1933); Eurythmic (1921); Wakeful (1902); La Carabine (1900); Wallace (1896); Carbine (1890, 1889); The Barb (1869, 1868).

Sydney Cup and the Melbourne Cup:
Melbourne Cup & Sydney Cup (same season): 4—Makybe Diva (Sydney Cup 2004); Galilee (1967); Straight Draw (1958); Lord Cardigan (1904).
Sydney Cup & Melbourne Cup (same year): 2—Carbine (1890); Makybe Diva (2004).

Sydney Cup winners to win key lead-up races:
Launceston Cup: 1—Streak (1999). Note: Ista Kareem won the 2008 Launceston Cup and the 2009 Sydney Cup.
Randwick City Stakes: 3—No Wine No Song (2008); Late Show (1985); Bankstream (1951).
Chipping Norton Stakes: 6—Tie The Knot (1999); Apollo Eleven (1983); General Command (1968); Prince Grant (1966); Carioca (1953); Carbon Copy (1949).
Sky High Stakes: 2—County Tyrone (2006); Cross Swords (1994).
Manion Cup: 4—The Offer (2014); Mahtoum (2005); Azzaam (1993); Marooned (1986).
Tancred Stakes: 4—Tie The Knot (1999); Kingston Town (1980); Apollo Eleven (1973); Maidenhead (1963). Note: Maidenhead (1963) is the only mare to complete the double, although Makybe Diva won The BMW in 2005 and the Sydney Cup in 2004.
Australian Derby (since 1978): 2—Our Paddy Boy (1981); Kingston Town (1980).
Tancred Stakes & Australian Derby: 1—Kingston Town (1980).
Chairman's Handicap: 8—The Offer (2014); Jessicabeel (2010); No Wine No Song (2008); Henderson Bay (2002); Linesman (1997); King Aussie (1990); Major Drive (1987); Marooned (1986).

Sydney Cup winners also won in same preparation:
Adelaide Cup: 2—Gallic (2007), Reckless (1977). Note: The Adelaide Cup was moved from May (after the Sydney Cup) to March in 2006.
Brisbane Cup: 1—Reckless.

Leading winning jockeys:
3 wins Jim Cassidy (Grand Marshal 2015, County Tyrone 2006, Marooned 1986); Peter Cook (Banderol 1988, Veloso 1983, Gallic Temple 1971); Tom Hales (Progress 1881, Petrea 1880; Savanaka 1879); George Moore (General Command 1968, Prince Grant 1966, Cordale 1946); Noel McGrowdie (Straight Draw 1958, Opulent 1952, Bankstream 1951); Darby Munro (Veiled Threat 1944, Abspear 1943, Mosaic 1940); Neville Sellwood (Grand Garry 1960, Sailor's Guide 1956, Gold Scheme 1954); Albert Wood (Prince Charles 1922, Kennaquhair 1920, The Fortune Hunter 1917).

Current winning jockeys:
2 wins Corey Brown (Polarisation 2017, Mr. Prudent 2001); Kerrin McEvoy (Gallante 2016, Honor Babe 2003).
1 win Steven Arnold (Gallic 2007); Tommy Berry (The Offer 2014); Glen Boss (Makybe Diva 2004); Hugh Bowman (Mourayan 2013); Larry Cassidy (Linesman 1997); Dwayne Dunn (Niwot 2012); Damien Oliver (No Wine No Song 2008); Brett Prebble (Daacha 1995); Craig Newitt (Jessicabeel 2010); Blake Shinn (Who Shot Thebarman 2018); Craig Williams (Ista Kareem 2009).

Leading winning trainers:
5 wins Dan Lewis (Proctor 1947, L'Aiglon 1938, Contact 1936, Akuna 1935, Crucis 1929).
4 wins James Wilson snr (Progress 1881, Petrea 1880, Savanaka 1879, Mermaid 1871).

Current winning trainers:
3 wins Chris Waller (Who Shot Thebarman 2018, Grand Marshal 2015, Stand To Gain 2011).
2 wins John Hawkes (Niwot 2012, Cross Swords 1994); Robert Hickmott (Gallante 2016; Mourayan 2013); John Meagher (Daacha 1995; Major Drive 1987); Graeme Rogerson (Gallic 2006; Just A Dancer 1991); Gai Waterhouse (The Offer 2014, Linesman 1997).
1 win Charlie Appleby (Polarisation 2017); Murray Baker (My Eagle Eye 1992); Lee Freedman (Count Chivas 1996); David Hall (Makybe Diva 2004); Michael, Wayne, John Hawkes (Niwot 2012); David Hayes (Azzaam 1993); Kris Lees (County Tyrone 2006); Colin Little (Ista Kareem 2009); Kim Moore (Mahtoum 2005); Kevin Moses (No Wine No Song 2008); John O'Shea (Jessicabeel 2010); Robert Smerdon (Streak 2000).

Points of interest:
The Barb—the "Black Demon"—won the Sydney Cup in 1868 and 1869, and his sister Barbelle (Sir Hercules-Fair Ellen) won in 1870.
The Barb's 10st 8lb (67kg), in 1869, is the most weight carried to win. Since Mosaic won his second cup in 1940 under 57.5kg, the only horses to lump more are Galilee (60.5kg, 1967), My Good Man (60kg, 1978), Battle Heights (58.5kg, 1974) and General Command (58.5kg, 1968).
The heaviest post-war weight carried in the Sydney Cup was Tulloch's 63kg when second behind Sharply in 1961.
The 2017 Sydney Cup, run on April 8, was declared a no race after Almoonqith fell soon after passing the winning post the first time. It was re-run on on April 22. Polarisation was first past the post in the first attempt, and also won the rerun. Polarisation (2017), trained in England by Charlie Appleby for Godolphin, is the first northern hemisphere-trained horse to win the Sydney Cup.

ATC Australian Oaks (2400m)—Randwick
Of $1,000,000. Group 1. Set Weights, 3YO Fillies. April 13, 2019.

2017-18 RESULT: Time: 2:27.21 (Good 4)

FP	NO	HORSE	TRAINER	JOCKEY	MARGIN	BAR.	WGT	SP
1	3	UNFORGOTTEN	Chris Waller	Hugh Bowman		7	56kg	$4f
2	2	HIYAAM	Mick Price	Michael Dee	1L	1	56kg	$4.60
3	11	MISS ADMIRATION	Mick Price	Damien Oliver	3.3L	11	56kg	$101
4	6	BRING ME ROSES	Tony McEvoy	Luke Currie	4.4L	12	56kg	$26
5	4	SAVVY COUP	Michael & Matthew Pitman	Chris Johnson	5.7L	2	56kg	$8
6	8	DANZDANZDANCE	Chris Gibbs	Michael Walker	6.3L	3	56kg	$17
7	1	ALOISIA	Ciaron Maher	Mark Zahra	6.9L	9	56kg	$5.50
8	9	CHILLY CHA CHA	Kris Lees	Jason Collett	12.5L	6	56kg	$21
9	7	CONTESSA VANESSA	Graeme Rogerson	Craig Williams	13.4L	5	56kg	$31
10	10	SHE'S A TREASURE	Tony Pike	Damian Lane	15.4L	4	56kg	$41
11	5	LUVALUVA	John Sargent	Kerrin McEvoy	15.8L	13	56kg	$6.50
12	13	WILD SEA	Michael Kent	Dwayne Dunn	19.8L	8	56kg	$71
13	12	NAIVASHA	Nigel Blackiston	Rhys McLeod	25.9L	10	56kg	$151

PAST WINNERS

YEAR	WINNER	JOCKEY	TRAINER	2ND	3RD	TIME
2018	Unforgotten	Hugh Bowman	Chris Waller	Hiyaam	Miss Admiration	2:27.2
2017	Bonneval	Hugh Bowman	Murray Baker & Andrew Forsman	Perfect Rhyme	Lasqueti Spirit	2:36.2
2016	Sofia Rosa	Hugh Bowman	Stephen Marsh	Ambience	Believe	2:34.2
2015	Gust Of Wind	Tye Angland	John Sargent	Winx	Candelara	2:32.4
2014	Rising Romance	James McDonald	Donna & Dean Logan	Zanbagh	Lucia Valentina	2:31.7
2013	Royal Descent	Nash Rawiller	Chris Waller	Dear Demi	Gondokoro	2:34.1
2012	Streama	Hugh Bowman	Guy Walter	Aliyana Tilde	Thy	2:31.3
2011	Absolutely	Brad Rawiller	Michael Kent	Shamrocker	Pinker Pinker	2:35.6
2010	Once Were Wild	Nash Rawiller	Gai Waterhouse	Faint Perfume	Run For Naara	2:30.4
2009	Daffodil	Hugh Bowman	Kevin Gray	Think Money	Miss Darcey	2:33.3
2008	Heavenly Glow	Robert Thompson	Allan Denham	Boundless	Galileo's Daughter	2:34.8
2007	Rena's Lady	Michael Rodd	Gary Portelli	Perfect Drop	Tuesday Joy	2:33.7
2006	Serenade Rose	Glen Boss	Lee Freedman	Flora Danica	Beauty Watch	2:28.6
2005	Dizelle	Corey Brown	John Hawkes	She's Justa Tad	Gee That's Tops	2:34.2
2004	Wild Iris	Larry Cassidy	Guy Walter	French Lady	Boulevard Of Dreams	2:30.5
2003	Sunday Joy	Len Beasley	Gai Waterhouse	Shower Of Roses	Bramble Rose	2:32.5
2002	Republic Lass	Glen Boss	Guy Walter	Elegant Fashion	Quays	2:31.0
2001	Rose Archway	Brian York	Clarry Conners	Tempest Morn	Asia	2:35.8
2000	Coco Cobanna	Shane Dye	Gai Waterhouse	Tributes	Miss Zoe	2:32.5
1999	Grand Archway	Shane Dye	Graeme Rogerson	Light Work	Camarena	2:33.0
1998	On Air	John Marshall	Anthony Cummings	Champagne	Star Alight	2:35.5
1997	Danendri	Glen Boss	Bart Cummings	Assertive Lass	Ellakapella	2:32.3

BACKGROUND
First run: 1885 (won by Uralla). Group 1 since 1979. Run over 2400m 1885-94, from 1956; Run over 1600m 1922-45 (run in January); 2000m 1946-55. Known as the Adrian Knox Stakes 1922-45 and the Adrian Knox Oaks 1946-62; AJC Oaks 1885-94, 1963-94; Australian Oaks from 1995. Not held 1894-1921. Held in the spring 1885-94.

Fastest time (2400m): Unforgotten (2018) 2:27.21.

Notable winners: Unforgotten (2018); Bonneval (2017); Streama (2012); Serenade Rose (2006); Sunday Joy (2003); Grand Archway (1999); Circles Of Gold (1995); Triscay (1991); Research (1989); Bounding Away (1987); Just Now (1986); November Rain (1981); Lowan Star (1980); Surround (1977); How Now (1976); Leilani (1974); Analie (1973); Gossiper (1972); Gay Poss (1970); Lowland (1968); Light Fingers (1965); Indian Summer (1962); Wenona Girl (1961); Chicola (1959); Evening Peal (1956); True Course (1951); Sweet Chime (1947); Flight (1944); Valicare (1926).

Australian Oaks winners to win key lead-up races:
Armanasco Stakes: 2—Serenade Rose (2006); Rose Archway (2001).
Kewney Stakes: 7—How Now (1976); Gossiper (1972); Gay Poss (1970); Lowland (1968); Dual Quest (1966); Gay Satin (1958); Sandara (1957).
Phar Lap Stakes: 1—Unforgotten (2018).
Storm Queen Stakes: 6—Heavenly Glow (2008); Serenade Rose (2006); Danendri (1997); Alcove (1994); Research (1989); Sheraco (1982).
VRC Oaks & Storm Queen Stakes: 2—Serenade Rose (2006); Research (1989).

Adrian Knox Stakes: 15—Royal Descent (2013); Rena's Lady (2007); Wild Iris (2004); Republic Lass (2002); Circles Of Gold (1995); Just Now (1986); Our Sophia (1985); Starzaan (1983); Leilani (1974); Lowland (1968); Light Fingers (1965); Jane Hero (1964); Sabah (1955); Edelweiss (1954); Persist (1949).
VRC Oaks & Adrian Knox Stakes: 1—Light Fingers (1965).
ATC Australian Derby: 1—Research (1989).
New Zealand Oaks: 2—Bonneval (2017); Domino (1990).
Australian Oaks winners went on to win:
Queensland Oaks: 6—Triscay (1991); November Rain (1981); Lowan Star (1980); Surround (1977); Analie (1972); Evening Peal (1956). Note: Evening Peal (1956) won the Queensland Oaks when it was run in the spring (now run in winter).
Melbourne Cup as a 4YO: 2—Light Fingers (1965); Evening Peal (1956).
Caulfield Cup as a 4YO: 2—How Now (1976); Leilani (1974).
Australian Oaks and the previous spring features:
Flight Stakes: 1—Streama (Oaks 2012).
Caulfield Guineas: 1—Surround (Oaks 1977)
Thousand Guineas: 3—Indian Summer (Oaks 1962); True Course (1951); Sweet Chime (1947).
Cox Plate: 1—Surround (Oaks 1977). Note: Surround is the only 3YO filly to win the Cox Plate.
VRC Oaks & Australian Oaks: 18—Serenade Rose (Australian Oaks 2006); Grand Archway (1999); Research (1989); November Rain (1981); Surround (1977); Farmer's Daughter (1967); Light Fingers (1965); Arctic Star (1963); Indian Summer (1962); Chicola (1959); Evening Peal (1956); True Course (1951); Sweet Chime (1947) Session (1941); Gallantic (1932); Spice (1889); Pearlshell (1888); Uralla (1885).
Leading winning jockeys:
6 wins Roy Higgins (Leilani 1974, Gossiper 1972, Gay Poss 1970, Lowland 1968, Light Fingers 1965, Indian Summer 1962).
5 wins Ted Bartle (Whisper Low 1942, Early Bird 1939, Leila Vale 1934, Roman Spear 1933, Gay Ballerina 1930); Hugh Bowman (Unforgotten 2018, Bonneval 2017, Sofia Rosa 2016, Streama 2012, Daffodil 2009); Jack Thompson (Gay Satin 1948, Wayside Bloom 1952, True Course 1951, Flight 1944, Flying Shuttle 1943).
4 wins Mick Dittman (Mahaya 1993, Triscay 1991, Research 1989, Bounding Away 1987); Neville Sellwood (Pique 1960, Edelweiss 1954, Persist 1949, Sweet Chime 1947).
Current winning jockeys:
5 wins Hugh Bowman (Unforgotten 2018, Bonneval 2017, Sofia Rosa 2016, Streama 2012, Daffodil 2009).
3 wins Glen Boss (Serenade Rose 2006, Republic Lass 2002, Danendri 1997).
2 wins Nash Rawiller (Royal Descent 2013, Once Were Wild 2010).
1 win Tye Angland (Gust Of Wind 2015); Corey Brown (Dizelle 2005); Larry Cassidy (Wild Iris 2004); James McDonald (Rising Romance 2014); Brad Rawiller (Absolutely 2011); Michael Rodd (Rena's Lady 2007); Robert Thompson (Heavenly Glow 2010).
Leading winning trainers:
7 wins Bart Cummings (Danendri 1997, Sheraco 1982, Invade 1978, Leilani 1974, Gay Poss 1970, Lowland 1968, Light Fingers 1965).
6 wins Tommy Smith (Bounding Away 1987, Lowan Star 1980, Analie 1973, Waikiki 1971, Flying Fable 1969, Waterlady 1953).
Current winning trainers:
3 wins Gai Waterhouse (Once Were Wild 2010; Sunday Joy 2003, Coco Cobanna 2000).
2 wins Clarry Conners (Rose Archway 2001, Research 1989); Chris Waller (Unforgotten 2018, Royal Descent 2013).
1 win Murray Baker & Andrew Forsman (Bonneval 2017); Grahame Begg (Mahaya 1993); Anthony Cummings (On Air 1998); Allan Denham (Heavenly Glow 2008); Lee Freedman (Serenade Rose 2006); Kevin Gray (Daffodil 2009); John Hawkes (Dizelle 2005); Tom Hughes Jnr (Alcove 1994); Mick Kent (Absolutely 2011); Donna Logan (Rising Romance 2014); Stephen Marsh (Sofia Rosa 2016); Gary Portelli (Rena's Lady 2007); Graeme Rogerson (Grand Archway 1999); John Sargent (Gust Of Wind 2015); Brian Smith (Circles Of Gold 1995).
Points of interest:
Circles Of Gold (1995) is the dam of outstanding multiple Group 1-winning gallopers Elvstroem (by Danehill) and Haradasun (by Fusaichi Pegasus), and the grand-dam of international champion Highland Reel (IRE).
Bounding Away (1987) is the only Australian Oaks winner to also win a Golden Slipper (1986).
Research (1989) was named Australian Champion Racehorse for season 1988-89; Bounding Away (1987) was named Australian Champion Racehorse for season 1985-86; Surround (1977) was named Australian Champion Racehorse for 1976-77.
No filly has won the Australasian Oaks or SA Fillies Classic (formerly SA Oaks) and the Australian Oaks.
Tamarisk and Crossfire dead-heated in 1886.
Roy Higgins, who rode six winners of the Oaks, died on March 8, 2014; Guy Walter, who trained three winners of the Oaks, died suddenly on May 22, 1914.
Murray Baker and Andrew Forsman (Bonneval 2017) became the first trainers to win the Australian Derby-Australian Oaks double since Clarry Conners (Research) in 1989. Baker-Forsman trained Jon Snow to win the Derby.

ATC Queen Of The Turf Stakes (1600m)—Randwick

Of $1,000,000. Group 1. Weight For Age, 3YO&Up Fillies & Mares. April 13, 2019.

2017-18 RESULT: Time: 1:34.94 (Good 4)

FP	NO	HORSE	TRAINER	JOCKEY	MARGIN	BAR.	WGT	SP
1	17	ALIZEE	James Cummings	Glyn Schofield		8	54.5kg	$8.50
2	4	PROMPT RESPONSE	Gai Waterhouse & Adrian Bott	Blake Shinn	2L	7	57kg	$12
3	6	HEAVENS ABOVE	Tim Martin	Tye Angland	2.5L	4	57kg	$15
4	9	OREGON'S DAY	Mick Price	Michael Dee	2.6L	12	57kg	$26
5	11	ABBEY MARIE	Michael Kent	Damian Lane	2.9L	3	57kg	$14
6	3	DIXIE BLOSSOMS	Ron Quinton	Corey Brown	3.1L	16	57kg	$7.50
7	13	ECKSTEIN	Kurt Goldman	Brenton Avdulla	3.3L	2	57kg	$21
8	2	FOXPLAY	Chris Waller	Kerrin McEvoy	3.4L	9	57kg	$15
9	16	NETTOYER	Wendy Roche	Dean Yendall	3.8L	11	57kg	$71
10	5	SILENT SEDITION	Andrew Noblet	Craig Williams	3.9L	10	57kg	$7ef
11	1	DAYSEE DOOM	Ron Quinton	Andrew Adkins	5.2L	17	57kg	$13
12	8	ZANBAGH	John P Thompson	Hugh Bowman	6.7L	5	57kg	$81
13	10	PAYROLL	Richard Laming	Damien Oliver	6.8L	1	57kg	$18
14	7	SPANISH REEF	Ken Keys	Mark Zahra	7.4L	15	57kg	$7ef
15	14	SAMOVARE	David & Ben Hayes & Tom Dabernig	Joao Moreira	7.5L	6	57kg	$21
16	12	AIDE MEMOIRE	Kris Lees	Jason Collett	8.4L	13	57kg	$41
17	15	PERFECT RHYME	Ron Leemon	Luke Currie	9L	14	57kg	$201

PAST WINNERS

YEAR	WINNER	JOCKEY	TRAINER	2ND	3RD	TIME
2018	Alizee	Glyn Schofield	James Cummings	Prompt Response	Heavens Above	1:34.9
2017	Foxplay	Kerrin McEvoy	Chris Waller	Zanbagh	Dixie Blossoms	1:39.6
2016	Azkadellia	Damien Oliver	Ciaron Maher	Heavens Above	Noble Protector	1:35.9
2015	Amanpour	Kerrin McEvoy	Gai Waterhouse	Catkins	Noble Protector	1:37.7
2014	Diamond Drille	Tommy Berry	Gai Waterhouse	Gypsy Diamond	Red Tracer	1:35.8
2013	Appearance	Kerrin McEvoy	Guy Walter	Red Tracer	Streama	1:30.7
2012	More Joyous	Nash Rawiller	Gai Waterhouse	Miss Keepsake	King's Rose	1:28.5
2011	More Joyous	Nash Rawiller	Gai Waterhouse	Melito	Happy Hippy	1:29.2
2010	Typhoon Tracy	Luke Nolen	Peter Moody	Illuminates	Montana Flyer	1:29.9
2009	Neroli	Darren Beadman	Peter Snowden	Hot Danish	Imananabaa	1:31.2
2008	Forensics	Danny Nikolic	Peter Snowden	Perfect Drop	Occurrence	1:31.5
2007	Divine Madonna	Glen Boss	Mark Kavanagh	Cheeky Choice	Beauty Watch	1:30.6
2006	Mnemosyne	Darren Beadman	John Hawkes	Regal Cheer	Shania Dane	1:28.2
2005	Ike's Dream	Darren Beadman	John Hawkes	Tui Song	Dannu Martine	1:28.7
2004	In A Bound	Chris Munce	Gai Waterhouse	Hec Of A Party	Ain't Seen Nothin'	1:28.0
2003	Hosannah	Corey Brown	John Hawkes	Arrabeea	Faith Hill	1:27.9
2002	Ugachaka	Scott Seamer	Lee Freedman	Miss Zoe	Snow Hero	1:28.4
2001	Sorrento	Chris Munce	John Size	Poppett	Belle Du Jour	1:27.7
2000	Danglissa	Chris Munce	Gai Waterhouse	Glided Angel	Zatella	1:28.2
1999	Camino Rose	Corey Brown	Marc Conners	Flickering Fire	Staging	1:28.5
1998	Arletty	Shane Dye	Dave O'Sullivan	Greeting	Camino Rose	1:28.6
1997	Kenbelle	Brian York	Kevin Robinson	Admiring Glances	Timeless Winds	1:27.8

BACKGROUND

First run: 1972 (won by Refulgence). Run over 1500m 1972-2007, 2009-2013. Listed 1979-84. Group 3 1985-90. Group 2 1991-2004. Group 1 from 2005. Held at Rosehill 1972-2013, except for 2008 when held at Canterbury (1550m). Moved to Randwick (1600m) in 2014 as part of The Championships. Also known as the Coolmore Legacy (2017-)
Most recent 3YO filly to win: Foxplay (2017). Note: 13 3YOs have won.
Multiple winners: 1—More Joyous (2012, 2011).
Fastest time (1600m, Randwick): Alizee (2018) 1:34.94.
Notable winners: Alizee (2018); Appearance (2013); More Joyous (2012, 2011); Typhoon Tracy (2010); Forensics (2008); Danglissa (2000); Camino Rose (1999); Kenbelle (1997); Shame (1996); Excited Angel

(1993); Romanee Conti (1992); Memphis Blues (1990); Shinakima (1987); Ducatoon (1981); Scomeld (1980); Visit (1976); Just Topic (1975); Millefleurs (1973).
Queen of the Turf Stakes winners won in the previous spring:
Myer Classic: 2—Appearance (QOTT 2013); Typhoon Tracy (2010). Note: Forensics (2008) won the double in the same year.
Queen Of The Turf winners won the lead-up races:
Light Fingers Stakes: 2—Alizee (2018); Forensics (2008).
Breeders' Classic: 2—More Joyous (2011); Arletty (1998).
Surround Stakes: 1—Shame (1996).
Birthday Card Stakes: 1—Light Up The World (1995).
Orr Stakes: 1—Typhoon Tracy (2010).
Futurity Stakes: 2—More Joyous (2011); Typhoon Tracy (2010).
Canterbury Stakes: 2—More Joyous (2012, 2011).
Coolmore Classic: 3—Appearance (2013); Camino Rose (1999); Favoured (1974).
Emancipation Stakes: Until 2014 the Emancipation Stakes was run after the Queen Of The Turf. The only winner of the double is Romanee Conti (1992).
Queen Of The Turf winners went on to win in the same preparation:
Doncaster Handicap: 1—More Joyous (2012). Note 1: Divine Madonna (2007) finished third in the 2007 Doncaster behind Haradasun and Mentality. Ducatoon (1981) finished second in the 1981 Doncaster behind Lawman. Note 2: from 2014, the Doncaster will be run before the Queen Of The Turf.
Queen Elizabeth Stakes: 1—More Joyous (2012).
Leading winning jockeys:
5 wins Darren Beadman (Neroli 2009, Mnemosyne 2006, Ike's Dream 2005, Shame 1996, Special Finish 1989).
3 wins Kerrin McEvoy (Foxplay 2017, Amanpour 2015, Appearance 2013); Chris Munce (In A Bound 2004, Sorrento 2001, Danglissa 2000).
Current winning jockeys:
3 wins Kerrin McEvoy (Foxplay 2017, Amanpour 2015, Appearance 2013).
2 wins Glen Boss (Divine Madonna 2007, The Perfume Garden 1994); Corey Brown (Hosannah 2003, Camino Rose 1999); Nash Rawiller (More Joyous 2012, 2011).
1 win Tommy Berry (Diamond Drille 2014); Chris Johnson (Harbour Flo 1986); Luke Nolen (Typhoon Tracy 2010); Damien Oliver (Azkadellia 2016); Glyn Schofield (Alizee 2018).
Leading winning trainers:
7 wins Gai Waterhouse (Amanpour 2015, Diamond Drille 2014, More Joyous 2012, 2011, In A Bound 2004, Danglissa 2000, Light Up The World 1995).
4 wins Bart Cummings (The Perfume Garden 1994; More Rain 1983; Scomeld 1980; Millefleurs 1973); John Hawkes (Mnemosyne 2006, Ike's Dream 2005, Hosannah 2003, Shame 1996).
Current winning trainers:
7 wins Gai Waterhouse (Amanpour 2015, Diamond Drille 2014, More Joyous 2012 & 2011, In A Bound 2004, Danglissa 2000, Light Up The World 1995).
4 wins John Hawkes (Mnemosyne 2006, Ike's Dream 2005, Hosannah 2003, Shame 1996).
2 wins Peter Snowden (Neroli 2009, Forensics 2008).
1 win Jim Conlan (Excited Angel 1992); Marc Conners (Camino Rose 1999); James Cummings (Alizee 2018); David Hall (Sorrento 2001); Mark Kavanagh (Divine Madonna 2007); Laurie Laxon (Romanee Conti 1992); Ciaron Maher (Azkadellia 2016); Paul O'Sullivan (Arletty 1998); Chris Waller (Foxplay 2017).
Point of interest:
Kenbelle (1997) won the Australian Oaks in 1996.

ATC All Aged Stakes (1400m)—Randwick
Of $600,000. Group 1. Weight For Age. April 20, 2019.

2017-18 RESULT: Time: 1:20.33 (Good 3)

FP	NO	HORSE	TRAINER	JOCKEY	MARGIN	BAR.	WGT	SP
1	10	TRAPEZE ARTIST	Gerald Ryan	Tye Angland		7	56.5kg	$2.30F
2	1	LE ROMAIN	Kris Lees	Jason Collett	0.2L	10	59kg	$11
3	11	SHOWTIME	Michael, Wayne & John Hawkes	Corey Brown	1.7L	8	56.5kg	$17
4	3	HARTNELL	James Cummings	Hugh Bowman	1.8L	9	59kg	$7.50
5	12	THE MISSION	Paul Perry	Brenton Avdulla	2.2L	3	56.5kg	$31
6	4	IT'S SOMEWHAT	James Cummings	Tim Clark	3.1L	1	59kg	$21
7	13	MURAAQEB	David & Ben Hayes & Tom Dabernig	Damien Oliver	3.4L	2	56.5kg	$17
8	8	TOM MELBOURNE	Chris Waller	Kerrin McEvoy	3.5L	4	59kg	$8.50
9	9	SATONO RASEN	Chris Waller	Blake Shinn	5.3L	6	59kg	$31
10	2	BRAVE SMASH	Darren Weir	Mark Zahra	9.7L	5	59kg	$6.50

PAST WINNERS

YEAR	WINNER	JOCKEY	TRAINER	2ND	3RD	TIME
2018	Trapeze Artist	Tye Angland	Gerald Ryan	Le Romain	Showtime	1:20.3
2017	Tivaci	Damien Oliver	Michael Moroney	Le Romain	Jungle Edge	1:26.9
2016	English	Sam Clipperton	Gai Waterhouse	Black Heart Bart	Kermadec	1:22.9
2015	Dissident	Jim Cassidy	Peter Moody	Wandjina	Chautauqua	1:24.6
2014	Hana's Goal	Nash Rawiller	Kazuhiro Kato	Weary	Tiger Tees	1:24.6
2013	All Too Hard	Dwayne Dunn	Michael, Wayne & John Hawkes	Rain Affair	Fiorente	1:22.8
2012	Atlantic Jewel	Michael Rodd	Mark Kavanagh	Rain Affair	Ofcourseican	1:21.8
2011	Hay List	Glen Boss	John Mcnair	Hinchinbrook	Heart Of Dreams	1:26.2
2010	Hot Danish	Tim Clark	Les Bridge	Melito	Beaded	1:22.0
2009	Danleigh	Damien Oliver	Chris Waller	Light Fantastic	Royal Discretion	1:24.8
2008	Racing to Win	Hugh Bowman	John O'Shea	Murtajill	Casino Prince	1:22.7
2007	Bentley Biscuit	Nash Rawiller	Gai Waterhouse	Black Ink	Malcolm	1:24.0
2006	Paratroopers	Darren Beadman	John Hawkes	Niconero	Shania Dane	1:21.5
2005	Shamekha	Darren Beadman	Gai Waterhouse	Only Words	Our Egyptian Raine	1:23.4
2004	Private Steer	Glen Boss	John O'Shea	Our Egyptian Raine	Defier	1:21.6
2003	Arlington Road	Jim Cassidy	Gai Waterhouse	Dash For Cash	Lord Essex	1:36.5
2002	Sunline	Greg Childs	Trevor Mckee	Cent Home	Dress Circle	1:34.3
2001	El Mirada	Brian York	John Size	Final Fantasy	Sunline	1:39.7
2000	Sunline	Greg Childs	Trevor Mckee	Georgie Boy	Over	1:35.7
1999	Intergaze	Craig Carmody	Rod Craig	Bonanova	Adam	1:36.0
1998	Des's Dream	Steven King	Chris Wood	Catalan Opening	Noise	1:36.3
1997	All Our Mob	Chris Munce	Gai Waterhouse	Shame	Catalan Opening	1:35.0

BACKGROUND

First run: 1866 (won by Falcon). Group 1 since 1980. Run over 1600m 1866-2003.
Most recent mare to win: English (2016).
Most recent 3YO to win: C&G—Trapeze Artist (2018); Filly—English (2016): Note: the other two 3YO fillies were Atlantic Jewel (2012) and Valicare (1926).
Multiple winners: 11—Sunline (2002, 2000); Rough Habit (1993, 1992); Dalrello (1977, 1976); Kilshery (1963, 1962); Yaralla (1943, 1942); Ajax (1940, 1939, 1938); Malt King (1912, 1911); Gladsome (1904, 1904); Marvel (1894, 1891); Carbine (18, 90, 1889); Tim Whiffler (1871, 1870).
Fastest time (1400m): Trapeze Artist (2018) 1:20.33
Notable winners: Trapeze Artist (2018); Dissident (2015); Hana's Goal (2014); All Too Hard (2013); Atlantic Jewel (2012); Hay List (2011); Racing To Win (2008); Sunline (2000, 2002); Flying Spur (1996); Rough Habit (1992-93); Shaftesbury Avenue (1991); Campaign King (1987); Emancipation (1984); Belmura Lad (1979); Tontonan (1974); Triton (1972); Abdul (1971); Tobin Bronze (1967); Wenona Girl (1964); Sky High (1961); Noholme (1960); Lord (1959); Tulloch (1958); Bernborough (1946); Ajax (1938-39-40); Peter Pan (1935); Chatham (1934); Amounis (1930); Mollison (1929); Limerick (1928); Desert Gold (1918); Wakeful (1902); Carbine (1889-90); Briseis (1976); Tim Whiffler (1870-71); Fireworks (1868).

All Aged Stakes winners won the lead-up races:
Orr Stake: 4—Dissident (2015); All Too Hard (2013); Tobin Bronze (1967); Lord (1959).
Futurity Stakes: 13—All Too Hard (2013); Vite Cheval (1985); Always Welcome (1978); Sky High (1961); Lord (1959); San Domenico (1952); Bernborough (1946); Ajax (1940, 1939, 1938); Winooka (1933); Amounis (1930); Gladsome (1905).
Chipping Norton Stakes: 5—Emancipation (1984); Tulloch (1958); Bernborough (1946); Katanga (1944); Limerick (1928).
Challenge Stakes: 3—English (2016); Hay List (2011); The Hawk (1925);
Coolmore Classic: 3—Sunline (2000, 2002); Emancipation (1984).
Canterbury Stakes: 4—Hot Danish (2010); Paratroopers (2006); Broker's Tip (1970); Yaralla (1942).
George Ryder Stakes: 7—Campaign King (1987); Emancipation (1984); All Shot (1973); Triton (1972); Foresight (1969); Fuji San (1927); Claro (1924).
Queen Of The Turf Stakes: None.
T J Smith Stakes: 3—Trapeze Artist (2018); Bentley Biscuit (2007); Shamekha (2005).
Doncaster Handicap: 14—Private Steer (2004); Sunline (2002); My Gold Hope (1982); Belmura Lad (1979); Tontonan (1974); Broker's Tip (1970); Unpainted (1968); Cuddle (1936); Chatham (1934); Winooka (1933); Sir Christopher (1931); Valicare (1926); Speciality (1921); Cremorne (1893).
All Aged Stakes also won in the same preparation:
Queen Elizabeth Stakes: 2—Rough Habit (1992); Tulloch (1958).
BRC Cup: 1—Bentley Biscuit (2007)
Doomben 10,000: 2—Hay List (2011); Bernborough (1946).
Stradbroke Hcp: 4—Rough Habit (1992); Triton (1972); Kilshery (1962); Kingster (1957).
Leading winning jockeys:
7 wins Jim Pike (Peter Pan 1935, Chatham 1934, Winooka 1933, Amounis 1930, Fujisan 1927, The Hawk 1925, Chrysolaus 1920).
5 wins Neville Sellwood (Sky High 1961, Noholme 1960, King's Fair 1956, Prince Morvi 1955, Prince Cortauld 1954).
4 wins Harold Badger (Ajax 1930, 1939, 1938, Viol D'Amour 1932); Jim Cassidy (Dissident 2015, Arlington Road 2003, Rough Habit 1993, 1992); Athol Mulley (Scottish Soldier 1965, Kingster 1957, Red Jester 1953, Bernborough 1946); Arthur Wood (Beauford 1922, Malt King 1912, 1911, Bobrikoff 1910).
Current winning jockeys:
3 wins Damien Oliver (Tivaci 2017, Danleigh 2009k, Hurricane Sky 1995).
2 wins Glen Boss (Hay List 2011, Private Steer 2004); Nash Rawiller (Hana's Goal 2014, Bentley Biscuit 2007)
1 win Tye Angland (Trapeze Artist 2018); Hugh Bowman (Racing To Win 2008); Tim Clark (Hot Danish 2010); Sam Clipperton (English 2016); Dwayne Dunn (All Too Hard 2013); Michael Rodd (Atlantic Jewel 2012).
Leading winning trainers:
5 wins Gai Waterhouse (English 2016, Bentley Biscuit 2007, Shamekha 2005, Arlington Road 2003, All Our Mob 1997).
4 wins Tom Lamond (Lady Betty 1888, Wheatear 1882, Tocal 1877, Fitz Yattendon 1874); Maurice McCarten (Wenona Girl 1964, Noholme 1960, Prince Morvi 1955, Prince Cortauld 1954); Tommy Smith (Unpainted 1968, Kilshery 1963, 1962, Tulloch 1957).
Current winning trainers:
5 wins Gai Waterhouse (English 2016; Bentley Biscuit 2007, Shamekha 2005, Arlington Road 2003, All Our Mob 1997).
3 win John Hawkes (All Too Hard 2013, Paratroopers 2006, El Mirada 2001).
2 wins Les Bridge (Hot Danish 2010, Drawn 1986); John O'Shea (Racing To Win 2008, Private Steer 2004); Gerald Ryan (Trapeze Artist 2018, Hurricane Sky 1995); John Wheeler (Rough Habit 1993, 1992).
1 win Rod Craig (Intergaze 1999); Lee Freedman (Flying Spur 1996); Michael, Wayne & John Hawkes (All Too Hard 2013); Kazuhiro Kato (Hana's Goal 2014); Mark Kavanagh (Atlantic Jewel 2012); Micheal Moroney (Tivaci 2017); Bruce Wallace (Prince Of Praise 1994); Chris Waller (Danleigh 2009); Chris Wood (Des's Dream 1998).
Points of interest:
Gerald Ryan, who trained Hurricane Sky to win in 1995, rode Bit Of A Skite to win in 1980.
Maurice McCarten trained four winners (see above) and rode Cuddle (1936) and Limerick (1928).
Matador (1887) dead-heated with Nelson, but was awarded the race in a run-off.
Hana's Goal (2104), trained by Japan's Kazuhiro Kato, is the only international winner of the All Aged Stakes.

ATC Champagne Stakes (1600m)—Randwick
Of $500,000. Group 1. Set Weights, 2YO. April 20, 2019.

2017-18 RESULT: Time: 1:34.47 (Good 3)

FP	NO	HORSE	TRAINER	JOCKEY	MARGIN	BAR.	WGT	SP
1	13	SEABROOK	Mick Price	Damien Oliver		12	54.5kg	$9
2	7	BONDI	Peter & Paul Snowden	Mark Zahra	0.5L	2	56.5kg	$7.50
3	12	EL DORADO DREAMING	Benjamin Smith	Jason Collett	1.3L	7	54.5kg	$7.50
4	11	GUERRIER	Jean Dubois	Jean Van Overmeire (a)	1.9L	1	56.5kg	$26
5	3	OUTRAGEOUS	Michael, Wayne & John Hawkes	Brenton Avdulla	2.8L	3	56.5kg	$6f
6	1	ENCRYPTION	James Cummings	Hugh Bowman	3.4L	10	56.5kg	$9.50
7	6	IRUKANDJI	Michael, Wayne & John Hawkes	Corey Brown	3.5L	4	56.5kg	$10
8	5	NOT A SINGLE CENT	Ciaron Maher	Blake Shinn	4.8L	5	56.5kg	$8
9	2	LONG LEAF	David & Ben Hayes & Tom Dabernig	Kerrin McEvoy	6.2L	9	56.5kg	$8
10	8	SEBERATE	David & Ben Hayes & Tom Dabernig	Tim Clark	6.4L	11	56.5kg	$17
11	9	AKKADIAN	Matt Cumani	Jordan Childs	8.8L	6	56.5kg	$21
12	4	RAGGED RASCAL	Paul Perry	Joshua Parr	10.4L	13	56.5kg	$51
13	10	BLAZING ISSUE	Gregory Hickman	Michael Walker	12.1L	8	56.5kg	$101

PAST WINNERS

YEAR	WINNER	JOCKEY	TRAINER	2ND	3RD	TIME
2018	Seabrook	Damien Oliver	Mick Price	Bondi	El Dorado Dreaming	1:34.4
2017	The Mission	Damian Lane	Paul Perry	Invader	Whispered Secret	1:41.0
2016	Prized Icon	Glyn Schofield	James Cummings	Chimboraa	Divine Prophet	1:36.8
2015	Pasadena Girl	Hugh Bowman	Peter Moody	Street Rapper	Tarquin	1:38.0
2014	Go Indy Go	Chad Schofield	Leon Macdonald & Andrew Gluyas	Zululand	Kumaon	1:40.2
2013	Guelph	Kerrin McEvoy	Peter Snowden	Fuerza	Equator	1:36.2
2012	Pierro	Nash Rawiller	Gai Waterhouse	Dear Demi	Tatra	1:35.0
2011	Helmet	Kerrin McEvoy	Peter Snowden	Pane In The Glass	Fast And Sexy	1:40.3
2010	Skilled	Josh Parr	Peter Snowden	Sasa	Divorces	1:36.3
2009	Onemorenomore	Peter Robl	Jason Coyle	Tickets	Manhattan Rain	1:39.4
2008	Samantha Miss	Hugh Bowman	Kris Lees	Sebring	Glowlamp	1:38.2
2007	Meurice	Nash Rawiller	Gai Waterhouse	Solo Flyer	Camarilla	1:37.6
2006	Mentality	Darren Beadman	John Hawkes	Miss Finland	Gallant Tess	1:35.0
2005	Carry On Cutie	Len Beasley	Graeme Rogerson	Fashions Afield	Media	1:36.2
2004	Dance Hero	Chris Munce	Gai Waterhouse	Wager	Savabeel	1:34.7
2003	Hasna	Len Beasley	Gai Waterhouse	Aim For Gold	Bushland	1:36.9
2002	Victory Vein	Danny Beasley	Bede Murray	Half Hennessy	Choisir	1:37.9
2001	Viscount	Rod Quinn	John Hawkes	Ustinov	Miss Bussell	1:37.4
2000	Assertive Lad	Shane Dye	Gai Waterhouse	Clonmel	Re Rinka	1:40.0
1999	Quick Star	Damien Oliver	Garry Frazer	Let's Rock Again	Shogun Lodge	1:38.0
1998	Dracula	Larry Cassidy	John Hawkes	Happyanunoit	Mossman	1:39.6
1997	Encounter	Shane Dye	Clarry Conners	Salty	Irish Air	1:36.9

BACKGROUND

First run: 1861 (won by Exeter). Group 1 since 1980. Run over 1000m in 1861; 1600m 1862-64. Run over 1400m in 1866; 1000m 1867-80; 1882; 1200m 1881; 1883-1971.

1600m from 1972 (won by Anjudy).

Most recent filly to win: Seabrook (2018). Note: 31 fillies have won since 1930.

Fastest time (1600m): Seabrook (2018) 1:34.47

Notable winners: Prized Icon (2016); Guelph (2013); Pierro (2012); Helmet (2011); Dance Hero (2004); Burst (1992); Red Anchor (1984); Luskin Star (1977); Baguette (1970); Vain (1969); Storm Queen (1966); Sky High (1960); Noholme (1959); Wiggle (1958); Todman (1957); True Course (1950); High Caste (1939); Ajax (1937); Hall Mark (1933); Mollison (1928); Heroic (1924); Furious (1921); Wolaroi (1916); Malt King (1909); Bobadil (1898); Chester (1877); Robinson Crusoe (1876); Fishhook (1866); Yattendon (1864).

Champagne Stakes winners won the lead-up races:
Skyline Stakes: 2—Dance Hero (2004); Viscount (2001).
Sweet Embrace Stakes: 3—Seabrook (2018); Carry On Cutie (2005); Victory Vein (2002).

SAJC Sires' Produce Stakes: 2—Go Indy Go (2014); Zasu (1974).
Todman Stakes: 4—Pierro (2012); Meurice (2007); Tierce (1991); Luskin Star (1977).
Reisling Stakes: 2—Burst (1992); Triscay (1990).
T.L. Baillieu Handicap: 5—The Mission (2017); Skilled (2010); Onemorenomore (2009); Mentality (2006); Select Prince (1989).
Fernhill Stakes: 2—Prized Icon (2016); Dracula (1998).
Golden Slipper: 10—Pierro (2012); Dance Hero (2004); Burst (1992); Tierce (1991); Luskin Star (1971); Vivarchi (1976); Baguette (1970); Storm Queen (1966); Sky High (1960); Todman (1957).
ATC Sires' Produce Stakes: 40—Guelph (2013); Pierro (2012); Helmet (2011); Dance Hero (2004); Hasna (2003); Victory Vein (2002); Viscount (2001); Assertive Lad (2000); Encounter (1997); Burst (1992); Tierce (1991); Luskin Star (1977); Baguette (1970); Time And Tide (1963); Bogan Road (1962); Lindbergh (1954); Ocean Bound (1951); True Course (1950); Temeraire (1947); Magnificent (1945); Ajax (1937); Young Idea (1935); Hall Mark (1933); Kuvera (1932); Mollison (1928); Furious (1921); Outlook (1918); Thrice (1917); Malt Queen (1908); Collarit (1906); Uralla (1885); Warwick (1883); Spinningdale (1881); His Lordship (1878); Chester (1877); Robinson Crusoe (1876); Kingsborough (1874); Rose d'Amour (1873); Lecturer (1872); Hamlet (1871).

Champagne Stakes winners went on to win in the same preparation:
BRC Sires' Produce: 2—Red Anchor (1984); Luskin Star (1977).
BRC JJ Atkins Stakes: 1—Luskin Star (1977).

Champagne Stakes and the spring 1600m features for 3YOs:
Flight Stakes: 5—Guelph (2013); Samantha Miss (2008); Triscay (1990); Bounding Away (1986); Wattle (1948).
Thousand Guineas: 2—Guelph (2013); True Course (1950).
Caulfield Guineas: 20—Helmet (2011); Encounter (1997); Red Anchor (1984); Luskin Star (1977); Vain (1969); Storm Queen (1966); Time And Tide (1963); High Caste (1939); Ajax (1937); Young Idea (1935); Rampion (1926); Heroic (1924); Thrice (1917); Malt King (1909); Ibex (1901); Bobadil (1898); Aurum (1897); Autonomy (1892); Rudolph (1889); Volley (1888).
Victoria Derby: 11—Prized Icon (2016); Red Anchor (1984); Sky High (1960); Hall Mark (1933); Rampion (1926); Manfred (1925); Furious (1921); Wolaroi (1916); Navigator (1882); Florence (1870); Fireworks (1867).

Leading winning jockeys:
6 wins Shane Dye (Assertive Lad 2000, Encounter 1997, Isolda 1995, March Hare 1993, Burst 1992, Tierce 1991).
5 wins Tom Hales (Rudolph 1889, Volley 1888, Uralla 1885, Bargo 1884, Navigator 1882).
4 wins Joe Morrison (Grand Prix 1880, His Lordship 1878, Robinson Crusoe 1876, Fenella 1868); Darby Munro (Lindbergh 1954, Wattle 1948, Tonga 1936, Chemosh 1930); Neville Sellwood (Noholme 1959, Todman 1957, Knave 1955, Cortauld 1953); Jack Thompson (Columbia Star 1961, Count Olin 1956, Lady Pirouette 1949, Persian Prince 1946).

Current winning jockeys:
2 wins Hugh Bowman (Pasadena Girl 2015, Samantha Miss 2008); Kerrin McEvoy (Guelph 2013, Helmet 2011); Damien Oliver (Seabrook 2018, Quick Star 1999); Nash Rawiller (Pierro 2012, Meurice 2007);
1 win Glen Boss (Intergaze 1996); Larry Cassidy (Dracula 1998); Damian Lane (The Mission 2017); Josh Parr (Skilled 2010); Chad Schofield (Go Indy Go 2014); Glyn Schofield (Prized Icon 2016); Robert Thompson (I Like Diamond 1982).

Leading winning trainers:
7 wins Etienne de Mestre (Navigator 1882, Grand Prix 1880, His Lordship 1878, Chester 1877, Robinson Crusoe 1876, Yattendon 1864, Exeter 1861); Tom Payten (Cider 1912, Lord Fitzroy 1904, Brakpan 1902, Coil 1896, Autonomy 1892, Rudolph 1889, Volley 1888).
6 wins Tom Lamond (Reviver 1899, Oxide 1891, Blairgowrie 1886, Spinningdale 1881, Hyperion 1875, Kingsborough 1874); Maurice McCarten (Farnworth 1964, Noholme 1959, Todman 1957, Knave 1955, Cortauld 1953, Ocean Bound 1951); Tommy Smith (Bounding Away 1986, Charity 1979, Parade 1978, Zasu 1974, Rajah 1968, Guilia 1967).
5 wins Gai Waterhouse (Pierro 2012, Meurice 2007, Dance Hero 2004, Hasna 2003, Assertive Lad 2000).

Current winning trainers:
5 wins Gai Waterhouse (Pierro 2012, Meurice 2007, Dance Hero 2004, Hasna 2003, Assertive Lad 2000).
4 wins Clarry Conners (Encounter 1997, Euphoria 1994, Burst 1992, Tierce 1991);
3 wins John Hawkes (Mentality 2006, Viscount 2001, Dracula 1998); Peter Snowden (Guelph 2013, Helmet 2011, Skilled 2010).
2 wins Rod Craig (Intergaze 1996, Lady Eclipse 1983); Graeme Rogerson (Carry On Cutie 200, Isolda 1995).
1 win James Cummings (Prized Icon 2016); Garry Frazer (Quick Star 1999); Kris Lees (Samantha Miss 2008); Leon Macdonald (Go Indy Go 2014); Paul Perry (The Mission 2017); Mick Price (Seabrook 2018); John Thompson (Onemorenomore 2009).

Points Of Interest:
Noholme (1959) and Todman (1957) are brothers. Both colts are by Star Kingdom from Oceana. Todman (1957) beat Tulloch in one of the best Champagne Stakes in history.
Dance Hero (2004) is the only Champagne Stakes winner to win the Magic Millions. He also won the Golden Slipper and ATC Sires' Produce Stakes.
Maurice McCarten trained six winners (see above) and rode three winners—High Caste 1939, Ajax 1937, Kuvera 1932.

SAJC Schweppes Oaks (2000m)—Morphettville

Of $500,000. Group 1. Set Weights, 3YO Fillies. May 4, 2019.

2017-18 RESULT: Time: 2:04.34 (Soft 5)

FP	NO	HORSE	TRAINER	JOCKEY	MARGIN	BAR.	WGT	SP
1	5	SOPRESSA	Darren Weir	Harry Coffey		1	56kg	$6.50
2	12	SHEEZDASHING	Mathew Ellerton & Simon Zahra	Damien Thornton	0.3L	6	56kg	$16
3	3	MISS ADMIRATION	Mick Price	Ben Melham	0.4L	4	56kg	$26
4	6	PLEASURING	Darren Weir	Damian Lane	0.7L	7	56kg	$21
5	4	THINK BLEUE	Darren Weir	John Allen	1.5L	14	56kg	$5.50
6	1	ALOISIA	Ciaron Maher	Mark Zahra	1.6L	12	56kg	$5.50
7	7	SAVACOOL	Chris Waller	Damien Oliver	2.5L	10	56kg	$5f
8	11	SEMARI	Trent Busuttin & Natalie Young	Dwayne Dunn	3.7L	8	56kg	$21
9	9	TEMPLE OF BEL	Tony McEvoy	Craig Williams	3.9L	9	56kg	$18
10	14	PURE SCOT	David & Ben Hayes & Tom Dabernig	Regan Bayliss	4.6L	2	56kg	$61
11	8	PRETTY TO SEA	Ciaron Maher	Michael Dee	4.7L	13	56kg	$41
12	13	EARTH ANGEL	David & Ben Hayes & Tom Dabernig	Joe Bowditch	5L	5	56kg	$51
13	10	VELOCITA	Chris Waller	Stephen Baster	5.6L	3	56kg	$31
14	2	BRING ME ROSES	Tony McEvoy	Luke Currie	7.2L	11	56kg	$12

PAST WINNERS

YEAR	WINNER	JOCKEY	TRAINER	2ND	3RD	TIME
2018	Sopressa	Harry Coffey	Darren Weir	Sheezdashing	Miss Admiration	2:04.3
2017	Egg Tart	Kerrin McEvoy	Chris Waller	Kenedna	Ana Royale	2:04.3
2016	Abbey Marie	Luke Nolen	Michael Kent	Silent Sedition	C'Est Beau La Vie	2:04.1
2015	Delicacy	Peter Hall	Grant Williams	Fenway	Bahamas	2:03.3
2014	May's Dream	Brad Rawiller	Darren Weir	Star Fashion	Scratchy Bottom	2:04.8
2013	Maybe Discreet	Dominic Tourneur	Phillip Stokes	Grand Daughter	La Zuma	2:07.0
2012	Invest	Peter Mertens	Clarry Conners	Our Miss Jones	Essence	2:06.9
2011	Lights Of Heaven	Luke Nolen	Peter Moody	Absolutely	Southern Speed	2:05.3
2010	Small Minds	Dean Holland	John P Thompson	No Evidence Needed	Ipioga	2:06.4
2009	Gallica	Craig Newitt	Mick Price	Estee	Miss Lily Rose	2:03.8
2008	Zarita	Greg Childs	Pat Hyland	Moment In Time	Queen Of Queens	2:04.3
2007	Anamato	Michael Rodd	David Hayes	Cancanelle	Devil Moon	2:02.2
2006	Marju Snip	Steven Arnold	Phillip Stokes	Zenarta	Fanciful Bella	2:04.4
2005	Irish Darling	Paul Harvey	Tony Vasil	Kylikwong	Hveger	2:04.4
2004	Rinky Dink	Greg Childs	Rick Hore-Lacy	Star Of Grechen	Dane Belltar	2:04.3
2003	Sound Action	Wayne Hokai	Roberta Maguire	Milanova	Great Anna	2:05.1
2002	Tully Thunder	Damien Oliver	Ross McDonald	Shes Archie	Arboretum	2:03.3
2001	Tempest Morn	Jim Cassidy	Gai Waterhouse	South Sea Pearl	Glitzy Guru	2:07.1
2000	Grand Echezeaux	Craig Williams	Lee Freedman	Umaline	Porto Roca	2:04.3
1999	Episode	Damien Oliver	David Hall	Grand Archway	Toy Carousel	2:04.2
1998	La Volta	Danny Brereton	Colin Alderson	Pavan	Madonna	2:07.0
1997	Minegold	Alf Matthews	Leon Macdonald	Prairie	Derobe	2:09.9

BACKGROUND

First run: 1982 (won by Rose of Kingston) Group 3 1982. Group 1 from 1983. Registered as SAJC Australasian Oaks.
Fastest time (2000m): Anamato (2007), Gatherneaux (1992) & Mannerism (1991) 2:02.20
Notable winners: Egg Tart (2017); Delicacy (2015); Lights Of Heaven (2011); Zarita (2008); Anamato (2007); Gallica (2005); Tully Thunder (2002); Tempest Morn (2001); Grand Echezeaux (2000); Episode (1999); Tristalove (1994); Mannerism (1991); Imposera (1988); Miss Clipper (1986); Centaurea (1985); Rose Of Kingston (1982).

Schweppes Oaks winners won the lead-up races:
Queen Of The South Stakes: 1—Rose Of Kingston (1982).
Auraria Stakes: 6—Sopressa (2018); Grand Echezeaux (2000); Episode (1999); La Volta (1998); Gatherneaux (1992); Miss Clipper (1986).
Adelaide Guineas: 2—Small Minds (2010); Tristalove (1994). Note: Marju Snip (2006) finished third in the Adelaide Guineas and won the Schweppes Oaks.
Angus Armanasco Stakes: 1—Zarita (2008).
Kewney Stakes: 6—Gallica (2009); Zarita (2008); Anamato (2007); Tristalove (1994); Mannerism (1991); Send Me An Angel (1987).
MV Fillies Classic: 2—Lights Of Heaven (2011); Anamato (2007).
WA Derby: 1—Delicacy (2015).
Schweppes Oaks winners went on to win in the same preparation:
South Australian Oaks (SAJC Fillies Classic): 3—Irish Darling (2005); Episode (1999); Our Tristalight (1993).
Auraria Stakes & SA Oaks: 1—Episode (1999).
South Australian Derby: 2—Delicacy (2015); Zarita (2008).
Australian Derby: 1—Rose Of Kingston (1982).
Doomben Roses: 1—Invest (2012).
Queensland Oaks: 1—Egg Tart (2017).
Schweppes Oaks winners and the "other" Oaks:
VRC Oaks: 1—Rose Of Kingston (1982). Note: Grand Archway (1998 VRC Oaks winner) finished second to Episode in the 2000 Schweppes Oaks.
ATC Australian Oaks: No horses have won both races. Note: Grand Archway (1999 Australian Oaks winner) finished second to Episode in the Schweppes Oaks; My Brilliant Star (1992 Australian Oaks winner) finished second to Gatherneaux in the Schweppes Oaks. Tempest Morn (2001) finished second in the Australian Oaks.
Queensland Oaks: 1—Egg Tart (2017).
WA Oaks: 2—Delicacy (2015); Send Me An Angel (1986).
Schweppes Oaks winners and the following spring:
Schweppes Oaks & Caulfield Cup (same year): 1—Imposera (1988). Note: Mannerism (1991) won the 1992 Caulfield Cup as a 5YO; Gatherneaux (1992) finished fifth in the 1992 Caulfield Cup behind stablemate Mannerism.
Leading winning jockeys:
3 wins Damien Oliver (Tully Thunder 2002, Episode 1999, Mannerism 1991).
2 wins Danny Brereton (La Volta 1998, Leica Smile 1996); Greg Childs (Zarita 2008, Rinky Dink 2004); John Letts (Miss Clipper 1986, Royal Regatta 1983); Luke Nolen (Abbey Marie 2016, Lights Of Heaven 2011).
Current winning jockeys:
3 wins Damien Oliver (Tully Thunder 2002, Episode 1999, Mannerism 1991).
2 wins Luke Nolen (Abbey Marie 2016, Lights Of Heaven 2011).
1 win Steven Arnold (Marju Snip 2006); Harry Coffey (Sopressa 2018); Paul Harvey (Irish Darling 2005); Peter Hall (Delicacy 2015); Dean Holland (Small Minds 2010); Kerrin McEvoy (Egg Tart 2017); Craig Newitt (Gallica 2009); Brad Rawiller (May's Dream 2014); Michael Rodd (Anamato 2007); Dominic Tourneur (Maybe Discreet 2013); Craig Williams (Grand Echezeaux 2000).
Leading winning trainers:
4 wins Bart Cummings (Tristalove 1994, Our Tristalight 1993, Stapleton Lass 1989, Royal Regatta 1983); Lee Freedman (Grand Echezeaux 2000, Gatherneaux 1992, Mannerism 1991, Miss Clipper 1986).
3 wins Ross McDonald (Tully Thunder 2002, Imposera 1988, Centaurea 1985).
Current winning trainers:
4 wins Lee Freedman (Grand Echezeaux 2000, Gatherneaux 1992, Mannerism 1991, Miss Clipper 1986).
2 wins Phillip Stokes (Maybe Discreet 2013, Marju Snip 2006); Darren Weir (Sopressa 2018, May's Dream 2014).
1 win Clarry Conners (Invest 2012); David Hall (Episode 1999); David Hayes (Anamato 2007); Pat Hyland (Zarita 2008); Mick Kent (Abbey Marie 2016); Leon Macdonald (Minegold 1997); Roberta Maguire (Sound Action 2003); Mick Price (Gallica 2009); John Thompson (Small Minds 2010); Tony Vasil (Irish Darling 2005); Chris Waller (Egg Tart 2017); Gai Waterhouse (Tempest Morn 2001); Grant Williams (Delicacy 2015).
Points of interest:
Miss Clipper (1986) is trainer Lee Freedman's first Group 1 winner.
Sound Action (2003) won the 2004 Group 1 Ranvet Stakes at Rosehill.
No MRC Armanasco Stakes winner has won the G1 Schweppes Oaks.
Centaurea (1985) was ridden by champion English rider Lester Piggott.
Anamato (2007) won the Schweppes Oaks before travelling to America to finish third in the Group 1 American Oaks (2000m) at Hollywood Park in California.
Delicacy (2015) won in four consecutive races, the G3 WA Oaks, G2 WA Derby, G1 Schweppes Oaks and G1 SA Derby.

SAJC Robert Sangster Stakes (1200m)—Morphettville

Of $1,000,000. Group 1. Weight For Age. Fillies & Mares. May 4, 2019.

2017-18 RESULT: Time: 1:09.19 (Soft 5)

FP	NO	HORSE	TRAINER	JOCKEY	MARGIN	BAR.	WGT	SP
1	14	SHOALS	Anthony Freedman	Tim Clark		15	55kg	$12
2	1	SECRET AGENDA	Mick Price	Damien Oliver	1.7L	13	56.5kg	$9.50
3	12	MICA LIL	Mark Minervini	Shayne Cahill	2.6L	9	56.5kg	$91
4	18	TRUE EXCELSIOR	Leon & Troy Corstens	Stephen Baster	2.9L	14	55kg	$151
5	7	WHISPERING BROOK	Darren Weir	Dean Yendall	2.9L	3	56.5kg	$8
6	13	MYSTIFIED	Ryan Balfour	Damien Thornton	3.3L	6	56.5kg	$151
7	15	CATCHY	David & Ben Hayes & Tom Dabernig	Dwayne Dunn	3.3L	7	55kg	$6.50
8	4	MISSROCK	Robbie Laing	Ben Melham	4L	10	56.5kg	$15
9	6	QUILISTA	Darren Weir	Damian Lane	4.1L	1	56.5kg	$4.80f
10	10	LEGLESS VEUVE	Henry Dwyer	Chris Parnham	4.3L	11	56.5kg	$31
11	3	SUPER CASH	Andrew Noblet	Craig Williams	4.4L	8	56.5kg	$13
12	9	PEDRENA	Mick Price	Michael Dee	4.6L	16	56.5kg	$31
13	5	DAINTY TESS	Daniel Morton	Jamie Kah	5.1L	4	56.5kg	$12
14	16	FORMALITY	David & Ben Hayes & Tom Dabernig	Kerrin McEvoy	6.1L	2	55kg	$9
15	17	TULIP	David & Ben Hayes & Tom Dabernig	Regan Bayliss	6.1L	17	55kg	$26
16	8	MISS GUNPOWDER	David & Ben Hayes & Tom Dabernig	Jason Holder	7L	5	56.5kg	$61
17	11	IT'S BEEN A BATTLE	Shane Oxlade	Justin Potter	8L	12	56.5kg	$101

PAST WINNERS

YEAR	WINNER	JOCKEY	TRAINER	2ND	3RD	TIME
2018	Shoals	Tim Clark	Anthony Freedman	Secret Agenda	Mica Lil	1:09.1
2017	Secret Agenda	Damien Oliver	Mick Price	Viddora	I Am A Star	1:09.1
2016	Precious Gem	Jake Noonan	Henry Dwyer	Sheidel	I Love It	1:09.4
2015	Miracles Of Life	Hugh Bowman	Peter & Paul Snowden	Gregers	I Love It	1:09.7
2014	Driefontein	Vlad Duric	Gai Waterhouse	Platelet	Gregers	1:09.2
2013	Platelet	Ben Melham	Darren Weir	Angelic Light	Yosei	1:11.0
2012	Black Caviar	Luke Nolen	Peter Moody	Sistine Angel	Power Princess	1:10.6
2011	Response	Dwayne Dunn	Mathew Ellerton & Simon Zahra	Beaded	Miss Octopussy	1:09.0
2010	Rostova	Steven King	Steve Richards	Velocitea	Sister Madly	1:09.4
2009	Bel Mer	Craig Newitt	Mick Price	Hidden Energy	Impressive Eagle	1:09.5
2008	Juste Momente	Steven Arnold	Danny O'Brien	Zipanese	Serious Speed	1:09.7
2007	Universal Queen	Corey Brown	Lee Freedman	Media	Flying Object	1:08.3
2006	Ellicorsam	Danny Nikolic	Lee Freedman	Social Glow	Truly Wicked	1:09.7
2005	Alinghi	Damien Oliver	Lee Freedman	Glamour Puss	Solar Antiquity	1:08.7
2004	French Bid	Stephen Baster	Mick Price	Fly For Me	Social Glow	1:09.0
2003	Our Egyptian Raine	Cathy Treymane	Kenny Rae	Brief Embrace	Dama De Noche	1:08.7
2002	Suzy Grey	Paul Gatt	Alan Bailey	Regal Kiss	Lady Belvedere	1:13.2
2001	Umaline	Shayne Cahill	John Hall	Fayrouz	Crixia	1:08.1
2000	Rain Dance Lady	Fabian Alescil	David Hall	Tapalinga	Daninkling	1:09.1
1999	Dantelah	Jim Cassidy	Paul Perry	My Millennium	Speedy Kids	1:07.9
1998	Spirit Of Love	Eddie Wilkinson	Mick Price	Will Fly	Rose Of Danehill	1:09.9
1997	Apple Danish	Michael Carson	Anthony Cummings	Bionic Bess	Zeya	1:10.5

BACKGROUND

First run: 1983 (won by Ranee's Palace). Listed 1984-85. Group 3 1986-2003. Group 2 in 2004. Group 1 from 2005. Set weights until 1987. Run at Cheltenham in 2002. Registered as the Robert Sangster Stakes. Also known as the Swettenham Stud Stakes and Ubet Stakes.
Most recent 3YO to win: Shoals (2018). Note: 10 3YO fillies have won.
Multiple winners: None.
Fastest time (1200m): Dantelah (1999) 1:07.90

Notable winners: Shoals (2018); Miracles Of Life (2015); Black Caviar (2012); Alinghi (2005); Our Egyptian Raine (2004); Dantelah (1999); With Me (1991).
Robert Sangster Stakes winners won the lead-up races:
MRC Anniversary Vase: 1—Precious Gem (2016).
Irwin Stakes: 2—Driefontein (2014); Leica Western (1990).
Surround Stakes: 1—Shoals (2018).
Lightning Stakes: 1—Black Caviar (2012).
Oakleigh Plate: 2—Dantelah (1999); With Me (1991).
Newmarket Handicap: 1—Alinghi (2005).
Sapphire Stakes: 1—Secret Agenda (2017).
Robert Sangster Stakes winners went on to win in the same preparation:
Euclase Stakes: 1—Universal Queen (2007).
The Goodwood: 2—Platelet (2013); Black Caviar (2012).
Leading winning jockey:
2 wins Shayne Cahill (Umaline 2001, Tarare 1994); Damien Oliver (Secret Agenda 2017, Alinghi 2005).
Current winning jockeys:
2 wins Shayne Cahill (Umaline 2001, Tarare 1994); Damien Oliver (Secret Agenda 2017, Alinghi 2005).
1 win Fabian Alesci (Rain Dance Lady 2000); Steven Arnold (Juste Momente 2008); Stephen Baster (French Bid 2004); Corey Brown (Universal Queen 2007); Michael Carson (Apple Danish 1997); Tim Clark (Shoals 2018); Dwayne Dunn (Response 2011); Vlad Duric (Driefontein 2014); Paul Gatt (2002); Ben Melham (2013); Craig Newitt (Bel Mer 2009); Luke Nolen (Black Caviar 2012); Jake Noonan (Precious Gem 2016); Brett Prebble (Mad Shavirl 1996).
Leading winning trainers:
3 wins Lee Freedman (Universal Queen 2007, Ellicorsam 2006, Alinghi 2005); Mick Price (Bel Mer 2009, French Bid 2004, Spirit Of Love 1998).
Current winning trainers:
3 wins Lee Freedman (Universal Queen 2007, Ellicorsam 2006, Alinghi 2005); Mick Price (Bel Mer 2009, French Bid 2004, Spirit Of Love 1998).
1 win Grahame Begg (Our Egyptian Raine 2003); Anthony Cummings (Apple Danish 1997); Colin Davies (Vatican Lass 1984); Henry Dwyer (Precious Gem 2016); Mathew Ellerton & Simon Zahra (Response 2011); Anthony Freedman (Shoals 2018); David Hall (Rain Dance Lady 2000); Tom Hughes jnr (Viminaria 1995); Neville Kennedy (Showport 1985); Danny O'Brien (Juste Momente 2008); Stuart Padman (Tree Of Renown 1989); Paul Perry (Dantelah 1999); Steve Richards (Rostova 2010); Peter & Paul Snowden (Miracles Of Life 2015); Terry Sullivan (Mad Shavirl 1996); Gai Waterhouse (Driefontein 2014); Darren Weir (Platelet 2013).
Points of interest:
Alinghi (2005) finished second to Fastnet Rock in the 2005 Lightning Stakes at Flemington, before winning both the Robert Sangster Stakes and the Newmarket Handicap. Viminaria (1995) also finished third to Mad Shavirl in 1996.
Black Caviar (2012) went on to win the 2012 G1 Diamond Jubilee Stakes (1200m) at Royal Ascot in June.

SAJC South Australian Derby (2500m)—Morphettville

Of $600,000. Group 1. Set Weights, 3YO. May 11, 2019.

2017-18 RESULT: Time: 2:38.95 (Good 4)

FP	NO	HORSE	TRAINER	JOCKEY	MARGIN	BAR.	WGT	SP
1	3	LEICESTER	Darren Weir	Damian Lane		7	56.5kg	$4F
2	10	REZEALIENT	David & Ben Hayes & Tom Dabernig	Jamie Kah	1.4L	4	56.5kg	$21
3	7	RUNAWAY	Gai Waterhouse & Adrian Bott	Stephen Baster	2.1L	12	56.5kg	$13
4	17	TROPICAL LIGHTNING	Travis Doudle	Todd Pannell	2.3L	5	56.5kg	$151
5	8	WON WON TOO	David & Ben Hayes & Tom Dabernig	Jordan Childs	2.9L	3	56.5kg	$51
6	13	HIGH 'N' DRY	Mathew Ellerton & Simon Zahra	Andrew Mallyon	4.1L	16	56.5kg	$6
7	12	INTO RIO	Mathew Ellerton & Simon Zahra	Damien Thornton	4.7L	6	56.5kg	$51
7	2	MONEY MAHER	Daniel & Ben Pearce	Jarrad Noske	4.7L	15	56.5kg	$31
9	5	MAIN STAGE	Trent Busuttin & Natalie Young	Damien Oliver	4.9L	8	56.5kg	$8
10	6	HIGH SHERRIF	Roger James	Leith Innes	5L	10	56.5kg	$9
11	15	NOTHIN' LEICA HIGH	Robbie Griffiths	Dom Tourneur	6.3L	9	56.5kg	$61
12	9	SAVAHEAT	Darren Weir	Dean Yendall	7.6L	1	56.5kg	$31
13	16	BOX ON COLLINS	Tony McEvoy	Luke Currie	8.9L	14	56.5kg	$61
14	1	TANGLED	Chris Waller	Michael Walker	9L	13	56.5kg	$5.50
15	4	CIVIL DISOBEDIENCE	Darren Weir	John Allen	9.1L	11	56.5kg	$14
16	11	SILENT COMMAND	Nick Smart	Shayne Cahill	13.1L	2	56.5kg	$101

PAST WINNERS

YEAR	WINNER	JOCKEY	TRAINER	2ND	3RD	TIME
2018	Leicester	Damian Lane	Darren Weir	Rezealient	Runaway	2:38.9
2017	Volatile Mix	John Allen	Darren Weir	Ruthven	Odeon	2:37.0
2016	Howard Be Thy Name	John Allen	Darren Weir	Etymology	Cool Chap	2:40.0
2015	Delicacy	Peter Hall	Grant Williams	Werther	Allergic	2:37.9
2014	Kushadasi	Steven Arnold	Richard Jolly	Scratchy Bottom	Best Case	2:41.9
2013	Escado	Ben Melham	Matt Laurie	Hioctdane	Shoreham	2:39.0
2012	Zabeelionaire	Damien Oliver	Leon Corstens	Sabrage	Westsouthwest	2:42.1
2011	Shadows In The Sun	Ben Melham	Anthony Cummings	Echoes Of Heaven	Lalla Rookh	2:39.8
2010	Kidnapped	Kerrin McEvoy	Peter Snowden	Red Colossus	Sea Galleon	2:37.2
2009	Rebel Raider	Clare Lindop	Leon Macdonald	Astro Gains	Fitoussi	2:40.3
2008	Zarita	Greg Childs	Pat Hyland	Zagreb	Neugine	2:39.5
2007	Lazer Sharp	Brad Rawiller	Jamie Edwards	Classic De Lago	Red Lord	2:37.8
2006	Testafiable	Greg Childs	Peter Moody	Empire Gold	Irazu	2:43.3
2005	Tails Of Triomphe	Paul Gatt	Terry O'Sullivan	Douro Valley	Kamsky	2:37.7
2004	Hard To Get	Joe Bowditch	Mark Kavanagh	On A Jeune	Better Jetsetter	2:37.1
2003	Mummify	Danny Nikolic	Lee Freedman	Vicksburgh	Lord Wooburn	2:38.7
2002	Pantani	Danny Nikolic	Robbie Laing	Silver Baron	Lester Thunderwing	2:37.8
2001	Big Pat	Peter Mertens	Peter Tulloch	Bush Padre	Adolescence	2:36.2
2000	Blue Murder	Matt Gatt	Cliff Brown	Mr Nelson	Voile D'Or	2:38.4
1999	Showella	Eddie Wilkinson	Frank Ritchie	Seasquill	Our Position	2:36.7
1998	Bulta	Nash Rawiller	Tim White	Prince Standaan	The Hind	2:39.2
1997	Markham	Jason Holder	Cliff Brown	Kings Landing	Derobe	2:39.8

BACKGROUND

First run: 1860 (won by Midnight). Group 1 since 1979. Run over 2400m 1860-1979. Run at Cheltenham in 1979; Victoria Park in 1980 (2600m). Not held 1869-75; 1885-89; 1942-43; 1983. Originally held on the first Saturday in October. Not held in 1983 when moved from the spring to the autumn.

3YO fillies to win (since 1935): 6—Delicacy (2015); Zarita (2008); Showella (1999); Mapperley Heights (1984); English Wonder (1982); Idle Banter (1948).

Fastest time (2500m): Big Pat (2001) 2:36.25

Notable winners: Delicacy (2015); Rebel Raider (2009); Zarita (2008); Mummify (2003); Our Pompeii (1993); Subzero (1992); Shiva's Revenge (1991); Brewery Boy (1981); Stormy Rex (1977); Dayana (1972); Ziema (1964); Gatum Gatum (1961); F.J.A. (1903); Auraria (1895); Tim Whiffler (1865).
SA Derby winners won the lead-up races:
VRC St Leger: 5—Lazer Sharp (2007); Big Pat (2001); Count Chivas (1995); Shiva's Revenge (1991); Shark's Fin (1987).
Lord Reims Stakes: 1—Auraria (1895).
Port Adelaide Guineas: 6—Howard Be Thy Name (2016); French Cotton (1985); English Wonder (1982); Waxwings (1940); Opera King (1931); Pindenda (1926).
Adelaide Guineas: 2—French Cotton (1985); Prince Of All (1975).
Auraria Stakes: none.
Chairman's Stakes: 5—Leicester (2018); Howard Be Thy Name (2016); Rebel Raider (2009); Mummify (2003); Markham (1997).
Schweppes Oaks: 2—Delicacy (2015); Zarita (2008).
Rain Lover Plate: None. Note: Mapperley Heights won the Derby in 1984 and the Rain Lover in 1985. Note 2: Dayana won the Derby in 1972, and the Rain Lover in 1975.
SA Derby and the Adelaide Cup:
3—Our Pompeii (1993); Subzero (1992); Vakeel (Derby 1892, Cup 1893). Note: Vakeel won the Derby when it was conducted in the spring. The Adelaide Cup has moved dates a number of times between March and May.
SA Derby winners and the Melbourne spring majors:
Melbourne Cup: 4—Subzero (1992); Gatum Gatum (Derby 1961, Cup 1963); Auraria (Derby 1895, Cup 1895); Tim Whiffler (Derby 1865, Cup 1867).
Caulfield Cup: 1—Mummify (2003).
Cox Plate: None.
Leading winning jockeys:
6 wins Mick Medhurst (Beau Cavalier 1951, Ladmond 1941, Maxwings 1940, Tempest 1938, Holden Hill 1937, Pinenda 1926).
4 wins Bobby Lewis (The Greek 1909, Tiercel 1908, Hainault 1898, Thunder Queen 1896).
Current winning jockeys:
2 wins John Allen (Volatile Mix 2017, Howard Be Thy Name 2016); Ben Melham (Escado 2013, Shadows In The Sun 2011).
1 win Steven Arnold (Kushadasi 2014); Jason Bowditch (Hard To Get 2004); Damian Browne (Cheviot 1996); Paul Gatt (Tails Of Triomphe 2005); Peter Hall (Delicacy 2015); Jason Holder (Markham 1997); Damian Lane (Leicester 2018); Clare Lindop (Rebel Raider 2009); Kerrin McEvoy (Kidnapped 2010); Damien Oliver (Zabeelionaire 2012); Brad Rawiller (Lazer Sharp 2007); Nash Rawiller (Bulta 1998).
Leading winning trainers:
10 wins Bart Cummings (Shiva's Revenge 1991, Shark's Fin 1987, Stormy Rex 1977, Vacuum 1976, Prince Of All 1975, Dayana 1972, Paradigm 1969, Perculator 1966, Ziema 1964, Stormy Passage 1958).
5 wins James Scobie (Wyncherley 1924, Kildalton 1913, F.J.A 1903, Rienzi 1902, Miltiades 1900).
4 wins Colin Hayes (Mapperley Heights 1984, Clear Prince 1970, Royal Chat 1960, Pandie Star 1954).
Current winning trainers:
3 wins Cliff Brown (Blue Murder 2000, Markham 1997, Cheviot 1996); Darren Weir (Leicester 2018, Volatile Mix 2017, Howard Be Thy Name 2016).
2 wins Lee Freedman (Mummify 2003, Subzero 1992); Leon Macdonald (Rebel Raider 2009, French Cotton 1986).
1 win Pat Conroy (Sea Brigand 1989); Leon Corstens (Zabeelionaire 2012); Anthony Cummings (Shadows In The Sun 2011); Jamie Edwards (Lazer Sharp 2007); John Hawkes (English Wonder 1982); Pat Hyland (Zarita 2008); Richard Jolly (Kushadasi 2014); Mark Kavanagh (Hard To Get 2004); Mick Kent (Bullwinkle 1994); Robbie Laing (Pantani 2002); Matt Laurie (Escado 2013); Terry O'Sullivan (Tails Of Triomphe 2005); Frank Ritchie (Showella 1999); Brian Smith (Sir Zephyr 1985); Peter Snowden (Kidnapper 2010); Grant Williams (Delicacy 2015).
Point of interest:
Delicacy (2015), in four consecutive starts, won the WA Oaks, WA Derby and the Schweppes Oaks before winning the SA Derby.
Bart Cummings trained 10 SA Derby winners (see above), and his father Jim trained three—Auteuil (1956), Opera King (1931) and Ethelton (1925). Bart's son Anthony trained Shadows In The Sun to win in 2011.

BRC Doomben 10,000 (1200m)—Eagle Farm

Of $700,000. Group 1. Weight For Age. May 11, 2019.

2017-18 RESULT: Time: 1:09.58   (Soft 5)

FP	NO	HORSE	TRAINER	JOCKEY	MARGIN	BAR.	WGT	SP
1	13	ENGLISH	Gai Waterhouse & Adrian Bott	Tim Clark		1	56.5kg	$11
2	2	IMPENDING	James Cummings	Damian Browne	0.2L	7	58.5kg	$12
3	3	LE ROMAIN	Kris Lees	Glyn Schofield	0.4L	11	58.5kg	$16
4	1	REDZEL	Peter & Paul Snowden	Kerrin McEvoy	0.6L	4	58.5kg	$2.50f
5	6	SPIETH	David & Ben Hayes & Tom Dabernig	Craig Williams	1.85L	8	58.5kg	$19
6	4	CARE TO THINK	Matthew Dunn	Jeff Lloyd	2.05L	10	58.5kg	$17
7	8	BURNING PASSION	Mark Newnham	Michael Cahill	2.15L	5	58.5kg	$51
8	5	MOST IMPORTANT	Tony Gollan	Jim Byrne	2.35L	3	58.5kg	$31
9	12	IN HER TIME	Benjamin Smith	Corey Brown	2.55L	6	56.5kg	$3.70
10	11	THE MISSION	Paul Perry	James Orman	5.3L	9	57kg	$81
11	7	MONSIEUR GUSTAVE	Darryl Hansen	Tiffani Brooker	6.05L	2	58.5kg	$41
12	14	HOUTZEN	Toby Edmonds	Regan Bayliss	7.8L	12	55kg	$26

PAST WINNERS

YEAR	WINNER	JOCKEY	TRAINER	2ND	3RD	TIME
2018	English	Tim Clark	Gai Waterhouse & Adrian Bott	Impending	Le Romain	1:09.5
2017	Redzel	Jim Byrne	Peter & Paul Snowden	Counterattack	Derryn	1:10.5
2016	Music Magnate	Kerrin McEvoy	Bjorn Baker	Azkadellia	Charlie Boy	1:17.7
2015	Boban	Glyn Schofield	Chris Waller	Charlie Boy	Generalife	1:19.1
2014	Spirit Of Boom	Michael Rodd	Tony Gollan	Temple Of Boom	Buffering	1:17.9
2013	Epaulette	Kerrin McEvoy	Peter Snowden	Sea Siren	Buffering	1:18.8
2012	Sea Siren	Jim Cassidy	John O'Shea	Buffering	Temple Of Boom	1:19.0
2011	Beaded	Corey Brown	Peter Snowden	Love Conquers All	Black Piranha	1:19.6
2010	Hot Danish	Tim Clark	Les Bridge	Whobegotyou	Melito	1:19.1
2009	Apache Cat	Damien Oliver	Greg Eurell	Black Piranha	All Silent	1:22.4
2008	Apache Cat	Corey Brown	Greg Eurell	Murtajil	Turffontein	1:17.9
2007	Takeover Target	Jay Ford	Joe Janiak	Gold Edition	Mitanni	1:18.5
2006	Undue	Steven Arnold	Shane Clarke	Impaler	Street Smart	1:18.0
2005	Red Oog	Hugh Bowman	Joseph Pride	Our Egyptian Raine	Takeover Target	1:18.6
2004	Super Elegant	Greg Childs	Tony Vasil	Our Egyptian Raine	Scenic Peak	1:17.7
2003	Bel Esprit	Nash Rawiller	John Symons	Private Steer	Spinning Hill	1:18.3
2002	Falvelon	Damien Oliver	Danny J Bougoure	Show A Heart	Lord Essex	1:18.8
2001	Falvelon	Michael Cahill	Danny J Bougoure	Spinning Hill	Mr Innocent	1:17.2
2000	Mr Innocent	Glen Colless	Mal Gerrard	Easy Rocking	Falvelon	1:18.8
1999	Lauries Lottery	Michael Peeling	Michael Nolan	Adam	Corporate James	1:19.0
1998	Chief De Beers	Ken Waller	Bill Calder	Staging	General Nediym	1:19.8
1997	Accomplice	Shane Dye	John Hawkes	Blazing Steel	Monopolize	1:18.5

BACKGROUND

First run: 1933 (won by Wallun) 1933-41 run down the Doomben straight 1200m; 1942-45 run at Albion Park over 1400m; run over 1350m 1946-2016. Reduced to 1200m in 2017. Previously known as the Doomben Newmarket Handicap (1933-42); Ahern Stakes (1943-46). Swapped placed on calendar with Kingsford-Smith (BTC) Cup in 2017.
Fastest Time (1200m, Doomben): English (2018) 1:09.58
Multiple winners: 5—Apache Cat (2009, 2008); Falvelon (2002, 2001); Chief De Beers (1998, 1995); Prince Trialia (1991, 1992); Black Onyx (1970, 1969).
Fillies and mares to win: 8—English (2018); Sea Siren (2012); Beaded (2011); Hot Danish (2010); Flitter (1994); Maybe Mahal (1977); Hamurah (1938); High Benia (1936). Note: Sea Siren (2012) is the only 3YO filly to win.
3YOs to win: 27—Epaulette (2013); Sea Siren (2012); Bel Esprit (2003); Laurie's Lottery (1999); Accomplice (1997); Chief De Beers (1995); Broad Reach (1987); Between Ourselves (1986); Ideal Planet (1982); Sovereign Red (1981); Hit It Benny (1980); Manikato (1979); Burwana (1976); Craigola (1973); Bengalla Lad (1972); Baguette (1971); Black Onyx (1969); Winfreux (1965); Second Earl (1959); Grey Ghost (1958); El Khobar (1956); Apple Bay (1955); Coniston (1951); Ungar (1949); The Image (1943); Pamelus (1935); Wallun (1933).

Note: Sea Siren (2012) is the only 3YO filly to win.
Notable winners: English (2018); Redzel (2017); Boban (2015); Sea Siren (2012); Hot Danish (2010); Apache Cat (2009, 2008); Takeover Target (2007); Bel Esprit (2003); Falvelon (2002, 2001); Chief De Beers (1998, 1994); Campaign King (1998); Lord Ballina (1985); Sovereign Red (1981); Manikato (1979); Maybe Mahal (1977); Baguette (1971); Black Onyx (1970, 1969); Pterylaw (1966); Winfreux (1965); Aquanita (1961); Grey Ghost (1958); Bernborough (1946); Lough Neagh 1934).
Doomben 10,000 winners won the lead-up races:
Canterbury Stakes: 3—Hot Danish (2010); Baguette (1971); Lough Neagh (1934).
TJ Smith Stakes: 1—Apache Cat (2008);
All Aged Stakes: 3—Hot Danish (2010); Murray Stream (1948); Bernborough (1946).
BRC Classic: 1—Chief De Beers (1995). Note: Chief De Beers also won the Doomben 10,000 in 1998.
BRC Sprint: 2—Chief De Beers (1998); Barrosa Boy (1992).
Sir Byrne Hart Stakes: No horse has won both races.
Doomben 10,000 winners won in the same preparation:
QTC Cup: None. Note: My Axeman (1983) won the Doomben 10,000 before finishing second in the QTC Cup to Nosey Parker.
WJ Healy Stakes: 6—Between Ourselves (1986); Ideal Planet (1982); Hit It Benny (1980); Blue's Finito (1978); Aquanita (1961); Second Earl (1959).
Kingsford-Smith Cup (run before Doomben 10,000 until 2017): 5—Sea Siren (2012); Apache Cat (2008); Accomplice (1997); Barrosa Boy (1992); Broad Reach (1987).
Stradbroke Handicap: 4—Campaign King (1988); Spedito (1975); Winfreux (1965); High Rank (1941).
Kingsford-Smith Cup & Stradbroke Handicap: None.
Doomben Cup: 1—Bernborough (1946). Note: Winfreux won the 1965 Doomben 10,000 and the 1966 Doomben Cup.
Leading winning jockeys:
5 wins George Moore (Baguette 1971, Black Onyx 1969, Teranyan 1957, True Leader 1953, Expressman 1940).
4 wins Mick Dittman (Chief De Beers 1995, Lord Ballina 1985, Sovereign Red 1981, Craigola 1973).
3 wins John Marshall (Campaign King 1988, Broad Reach 1987, Between Ourselves 1986); Noel McGrowdie (Highlea 1952, Coniston 1951, Highstrung 1947); Michael Pelling (Laurie's Lottery 1999, Suntain 1996, Unequalled 1993).
Current winning jockeys:
2 wins Corey Brown (Beaded 2011, Apache Cat 2008); Tim Clark (English 2018; Hot Danish 2010); Kerrin McEvoy (Music Magnate 2016, Epaulette 2013); Damien Oliver (Apache Cat 2009, Falvelon 2002).
1 win Steven Arnold (Undue 2006); Hugh Bowman (Red Oog 2005); Jim Byrne (Redzel 2017); Michael Cahill (Falvelon 2001); Glen Colless (Mr. Innocent 2000); Jay Ford (Takeover Target 2007); Nash Rawiller (Bel Esprit 2003); Michael Rodd (Spirit Of Boom 2014); Glyn Schofield (Boban 2015).
Leading winning trainers:
6 wins Tommy Smith (Lord Ballina 1985, Ideal Planet 1982, Black Onyx 1970, 1969, The Tempest 1964, Apple Bay 1955).
3 wins Bart Cummings (Campaign King 1988, Broad Reach 1987, Maybe Mahal 1977); Harry Plant (High Lea 1952, Coniston 1951, Bernborough 1946).
Current winning trainers:
2 wins Danny Bougoure (Falvelon 2002, 2001); Greg Eurell (Apache Cat 2009, 2008); Peter Snowden (Epaulette 2013, Beaded 2011).
1 win Bjorn Baker (Music Magnate 2016); Les Bridge (Hot Danish 2010); Shane Clarke (Undue 2006); Tony Gollan (Spirit Of Boom 2014); John Hawkes (Accomplice 1997); Joe Janiak (Takeover Target 2007); Joe Pride (Red Oog 2005); John O'Shea (Sea Siren 2012); Peter & Paul Snowden (Redzel 2017); John Symons (Bel Esprit 2003); Tony Vasil (Super Elegant 2004); Chris Waller (Boban 2015); Gai Waterhouse & Adrian Bott (English 2018).
Points of interest:
Barrosa Boy (1992) is the only horse to win the Doomben sprint treble—the BRC Sprint, BTC Cup and Doomben 10,000. Doomben specialist Chief De Beers won all three sprints but not in the same year—BRC Sprint (1998), BTC Cup (1996); Doomben 10,000 (1995, 1998). Falvelon won the BTC Cup in 2000 and 2003, and the Doomben 10,000 in 2001 and 2002.

SAJC The Goodwood (1200m)—Morphettville

Of $1,000,000. Group 1. Set Weights plus Penalties, 3YO&Up. May 18, 2019.

2017-18 RESULT: Time: 1:09.88 (Soft 6)

FP	NO	HORSE	TRAINER	JOCKEY	MARGIN	BAR.	WGT	SP
1	2	SANTA ANA LANE	Anthony Freedman	Ben Melham		9	58.5kg	$26
2	18	MISSROCK	Robbie Laing	Ben Thompson	1.2L	6	52.5kg	$17
3	17	I'LL HAVE A BIT	John McArdle	Chris Parnham	1.6L	3	53.5kg	$51
4	13	FLAMBERGE	Mathew Ellerton & Simon Zahra	Damian Lane	2L	4	54.5kg	$19
4	8	SUPER CASH	Andrew Noblet	Jamie Kah	2L	7	55.5kg	$18
6	11	STEEL FROST	Will Clarken	Todd Pannell	2.3L	8	55.5kg	$18
7	14	HANDSOME THIEF	Darren Weir	Dean Yendall	2.6L	12	54.5kg	$12
8	1	VEGA MAGIC	David & Ben Hayes & Tom Dabernig	Damien Oliver	4.2L	14	59kg	$4f
9	16	EXALTED ADAM	Grant Young	Clare Lindop	4.4L	13	54.5kg	$151
10	6	VOODOO LAD	Darren Weir	Ben Allen (a)	4.6L	1	56.5kg	$16
11	15	OVERSHARE	Michael, Wayne & John Hawkes	James Winks	5.3L	16	54.5kg	$71
12	19	MICA LIL	Mark Minervini	Damien Thornton	6.5L	10	52.5kg	$41
13	5	VIDDORA	Lloyd Kennewell	Joe Bowditch	6.9L	11	56.5kg	$8.50
14	9	STELLAR COLLISION	Darren Weir	Luke Currie	7.1L	17	55.5kg	$26
15	20	NIPPERKIN	Barry Brook	Krystal Bishop	7.4L	18	52.5kg	$201
16	4	SECRET AGENDA	Mick Price	Dwayne Dunn	8.9L	19	56.5kg	$13
17	10	VIRIDINE	James Cummings	Regan Bayliss	10.4L	20	55.5kg	$9
18	12	LOPE DE CAPIO	Wayne Francis & Glen Kent	Kayla Crowther (a)	10.7L	15	55.5kg	$151
19	7	FERRANDO	Graeme Rogerson	Stephen Baster	18.2L	2	56kg	$61
20	3	THRONUM	David & Ben Hayes & Tom Dabernig	Tim Clark	28.4L	5	57kg	$11

PAST WINNERS

YEAR	WINNER	JOCKEY	TRAINER	2ND	3RD	TIME
2018	Santa Ana Lane	Ben Melham	Anthony Freedman	Missrock	I'll Have A Bit	1:09.8
2017	Vega Magic	Craig Williams	David & Ben Hayes & Tom Dabernig	Missrock	Casino Wizard	1:09.3
2016	Black Heart Bart	Brad Rawiller	Darren Weir	Under The Louvre	Supido	1:10.0
2015	Flamberge	Vlad Duric	Peter Moody	Lord Of The Sky	Under The Louvre	1:09.3
2014	Smokin' Joey	Ben Melham	Wez Hunter	Platelet	Riziz	1:11.6
2013	Platelet	Ben Melham	Darren Weir	Conservatorium	Altar	1:09.6
2012	Black Caviar	Luke Nolen	Peter Moody	We're Gonna Rock	Stirling Grove	1:10.3
2011	Lone Rock	Clare Lindop	Robert Smerdon	Crystal Lily	Pinwheel	1:09.0
2010	Velocitea	Craig Newitt	Mick Price	Catapulted	Very Discreet	1:09.0
2009	Takeover Target	Jay Ford	Joe Janiak	I Am Invincible	Commanding Hope	1:10.7
2008	Shadoways	Mark Pegus	Gwenda Johnstone	Cargo Cult	Diplomatic Force	1:09.3
2007	Let Go Thommo	Steven King	Steven J Ryan	Tesbury Jack	Royal Ida	1:09.3
2006	Perfectly Ready	Stephen Baster	Mick Price	Sassbee	Squiliani	1:10.7
2005	Glamour Puss	Steven King	Danny O'Brien	Solar Antiquity	Shablec	1:09.1
2004	Super Elegant	Greg Childs	Tony Vasil	Recurring	Danabaa	1:09.2
2003	Bomber Bill	Steven Arnold	Robert Smerdon	Squillani	Debrief	1:09.4
2002	Zip Zip Aray	Brian Park	David Jolly	Libidinious	The Big Chill	1:11.1
2001	Keeper	Brett Prebble	Myles Plumb	Sudurka	Ateaters	1:10.4
2000	Marstic	Aaron Spiteri	Tony Vasil	Czar Hero	Strident	1:13.9
1999	French Clock	Damien Holland	Pat Hyland	Any Rhythm	Loafer	1:10.8
1998	Spectrum	Paul Harvey	George Hanlon	Scandinavia	Its My Sin	1:08.3
1997	Bellzevir	Michael Carson	Jim Houlahan	Another Excuse	Clang	1:10.3

BACKGROUND

First run: 1881 (won by D.O.D). Group 1 since 1980. Run over 1600m 1881-85; 1450 1980. Not held 1886-88; 1942-43. Also known as the Marlboro Plate, Goodwood Stakes and The Goodwood. Registered name SAJC Goodwood.

Fillies & mares to win (since 1960): 11—Platelet (2013); Black Caviar (2012); Lone Rock (2011); Velocitea (2010); Glamour Puss (2005); Centisle (1995); Boardwalk Angel (1989); Wise Virgin (1973); Tango Miss (1972); Queen Dassie (1963); Scenic Star (1960).
3YOs to win (since 1940): 14—*Lone Rock (2011); Perfectly Ready (2006); Zip Zip Aray (2002); *Boardwalk Angel (1989); Daring Jon (1987); Romantic Dream (1977); Puncheon (1976); Kenmark (1975); *Wise Virgin (1973); Kiltrice (1964); Hunter's Sight (1957); Power's Hope (1950); Galway Pipe (1947); Royal Gem (1946). *Fillies
Multiple winners: 2—Musket Belle (1912, 1911); Mostyn (1895, 1894).
Fastest time (1200m): Spectrum (1998) 1:08.33
Notable winners: Santa Ana Lane (2018); Black Heart Bart (2016); Black Caviar (2012); Takeover Target (2009); Bomber Bill (2003); Euclase (1992); Tango Miss (1972); Matrice (1956); Royal Gem (1946); Aurie's Star (1940).
The Goodwood winners won the lead-up races.
Rubiton Stakes: 1—Super Elegant (2004).
Oakleigh Plate: None. Note: Aurie's Star won the Goodwood in the 1940 after winning the 1937 and 1939 Oakleigh Plates.
Newmarket Handicap: None. Note: Royal Gem won the Goodwood in 1946 and the Newmarket in 1948. Brague won the Newmarket in 1915 and Goodwood in 1916.
Irwin Stakes: 2—Bomber Bill (2003); Sleep Tight (1958).
Victoria Handicap: 4—Black Heart Bart (2016); Keeper (2001); Kenmark (1975); Romantic Son (1971).
McKay Stakes: 5—Boardwalk Angel (1989); Lord Galaxy (1986); Comaida Boy (1979); Wise Virgin (1973); Grey John (1969).
Lightning Stakes: 1—Black Caviar (2012).
Robert Sangster Stakes: 2—Platelet (2013); Black Caviar (2012).
The Goodwood winners went on to win in the same preparation:
Doomben 10,000: 1—Super Elegant (2004).
Stradbroke Handicap: 1—Santa Ana Lane (2018).
Diamond Jubilee Stakes (Royal Ascot): 1—Black Caviar (2012).
Leading winning jockeys:
5 wins John Letts (Leica Planet 1984, Romantic Dream 1977, Wise Virgin 1973, Tango Miss 1972, Mikadis 1961).
4 wins Mick Medhurst (Cellarman 1949, Hegemonic 1938, Second Dale 1928, Denacre 1923).
Current winning jockeys:
3 wins Ben Melham (Santa Ana Lane 2018, Smokin' Joey 2014, Platelet 2013).
1 win Steven Arnold (Bomber Bill 2003); Stephen Baster (Perfectly Ready 2006); Michael Carson (Bellzevir 1997); Vlad Duric (Flamberge 2015); Jay Ford (Takeover Target 2009); Paul Harvey (Spectrum 1998); Jason Holder (Ambala 1994); Clare Lindop (Lone Rock 2011); Craig Newitt (Velocitea 2010); Luke Nolen (Black Caviar 2012); Brett Prebble (Keeper 2001); Brad Rawiller (Black Heart Bart 2016); Craig Williams (Vega Magic 2017).
Leading winning trainers:
6 wins Walter Hickenbotham (Lord Derby 1910, True Scot 1909, Step Out 1906, Footbolt 1902, Finland 1901, Mostyn 1895).
5 wins George Hanlon (Spectrum 1998, Centisle 1995, Boardwalk Angel 1989, Marjoleo 1980, Comaida Boy 1979).
4 wins Bart Cummings (Leica Planet 1984, Romantic Dream 1977, Kenmark 1975, Wise Virgin 1973); John James (Musket Belle 1912, 1911, Lord Carlyon 1908, Goldstream 1890).
Current winning trainers:
2 wins John Hawkes (Cameronic 1988, Lord Galaxy 1986); Mick Price (Velocitea 2010, Perfectly Ready 2006); Robert Smerdon (Lone Rock 2011, Bomber Bill 2003); Tony Vasil (Super Elegant 2004, Marstic 2000); Darren Weir (Black Heart Bart 2016, Platelet 2013).
1 win Barry Brook (Ambala 1994); Allan Denham (Euclase 1992); Stuart Dodd (Puncheon 1976); David & Ben Hayes & Tom Dabernig (Vega Magic 2017); Anthony Freedman (Santa Ana Lane 2018); Wez Hunter (Smokin' Joey 2014); Pat Hyland (French Clock 1999); Joe Janiak (Takeover Target 2009); Gwenda Johnstone (Shadoways 2008); David Jolly (Zip Zip Aray 2002); John Meagher (Daring Jon 1987); Danny O'Brien (Glamour Puss 2005); Steven Ryan (Let Go Thommo 2007); John Sadler (Jolly Old Mac 1993).
Points of interest:
The heaviest weight carried by a winner is Aurie's Star (1940) who lumped 63.5 kg (10 stone).
Super Elegant's (2004) winning weight of 57kg is the heaviest since metrics in 1973.
Royal Gem (1946) went on to win the Caulfield Cup that year. He also sired the 1953 Kentucky Derby winner Dark Star.

BRC Doomben Cup (2000m)—Doomben
Of $650,000. Group 1. Weight For Age. May 19, 2019.

2017-18 RESULT: Time: 2:01.43 (Good 4)

FP	NO	HORSE	TRAINER	JOCKEY	MARGIN	BAR.	WGT	SP
1	2	COMIN' THROUGH	Chris Waller	Michael Walker		11	59kg	$9
2	11	EGG TART	Chris Waller	Leith Innes	0.2L	6	57kg	$15
3	3	AMBITIOUS	Anthony Freedman	Craig Williams	1.45L	7	59kg	$9.50
4	13	ABBEY MARIE	Michael Kent	Matthew McGillivray	1.85L	5	57kg	$12
5	12	OREGON'S DAY	Mick Price	Jim Byrne	2.05L	2	57kg	$3.80f
6	8	LIFE LESS ORDINARY	Chris Waller	Opie Bosson	3.55L	10	59kg	$11
7	7	SATONO RASEN	Chris Waller	Glyn Schofield	6.3L	4	59kg	$6.50
8	4	TOM MELBOURNE	Chris Waller	Corey Brown	9.55L	8	59kg	$9
9	10	TRADESMAN	Darren Weir	John Allen	10.3L	3	59kg	$9
10	6	MAN OF HIS WORD	Bruce Hill	Brad Stewart	12.55L	1	59kg	$21
11	9	VIOLATE	Brent Stanley	Mark Du Plessis	26.55L	9	59kg	$151

PAST WINNERS

YEAR	WINNER	JOCKEY	TRAINER	2ND	3RD	TIME
2018	Comin' Through	Michael Walker	Chris Waller	Egg Tart	Ambitious	2:01.4
2017	Sense Of Occasion	Corey Brown	Kris Lees	Star Exhibit	Rudy	2:06.6
2016	Our Ivanhowe	Kerrin McEvoy	Lee & Anthony Freedman	Hauraki	It's Somewhat	2:01.4
2015	Pornichet	Blake Shinn	Gai Waterhouse	Weary	I'm Imposing	2:02.5
2014	Streama	Blake Shinn	Guy Walter	Leebaz	Junoob	2:01.7
2013	Beaten Up	Leith Innes	Chris Waller	Foreteller	Secret Admirer	2:04.3
2012	Mawingo	Nash Rawiller	Anthony Freedman	Lights Of Heaven	Manighar	2:02.0
2011	Scenic Shot	Shane Scriven	Daniel Morton	My Kingdom Of Fife	Glass Harmonium	2:03.7
2010	Metal Bender	Kerrin McEvoy	Chris Waller	Gold Water	Triple Honour	2:02.6
2009	Scenic Shot	Shane Scriven	Daniel Morton	Racing To Win	Sir Slick	2:02.8
2008	Sarrera	Damien Oliver	Michael Moroney	Rampant Lion	Like It Is	2:03.3
2007	Cinque Cento	Steven Arnold	Peter Moody	Gaze	Pentathon	2:01.8
2006	Above Deck	Mark Zahra	Jim Conlan	Octapussy	Roman Arch	2:13.8
2005	Perlin	Danny Nikolic	Graeme Rogerson	Platinum Scissors	Natural Blitz	2:15.0
2004	Defier	Hugh Bowman	Guy Walter	Pentastic	Upsetthym	2:11.6
2003	Bush Padre	Michael Rodd	Lee Freedman	Freemason	Maguire	2:13.0
2002	Mr Bureaucrat	Alan Robinson	Warwick Hailes	Galroof	Freemason	2:14.0
2001	King Keitel	Brian York	Paul Jenkins	Shogun Lodge	Kasakh Belle	2:01.9
2000	Akhenaton	Glen Boss	Bill Mitchell	Integrate	Cruzeiro	2:04.7
1999	Intergaze	Craig Carmody	Rod Craig	Lahar	Joss Sticks	2:03.7
1998	Might And Power	Brian York	Jack Denham	Intergaze	I Like Him	2:00.5
1997	Sapio	Darryl Bradley	Sylvia Kay	Pakaraka Star	Shame	2:05.5

BACKGROUND

First run: 1933 (won by Penthaus). 1933-37 2000m; 1938-41 2200m; 1942-45 run at Albion Park over 2000m; 1946-1989, 2002-06 2200m; from 1990 2020m, except for 1996 when 2040m, to 2001; 2007-11. From 2008 run over 2000m.
Mares to win: 5—Streama (2014); Cinque Cento (2007); Dream (1950); Qualeta (1943); Cooranga (1939).
3YOs to win: 12—Akhenaton (2000); Danewin (1995); Dandy Andy (1987); Marceau (1978); Cheyne Walk (1976); Divide And Rule (1979); Striking Force (1964); Earlwood (1959); French Echo (1953); Forge (1948); Dark Marne (1947); Beaulivre (1940). Note: No 3YO filly as won a Doomben Cup.
Multiple winners: 3—Scenic Blast (2011, 2009); Rough Habit (1993, 1992, 1991); Earkwood (1960, 1959).
Notable winners: Our Ivanhowe (2016); Streama (2014); Scenic Shot (2011, 2009); Metal Bender (2010); Defier (2004); Intergaze (1999); Might And Power (1998); Juggler (1996); Danewin (1995); Durbridge (1994); Rough Habit (1993, 1992, 1991); Dandy Andy (1987); Marceau (1978); Tails (1971); Divide And Rule (1970); Bore Head (1967); Winfreux (1966); River Seine (1965); Samson (1962); Prince Delville (1957); Dark Marne (1947); Bernborough (1946); Beaulivre (1940).
Fastest time (Doomben 2000m): Our Ivanhowe (2016) 2:01.41.
Doomben Cup winners won the lead-up races:
Australian Cup (since 1964 when Australian Cup reduced to 2000m): 2—Durbridge (1994); Bore Head (1967).
Chipping Norton Stakes: 2—Juggler (1996); Bernborough (1946).
ATC Queen Elizabeth Stakes: 4—Sarrera (2008); Intergaze (1999); Might And Power (1998); Rough Habit (1992).

Hollindale Stakes: 9—Streama (2014); Above Deck (2006); Bush Padre (2003); Mr. Bureaucrat (2002); Might And Power (1998); Danewin (1995); Durbridge (1994); Rough Habit (1992, 1991). Note: Rough Habit also won the Doomben Cup in 1993 (after finishing second in the Hollindale). Eye Of The Sky won the Hollindale in 1989, and the Doomben Cup in 1990.
Doomben Classic: 1—Akhenaton (2000). Note: No Doomben Classic winner has won the G1 Qld Derby or the G1 Qld Oaks (see notes below).
Chairman's Handicap: 2—Juggler (1996); Lord Seaman (1983).
Sir Byrne Hart Stakes: 3—Mr. Bureaucrat (2002); Rough Habit (1991); Golden Rhapsody (1980).
Doomben Cup winners went on to win:
Brisbane Cup: 2—Scenic Shot (2009); Lord Hybrow (1988).
O'Shea Stakes: 2—Scenic Shot (2009); Lord Hybrow (1988). Note: Lord Hybrow (1988) is the only horse to win the Doomben Cup, O'Shea Stakes and Brisbane Cup in the same year.
O'Shea Stakes & Brisbane Cup: 2—Scenic Shot (2009); Lord Hybrow (1988).
Tattersall's Cup: 8—Sapio (1997); Eye Of The Sky (1990); Golden Rhapsody (1980); Winfreux (1966); High Society (1961); Elwood (1959); Euphrates (1954); Repshot (1945).
Cox Plate (same year): 1—Might And Power (1998).
Leading winning jockeys:
3 wins Jim Cassidy (Rough Habit 1993, 1992, 1991); Maurice McCarten (Beaulivre 1940, Whittingham 1934, Pentheus 1933); George Moore (Book Link 1958, French Echo 1953, Rio Fe 1949).
Current winning jockeys:
2 wins Kerrin McEvoy (Our Ivanhowe 2016, Metal Bender 2010); Blake Shinn (Pornichet 2015; Streama 2014).
1 win Steven Arnold (Cinque Cento 2007); Glen Boss (Akhenaton 2000); Hugh Bowman (Defier 2004); Darryl Bradley (Sapio 1997); Corey Brown (Sense Of Occasion 2017); Leith Innes (Beaten Up 2013); Damien Oliver (Sarrera 2008); Nash Rawiller (Mawingo 2012); Michael Rodd (Bush Padre 2003); Michael Walker (Comin' Through 2018); Mark Zahra (Above Deck 2006).
Leading winning trainers:
4 wins Lee Freedman (Our Ivanhowe 2016, Bush Padre 2003, Durbridge 1994, Abstraction 1989).
3 wins Tommy Smith (Marceau 1978, Cheyne Walk 1976, Lord Nelson 1973); John Wheeler (Rough Habit 1993, 1992, 1991).
Current winning trainers:
4 wins Lee Freedman (Our Ivanhowe 2016, Bush Padre 2003, Durbridge 1994, Abstraction 1989).
3 wins Chris Waller (Comin' Through 2018, Beaten Up 2013, Metal Bender 2010); John Wheeler (Rough Habit 1993, 1992, 1991).
2 wins Anthony Freedman (Our Ivanhowe 2016, Mawingo 2012); Daniel Morton (Scenic Shot 2011, 2009); Gai Waterhouse (Pornichet 2015; Juggler 1996).
1 win Grahame Begg (Eye Of The Sky 1990); Jim Conlan (Above Deck 2006); Rod Craig (Intergaze 1999); Lee and Anthony Freedman (Our Ivanhowe 2016); Paul Jenkins (King Keitel 2001); Sylvia Kay (Sapio 1997); Kris Lees (Sense Of Occasion 2017); Bruce Marsh (Double You Em 1982); Michael Moroney (Sarrera 2008); Graeme Rogerson (Perlin 2005).
Points of interest:
Jack Denham and Maurice McCarten rode and trained winners of the Doomben Cup.
Might And Power (1998) is the only Melbourne Cup winner to win a Doomben Cup. He won the Melbourne Cup in the same season in 1997. He also is the only Cox Plate winner to win a Doomben Cup (same year 1998).
Bore Head (1967) won the Caulfield Cup in 1965. Might And Power (1998) won the Caulfield Cup in 1997. Beaulivre won the Caulfield Cup and Doomben Cup in 1940.

BRC Kingsford Smith Cup (1300m)—Eagle Farm
Of $700,000. Group 1. Weight For Age. May 26, 2019.

2017-18 RESULT: Time: 1:19.51   (Soft 6)

FP	NO	HORSE	TRAINER	JOCKEY	MARGIN	BAR.	WGT	SP
1	1	IMPENDING	James Cummings	Damian Browne		7	59kg	$4.20EF
2	2	LE ROMAIN	Kris Lees	Glyn Schofield	0.1L	4	59kg	$4.20ef
3	11	CHAMPAGNE CUDDLES	Bjorn Baker	Corey Brown	1.35L	8	55kg	$6
4	9	ENGLISH	Gai Waterhouse & Adrian Bott	Tim Clark	1.75L	1	57kg	$6
5	8	ENDLESS DRAMA	Chris Waller	Tye Angland	3L	3	59kg	$9.50
6	10	VOLPE VELOCE	Graham Richardson & Gavin Parker	Jake Bayliss	3.2L	6	57kg	$26
7	3	CARE TO THINK	Matthew Dunn	James McDonald	3.5L	9	59kg	$9
8	6	MONSIEUR GUSTAVE	Darryl Hansen	Jeff Lloyd	13.5L	5	59kg	$41
9	4	MOST IMPORTANT	Tony Gollan	Jim Byrne	15L	2	59kg	$15

PAST WINNERS

YEAR	WINNER	JOCKEY	TRAINER	2ND	3RD	TIME
2018	Impending	Damian Browne	James Cummings	Le Romain	Champagne Cuddles	1:19.5
2017	Clearly Innocent	Hugh Bowman	Kris Lees	Jungle Edge	Counterattack	1:19.0
2016	Malaguerra	Glen Colless	Lee & Anthony Freedman	Dothraki	Japonisme	1:08.7
2015	Hot Snitzel	Blake Shinn	P & P Snowden	Knoydart	Our Boy Malachi	1:09.4
2014	Famous Seamus	Ryan Wiggins	Noel Mayfield-Smith	Spirit Of Boom	Buffering	1:09.0
2013	Your Song	Peter Robl	Anthony Cummings	Rain Affair	Better Than Ready	1:11.2
2012	Sea Siren	Jim Cassidy	John O'Shea	Scenic Blast	Beaded	1:08.3
2011	Black Caviar	Luke Nolen	Peter Moody	Hay List	Buffering	1:08.8
2010	Albert The Fat	Damian Browne	Eden Petrie	Melito	Latin News	1:09.2
2009	Duporth	Luke Nolen	Anthony Cummings	Bank Robber	Apache Cat	1:08.9
2008	Apache Cat	Corey Brown	Greg Eurell	Vormista	Swiss Ace	1:09.3
2007	Bentley Biscuit	Nash Rawiller	Gai Waterhouse	Takeover Target	Mitanni	1:08.5
2006	Gee I Jane	Scott Seamer	Neville Couchman	Daunting Lad	All Bar One	1:08.6
2005	Spark Of Life	Chris Munce	Allan Denham	St Basil	Regimental Gal	1:09.0
2004	Thorn Park	Danny Nikolic	Bob Thomsen	Star Of Florida	Regimental Gal	1:08.7
2003	Falvelon	Alan Russell	Danny J Bougoure	Make Mine Magic	Diamond Dane	1:10.0
2002	Lord Essex	Scott Galloway	John Hawkes	Falvelon	Phoenix Park	1:08.3
2001	Fritz	Noel Harris	Neil Coulbeck	Show A Heart	King Lotto	1:09.1
2000	Falvelon	Michael Cahill	Daniel Bougoure	Mr Innocent	Toledo	1:08.4
1999	Staging	Glen Boss	Clarry Conners	Pimpala Prince	Ab Initio	1:09.0
1998	General Nediym	Grant Cooksley	Bill Mitchell	Mulugwa	Sahara Zed	1:10.9
1997	Accomplice	Shane Dye	John Hawkes	Chief De Beers	Poetic King	1:09.3

BACKGROUND
First run: 1964 (won by Rashlore). Quality Handicap until 1990. WFA from 1991. Group 3 1979-86; Group 2 1987-2005. Group 1 from 2006. Raced over 1400m 1964-72; 1200m 1973-79; 1350m 1980-1990; 1200m from 1991; 1350m from 2017-18. Run at Doomben 1964-2018. Originally known as the J.T. Delaney Quality Handicap. Previously known as the Tourist Minister's Cup, Robin's Kitchen Cup, Foster's Cup and Carlton Cup, Wynham Estate Cup and Richmond Grove Cup. Registered as the BRC BTC Cup—renamed the Kingsford Smith Stakes in 2017; swapped places on the calendar with the Doomben 10,000.
Fastest time (1350m, Doomben): Clearly Innocent (2017) 1:19.09
Most recent filly or mare to win: Sea Siren (2012).
Most recent 3YO to win: C&G—Your Song (2013). Filly—Sea Siren (2012). Note: Sea Siren is the first 3YO filly to win the Kingsford Smith Cup.
Multiple winners: 2—Falvelon (2003, 2000); Buck's Pride (1994, 1993).
Notable winners: Impending (2018); Malaguerra (2016); Sea Siren (2012); Black Caviar (2011); Apache Cat (2008); Thorn Park (2004); Falvelon (2000, 2003); General Nediym (1998); Chief De Beers (1996); St. Jude (1991); Strawberry Road (1983); Magari (1982); Tontonan (1974); Triton (1973); Ricochet (1971), Cabochon (1970); Eye Liner (1967).

Kingsford Smith Stakes winners won the lead-up races:
Victory Stakes: 1—Impending (2018).
AJC The Galaxy: 2—Accomplice (1997); Mr. Illusion (1984).
TJ Smith Stakes: 1—Black Caviar (2011). Note: Black Caviar also won the 2011 Lightning Stakes and Newmarket Handicap before she won the TJ Smith.
BRC Sprint: 1—Barossa Boy (1992).
Luskin Star Stakes (Scone): 1—Clearly Innocent (2017).
Doomben 10,000: None. Note: The Kingsford Smith swapped places with the Doomben 10,000 in 2017, and is now run between the 10,000 and the Stradbroke Handicap. Five horses have previously won the double: Sea Siren (2012); Apache Cat (2008); Accomplice (1997); Barrosa Boy (1992); Broad Reach (1987).
Kingsford Smith Stakes winners went on to win in the same preparation:
Stradbroke Handicap: 1—Thorn Park (2004).
Doomben Cup: 1—Dual Control (1969).
Leading winning jockeys:
2 wins Neil Birrer (Charlton Boy 1972, Todwana 1965); Damian Browne (Impending 2018, Albert The Fat 2010); Mick Dittman (Chief De Beers 1996, Strawberry Road 1983); Roy Higgins (Martindale 1975, Tontonan 1974); Len Hill (Dual Control 1969, Prince Gauntlet 1968); Chris Munce (Spark Of Life 2005, Barrosa Boy 1992); Luke Nolen (Black Caviar 2011, Duporth 2009); Shane Scriven (Buck's Pride 12994, 1993); Neil Williams (Cool Report 1988, Goldorme 1986).
Current winning jockeys:
2 wins Damian Browne (Impending 2018, Albert The Fat 2010); Luke Nolen (Black Caviar 2011, Duporth 2009).
1 win Hugh Bowman (Clearly Innocent 2017); Corey Brown (Apache Cat 2008); Jim Byrne (Seawinnie 1995); Michael Cahill (Falvelon 2000); Glen Colless (Malaguerra 2016); Grant Cooksley (General Nediym 1998); Scott Galloway (Lord Essex 2002); Nash Rawiller (Bentley Biscuit 2007); Blake Shinn (Hot Snitzel 2015); Ryan Wiggins (Famous Seamus 2014).
Leading winning trainers:
3 wins Bart Cummings (Broad Reach 1987, Martindale 1975, Tontonan 1974).
2 wins Danny Bougoure (Falvelon 2003, 2000); Doug Bougoure (Gypsy Rogue 1990, Strawberry Road 1983); Anthony Cummings (Your Song 2013, Duporth 2009); Tom Dawson (Ima Shadow 1976; Charlton Boy 1972); Jack Denham (High Regard 1989; Ricochet 1971); John Hawkes (Lord Essex 2002; Accomplice 1997); Barry Higgins (Buck's Pride 1994, 1993).
Current winning trainers:
2 wins Danny Bougoure (Falvelon 2003, 2000); Anthony Cummings (Your Song 2013, Duporth 2009); John Hawkes (Lord Essex 2002; Accomplice 1997).
1 win Clarry Conners (Staging 1999); Neil Coulbeck (Fritz 2001); James Cummings (Impending 2018); Allan Denham (Spark Of Life 2005); Greg Eurell (Apache Cat 2008); Lee & Anthony Freedman (Malaguerra 2016); Kris Lees (Clearly Innocent 2017); Bruce Marsh (Mr. Illusion 1984); Noel Mayfield-Smith (Famous Seamus 2014); Eden Petrie (Albert The Fat 2010); John O'Shea (Sea Siren 2012); Peter & Paul Snowden (Hot Snitzel 2015); Gai Waterhouse (Bentley Biscuit 2007).
Points of interest:
Barrosa Boy (1992) is the only horse to win the Doomben winter sprint treble—the BTC Sprint, BTC Cup (Kingsford Smith Stakes) and Doomben 10,000.
Doomben specialist Chief De Beers won all three sprints but not in the same year—BTC Sprint (1998), BTC Cup (1996); Doomben 10,000 (1995 & 1998). Falvelon won the BTC Cup in 2000 and 2003, and the Doomben 10,000 in 2001 & 2002.
James Cummings (Impending 2018); is the third generation of his family to train the winner of the Kingsford Smith Cup. His grandfather Bart Cummings won three times (see above) and his father Anthony Cummings won twice (see above).

BRC Queensland Oaks (2400m)—Eagle Farm
Of $500,000. Group 1 Set Weights, 3YO Fillies. June 1, 2019.

2017-18 RESULT: Time: 2:17.47 (Soft 6)

FP	NO	HORSE	TRAINER	JOCKEY	MARGIN	BAR.	WGT	SP
1	3	YOUNGSTAR	Chris Waller	Kerrin McEvoy		4	56.5kg	$3.70f
2	5	ANOTHER DOLLAR	Chris Waller	Glyn Schofield	0.1L	2	56.5kg	$6.50
3	2	SHEEZDASHING	Mathew Ellerton & Simon Zahra	Damien Thornton	0.2L	3	56.5kg	$8
4	10	CORAL COAST	Anthony Freedman	Mark Zahra	2.95L	16	56.5kg	$19
5	13	MISS SHANTI	Chris Waller	Tye Angland	3.7L	1	56.5kg	$41
6	11	TERRA SANCTA	Tony Pike	Jim Byrne	4L	8	56.5kg	$61
7	9	PLAY THAT SONG	Michael Moroney	Michael Cahill	5.75L	15	56.5kg	$61
8	1	ALOISIA	Ciaron Maher	Damian Browne	5.95L	7	56.5kg	$4.60
9	16	SHE'S RELIABLE	Kelly Schweida	James Orman	7.45L	11	56.5kg	$151
10	15	PROTEST	Bryan & Daniel Guy	Craig Williams	7.55L	13	56.5kg	$101
11	14	DELANEY'S DESIRE	Matt Kropp	Tegan Harrison	10.05L	14	56.5kg	$201
12	6	TINKERMOSA	John Sargent	Jeff Lloyd	10.25L	9	56.5kg	$19
13	7	HIGHWAY	Steve Englebrecht	Deanne Panya	11.5L	10	56.5kg	$51
14	8	JOYFILLY OURS	Gai Waterhouse & Adrian Bott	Tim Clark	12.25L	5	56.5kg	$61
15	12	IMPULSIVE	Chris Waller	Corey Brown	13.5L	6	56.5kg	$101
16	4	SAVACOOL	Chris Waller	James McDonald	34.5L	12	56.5kg	$6

PAST WINNERS

YEAR	WINNER	JOCKEY	TRAINER	2ND	3RD	TIME
2018	Youngstar	Kerrin McEvoy	Chris Waller	Another Dollar	Sheezdashing	2:17.4
2017	Egg Tart	Kerrin McEvoy	Chris Waller	Pygmy	Oklahoma Girl	2:16.0
2016	Provocative	Leith Innes	Tony Pike	Ambience	Falkenberg	2:32.6
2015	Winx	Hugh Bowman	Chris Waller	Ungrateful Ellen	Imperial Lass	2:14.0
2014	Tinto	Timothy Bell	Rex Lipp	Arabian Gold	Sister Souss	2:29.4
2013	Gondokoro	Rhys McLeod	Pat Carey	Miss Zenella	Vaquera	2:32.1
2012	Quintessential	Damian Browne	John Sargent	Eliza Blues	Vittoria	2:38.4
2011	Scarlett Lady	James McDonald	Graeme & Debbie Rogerson	Becerra Shez	Shez Sinsational	2:29.6
2010	Miss Keepsake	Chris Munce	Andrew Scott	Marheta	Danaupair Starlet	2:29.4
2009	Purple	Kerrin McEvoy	Peter Snowden	Nothin Leica Cat	Walk In The Park	2:34.3
2008	Riva San	Scott Seamer	Peter Moody	Rathsallagh	Heavenly Glow	2:36.4
2007	Eskimo Queen	Greg Childs	Michael Moroney	Dougs Mate	Rose Of Sharon	2:32.6
2006	Allow	Stathi Katsidis	Clarry Conners	Vietnam	Stars In Flight	2:31.4
2005	Vitesse Dane	Hugh Bowman	Kris Lees	Cinque Cento	Tick By	2:27.4
2004	Vouvray	Chris Munce	Paul Sullivan	Zumanity	Winning Belle	2:27.0
2003	Zagalia	Chris Munce	Clarry Conners	The Jewel	Penny Gem	2:29.2
2002	Mon Mekki	Paul Hammersley	Gerald Ryan	Night Chaser	Quays	2:28.8
2001	Ethereal	Scott Seamer	Sheila Laxon	Tempest Morn	Altiero	2:28.5
2000	Giovana	Chris Munce	Roger James	Citirecruit	Figurante	2:27.3
1999	Miss Danehill	Eddie Wilkinson	Lee Freedman	Episode	Lady Elsie	2:34.0
1998	Zacheline	Shane Dye	Gai Waterhouse	Midnight Babe	Melora	2:28.0
1997	Crystal Palace	Brian York	Stephen Autridge	Royal Sencherec	Calm Abiding	2:35.7

BACKGROUND

First run: 1951 (won by Maltmaid). Conducted in the spring 1951-56. Not run in 1957. Run in the winter from 1958. Run at Doomben (2200m) in 2015 and 2017-18.
Fastest time (2400m): Vouvray (2004) & Arctic Scent (1996) 2:27.00: Note: the 2015 Queensland Oaks was run at Doomben over 2200m. The winner, Winx, ran 2:14.09 on a track rated Good 3.
Notable winners: Egg Tart (2017); Winx (2015); Eskimo Queen (2007); Ethereal (2001); Arctic Scent (1996); Slight Chance (1993); Triscay (1991); Show Ego (1978); Surround (1977); Denise's Joy (1976); Analie (1973); Mode (1971); Evening Peal (1955).

Queensland Oaks winners won the lead-up races:
Vinery Stud Stakes: 3—Purple (2009); Slight Chance (1993); A Little Kiss (1990).
Gold Coast Bracelet: 1—Tinto (2014).
Sunshine Coast Guineas: 1—Winx (2015).
Doomben Roses: 3—Youngstar (2018); Scarlett Lady (2011); Ethereal (2001).
Queensland Guineas: 1—Triscay (1991).
Queensland Oaks winners went on to win in the same preparation:
Queensland Derby: 4—Riva San (2008); Royal Magic (1992); Bravery (1988); Analie (1973).
Brisbane Cup: None. Note: Mode is the only Queensland Oaks winner (1971) to win the Brisbane Cup (as a 4YO in 1972).
Queensland Oaks winners and the "other" Oaks:
Australian Oaks: 6—Triscay (1991); November Rain (1981); Lowan Star (1980); Surround (1977); Analie (1972); Evening Peal (1955). Note: Evening Peal won the Queensland Oaks in the spring and the AJC Oaks (1956) in the autumn.
VRC Oaks (spring): 7—Slight Chance (Qld Oaks 1993); November Rain (1981); Show Ego (1978); Surround (1977); Denise's Joy (1976); Bonnybel (1974); Evening Peal (1955—both races run in spring).
VRC Oaks & AJC Oaks: 3—November Rain (Qld Oaks 1981); Surround (1977); Evening Peal (1955 VRC Oaks and Qld Oaks run in the spring).
Australasian Oaks: 1—Egg Tart (2017). Note: Episode (1999) won the Australasian Oaks, and finished 2nd to Miss Danehill in the Queensland Oaks.
SA Fillies Classic (formerly SA Oaks): 1—Zacheline (1998). Note: Episode (1999) won the SA Oaks, and finished 2nd to Miss Danehill in the Queensland Oaks.
Queensland Oaks winners and the Melbourne spring majors:
Melbourne Cup: 2—Ethereal (2001); Evening Peal (Oaks 1955, Cup 1956).
Caulfield Cup: 2—Ethereal (2001); Arctic Scent (1996).
Cox Plate: 2—Winx (2015); Surround (Cox Plate 1976; Oaks 1977). Note: Surround is the only 3YO filly to win a Cox Plate.
Leading winning jockeys:
4 wins Chris Munce (Miss Keepsake 2010, Vouvray 2004, Zagalia 2003, Giovana 2000).
3 wins Neil Birrer (Meanmi Shadow 1972, Kazan Retto 1969, Hoa Hine 1962); Mick Dittman (Triscay 1991, A Little Kiss 1990, Denise's Joy 1976); Kerrin McEvoy (Youngstar 2018, Egg Tart 2017, Purple 2009); Andy Tindall (Mian Mir 1954, Lady Hannah 1952, Maltmaid 1951).
Current winning jockeys:
3 wins Kerrin McEvoy (Youngstar 2018, Egg Tart 2017, Purple 2009).
2 wins Hugh Bowman (Winx 2015, Vitesse Dane 2005).
1 win Damian Browne (Quintessential (2012); Larry Cassidy (Arctic Scent 1996); Grant Cooksley (Booked 1994); Paul Hammersley (Mon Mekki 2002); Leith Innes (Provocative 2016); James McDonald (Scarlett Lady 2011); Rhys McLeod (Gondokoro 2013).
Leading winning trainers:
8 wins Tommy Smith (A Little Kiss 1990, Lowan Star 1980, Show Ego 1978, Denise's Joy 1976, Zasu 1975, Analie 1973, Winnipeg II 1961, Orient 1958).
4 wins Neville Begg (Travel Light 1986, Tristram Rose 1985, November Rain 1981, Affectionate 1970).
3 wins Mick Kenny (Mian Mir 1954, Lady Hannah 1952, Maltmaid 1951); Chris Waller (Youngstar 2018, Egg Tart 2017, Winx 2015).
Current winning trainers:
3 wins Chris Waller (Youngstar 2018, Egg Tart 2017, Winx 2015).
2 wins Clarry Conners (Allow 2006, Zagalia 2003); Gerald Ryan (Mon Mekki 2002, Arctic Scent 1996).
1 win Stephen Autridge (Crystal Palace 1997); Les Bridge (Joie Denise 1995); Pat Carey (Gondokoro 2013); Lee Freedman (Miss Danehill 1999); John Hawkes (Booked 1994); Roger James (Giovana 2000); Sheila Laxon (Ethereal 2001); Kris Lees (Vitesse Dane 2005); Rex Lipp (Tinto 2014); Michael Moroney (Eskimo Queen 2007); Paul O'Sullivan (Vouvray 2004); Tony Pike (Provocative 2016); Graeme & Debbie Rogerson (Miss Scarlett 2011); Andrew Scott (Miss Keepsake 2010); Peter Snowden (Purple 2009); John Wallace (Mother Of Pearl 1982); Gai Waterhouse (Zacheline 1998).
Point of interest:
Denise's Joy, who won the Queensland Oaks in 1976, is the dam of 1995 winner Joie Denise, and the granddam of 1999 winner Miss Danehill.

BRC Stradbroke Handicap (1400m)—Eagle Farm
Of $1,500,000. Group 1, Handicap, Minimum Weight 50.5kg. June 8, 2019.

2017-18 RESULT: Time: 1:19.95 (Heavy 8)

FP	NO	HORSE	TRAINER	JOCKEY	MARGIN	BAR.	WGT	SP
1	2	SANTA ANA LANE	Anthony Freedman	Ben Melham		3	55.5kg	$14
2	13	SUPER CASH	Andrew Noblet	Jamie Kah	1.75L	10	51.5kg	$31
3	16	CHAMPAGNE CUDDLES	Bjorn Baker	Corey Brown	1.95L	1	51kg	$5
4	3	CRACK ME UP	Liam Birchley	Jim Byrne	2.15L	4	53.5kg	$21
5	15	PERAST	Paul Perry	Jeff Lloyd	2.25L	9	50kg	$6.50
6	10	SHILLELAGH	Chris Waller	Michael Dee	3.25L	8	52.5kg	$16
7	1	IMPENDING	James Cummings	Damian Browne	3.45L	7	57.5kg	$6.50
8	6	SPIETH	David & Ben Hayes & Tom Dabernig	Craig Williams	3.65L	16	53.5kg	$19
9	14	INVINCIBLE GEM	Kris Lees	Brenton Avdulla	3.95L	13	52kg	$15
10	4	ENDLESS DRAMA	Chris Waller	Glyn Schofield	4.05L	15	53.5kg	$26
11	8	MOST IMPORTANT	Tony Gollan	Mark Du Plessis	5.05L	2	53kg	$61
12	7	FOXPLAY	Chris Waller	Kerrin McEvoy	6.8L	14	53kg	$21
13	9	THE MONSTAR	Brett Cavanough	Skye Bogenhuber	7.55L	6	52.5kg	$21
14	11	CARE TO THINK	Matthew Dunn	Tim Clark	7.95L	12	52.5kg	$12
15	5	VOODOO LAD	Darren Weir	Chris Parnham	8.15L	5	53.5kg	$18
16	12	BURNING PASSION	Mark Newnham	Michael Cahill	10.65L	11	52kg	$26

PAST WINNERS

YEAR	WINNER	JOCKEY	TRAINER	2ND	3RD	TIME
2018	Santa Ana Lane	Ben Melham	Anthony Freedman	Super Cash	Champagne Cuddles	1:19.9
2017	Impending	Corey Brown	Darren Beadman	In Her Time	Clearly Innocent	1:17.9
2016	Under The Louvre	Dwayne Dunn	Robert Smerdon	Black Heart Bart	The Virginian	1:23.7
2015	Srikandi	Kerrin McEvoy	Ciaron Maher	Boban	Generalife	1:18.2
2014	River Lad	Damien Oliver	Natalie Mccall	Temple Of Boom	Srikandi	1:21.6
2013	Linton	Nicholas Hall	John Sadler	Buffering	Streama	1:22.0
2012	Mid Summer Music	Luke Nolen	Peter Moody	Buffering	Happy Zero	1:23.0
2011	Sincero	Jason Taylor	Stephen Farley	Beaded	Zero Rock	1:22.8
2010	Black Piranha	Nash Rawiller	Con Karakatsanis	Melito	Mic Mac	1:21.1
2009	Black Piranha	Tye Angland	Con Karakatsanis	Danleigh	Ortensia	1:25.5
2008	Mr Baritone	Sebastian Murphy	Michael Moroney	Hard To Catch	Double Dare	1:26.4
2007	Snipers Bullet	Craig Williams	Tracey Bartley	Gold Edition	Bendetti	1:23.1
2006	La Montagna	Craig Newitt	Barry Baldwin	Gee I Jane	Cog Hill	1:22.9
2005	St Basil	Michael Cahill	Bevan Laming	Perfect Promise	Shamekha	1:20.7
2004	Thorn Park	Danny Nikolic	Bob Thomsen	Consular	St Basil	1:21.3
2003	Private Steer	Glen Boss	John O'Shea	Diamond Dane	Into The Night	1:21.6
2002	Show A Heart	Danny Nikolic	Barry Miller	Falvelon	Kingsgate	1:21.7
2001	Crawl	Darren Gauci	John Hawkes	Hire	Mr Innocent	1:20.5
2000	Landsighting	Chris Munce	Noel Mayfield-Smith	Mr Innocent	Brighter Scene	1:21.4
1999	Adam	Jim Byrne	Ray Brock	City Fair	Staging	1:23.9
1998	Toledo	Brian York	Russell Cameron	Monopolize	Blazing Steel	1:20.2
1997	Dane Ripper	Chris Munce	Bart Cummings	Quick Flick	Celestial Choir	1:23.1

BACKGROUND

First run: 1890 (won by Pyrrhus). Group 1 since 1980. Run over 1200m 1890-1953. Previously known as the Elders Handicap. Run at Doomben (1350m) in 2015 due to Eagle Farm renovations, and also in 2017 & 2018 due to state of Eagle Farm track.
Fastest time (1400m): Crawl (2001) 1:20.50
Multiple winners: 8—Black Piranha (2010, 2009); Rough Habit (1992, 1991); Daybreak Lover (1986, 1984); Lucky Ring (1950, 1949); Petrol Lager (1935, 1934); Highland (1926, 1925); Gold Tie (1919, 1918); Babel (1896, 1895).
Fillies & mares to win (since 1930): 9—Srikandi (2015); Mid Summer Music (2012); La Montagna (2006); Private Steer (2003); Dane Ripper (1999); Canterbury Belle (1985); Cele's Image (1964); Wiggle (1958); Capri (1931). Note: Capri (1931) is the only mare (4YO). All the others are 3YO fillies, except for 2YO Wiggle (1958).

3YOs to win: 32—Impending (2017); Sniper's Bullet (2007); *La Montagna (2006); *Private Steer (2003); *Dane Ripper (1997); Never Undercharge (1993); *Canterbury Belle (1985); Daybreak Lover (1984); Bemboka Yacht (1980); Imposing (1979); Divide And Rule (1970); Mister Hush (1967); Winfreux (1965); *Cele's Image (1964); Kilshery (1962); Persian Lyric (1961); Knave (1956); Suncup (1953); Lucky Ring (1949); Thurles Lad (1938); King Merlin (1937); Highland (1925); *Lady Aura (1923); Laneffe (1922); *Syceonelle (1921); Gold Tie (1918); Malt Mark (1914); *Lady Hope (1911); Bright Laddie (1910); *Jessie's Dream (1907); Babel (1896); Dan O'Connell (1891). *Fillies.

2YOs to win: 8—*Wiggle (1958); Laneffe (1922); *Sydney Damsel (1917); Amberdown (1916); *Line Gun (1913); Fitz Grafton (1903); Sweetheart (1899); Boreas II (1898). *Fillies.

Notable winners: Santa Ana Lane (2018); Impending (2017); Private Steer (2003); Show A Heart (2002); Dane Ripper (1997); Rough Habit (1992, 1991); Campaign King (1988); Triton (1972); Divide And Ruler (1970); Winfreux (1965); Wiggle (1958); Kingster (1957); Highland (1926, 1925); Gold Tie (1919, 1918); Fitz Grafton (1903); Boreas II (1898); Babel (1896, 1895).

Stradbroke Handicap winners won the lead-up races:

George Ryder Stakes: 2—Campaign King (1988); Triton (1972).

Doncaster Handicap: 1—Karendi (1954).

All Aged Stakes: 4—Rough Habit (1992); Triton (1972); Kilshery (1962); Kingster (1957).

QTC Goldmarket: 1—Black Piranha (2009).

Sunshine Coast Cup: 1—Black Piranha (2009).

BRC Sprint: 1—River Lad (2014).

BTC Classic: 1—La Montagna (2006).

Kingsford Smith (BTC) Cup: 1—Thorn Park (2004).

The Goodwood: 1—Santa Ana Lane (2018).

Doomben 10,000: 4—Campaign King (1988); Spedito (1975); Winfreux (1965); High Rank (1941).

Doomben Cup: 3—Rough Habit (1992, 1991); Divide And Rule (1970).

Stradbroke Handicap winners went on to win in the same preparation:

WJ Healy Stakes: None. Note: No horse has won both races, but four horses have won the Healy after finishing second in the Stradbroke—Harmonize (1965); Samson (1962); Second Earl (1959); Grand Topic (1955).

Tatt's Tiara: 1—Srikandi (2015).

Leading winning jockeys:

4 wins Johno Stone (Line Gun 1913, Storm King 1909, Jessie's Dream 1907, Darelong 1906).

3 wins Billy Camer (Divide And Rule 1970, Wiggle 1958, Karendi 1954); Myles Connell (Amberdown 1916, Cairn Wallace 1915, Malt Mark 1914); Darby McCarthy (Castanea 1966, Cele's Image 1964, Mullala 1963); George Moore (Kilshery 1962, Persian Lyric 1961, Aqua Regis 1951).

Current winning jockeys:

1 win Tye Angland (Black Piranha 2009); Glen Boss (Private Steer 2003); Corey Brown (Impending 2017); Michael Cahill (St. Basil 2005); Grant Cooksley (Canterbury Belle 1985); Dwayne Dunn (Under The Louvre 2016); Nicholas Hall (Linton 2013); Kerrin McEvoy (Srikandi 2015); Ben Melham (Santa Ana Lane 2018); Craig Newitt (La Montagna 2006); Luke Nolen (Mid Summer Music 2012); Damien Oliver (River Lad 2014); Nash Rawiller (Black Piranha 2010); Jason Taylor (Sincero 2011); Craig Williams (Sniper's Bullet 2007).

Leading winning trainers:

6 wins Watty Blacklock (Gold Tie 1919, 1918, Blunderer 1902, Boreas II 1898, Babel 1896, 1895).

4 wins Bart Cummings (Dane Ripper 1997, Never Undercharge 1993, Robian Steel 1989, Campaign King 1988); John Stone snr (Line Gun 1913, Satisfaire 1908, Darelong 1906, Rosy Dawn 1893).

Current winning trainers:

2 wins Con Karakatsanis (Black Piranha 2010, 2009); John Wheeler (Rough Habit 1992, 1991).

1 win Barry Baldwin (La Montagna 2006); Tracey Bartley (Sniper's Bullet 2007); Darren Beadman (Impending 2017); Russell Cameron (Toledo 1998); Steve Farley (Sincero 2011); Anthony Freedman (Santa Ana Lane 2018); Lee Freedman (Danasinga 1996); Bryan Guy (All Our Mob 1994); John Hawkes (Crawl 2001); Bevan Laming (St. Basil 2005); Ciaron Maher (Srikandi 2015); Noel Mayfield-Smith (Landsighting 2000); Natalie McCall (River Lad 2014); Michael Moroney (Mr Baritone 2008); John O'Shea (Private Steer 2003); Graeme Rogerson (Brenlaine 1983); John Sadler (Linton 2013); Robert Smerdon (Under The Louvre 2016).

Points of interest:

Ducatoon was first past the post in 1980, but later disqualified for a positive swab. Bemboka Yacht was declared the winner. The heaviest weight carried to win since metrics in 1973: Rough Habit (1992) and Campaign King (1988) 58.5kg. Babel (1895) carried 69kg (10 stone 12 lbs) to win.

John Stone trained three winners and his son John jnr (Johno) rode four winners, including Line Gun (2013) and Darelong (1906), who were trained by his father.

BRC JJ Atkins (1600m)—Eagle Farm
Of $600,000. Group 1. Set Weights, 2YO. June 8, 2019.

2017-18 RESULT: Time: 1:38.89 (Heavy 8)

FP	NO	HORSE	TRAINER	JOCKEY	MARGIN	BAR.	WGT	SP
1	5	THE AUTUMN SUN	Chris Waller	Kerrin McEvoy		6	57kg	$4f
2	2	ZOUSAIN	Chris Waller	James McDonald	0.3L	14	57kg	$6
3	11	FUNDAMENTALIST	David & Ben Hayes & Tom Dabernig	Craig Williams	1.8L	7	55kg	$5
4	4	SESAR	Steven O'Dea	Damian Lane	2.1L	13	57kg	$13
5	7	HOME GROUND	John Sargent	Travis Wolfgram	3.35L	10	57kg	$71
6	6	GRIM REAPER	Steven O'dea	Brenton Avdulla	3.65L	4	57kg	$51
7	12	PLUMARO	Kevin Kemp	Tim Clark	3.85L	3	55kg	$9.50
8	13	MISS SARA	Les Ross	Ryan Wiggins	5.1L	2	55kg	$151
9	14	SIZZLING ACE	Toby Edmonds	Glyn Schofield	5.2L	1	55kg	$9.50
10	3	BOOMSARA	Chris Munce	Matthew McGillivray	5.95L	8	57kg	$18
11	1	LEAN MEAN MACHINE	Chris Waller	Corey Brown	6.95L	9	57kg	$7
12	10	PEPPI LA FEW	Liam Birchley	Damian Browne	10.45L	5	57kg	$91
13	8	CHAMPAGNE GARDEN	John Zielke	Tegan Harrison	10.85L	12	57kg	$151
14	9	HOME MADE	John Sargent	Mark Zahra	14.1L	11	57kg	$151

PAST WINNERS

YEAR	WINNER	JOCKEY	TRAINER	2ND	3RD	TIME
2018	The Autumn Sun	Kerrin McEvoy	Chris Waller	Zousain	Fundamentalist	1:38.8
2017	Capital Gain	Jim Byrne	Paul Butterworth	Aloisia	Taking Aim	1:36.2
2016	Sacred Elixir	Zac Purton	Tony Pike	Charnley River	Heart Skipt A Beat	1:37.8
2015	Press Statement	Tye Angland	Chris Waller	Sagaronne	Look To The Stars	1:35.4
2014	Almalad	Tommy Berry	Gai Waterhouse	Brazen Beau	Looks Like The Cat	1:35.3
2013	Romantic Touch	Nash Rawiller	Gai Waterhouse	Zoustar	Paximadia	1:36.5
2012	Sizzling	Chris Munce	Kelso Wood	Kabayan	Academus	1:37.0
2011	Benfica	Kerrin McEvoy	Peter Snowden	Hot Snitzel	Playtime	1:36.0
2010	Pressday	Nash Rawiller	Chris Waller	Ringa Ringa Rosie	American Crew	1:35.0
2009	Linky Dink	Peter Robl	Jason Coyle	Spot On Target	Southport	1:39.9
2008	Rockdale	Mark Zahra	John Morrisey	Baci Amore	Fravashi	1:40.3
2007	Apercu	Darren Beadman	Clarry Conners	Tripitz	Masked Assassin	1:37.9
2006	Reigning To Win	Chris Munce	John O'Shea	Danleigh	Carry To Glory	1:37.4
2005	Darci Brahma	Scott Seamer	Mark Walker	Ready As	Daemons	1:34.9
2004	Outback Prince	Corey Brown	Anthony Cummings	Star Shiraz	Lords A Leaping	1:34.1
2003	Picaday	Scott Seamer	Bruce McLachlan	Promoted	Ambulance	1:35.8
2002	Lovely Jubly	Brett Prebble	David Throsby	Top Echelon	Big Breakfast	1:35.3
2001	Juanmo	Kerrin McEvoy	Alan Bailey	Barawin	Evander	1:35.1
2000	Show A Heart	Stathi Katsidis	Barry Miller	Lady Mulan	Rapid Man	1:36.8
1999	Freemason	Darren Gauci	John Hawkes	Perfect Paradise	I Realise	1:37.4
1998	Mossman	Mick Dittman	Clarry Conners	Lease	Curio Jade	1:34.6
1997	Al Mansour	Danny Brereton	Bruce Mclachlan	Evader	Freedom Road	1:37.0

BACKGROUND

First run: 1976 (won by Romantic Dream). Group 2 1980-1984, Group 1 from 1985. Registered name is BRC TJ Smith Stakes. Previously known as the Claret Stakes, Sir Robert Herbert Stakes, QTC Stakes, Marlboro Stakes, Castlemaine Stakes, TJ Smith Classic. Run at Doomben (1600m) in 2015 and 2017-18.
Most recent filly to win: Linky Dink (2009)
Fastest time (1600m): Just A Printer (1994) 1:33.00 (Australian record for 2YO).
Notable winners: Press Statement (2015); Sizzling (2012); Pressday (2010); Darci Brahma (2005); Lovely Jubly (2002); Show A Heart (2000); Mossman (1998); Mahogany (1993); Slight Chance (1992); Prince Salieri (1989); Zeditave (1988); Zephyr Zip (1979); Scomeld (1978); Luskin Star (1977).
JJ Atkins Stakes winners won the lead-up races:
Hampden Stakes (Hardy Brothers): 3—Benfica (2011); Apercu (2007); Show A Heart (2000).
Doomben Slipper: 3—Picaday (2003); Show A Heart (2000); Al Mansour (1997).
Champagne Classic: 3—Sizzling (2012); Pressday (2010); Lovely Jubly (2002).
BRC Sires' Produce (since 1975): 10—Sizzling (2012); Pressday (2010); Lovely Jubly (2002); Anthems (1996); Mahogany (1993); Slight Chance (1992); Flotilla (1987); Zephyr Zip (1979); Luskin Star (1977); Romantic Dream (1976).

JJ Atkins Stakes and the other 2YO majors:
Magic Millions Gold Coast Classic: 1—Lovely Jubly (2002).
Blue Diamond Stakes: 1—Zeditave (1988).
Golden Slipper: 1—Luskin Star (1977).
Golden Slipper & BRC Sires' Produce: 1—Luskin Star (1977).
JJ Atkins Stakes winners went on to win as spring 3YOs.
Caulfield Guineas: 3—Press Statement (2015); Show A Heart (2000); Mahogany (1993).
Victoria Derby: 1—Mahogany (1993).
Leading winning jockeys:
3 wins Mick Dittman (Mossman 1998, Just A Printer 1994, Scomeld 1978); Kerrin McEvoy (The Autumn Sun 2018, Benfica 2011, Juanmo 2001).
Current winning jockeys:
3 wins Kerrin McEvoy (The Autumn Sun 2018, Benfica 2011, Juanmo 2001); Nash Rawiller (Romantic Touch 2013, Pressday 2010).
1 win Tye Angland (Press Statement 2015); Tommy Berry (Almalad 2014); Corey Brown (Outback Prince 2004); Jm Byrne (Capital Gaion 2017); Larry Cassidy (Ravarda 1995); Brett Prebble (Lovely Jubly 2002); Zac Purton (Sacred Elixir 2016); Mark Zahra (Rockdale 2008).
Leading winning trainers:
3 wins Chris Waller (The Autumn Sun 2018, Press Statement 2015, Pressday 2010).
2 wins Jim Atkins (Tristram's Edition 1985; Prince Frolic 1984); Clarry Conners (Apercu 2007; Mossman 1998); John Hawkes (Freemason 1999; Anthems 1996); Bruce McLachlan (Picaday 2003; Al Mansour 1997); Bob Thomsen (Slight Chance 1992; Zinders 1991); Gai Waterhouse (Almalad 2014, Romantic Touch 2013).
Current winning trainers:
3 wins Chris Waller (The Autumn Sun 2018, Press Statement 2015, Pressday 2010).
2 wins Clarry Conners (Apercu 2007, Mossman 1998); John Hawkes (Freemason 1999, Anthems 1996); Gai Waterhouse (Almalad 2014, Romantic Touch 2013).
1 win Paul Butterworth (Capital Gain 2017); Jason Coyle (Linky Dink 2009); Anthony Cummings (Outback Prince 2004); Lee Freedman (Mahogany 1993); Bryan Guy (Ravarda 1995); Tony Pike (Sacred Elixir 2016); John O'Shea (Reigning To Win 2006); Peter Snowden (Benfica 2011); Mark Walker (Darci Brahma 2005).
Points of interest:
Bob Thomsen rode Romantic Dream (1976) to win and trained Slight Chance (1992) and Zinders (1991).
Luskin Star also won the Sydney 2YO Triple Crown – Golden Slipper, AJC Sires' Produce and Champagne Stakes.
Mahogany (1993) won the Caulfield Guineas and Victoria Derby in the 1993 spring, and then went on to win the Australian Guineas and Australian Derby in the autumn of 1994.
Press Statement (2015) and Pressday (2010) are half-brothers, out of the broodmare Kaaptive Empress, by Kaaptive Edition. Press Statement is by Hinchinbrook; Pressday is by Domesday. Both horses were trained by Chris Waller.

BRC Queensland Derby (2400m)—Eagle Farm
Of $600,000. Group 1. Set Weights, 3YO. June 8, 2019.

2017-18 RESULT: Time: 2:19.31 (Heavy 8)

FP	NO	HORSE	TRAINER	JOCKEY	MARGIN	BAR.	WGT	SP
1	1	DARK DREAM	Kerry Parker	Tim Clark		3	57kg	$4.20f
2	2	HEAVENLY THOUGHT	Darren Weir	Brad Rawiller	0.2L	1	57kg	$8
3	16	YOUNGSTAR	Chris Waller	Kerrin McEvoy	2.95L	16	55kg	$6.50
4	13	AUGUSTUS	Chris Waller	Brenton Avdulla	3.25L	6	57kg	$101
5	4	MAHAMEDEIS	Nick Ryan	James Winks	3.75L	15	57kg	$21
6	5	REZEALIENT	David & Ben Hayes & Tom Dabernig	Jamie Kah	4.5L	12	57kg	$51
7	11	LUCKY FOR ALL	Darren Weir	Damian Lane	4.8L	14	57kg	$4.40
8	8	HAN XIN	Gai Waterhouse & Adrian Bott	Mark Zahra	4.9L	13	57kg	$14
9	10	ALMIGHTY CROWN	Chris Waller	Ben Melham	5.65L	7	57kg	$151
10	12	MEROVEE	Chris Waller	Blake Shinn	6.9L	11	57kg	$31
11	14	BANNER SEASON	Kris Lees	Jeff Lloyd	12.4L	5	57kg	$41
12	15	TURNBERRY	Kris Lees	Damian Browne	13.65L	10	57kg	$151
13	7	LIVE AND FREE	John O'Shea	James McDonald	14.9L	8	57kg	$5.50
14	17	CAPTIVATOR	Les Kelly	Leith Innes	18.15L	4	57kg	$201
15	6	CALIFORNIA TURBO	Peter & Paul Snowden	Corey Brown	22.65L	9	57kg	$91
16	9	WON WON TOO	David & Ben Hayes & Tom Dabernig	Jim Byrne	25.65L	2	57kg	$91

PAST WINNERS

YEAR	WINNER	JOCKEY	TRAINER	2ND	3RD	TIME
2018	Dark Dream	Tim Clark	Kerry Parker	Heavenly Thought	Youngstar	2:19.3
2017	Ruthven	Hugh Bowman	Ciaron Maher	Rockstar Rebel	Ana Royale	2:14.4
2016	Eagle Way	Tommy Berry	Bryan Guy	Rodrico	I'm Belucci	2:32.8
2015	Magicool	James Winks	Mark Kavanagh	Werther	Jumbo Prince	1:35.4
2014	Sonntag	Chad Schofield	Henry Dwyer	Pinstripe Lane	Vilanova	2:28.3
2013	Hawkspur	Jim Cassidy	Chris Waller	Electric Fusion	Honorius	2:27.8
2012	Brambles	Brad Rawiller	Peter Moody	Quintessential	Westsouthwest	2:29.7
2011	Shootoff	Michael Rodd	Graeme Rogerson	Shez Sinsational	Heidilicious	2:28.7
2010	Dariana	Michael Rodd	Bart Cummings	Kutchinsky	Miss Keepsake	2:26.4
2009	Court Ruler	Larry Cassidy	John Wheeler	Shocking	Larry's Never Late	2:34.4
2008	Riva San	Jim Byrne	Peter Moody	Petushki	Moatize	2:36.9
2007	Empires Choice	Damien Oliver	Bart Cummings	Volcanic Star	Sirmione	2:32.9
2006	Ice Chariot	Glen Lynch	Ron Maund	Cape Breton	Loanhead	2:30.6
2005	Lachlan River	Glen Boss	John Morrisey	Lords A Leaping	Vitesse Dane	2:26.5
2004	Toulouse Lautrec	Corey Brown	John Hawkes	Devastating	Set Up	2:26.5
2003	Half Hennessy	Scott Seamer	Bede Murray	Schumpeter	King Of Them All	2:27.7
2002	County Tyrone	Corey Brown	Max Lees	Galroof	Miss Bussell	2:29.0
2001	De Gaulle Lane	Brett Prebble	Colin Alderson	Tempest Morn	Lottery Prize	2:25.2
2000	Freemason	Larry Cassidy	John Hawkes	Citras Prince	Maguire	2:27.3
1999	Camarena	Glen Boss	John Morrisey	Figurehead	Skoozi Please	2:33.6
1998	Dodge	Larry Cassidy	John Hawkes	Melora	Bluebird The Word	2:29.1
1997	Yippyio	Jim Cassidy	Jack Denham	Marble Halls	Summer Beau	2:31.9

BACKGROUND

First run: 1868 (won by Hermit). Group 1 since 1980. Run twice in 1870. Run at Gayndah 1868-70. Not held 1873-77; 1942-45. Switched from spring to winter in 1973. Run at Doomben (2200m) in 2015, 2017-18.
Most recent filly to win: Dariana (2010).
Notable winners: Eagle Way (2016); County Tyrone (2002); Freemason (2000); Camarena (1999); Yippyio (1997); Rough Habit 1992; Bravery (1988); Strawberry Road (1983); Kingston Town (1980); Double Century (1979); Analie (1973); Silver Sharpe (1970); Tails (1968); Royal Sovereign (1964); Tulloch (1957); Book Link (1956); Basha Felika (1950); Spear Chief (1937); Lough Neagh (1931); High Syce (1927); Fitz Grafton (1903); Florence (1870);
Fastest time (2400m, Eagle Farm): De Gaulle Lane (2001): 2:25.20.

Queensland Derby winners won the lead-up races:
Frank Packer Plate: 4—Shootoff (2011); Dariana (2010); Freemason (2000); Dodge (1998).
Lord Mayor's Cup: None. Note: Book Link (1958) won the Derby in 1956. He is the only horse to win both races.
Queensland Guineas: 19—Camarena (1999); Yippyio (1997); Confidence (1963); Book Link (1956); Blue Slipper (1948); Sefiona (1947); Spearace (1937); Lough Neagh (1931); Bernfield (1929); High Syce (1927); Ardglen (1923); Kingslot (1922); Lordacre (1916); Flaxen (1908); Euroa (1907); Alexis (1905); Joyance (1904); Fitz Grafton (1903); Boreas (1898).
Rough Habit Plate: 6—Dark Dream (2018); Hawkspur (2013); Brambles (2012); De Gaulle Lane (2001); Dodge (1998); Tenor (1994).
Grand Prix: 14—Hawkspur (2013); Brambles (2012); Ice Chariot (2006); Half Hennessy (2003); Air Seattle (1993); Dorset Downs (1991); Hidden Rhythm (1989); Handy Proverb (1986); Librici (1984); Our Planet (1982); Mr. Cromwell (1981); Kingston Town (1980); Double Century (1979); Lefroy (1978).
Queensland Oaks: 4—Riva San (2008); Royal Magic (1992); Bravery (1988); Analie (1973).
Queensland Derby and the "other" Derbys:
Victoria Derby: 4—Silver Sharpe (1970); Royal Sovereign (1964); Tulloch (1957); Florence (1870). Note: No horse has completed the double since the Queensland Derby was moved to the winter in 1973.
Australian Derby: 7—Strawberry Road (1983); Kingston Town (1980); Silver Sharpe (1970); Royal Sovereign (1964); Persian Lyric (1960); Tulloch (1957); Florence (1870).
The Treble: Victoria Derby, Australian Derby & Queensland Derby: 4—Silver Sharpe (1970); Royal Sovereign (1964); Tulloch (1957); Florence (1870). Note: Queensland Derby was moved from spring to the winter in 1973.
Queensland Derby and the Melbourne spring majors:
Caulfield Cup as a 4YO: 1—Basha Felika (1951).
Cox Plate (as a 4YO): 2—Strawberry Road (1983); Kingston Town (1980). Note: Kingston Town also won the Cox Plate in 1981 and 1982. Tulloch (1957) won the Cox Plate in 1960.
No Queensland Derby winner has won a Melbourne Cup.
Leading winning jockeys:
4 wins Jim Cassidy (Hawkspur 2013, Yippyio 1997, Bravery 1988, Handy Proverb 1986).
3 wins Larry Cassidy (Court Ruler 2009, Freemason 2000, Dodge 1998); Mick Dittman (Turridu 1995, Strawberry Road 1983, Cheyne Walk 1976); George Moore (Persian Lyric 1960, Tulloch 1957, Forest Beau 1951); Johno Stone (Maritoria 1911, Braw Laddie 1909, Joyance 1904); Ted Tanwan (Auto Buz 1935, Waikare 1933, Lough Neagh 1931); Edward "Georgie" Tucker (High Syce 1927, Wee Glen 1925, Ardglen 1923);
Current winning jockeys:
3 wins Larry Cassidy (Court Ruler 2009, Freemason 2000, Dodge 1998).
2 wins Glen Boss (Lachlan River 2005, Camarena 1999); Corey Brown (Toulouse Lautrec 2004, County Tyrone 2002); Michael Rodd (Shootoff 2011, Dariana 2010);
1 win Tommy Berry (Eagle Way 2016); Hugh Bowman (Ruthven 2017); Jim Byrne (Riva San 2008); Tim Clark (Dark Dream 2018); Grant Cooksley (Tenor 1994); Damien Oliver (Empire's Choice 2007); Brad Rawiller (Brambles 2012); Chad Schofield (Sonntag 2014); James Winks (Magicool 2015).
Leading winning trainers:
12 wins Tommy Smith (Dorset Downs 1991, Our Planet 1982, Kingston Town 1980, Cheyne Walk 1976, Analie 1973, Silver Sharpe 1970, Dark Briar 1966, Bahram Star 1965, Travel Boy 1959, Tulloch 1957, Castillo 1953, Forest Beau 1951).
7 wins Harry Walsh (Czarina 1894, Greywing 1888, Lord Headington 1887, Legerdemain 1881, Waterloo 1880, Elastic 1879, Whisker 1878).
5 wins John Stone snr (Maritoria 1911, Braw Laddie 1909, Joyance 1904, The Guard 1897, Garuda 1890).
4 wins Watty Blacklock (Lordacre 1916, Togo 1906, Balfour 1902, Boreas II 1898); John Hawkes (Toulouse Lautrec 2004, Freemason 2000, Dodge 1998, Tenor 1994).
Current winning trainers:
4 wins John Hawkes (Toulouse Lautrec 2004, Freemason 2000, Dodge 1998, Tenor 1994).
2 wins John Morrisey (Lachlan River 2005; Camarena 1999); John Wheeler (Court Ruler 2009, Rough Habit 1990).
1 win Clarry Conners (Air Seattle 1993); Henry Dwyer (Sonntag 2014); Peter Eggleston (Valance 1996); Garry Frazer (Turridu 1995); Bryan Guy (Eagle Way 2016); Mark Kavanagh (Magicool 2015); Carion Maher (Ruthven 2017); Kerry Parker (Dark Dream 2018); Graeme Rogerson (Shootoff 2011); Chris Waller (Hawkspur 2012).
Points of interest:
Spear Chief won the Qld Derby in 1937, and the Brisbane Cup in 1938 (as a 3YO) and again 1939.
Harry Walsh, who trained seven winners of the Derby, also rode two of them—Waterloo 1880 and Elastic 1879—when he was the private trainer and rider for Queensland racing's pioneer breeder and owner Sir Joshua P. Bell. Walsh also rode Strop to finish second behind Glencoe in the 1868 Melbourne Cup.

Tattersall's RC Tatt's Tiara (1400m)—Eagle Farm

Of $500,000. Group 1. Weight For Age Fillies & Mares. June 23, 2018.

2017-18 RESULT: Time: 1:18.51   (Good 4)

FP	NO	HORSE	TRAINER	JOCKEY	MARGIN	BAR.	WGT	SP
1	4	PROMPT RESPONSE	Gai Waterhouse & Adrian Bott	Blake Shinn		3	57kg	$4.20f
2	6	SHILLELAGH	Chris Waller	Michael Walker	1.25L	7	57kg	$14
3	5	SUPER CASH	Andrew Noblet	Jamie Kah	1.35L	13	57kg	$10
4	10	SAVANNA AMOUR	Chris Meagher	Ben Melham	1.55L	1	57kg	$10
5	1	INVINCIBELLA	Chris Waller	Kerrin McEvoy	1.75L	11	57kg	$13
5	3	DAYSEE DOOM	Ron Quinton	Andrew Adkins	1.75L	15	57kg	$20
7	9	INVINCIBLE GEM	Kris Lees	Jeff Lloyd	2.05L	10	57kg	$14
8	14	SIREN'S FURY	Jason Coyle	Tegan Harrison	2.25L	2	57kg	$20
9	16	MOSS TRIP	Peter & Paul Snowden	Brenton Avdulla	2.65L	16	55.5kg	$13
10	11	VOLPE VELOCE	Graham Richardson & Gavin Parker	Jake Bayliss	2.85L	12	57kg	$41
11	15	CHAMPAGNE CUDDLES	Bjorn Baker	Corey Brown	3.05L	4	55.5kg	$6
12	13	JUST DREAMING	Kris Lees	Damian Browne	4.3L	6	57kg	$41
13	8	FRENCH EMOTION	Chris Waller	Glen Colless	4.4L	5	57kg	$101
14	7	MISSROCK	Robbie Laing	Michael Cahill	4.7L	14	57kg	$26
15	12	PEDRENA	Mick Price	Michael Dee	6.2L	9	57kg	$21
16	2	MISS WILSON	John Bary	Vinnie Colgan	7.45L	8	57kg	$41

PAST WINNERS

YEAR	WINNER	JOCKEY	TRAINER	2ND	3RD	TIME
2018	Prompt Response	Blake Shinn	Gai Waterhouse & Adrian Bott	Shillelagh	Super Cash	1:18.5
2017	Tycoon Tara	Kerrin McEvoy	Peter & Paul Snowden	Prompt Response	In Her Time	1:19.3
2016	Miss Cover Girl	Damian Browne	Kelly Schweida	Azkadellia	Sultry Feeling	1:24.9
2015	Srikandi	Kerrin McEvoy	Ciaron Maher	Avoid Lightning	Lumosty	1:24.3
2014	Cosmic Endeavour	Tommy Berry	Gai Waterhouse	Angel Of Mercy	Avoid Lightning	1:22.0
2013	Red Tracer	Nash Rawiller	Chris Waller	Streama	Floria	1:24.2
2012	Pear Tart	Jeff Lloyd	John P Thompson	Skyerush	Gai's Choice	1:23.3
2011	Yosei	Michelle Payne	Stuart Webb	Beaded	Born To Rock	1:22.2
2010	Melito	Corey Brown	Gerald Ryan	Wealth Princess	Beaded	1:21.8
2009	Russeting	Michael Cahill	Bart Cummings	Prima Nova	Subtle Cove	1:22.6
2008	Absolut Glam	James Winks	Danny O'Brien	Fritzs Princess	Alverta	1:24.0
2007	Nova Star	Stathi Katsidis	Kelly Schweida	Fashions Afield	J Adane	1:22.0
2006	La Sizeranne	Michael Rodd	Roger James	Gee I Jane	Villa Bled	1:31.2
2005	Charmview	Brian Stewart	Tony Wildman	Tui Song	Yvonne	1:28.9
2004	Miss Potential	Barry Jones	Bill Borrie	Paraca	Rodrigo Rose	1:28.1
2003	Mon Mekki	Michael Rodd	Gerald Ryan	With My	Recurring	1:27.7
2002	Heptonstall	Scott Galloway	John Hawkes	Princess Clang	Omens	1:28.6
2001	Porto Roca	Nash Rawiller	Danny O'Brien	Dynamic Love	Heather	1:28.7
2000	Bonanova	Chris Munce	Grahame Begg	Crestfallen	Stella Maree	1:28.6
1999	Bonanova	Jim Cassidy	Grahame Begg	Staging	Amnesia	1:31.3
1998	Razer Blade	Shane Dye	Guy Walter	Zalinda	Gunalda	1:28.5
1997	Dane Ripper	Darren Beadman	Bart Cummings	Amber	Monica	1:34.1

BACKGROUND

First run: 1989 (won by La Posette). Listed from 1992-95. Group 3 1996-2005. Group 2 2006. Group 1 2007. Set weights and penalties to 2006. WFA from 2007. Run over 1500m 1989-2006. Registered name: Tattersall's Tiara. Conducted by the Tatts Racing Club Qld. Run at the Gold Coast (1400m) in 2015 due to renovations at Eagle Farm. Run at Doomben (1350m) in 2017-18 due to Eagle Farm track issues.
3YO fillies to win: 15—Cosmic Endeavour (2014); Pear Tart (2012); Yosei (2011); Melito (2010); Absolut Glam (2008); Heptonstall (2002); Razor Blade (1998); Dane Ripper (1997); Tripping (1996); Mamzelle Pedrille (1995); Rich Pageantry (1993); Blushing Bijou (1992); Rose Road (1991); Piper's Belle (1990); La Posette (1989).
Multiple winners: 1—Bonanova (2000, 1999).
Fastest time (1400m): Melito (2010) 1:21.83.

Notable winners: Tycoon Tara (2017); Srikandi (2015); Cosmic Endeavour (2014); Red Tracer (2013); Yosei (2011); Melito (2010); Miss Potential (2004); Porto Roca (2001); Bonanova (2000, 1999); Dane Ripper (1997).

Tattersall's Tiara winners won the lead-up races:
ATC Sapphire Stakes: 1—Cosmic Endeavour (2014).
Juanmo Stakes: 1—Russeting (2009).
Queensland Guineas: 1—Pear Tart (2012);
Dane Ripper Stakes: 3—Cosmic Endeavour (2014); Dane Ripper (2013); Tripping (1996).
Coolmore Classic: 1—Porto Roca (2001). Note: Bonanova finished second to Camino Rose in the 1999 Coolmore Classic before winning the Winter Stakes in 1999 and 2000.
ATC TJ Smith Stakes: 1—Melito (2010).
Stradbroke Handicap: 1—Srikandi (2015).

Tattersall's Tiara winners went on to win in the following spring:
Myer Classic: 2—Red Tracer (2013); Miss Potential (2004). Note: Bonanova won the Myer Classic in 1998, and then the Winter Stakes in 1999 and 2000.

Leading winning jockey:
2 wins Kerrin McEvoy (Tycoon Tara 2017, Srikandi 2015); Michael Rodd (La Sizeranne 2006; Miss Potential 2004).

Current winning jockeys:
2 wins Kerrin McEvoy (Tycoon Tara 2017, Srikandi 2015); Michael Rodd (La Sizeranne 2006, Miss Potential 2004).
1 win Tommy Berry (Cosmic Endeavour 2014); Corey Brown (Melito 2010); Damian Browne (Miss Cover Girl 2016); Michael Cahill (Russeting 2009); Larry Cassidy (Tripping 1996); Barry Jones (Miss Potential 2004); Jeff Lloyd (Pear Tart 2012); Michelle Payne (Yosei 2011); Nash Rawiller (Red Tracer 2013); Blake Shinn (Prompt Response 2018); Brad Stewart (Charmview 2005); James Winks (Absolut Glam 2008).

Leading winning trainers:
3 wins Gerald Ryan (Melito 2010, Mon Mekki 2003, Blushing Bijou 1992).
2 wins Grahame Begg (Bonanova 2000, 1999); Bart Cummings (Russeting 2009, Dane Ripper 1997); Danny O'Brien (Absolut Glam 2008, Porto Roca 2001); Kelly Schweida (Miss Cover Girl 2016, Nova Star 2007); Gai Waterhouse (Prompt Response 2018, Cosmic Endeavour 2014).

Current winning trainers:
3 wins Gerald Ryan (Melito 2010, Mon Mekki 2003, Blushing Bijou 1992).
2 wins Grahame Begg (Bonanova 2000, 1999); Danny O'Brien (Absolut Glam 2008, Porto Roca 2001); Kelly Schweida (Miss Cover Girl 2016, Nova Star 2007); Gai Waterhouse (Prompt Response 2018, Cosmic Endeavour 2014).
1 win Clarry Conners (Tripping 1996); Roger James (La Sizeranne 2006); John Hawkes (Heptonstall 2002); Ciaron Maher (Srikandi 2015); Ron Quinton (Mamzelle Pedrille 1995); Peter & Paul Snowden (Tycoon Tara 2017); John Thompson (Pear Tart 2012); Chris Waller (Red Tracer 2013); Gai Waterhouse & Adrian Bott (Prompt Response 2018); Stuart Webb (Yosei 2011).

Points of interest:
In 2006, Gee I Jane won the G1 Kingsford Smith (BTC) Cup. She finished second to La Montagna in the G1 Stradbroke Hcp, and then finished second to La Sizeranne in the Tattersall's Tiara. Dane Ripper won the Tiara and the Cox Plate in 1997.
Yosei won the G1 Thousand Guineas (in 2010) in the same season she won the Tattersall's Tiara (2011).

ATC Missile Stakes (1200m)—Randwick
$175,000 Group 2 3YO&Up WFA. August 4, 2018.

YEAR	WINNER	JOCKEY	TRAINER	2ND	3RD	TIME
2017	Invincible Gem	Corey Brown	Kris Lees	Le Romain	The Monstar	1:11.8
2016	Tycoon Tara	Blake Shinn	Peter & Paul Snowden	Rebel Dane	Mount Nero	1:15.6
2015	Burbero	Rory Hutchings	Bjorn Baker	Weary	Temple Of Boom	1:09.1
2014	Sweet Idea	Tommy Berry	Gai Waterhouse	Messene	Rebel Dane	1:09.4
2013	Rain Affair	Nash Rawiller	Joseph Pride	Mic Mac	Title	1:10.8
2012	Pinwheel	Kerrin McEvoy	Peter Snowden	Centennial Park	Rolling Pin	1:09.7
2011	Rain Affair	Corey Brown	Joseph Pride	Winter King	Pinwheel	1:10.7
2010	Love Conquers All	Jim Cassidy	Michael, Wayne & John Hawkes	Danleigh	Sniper's Bullet	1:12.4
2009	Teasing	Chris Munce	Tim Martin	Gold Trail	Typhoon Zed	1:04.4
2008	Captain Bax	Tim Clark	Kris Lees	Typhoon Zed	Interfere	1:05.4
2007	German Chocolate	Zac Purton	Paul Cave	La Montagna	Vionneto	1:04.6
2006	Imprisoned	Michael Rodd	John O'Shea	Crimson Reign	Mac'S Tune	1:06.3
2005	Dance Hero	Len Beasley	Gai Waterhouse	Snippetson	Spark Of Life	1:02.8
2004	Spark Of Life	Chris Munce	Allan Denham	Into The Night	Dane Shadow	1:02.8
2003	Pompeii	Corey Brown	Garry White	Academe	Our Egyptian Raine	1:03.7
2002	Lonhro	Darren Beadman	John Hawkes	Ancient Song	Notoire	1:03.5
2001	Sportsbrat	Hugh Bowman	Gary Portelli	Air She Goes	Lonhro	1:06.7

BACKGROUND

First run: 1978 (won by Idol). Group 3 1980-2013. Run at Canterbury 1978, 1980 & 1983.
Run at Rosehill all other times until 2009. Not held 1981. 1100m 1878-2009.
Note: This race is run on the last weekend of July or early August.
Most recent mare to win: Invincible Gem (2017).
Most recent 2YO to win: C&G–Commands (1999); Filly–None.
Most recent 3YO to win: C&G–Dance Hero (2005); Filly–Klokka (1993)
Multiple Winners: 4–Rain Affair (2013, 2011); Klokka (1994, 1993); Joanne (1992, 1991); Campaign King (1988, 1987)
Fastest Time (1200m): Burbero (2015) 1:09:13.
Notable Winners: Tycoon Tara (2016); Sweet Idea (2014); Dance Hero (2005); Spark Of Life (2004); Lonhro (2002); Padstow (2000); Guineas (1997); Potrero (1990); Select Prince (1989); Campaign King (1988, 1987); Shankhill Lass (1986); Row Of Waves (1985); Razor Sharp (1982)—all winners at Group 1 level.
Missile Stakes winner went on to win in the same preparation:
Up And Coming Stakes: None.
San Domenico Stakes: None.
Concorde Stakes: 1 – Joanne (1991). Note: Guineas (1997) won the Concorde Stakes in 1999.
Warwick Stakes: 1—Pinwheel (2012).
Premiere Stakes: 7—German Chocolate (2007); Spark Of Life (2004); Legal Agent (1996); Klokka (1993); Joanne (1992, 1991); Campaign King (1987).
VRC Sprint Classic Stakes: 1—Brawny Spirit (1995). Note: Dance Hero (2005) won the VRC Sprint Classic in 2006.
Chelmsford Stakes: 3 – Lonhro (2002); Campaign King (1987); Shankhill Lass (1986).
Missile Stakes and the Golden Slipper: 2—Dance Hero (Missile 2005, GS 2004); Guineas (1997).
Leading winning jockeys: 3 wins Darren Beadman (Lonhro 2002, Legal Agent 1996, Brawny Spirit 1995); Corey Brown (Invincible Gem 2017, Rain Affair 2011, Pompeii 2003); Jim Cassidy (Love Conquers All 2010, Klokka 1994, Potrero 1990); John Marshall (Camp;aign king 1988, 1987, Shankhill Lass 1986).
Current winning jockeys: 3 wins Corey Brown (Invincible Gem 2017, Rain Affair 2011, Pompeii 2003).
2 wins Larry Cassidy (Commands 1999, Guineas 1997).
1 win Tommy Berry (Sweet Idea 2014); Hugh Bowman (Sportsbrat 2001); Tim Clark (Captain Bax 2008); Rory Hutchings (Burbero 2015); Kerrin McEvoy (Pinwheel 2012); Zac Purton (German Chocolate 2007); Nash Rawiller (Rain Affair 2013); Michael Rodd (Imprisoned 2006); Blake Shinn (Tycoon Tara 2016).
Leading winning trainers: 4 wins John Hawkes (Love Conquers All 2010, Lonhro 2002, Commands 1999, Guineas 1997).
3 wins Bart Cummings (Campaign King 1988, 1987, Plus Vite 1984); Jack Denham (Joanne 1992, 1991, Macho 1980).
Current winning trainers: 4 wins John Hawkes (Love Conquers All 2010, Lonhro 2002, Commands 1999, Guineas 1997).
2 wins Kris Lees Invincible Gem 2017, Captain Bax 2008); Joe Pride (Rain Affair 2013, 2011); Peter Snowden (Tycoon Tara 2016, Pinwheel 2012);
Gai Waterhouse (Sweet Idea 2014, Dance Hero 2005).

1 win Bjorn Baker (Burbero 2015); Les Bridge (Row Of Waves 1985); Paul Cave (German Chocolate 2007); Allan Denham (Spark Of Life 2004); Michael, Wayne, John Hawkes (Love Conquers All 2010); Tim Martin (Teasing 2009); John O'Shea (Imprisoned 2006); Gary Portelli (Sportsbrat 2001); John Size (Padstow 2000); Peter & Paul Snowden (Tycoon Tara 2016);
Point of interest: Commands (1999) finished second past the post behind Padstow, but won the race on protest. Padstow (2000) won the race the following year.

MRC PB Lawrence Stakes (1400m)—Caulfield
$200,000 Group 2 3YO&Up WFA. August 18, 2018.

YEAR	WINNER	JOCKEY	TRAINER	2ND	3RD	TIME
2017	Hartnell	Craig Williams	James Cummings	Charmed Harmony	Black Heart Bart	1:24.0
2016	Miss Rose De Lago	Damien Oliver	Danny O'Brien	Jacquinot Bay	Entirely Platinum	1:24.8
2015	Mourinho	Vlad Duric	Darryl Blackshaw	The Cleaner	Dibayani	1:23.5
2014	Star Rolling	Stephen Baster	Peter Morgan & Craig Widdison	Spillway	Gig	1:24.3
2013	Puissance De Lune	Glen Boss	Darren Weir	Ajeeb	Second Effort	1:24.2
2012	Second Effort	Chris Symons	Clinton McDonald	Zamorar	Ready To Rip	1:27.6
2011	Whobegotyou	Damien Oliver	Mark Kavanagh	Lights Of Heaven	Prince Obama	1:23.9
2010	Shoot Out	Stathi Katsidis	John Wallace	Predatory Pricer	Heart Of Dreams	1:27.2
2009	Predatory Pricer	Steven King	Paul Murray	Whobegotyou	Typhoon Tracy	1:23.4
2008	Light Fantastic	Craig Newitt	Mick Price	Weekend Hussler	Maldivian	1:24.7
2007	Apache Cat	Michael Rodd	Greg Eurell	Marasco	Maldivian	1:22.1
2006	Pompeii Ruler	Nash Rawiller	Mick Price	Red Dazzler	Our Smoking Joe	1:23.6
2005	Lad Of The Manor	Greg Childs	Roger Hoysted	Our Smoking Joe	Super Elegant	1:27.9
2004	Regal Roller	Mark Flaherty	Clinton McDonald	Amtrak	Le Zagaletta	1:26.3
2003	Super Elegant	Greg Childs	Tony Vasil	Vocabulary	Walk On Air	1:24.4
2002	Sports	Brendan Fenech	John Hawkes	Le Zagaletta	Tully Thunder	1:23.2
2001	Le Zagaletta	Damien Oliver	Lee Freedman	Inaflury	Umrum	1:25.5

BACKGROUND
First run: 1949 (won by One Up). Group 2 since 1979. Run over 1600m 1949-50; Run over 1400m from 1951. Run at Flemington 1949-62; Sandown 1985-2001. Registered as the JJ Liston Stakes.
Most recent mare to win: Miss Rose De Lago (2016). Seven mares have won the Lawrence.
Most recent 3YO to win: C&G—Clear Springs (1954). Note: Clear Springs is the only 3YO to win the Lawrence.
Multiple winners: 2—Tauto (1972, 1971); My Peak (1962, 1960).
Fastest time (Caulfield 1400m): Apache Cat (2007) 1:22:19.
Notable winners: Hartnell (2017); Whobetgotyou (2011); Shoot Out (2010); Pompeii Ruler (2006); Mahogany (1994); Dr. Grace (1991); Sydeston (1990); Military Plume (1987); Sovereign Red (1981); So Called (1978); Vice Regal (1977); Tauto (1971-72); Regal Vista (1970); Winfreux (1968); Tobin Bronze (1966); Craftsman (1964); Lord (1958); Chicquita (1951).
Lawrence Stakes winners won the lead-up races:
Monash Stakes: 1—Delsole (1996).
Bletchingly Stakes: 3—Shoot Out (2010); Apache Cat (2007); Super Elegant (2003).
Lawrence Stakes winners went on to win in the same campaign:
Memsie Stakes: 4—Regal Roller (2004), Zambari (1973); Lord (1958), Syntax (1957).
Note: Regal Roller is the only horse to win the double since the Memsie became a 1400m event in 1979.
Dato Tan Chin Nam Stakes: 5—Lad Of The Manor (2005); Inaflury (1999); King Delamere (1985); So Called (1978); Vice Regal (1977).
Makybe Diva Stakes: 8—Pompeii Ruler (2006); Mahogany (1994); Military Plume (1987); Pleach (1983); Sovereign Red (1981); Stellar Belle (1967); Tobin Bronze (1966); Cromis (1955).
Underwood Stakes: 6—So Called (1978); Tobin Bronze (1966); Lord (1958); Syntax (1957); Cromis (1955); Ellerslie (1952).
Turnbull Stakes: 3—Stellar Belle (1967); Tobin Bronze (1966); Syntax (1957).
Caulfield Stakes: 1—Lord (1958).
Caulfield Cup: 1—Sydeston (1990).
Cox Plate: 3—So Called (1978); Tauto (1971); Tobin Bronze (1966).
Melbourne Cup: None.
Leading winning jockey: 4 wins Greg Childs (Lad Of The Manor 2001, Super Elegant 2003, Happy Star 1997, Bundy Lad 1993).
3 wins Jim Johnson (Winfreux 1968, Tobin Bronze 1966, Samson 1965); Damien Oliver (Miss Rose De Lago 2016, Whobegotyou 2011, La Zagaletta 2001).

Current winning jockeys: 3 wins Damien Oliver (Miss Rose De Lago 2016, Whobegotyou 2011, La Zagaletta 2001).
1 win Stephen Baster (Star Rolling 2014); Glen Boss (Puissance De Lune 2013); Vlad Duric (Mourinho 2015); Craig Newitt (Light Fantastic 2009); Brett Prebble (Skoozi Please 2000); Nash Rawiller (Pompeii Ruler 2006); Michael Rodd (Apache Cat 2007); Chris Symons (Second Effort 2012); Craig Williams (Hartnell 2017).
Leading winning trainer: 3 wins Brian Courtney (Regal Vista 1970, My Peak 1962, 1960).
Current winning trainers: 2 wins Lee Freedman (Le Zagaletta 2001, Mahogany 1994); Mick Price (Light Fantastic 2008, Pompeii Ruler 2006); Clinton McDonald (Second Effort 2012, Regal Roller 2004); Allan Sharrock (Jim's Mate 1992, Kairau Lad 1989).
1 win Darryl Blackshaw (Mourinho 2015); James Cummings (Hartnell 2017); Greg Eurell (Apache Cat 2007); Tony Gillies (My Steely Dan 1988); John Hawkes (Sports 2002); Mark Kavanagh (Whobegotyou 2011); Peter Morgan & Craig Widdison (Star Rolling 2014); Mike Moroney (Happy Star 1997); Paul Murray (Predatory Price 2009); Danny O'Brien (Miss Rose De Lago 2016); Bruce Purcell (Vonanne 1998); Graeme Rogerson (Skoozi Please 2000); Gerald Ryan (Baryshnikov 1995); Tony Vasil (Super Elegant 2003); John Wallace (Shoot Out 2010); Wayne Walters (Cobra 1982); Darren Weir (Puissance De Lune 2013).
Points of interest: No Lawrence Stakes winner has won the Melbourne Cup in the same year. Subzero (1992) is the most recent Melbourne Cup winner to contest the Larence in the same preparation. Maldivian (third behind Light Fantastic) in 2009, is the most recent Cox Plate winner to contest the Lawrence in the same year. Before that it was Better Loosen Up in 1990.

ATC Silver Shadow Stakes (1200m)—Randwick
$175,000 Group 2 3YO Fillies. SWP. August 18, 2018.

YEAR	WINNER	JOCKEY	TRAINER	2ND	3RD	TIME
2017	Formality	Kerrin McEvoy	David & Ben Hayes & Tom Dabernig	Alizee	Champagne Cuddles	1:08.8
2016	Omei Sword	Brenton Avdulla	Chris Waller	Bacarella	Quick Feet	1:09.6
2015	Speak Fondly	Kerrin McEvoy	Gai Waterhouse	Kimberley Star	Lake Geneva	1:09.4
2014	Bring Me The Maid	Luke Nolen	Peter Moody	Memorial	Clover Lane	1:12.3
2013	Thump	Jim Cassidy	John P Thompson	Sweet Idea	Montsegur	1:09.6
2012	Nechita	Christian Reith	John P Thompson	Meidung	Ichihara	1:09.4
2011	Pane In The Glass	Craig Williams	John P Thompson	Florentina	Streama	1:13.4
2010	Parables	Tim Clark	Peter Snowden	Solar Charged	Chance Bye	1:09.9
2009	Deer Valley	Daniel Ganderton	Chris Waller	Melito	Hurtle Myrtle	1:10.3
2008	Samantha Miss	Hugh Bowman	Kris Lees	Glowlamp	Love and Kisses	1:12.4
2007	Race not run					
2006	Gold Edition	Glen Lynch	Ron Maund	Montmelo	Heat Of The Fire	1:10.6
2005	Mnemosyne	Darren Beadman	John Hawkes	Fashions Afield	Paulini	1:09.6
2004	Our Sweet Moss	Jim Byrne	Gerald Ryan	Wager	Trezevant	1:10.7
2003	Regimental Gal	Michael Rodd	Shaun Dwyer	Legally Bay	Dorky	1:12.0
2002	Victory Vein	Danny Beasley	Bede Murray	Chantelaine	Calaway Gal	1:09.9
2001	Ha Ha	Jim Cassidy	Gai Waterhouse	Hosannah	Oomph	1:11.3

BACKGROUND
First run: 1980 (won by Moabite). Group 3 1980-92. Group 2 1993-2004. Group 3 from 2005.
Run at Randwick 1980, 1981, 1993, 2003 & 2005. Run at Rosehill 1997. Run at Canterbury 2000.
Fastest time (1200m): Formality (2017) 1:08.83
Notable winners: Nechita (2012); Samantha Miss (2008); Gold Edition (2006); Mnemosyne (2005); Regimental Gal (2003); Victory Vein (2002); Ha Ha (2001); Aragen (1994); Angst (1993); Skating (1992); Triscay (1990); Diamond Shower (1986); Shankhill Lass (1985); Satin Sand (1984); Black Shoes (1981).
Silver Shadow Stakes winners won the lead-up races:
San Domenico Stakes: 4—Gold Edition (2006); Regimental Gal (2003); Rosebrook (1982); Black Shoes (1981).
Silver Shadow Stakes winners went on to win in the same preparation:
Furious Stakes: 6—Formality (2017); Speak Fondly (2015); Samantha Miss (2008); Mnemosyne (2005); Victory Vein (2002); Angst (1993).
Tea Rose: 6—Samantha Miss (2008); Mnemosyne (2005); Victory Vein (2002); Ha Ha (2001); Angst (1993); Black Shoes (1981).
Flight Stakes: 5—Speak Fondly (2015); Samantha Miss (2008); Ha Ha (2001); Angst (1993); Triscay (1990).
Thousand Guineas: 2—Mnemosyne (2005); Shankhill Lass (1985).
Coolmore Stud Stakes: 1—Nechita (2012).
VRC Oaks: 2—Samantha Miss (2008); Diamond Shower (1986).

Leading winning jockeys: 3 wins Jim Cassidy (Thump 2013, Ha Ha 2001, Soda Springs 1987); Mick Dittman (Adeewin 1997, Triscay 1990, Shankhill Lass 1985).
Current winning jockeys: 2 wins Kerrin McEvoy (Formality 2017, Speak Fondly 2015).
1 win Brenton Avdulla (Omei Sword 2016); Glen Boss (Cashier 1996); Hugh Bowman (Samantha Miss 2008); Jim Byrne (Our Sweet Moss 2004); Larry Cassidy (Seika 1995); Tim Clark (Parables 2010); Grant Cooksley (Aragen 1994); Daniel Ganderton (Deer Valley 2009); Luke Nolen (Bring Me The Maid 2014); Christian Reith (Nechita 2012); Michael Rodd (Regimental Gal 2003); Craig Williams (Pane In The Glass 2011).
Leading winning trainer: 3 wins John Thompson (Thump 2013, Nechita 2012, Pane In The Glass 2011).
Current winning trainers: 3 wins John Thompson (Thump 2013, Nechita 2012, Pane In The Glass 2011).
2 wins John Hawkes (Mnemosyne 2005, Seika 1995); Chris Waller (Omei Sword 2016, Deer Valley 2009); Gai Waterhouse (Speak Fondly 2015, Ha Ha 2001).
1 win Shaun Dwyer (Regimental Gal 2003); David & Ben Hayes & Tom Dabernig (Formality 2017); Kris Lees (Samantha Miss 2008); Noel Mayfield-Smith (Angst 1993); Gary Portelli (Ateates 2000); Graeme Rogerson (Skating 1992); Gerald Ryan (Our Sweet Moss 2004); Peter Snowden (Parables 2010).
Points of interest: Brothers Brian Mayfield-Smith (Soda Springs 1987; Diamond Shower 1986) and Noel Mayfield-Smith (Angst 1993) have both trained winners of the Silver Slipper Stakes.
Samantha Miss (2008) and Angst (1993) are the only fillies to win the four Sydney spring 3YO filly features—Silver Shadow, Furious, Tea Rose and Flight Stakes.
Ha Ha (2001) is the only Golden Slipper winner to win the Silver Shadow Stakes.

Tattersalls Chelmsford Stakes (1600m)—Randwick
$250,000 Group 2 3YO&Up WFA. September 1, 2018.

YEAR	WINNER	JOCKEY	TRAINER	2ND	3RD	TIME
2017	Winx	Hugh Bowman	Chris Waller	Red Excitement	Chocante	1:34.1
2016	Hartnell	James McDonald	John O'Shea	Grand Marshal	Storm The Stars	1:39.1
2015	Complacent	Sam Clipperton	John O'Shea	Kermadec	Royal Descent	1:37.6
2014	Hawkspur	Jim Cassidy	Chris Waller	Royal Descent	Bagman	1:39.3
2013	Hawkspur	Jim Cassidy	Chris Waller	Beaten Up	Lightinthenite	1:34.7
2012	Danleigh	Hugh Bowman	Chris Waller	Secret Admirer	Lamasery	1:36.2
2011	Trusting	Joao Moreira	John P Thompson	My Kingdom Of Fife	Strike The Stars	1:37.1
2010	Theseo	Nash Rawiller	Gai Waterhouse	Metal Bender	Purple	1:39.6
2009	O'lonhro	Jay Ford	Michael, Wayne & John Hawkes	Miss Marielle	Triple Honour	1:34.5
2008	Galiant Tess	Jeff Lloyd	David Payne	Triple Honour	Kishkat	1:39.3
2007	Race not run					
2006	Eremein	Glen Boss	Allan Denham	Newton's Rings	Aqua d' Amore	1:35.5
2005	Nevis	Hugh Bowman	David Payne	Sir Dex	Natural Blitz	1:35.7
2004	Unearthly	Corey Brown	David Payne	So Assertive	Niello	1:37.9
2003	Lonhro	Darren Beadman	John Hawkes	Platinum Scissors	Excellerator	1:35.1
2002	Lonhro	Darren Beadman	John Hawkes	Platinum Scissors	Republic Lass	1:36.3
2001	Brave Prince	Jamie Innes	Sterling M Smith	Zabeels Angel	The Man	1:24.5

BACKGROUND
First run: 1895 (won by Newman). Group 2 since 1979. 1800m before 1985. Run over 9 furlongs 1945, 1950 & 1951; 1500m 2000; 1400m 2001. Run at Rosehill 2000; Randwick inner track 2001; Warwick Farm 2004. Not held in 2007 due to Equine Influenza outbreak.
Most recent mare to win: Winx (2017).
Most recent 3YO to win: C&G—Mighty Kingdom (1979); Filly—Pique (1959).
Multiple winners: 12—Hawkspur (2014, 2013); Lonhro (2003, 2002); Stargazer (1991, 1990); Kingston Town (1981, 1980); Roman Consul (1969, 1968 & 1967); Prince Darius (1958, 1957); Delta (1952, 1951 & 1950); Rogilla (1934, 1933); Limerick (1928, 1927 & 1926); Duke Foote (1913, 1912); Prince Foote (1910, 1909); The Chief (1899, 1898).
Fastest time (1600m): Winx (2017) 1:34.11.
Notable winners: Winx (2017); Lonhro (2003, 2002); Might And Power (1998); Campaign King (1987); Emancipation (1983); Kingston Town (1981, 1980); Ming Dynasty (1978); Gunsynd (1970); Roman Consul (1969, 1968, 1967); Tulloch (1960); Delta (1952, 1951, 1950); Bernborough (1946); Phar Lap (1930); Limerick (1928, 1927, 1926); Heroic (1924).
Chelmsford Stakes winners won the lead-up races:
Warwick Stakes: 11—Winx (2017); Lonhro (2003); Filante (1996); March Hare (1994); Kingston Town (1981,

1980); Purple Patch (1976); Longfella (1973); Bernborough (1946); Beaulivre (1940); Defaulter (1939); Limerick (1928, 1927).
Chelmsford Stakes winners went on to win in the same preparation:
George Main Stakes: 6—Winx (2017); Lonhro (2003); Campaign King (1987); Emancipation (1983); Kingston Town (1981); Purple Patch (1976).
Underwood Stakes: 1—Intergaze (1999).
Epsom Handicap: 1—Filante (1996).
Hill Stakes: 9—Hartnell (2016); Trusting (2011); Pasta Express (2000); Emancipation (1983); Prince Cortauld (1954); Bernborough (1946); Phar Lap (1930); Limerick (1928, 1927).
Cox Plate: 7—Might And Power (1998); Kingston Town (1981, 1980); Tulloch (1960); Beau Vite (1941); Rogilla (1933); Phar Lap (1930).
Leading winning jockeys: 6 wins Neville Sellwood (Tulloch 1960, Prince Cortauld 1954, Delta 1952, 1951, 1950, Bernbrook 1948).
5 wins Jim Cassidy (Hawkspur 2014, 2013, March Hare 1994, Soho Square 1993, High Regard 1989); Maurice McCarten (Mala 1937, Gold Rod 1936, Limerick 1928, 1927, 1926); Darby Munro (Sleepy Fox 1945, Beau Vite 1941, Beaulivre 1940, Rogilla 1934, 1933).
Current winning jockeys: 3 wins Hugh Bowman (Winx 2017, Danleigh 2012, Nevis 2005).
2 wins Glen Boss (Eremein 2006, Juggler 1997).
1 win Corey Brown (Unearthly 2004); Sam Clipperton (Complacent 2015); Jay Ford (O'Lonhro 2009); Jamie Innes (Brave Prince 2001); Jeff Lloyd (Gallant Tess 2008); James McDonald (Hartnell 2016); Joao Moreira (Trusting 2011); Nash Rawiller (Theseo 2010).
Leading winning trainers: 16 wins Tommy Smith (Stargazer 1991, 1990, Shankhill Lass 1986, Lord Of Camelot 1985, Kingston Town 1981, 1980, Mighty Kingdom 1979, Flirting Prince 1977, Passetreul 1974, Longfella 1973, Roman Consul 1969, 1968, 1967, Pyramus 1965, Burgos 1962, Tulloch 1960).
5 wins Maurice McCarten (Prince Cortauld 1954, Delta 1952, 1951, 1950, Columnist 1949).
4 wins Bart Cummings (Sky Chase 1988, Campaign King 1987, Ming Dynasty 1978, Leica Lover 1975); Chris Waller (Winx 2017, Hawkspur 2014, 2013, Danleigh 2012).
Current winning trainers: 4 wins Chris Waller (Winx 2017, Hawkspur 2014, 2013, Danleigh 2012).
3 wins John Hawkes (O'Lonhro 2010, Lonhro 2003, 2002); David Payne (Gallant Tess 2008, Neis 2005, Unearthly 2004).
2 wins John O'Shea (Hartnell 2016, Complacent 2015); Gai Waterhouse (Theseo 2010, Juggler 1997).
1 win Paul Cave (Pasta Express 2000); Rod Craig (Intergaze 1999); Allan Denham (Eremein 2006); Jim Lee (Hayai 1984); John Thompson (Trusting 2011).
Points of Interest: Phar Lap finished second behind Mollison in the Chelmsford Stakes as a 3YO in 1929. He won in 1930.
Allan Denham rode Purple Patch (1976) and trainer Eremein (2006). Purple Patch was trained by his father Jack Denham, who trained three winners of the Chelmsford Stakes.
Maurice McCarten rode five winners of the Chelmsford Stakes (see above), and trained five winners—Prince Cortauld (1954) and Delta (1952, 1951, 1950) and Columnist (1949).
It is believed that Tommy Smith's 16 Chelmsford Stakes wins is a world record for a trainer in a Group race.
Winx (2017) won her 19th consecutive race.

Tattersalls Furious Stakes (1200m)—Randwick
$175,000 Group 2 3YO Fillies SWP. September 1, 2018.

YEAR	WINNER	JOCKEY	TRAINER	2ND	3RD	TIME
2017	Formality	Kerrin McEvoy	David & Ben Hayes & Tom Dabernig	Champagne Cuddles	A Am Excited	1:09.9
2016	Foxplay	Hugh Bowman	Chris Waller	Bararella	Global Glamour	1:12.5
2015	Speak Fondly	Kerrin McEvoy	Gai Waterhouse	Perignon	Ottoman	1:10.6
2014	Winx	Hugh Bowman	Chris Waller	Alpha Miss	Earthquake	1:11.9
2013	Bound For Earth	Nicholas Hall	John O'Shea	Guelph	Thump	1:09.0
2012	Dear Demi	James McDonald	Clarry Conners	Meidung	Jade Marauder	1:22.9
2011	Streama	Hugh Bowman	Guy Walter	Florentina	Detours	1:25.0
2010	More Strawberries	Nash Rawiller	Gai Waterhouse	Divorces	Parables	1:27.0
2009	Melito	Corey Brown	Gerald Ryan	Hurtle Myrtle	Lovemelikearock	1:21.5
2008	Samantha Miss	Hugh Bowman	Kris Lees	Love and Kisses	Portillo	1:26.2
2007	Race Not Run					
2006	Just Dancing	Jim Cassidy	Grahame Begg	My Lady's Chamber	Gallant Tess	1:26.6
2005	Mnemosyne	Darren Beadman	John Hawkes	Media	Permissive	1:22.6
2004	Prisoner of Love	Glen Boss	Guy Walter	Wager	Our Sweet Moss	1:23.1
2003	Shamekha	Jim Cassidy	Gai Waterhouse	Regimental Gal	Spurcent	1:22.4
2002	Victory Vein	Danny Beasley	Bede Murray	Royal Purler	Lavishly	1:24.2
2001	Moonflute	Darren Beadman	Graeme Rogerson	Hosannah	Ha Ha	1:25.1

BACKGROUND
First run: 1982 (won by Explicit). Listed 1986-94. Group 3 1995-2004. Group 2 from 2005. Run over 1400m from 1975-1999, 2001-2012; 1350m 2000; 1200m from 2013. Run at Rosehill 2000; Randwick inner track 2001; Warwick Farm 2004. Also known as the AJC Sharp Stakes. Not held in 2007 due to EI outbreak.
Fastest time (1200m): Bound To Earth (2013) 1:09.07.
Notable winners: Winx (2014); Dear Demi (2012); Streama (2011); Melito (2009); Samantha Miss (2008); Mnemosyne (2005); Shamekha (2003); Victory Vein (2002); Unworldly (2000); Sunline (1998); Dashing Eagle (1996); Angst (1993); Bold Promise (1991); Twiglet (1990); Tristanagh (1989).
Furious Stakes winners won the lead-up races:
Silver Shadow Stakes: 6—Formality (2017); Speak Fondly (2015); Samantha Miss (2008); Mnemosyne (2005); Victory Vein (2002); Angst (1993).
Furious Stakes winners went on to win in the same preparation:
Tea Rose Stakes: 17—Foxplay (2016); Streama (2011); More Strawberries (2010); Samantha Miss (2008); Mnemosyne (2005); Prisoner Of Love (2004); Shamekha (2003); Victory Vein (2002); Unworldly (2000); Danglissa (1999); Sunline (1998); Stella Cadente (1997); Danarani (1994); Angst (1993); Bold Promise (1991); Tristanagh (1989); Glory Girl (1987).
Flight Stakes: 10—Streama (2011); Samantha Miss (2008); Unworldly (2000); Danglissa (1999); Sunline (1998); Dashing Eagle (1996 dead-heat); Danarani (1994); Angst (1993); Research (1988); Tingo Tango (1985).
The Princess Series clean sweep:
Silver Shadow, Furious, Tea Rose & Flight Stakes: 2—Samantha Miss (2008); Angst (1993).
Furious Stakes winners and the Melbourne spring:
Thousand Guineas: 3—Mnemosyne (2005); Dashing Eagle (1996); Tristanagh (1989).
VRC Oaks: 2—Dear Demi (2012); Samantha Miss (2008).
Leading winning jockeys: 4 wins Hugh Bowman (Foxplay 2016, Winx 2014, Streama 2011, Samantha Miss 2008); Jim Cassidy (Just Dancing 2006, Shamekha 2003, Bold Promise 1991, Glory Girl 1987)
Current winning jockeys: 4 wins Hugh Bowman (Foxplay 2016, Winx 2014, Streama 2011, Samantha Miss 2008). 3 wins Larry Cassidy (Unworldly 2000, Sunline 1998, Stella Cadente 1997).
2 wins Kerrin McEvoy (Formality 2017, Speak Fondly 2015).
1 win Glen Boss (Prisoner Of Love 2004); Corey Brown (Melito 2009); Grant Buckley (Dear Demi 2012); Nicholas Hall (Bound For Earth 2013); John Powell (Dashing Eagle 1996); Nash Rawiller (More Strawberries 2010); Robert Thompson (Twiglet 1990).
Leading winning trainers: 4 wins Bart Cummings (Dashing Eagle 1996, Danarani 1994, Tristanagh 1989, Explicit 1982); Gai Waterhouse (Speak Fondly 2015, More Strawberries 2010, Shamekha 2003, Danglissa 1999).
Current winning trainers: 4 wins Gai Waterhouse (Speak Fondly 2015, More Strawberries 2010, Shamekha 2003, Danglissa 1999).
2 wins Grahame Begg (Just Dancing 2006, Twiglet 1990); Clarry Conners (Dear Demi 2012, Research 1988); John Hawkes (Mnemosyne 2005, Unworldly 2000); Chris Waller (Foxplay 2016, Winx 2014).
1 win David & Ben Hayes & Tom Dabernig (Formality 2017); Jim Lee (Seattle Gem 1995); Kris Lees (Samantha Miss 2008); Noel Mayfield-Smith (Angst 1993); John O'Shea (Bound For Earth 2013); Graeme Rogerson (Moonflute 2001); Gerald Ryan (Melita 2009).
Point of interest: No Golden Slipper winner has won the Furious Stakes.

Tattersalls Tramway Stakes (1400m)—Randwick
$175,000 Group 2 3YO&Up SWP. September 1, 2018.

YEAR	WINNER	JOCKEY	TRAINER	2ND	3RD	TIME
2017	Happy Clapper	Josh Adams	Pat Webster	Tom Melbourne	Invincible Gem	1:21.9
2016	Hauraki	James McDonald	John O'Shea	Le Romain	Dibayani	1:25.9
2015	Hooked	Tye Angland	John P Thompson	Ecuador	Rudy	1:24.4
2014	Lucia Valentina	Kerrin McEvoy	Kris Lees	Tiger Tees	Toydini	1:26.6
2013	Malavio	Nathan Berry	Steve Englebrecht	Bello	Royal Descent	1:21.3
2012	Tagus	Jim Cassidy	John P Thompson	Kontiki Park	Moment Of Time	1:22.5
2011	Sincero	Chris O'Brien	Stephen Farley	Secret Admirer	Thankgodyou'rehere	1.22.2
2010	Neeson	Peter Robl	Joseph Pride	Cannonball	Herculian Prince	1:26.1
2009	Rangirangdoo	Corey Brown	Chris Waller	Strat's Flyer	Murray's Sun	1:21.9
2008	Bank Robber	Blake Shinn	Gai Waterhouse	Kick 'N Chase	Vecchia Roma	1:25.7
2007	Race Not Run					
2006	Primus	Hugh Bowman	John O'Shea	Stormhill	Flaming	1:25.6
2005	Shania Dane	Rod Quinn	John Hawkes	Lotteria	Utzon	1:22.7
2004	Nips	Jamie Innes	Clarry Conners	West Country	Desert War	1:22.9
2003	Sportsman	Zac Purton	Gregory Hickman	Britt's Best	Boreale	1:21.8
2002	Gordo	Corey Brown	John Hawkes	Shot Of Thunder	Universal Prince	1:24.0
2001	Diamond Dane	Corey Brown	Bruce McLachlan	Maitland Gold	Kootoomootoo	1:18.3

BACKGROUND

First run: 1886 (won by Burrilda). Listed race 1979-83. Group 3 from 1984. Run over 1300m 2001. Run at Warwick Farm 1983 & 2004.
Most recent mare to win: Lucia Valentina (2014).
Most recent 3YO to win: C&G—Farnworth (1964); Filly—Marvel Loch (1903).
Multiple winners: 3—Grenoble (1960, 1959); Lough Neagh (1938, 1936); Gigandra (1913, 1912).
Fastest time (1400m): Mr Innocent (2000) 1:20.60
Notable winners: Lucia Valentina (2014); Rangirangdoo (2009); Mr Innocent (2000); Peruzzi (1996); Shaftesbury Avenue (1990); Cole Diesel (1989); Imposing (1979); Black Onyx (1969); Wenona Girl (1961); Grenoble (1959-60); Lough Neagh (1935 & 1937); Amounis (1928).
Tramway Handicap winners won the lead-up races.
Show County Quality: 3—Bank Robber (2008); Primus (2006); Sportsman (2003).
Tramway Handicap winners went on to win in the same preparation:
Bill Ritchie Handicap: None.
Cameron Handicap: None. Note: Tandrio (1984) won the Cameron Hcp in 1983.
Turnbull Stakes: 1—Lucia Valentina (2014).
Epsom Handicap: 12—Happy Clapper (2017); Chanteclair (1986); Imposing (1979); High Law (1952); De La Salle (1948); Shannon (1945); Chatham (1932); Amounis (1928); Rostrum (1922); Beauford (1921); Wolaroi (1919); Melodrama (1908). Note: Amounis (1928) also won the 1926 Epsom Handicap and Melodrama (1908) also won the 1907 Epsom Handicap.
George Main Stakes: 5—Sincero (2011); Shaftesbury Avenue (1990); Tullmax (1980); Imposing (1979); Landy (1957).
Toorak Handicap: 1—Cole Diesel (1989).
Leading winning jockey: 6 wins Darby Munro (Shannon 1945, Dewar 1943, Mohican 1938, The Marne 1936, Sir Duninald 1932, Rogilla 1932).
Current winning jockeys: 3 wins Corey Brown (Rangirangdoo 2009, Gordo 2002, Diamond Dane 2001).
1 win Josh Adams (Happy Clapper 2017); Tye Angland (Hooked 2015); Glen Boss (Big Dreams 1994); Hugh Bowman (Primus 2006); Glen Colless (Mr Innocent 2000); Jamie Innes (Nips 2004); James McDonald (Hauraki 2016); Kerrin McEvoy (Lucia Valentina 2014); Chris O'Brien (Sincero 2011); Zac Purton (Sportsman 2003); Blake Shinn (Bank Robber 2008).
Leading winning trainers: 4 wins Tommy Smith (Chanteclair 1986, Imposing 1979, Black Onyx 1969, Landy 1957); Tom Payten (Melodrama 1908, Pompous 1906, Mimer 1904, Blue Cap 1895).
3 wins Maurice McCarten (Farnworth 1964, Wenona Girl 1962, French Cavalier 1951).
Current winning trainers: 2 wins John Hawkes (Shania Dane 2005, Gordo 2002); John O'Shea (Hauraki 2016; Primus 2006); John Size (Kinzaffra 1999, Peruzzi 1996); John Thompson (Hooked 2015, Tagus 2012).
1 win Clarry Conners (Nips 2004); Allan Denham (Ghost Story 1993); Steve Englebrecht (Malavio 2013); Steve Farley (Sincero 2011); Lee Freedman (Cobbora 1992); Greg Hickman (Sportsman 2003); Kris Lees (Lucia Valentina 2014); Joe Pride (Neeson 2010); Ron Quinton (Big Dreams 1994); Chris Waller (Rangirangdoo 2009); Gai Waterhouse (Bank Robber 2008); Pat Webster (Happy Clapper 2017).
Points of interest: The Tramway Handicap is run under the banner of the Sydney Tattersalls Club.
In 2000, Mr. Innocent survived a protest from Eau D'Scay. In 1932, Chatham dead-heated with Rogilla. The Tramway Handicap was held twice in 1932 and 1931.
Rogilla (1932) dead heated with Chatham.

ATC The Run To The Rose (1200m)—Rosehill
$175,000 Group 2 3YO SWP. September 8, 2018.

YEAR	WINNER	JOCKEY	TRAINER	2ND	3RD	TIME
2017	Menari	Josh Parr	Gerald Ryan	Pariah	Perast	1:08.5
2016	Astern	James McDonald	John O'Shea	Star Turn	Impending	1:10.9
2015	Exosphere	Sam Clipperton	John O'Shea	Press Statement	Holler	1:10.6
2014	Hallowed Crown	Josh Parr	Bart & James Cummings	Kumaon	Ygritte	1:12.9
2013	Va Pensiero	Nathan Berry	Jason Coyle	Dissident	Marseille Roulette	1:09.6
2012	Pierro	Nash Rawiller	Gai Waterhouse	Your Song	Epaulette	1:09.8
2011	Smart Missile	Glen Boss	Anthony Cumming	Foxwedge	Helmet	1:10.5
2010	Squamosa	Blake Spriggs	Gai Waterhouse	Masquerader	Testarhythm	1:18.2
2009	Denman	Kerrin McEvoy	Peter Snowden	More Than Great	Bombay Sling	1:16.6
2008	Desuetude	Kerrin McEvoy	Peter Snowden	Maybe I	Emperor Bonaparte	1:18.1
2007	El Cambio	Darren Beadman	John Hawkes	Rapid Jacko	Turffontein	1:16.2
2006	Mentality	Darren Beadman	John Hawkes	He'S No Pie Eater	Boncoeur	1:17.6
2005	Paratroopers	Darren Beadman	John Hawkes	Pendragon (Nz)	Thunderbird Hill	1:16.3
2004	Eremein	Glen Boss	Allan Denham	Uber	Econsul (Nz)	1:18.3
2003	Gilded Youth	Robbie Brewer	Frank Cleary	Charmview	Confectioner	1:16.7

BACKGROUND
First run: 2006 (won by Mentality). Listed in 2006. Group 3 2007-2014. Group 2 from 2015. Run as a handicap. 2006-2010 1300m; since 2011 1200m.
No filly has won The Run To Rose.
Fastest time (1200m): Menari (2017) 1:08.59
Notable winners: Menari (2017); Astern (2016); Exosphere (2015); Hallowed Crown (2014); Pierro (2012); Smart Missile (2011); Denman (2009); Mentality (2006).
The Run To The Rose winner won the lead-up races:
San Domenico Stakes: 1—Va Pensiero (2013).
The Rosebud: 1—Menari (2017).
The Run To The Rose winners went on to win in the same preparation:
Golden Rose: 4—Astern (2016); Exosphere (2015); Hallowed Crown (2014); Denman (2009).
Roman Consul Stakes: 1—Exosphere (2015).
Stan Fox Stakes: 1—Denman (2009).
Bill Stutt Stakes: 1—Pierro (2012).
Caulfield Guineas: None.
Coolmore Stud Stakes: None.
Leading winning jockeys: 2 wins Darren Beadman (El Cambio 2007, Mentality 2006); Kerrin McEvoy (Denman 2009, Desuetude 2008); Josh Parr (Menari 2017, Hallowed Crown 2014).
Current winning jockeys: 2 wins Josh Parr (Menari 2017, Hallowed Crown 2014).
1 win Glen Boss (Smart Missile 2011); Sam Clipperton (Exosphere 2015); James McDonald (Astern 2016); Nash Rawiller (Pierro 2012); Blake Spriggs (Squamosa 2010).
Leading winning trainers: 2 wins John Hawkes (El Cambio 2007, Mentality 2006); John O'Shea (Astern 2016, Exosphere 2015); Peter Snowden (Denman 2009, Desuetude 2008); Gai Waterhouse (Pierro 2012, Squamosa 2010).
Current winning trainers: 2 wins John Hawkes (El Cambio 2007, Mentality 2006); John O'Shea (Astern 2016, Exosphere 2015); Peter Snowden (Denman 2009, Desuetude 2008); Gai Waterhouse (Pierro 2012, Squamosa 2010).
1 win Jason Coyle (Va Pensiero 2013); Anthony Cummings (Smart Missile 2011); James Cummings (Hallowed Crown 2014, in partnership with Bart Cummings); Gerald Ryan (Menari 2017).
Points of interest: Mentality (Randwick Guineas) and He's No Pie Eater (Chipping Norton Stakes and Rosehill Guineas), first and second in 2006, were both Group 1 winners in the 2007 autumn.
Hallowed Crown (2014) won the 2015 G1 Randwick Guineas.
Pierro (2012) won the 2012 G1 Golden Slipper.

ATC Theo Marks Quality (1300m)—Rosehill
$200,000 Group 2 3YO&Up Quality Handicap. September 8, 2018.

YEAR	WINNER	JOCKEY	TRAINER	2ND	3RD	TIME
2017	Deploy	Josh Parr	Gerald Ryan	Egg Tart	Euro Angel	1:14.9
2016	Mackintosh	Joao Moreira	Chris Waller	Counterattack	Southern Legend	1:17.1
2015	Winx	James McDonald	Chris Waller	Sons Of John	Ninth Legion	1:15.7
2014	Cluster	Tim Clark	Peter & Paul Snowden	Bull Point	Ninth Legion	1:23.2
2013	Riva De Lago	Jim Cassidy	Chris Waller	Solzhenitsyn	Your Honour	1:21.6
2012	Ambidexter	Kerrin McEvoy	Peter Snowden	Fat Al	Dystopia	1:22.2
2011	Master Of Design	Christian Reith	David Payne	Torio's Quest	Fast Clip	1:16.7
2010	More Joyous	Corey Brown	Gai Waterhouse	Rothesay	Drumbeats	1:22.1
2009	Racing To Win	Hugh Bowman	John O'Shea	Rock Kingdom	Triple Honour	1:22.1
2008	Hurried Choice	Jeff Lloyd	David Payne	Forensics	Ice Chariot	1:17.1
2007	Race Not Run					
2006	Racing To Win	Glen Boss	John O'Shea	New Edge	Regal Cheer	1:16.5
2005	Paratroopers	Darren Beadman	John Hawkes	Perfect Promise	Outback Prince	1:16.8
2004	Falkirk	Darren Beadman	John O'Shea	Grand Armee	Private Steer	1:17.7
2003	Fiery Venture	Len Beasley	Gai Waterhouse	Grand Armee	Osca Warrior	1:16.3
2002	Defier	Chris Munce	Guy Walter	Phoenix Park	Carael Boy	1:15.7
2001	Shogun Lodge	Glen Boss	Bob Thomsen	Fouardee	Belle Du Jour	1:16.8

BACKGROUND

First run: 1946 (won by Shannon). Group 2 from 1979. Run over 1400m 1946-84, 2009-10, from 2012; 1300m 1985-89; 1992-2008, 2011; 1280m 1990-91. Run at Randwick 1960; Canterbury 1991, 2009-10. Not held in 2007 due to EI outbreak. Also known as the Theo Marks Quality and the Sebring Sprint.

Most recent mare to win: Winx (2015).

Most recent 3YO to win: C&G—Paratroopers (2005); Filly—None. Only two other 3YOs have won: the geldings Inspired (1984) and Time And Tide (1963).

Multiple winners: 2—Racing To Win (2009, 2006); Time And Tide (1966, 1965 & 1963).

Fastest time (1300m, Rosehill): Deploy (2017) 1:14.92

Notable winners: Winx (2015); More Joyous (2010); Racing To Win (2009, 2006); Defier (2002); Shogun Lodge (2001); Ivory's Irish (1995); Joanne (1991); Groucho (1987); Time And Tide (1966, 1965 & 1963); Shannon (1946).

Theo Marks Stakes winners won the lead-up races:
Premiere Stakes: 2—Joanne (1991); Silver Wraith (1980).
Concorde Stakes: 2—Final Card (1992); Joanne (1991).
Show County Quality: 1—Deploy (2017).

Theo Marks Stakes winners went on to win in the same preparation:
George Main Stakes: 9—More Joyous (2010); Racing To Win (2006); Defier (2002); Inspired (1984); Party's Pride (1978); Blockbuster (1977); Ricochet (1970); Martello Towers (1961); Shannon (1946).
Epsom Handicap: 6—Winx (2015); Racing To Win (2006); From The Planet (1989); Ricochet (1970); Cabochon (1967); Hans (1955).
Bill Ritchie Handicap: 2—Mamzelle Pedrille (1996); Rouslan (1994).
Cox Plate: 1—Winx (2015).

Leading winning jockeys: 6 wins Peter Cook (Ksar Royal 1982, Arbogast 1981, Silver Wraith 1980, Scomeld 1979, Ease To Squeeze 1976, Beaches 1972).
5 wins Darren Beadman (Paratroopers 2005, Falkirk 2004, Catalan Opening 1997, Alquoz 1990, Inspired 1984); George Moore (Game Prince 1964, Time And Tide 1963, Martello Towers 1961, French Charm 1956, Shannon 1946).
3 wins Glen Boss (Racing To Win 2006, Shogun Lodge 2001, Double Your Bet 1993); Mick Dittman (Mamzelle Pedrille 1996, Joanne 1991, From The Planet 1989).

Current winning jockeys: 3 wins Glen Boss (Racing To Win 2006, Shogun Lodge 2001, Double Your Bet 1993); 2 wins Hugh Bowman (Winx 2015, Racing To Win 2009); Larry Cassidy (Hire 2000, Ivory's Irish 1995). 1 win Corey Brown (More Joyous 2010); Tim Clark (Cluster 2014); Grant Cooksley (Rouslan 1994); Jeff Lloyd (Hurried Choice 2008); Kerrin McEvoy (Ambidexter 2012); Joao Moreira (Mackintosh 2016); Josh Parr (Deploy 2017); Christian Reith (Master Of Design 2011).

Leading winning trainers: 5 wins Tommy Smith (Zip Home 1986, Silver Wraith 1980, Scomeld 1979, Martello Towers 1961, The Groom 1948).
3 wins Harry Plant (Time And Tide 1966, 1965, 1963); Chris Waller (Mackintosh 2016, Winx 2015, Riva De Lago 2013).

Current winning trainers:
3 wins Chris Waller (Mackintosh 2016, Winx 2015, Riva De Lago 2013).
2 wins John Hawkes (Paratroopers 2005, Hire 2000); John O'Shea (Racing To Win 2009, 2006); Peter Snowden (Cluster 2014, Ambidexter 2012); Gai Waterhouse (More Joyous 2010, Fiery Venture 2003).
1 win Ray Brock (Adam 1999); Anthony Cummings (Final Card 1992); David Hayes (Alquoz 1990); Ron Quinton (Mamzelle Pedrille 1996); David Payne (Master Of Design 2011); Gerald Ryan (Deploy 2017); Peter & Paul Snowden (Cluster 2014); Bruce Wallace (Another Phenomenon 1983).

ATC Stan Fox Stakes (1500m)—Rosehill
$200,000 Group 2 3YO SW. September 8, 2018.

YEAR	WINNER	JOCKEY	TRAINER	2ND	3RD	TIME
2017	Gold Standard	Josh Parr	Gai Waterhouse & Adrian Bott	Sanctioned	Addictive Nature	1:28.4
2016	Impending	James McDonald	John O'Shea	Divine Prophet	Good Standing	1:29.2
2015	Press Statement	Hugh Bowman	Chris Waller	Shards	Rageese	1:31.9
2014	Shooting To Win	Tim Clark	Peter & Paul Snowden	Scissor Kick	Valentia	1:29.1
2013	Eurozone	Hugh Bowman	Bart & James Cummings	Criterion	Aussies Love Sport	1:30.1
2012	Kabayan	Nash Rawiller	Gai Waterhouse	Albrecht	Divine Moon	1:31.6
2011	Manawanui	Glyn Schofield	Ron Leemon	Roma Giaconda	Cocky Raider	1:21.4
2010	Decision Time	Craig Williams	Clarry Conners	Top Drop	Halekulani	1:23.1
2009	Denman	Kerrin McEvoy	Peter Snowden	Run For Naara	More Than Great	1:23.8
2008	Dreamscape	Nash Rawiller	Gai Waterhouse	Whitefriars	Judge Me Not	1:22.4
2007	Race Not Run					
2006	Court Command	Darryl Mclellan	Darren Smith	Antidotes	Cinque	1:22.1
2005	Paratroopers	Darren Beadman	John Hawkes	Primus	Testafiable	1:22.3
2004	Wager	Glen Boss	Gai Waterhouse	Spirit of Tara	Swick	1:22.5
2003	Ambulance	Rod Quinn	John Hawkes	Classy Dane	Hasna	1:22.9
2002	Rare Insight	Darren Beadman	John Hawkes	Magic Marvo	Choisir	1:24.0
2001	Lonhro	Rod Quinn	John Hawkes	Magic Albert	Stylish Lass	1:24.0

BACKGROUND
First run: 1975 (won by Hydahban). Listed 1985-88. Group 3 1989-95. Group 2 from 1996. Run over 1200m 1975-1980; 1400m 1981-2010; 1500m from 2011. Run on Randwick inner track 2001; Warwick Farm 2004.
Most recent filly to win: Wager (2004).
Fastest time (1500m): Gold Standard (2017) 1:28.46.
Notable winners: Impending (2016); Press Statement (2015); Shooting To Win (2014); Denman (2009); Paratroopers (2005); Lonhro (2001); Pins (1999); Kenwood Melody (1998); General Nediym (1997); Octagonal (1995); Show County (1989); From The Planet (1988).
Stan Fox Stakes winners won the lead-up races:
Theo Marks Stakes: 1—Paratroopers (2005).
Up And Coming Stakes: 4—Manawanui (2011); Dreamscape (2008); Court Command (2006); General Nediym (1997).
The Rosebud: 1—Eurozone (2013).
Run To The Rose: 1—Denman (2009).
Golden Rose: 2—Manawanui (2011); Denman (2009).
Stan Fox Stakes winners went on to win in the same preparation:
Caulfield Guineas: 4—Press Statement (2015); Shooting To Win (2014); Lonhro (2001); Kenwood Melody (1998).
Thousand Guineas: None.
Spring Champion Stakes: None.
Moonee Valley Vase: 1—Manawanui (2011).
Leading winning jockeys: 4 wins Rod Quinn (Ambulance 2003, Lonhro 2001, From The Planet 1988, Big Treat 1977).
3 wins Shane Dye (Pins 1999, West Point 1996, Campaign Warrior 1993).
Current winning jockeys: 2 wins Hugh Bowman (Press Statement 2015, Eurozone 2013); Nash Rawiller (Kabayan 2012, Dreamscape 2008).
1 win Glen Boss (Wager 2004); Corey Brown (Kenwood Melody 1998); Tim Clark (Shooting To Win 2014); Glen Colless (Dynamic Love 2000); Grant Cooksley (Octagonal 1995); James McDonald (Impending 2016); Kerrin McEvoy (Denman 2009); Josh Parr (Gold Standard 2017); Glyn Schofield (Manawanui 2011); Robert Thompson (Burraboolee 1984); Craig Williams (Decision Time 2010).
Leading winning trainers: 5 wins Gai Waterhouse (Gold Standard 2017); Kabayan 2012, Dreamscape 2008, Wager 2004, West Point 1996).
4 wins John Hawkes (Paratroopers 2005, Ambulance 2003, Rare Insight 2002, Lonhro 2001).
3 wins Brian Mayfield-Smith (Top Avenger 1986, Wild Rice 1982, Pink Posy 1979).
Current winning trainers: 5 wins Gai Waterhouse (Gold Standard 2017); Kabayan 2012, Dreamscape 2008, Wager 2004, West Point 1996).
4 wins John Hawkes (Paratroopers 2005, Ambulance 2003, Rare Insight 2002, Lonhro 2001).
2 wins Clarry Conners (Decision Time 2010, Pins 1999); Peter Snowden (Shooting To Win 2014, Denman 2009).
1 win Liam Birchley (Court Command 2006); Ken Callaughan (Campaign Warrior 1993); James Cummings (Eurozone 2013, in partnership with Bart Cummings); Allan Denham (Ghost Story 1992); Ron Leemon (Manawanui 2011); John O'Shea (Impending 2016); Paul Perry (Crossroads 1985); Peter & Paul Snowden (Shooting To Win 2014); John Wallace (Dynamic Love 2000); Chris Waller (Press Statement 2015); Gai Waterhouse & Adrian Bott (Gold Standard 2017).
Point of interest: No Golden Slipper winner has won a Stan Fox Stakes.

MVRC McEwen Stakes (1000m)—Moonee Valley

$200,000 Group 2 Open WFA. September 9, 2018.

YEAR	WINNER	JOCKEY	TRAINER	2ND	3RD	TIME
2017	Russian Revolution	Mark Zahra	Peter & Paul Snowden	Heatherly	Houtzen	0:58.1
2016	Wild Rain	Stephen Baster	Mark Kavanagh	Furnaces	Heatherly	0:58.8
2015	Chautauqua	Dwayne Dunn	Michael, Wayne & John Hawkes	Flamberge	Furnaces	0:58.2
2014	Angelic Light	Ryan Maloney	Robbie Griffiths	Lankan Rupee	Eloping	0:57.5
2013	Kuroshio	Craig Newitt	Peter Snowden	Moment Of Change	General Truce	0:57.8
2012	Bel Sprinter	Ben Melham	Jason Warren	Platelet	Snitzem	0:57.3
2011	Buffering	Damian Browne	Robert Heathcote	Crystal Lily	Atomic Force	0:58.5
2010	Hay List	Glyn Schofield	John Mcnair	Catapulted	Reward For Effort	0:59.6
2009	Nicconi	Craig Williams	David Hayes	Morgan Dollar	Secret Flyer	0:57.4
2008	Kaphero	Vlad Duric	Leon Corstens	Morgan Dollar	Lucky Secret	0:59.4
2007	Here De Angels	Corey Brown	Lee Freedman	Gold Edition	Dr Nipandtuck	0:57.4
2006	Miss Andretti	Craig Newitt	Lee Freedman	Sassbee	Cargo Cult	0:58.8
2005	Strikeline	Peter Mertens	Brian Mayfield-Smith	Truly Wicked	Titanic Jack	0:59.9
2004	Edgeton	Stephen Baster	Brendon Hearps	Reactive	Mistegic	1:01.8
2003	Yell	Darren Gauci	John Hawkes	The Big Chill	Dantana	0:59.6
2002	Mistegic	Damien Oliver	Lee Curtis	Shaye Spice	Aragonce	1:00.2
2001	Strategic Image	Scott Seamer	Peter Moody	Sports	Ateates	0:58.4

BACKGROUND

First run: 1995 (won by Sequalo). Listed race until 2005. Run at Caulfield in 1995 and 2007. Run over 1200m in 2000. Registered as the Ian McEwen Trophy.

Most recent mare to win: Wild Rain (2016).

Fastest time (1000m): Bel Sprinter (2012) 57.32

Most recent 3YO to win: C&G—Kuroshio (2013). No filly has won. Note: Strategic Image (2001) is the only other 3YO to win.

Notable winners: Russian Revolution (2017); Chautauqua (2015); Bel Sprinter (2012); Buffering (2011); Hay List (2010); Nicconi (2009); Miss Andretti (2006); Yell (2003); Mistegic (2002); Testa Rossa (2000); Flavour (1998); Sequalo (1995). McEwen Stakes winners and the lead-up races:

SAJC Spring Stakes: None. Note: Strategic Image (2001) won the Spring Stakes as a 4YO in 2002.

Sir John Monash Stakes: 1—Wild Rain (2016).

Bletchingly Stakes: None.

McEwen Stakes winners went on to win in the same preparation:

Gilgai Stakes: 2—Chautauqua (2015); Hay List (2010).

Manikato Stakes: 3—Chautauqua (2015); Hay List (2010); Miss Andretti (2006).

Moir Stakes: None: Note: Buffering (2011) won the Moir in 2012, 2014 and 2015.

Leading winning jockeys: 2 wins Stephen Baster (Wild Rain 2016, Edgeton 2004); Craig Newitt (Kuroshio 2013, Miss Andretti 2006).

Current winning jockeys: 2 wins Stephen Baster (Wild Rain 2016, Edgeton 2004); Craig Newitt (Kuroshio 2013, Miss Andretti 2006).

1 win Corey Brown (Here De Angels 2007); Dwayne Dunn (Chautauqua 2015); Vlad Duric (Kaphero 2008); Ryan Maloney (Angelic Light 2014); Ben Melham (Bel Sprinter 2012); Damien Oliver (Mistegic 2002); Brett Prebble (Testa Rossa 2000); Nash Rawiller (Theatre 1999); Glyn Schofield (Hay List 2010); Craig Williams (Nicconi 2009); Mark Zahra (Russian Revolution 2017).

Leading winning trainers: 3 wins John Hawkes (Chautauqua 2015, Yell 2003, Flavour 1998).

2 wins Lee Freedman (Here De Angels 2007, Miss Andretti 2006); Mark Kavanagh (Wild Rain 2016, Red Hope 1996).

Current winning trainers: 3 wins John Hawkes (Chautauqua 2015, Yell 2003, Flavour 1998).

2 wins Lee Freedman (Here De Angels 2007, Miss Andretti 2006); Mark Kavanagh (Wild Rain 2016, Red Hope 1996); Peter Snowden (Russian Revolution 2017, Kuroshio 2013).

1 win Leon Corstens (Kaphero 2008); Robbie Griffiths (Angelic Light 2014); Michael, Wayne, John Hawkes (Chautauqua 2015); David Hayes (Nicconi 2009); Brendon Hearps (Edgeton 2004); Rob Heathcote (Buffering 2011); John McNair (Hay List 2010); Peter & Paul Snowden (Russian Revolution 2017); Jason Warren (Bel Sprinter 2012).

Point of interest: Brian Mayfield-Smith quinellaed the race in 2005 when Strikeline beat Truly Wicked.

MVRC Dato' Tan Chin Nam Stakes (1600m)—Moonee Valley
$250,000 Group 2 Open WFA. September 9, 2018.

YEAR	WINNER	JOCKEY	TRAINER	2ND	3RD	TIME
2017	Bonneval	Damian Lane	Murray Baker & Andrew Forsman	Abbey Marie	Rhythm To Spare	1:37.3
2016	Awesome Rock	Stephen Baster	Leon & Troy Corstens	Real Love	Set Square	1:37.0
2015	The Cleaner	Noel Callow	Mick Burles	Bagman	Dibayani	1:36.3
2014	The Cleaner	Steven Arnold	Mick Burles	Mourinho	Foreteller	1:35.9
2013	Fiorente	Nash Rawiller	Gai Waterhouse	Spacecraft	Lidari	1:37.2
2012	Happy Trails	Glen Boss	Paul Beshara	Green Moon	Rekindled Interest	1:35.5
2011	Rekindled Interest	Dwayne Dunn	Jim Conlan	Alcopop	Whobegotyou	1:37.6
2010	Whobegotyou	Michael Rodd	Mark Kavanagh	Typhoon Tracy	Shoot Out	1:39.6
2009	Whobegotyou	Damien Oliver	Mark Kavanagh	Mic Mac	Jolie's Shinju	1:37.3
2008	Guillotine	Craig Williams	David Hayes	Casual Pass	Tears I Cry	1:35.9
2007	El Segundo	Luke Nolen	Colin Little	Haradasun	Cinque Cento	1:36.2
2006	Lad Of The Manor	Greg Childs	Roger Hoysted	Apache Cat	Spinney	1:35.8
2005	Lad Of The Manor	Greg Childs	Roger Hoysted	Makybe Diva	Fields of Omagh	1:37.6
2004	Delzao	Steven King	Greg Kavanagh	Makybe Diva	Studebaker	1:42.5
2003	Natural Blitz	Kerrin McEvoy	Doug Harrison	Vocabulary	De Gaulle Lane	1:36.7
2002	Fields Of Omagh	Damien Oliver	Tony Mc Evoy	Magical Miss	Le Zagaletta	1:40.4
2001	Northerly	Damien Oliver	Fred Kersley	Sunline	Sir Clive	1:37.1
2000	Sunline	Greg Childs	Trevor Mckee	Le Zagaletta	Citra's Prince	1:37.9

BACKGROUND

First run: 1948 (won by Phoibos). Group 2 since 1979. WFA 1949-55 & since 1975. Run at Sandown in 1976, Caulfield in 1995. Not held in 1960 and 1966 due to rain. From 2005 named after Malaysian-based owner Dato Tan Chin Nam. Also known as the Glenroy Stakes, Centennial Stakes. Registered name is the John F Feehan Stakes.
Most recent mare to win: Bonneval (2017). Nine mares have won.
Most recent 3YO to win: Phoibus (1948).
Multiple winners: 5—The Cleaner (2015, 2014); Whobegotyou (2010, 2009); Lad of the Manor (2006, 2005); Lawman (1982, 1981); Shorengro (1970, 1969, 1968).
Fastest time (1600m): Our Westminster (1989) & Our Poetic Prince (1988) 1:33:10.
Notable winners: Bonneval (2017); Awesome Rock (2016); Fiorente (2013); Happy Trails (2012); Whobegotyou (2010, 2009); El Segundo (2007); Fields Of Omagh (2002); Northerly (2001); Sunline (2000); Tristalove (1994); Naturalism (1992); Mannerism (1991); Better Loosen Up (1990); Our Poetic Prince (1988); Rubiton (1987); Strawberry Road (1983); So Called (1978); Tontonan (1975); Shorengro (1970, 1969, 1968); Winfreux (1965); Sometime (1963); Rising Fast (1964); Chicquita (1950).
Dato Tan Chin Nam Stakes winners:
PB Lawrence Stakes: 5—Lad Of The Manor (1995); Influry (1999); King Delamere (1985); So Called (1978); Vice Regal (1977).
Memsie Stakes: 5—Sunline (2000); Palace Reign (1993); Naturalism (1992); Rubiton (1987); Dazzling Duke (1986).
Dato Tan Chin Nam Stakes winners went on to win in the same preparation:
JRA Cup: 1—The Cleaner (2014).
Underwood Stakes: 4—Bonneval (2017); Northerly (2001); Rubiton (1987); So Called (1978).
Caulfield Stakes: 4—Whobegotyou (2009); Northerly (2001); Winfreux (1965); Rising Fast (1954).
Cox Plate: 9—El Segundo (2007); Northerly (2001); Sunline (2000); Better Loosen Up (1990); Our Poetic Prince (1988); Rubiton (1987); Strawberry Road (1983); So Called (1978); Rising Fast (1954).
Caulfield Cup: 2—Sometime (1963); Rising Fast (1954).
Melbourne Cup: 2—Fiorente (2013); Rising Fast (1954).
Cantala Stakes: 1—Happy Trails (2012).
Leading winning jockeys: 6 wins Harry White (Our Westminster 1989, Rubiton 1987, Arama 1974, Shorengro 1968, 1969, Bellition 1967).
4 wins Greg Childs (Lad Of The Manor 2006, 2005, Sunline 2000, Aerosmith 1998); Damien Oliver (Whobegotyou 2009, Northerly 2001, Fields Of Omagh 2002, Tristalove 1994).
3 wins Ron Hutchinson (Summall 1958, Arlunya 1956, Iron Duke 1951).
Current winning jockeys: 4 wins Damien Oliver (Whobegotyou 2009, Northerly 2001, Fields Of Omagh 2002, Tristalove 1994).
1 win Stephen Baster (Awesome Rock 2016); Steven Arnold (The Cleaner 2014); Glen Boss (Happy Trails 2012); Noel Callow (The Cleaner 2015); Dwayne Dunn (Rekindled Interest 2011); Damian Lane (Bonneval 2017); Kerrin McEvoy (Natural Blitz 2003); Luke Nolen (El Segundo 2007); Nash Rawiller (Fiorente 2013); Michael Rodd (Whobegotyou 2010); Craig Williams (Guillotine 2008).

Leading winning trainers: 4 wins David Hayes (Guillotine 2008, Tristalove 1994, Palace Reign 1993, Better Loosen Up 1990); Maurie Willmott (Grand Scale 1972, Shorengro 1970, 1969, 1968)
Current winning trainers: 4 wins David Hayes (Guillotine 2008, Tristalove 1994, Palace Reign 1993, Better Loosen Up 1990).
2 wins Lee Freedman (Naturalism 1992, Mannerism 1991); Mark Kavanagh (Whobegotyou 2010, 2009).
1 win Murray Baker & Andrew Forsman (Bonneval 2017); Paul Beshara (Happy Trails 2012); Jim Conlan (Rekindled Interest 2011); Leon & Troy Corstens (Awesome Rock 2016); Doug Harrison (Natural Blitz 2003); Peter Hurdle (Aerosmith 1998); Fred Kersley (Northerly 2001); Colin Little (El Segundo 2007); Tony McEvoy (Fields Of Omagh 2002); Gai Waterhouse (Fiorente 2013); John Wheeler (Our Poetic Prince 1988).
Points of interest: In 1972, the Dato Tan Chin Nam (Feehan Stakes) was run in two divisions: lst Division won by Jan's Beau; 2nd Division won by Grand Scale.
No Caulfield Cup winner has contested the Dato Tan Chin Nam Stakes in the past 28 years. In 1954, Rising Fast won the Feehan Stakes, Caulfield Stakes, Caulfield Cup, Cox Plate, Mackinnon Stakes and Melbourne Cup.
Fiorente (2013) is the most Melbourne Cup winner to run in the Dato Tan Chin Nam.
Bonneval (2017) is the only horse to win the race first-up.

VRC Danehill Stakes (1200m)—Flemington
$200,000 Group 2 3YO SWP. September 15, 2018.

YEAR	WINNER	JOCKEY	TRAINER	2ND	3RD	TIME
2017	Catchy	Regan Bayliss	David & Ben Hayes & Tom Dabernig	Jukebox	Booker	1:10.3
2016	Saracino	Damien Oliver	Murray Baker & Andrew Forsman	Archives	Samara Dancer	1:09.8
2015	Kinglike	Glen Boss	Peter Moody	Raphael's Cat	Ready For Victory	1:09.0
2014	Rich Enuff	Michael Rodd	Ken Keys	Looks Like The Cat	Ghibellines	1:08.1
2013	Charlie Boy	Michael Rodd	Gerald Ryan	Kiss A Rose	Eclair Big Bang	1:10.0
2012	Snitzerland	Damien Oliver	Gerald Ryan	Stralia	Rusambo	1:10.5
2011	Sepoy	Kerrin McEvoy	Peter Snowden	Hallowell Belle	Unique Quality	1:08.7
2010	Soul	Mark Zahra	Peter Snowden	Buffering	General Truce	1:11.6
2009	Black Caviar	Luke Nolen	Peter Moody	Wanted	Rarefied	1:09.9
2008	Aichi	Michael Rodd	Peter Snowden	Time Chief	Niccconi	1:10.4
2007	Tan Tat de Lago	Luke Nolen	Peter Moody	Scenic Blast	Purrealist	1:10.9
2006	The One	Greg Childs	Michael Moroney	Anamato	Sharkbite	1:10.4
2005	Jet Spur	Glen Boss	John O'Shea	Queen of the Hill	Stratum	1:09.5
2004	Fastnet Rock	Glen Boss	Paul Perry	Brannigan	Assafa	1:09.2
2003	Abdullah	Nash Rawiller	Tony Noonan	Critical List	Bronc	1:12.0
2002	Planchet	Darren Gauci	John Hawkes	Blur	Choisir	1:08.7
2001	Chong Tong	Danny Nikolic	Lee Freedman	North Boy	Spectatorial	1:09.0

BACKGROUND
First run: 1982 (won by Fiesta Star). Listed 1982-84. Group 3 from 1985. Run over 1100m 1982-87; 1200m from 1988. Prior to 2006, run on Derby Day. Switched to September in 2006, with the Ascot Vale Stakes. Previously known as Black Douglas Plate, Hilton On The Park, Crown Casino Stakes, Chivas Regal Stakes, Rory's Jester Stakes.
Most recent filly to win: Catchy (2017). Note: Eight fillies have won.
Fastest time (1200m): Armidale (1996) 1:08:10.
Notable winners: Catchy (2017); Snitzerland (2012); Sepoy (2011); Black Caviar (2009); Fastnet Rock (2004); Chong Tong (2001); Falvelon (1999); Dantelah (1997); Gold Ace 91995); Kenfair (1992); Umatilla (1991); Wrap Around (1990); Grandiose (1987); Rory's Jester (1985).
Danehill Stakes winners won the lead-up races:
San Domenico Stakes: 1—Snitzerland (2012).
Mitchell McKenzie Stakes: 1—Rich Enuff (2014).
William Crockett Stakes: 1—Black Caviar (2009).
McNeil Stakes: 1—Gold Ace (1995).
Blue Sapphire Classic: 1—Black Caviar (2009).
Danehill Stakes winners went on to win in the same preparation:
Caulfield Guineas Prelude: 1—Rich Enuff (2014).
Caulfield Sprint: 1—Sepoy (2011).

Manikato Stakes: 1—Sepoy (2011).
Coolmore Stud Stakes: 1—Sepoy (2011).
Leading winning jockeys: 4 wins Darren Gauci (Planchet 2002; Umatilla 1991, Sculptor 1983, Rory's Jester 1985); Damien Oliver (Saracino 2016, Snitzerland 2012, Gold Ace 1995, I Love Sydney 1994).
3 wins Glen Boss (Kinglike 2015, Jet Spur 2005, Fastnet Rock 2004); Michael Rodd (Rich Enuff 2014, Charlie Boy 2013, Aichi 2008).
Current winning jockeys: 4 wins Damien Oliver (Saracino 2016, Snitzerland 2012, Gold Ace 1995, I Love Sydney 1994).
3 wins Glen Boss (Kinglike 2015, Jet Spur 2005, Fastnet Rock 2004); Michael Rodd (Rich Enuff 2014, Charlie Boy 2013, Aichi 2008).
2 wins Luke Nolen (Black Caviar 2009, Tan Tat De Lago 2007).
1 win Stephen Baster (St Petersburg 2000); Regan Bayliss (Catchy 2017); Kerrin McEvoy (Sepoy 2011); Danny Nikolic (Chong Tong 2001); Brett Prebble (Point Danger 1998); Nash Rawiller (Abdullah 2003); Mark Zahra (Soul 2010).
Leading winning trainers: 3 wins Lee Freedman (Chong Tong 2001, Gold Ace 1995, I Love Sydney 1994); Peter Moody (Kinglike 2015, Black Caviar 2009, Tan Tat De Lago 2007); Peter Snowden (Sepoy 2011, Soul 2010, Aichi 2008).
Current winning trainers: 3 wins Lee Freedman (Chong Tong 2001, Gold Ace 1995, I Love Sydney 1994); Peter Snowden (Sepoy 2011, Soul 2010, Aichi 2008).
2 wins David Hayes (Catchy 2017, Wrap Around 1990); Paul Perry (Fastnet Rock 2004, Dantelah 1997); Gerald Ryan (Charlie Boy 2013, Snitzerland 2012).
1 win Murray Baker & Andrew Forsman (Saracino 2016); Danny Bougoure (Falvelon 1999); John Hawkes (Planchet 2002); David & Ben hayes & Tom Dabernig (Catchy 2017); Tony McEvoy (St Petersburg 2000); Michael Moroney (The One 2006); Tony Noonan (Abdullah 2003); John O'Shea (Jet Spur 2005); Ron Quinton (Dancing Dynamite 1993).
Points of interest: Star filly Special finished second to Cavalry in 1986.
Gold Ace won in 1995. His half-brother Final Card finished second to Wrap Around in 1990.
Choisir was first past the post in 2002, but he was relegated to third, behind Planchet and Blur, after causing interference in the final 200 metres.
Rory's Jester (1985) and Sepoy (2011) also won the Golden Slipper.

VRC Let's Elope Stakes (1400m)—Flemington
$200,000 Group 2 Mares 4YO&Up SWP. September 15, 2018.

YEAR	WINNER	JOCKEY	TRAINER	2ND	3RD	TIME
2017	Sword Of Light	Damian Lane	Mathew Ellerton & Simon Zahra	Swampland	Lovani	1:23.5
2016	Don't Doubt Mamma	Dwayne Dunn	Tony McEvoy	Thames Court	Manageress	1:24.5
2015	Amicus	Craig Newitt	Chris Waller	Precious Gem	May's Dream	1:23.0
2014	Commanding Jewel	Damien Oliver	Leon & Troy Corstens	Dear Demi	Nautical	1:23.6
2013	Commanding Jewel	Ben Melham	Leon Corstens	Catkins	A Time For Julia	1:22.5
2012	Zurella	Craig Newitt	Shaune Ritchie	Hi Belle	Total Attraction	1:23.3
2011	Pinker Pinker	Glen Boss	Greg Eurell	Mid Summer Music	Parables	1:23.8
2010	No Evidence Needed	James Winks	John P Thompson	Response	Live In Sin	1:26.8
2009	Cats Whisker	Steven King	Mark Kavanagh	Romneya	Symphony Miss	1:25.0
2008	Mimi Lebrock	Michael Rodd	Bart Cummings	Bellini Rose	Devil Moon	1:28.2
2007	Devil Moon	Michael Rodd	Mark Kavanagh	Eskimo Queen	Bellini Rose	1:23.4
2006	Rewaaya	Dwayne Dunn	David Hayes	Be Delicious	Celtic Bloom	1:24.2
2005	Dea	Stephen Baster	Kevin Corstens	Timbourina	Catscan	1:23.3
2004	Beautiful Gem	Nick Ryan	Lee Freedman	Galvanized	Demerger	1:24.4
2003	Ain't Seen Nothin	Damien Oliver	Barbara Joseph	Classic Patches	Reactive	1:24.4
2002	Purple Groove	Nash Rawiller	Tony Noonan	Tickle My	Crimson Gem	1:24.9
2001	Flushed	Noel Callow	Ken Keys	Miss Power Bird	Lolita Star	1:24.5

BACKGROUND
First run: 1987 (won by Take My Picture). Listed 1987-2004. Group 3 from 2005. Registered as the Milady Stakes.
Multiple winners: 1—Commanding Jewel (2014, 2013).
Notable winners: Amicus (2015); Commanding Jewel (2014, 2013); Pinker Pinker (2011); Devil Moon (2007); Rewaaya (2006); Ain't Seen Nothin' (2003); Tickle My (2000); Derobe (1997); Rose Of Portland (1996); Tolanda (1995); Mannerism (1993); Shavano Miss (1991).

Let's Elope Stakes winners won the lead-up races:
Cockram Stakes: 2—Dea (2005); Tickle My (2000).
Let's Elopes Stakes winners went on to win in the same preparation:
Stocks Stakes: 1—Devil Moon (2007)
Jayco Stakes: 1—Tolanda (1995).
Dubai Racing Club Cup: 1—Mannerism (1992).
Toorak Handicap: 1—Rewaaya (2006).
Caulfield Cup: —Mannerism (1992).
Myer Classic: 2—Rose Of Portland (1996); Natural Wonder (1990).
Leading winning jockeys: 6 wins Damien Oliver (Commanding Jewel 2014, Ain't Seen Nothin' 2003, Skyrocket 1998, Derobe 1997, Tolanda 1995, Mannerism 1992).
4 wins Steven King (Cats Whisker 2009, Rose Of Portland 1996, Amuse Us 1994, Rose Of Marizza 1993).
Current winning jockeys: 6 wins Damien Oliver (Commanding Jewel 2014, Ain't Seen Nothin' 2003, Skyrocket 1998, Derobe 1997, Tolanda 1995, Mannerism 1992).
2 wins Dwayne Dunn (Don't Doubt Mamma 2016, Rewaaya 2006); Craig Newitt (Amicus 2015, Zurella 2012); Michael Rodd (Mimi Lebrock 2008, Devil Moon 2007).
1 win Stephen Baster (Dea 2005); Glen Boss (Pinker Pinker 2011); Noel Callow (Flushed 2001); Damian Lane (Sword Of Light 2017); Ben Melham (Commanding Jewel 2013); Nash Rawiller (Purple Groove 2002); James Winks (No Evidence Needed 2010).
Leading winning trainer: 6 wins Lee Freedman (Beautiful Gem 2004, Skyrocket 1998, Derobe 1997, Rose Of Portland 1996, Tolanda 1995, Mannerism 1992).
Current winning trainers: 6 wins Lee Freedman (Beautiful Gem 2004, Skyrocket 1998, Derobe 1997, Rose Of Portland 1996, Tolanda 1995, Mannerism 1992).
2 wins Leon Corstens (Commanding Jewel 2014, 2013); Mark Kavanagh (Cats Whiskers 2009, Devil Moon 2007).
1 win Russell Cameron (Shavano Miss 1991); Leon & Troy Corstens (Commanding Jewel 2014); Mathew Ellerton & Simon Zahra (Sword Of Light 2017); Greg Eurell (Pinker Pinker 2011); David Hayes (Rewaaya 2006); Peter Hurdle (Sapeace 1999); Barbara Joseph (Ain't Seen Nothin' 2003); Ken Keys (Flushed 2001); Tony McEvoy (Don't Doubt Mamma 2016); Tony Noonan (Purple Groove 2002); Bruce Purcell (Tickle My 2000); Shaune Ritchie (Zurella 2012); John Thompson (No Evidence Needed 2010); Chris Waller (Amicus 2015).
Point of interest: Let's Elope finished third to Shavano Miss in 1991.

VRC Bobbie Lewis Quality (1200m)—Flemington
$200,000 Group 2 4YO&Up Quality Handicap. September 15, 2018.

YEAR	WINNER	JOCKEY	TRAINER	2ND	3RD	TIME
2017	Redkirk Warrior	Regan Bayliss	David & Ben Hayes & Tom Dabernig	Scales Of Justice	Land Of Plenty	1:09.9
2016	Faatinah	Regan Bayliss	David & Ben Hayes & Tom Dabernig	Tivaci	We've Got This	1:09.1
2015	Churchill Dancer	Michael Dee	David Hayes & Tom Dabernig	Under The Louvre	Gregers	1:08.8
2014	Chautauqua	Dwayne Dunn	Michael, Wayne & John Hawkes	Temple Of Boom	In Cahoots	1:08.1
2013	Speediness	Craig Williams	Colin Scott	Temple Of Boom	Albrecht	1:09.4
2012	We're Gonna Rock	Michael Rodd	Mark Kavanagh	Spirit Of Boom	Title	1:10.8
2011	Lone Rock	Mark Zahra	Robert Smerdon	Bel Sprinter	Danzylum	1:08.8
2010	Doubtful Jack	Luke Nolen	Peter Moody	Beltrois	About Ready	1:11.4
2009	Swift Alliance	Blake Shinn	Gai Waterhouse	Gold Salute	Chasm	1:09.9
2008	Bon Hoffa	Vlad Duric	Wendy Kelly	Grand Duels	Orange County	1:09.8
2007	Bon Hoffa	Vlad Duric	Wendy Kelly	Swick	Flash Trick	1:10.3
2006	Bel Danoro	Craig Newitt	Lee Freedman	Perfectly Ready	Volitant	1:09.6
2005	Wildly	Greg Childs	John McArdle	Calveen	Classiconi	1:09.3
2004	Face Value	Nick Ryan	Bevan Laming	Via De Lago	Scaredee Cat	1:11.0
2003	Titanic Jack	Brett Prebble	Tom Hughes (Jnr)	Bomber Bill	The Big Chill	1:09.8
2002	Chong Tong	Damien Oliver	Lee Freedman	Rubitano	Royal Code	1:10.9
2001	Scenic Peak	Rhys Mcleod	Danny J Bougoure	DH Calm Smytzer/ Dash For Cash		1:06.7

BACKGROUND
First run: 1974 (won by Citadel). Listed 1979-85. Group 3 1986-2015. Previously known as the Pat Lalor Quality, Sebel Of Melbourne Quality, Gateway Suites Quality.
Most recent mare to win: Lone Rock (2011). Note: Five mares have won.

Most recent 3YO to win: None. Note: 3YO Dash For Cash (2001) finished second (dead-heat) behind Scenic Peak.
Fastest time (1200m): Chautauqua (2014). 1:08:11
Multiple winners: 1—Bon Hoffa (2008, 2007).
Notable winners: Redkirk Warrior (2017); Chautauqua (2014); Lone Rock (2011); Bon Hoffa (2008, 2007); Titanic Jack (2003); Chong Tong (2002); Le Zagaletta (1999); El Mirada (1998); Hareeba (1994); Golden Sword (1993); Street Ruffian (1991); Placid Ark (1988); Special (1987); Magari (1982); Mr. Magic (1980); Bit Of A Skite (1979); Quiet Snort (1978).
Bobbie Lewis Quality winners won the lead-up races:
Show County Quality: 1—Swift Alliance (2009).
Bobbie Lewis Quality winners went on to win in the same preparation:
Gilgai Stakes: 2—Chautauqua (2014); Hareeba (1994). Note: Placid Ark (1988) won the Gilgai in 1987.
Sir Rupert Clarke Stakes: 3—Bon Hoffa (2007); Magari (1982); Soldier of Fortune (1981).
Longines Mile: 3—Titanic Jack (2003); Magari (1982); Bit Of A Skite (1979).
VRC Sprint Classic: 2—Hareeba (1994); Taj Quillo (1986).
The Bobbie Lewis and the Newmarket Handicap:
4—Redkirk Warrior (Bobbie Lewis 2017; Newmarket 2018, 2017); Special (Bobbie Lewis 1987; Newmarket 1988); Placid Ark (Bobbie Lewis 1988; Newmarket 1987). Note: Redkirk Warrior and Special won the double in the same season.
Leading winning jockeys: 2 wins Regan Bayliss (Redkirk Warrior 2017, Faatinah 2016); Michael Clarke (Hareeba 1994, Special 1987); Vlad Duric (Bon Hoffa 2008, 2007); Damien Oliver (Chong Tong 2002, Le Zagaletta 1999); Harry White (Base Fee 1985, Sports Ruler 1984).
Current winning jockeys: 2 wins Regan Bayliss (Redkirk Warrior 2017, Faatinah 2016); Vlad Duric (Bon Hoffa 2008, 2007); Damien Oliver (Chong Tong 2002, Le Zagaletta 1999).
1 win Stephen Baster (Ruthless Tycoon 2000); Michael Dee (Churchill Dancer 2015); Dwayne Dunn (Chautauqua 2014); Kevin Forrester (Holiday Lover 1992); Rhys McLeod (Scenic Peak 2001); Craig Newitt (Bel Danoro 2006); Luke Nolen (Doubtful Jack 2010); Brett Prebble (Titanic Jack 2003); Michael Rodd (We're Gonna Rock 2012); Blake Shinn (Swift Alliance 2009); Brian Werner (Temperate Pug 1996); Eddie Wilkinson (El Mirada 1998); Craig Williams (Speediness 2013); Mark Zahra (Lone Rock 2011).
Leading winning trainer: 3 wins Lee Freedman (Bel Danoro 2006, Chong Tong 2002, Le Zagaletta 1999); David Hayes & Tom Dabernig (Redkirk Warrior 2017, Faatinah 2016, Churchill Dancer 2015).
Current winning trainers: 3 wins Lee Freedman (Bel Danoro 2006, Chong Tong 2002, Le Zagaletta 1999); David Hayes & Tom Dabernig (Redkirk Warrior 2017, Faatinah 2016, Churchill Dancer 2015).
2 wins: David & Ben Hayes & Tom Dabernig (Redkirk Warrior 2017, Faatinah 2016); Wendy Kelly (Bon Hoffa 2008, 2007); John Meagher (Golden Sword 1993, Undoubted 1989).
1 win Danny Bougoure (Scenic Peak 2001); Michael, Wayne, John Hawkes (Chautauqua 2014); Tom Hughes Jnr (Titanic Jack 2003); Mark Kavanagh (We're Gonna Rock 2012); Robbie Laing (Temperate Pug 1996); Bevan Laming (Face Value 2004); John McArdle (Wildly 2005); Wally Mitchell (Placid Ark 1988); Steve Richards (Holiday Lover 1992); Colin Scott (Speediness 2013); Gai Waterhouse (Swift Alliance 2009).
Points of interest: Champion sire Bletchingly (1974) finished second to Citadel in the first Bobbie Lewis Quality. Calm Smytzer and Dash For Cash dead-heated for second behind Scenic Peak in 2001.

ATC The Shorts (1100m)—Randwick
$200,000 Group 2 3YO&Up SWP. September 15, 2018

YEAR	WINNER	JOCKEY	TRAINER	2ND	3RD	TIME
2017	Redzel	Hugh Bowman	Peter & Paul Snowden	Ball Of Muscle	Nieta	1:01.8
2016	Takedown	Tim Clark	Gary Moore	Ball Of Muscle	Kaepernick	1:03.2
2015	Rebel Dane	Brenton Avdulla	Gary Portelli	Ball Of Muscle	Shiraz	1:04.6
2014	Terravista	Corey Brown	Joseph Pride	I'm All The Talk	Famous Seamus	1:02.4
2013	Sessions	Josh Parr	Peter Snowden	Aeronautical	Spirit Of Boom	1:03.2
2012	Pampelonne	Hugh Bowman	Tim Martin	Satin Shoes	Appearance	1:09.6
2011	Love Conquers All	Jim Cassidy	Michael, Wayne & John Hawkes	Albert The Fat	Winter King	1:08.7
2010	Hot Danish	Tim Clark	Les Bridge	Whitefriars	Shellscrape	1:09.5
2009	Gold Trail	Nash Rawiller	Gary Portelli	Fritz's Princess	Sniper's Bullet	1:04.8
2008	Fritz's Princess	Jim Cassidy	Kris Lees	Hot Danish	Keen Commander	1:04.0
2007	Race Not Run					
2006	Bentley Biscuit	Hugh Bowman	Gai Waterhouse	Magnus	Spark Of Life	1:03.4
2005	Black Ink	Michael Cahill	Les Kelly	Mustard	Fumble	1:03.4
2004	Dance the Waves	Danny Beasley	Grahame Begg	Secret Land	Legally Bay	1:04.6
2003	Lucky Night	Chris Munce	Pat Farrell	Fair Embrace	Poetic Papal	1:04.8
2002	Empire	Hugh Bowman	Max Lees	Shags	Fouardee	1:04.1
2001	Oamaru Force	Glen Boss	David Hall	Pembleton	Fair Embrace	1:03.5

BACKGROUND
First run: 1867 (won by Gunilda). Listed 1979-93. Group 3 1994-2006. Group 2 from 2008.
Run over 1400m in 1944. Run over 1200m to 1972; 2010-12. Run at Warwick Farm 1983; Rosehill 2011.
Not held in 2007 due to the equine influenza outbreak.
Most recent mare to win: Hot Danish (2010).
Most recent 3YO to win: C&G–Tipperary Star (1961); Filly–Mother Duck (1987).
Multiple winners: 6—Kings Favourite (1977, 1976); Nagpuni (1954, 1953); Winnipeg (1944, 1941); Calmest (1927, 1926); Greenstead (1921, 1919); Gigandra (1915, 1914 & 1912).
Fastest time (1100m): Redzel (2017) 1:01.83 (track record)
Notable winners: Redzel (2017); Rebel Dane (2015); Terravista (2014); Hot Danish (2010); Bentley Biscuit (2006); Euclase (1991); Nagpuni (1954); Comedy Prince (1948); Greenstead (1921,1919); Gigandra (1915, 1914 & 1912).
The Shorts winners won the lead-up races:
Concorde Stakes: 1—Redzel (2017).
The Shorts winners went on to win in the same preparation:
Premiere Stakes: 2—Takedown (2016); Hot Danish (2010).
Caulfield Sprint: 2—Euclase (1991); Rise 'n' Shine (1990).
Moonga Stakes: 1—Love Conquers All (2011).
VRC Stakes: 1—Welsh Prince (1971). Note: The VRC Stakes was then run as a handicap
(named Craven A Stakes). WFA since 2007.
Linlithgow Stakes: 1—Wolaroi (1918). Note: In 1918, the Linlithgow Stakes was WFA 1600m.
Now run on Derby Day as a 1200m handicap.
Leading winning jockeys (since 1900): 6 wins Billy Cook (Nagpuni 1954, 1953, Some Boy 1936, High Disdain 1931, Panola 1930, Figure 1929).
5 wins Athol Mulley (Redcap 1966, Ferguson 1964, Merry Polly 1960, Chaperone 1946, Sogo 1942).
4 wins Hugh Bowman (Redzel 2017, Pamperlone 2012, Bentley Biscuit 2006, Empire 2002); George Moore (Rush Bye 1962, Free Rule 1951, Native Son 1947, Winnipeg 1944).
Current winning jockeys: 4 wins Hugh Bowman (Redzel 2017, Pamperlone 2012, Bentley Biscuit 2006, Empire 2002).
2 wins Glen Boss (Oamaru Force 2001, Bradshaw 2000); Corey Brown (Terravista 2014, Mulugwa 1998); Michael Cahill (Black Ink 2005, Madison Point 1996); Tim Clark (Takedown 2016, Hot Danish 2010).
1 win Brenton Avdulla (Rebel Dane 2015); Josh Parr (Sessions 2013); Nash Rawiller (Gold Trail 2009); Robert Thompson (Moss Rocket 1995).
Leading winning trainer (since 1900): 6 wins Tommy Smith (Potter McQueen 1988, Biscawong 1979, Welsh Prince 1971, Redcap 1966, Rush Bye 1962, Merry Polly 1960)
Current winning trainers: 3 wins John Hawkes (Love Conquers All 2011, Bradshaw 2000, Chiliad 1993).
2 wins Gary Portelli (Rebel Dane 2015, Gold Trail 2009); Peter Snowden (Redzel 2017, Sessions 2013).
1 win Grahame Begg (Dance The Waves (2004); Les Bridge (Hot Danish 2010); Ken Callaughan (Classic Magic 1992); Allan Denham (Euclase 1991); David Hall (Oamaru Force 2001); Michael, Wayne & John Hawkes (Love Conquers All 2011); Kris Lees (Fritz's Princess 2008); Les Kelly (Black Ink 2005); Tim Martin (Pampelonne 2012); Gary Moore (Takedown 2016); John Morrisey (Madison Point 1996); Joe Pride (Terravista 2014); Peter & Paul Snowden (Redzel 2017); Gai Waterhouse (Bentley Biscuit 2006); Pat Webster (Ab Initio 1999).
Point of interest: In 1939, The Albatross survived a protest from Caesar.

ATC Tea Rose Stakes (1400m)—Randwick
$175,000 Group 2 3YO Fillies. SWP. September 15, 2018.

YEAR	WINNER	JOCKEY	TRAINER	2ND	3RD	TIME
2017	Alizee	Glyn Schofield	James Cummings	Champagne Cuddles	Cellargirl	1:22.5
2016	Foxplay	Hugh Bowman	Chris Waller	Skylight Glow	Quick Feet	1:23.9
2015	Pearls	Sam Clipperton	John O'Shea	Honesta	Kimberley Star	1:24.4
2014	First Seal	Blake Shinn	John P Thompson	Winx	Earthquake	1:22.8
2013	Guelph	Hugh Bowman	Peter Snowden	Arabian Gold	Bound For Earth	1:22.1
2012	Longport	Jim Cassidy	John P Thompson	Norzita	Jade Marauder	1:29.3
2011	Streama	Hugh Bowman	Guy Walter	Pane In The Glass	Florentina	1:30.3
2010	More Strawberries	Jim Cassidy	Gai Waterhouse	Parables	Ambers Waltz	1:29.7
2009	More Joyous	Nash Rawiller	Gai Waterhouse	Melito	Deer Valley	1:28.7
2008	Samantha Miss	Hugh Bowman	Kris Lees	Kamillsy	Glowlamp	1:30.6
2007	Race Not Run					
2006	Cheeky Choice	Hugh Bowman	Gai Waterhouse	Gallant Tess	My Lady's Chamber	1:30.0
2005	Mnemosyne	Darren Beadman	John Hawkes	Fashions Afield	Sydney Owner	1:32.2
2004	Prisoner Of Love	Hugh Bowman	Guy Walter	Wager	Covertly	1:29.5
2003	Shamekha	Jim Cassidy	Gai Waterhouse	Unearthly	Miss Ivy	1:30.0
2002	Victory Vein	Danny Beasley	Bede Murray	Ms Bowie	Quiet As	1:29.0
2001	Ha Ha	Jim Cassidy	Gai Waterhouse	Lady Cay	Hosannah	1:29.8

BACKGROUND
First run: 1980 (won by Dark Eclipse). Listed 1980-82. Group 3 1983 & 1984. Group 2 since 1985.
Run over 1400m 1980-84, from 2013. Run over 1550m at Canterbury 1991. Run at Rosehill 1980-1990, 1992-2012. Randwick from 2013.
Fastest time (1400m): Guelph (2013) 1:22.10.
Notable winners: Foxplay (2016); First Seal (2014); Guelph (2013); Samantha Miss (2008); Shamekha (2003); Ha Ha (2001); Unworldly (2000); Sunline (1998); Assertive Lass (1996); Danarani (1994); Angst (1993); Burst (1992); Tristanagh (1989); Emancipation (1982); Black Shoes (1981).
Tea Rose Stakes winners also won the lead-up races:
Silver Shadow Stakes: 6— Samantha Miss (2008); Mnemosyne (2005); Victory Vein (2002); Ha Ha (2001); Angst (1993); Black Shoes (1981).
Furious Stakes: 17—Foxplay (2016); Streama (2011); More Strawberries (2010); Samantha Miss (2008); Mnemosyne (2005); Prisoner Of Love (2004); Shamekha (2003); Victory Vein (2002); Unworldly (2000); Danglissa (1999); Sunline (1998); Stella Cadente (1997); Danarani (1994); Angst (1993); Bold Promise (1991); Tristanagh (1989); Glory Girl (1987).
Tea Rose Stakes winners went on to win in the same preparation:
Flight Stakes: 15—Alizee (2017); First Seal (2014); Guelph (2013); Streama (2011); More Joyous (2009); Samantha Miss (2008); Cheeky Choice (2006); Ha Ha (2001); Unworldly (2000); Danglissa (1999); Sunline (1998); Assertive Lass (1996); Pontal Lass (1995); Danarani (1994); Angst (1993).
Furious Stakes & Flight Stakes: 5—Streama (2011); Samantha Miss (2008); Danglissa (1999); Sunline (1998); Angst (1993).
Thousand Guineas: 4—Guelph (2013); Mnemosyne (2005); Whisked (1990); Tristanagh (1989).
VRC Oaks: 2—Samantha Miss (2008); Tristanagh (1989).
The Princess Series:
Silver Shadow Stakes, Furious Stakes, Tea Rose Stakes & Flight Stakes: 2—Samantha Miss (2008); Angst (1993).
Leading winning jockeys: 6 wins Hugh Bowman (Foxplay 2016, Guelph 2013, Streama 2011, Samantha Miss 2008, Cheeky Choice 2006, Prisoner Of Love 2004).
5 wins Jim Cassidy (Longport 2012, More Strawberries 2010, Shamekha 2003, Ha Ha 2001, Glory Girl 1987).
3 wins Larry Cassidy (Unworldly 2000, Sunline 1998, Stella Cadente 1997).
Current winning jockeys: 6 wins Hugh Bowman (Foxplay 2016, Guelph 2013, Streama 2011, Samantha Miss 2008, Cheeky Choice 2006, Prisoner Of Love 2004).
3 wins Larry Cassidy (Unworldly 2000; Sunline 1998, Stella Cadente 1997).
1 win Glen Boss (Assertive Lass 1996); Sam Clipperton (Pearls 2015); Nash Rawiller (More Joyous 2009); Glyn Schofield (Alizee 2017); Blake Shinn (First Seal 2014).
Leading winning trainers: 7 wins Gai Waterhouse (More Strawberries 2010, More Joyous 2009, Cheeky Choice 2006, Shamekha 2003, Ha Ha 2001, Danglissa 1999, Assertive Lass 1996).
3 wins Neville Begg (Sabre Dancer 1983, Emancipation 1982, Dark Eclipse 1980); Bart Cummings (Danarani 1994, Tristanagh 1989, Glenview 1988).
Current winning trainers: 7 wins Gai Waterhouse (More Strawberries 2010, More Joyous 2009,

Cheeky Choice 2006, Shamekha 2003, Ha Ha 2001, Danglissa 1999, Assertive Lass 1996).
2 wins Clarry Conners (Pontal Lass 1995, Burst 1992); John Hawkes (Mnemosyne 2005, Unwordly 2000); John Thompson (First Seal 2014, Longport 2012).
1 win Grahame Begg (Whisked 1990); James Cummings (Alizee 2017); Kris Lees (Samantha Miss 2008); Noel Mayfield-Smith (Angst 1993); John O'Shea (Pearls 2015); Peter Snowden (Guelph 2013); Chris Waller (Foxplay 2016).
Points of interest: Dark Eclipse (1980), Burst (1992) and Ha Ha (2001) are the only Golden Slipper winners to win the Tea Rose.
Neville Begg trained three winners of the Tea Rose Stakes—Sabre Dancer 1983, Emancipation 1982, Dark Eclipse 1980—and his son, Grahame, trained Whisked to win in 1990.

ATC Golden Pendant (1400m)—Rosehill
$400,000 Group 2 3YO&Up Fillies & Mares SWP. September 22, 2018.

YEAR	WINNER	JOCKEY	TRAINER	2ND	3RD	TIME
2017	Daysee Doom	Andrew Adkins	Ron Quinton	Dixie Blossoms	Omei Sword	1:23.7
2016	Tycoon Tara	Josh Parr	Peter & Paul Snowden	Dixie Blossoms	Pearls	1:22.6
2015	Peeping	Sam Clipperton	Ron Quinton	Two Blue	Berry Delicious	1:23.0
2014	Arabian Gold	Blake Shinn	David Vandyke	Catkins	My Sabeel	1:22.6
2013	Sharnee Rose	Brenton Avdulla	Kris Lees	Red Tracer	Bennetta	1:23.0
2012	More Joyous	Nash Rawiller	Gai Waterhouse	Skyerush	Forarainyday	1:25.3
2011	Screen	Blake Shinn	Peter Snowden	Gybe	Ofcourseican	1:09.9
2010	Trim	Tim Clark	Peter Snowden	Montana Flyer =2	Girl Hussler =2	1:09.8
2009	Hot Danish	Corey Brown	Les Bridge	Madame Pedrille	Beaucoup	1:10.6
2008	Judged	Zac Purton	Joseph Pride	Illuminates	Nediyms Dream	1:11.0
2007	Race Not Run					
2006	Coolroom Candidate	Larry Cassidy	Keith Dryden	Napa Sky	Kakakakatie	1:11.1
2005	Fumble	Darren Beadman	Gai Waterhouse	Battle Maiden	One In A Million	1:09.5
2004	Besame Mucho	Glen Boss	Bart Cummings	Chatelaine	Covet Thee	1:10.6
2003	Classy Dane	Robert Thompson	Peter Dombkins	Forum Floozie	Gold Lottey	1:10.4
2002	Mica's Pride	Mark Newhman	Les Bridge	Ancient Song	Rare Insight	1:09.2
2001	La Rieuse	Darren Beadman	Ron Quinton	Winona	Gentle Genius	1:10.7

BACKGROUND
First run: 1996 (won by Fiddlestick). Listed 1998-2000. Group 3 from 2001. 1996-2012 1200m; from 2013 1400m. Was named the Research Stakes until 2013. Not run in 2007 due to EI outbreak.
Most recent 3YO to win: Classy Dane (2003). Note: the only 3YO to win.
Multiple winners: None. Note: Dantelah (1998) finished second in the 1999 Research Stakes.
Fastest time (1400m): Tycoon Tara (2016) 1:22.60
Notable winners: Tycoon Tara (2016); Peeping (2015); Arabian Gold (2014); More Joyous (2012); Hot Danish (2009); Spinning Hill (2000); Dantelah (1998).
Golden Pendant Stakes winners won the lead-up races:
Missile Stakes: 1—Tycoon Tara (2016).
Sheraco Stakes: 1—More Joyous (2012).
Show County Quality: 1—Tycoon Tara (2016).
Golden Pendant Stakes winners went on to win in the same preparation:
Angst Quality: 1—Sharnee Rose (2013).
Myer Classic: None.
Leading winning jockeys: 2 wins Darren Beadman (Besame Mucho 2004, Spinning Hill 2000); Blake Shinn (Arabian Gold 2014, Trim 2010).
Current winning jockeys: 2 wins Blake Shinn (Arabian Gold 2014, Trim 2010).
1 win Andrew Adkins (Daysee Doom 2017); Brenton Avdulla (Sharnee Rose 2013); Glen Boss (Classy Dane 2003); Corey Brown (Judged 2008); Larry Cassidy (Fumble 2005); Tim Clark (Hot Danish 2009); Sam Clipperton (Peeping 2015); Josh Parr (Tycoon Tara 2016); Zac Purton (Coolroom Candidate 2006); Robert Thompson (Mica's Pride 2002).
Leading winning trainer: 3 wins Ron Quinton (Peeping 2015, La Rieuse 2001, Brief Kiss 1999); Peter Snowden (Tycoon Tara 2016, Screen 2011, Trim 2010).
Current winning trainers: 4 wins Ron Quinton (Daysee Doom 2017, Peeping 2015, La Rieuse 2001, Brief Kiss 1999).
3 wins Peter Snowden (Tycoon Tara 2016, Screen 2011, Trim 2010).

2 wins Les Bridge (Hot Danish 2009, Mica's Pride 2002); Gai Waterhouse (More Joyous 2012, Fumble 2005).
1 win Clarry Conners (Unison 1997); Keith Dryden (Coolroom Candidate 2006); Kris Lees (Sharnee Rose 2013); Paul Perry (Dantelah 1998); Joe Pride (Judged 2008); Peter & Paul Snowden (Tycoon Tara 2016); David Vandyke (Arabian Gold 2014).
Points of interest: Dane Ripper finished third to Fiddlestick (1996). Dane Ripper won the Group 1 Cox Plate (2040m) at Moonee Valley in 1977.
Ancient Song finished second to Mica's Pride (2002). In 2003, she won the Group 1 Salinger Stakes (1200m) at Flemington.
Mica's Pride (2002) is the dam of champion Criterion.

ATC Shannon Stakes (1500m)—Rosehill
$175,000 Group 2 3YO&Up Quality Handicap. September 22, 2018.

YEAR	WINNER	JOCKEY	TRAINER	2ND	3RD	TIME
2017	Washington Heights	Kerrin McEvoy	Gerald Ryan	Mighty Lucky	Imposing Lass	1:28.8
2016	Moral Victory	Jason Collett	Tim Martin	Caped Crusader	Cosmic Cubed	1:28.0
2015	Vashka	Sam Clipperton	John O'Shea	God's In Him	Messene	1:29.2
2014	Rock Sturdy	Corey Brown	Joseph Pride	Liberty's Choice	Ninth Legion	1:28.8
2013	Rain Drum	Peter Robl	Gai Waterhouse	Centennial Park	Our Desert Warrior	1:29.3
2012	Rolling Pin	Corey Brown	Gwenda Markwell	Offenders	Fat Al	1:31.1
2011	King Lionheart	Tommy Berry	Gai Waterhouse	Fast Clip	Lone Command	1:29.9
2010	Firebolt	Daniel Ganderton	Roger James	Centennial Park	Sacred Choice	1:28.5
2009	Drumbeats	Kerrin McEvoy	Peter Snowden	Rangirangdoo	Strat's Flyer	1:30.1
2008	Musket	Corey Brown	Peter Snowden	Black Piranha	Ice Chariot	1:30.5
2007	Race Not Run					
2006	Stormhill	Jim Cassidy	Tim Martin	Temple Hills	Newton's Rings	1:28.4
2005	Lotteria	Len Beasley	Gai Waterhouse	Studebaker	Swick	1:30.2
2004	Nips	Jamie Innes	Clarry Conners	Whoc	Irongail	1:28.3
2003	Sportsman	Zac Purton	Gregory Hickman	Amex	Nips	1:28.1
2002	Gordo	Corey Brown	John Hawkes	Shot Of Thunder	Evander	1:29.7
2001	On Type	Len Beasley	Gai Waterhouse	Century Kid	Diamond Dane	1:22.4

BACKGROUND
First run: 1978 (won by For All Seasons). Listed 1979-84. Group 3 1985-2000. Group 2 from 2001.
Run over 1400m 1978-81 & 2001. Run over 1550m at Canterbury 1991.
Not held in 2007 due to Equine Influenza outbreak.
Most recent mare to win: Vashka (2015). Note: Only six mares have won the Shannon Stakes.
Most recent 3YO to win: None.
Multiple winners: 1—Never Quit (1989, 1988).
Fastest time (1500m): Moral Victory (2016) 1:28.06.
Notable winners: Lotteria (2005); Al Mansour (2000); Referral (1999); Quick Flick (1997); Juggler (1996); Sprint By (1995); Soho Square (1993); Cole Diesel (1989).
Shannon Stakes winners won the lead-up races:
Show County Quality: 2—Lotteria (2005); Sportsman (2003).
Warwick Stakes: 1—Al Mansour (2000).
Tramway Handicap: 5—Nips (2004); Sportsman (2003); Gordo (2002); Cole Diesel (1989); Double Dandy (1985).
Cameron Handicap: 1—Rolling Pin (2012).
Shannon Stakes winners went on to win in the same preparation:
Epsom Handicap: 1—Dalmacia (1982).
George Main Stakes: 1—Juggler (1996).
Chelmsford Stakes: 1—Soho Square (1993).
Toorak Handicap: 1—Cole Diesel (1989).
Caulfield Stakes: 1—Juggler (1996).
Caulfield Cup: 1—Cole Diesel (1989).
Leading winning jockeys: 5 wins Corey Brown (Rock Sturdy 2014, Rolling Pin 2012, Musket 2008, Gordo 2002, Referral 1999).
4 wins Len Beasley (Lotteria 2005, On Type 2001, Al Mansour 2000, Quick Flick 1997); Ron Quinton (Never Quit 1987, Eastern Bay 1984, Dalmacia 1982, For All Seasons 1978).
Current winning jockeys: 5 wins Corey Brown (Rock Sturdy 2014, Rolling Pin 2012, Musket 2008, Gordo 2002, Referral 1999).

2 wins Kerrin McEvoy (Washington Heights 2017); Drumbeats 2009).
1 win Tommy Berry (King Lionheart 2011); Glen Boss (Juggler 1996); Jason Collett (Moral Victory 2016); Daniel Ganderton (Firebolt 2010); Jamie Innes (Nips 2004); James McDonald (Vashka 2015); Zac Purton (Sportsman 2003).
Leading winning trainers: 6 wins Neville Begg (Never Quit 1988, 1987, Eastern Bay 1984, Dalmacia 1982, Stylee 1979, For All Seasons 1978); Gai Waterhouse (Rain Drum 2013, King Lionheart 2011, Lotteria 2005, On Type 2001, Juggler 1996, Sprint By 1995).
Current winning trainers: 6 wins Gai Waterhouse (Rain Drum 2013, King Lionheart 2011, Lotteria 2005, On Type 2001, Juggler 1996, Sprint By 1995).
2 wins John Hawkes (Gordo 2002, Deposition 1991); Tim Martin (Moral Victory 2016, Stormhill 2006); Peter Snowden (Drumbeats 2009, Musket 2008).
1 win Les Bridge (Drawn 1984); Clarry Conners (Nips 2004); Tim Donnelly (Quick Flick 1997); Steve Englebrecht (Referral 1999); Greg Hickman (Sportsman 2003); Roger James (Firebolt 2010); Gwenda Markwell (Rolling Pin 2012); John O'Shea (Vashka 2015); Joe Pride (Rock Sturdy 2014); Gerald Ryan (Washington Heights 2017); John Size (Al Mansour 2000); John Wilcock (Armed For Action 1998).

MVRC W.H. Stock Stakes (1600m)—Moonee Valley
$200,000 Group 2 4YO&Up Mares WFA. September 28, 2018.

YEAR	WINNER	JOCKEY	TRAINER	2ND	3RD	TIME
2017	I Am A Star	Ben Melham	Shane Nichols	Flying Jess	Hell Or Highwater	1:37.3
2016	Don't Doubt Mamma	Dwayne Dunn	Tony McEvoy	Kaniana	Miss Rose De Lago	1:38.7
2015	Fenway	Blake Shinn	Lee & Shannon Hope	May's Dream	Scratchy Bottom	1:34.9
2014	Dear Demi	Jim Cassidy	Clarry Conners	Solicit	Commanding Jewel	1:37.8
2013	Atlantic Jewel	Michael Rodd	Mark Kavanagh	Oasis Bloom	Oriental Ruby	1:36.8
2012	Oasis Bloom	Glen Boss	Peter Morgan & Craig Widdison	Spirit Song	Chateau Margaux	1:36.9
2011	King's Rose	Luke Nolen	Peter Moody	Pinker Pinker	Lady Lynette	1:37.0
2010	Avienus	Craig Williams	Mark Webb	Belscenica	Lady Lynette	1:38.3
2009	Zarita	Dwayne Dunn	Pat Hyland	Cats Whisker	Soul Diva	1:37.0
2008	Tuesday Joy	Nash Rawiller	Gai Waterhouse	Devil Moon	Bird of Fire	1:36.3
2007	Devil Moon	Michael Rodd	Mark Kavanagh	Brom Felinity	Hidden Strings	1:36.4
2006	Astrodame	Kerrin McEvoy	Lee Freedman	Brockman's Lass	Belle Bizaare	1:36.1
2005	Flowerdrum	Daniel Moor	Brian Mayfield-Smith	Honest Politician	Taken	1:38.5
2004	She's Archie	Nick Ryan	John Sadler	Annie La Vie	Zumanity	1:41.9
2003	Sunday Joy	Brad Rawiller	Darren Weir	Liberty Rose	Monde Special	1:36.8
2002	Gold Lottey	Damien Oliver	Gai Waterhouse	Tyrolean	Visage	1:38.7
2001	Lady Marion	Steven King	Graeme Rogerson	Tickle My	Tyrolean	1:38.7

BACKGROUND
First run: 1973 (won by Mellition). Listed 1979-92. Group 3 1994-2004. Group 3 since 2005. WFA since 1990. Not held in 1977. Run at Sandown in 1976. Conducted at night in 1998-99. Formerly called the Dallas Handicap (1974-79) and Royal Park Handicap (1973).
Multiple winners: None.
Fastest time (1600m): Fenway (2015) 1:34.98
Notable winners: I Am A Star (2017); Dear Demi (2014); Atlantic Jewel (2013); King's Rose (2011); Dear Demi (2014); Atlantic Jewel (2013); King's Rose (2011); Zarita (2009); Tuesday Joy (2008); She's Archie (2004); Sunday Joy (2003); Arctic Scent (1996); Alcove (1994).
Stocks Stakes winners won the lead-up races:
Cockram Stakes: None.
Memsie Stakes: 2—Atlantic Jewel (2013); King's Rose (2011).
Let's Elope Stakes: 3—Don't Doubt Mamma (2016); Devil Moon (2007); Natural Wonder (1990).
Tranquil Star Stakes: None.
How Now Stakes: None.
Stocks Stakes winners went on to win in the same preparation:
Turnbull Stakes: 1—Devil Moon (2007).
Caulfield Stakes: 1—Atlantic Jewel (2013).
Caulfield Cup: 1—Arctic Scent (1996).
Myer Classic: 1—Natural Wonder (1990).
Leading winning jockeys: 2 wins Dwayne Dunn (Don't Doubt Mamma 2016, Zarita 2009); Damien Oliver

(Gatherneaux 1992, Sunday Joy 2003); Michael Rodd (Atlantic Jewel 2013, Devil Moon 2007); Craig Williams (Avienus 2010, Sweet Delight 1997).
Current winning jockeys: 2 wins Dwayne Dunn (Don't Doubt Mamma 2016, Zarita 2009); Damien Oliver (Gatherneaux 1992, Sunday Joy 2003); Michael Rodd (Atlantic Jewel 2013, Devil Moon 2007); Craig Williams (Avienus 2010, Sweet Delight 1997).
1 win Stephen Baster (The Penny 1995); Glen Boss (Oasis Bloom 2012); Ben Melham (I Am A Star 2017); Daniel Moor (Astrodame 2006); Luke Nolen (King's Rose 2011); Brett Prebble (Lady Marion 2001); Brad Rawiller (She's Archie 2004); Nash Rawiller (Tuesday Joy 2008); Blake Shinn (Fenway 2015).
Leading winning trainer: 3 wins Colin Hayes (Change The Tune 1984, Dondal 1980, Princess Veronica 1976).
Current winning trainers: 2 wins Pat Hyland (Zarita 2009, Londolozi 1998); Mark Kavanagh (Atlantic Jewel 2013, Devil Moon 2007); Gai Waterhouse (Tuesday Joy 2008, Sunday Joy 2003).
1 win Clarry Conners (Dear Demi 2014); Lee Freedman (Gatherneaux 1992); David Hayes (Pacific 1991); Lee and Shannon Hope (Fenway 2015); Tom Hughes Jnr (Alcove 1994); Tony McEvoy (Don't Doubt Mamma 2016); Peter Morgan & Craig Widdison (Oasis Bloom 2012); Shane Nichols (I Am A Star 2017); Graeme Rogerson (Gold Lottey 2002); John Sadler (Flowerdrum 2005); John Size (Sorrento 1999); Mark Webb (Avienus 2010); Darren Weir (She's Archie 2004).
Points of interest: She's Archie (2004) finished second to Makybe Diva in the 2003 Melbourne Cup.
Tuesday Joy (2008), by Carnegie, is a half-sister to Sunday Joy (2003), by Sunday Silence. Both are from Joie Denise, by Danehill.
Hula Wonder (2000) is a daughter of Natural Wonder (1990).
Jockeys Darryn Murphy (Digger's Lass 1985) and Garry Murphy (Dowling Lass 1974) are brothers.
Jockey Midge Didham won in Mellition (1973), trained by brother A.E. Didham. Midge's son John won on Hazy Pond (1988).
Roger Hoysted, who trained daughter and mother winners, Hula Wonder (2000) and Natural Wonder (1990), is the son of Hal Hoysted, who trained Hot Cross to win in 1975.
Tom Hughes Jnr (Alcove 1994) is the son of T.J "Tommy" Hughes, who trained Bold Bridget to win in 1978.
David Hayes (Pacific 1991) is the son of Colin Hayes, who trained three winners—Change The Tune 1984, Dondal 1980 and Princess Veronica 1976.

MVRC Stutt Stakes (1600m)—Moonee Valley
$200,000 Group 2 3YO Open SW. September 28, 2018.

YEAR	WINNER	JOCKEY	TRAINER	2ND	3RD	TIME
2017	Showtime	Beau Mertens	Michael, Wayne & John Hawkes	Salsamor	Holy Snow	1:37.1
2016	Hey Doc	Luke Currie	Tony McEvoy	Land Of Plenty	Kaching	1:37.4
2015	Sovereign Nation	Michael Walker	David Hayes & Tom Dabernig	Get The Picture	Gredington	1:36.1
2014	Almalad	Tommy Berry	Gai Waterhouse	Moonovermanhattan	Kumaon	1:38.8
2013	Divine Calling	Damien Oliver	Gai Waterhouse	Shamus Award	Cluster	1:37.2
2012	Pierro	Nash Rawiller	Gai Waterhouse	Carringbush Jack	Jimando	1:36.3
2011	Chase The Rainbow	Dean Yendall	Rick Hore-Lacy	Cute Emily	Sabrage	1:38.3
2010	Hollowlea	Blake Shinn	Terry & Karina O'sullivan	Run For Levi	Bullbars	1:37.2
2009	Carrara	Craig Williams	Tony Vasil	Extra Hero	Miss With Attitude	1:39.5
2008	Whobegotyou	Michael Rodd	Mark Kavanagh	All American	Carnero	1:36.3
2007	Barbaricus	Steven Arnold	Danny O'Brien	Davcon	Cecconi	1:36.0
2006	Churchill Downs	Craig Williams	David Hayes	Magic Jet	Ankh Morpork	1:36.7
2005	Red Dazzler	Danny Nikolic	Mick Price	Stratum	Maybe Better	1:38.0
2004	Mr Martini	Stephen Baster	Leon Corstens	Under Command	Danaurum	1:37.8
2003	Casual Pass	Noel Callow	Mathew Ellerton	Special Harmony	Face Value	1:37.2
2002	Helenus	Steven King	Leon Corstens	Aint Here	Half Hennessy	1:39.6
2001	Viscount	Kerrin McEvoy	John Hawkes	Dash For Cash	Amalfi	1:38.1

BACKGROUND

First run: 1934 (won by Titanium). Group 2 since 1979. Run over 1500m 1934-36. Run at Sandown in 1976. Also known as the Moonee Valley Stakes. Conducted at night since 1999.
Most filly to win: St. Clemens Belle (1998): Note: St. Clemens Belle dead-heated with Helm.
Fastest time (1600m): Almurtajaz (1988) 1:34.70.
Notable winners: Pierro (2012); Whobegotyou (2008); Casual Pass (2003); Helenus (2002); Viscount (2001); Diatribe (1999); Encosta De Lago (1996); Blevic (1994); Canny Lad (1990); Zabeel (1989); Sky Chase (1987); Red Anchor (1984); Karaman (1978); Surround (1976); Denise's Joy (1975); Plush (1974); Taj Rossi (1973); Century (1972); Daryl's Joy (1969); Always There (1968); Storm Queen (1966), Star Affair (1965); Skipton (1941); Valiant Chief (1935).
Stutt Stakes winners won the lead-up races:
Mitchell McKenzie Stakes: 1—Carrara (2009).
Run To The Rose: 1—Pierro (2012).
Exford Plate: 2—Hollowlea (2010; Carrara (2009).
Stutt Stakes winners went on to win in the same preparation:
Caulfield Guineas: 10—Whobegotyou (2008); Helenus (2002); Red Anchor (1984); Surround (1976); Beau Sovereign (1971); Storm Queen (1066); Star Affair (1965); Lady Sybil (1960); Phoibus (1948); Attley (1945).
Victoria Derby: 9—Helenus (2002); Blevic (1994); Red Anchor (1984); Taj Rossi (1973); Daryl's Joy (1969); Always There (1968); New Statesman (1961); Precept (1943); Skipton (1941).
Caulfield Guineas & Victoria Derby: 2—Helenus (2002), Red Anchor (1984).
Moonee Valley Vase: 4—Whobegotyou (2008); Helenus (2002); Diatribe (1999); Blevic (1994).
Moonee Valley Vase & Victoria Derby: 2—Helenus (2002), Blevic (1994).
Cox Plate: 6—Red Anchor (1984); Surround (1976); Taj Rossi (1973); Daryl's Joy (1969); Star Affair (1965); Chanak (1947).
Thousand Guineas: None.
VRC Oaks: 3—Surround (1976), Denise's Joy (1975); Lady Sybil (1960).
Leading winning jockeys: 5 wins Roy Higgins (Taj Rossi 1973, Century 1972, Storm Queen 1966, Star Affair 1965, Lady Sybil 1960).
4 wins Steven King (Helenus 2002, Schubert 1997, Encosta De Lago 1996, Ready To Explode 1991).
3 wins Scobie Breasley (Phoibos 1948, Chanak 1947, Bold Beau 1946); Ted Preston (Friar's Hope 1951, Precept 1943, Sun Valley 1940).
Current winning jockeys: 2 wins Stephen Baster (Mr Martini 2004, Sarson Trail 2000); Craig Williams (Carrara 2009, Churchill Downs 2006);
1 win Steven Arnold (Barbaricus 2007); Noel Callow (Casual Pass 2003); Luke Currie (Hey Doc 2016); Dwayne Dunn (St. Clemen's Belle 1998*); Kerrin McEvoy (Viscount 2001); Beau Mertens (Showtime 2017); Damien Oliver (Divine Calling 2013); Tommy Berry (Almalad 2014); Nash Rawiller (Pierro 2012); Michael Rodd (Whobegotyou 2008); Michael Walker (Sovereign Nation 2015); Blake Shinn (Hollowlea 2010); Dean Yendall (Chase The Rainbow 2011).
Leading winning trainers: 6 wins Bart Cummings (Sky Chase 1987, Broad Reach 1986, Taj Rossi 1973,

Century 1972, Storm Queen 1966, L'Orage Boy 1964).
4 wins Geoff Murphy (Albany Bay 1983, Guns Away 1977, Surround 1976, Beau Sovereign 1971).
Current winning trainers: 4 wins John Hawkes (Showtime 2017, Viscount 2001, Helm 1998*, Burrito 1995).
3 wins David Hayes (Sovereign Nation 2015, Churchill Downs 2006, Blevic 1994); Gai Waterhouse (Almalad 2014, Divine Calling 2013, Pierro 2012).
2 wins Leon Corstens (Mr Martini 2004, Helenus 2002).
1 win Russell Cameron (St Clemen's Belle 1998*); Mathew Ellerton (Casual Pass 2003); Lee Freedman (Encosta De Lago 1996); Michael, Wayne & John Hawkes (Showtime 2017); David Hayes & Tom Dabernig (Sovereign Nation 2015); Mark Kavanagh (Whobegotyou 2008); Tony McEvoy (Hey Doc 2016); John Meagher (Ready To Explode 1991); Mick Price (Red Dazzler 2005); Terry and Katrina O'Sullivan (Hollowlea 2010); Allan Williams (Pearl Prince 1993); Tony Vasil (Carrara 2009).
* dead heat
Points of interest: Helenus (2002) is the only horse to win the Stutt Stakes, Caulfield Guineas, Moonee Valley Vase and Victoria Derby.
Diatribe (1999) won the 2000 Caulfield Cup.
Canny Lad (1990) and Storm Queen (1966) are the only Golden Slipper winners to win the Stutt Stakes.

ATC Hill Stakes (1800m)—Randwick
$500,000 Group 2 3YO&Up WFA. September 29, 2018

YEAR	WINNER	JOCKEY	TRAINER	2ND	3RD	TIME
2017	Classic Uniform	Michael Walker	Gary Moore	Embley	Mackintosh	1:49.9
2016	Hartnell	James McDonald	John O'Shea	Who Shot Thebarman	Storm The Stars	2:04.1
2015	Preferment	Hugh Bowman	Chris Waller	Magic Hurricane	Complacent	2:06.8
2014	Junoob	Blake Shinn	Chris Waller	Criterion	Bagman	2:06.1
2013	Moriarty	Nash Rawiller	Chris Waller	Glencadam Gold	Masked Marvel	2:03.6
2012	Lamasery	Peter Robl	David Vandyke	Mourayan	Lights Of Heaven	2:06.2
2011	Trusting	Joao Moreira	John P Thompson	Hawk Island	Tullamore	2:02.9
2010	Descarado	Peter Robl	Gai Waterhouse	Triple Honour	Purple	1:56.4
2009	Miss Marielle	Peter Robl	Joseph Pride	Pacino	Roman Emperor	1:56.1
2008	Fiumicino	Glen Boss	John Hawkes	Dealer Principal	Hurrah	1:57.3
2007	Race Not Run					
2006	Desert War	Larry Cassidy	Gai Waterhouse	Eremein	Grand Zulu	1:56.3
2005	Desert War	Jim Byrne	Gai Waterhouse	Portland Singa	Dizelle	1:56.7
2004	Natural Blitz	Danny Beasley	Doug Harrison	Vouvray	Just Polite	1:56.6
2003	Excellerator	Jim Cassidy	Gai Waterhouse	Platinum Scissors	Carnegie Express	1:56.8
2002	Dress Circle	Len Beasley	Gai Waterhouse	Bedouin	Republic Lass	1:56.6
2001	Mulan Princess	Chris Munce	Gai Waterhouse	Altiero	Dottoressa	1:47.0

BACKGROUND
First run: 1921 (won by Beauford). Group 2 from 1979. Run over 1600m 1921-1940, 1960. Run over 1700m 1941-1959, 1961-1971; 1750 1972-1990, 2001; 1900m 1991-2000, 2002-2010. 2000m 2011-16; 1800m from 2017. Run at Rosehill 1921-1990, 1992-2011; Randwick 1960, from 2012; Canterbury 1991. Not held in 2007 due to Equine Influenza outbreak.
Most recent mare to win: Miss Marielle (2009).
3YOs to win: 9—Arena (1998); Muirfield Village (1992); Beau Zam (1987); Cossack Prince (1982); Canarthus (1981); Grand Cidium (1972); Noholme (1959); Skyline (1958); Peter Pan (1932). Note: no 3YO filly has won the Hill Stakes.
Multiple winners: 11—Desert War (2006, 2005); Toi Port (1964, 1963); Redcraze (1957, 1956); Hydrogen (1953, 1952); Yaralla (1943, 1942); Gold Rod (1939, 1938); Peter Pan (1935, 1932); Chatham (1934, 1933); Phar Lap (1931, 1930); Limerick (1928, 1927); The Hawk (1925, 1923); Gloaming (1922).
Fastest time (1800m, Randwick): Classic Uniform (2017) 1:49.98.(First time run at this distance).
Notable winners: Hartnell (2016); Preferment (2015); Descarado (2010); Desert War (2006, 2005); Tie The Knot (1999); Saintly (1996); Super Impose (1991); Beau Zam (1987); Emancipation (1983); Gunsynd (1972); Baguette (1971); Eskimo Prince (1965); Sky High (1962); Noholme (1959); Skyline (1958); Redcraze (1957, 1956); Bernborough (1946); Shannon (1945); High Caste (1941); Beau Vite (1940); Peter Pan (1935, 1932); Chatham (1934, 1933); Phar Lap (1931, 1930); Limerick (1928, 1927).
Hill Stakes winners won the lead-up races:
Warwick Stakes: 10—Super Impose (1991); Sky High (1962); San Domenico (1951); Bernborough (1946); Yaralla (1942); High Caste (1941); Chatham (1934, 1933); Limerick (1928, 1927).

Chelmsford Stakes: 9—Hartnell (2016); Trusting (2011); Pasta Express (2000); Emancipation (1983); Prince Courtauld (1954); Bernborough (1946); Phar Lap (1930); Limerick (1928, 1927).
Warwick Stakes & Chelmsford Stakes: 3—Bernborough (1946); Limerick (1928, 1927).
George Main Stakes: 3—Emancipation (1983); Imposing (1979); Baguette (1971).

Hill Stakes winners went on to win in the same preparation:
Craven Plate: 18—Miss Marielle (2009); Tie The Knot (1999); Stony Bay (1995); Leica Lover (1974); Winfreux (1967); Prince Cortauld (1954); Hydrogen (1952); Playboy (1950); Yaralla (1942); Beau Vite (1940); Talking (1937); Peter Pan (1935); Chatham (1934, 1933); Phar Lap (1931, 1930); Limerick (1927); Gloaming (1922).
Epsom Handicap: 8—Desert War (2005); Super Impose (1991); Imposing (1979); Toi Port (1964, 1963); Noholme (1959); Shannon (1945); Chatham (1933).
The Metropolitan: 3—Junoob (2014); Redcraze (1956); Beau Vite (1940).
Turnbull Stakes: 1—Preferment (2015).
Cox Plate: 10—Saintly (1996); Gunsynd (1972); Noholme (1959); Redcraze (1957); Hydrogen (1953, 1952); Beau Vite (1940); Chatham (1934); Phar Lap (1931, 1930).
Caulfield Cup: 3—Descarado (2010); Redcraze (1956); Columnist (1947).
Melbourne Cup: 4—Saintly (1996); Lord Fury (1961); Peter Pan (1932); Phar Lap (1930).
Leading winning jockeys: 8 wins Jim Pike (Peter Pan 1935, Chatham 1934, 1933, Phar Lap 1931, 1930, Winalot 1929, The Hawk 1925, 1923).
6 wins George Moore (Baguette 1971, Black Onyx 1969, Prince Grant 1966, Eskimo Prince 1965, Sky High 1962, Playboy 1950).
5 wins Peter Cook (Cossack Prince 1982, Silver Wraith 1980; Marceau 1978, Skyjack 1975, Leica Lover 1974).
4 wins Shane Dye (Tie The Knot 1999, Ebony Grosve 1997, Stony Bay 1995, Muirfield Village 1992); Maurice McCarten (Gold Rod 1939, 1938, Talking 1937, Limerick 1927); Neville Sellwood (Noholme 1959, Prince Cortauld 1954, Hydrogen 1953, Vagabond 1949); Arthur Ward (Redcraze 1957, 1956, San Domenico 1951, Dark Marne 1948).
3 wins John Marshall (Pasta Express 2000, Beau Zam 1987, Trissaro 1984); Ted McMenamin (Yaralla 1943, 1942, Beau Vite 1940); Peter Robl (Lamasery 2012, Descarado 2010, Miss Marielle 2009).
Current winning jockeys: 2 wins Larry Cassidy (Desert War 2006, Arena 1998).
1 win Glen Boss (Fiumicino 2008); Hugh Bowman (Preferment 2015); Jim Byrne (Desert War 2005); Grant Cooksley (Slight Chance 1994); James McDonald (Hartnell 2016); Joao Moreira (Trusting 2011); Nash Rawiller (Moriarty 2013); Black Shinn (Junoob 2014); Michael Walker (Classic Uniform 2017).
Leading winning trainers: 9 wins Tommy Smith (Silver Wraith 1980, Imposing 1979, Marceau 1978, Gunsynd 1972, Black Onyx 1969, Playboy 1950, Prince Grant 1966, Redcraze 1957, 1956).
7 wins Bart Cummings (Saintly 1996, Muirfield Village 1992, Beau Zam 1987, Trissaro 1984, Ngawyni 1976, Skyjack 1975, Leica Lover 1974); Gai Waterhouse (Descarado 2010, Desert War 2006, 2005; Excellerator 2003; Dress Circle 2002; Mulan Princess 2001, Stony Bay 1995).
Current winning trainers: 7 wins Gai Waterhouse (Descarado 2010, Desert War 2006, 2005; Excellerator 2003; Dress Circle 2002; Mulan Princess 2001, Stony Bay 1995).
3 wins Chris Waller (Preferment 2015, Junoob 2014, Moriarty 2013).
2 wins John Hawkes (Fiumicino 2008, Arena 1998).
1 win Paul Cave (Pasta Express 2000); Lee Freedman (Super Impose 1991); Doug Harrison (Natural Blitz 2004); Michael, Wayne & John Hawkes (Fiumicino 2008); David Hayes (Eastern Classic 1990); Gary Moore (Classic Uniform 2017); John O'Shea (Hartnell 2016); Joe Pride (Miss Marielle 2009); Graeme Rogerson (Ebony Grosve 1997); John Thompson (Trusting 2011); David Vandyke (Lamasery 2012).
Points of interest: Imposing (1979) is the sire of Super Impose (1991).
Sky High (1962) is the brother to Skyline (1958). Both are by Star Kingdom from Flight's Daughter.
Father-daughter trainers—Tommy Smith and Gai Waterhouse—have won 16 Hill Stakes since Smith won his first of nine with Playboy in 1950.
Maurice McCarten rode four Hill Stakes winners (see leading winning jockeys) and trained Prince Cortauld to win in 1954.

ATC Premiere Stakes (1200m)—Randwick
$500,000 Group 2 3YO&Up WFA. September 29, 2018.

YEAR	WINNER	JOCKEY	TRAINER	2ND	3RD	TIME
2017	In Her Time	Corey Brown	Ben Smith	English	Clearly Innocent	1:08.2
2016	Takedown	Blake Shinn	Gary Moore	Our Boy Malachi	Danish Twist	1:08.2
2015	Terravista	Hugh Bowman	Joseph Pride	Rebel Dane	That's A Good Idea	1:09.1
2014	Famous Seamus	Tim Clark	Noel Mayfield-Smith	Charlie Boy	Wouldnt It Be Nice	1:09.8
2013	Arinosa	Brenton Avdulla	Chris Waller	Dystopia	Famous Seamus	1:09.3
2012	Red Tracer	Nash Rawiller	Chris Waller	Satin Shoes	Emotional Circus	1:09.6
2011	Neeson	Michael Rodd	Joseph Pride	Hurtle Myrtle	Love Conquers All	1:10.2
2010	Hot Danish	Tim Clark	Les Bridge	Trader	Cardinal Virtue	1:09.8
2009	=1 Mentality	Blake Shinn	Bart Cummings	=1 Kroner	Phelan Ready	1:10.4
2008	Triple Honour	Jay Ford	Michael, Wayne & John Hawkes	Captain Bax	Reigning to Win	1:10.1
2007	German Chocolate	Glen Boss	Chris Waller	Solo Flyer	Fashions Afield	1:09.9
2006	Paratroopers	Zac Purton	Paul Cave	Imana	Johan'S Toy	1:10.3
2005	Shania Dane	Darren Beadman	John Hawkes	Dance Hero	Spark Of Life	1:08.8
2004	Spark Of Life	Rod Quinn	John Hawkes	Into The Night	Century Kid	1:09.8
2003	Thorn Park	Chris Munce	Allan Denham	Patezza	Excellerator	1:09.0
2002	Century Kid	Glen Boss	Bob Thomsen	Ancient Song	Shogun Lodge	1:09.4
2001	On Type	Justin Sheehan	Graeme Rogerson	Padstow	Century Kid	1:10.3

BACKGROUND
First run: 1972 (won by Outback). Group 3 1979-96. Group 2 since 1997. Run over 1300m 1972-74. Run at Rosehill 1972-75, 1979-81, 1983, 1985-92, 1994-2010. Canterbury 1976-78, 1982, 1984 & 1993. Randwick from 2011. (Note the Premiere Stakes was moved from mid August to late September/early October in 2011).
Most recent mare to win: In Her Time (2017).
3YOs to win: 3—Integra (1990); Imperial Baron (1986); Outback (1972). Note: No 3YO filly has won.
Multiple winners: 2—Mr. Innocent (2000, 1999); Joanne (1992, 1991).
Fastest time (1200m, Randwick): In Her Time (2017) 1:08.20.
Notable winners: Terravista (2015); Red Tracer (2012); Hot Danish (2011); Mentality (dead-heat 2009); Paratrooper (2006); Spark Of Life (2004); Thorn Park (2003); Mr. Innocent (2000, 1999); Joanne (1992, 1991); Sky Chase (1988); Campaign King (1987); Emancipation (1983); Kingston Town (1981).
Premiere Stakes winners won the lead-up races:
Missile Stakes: 7—German Chocolate (2007); Spark Of Life (2004); Legal Agent (1996); Klokka (1993); Joanne (1992, 1991); Campaign King (1987).
Show County Stakes: None.
The Shorts: 2—Takedown (2016); Hot Danish (2010).
Premiere Stakes winners also won in the same preparation:
Manikato Stakes: 1—Spark Of Life (2004).
Theo Marks Stakes: 2—Joanne (1991); Silver Wraith (1980).
Warwick Stakes: 2—Kingston Town (1981); Purple Patch (1976).
Concorde Stakes: 1—Joanne (1991).
Cox Plate: 1—Kingston Town (1981).
Leading winning jockeys: 4 wins Mick Dittman (Mr. Innocent 1999, Joanne 1992, 1991, March Magic 1984).
3 wins Glen Boss (Triple Honour 2008, Thorn Park 2003, Legal Agent 1996); Jim Cassidy (King Ivor 1997, High Regard 1989, Imperial Baron 1986); Malcolm Johnston (Latin Saint 1982, Kingston Town 1981, Salaam 1979).
Current winning jockeys: 3 wins Glen Boss (Triple Honour 2008, Thorn Park 2003, Legal Agent 1996).
2 wins Tim Clark (Famous Seamus 2014, Hot Danish 2010); Blake Shinn (Takedown 2016, Kroner 2009).
1 win Brenton Avdulla (Arinosa 2013); Hugh Bowman (Terravista 2015); Corey Brown (In Her Time 2017); Larry Cassidy (Stormy Regent 1994); Jay Ford (Mentality 2009); Zac Purton (German Chocolate 2007); Nash Rawiller (Red Tracer 2012); Michael Rodd (Neeson 2011).
Leading winning trainers: 7 wins Jack Denham (King Ivor 1997, Joanne 1992, 1991, High Regard 1989, Purple Patch 1976, Favoured 1974, Outback 1972).
4 wins Bart Cummings (Kroner 2009, Sky Chase 1988, Campaign King 1987, Monakea 1978); John Hawkes (Neeson 2011, Mentality 2009, Paratroopers 2006, Shania Dane 2005); Tommy Smith (Latin Saint 1982, Kingston Town 1981, Silver Wraith 1980, Zambari 1973).
Current winning trainers: 4 wins John Hawkes (Neeson 2011, Mentality 2009, Paratroopers 2006, Shania Dane 2005).
3 wins Chris Waller (Arinosa 2013, Red Tracer 2012, Triple Honour 2008).

2 wins Michael, Wayne & John Hawkes (Neeson 2011, Mentality 2009); Graeme Rogerson (Century Kid 2002, Masked Party 1998).
1 win Les Bridge (Hot Danish 2010); Ken Callaughan (Stormy Regent 1994); Paul Cave (German Chocolate 2007); Noel Mayfield-Smith (Famous Seamus 2014); Gary Moore (Takedown 2016); Joe Pride (Terravista 2015); Benjamin Smith (In Her Time 2017); Gai Waterhouse (Light Up The World 1995).
Points of interest: 2004 Golden Slipper winner Dance Hero was second to Shania Dane in the 2004 Premiere Stakes. Kroner and Mentality dead-heated in 2009.
Allan Denham rode Purple Patch (1976), trained by his father Jack. Allan went on to train Spark Of Life to win in 2004. Jack trained seven winners of the Premiere Stakes.

MRC Thousand Guineas Prelude (1400m)—Caulfield
$200,000 Group 2 3YO Fillies SWP. September 30, 2018.

YEAR	WINNER	JOCKEY	TRAINER	2ND	3RD	TIME
2017	Booker	Dwayne Dunn	Mathew Ellerton & Simon Zahra	Shoals	Catchy	1:23.4
2016	Legless Veuve	Mark Zahra	Stuart Webb	La Luna Rossa	Sword Of Light	1:25.2
2015	Miss Gunpowder	Craig Williams	Phillip Stokes	Payroll	Jameka	1:23.2
2014	Afleet Esprit	Damien Oliver	David Hayes & Tom Dabernig	Amicus	Go Indy Go	1:24.5
2013	Gregers	Chad Schofield	David Hayes	Marianne	Politeness	1:29.5
2012	Lady Of Harrods	Steven Arnold	Russell Cameron	Commanding Jewel	Molto Bene	1:24.9
2011	Bliss Street	Steven Arnold	Daniel Morton	Hallowed Belle	Mosheen	1:24.4
2010	Divorces	Mark Zahra	Peter Snowden	Sistine Angel	Panipique	1:24.2
2009	Irish Lights	Glen Boss	David Hayes	Set For Fame	Mont Fleuri	1:26.1
2008	Ortensia	Danny Nikolic	Tony Noonan	Romneya	Sugar Babe	1:26.0
2007	Gabbidon	Stathi Katsidis	Gary Kennewell	Jestatune	Sleek Chassis	1:23.9
2006	Miss Finland	Craig Williams	David Hayes	Anamato	My Only Hope	1:24.3
2005	Doubting	Steven King	Mick Price	Pinezero	Isanami	1:27.4
2004	Hollow Bullet	David Taggart	John McArdle	Ballet Society	Astradame	1:24.3
2003	Hinting	Brett Prebble	Bill Mitchel	Ashenti	Portland Damask	1:22.9
2002	La Bella Dame	Danny Nikolic	Mick Price	Toast Of The Coast	Lashed	1:24.2
2001	Haste Ye Back	Brett Prebble	Leon Corstens	Malagra Miss	Special Grange	1:25.0

BACKGROUND
First run: 1965 (won by Bounteous (1st Div), On Point (2nd Div)). Listed until 1999. Group 3 from 2000. Run over 1400m 1965 & 1966 and since 1990; 1600m 1967-1989. Registered the Tranquil Star Stakes. Also known as the Jumeirah International Stakes and the Heath Stakes. Run in two divisions in 1965, 1977 & 1978.
Fastest time (1400m): Miss Pennymoney (1999) 1:22.58.
Notable winners: Irish Lights (2009); Ortensia (2008); Miss Finland (2006); Hollow Bullet (2004); Miss Pennymoney (1999); Danelagh (1998); Derobe (1996); Azzurro (1992); Bianco Flyer (1987); Shackle (1986); Sanderae (1970); Gay Poss (1969); Eld (1967).
Thousand Guineas Prelude winners won the lead-up races:
McNeil Stakes: 2—Lady Of Harrods (2012); Miss Finland (2006).
Cap d'Antibes Stakes: 1—Afleet Esprit (2014).
Thousand Guineas Prelude winners went on to win in the same preparation:
Thoroughbred Club Stakes: 1—Cornwall Queen (1997).
Thousand Guineas: 5—Irish Lights (2009); Miss Finland (2006); Azzurro (1992); Bianco Flyer (1987); Biscadale (1980).
Edward Manifold Stakes: 4—So Gorgeous (2000); Rubidium (1995); Brompton Cross (1993); Azzurro (1992).
Wakeful Stakes: 3—Hollow Bullet (2004); Sanderae (1970); Eld (1967).
VRC Crown Oaks: 3—Miss Finland (2006); Hollow Bullet (2004); Sanderae (1970).
Leading winning jockeys: 3 wins Greg Hall (Aerobe 1996, Majestic Dawn 1994, Fiery Belle 1978); Roy Higgins (As You Like It 1976, Sandarae 1970, Gay Poss 1969); Damien Oliver (Afleet Esprit 2014, Danelagh 1998, Azzurro 1992); Brett Prebble (Hinting 2003, Haste Ye Back 2001, Cornwall Queen 1997); Harry White (Torn Monarch 1982, Tregal 1971, Eld 1967).
Current winning jockeys: 3 wins Damien Oliver (Afleet Esprit 2014, Danelagh 1998, Azzurro 1992);
Brett Prebble (Hinting 2003, Haste Ye Back 2001, Cornwall Queen 1997).
2 wins Steven Arnold (Lady Of Harrods 2012, Bliss Street 2011); Craig Williams (Miss Gunpowder 2015, Miss Finland 2006); Mark Zahra (Legless Veuve 2016, Divorces 2010).
1 win Glen Boss (Irish Lights 2009); Dwayne Dunn (Booker 2017); Nash Rawiller (So Gorgeous 2000); Chad Schofield (Gregers 2013).

Leading winning trainers: 5 wins David Hayes (Afleet Esprit 2014, Gregers 2013, Irish Lights 2009, Miss Finland 2006, Majestic Dawn 1994).
4 wins Lee Freedman (Danelagh 1998, Derobe 1996, Azzurro 1992, Shackle 1986).
Current winning trainers: 5 wins David Hayes (Afleet Esprit 2014, Gregers 2013, Irish Lights 2009, Miss Finland 2006, Majestic Dawn 1994).
4 wins Lee Freedman (Danelagh 1998, Derobe 1996, Azzurro 1992, Shackle 1986).
2 wins Mick Price (Doubting 2006, La Bella Dame 2002).
1 win Russell Cameron (Lady of Harrods 2012); Jim Conlan (Miss Pennymoney 1999); Leon Corstens (Haste Ye Back 2001); Mathew Ellerton & Simon Zahra (Booker 2017); David Hayes & Tom Dabernig (Afleet Esprit 2014); Gary Kennewell (Gabbidon 2007); John McArdle (Hollow Bullet 2004); John Meagher (Chador 1991); Daniel Morton (Bliss Street 2011); Tony Noonan (Ortensia 2008); Dan O'Sullivan (So Gorgeous 2000); Steve Richards (Cornwall Queen 1997); Peter Snowden (Divorces 2010); Phillip Stokes (Miss Gunpowder 2015); Stuart Webb (Legless Veuve 2016).
Points of interest: Miss Finland (2006) is the only Golden Slipper winner to win the Thousand Guineas Prelude. Danelagh (1998) is the only Blue Diamond Stakes winner to win the Thousand Guineas Prelude.

ATC Roman Consul Stakes (1200m)—Randwick
$300,000 Group 2 3YO Open SW. October 6, 2018.

YEAR	WINNER	JOCKEY	TRAINER	2ND	3RD	TIME
2017	Viridine	Brenton Avdulla	James Cummings	Single Bullet	Beau Geste	1:10.2
2016	Russian Revolution	Kerrin McEvoy	Peter & Paul Snowden	Astern	Capitalist	1:09.0
2015	Exosphere	James McDonald	John O'Shea	Zoutenant	Japonisme	1:08.5
2014	Brazen Beau	Joao Moreira	Chris Waller	Nostradamus	Delectation	1:09.0
2013	Zoustar	Jim Cassidy	Chris Waller	Barbed	Open Book	1:09.4
2012	Jolie Bay	Jay Ford	Michael, Wayne & John Hawkes	Knight Exemplar	Your Song	1:09.6
2011	Foxwedge	Nash Rawiller	John O'Shea	Masthead	Do You Think	1:11.1
2010	Buffering	Nash Rawiller	Robert Heathcote	Obsequious	Parriwi	1:09.0
2009	Shellscrape	Blake Shinn	Chris Waller	Honest Truth	Shadow Assassin	1:09.9
2008	Montana Flyer	Peter Robl	Gai Waterhouse	Drumbeats	Silent But Deadly	1:11.6
2007	Race Not Run					
2006	Reigning to Win	Glen Boss	John O'Shea	Gold Edition	Mute	1:10.7
2005	Denmarket	Stathi Katsidis	Gerald Ryan	Stratum	De Beers	1:10.5
2004	Fastnet Rock	Glen Boss	Paul Perry	Charge Forward	Star Cat	1:09.3
2003	Exceed and Excel	Hugh Bowman	Tim Martin	Hasna	Ambulance	1:09.1
2002	Snowland	Chris Munce	Gai Waterhouse	Force Apollo	Bollinger	1:10.6
2001	Stylish Lass	Len Beasley	Gai Waterhouse	Fair Embrace	Mistegic	1:04.9

BACKGROUND

First run: 1979 (won by Meriville). Listed 1979-84. Group 3 1985-2004. Group 2 from 2005. Run over 1100m 2001. Run at Rosehill 2000; Randwick inner track 2001; Warwick Farm 2004. Not held in 2007 due to Equine Influenza.
Most recent filly to win: Jolie Bay (2009).
Fastest time (1200m): Exosphere (2015) 1:08:52.
Notable winners: Russian Revolution (2016); Exosphere (2015); Zoustar (2013); Foxwedge (2011); Buffering (2010); Fastnet Rock (2004); Exceed And Excel (2003); Snowland (2002); Easy Rocking (1999); Encounter (1997); Our Maizcay (1995); Jetball (1993); Slight Chance (1992); Heat Of The Moment (1985); Red Anchor (1984).
Roman Consul Stakes winners won the lead-up races:
Up And Coming Stakes: 4—Fastnet Rock (2004); Exceed And Excel (2003); Snowland (2002); Our Maizcay (1995).
San Domenico Stakes: 4—Foxwedge (2011); Shellscrape (2009); Our Maizcay (1995); Show County (1989).
Vain Stakes: 1—Russian Revolution (2016).
Heritage Stakes: 4—Viridine (2017); Laurie's Legacy (1998); Show County (1989); Rendoo (1986).
Golden Rose: 2—Exosphere (2015); Zoustar (2013).
Stan Fox Stakes: 2—Marwina (1994); Show County (1989). Note: The Roman Consul Stakes was previously run on the first Saturday in September.
Roman Consul Stakes winners went on to win in the same preparation:
Coolmore Stud Stakes: 3—Zoustar (2013); Our Maizcay (1995); Bureaucracy (1990).
Cox Plate: 1—Red Anchor (1984).
Victoria Derby: 1—Red Anchor (1984).
VRC Oaks: 1—Slight Chance (1992).
Leading winning jockeys: 3 wins Jim Cassidy (Zoustar 2013, Laurie's Lottery 1998, Marwina 1994);

Mick Dittman (Easy Rocking 1999, Bureaucracy 1990, Red Anchor 1984).
Current winning jockeys: 2 wins Glen Boss (Reigning To Win 2006, Fastnet Rock 2004); Nash Rawiller (Foxwedge 2011, Buffering 2010).
1 win Brenton Avdulla (Viridine 2017); Hugh Bowman (Exceed And Excel 2003); James McDonald (Exosphere 2015); Kerrin McEvoy (Russian Revolution 2016); Joao Moreira (Brazen Beau 2014); Blake Shinn (Shellscrape 2009).
Leading winning trainers: 4 wins Jack Denham (Kootoomootoo 2000, Marwina 1994, Jetball 1993, Bureaucracy 1990); Tommy Smith (Wonder Dancer 1988, Christmas Tree 1987, Red Anchor 1984, Swift Gun 1981).
3 wins John O'Shea (Exosphere 2015, Foxwedge 2011, Reigning To Win 2006); Chris Waller (Brazen Beau 2014, Zoustar 2013, Shellscrape 2009); Gai Waterhouse (Montana Flyer 2008, Snowland 2002, Stylish Lass 2001).
Current winning trainers: 3 wins John O'Shea (Exosphere 2015, Foxwedge 2011, Reigning To Win 2006); Chris Waller (Brazen Beau 2014, Zoustar 2013, Shellscrape 2009); Gai Waterhouse (Montana Flyer 2008, Snowland 2002, Stylish Lass 2001).
2 wins John Hawkes (Jolie Bay 2012, Anthems 1996).
1 win James Cummings (Viridine 2017); Michael, Wayne, John Hawkes (Jolie Bay 2012); Rob Heathcote (Buffering 2010); Tim Martin (Exceed And Excel 2003); Mick Nolan (Laurie's Lottery 1998); Paul Perry (Fastnet Rock 2004); Ron Quinton (Easy Rocking 1999); Gerald Ryan (Denmarket 2005); Grant Searle (Our Maizcay 1995); Peter & Paul Snowden (Russian Revolution 2016); Bruce Wallace (Prince Of Praise 1991).
Points of interest: Fastnet Rock (2004) and Exceed And Excel (2003) went on to win Australia's Champion Stallion title.
Exceed And Excel (2003) won the 2004 G1 Newmarket Handicap at Flemington; Fastnet Rock (2004) won the G1 Lightning Stakes at Flemington and the G1 Oakleigh Plate at Caulfield before finishing second behind Alinghi in the Newmarket.
Jetball (1993) and Marwina (1994) are brothers— colts by Marscay from Orwhina.

VRC Edward Manifold Stakes (1600m)—Flemington
$200,000 Group 2 3YO Fillies SW. October 6, 2018.

YEAR	WINNER	JOCKEY	TRAINER	2ND	3RD	TIME
2017	Bring Me Roses	Luke Currie	Tony McEvoy	Hiyaam	Leather'n'Lace	1:38.3
2016	Serenely Discreet	Luke Nolen	Phillip Stokes	Bella Sorellastra	Waterloo Sunset	1:37.5
2015	Badawiya	Damien Oliver	Mick Price	Sacred Eye	My Poppette	1:36.4
2014	Fontein Ruby	Mark Zahra	Robert Smerdon	Maastricht	Crafty	1:37.6
2013	Su Sauver	Damian Lane	Matt Laurie	Star Fashion	Solicit	1:39.5
2012	Maybe Discreet	Luke Nolen	Phillip Stokes	Members Joy	Commanding Jewel	1:37.6
2011	Mosheen	Danny Nikolic	Robert Smerdon	Bliss Street	Celebrity Girl	1:39.4
2010	Sistine Angel	Craig Williams	Andrew Noblet	Brazilian Pulse	Shamrocker	1:38.1
2009	Majestic Music	Clare Lindop	Leon Macdonald	Fomalite	Silent Surround	1:38.3
2008	Gallica	Damien Oliver	Mick Price	Cats Whisker	Sparks Fly	1:38.0
2007	El Daana	Dwayne Dunn	David Hayes	Serious Speed	Absolut Glam	1:40.1
2006	She Will Be Loved	Nash Rawiller	Mathew Ellerton	Miss Finland	My Only Hope	1:37.0
2005	Serenade Rose	Steven King	Lee Freedman	Empress Lily	Mary Marvel	1:37.2
2004	Alinghi	Damien Oliver	Lee Freedman	Ballet Society	Kylikwong	1:36.4
2003	Special Harmony	Luke Currie	Lee Freedman	Ashenti	Bahamian Star	1:38.2
2002	Coupe	Vin Hall	Mathew Ellerton	Fuji Dancer	Lashed	1:39.4
2001	Ugachuka	Damien Oliver	Lee Freedman	Li Lo Lill	Hot Beat	1:38.7

BACKGROUND
First run: 1932 (won by Dutchie). Group 2 since 1979.
Fastest time (1600m): Rubidium (1995) 1:35.70
Notable winners: Mosheen (2011); Serenade Rose (2005); Alinghi (2004); Special Harmony (2003); Azzurro (1992); Richfield Lady (1991); Midnight Fever (1987); Spirit Of Kingston (1984); Taj Eclipse (1983); Emancipation (1982); Stage Hit (1979); Dual Choice (1970); Storm Queen (1966); Light Fingers (1964); Indian Summer (1961); Lady Sybil (1960); Wiggle (1958); Chicquita (1949); Tranquil Star (1940).
Edward Manifold Stakes winners won the lead-up races:
McNeil Stakes: 1—Sistine Angel (2010).
Tranquil Star Stakes: 3—So Gorgeous (2000); Rubidium (1995); Azzurro (1992).
Morphettville Guineas: 2—Maybe Discreet (2012), Majestic Music (2009).
Edward Manifold Stakes winners went on to win in same preparation:
Thousand Guineas: 14—Gallica (2008); Alinghi (2004); Special Harmony (2003), Inaflury (1998);

Azzurro (1992); Richfield Lady (1991); Riverina Charm (1988); Princess Talaria (1977); Gipsy Queen (1965); Indian Summer (1961); Chicquita (1949); Goldenway (1957); Bendrum (1956); Siren Song (1948).
Wakeful Stakes: 7—Serenade Rose (2005); My Sienna (1999); Richfield Lady (1991); Light Fingers (1994); Indian Summer (1961); Siren (1936); Arachne (1934).
VRC Oaks: 17—Mosheen (2011); Serenade Rose (2005); Special Harmony (2004); Richfield Lady (1991); Spirit Of Kingston (1984); Taj Eclipse (1983); Chosen Lady (1967); Gipsy Queeen (1965); Light Fingers (1964); Arctic Star (1962); Indian Summer (1961); Lady Sibyl (1960); Mintaway (1959); Lady Havers (1951); Chicquita (1949); Primavera (1941); Siren (1936).
Thousand Guineas & VRC Oaks: 3—Richfield Lady (1991); Indian Summer (1961); Chicquita (1949).
Thousand Guineas & Wakeful Stakes & VRC Oaks: 2—Richfield Lady (1991), Indian Summer (1961).
Leading winning jockeys: 6 wins Bill Williamson (Mintaway 1959, Goldenway 1957, Bendrum 1956, Lady Havers 1951, Perm 1947, Delina 1944).
5 wins Damien Oliver (Badawiya 2015, Gallica 2008, Alinghi 2004, Ugachaka 2001, Azzurro 1992).
Current winning jockeys: 5 wins Damien Oliver (Badawiya 2015, Gallica 2008, Alinghi 2004, Ugachaka 2001, Azzurro 1992).
2 wins Luke Currie (Bring Me Roses 2017, Special Harmony 2003); Luke Nolen (Serenely Discreet 2016, Maybe Discreet 2012); Nash Rawiller (She Will Be Loved 2006, So Gorgeous 2000).
1 win Dwayne Dunn (El Daana 2007); Damian Lane (Se Sauver 2013); Clare Lindop (Majestic Music 2009); Brian Werner (Rebecca Gay 1985); Craig Williams (Sistine Angel 2010); Mark Zahra (Fontein Ruby 2014).
Leading winning trainer: 7 wins Lee Freedman (Serenade Rose 2005, Alinghi 2004, Special Harmony 2003, Ugachaka 2001, Rose Of Danehill 1997, Love Of Mary 1994, Azzurro 1992).
Current winning trainers: 7 wins Lee Freedman (Serenade Rose 2005, Alinghi 2004, Special Harmony 2003, Ugachaka 2001, Rose Of Danehill 1997, Love Of Mary 1994, Azzurro 1992).
2 wins David Hayes (El Daana 2007, She Will Be Loved 2006); Mick Price (Badawiya 2015, Gallica 2008); Robert Smerdon (Fontein Ruby 2014, Mosheen 2011); Phillip Stokes (Serenely Discreet 2016, Maybe Discreet 2012).
1 win Grahame Begg (Twiglet 1990); Mat Ellerton (Coupe 2002); Matt Lawrie (Se Sauver 2013); Dean Lawson (Ascorbic 1996); Leon Macdonald (Majestic Music 2009); Tony McEvoy (Bring Me Roses 2017); Andrew Noblett (Sistine Angel 2010); Dan O'Sullivan (So Gorgeous 2000).
Points of interest: 2006 Golden Slipper winner Miss Finland finished second behind She Will Be Loved in 2006, and then won the Thousand Guineas and VRC Oaks.
Storm Queen (1966) is the only Golden Slipper winner to win the Edward Manifold.
Alinghi (2004) and Midnight Fever (1987) are the only Blue Diamond Stakes winners to win the Edward Manifold.
Light Fingers (1964) is the only Edward Manifold winner to win a Melbourne Cup (1965).
Tranquil Star (1940) is the only Edward Manifold winner to win a Cox Plate (1944 & 1942).

VRC Gilgai Stakes (1200m)—Flemington
$200,000 Group 2 Open SWP. October 6, 2018.

YEAR	WINNER	JOCKEY	TRAINER	2ND	3RD	TIME
2017	Keen Array	Mark Zahra	Davidd & Ben Hayes & Tom Dabernig	Sold For Song	Malibu Style	1:09.2
2016	The Quarterback	Matthew Allen	Robbie Griffiths	We've Got This	Durendal	1:09.0
2015	Chautauqua	Dwayne Dunn	Michael, Wayne & John Hawkes	Delectation	Knoydart	1:09.8
2014	Chautauqua	Dwayne Dunn	Michael, Wayne & John Hawkes	Bounding	Final Crescendo	1:08.2
2013	Platelet	Michelle Payne	Darren Weir	Spirit Of Boom	Steps In Time	1:10.1
2012	Hallowell Belle	Vlad Duric	Gai Waterhouse	King's Rose	Spirit Of Boom	1:08.8
2011	Temple Of Boom	James McDonald	Tony Gollan	Sistine Angel	Response	1:10.5
2010	Hay List	Glyn Schofield	John Mcnair	Catapulted	Chasm	1:08.2
2009	All Silent	Nicholas Hall	Grahame Begg	First Command	Light Fantastic	1:09.8
2008	El Cambio	Kerrin McEvoy	Peter Snowden	Swick	Murtajill	1:10.1
2007	Stanzout	Nash Rawiller	Colin Davies	Shadoways	Valedictum	1:10.4
2006	Fast N Famous	Danny Nikolic	John O'Shea	Shadoways	Dance Hero	1:08.3
2005	Falkirk	Noel Callow	Lee Freedman	Glamour Puss	Recapitalize	1:07.9
2004	Recapitalize	Vin Hall	Mathew Ellerton	Falkirk	Amtrak	1:09.2
2003	Bomber Bill	Steven Arnold	Robert Smerdon	Mr. Magoo	Red Labelle	1:09.7
2002	Cosmic Strike	Jason Patton	Dan O'sullivan	Strategic Image	Rubitano	1:09.3
2001	Belle Du Jour	Patrick Payne	Clarry Conners	Point Danger	Gold Class	1:10.4

BACKGROUND

First run: 1984 (won by Royal Troubadour). Listed 1984-86. Group 3 from 1987. Previously known as the Rupert Steele Stakes. Registered as the Baguette Stakes.
Most recent mare to win: Platelet (2013). Note: three mares have won.
Most recent 3YO to win: C&G–Royal Troubadour (1984) – the only 3YO to win.
Multiple winners: 2—Chautauqua (2015, 2014); Bomber Bill (2003, 2000).
Fastest time (1200m): Falkirk (2005) 1:07:96.
Notable winners: The Quarterback (2016); Chautauqua (2015, 2014); Bomber Bill (2003, 2000); Hay List (2010); All Silent (2009); Belle Du Jour (2001); Black Bean (1999); Poetic King (1996); Racer's Edge (1995); Hareeba (1994); Joanne (1990); Grandiose (1989); Redelva (1988); Placid Ark (1987); Campaign King (1986).

Gilgai Stakes winners also won the lead-up races:
Aurie's Star Handicap: 1—Temple Of Boom (2011).
McEwen Stakes: 2—Chautauqua (2015); Hay List (2010).
Bobbie Lewis Quality: 2—Chautauqua (2014); Hareeba (1994). Note: Placid Ark won the Gilgai in 1987, and the Bobbie Lewis in 1988.

Gilgai Stakes winners went on to win in the same preparation:
Manikato Stakes: 1—Chautauqua (2015). Note: Hay List (2010) and Poetic King (1996) won the double when the Manikato was run before the Gilgai.
VRC Classic Stakes: 2—All Silent (2009); Hareeba (1994).
Schillaci Stakes: None.
Yallambee Stakes: 1—Black Bean (1999).

Gilgai Stakes and Flemington autumn G1 sprints:
Newmarket Handicap: 4—The Quarterback (2016); Belle Du Jour (Gilgai 2001; Newmarket 2003); Grandiose (1989); Placid Ark (1987).
Lightning Stakes: 3—Chautauqua (Lighting 2016, Gilgai 2015, 2014); Redelva (Gilgai 1988, Lightning 1990); Placid Ark (Lightning 1987; Gilgai 1987).
Leading winning jockey: 3 wins Damien Oliver (Rock You 1997, Simonstad 1993, Storaia 1992).
Current winning jockeys: 3 wins Damien Oliver (Rock You 1997, Simonstad 1993, Storaia 1992).
2 wins Steven Arnold (Bomber Bill 2003, 2000); Dwayne Dunn (Chautauqua 2015, 2014).
1 win Matthew Allan (The Quarterback 2016); Noel Callow (Falkirk 2005); Vlad Duric (Hallowell Belle 2012); Nick Hall (All Silent 2009); James McDonald (Temple Of Boom 2011); Kerrin McEvoy (El Cambio 2008); Michelle Payne (Platelet 2013); Nash Rawiller (Stanzout 2007); Glyn Schofield (Hay List 2010); Mark Zahra (Keen Array 2017).
Leading winning trainer: 5 wins Lee Freedman (Falkirk 2005; Rock You 1997; Poetic King 1996; Simonstad 1993; Storaia 1992).
Current winning trainers: 5 wins Lee Freedman (Falkirk 2005; Rock You 1997; Poetic King 1996; Simonstad 1993; Storaia 1992).
2 wins Mathew Ellerton (Recapitalize 2004, Black Bean 1999); Michael, Wayne & John Hawkes (Chautauqua 2015, 2014).
1 win Grahame Begg (All Silent 2009); Russell Cameron (Bomber Bill 2000); Clarry Conners (Belle Du Jour 2001); Colin Davies (Stanzout 2007); Tony Gollan (Temple Of Boom 2011); Robbie Griffiths (The Quarterback 2016); David & Ben Hayes & Tom Dabernig (Keen Array 2017); John McNair (Hay List 2010); John O'Shea (Fast 'N' Famous 2006); Dan O'Sullivan (Cosmic Strike 2002); Gerald Ryan (Racer's Edge 1995); Robert Smerdon (Bomber Bill 2003); Peter Snowden (El Cambio 2008); Gai Waterhouse (Hallowell Belle 2012); Darren Weir (Platelet 2013).
Points of interest: The highest weight carried to win: Bomber Bill (2003) 60.5kg.
Redelva won in 1988, but he also finished second in three consecutive years, 1989-91.
Stanzout (2007) survived a protest from Shadoways.

VRC Rose Of Kingston Stakes (1400m)—Flemington
$200,000 Group 2 4YO&Up Mares SWP. October 6, 2018.

YEAR	WINNER	JOCKEY	TRAINER	2ND	3RD	TIME
2017	Now Or Later	Ryan Maloney	Robert Smerdon	Merriest	Payroll	1:24.3
2016	French Emotion	Ben Melham	Chris Waller	Pure Pride	Vibrant Rouge	1:24.3
2015	La Passe	Michelle Payne	Darren Weir	Manageress	Lucky Lago/Jessy Belle	1:22.9
2014	Forever Loved	Vlad Duric	Gai Waterhouse	Enquare	May's Dream	1:24.8
2013	Fire Up Fifi	Damian Browne	Robert Heathcote	Peron	Catkins	1:23.8
2012	Mosheen	Nicholas Hall	Robert Smerdon	Bonaria	Miss Stellabelle	1:23.4
2011	Lady Lynette	Nicholas Hall	David & Scott Brunton	Booklet	Dysphonia	1:24.1
2010	Palacio De Cristal	Dwayne Dunn	Grahame Begg	No Evidence Needed	Strawberry Field	1:23.9
2009	Cats Whisker	Hugh Bowman	Mark Kavanagh	Gold Water	Dane Julia	1:22.4
2008	Bellini Rose	Chris Symons	Mathew Ellerton	Absolute Glam	Viking Turf Belle	1:24.1
2007	Vormista	Dwayne Dunn	Mark Minervini	Bellini Rose	El Pauji	1:23.9
2006	Divine Madonna	Mark Zahra	Mark Kavanagh	Imana	Open Cut	1:23.3
2005	Sky Cuddle	Luke Nolen	Peter Moody	Dea	Astrodame	1:23.5
2004	Skewiff	Brad Rawiller	Darren Weir	Infinite Grace	Light Sweeper	1:22.4
2003	Vocabulary	Danny Nikolic	Mick Price	Gazania	Galipagos Girl	1:24.1
2002	Hosannah	Darren Gauci	John Hawkes	Gentle Genius	Purple Groove	1:23.8
2001	Tickle My	Mark Flaherty	Bruce Purcell	Hula Wonder	Calm Smytzer	1:25.7

BACKGROUND
First run: 1989 (won by Lady Jess). Listed 1990-96. Group 3 1997-2005. Group 2 from 2006. Registered as the Rose of Kingston Stakes. Also known as the Jayco Stakes, Melbourne Carnival Stakes, Hardy Brothers, Honda Prelude, The Gillette Stakes, The Flag International, UCI Stakes and Blazer Stakes.
Multiple winners: None.
Fastest time (1400m): Skewiff (2004) 1:22:40.
Notable winners: Mosheen (2012); Vormista (2007); Divine Madonna (2006); Sky Cuddle (2005); Skewiff (2004); Will Fly (1997); Chlorophyll (1996); Excited Angel (1993).
Rose Of Kingston Stakes winners won the lead-up races:
Cockram Stakes: 1—Cats Whisker (2009)
Let's Elope Stakes: 2—Cats Whisker (2009); Tolanda (1995).
Rose Of Kingston Stakes winners went on to win in the same preparation:
Tristarc Stakes: 4—La Passe (2015); Will Fly (1997); Chlorophyll (1996); Danjiki (1992).
Myer Classic: 1—Sedately (1994).
Emirates Stakes: 1—Divine Madonna (2006).
Leading winning jockeys: 2 wins Dwayne Dunn (Palacio De Cristal 2010, Vormista 2007); Steven King (Exciting Angel 1993, Lady Jess 1989); Nicholas Hall (Mosheen 2012, Lady Lynette 2011).
Current winning jockeys: 2 wins Dwayne Dunn (Palacio De Cristal 2010, Vormista 2007); Nicholas Hall (Mosheen 2012, Lady Lynette 2011).
1 win Hugh Bowman (Cats Whisker 2009); Damien Browne (Fire Up Fifi 2013); Noel Callow (Ramano's Star 2000); Vlad Duric (Forever Loved 2014); Ryan Maloney (Now Or Later 2017); Ben Melham (French Emotion 2016); Luke Nolen (Sky Cuddle 2005); Damien Oliver (Tolanda 1995); Brett Prebble (Hula Wonder 1999); Brad Rawiller (Skewiff 2004); Craig Williams (Will Fly 1997); Mark Zahra (Divine Madonna 2006).
Leading winning trainer: 2 wins Mark Kavanagh (Cats Whisker 2009, Divine Madonna 2006); Robert Smerdon (Now Or Later 2017, Mosheen 2012).
Current winning trainers: 2 wins Mark Kavanagh (Cats Whisker 2009, Divine Madonna 2006); Robert Smerdon (Now Or Later 2017, Mosheen 2012).
1 win Grahame Begg (Palacio De Cristal 2010); Ricky Bruhn (Sedately 1994); David & Scott Brunton (Lady Lynette 2011); Jim Conlan (Excited Angel 1993); Mat Ellerton (Bellini Rose 2008); Lee Freedman (Tolanda 1995); John Hawkes (Hosannah 2002); Rob Heathcote (Fire Up Fifi 2013); Leon Macdonald (Will Fly 1997); Mark Minervini (Vormista 2007); Mick Price (Vocabulary 2003); Robert Priscott (Danjiki 1992); Bruce Purcell (Tickle My 2001); Steve Richards (Holiday Lover 1991); Gai Waterhouse (Forever Loved 2014); Chris Waller (French Emotion 2016); Darren Weir (Skewiff 2004).
Points of interest: Sky Cuddle (2005) won the Group 1 Emirates Stakes in 2004.
Vormista (2007) finished second to Gold Edition in the Group 1 Manikato Stakes (1200m) at Moonee Valley before winning the Blazer Stakes.

MRC Schillaci Stakes (1100m)—Caulfield
$400,000 Group 2 3YO&Up WFA. October 13, 2018.

YEAR	WINNER	JOCKEY	TRAINER	2ND	3RD	TIME
2017	Super Cash	Katelyn Mallyon	Andrew Noblet	Illustrious Lad	Rock Magic	1:03.2
2016	Star Turn	Craig Williams	Michael, Wayne & John Hawkes	Malaguerra	Fell Swoop	1:02.8
2015	Alpha Miss	Craig Williams	Robert Smerdon	Cashed	Lankan Rupee	1:03.5
2014	Rubick	Kerrin McEvoy	Gerald Ryan	Platelet	Overreach	0:56.6
2013	Unpretentious	Damien Oliver	Nikki Burke	Pago Rock	Kuroshio	0:57.6
2012	Buffering	Hugh Bowman	Robert Heathcote	Golden Archer	Stirling Grove	0:56.9
2011	Black Caviar	Luke Nolen	Peter Moody	Karuta Queen	Stirling Grove	0:56.7
2010	Black Caviar	Luke Nolen	Peter Moody	Winter King	General Truce	0:56.6
2009	Lucky Secret	Nash Rawiller	Tony Vasil	Apache Cat	Wanted	0:55.9
2008	Wilander	Kerrin McEvoy	Lee Freedman	Lucky Secret	Gamble Me	0:58.0
2007	Gold Edition	Stathi Katsidis	Ron Maund	Royal Asscher	Let Go Thommo	0:57.3
2006	Miss Andretti	Damien Oliver	Lee Freedman	Green Birdie	Nediyms Glow	0:57.2
2005	Segments	Scott Seamer	Peter Moody	Danerich	Miss Mooney Mooney	0:57.6
2004	Patpong	Damien Oliver	Tony Wildman	Alizes	Regimental Gal	0:58.2
2003	Halibery	Craig Newitt	Mick Price	Dantana	Spinning Hill	0:56.7
2002	Spinning Hill	Patrick Payne	Guy Walter	Falvelon	Mistegic	0:57.1
2001	Mistegic	Glen Boss	Lee Curtis	Windigo	Falvelon	0:57.6

BACKGROUND

First run: 1970 (won by Regal Vista). Group 2 since 1979. Run over 1200m 1970-1986; 1000m 1987-2014. Run at Sandown in 1986. Also known as the Chirnside Stakes.
Most recent mare to win: Super Cash (2017). Note: 15 mares have won.
Most recent 3YO to win: C&G – Star Turn (2016); Filly – Halibery (2003); Note: Seven 3YOs have won the Schillaci.
Multiple winners: 2—Black Caviar (2011, 2010); Street Ruffian (1991, 1990).
Fastest time (1100m): Star Turn (2016) 1:02:89.
Notable winners: Buffering (2012); Black Caviar (2011, 2010); Gold Edition (2007); Miss Andretti (2006); Spinning Hill (2002); Falvelon (2000); Mahogany (1997); Sequalo (Dead heat 1996); Bint Marscay (1994); Rancho Ruler (1988); Mr. Magic (1979); The Judge (1978); Desirable (1977); Tontonan (1975); Tolerance (1972).
Schillaci Stakes winners won the lead-up races:
San Domenico Stakes: 2—Star Turn (2016); Mistegic (2001).
Ian McEwen Stakes: 1—Miss Andretti (2006).
Bobbie Lewis Quality: 1—Street Ruffian (1991).
Gilgai Stakes: None.
Moir Stakes: 6—Spinning Hill (2002); Mistegic (2001); Falvelon (2000); Magic Music (1999); Show No Emotion (1998); The Judge (1978). Note: before 2013 the Moir was run on Cox Plate day, after the Schillaci Stakes.
Schillaci Stakes winners went on to win in the same preparation:
Manikato Stakes: 6—Gold Edition (2007); Miss Andretti (2006); Spinning Hill (2002); King Marauding (1992); Street Ruffian (1990); Rancho Ruler (1988). Note: from 2013, the Manikato was moved from before the Schillaci Stakes to Cox Plate Eve.
Linlithgow Stakes: 1—Galleon (1982).
VRC Classic: 2—Black Caviar (2011, 2010).
Leading winning jockey: 5 wins Damien Oliver (Unpretentious 2013, Miss Andretti 2006, Patpong 2004, Falvelon 2000, Magic Music 1999).
Current winning jockeys: 5 wins Damien Oliver (Unpretentious 2013, Miss Andretti 2006, Patpong 2004, Falvelon 2000, Magic Music 1999).
2 wins Kerrin McEvoy (Rubick 2014, Wilander 2008); Luke Nolen (Black Caviar 2011, 2010); Nash Rawiller (Lucky Secret 2009, Show No Emotion 1998); Craig Williams (Star Turn 2016, Alpha Miss 2015).
1 win Glen Boss (Mistegic 2001); Hugh Bowman (Buffering 2012); Dwayne Dunn (Toledo 1998); Kevin Forrester (Belle Spirit 1986); Katelyn Mallyon (Super Cash 2017); Craig Newitt (Halibery 2003).
Leading winning trainers: 4 wins Lee Freedman (Wilander 2008, Miss Andretti 2006, Mahogany 1997, Bint Marscay 1994).
3 wins Colin Hayes (Scarlet Bisque 1989, Galleon 1982, Desirable 1977); Peter Moody (Black Caviar 2011, 2010, Segments 2005).
Current winning trainers: 4 wins Lee Freedman (Wilander 2008, Miss Andretti 2006, Mahogany 1997, Bint Marscay 1994).
2 wins Russell Cameron (Toledo 1998, 1997).
1 win Danny Bougoure (Falvelon 2000); Nikki Burke (Unpretentious 2013); Leon Corstens (Magic Music 1999); Michael, Wayne & John Hawkes (Star Turn 2016); Robert Heathcote (Buffering 2012); Andrew Noblet (Super

Cash 2017); Paul Perry (Notoire 1999); Mick Price (Halibery 2003); Gerald Ryan (Rubick 2014); Robert Smerdon (Alpha Miss 2015); Tony Vasil (Lucky Secret 2009).
Points of interest: Bint Marscay (1994) and Tontonan (1975) are the only Golden Slipper winners to win the Schillaci Stakes. Tolerance (1972) is the only Blue Diamond Stakes winner to win the Schillaci. Champion sprinter Schillaci did not win a Schillaci (formerly Chirnside) Stakes.
Sequalo and Sword dead-heated for first in 1996. In 2001, Mistegic was disqualified for returning a positive swab, but reinstated on appeal.

MRC Herbert Power Stakes (2400m)—Caulfield
$400,000 Group 2 Quality Handicap. October 13, 2018.

YEAR	WINNER	JOCKEY	TRAINER	2ND	3RD	TIME
2017	Lord Fandango	Ben Allen	Archie Alexander	Wall Of Fire	Gallic Chieftain	2:27.6
2016	Assign	Katelyn Mallyon	Robert Hickmott	Big Memory	Pemberley	2:29.1
2015	Amralah	Hugh Bowman	Robert Hickmott	Excess Knowledge	Bohemian Lily	2:27.7
2014	Big Memory	Tommy Berry	Tony McEvoy	Signoff	Let's Make A Deal	2:26.6
2013	Sea Moon	Hugh Bowman	Robert Hickmott	Oasis Bloom	Simenon	2:29.9
2012	Shahwardi	Kerrin McEvoy	Alain De Royer Dupre	Excluded	Exceptionally	2:28.8
2011	Shewan	Chris Symons	Robert Smerdon	Tanby	Moyenne Corniche	2:30.7
2010	Linton	Nicholas Hall	Robert Hickmott	Cedarberg	Precedence	2:29.4
2009	Alcopop	Dom Tourneur	Jake Stephens	Shocking	Hissing Sid	2:27.2
2008	Dolphin Jo	Clare Lindop	Terry & Karina O'sullivan	The Wolverine	Cefalu	2:30.2
2007	Master O'reilly	Vlad Duric	Danny O'Brien	Zavite	Reggie	2:30.0
2006	Growl	Craig Williams	David Hayes	Dracs Back	Siamun	2:29.3
2005	Leica Falcon	Craig Williams	Richard Freyer	Sarrera	Hugs Dancer (Fr)	2:29.5
2004	Rizon	Corey Brown	Cliff Brown	Grey Song	Zazzman	2:31.7
2003	Yakama	Damien Oliver	Bevan Laming	Physique	Vicksburg	2:30.7
2002	The Secondmortgage	Kerrin McEvoy	Michael Moroney	Requiem	Thong Classic	2:29.8
2001	Freemason	Darren Gauci	John Hawkes	The Secondmortgage	Rain Gauge	2:30.7

BACKGROUND
First run: 1898 (won by Cocos). Group 1979 & 1980. Group 2 since 1981. Run at weight for age with penalties and allowances from 1898 to 1934. Handicap from 1935. Run over 1600m 1898-99; 2200m 1900-19. Also known as the Quick-Eze Stakes, Perrier Mineral Water Stakes and, originally, the Eclipse Stakes (1898-1919).
Most recent mare to win: Yakama (2003).
Most recent 3YO to win: C&G—Taisho (1929); No filly has won.
Multiple winners: 8—Durham (1952, 1951); Dashing Beau (1950, 1949); Royal Charter (1927, 1925); Easingwold (1924, 1923); Anna Carlovna (1914, 1913); Alawa (1909, 1908); Poseidon (1907, 1906); Wakeful (1903, 1902).
Fastest time (2400m): Rogan Josh (1999) 2:27.63
Notable winners: Sea Moon (2013); Linton (2010); Rogan Josh (1999); Just A Dancer (1990); Arwon (1978); Van Der Hum (1976); Gala Supreme (1973); Gala Crest (1966); Rising Fast (1955); Wodalla (1954); Sirius (1944); Colonus (1942); Shadow King (1931); Easingwold (1924, 1923); Eurythmic (1921); Comedy King (1911); Poseidon (1907, 1906); Wakeful (1903, 1902).
Herbert Power Handicap winners won the lead-up races:
JRA Cup: 1—Alcopop (2009).
Heatherlie Handicap: 2—Growl (2006); Gala Supreme (1973).
Naturalism Stakes: 1—Just A Dancer (1990).
Caulfield Cup: 6—Master O'Reilly (2007); Beer Street (1970); Rising Fast (1955); My Hero (1953); Poseidon (1907); Marvel Loch (1905).
Lexus Stakes: 5—Scotch And Dry (1972); Fighting Force (1956); My Hero (1953); Howe (1948); Sirius (1944).
Melbourne Cup: 6—Rogan Josh (1999); Arwon (1978); Van Der Hum (1976); Gala Supreme (1973); Colonus (1942); Poseidon (1906).
Leading winning jockeys: 5 wins Bobby Lewis (Second Wind 1930, Outlook 1918, Cyklon 1916, Alawa 1909, Cocos 1898); Jack Purtell (Fighting Force 1956, Wodalla 1954, Durham 1952, 1951, Dashing Beau 1950).
3 wins Hughie Cairns (The Banker 1926, Easingwold 1923, Purser 1922); Billy Duncan (Scalpel 1932, Royal Charter 1927, 1925); Darren Gauci (Freemason 2001, Rogan Josh 1999, Congressman 1988).
Current winning jockeys: 2 wins Hugh Bowman (Amralah 2015, Sea Moon 2013); Kerrin McEvoy (Shahwardi 2012, The Secondmortgage 2002); Craig Williams (Growl 2006, Leica Falcon 2005).
1 win Ben Allan (Lord Fandango 2017); Tommy Berry (Big Memory 2014); Glen Boss (Majestic Avenue 2000);

Corey Brown (Rizon 2004); Vlad Duric (Master O'Reilly 2007); Nick Hall (Linton 2010); Clare Lindop (Dolphin Jo 2008); Katelyn Mallyon (Assign 2016); Damien Oliver (Yakama 2003); Chris Symons (Shewan 2011); Dom Tourneur (Alcopop 2009).
Leading winning trainers: 8 wins Jack Holt (Mac Rob 1943, Second Wind 1930, Royal Charter 1927, 1925, Easingwold 1924, 1923, Eurythmic 1921, Tangalooma 1920).
4 wins Colin Hayes (Cossack Warrior 1987, Colonial Flag 1984, Impetus 1968, Pandie Sun 1957); Robert Hickmott (Assign 2016, Amralah 2015; Sea Moon 2013, Linton 2010); Ernie Willmott (Durham 1952, 1951, Dashing Beau 1950, 1949).
Current winning trainers: 4 wins Robert Hickmott (Assign 2016, Amralah 2015; Sea Moon 2013, Linton 2010).
2 wins Tony Noonan (Majestic Avenue 2000, Magneto 1998); Graeme Rogerson (Just A Dancer 1990, Nostradamus 1983).
1 win Archie Alexander (Lord Fandango 2017); Cliff Brown (Rizon 2004); Alain de Royer Dupre (Shahwardi 2012); Lee Freedman (Solo Show 1994); John Hawkes (Freemason 2001); David Hayes (Growl 2006); Bevan Laming (Yakama 2003); Tony McEvoy (Big Memory 2014); John Meagher (Nayrizi 1989); Mike Moroney (The Secondmortgage 2002); Danny O'Brien (Master O'Reilly 2007); Katrina & Terry O'Sullivan (Dolphin Jo 2008); Robert Smerdon (Shewan 2011); Brian Smith (Pharostan 1986); Jake Stevens (Alcopop 2009); John Wheeler (The Bandette 1996).
Points of interest: Arwon went close to winning the Herbert Power, Caulfield Cup and Melbourne Cup treble in 1978. He won the Herbert Power and the Melbourne Cup, but he was beaten a lip by Taksan in the Caulfield Cup.
The heaviest weight carried to win: Royal Charter (1927) 62kg (SW&P). Rising Fast's 61kg (handicap) to win is the Herbert Power Handicap is the heaviest since 1940.
Billy Duncan rode four winners (see above) and trained Rex Felt to win in 1940.

MRC Caulfield Sprint (1100m)—Caulfield
$200,000 Group 2 Open Handicap. October 20, 2018.

YEAR	WINNER	JOCKEY	TRAINER	2ND	3RD	TIME
2017	Snitty Kitty	Beau Mertens	Henry Dwyer	Super Too	Faatinah	0:56.2
2016	Our Boy Malachi	Dwayne Dunn	Michael, Wayne & John Hawkes	Faatinah	Lankan Rupee	0:57.7
2015	DH Lumosty/Éclair Choice	Dwayne Dunn/Dom Tourneur	Robert Smerdon/Phillip Stokes	Ball Of Muscle		0:57.4
2014	DH Miracles Of Life/Bel Sprinter	Hugh Bowman/Ben Melham	Peter & Paul Snowden/Jason Warren	Shamal Wind		1:04.3
2013	Spirit Of Boom	Nicholas Hall	Ton Gollan	Shamal Wind	Ready To Rip	1:04.7
2012	Howmuchdoyouloveme	Brenton Avdulla	Con Karakatsanis	Canali	Latin News	1:03.1
2011	Sepoy	Kerrin McEvoy	Peter Snowden	Curtana	Mid Summer Music	1:03.1
2010	Set For Fame	Luke Nolen	Peter Moody	Dubleanny	Soul	1:05.4
2009	First Command	Dwayne Dunn	Lee Freedman	Turffontein	Happy Glen	1:04.2
2008	Sunburnt Land	Chris Symons	Mathew Ellerton	Aichi	Biscayne Bay	1:03.6
2007	Tesbury Jack	Darren Gauci	Julie Scott	Typhoon Zed	Let Go Thommo	1:02.5
2006	Biscayne Bay	Greg Childs	Paul Perry	Magnus	Rightson	1:02.4
2005	Jet Spur	Stephen Baster	John O'Shea	Dance The Waves	Mustard	1:02.1
2004	Lilando	Corey Brown	Andrew Noblet	Dilly Dally	Strikeline	1:04.0
2003	Blur	Steven King	Colin Little	Ancient Song	Suit	1:03.5
2002	Rubitano	Nash Rawiller	Brian Mayfield-Smith	Intelligent Star	Pembleton	1:03.0
2001	Windigo	Nash Rawiller	Ramon Goldsmith	Crystal Finale	Point Danger	1:04.0

BACKGROUND
First run: 1983 (won by Bow Mistress). Listed 1983-92. Group 3 1993-98. Group 2 from 1999.
Run over 1100m 1983-2014. Also known as the Thai Airways International Stakes.
Most recent mare to win: Snitty Kitty (2017). Note: six mares have won.
Most recent 3YO to win: C & G—Sepoy (2011); No filly has won. Note: Jet Spur (2005) and Campaign King (1985) is the only other 3YOs to win.
Multiple winners: 1—Toledo (1998, 1997).
Fastest time (1000m): Snitty Kitty (2017) 56.28 secs
Notable winners: Miracles Of Life (DH 2014); Sepoy (2011); Rubitano (2002); Toledo (1998, 1997); Ruffles (1996); Schillaci (1994); Euclase (1991); Campaign King (1985); River Rough (1984).
Caulfield Sprint winners won the lead-up races:
Danehill Stakes: 1—Sepoy (2011).

Gilgai Stakes: None
Schillaci Stakes: None
Caulfield Sprint winners went on to win in the same preparation:
VRC Sprint Classic: 2—Rubitano (2002); River Rough (1984).
Linlithgow Stakes: 3—Eclair Choice (2015); Toledo (1998); Tanjian Prince (1992).
Leading winning jockeys: 4 wins Dwayne Dunn (Our Boy Malachi 2016, Lumosty 2015, First Command 2009, Toledo 1997);
3 wins Darren Gauci (Tesbury Jack 2007, Bullion Broker 1986, River Rough 1984).
Current winning jockeys: 4 wins Dwayne Dunn (Our Boy Malachi 2016, Lumosty 2015, First Command 2009, Toledo 1997).
2 wins Stephen Baster (Jet Spur 2005, Royal Discard 2003); Nash Rawiller (Rubitano 2002, Windago 2001);
1 win Brenton Avdulla (Howmuchdoyouloveme 2012); Hugh Bowman (Miracles Of Life 2014); Corey Brown (Lilando 2004); Jim Byrne (Camena 2000); Nick Hall (Spirit Of Boom 2013); Kerrin McEvoy (Sepoy 2011); Ben Melham (Bel Sprinter 2015*); Beau Mertens (Snitty Kitty 2017); Damien Oliver (Schillaci 1994); Luke Nolen (Set For Fame 2010); Chris Symons (Sunburnt Lad 2008); Domenic Tourneur (Eclair Choice 2015*)
Leading winning trainers: 2 wins Russell Cameron (Toledo 1998, 1997); Lee Freedman (First Command 2009, Schillaci 1994); Paul Perry (Biscayne Bay 2006, Notoire 1999); Peter Snowden (Miracles Of Life 2014*, Sepoy 2011).
Current winning trainers: 2 wins Russell Cameron (Toledo 1998, 1997); Lee Freedman (First Command 2009, Schillaci 1994); Paul Perry (Biscayne Bay 2006, Notoire 1999); Peter Snowden (Miracles Of Life 2014*, Sepoy 2011).
1 win Henry Dwyer (Snitty Kitty 2017); Mat Ellerton (Sunburnt Lad 2008); Tony Gollan (Spirit Of Boom 2013); Michael, Wayne & John Hawkes (Our Boy Malachi 2016); Con Karakatsanis (Howmuchdoyouloveme 2012); Colin Little (Blur 2003); Tony Logan (Lord Scotia 1987); Andrew Noblet (Lilando 2004); John O'Shea (Jet Spur 2005); Gerald Ryan (Camena 2000); Julie Scott (Tesbury Jack 2007); Robert Smerdon (Lumosty 2015*); Peter & Paul Snowden (Miracles Of Life 2014*); Phillip Stokes (Eclair Choice 2015*); Jason Warren (Bel Sprinter 2014*). *dead-heat
Point of interest: Heaviest weight carried to win: Toledo (1998) & River Rough (1984) 58.5kg.
Consecutive dead-heats for first in 2014 and 2014 (see past winners table).

MRC Tristarc Stakes (1400m)—Caulfield
$200,000 Group 2 4YO&Up Mares SWP. October 20, 2018.

YEAR	WINNER	JOCKEY	TRAINER	2ND	3RD	TIME
2017	Global Glamour	Tim Clark	Gai Waterhouse & Adrian Bott	Cool Passion	Shillelagh	1:23.8
2016	First Seal	Blake Shinn	John Thompson	Tycoon Tara	Pearls	1:25.1
2015	La Passe	Michelle Payne	Darren Weir	Solicit	Jessy Belle	1:23.7
2014	Sweet Idea	Tommy Berry	Gai Waterhouse	Girl Guide	Catkins	1:25.4
2013	Red Tracer	Nash Rawiller	Chris Waller	Koonoomoo	Ava's Delight	1:23.1
2012	Streama	Hugh Bowman	Guy Walter	Pear Tart	Red Tracer	1:24.7
2011	More Joyous	Nash Rawiller	Gai Waterhouse	Sister Madly	Response	1:22.8
2010	Culminate	Michael Walker	Darren Weir	Jersey Lily	Marquardt	1:26.5
2009	Typhoon Tracy	Luke Nolen	Peter Moody	Hot Danish	Glowlamp	1:22.8
2008	Mimi Lebrock	Michael Rodd	Bart Cummings	Tan Tat De Lago	Absolutely Fabulous	1:23.3
2007	Miss Fantabulous	Michael Rodd	David Hayes	Bellini Rose	Like It Is	1:23.0
2006	Nuclear Free	Darren Beadman	John Blacker	Belle Bizarre	Divine Madonna	1:23.0
2005	Infinite Grace	Scott Seamer	John Symons	Candy Vale	Storm Alert	1:22.1
2004	Our Egyptian Raine	Nash Rawiller	Grahame Begg	Infinite Grace	Skewiff	1:24.5
2003	Infinite Grace	Greg Childs	John Symons	Forum Floozie	Faith Hill	1:23.0
2002	Reactive	Reece Wheeler	Brian Mayfield-Smith	Gentle Genius	Taimana	1:23.6
2001	Pernod	Kerrin McEvoy	Michael Moroney	Kaemess	Calm Smyzer	1:24.2

BACKGROUND
First run: 1987 (won by Canny Lass). Listed 1987-93. Group 3 1994-2005. Group 2 since 2006.
Multiple winners: 1—Infinite Grace (2005, 2003).
Fastest time (1400m): Infinite Grace (2005) 1:22.19
Notable winners: Global Glamour (2017); First Seal (2016); Sweet Idea (2014), Red Tracer (2012), More Joyous (2011); Typhoon Tracy (2009); Infinite Grace (2005, 2003); Our Egyptian Raine (2004); Reactive (2002); Pernod (2001); Bonanova (1999); Camino Rose (1998); Chlorophyll (1996); Procrastinate (1994); Danjiki (1992); Whistling (1989); Canny Lass (1987).
Tristarc Stakes winners won the lead-up races:
Cockram Stakes: 1—Pernod (2002).

Let's Elope Stakes: 1—Mimi Lebrock (2008).
Rose Of Kingston (Blazer) Stakes: 4—La Passe (2015); Will Fly (1997); Chlorophyll (1996); Danjiki (1992).
Tristarc Stakes winners went on to win in the same preparation:
Myer Classic: 3—Typhoon Tracy (2009); Red Tracer (2013) Mingling Glances (1993).
Leading winning jockeys: 3 wins Nash Rawiller (Red Tracer 2013), More Joyous 2011, Our Egyptian Raine 2004).
2 wins Darren Beadman (Nuclear Free 2006, Whistling 1989); Simon Marshall (Chlorophyll 1996, Ice Cream Sundae 1990); Kerrin McEvoy (Pernod 2001, Lady Marion 2000); Michael Rodd (Mimi Lebrock 2008, Miss Fantabulous 2007).
Current winning jockeys: 3 wins Nash Rawiller (Red Tracer 2013), More Joyous 2011, Our Egyptian Raine 2004).
2 wins Kerrin McEvoy (Pernod 2001, Lady Marion 2000); Michael Rodd (Mimi Lebrock 2008, Miss Fantabulous 2007).
1 win Tommy Berry (Sweet Idea 2014); Glen Boss (Bionic Bess 1995); Hugh Bowman (Streama 2012); Tim Clark (Global Glamour 2017); Luke Nolen (Typhoon Tracy 2009); Michelle Payne (La Passe 2015); Blake Shinn (First Seal 2016); Michael Walker (Culminate 2010); Reece Wheeler (Reactive 2002); Craig Williams (Will Fly 1997); Eddie Wilkinson (Camino Rose 1998).
Leading winning trainers: 3 wins Gai Waterhouse (Global Glamour 2017, Sweet Idea 2014, More Joyous 2011).
2 wins Grahame Begg (Our Egyptian Raine 2004, Bonanova 1999); Darren Weir (La Passe 2015, Culminate 2010).
Current winning trainers: 3 wins Gai Waterhouse (Global Glamour 2017, Sweet Idea 2014, More Joyous 2011).
2 wins Grahame Begg (Our Egyptian Raine 2004, Bonanova 1999); Darren Weir (La Passe 2015, Culminate 2010).
1 win John Blacker (Nuclear Free 2006); Paul Cave (Mingling Glances 1993); Marc Conners (Camino Rose 1998); David Hall (Procrastinate 1994); David Hayes (Miss Fantabulous 2007); Leon Macdonald (Will Fly 1997); Mike Moroney (Pernod 2001): Tony Noonan (Bionic Bess 1995); Robert Priscott (Danjiki 1992); John Symons (Infinite Grace 2005); John Thompson (First Seal 2016); Chris Waller (Red Tracer 2013); Gai Waterhouse & Adrian Bott (Global Glamour 2017).
Point of interest: Infinite Grace (2005, 2003) also finished second to Our Egyptian Raine in 2004.

MVRC The MV Vase (2040m)—Moonee Valley
$200,000 Group 2 3YO Open SWP. October 27, 2018.

YEAR	WINNER	JOCKEY	TRAINER	2ND	3RD	TIME
2017	Aloisia	Luke Nolen	Aaron Purcell	Cliff's Edge	Salsamor	2:04.2
2016	Sacred Elixir	Damian Lane	Tony Pike	Morvada	So Si Bon	2:10.9
2015	Jameka	Damien Oliver	Ciaron Maher	Shards	Tarzino	2:06.0
2014	Moonovermanhattan	Craig Newitt	Mick Price	Atmosphere	Go Indy Go	2:06.4
2013	Savvy Nature	James McDonald	John O'Shea	All Rigged Up	Pinstripe Lane	2:05.0
2012	Super Cool	Michael Rodd	Mark Kavanagh	It's A Dundeel	Viking Star	2:08.2
2011	Manawanui	Glyn Schofield	Ron Leemon	Collar	Scelto	2:07.1
2010	Rekindled Interest	Dwayne Dunn	Jim Conlan	Lion Tamer	Hollowlea	2:07.0
2009	Hanks	Luke Nolen	Peter Moody	Spacecraft	Viking Legend	2:06.2
2008	Whobegotyou	Michael Rodd	Mark Kavanagh	Buffett	Orca	2:05.3
2007	Marching	Damien Oliver	John Hawkes	Kibbutz	Barbaricus	2:06.5
2006	Efficient	Michael Rodd	Graeme Rogerson	The One	Excites	2:05.2
2005	Duelled	Kerrin McEvoy	Graeme Rogerson	Manton	Benicio	2:14.1
2004	Plastered	Paul Harvey	Lindsey Smith	Mr Martini	Count Ricardo	2:07.6
2003	Kempinsky	Kerrin McEvoy	Mick Price	Elvstroem	Lifes A Bounty	2:07.1
2002	Helenus	Steven King	Leon Corstens	Macedon Lady	Wild Heart	2:08.0
2001	Ustinov	Patrick Payne	Bart Cummings	Viking Ruler	Pure Theatre	2:06.3
2000	Skalato	Patrick Payne	Clarry Conners	Universal Prince	Sale Of Century	2:09.2

BACKGROUND
First run: 1981 (won by Vinaka). Listed 1983-88. Group 3 1989-96. Group 2 since 1997.
Run over 1600m 1983-85. Also known as the AAMI Vase and the The Herald Vase.
Most recent filly to win: Aloisia (2017). Note: Jameka (2015) and Rockets Galore (1990) is the only other fillies to win.
Fastest time (2040m): Blevic (1994) 2:02.80
Notable winners: Aloisia (2017); Jameka (2015); Whobegotyou (2008); Efficient (2006); Plastered (2004); Helenus (2002); Diatribe (1999); Gold Guru (1997); Alfa (1996); Blevic (1994); Naturalism (1991); Raveneaux (1986); Centaine (1983).
The MV Vase winners also won the lead-up races:

The Golden Rose: 1—Manawanui (2011).
Newcastle Spring Stakes: 1—Savvy Nature (2013).
Guineas Prelude: 1—Sacred Elixir (2016).
Stutt Stakes: 4—Whobegotyou (2008); Helenus (2002); Diatribe (1999); Blevic (1994).
Caulfield Guineas: 3—Whobegotyou (2008); Helenus (2002); Alfa (1996).
Thousand Guineas: 1—Aloisia (2017).
Caulfield Classic: None.
The MV Vase winners went on to win in the same preparation:
Victoria Derby: 5—Efficient (2006); Plastered (2004); Helenus (2002); Blevic (1994); Raveneaux (1986).
VRC Oaks: 1—Jameka (2015).
The MV Vase and the autumn features:
Australian Cup: 1—Super Cool (season 2012-13).
ATC Australian Derby (following April): 2—Gold Guru (season 1997-98); Naturalism (1991-92).
Leading winning jockeys: 4 wins Damien Oliver (Jameka 2015, Marching 2007, Gold Guru 1997, Naturalism 1991)
3 wins Mick Dittman (Blevic 1994, Kenny's Best Pal 1992, Big Grey Roo 1988); Greg Hall (Diatribe 1999, Crush 1987, Brash Son 1984); Michael Rodd (Super Cool 2012, Whobegotyou 2008, Efficient 2006)
Current winning jockeys: 4 wins Damien Oliver (Jameka 2015, Marching 2007, Gold Guru 1997, Naturalism 1991)
3 wins Michael Rodd (Super Cool 2012, Whobegotyou 2008, Efficient 2006)
2 wins Kerrin McEvoy (Duelled 2005, Kempsinky 2003); Luke Nolen (Aloisia 2017, Hanks 2009).
1 win Dwayne Dunn (Rekindled Interest 2010); Paul Harvey (Plastered 2004); Damian Lane (Sacred Elixir 2016); James McDonald (Savvy Nature 2013); Craig Newitt (Moonovermanhattan 2014); Glyn Schofield (Manawanui 2011).
Leading winning trainers: 3 wins Bart Cummings (Ustinov 2001, Alfa 1996, Zamoff 1989).
2 wins Clarry Conners (Skalato 2000, Mossman 1998); John Hawkes (Marching 2007, Donar 1995); Mark Kavanagh (Super Cool 2012, Whobegotyou 2008); John Meagher (Rockets Galore 1990, Crush 1987); Mick Price (Moonovermanhattan 2014, Kempinsky 2003); Graeme Rogerson (Efficient 2006, Duelled 2005).
Current winning trainers: 2 wins Clarry Conners (Skalato 2000, Mossman 1998); John Hawkes (Marching 2007, Donar 1995); Mark Kavanagh (Super Cool 2012, Whobegotyou 2008); John Meagher (Rockets Galore 1990, Crush 1987); Mick Price (Moonovermanhattan 2014, Kempsinky 2003); Graeme Rogerson (Efficient 2006, Duelled 2005).
1 win Jim Conlan (Rekindled Interest 2010); Leon Corstens (Helenus 2002); Lee Freedman (Naturalism 1991); David Hayes (Blevic 1994); Ron Leemon (Manawanui 2011); Leon Macdonald (Gold Guru 1997); Ciaron Maher (Jameka 2015); Tony Pike (Sacred Elixir 2016); Aaron Purcell (Aloisia 2017); John O'Shea (Savvy Nature 2013); Lindsey Smith (Plastered 2004).
Points of interest: Since the AAMI Vase was increased from 1600m to 2040m in 1986, 15 Victoria Derby winners have had their final lead-up run in the Vase—the most recent was Tarzino in 2015.
Diatribe (1999) won the 2000 Caulfield Cup.

MVRC Moonee Valley Fillies Classic (1600m)—Moonee Valley
$200,000 Group 2 3YO Fillies SW. October 27, 2018.

YEAR	WINNER	JOCKEY	TRAINER	2ND	3RD	TIME
2017	Banish	Craig Williams	James Cummings	I'll Have A Bit	Touch Of Mink	1:36.5
2016	Nurse Kitchen	Kerrin McEvoy	David Brideoake	Sezanne	I Am A Star	1:40.0
2015	My Poppette	Mark Zahra	Robert Smerdon	Bengal Cat	Thames Court	1:36.3
2014	Lumosty	Nicholas Hall	Robert Smerdon	Tahni Dancer	Berimbau	1:37.3
2013	Gypsy Diamond	James McDonald	John O'Shea	Gregers	Lady Tatia	1:38.7
2012	Kazanluk	Kerrin McEvoy	Anthony Freedman	Stella Lante	Moreau	1:38.3
2012	Empress Rock	Steven Arnold	Bart Cummings	Toal Attraction	Our Miss Jones	1:36.8
2011	Lights Of Heaven	Luke Nolen	Peter Moody	Always Discreet	Absolutely	1:35.6
2010	My Emotion	Craig Williams	Mick Kent	Speedy Natalie	Aloha	1:36.4
2009	Romneya	Kerrin McEvoy	Lee Freedman	Lamarr	Turquia	1:30.6
2008	Absolut Glam	Steven King	Danny O'Brien	Miss Marielle	Arapaho Miss	1:30.3
2007	Anamato	Michael Rodd	David Hayes	Deloraine	De Lago Mist	1:31.0
2006	Pure Harmony	Noel Callow	Mick Price	Pinezero	Pasikatera	1:30.8
2005	Dizelle	Darren Gauci	John Hawkes	Hollow Bullet	Truly Wicked	1:37.2
2004	Special Harmony	Brett Prebble	Lee Freedman	Demerger	Sunnah	2:07.2
2003	Ribe	Danny Nikolic	Lee Freedman	Lashed	Thurman	2:09.9
2002	Elegant Fashion	Greg Childs	Tony McEvoy	Damaschino	Gold Lottery	2:07.8
2001	Dandify	Brett Prebble	Jack Denham	Tanith	Lovelorn	2:10.5

BACKGROUND

First run: 1996 (won by Just A Runner). Listed in 1998. Group 3 1999-2000. Group 2 from 2001.
Run over 2040m 1996-2004; 1600m 2005. Previously known as the Moonee Valley Oaks. Run in March until 2005 when moved to February. Moved to Cox Plate day in October in 2012—run twice in 2012.
Fastest time (1500m): Absolut Glam (2008) 1:30:31.
Notable winners: Lumosty (2014); Lights Of Heaven (2011); Anamato (2007); Dizelle (2005); Special Harmony (2004); Elegant Fashion (2002); Sunline (1999); Champagne & Kensington Palace (dead-heat 1998).
MV Fillies Classic and the VRC Oaks:
VRC Oaks (spring) & MV Fillies Classic (autumn): 2—Special Harmony (2004); Kensington Palace (1998).
MV Fillies Classic winners won the lead-up races:
Kevin Hayes Stakes: 1—Absolut Glam (2008)
The Vanity: 1—Romneya (2009).
MV Fillies Classic winners went on to win in the same preparation (information relates to time before the race was moved from the autumn to the spring in 2012):
Kewney Stakes: 2—Empress Rock (2012); Anamato (2007). Note: Special Harmony (2004), Elegant Fashion (2002) and Sunline (1999) won the double when the Kewney was run before the MV Fillies Classic, which then was run over 2040m.
Armanasco Stakes: None. Note: Special Harmony (2004), Elegant Fashion (2002) and Champagne (1998) won the double when the Armanasco was run before the MV Fillies Classic (1500m), which then was run over 2040m.
Australian Oaks: 1—Dizelle (2005).
Australasian Oaks: 2—Lights Of Heaven (2011); Anamato (2007).
Leading winning jockeys: 3 wins Greg Childs (Elegant Fashion 2002, Sunline 1999, Champagne 1998); Brett Prebble (Special Harmony 2004, Dandify 2001, Hill Of Grace 2000).
Current winning jockeys: 3 wins Kerrin McEvoy (Nurse Kitchen 2016, Kazanluk Oct. 2012, Romneya 2009); Brett Prebble (Special Harmony 2004, Dandify 2001, Hill Of Grace 2000).
2 wins Craig Williams (Banish 2017, My Emotion 2010).
1 win Steven Arnold (Empress Rock Mar. 2012); Noel Callow (Pure Harmony 2006); Nick Hall (Lumosty 2015); James McDonald (Gypsy Diamond 2014); Luke Nolen (Lights Of Heaven 2011); Michael Rodd (Anamato 2007); Mark Zahra (My Poppette 2016).
Leading winning trainer: 5 wins Lee Freedman (Romneya 2009, Special Harmony 2004, Ribe 2003, Kensington Palace 1998, Just A Runner 1996).
Current winning trainers: 5 wins Lee Freedman (Romneya 2009, Special Harmony 2004, Ribe 2003, Kensington Palace 1998, Just A Runner 1996).
2 wins Robert Smerdon (My Poppette 2016, Lumosty 2015).
1 win David Brideoake (Nurse Kitchen 2016); James Cummings (Banish 2017); Anthony Freedman (Kazanluk Oct. 2012); David Hall (Star Cossack 1997); David Hayes (Anamato 2007); John Hawkes (Dizelle 2005); Mick Kent (My Emotion 2010); Laurie Laxon (Champagne 1998); Tony McEvoy (Elegant Fashion 2002); Danny O'Brien (Absolut Glam 2008); Mick Price (Pure Harmony 2006); Robert Priscott (Hill Of Grace 2000); John O'Shea (Gypsy Diamond 2014).
Point of interest: Anamato (2007) went on to finish third in the Group 1 American Oaks (2000m) at Hollywood Park in July 2007.

MVRC Crystal Mile (1600m)—Moonee Valley
$200,000 Group 2 Open Handicap. October 27, 2018.

YEAR	WINNER	JOCKEY	TRAINER	2ND	3RD	TIME
2017	Lucky Hussler	Blake Shinn	Darren Weir	Religify	It's Somewhat	1:34.5
2016	The United States	Kerrin McEvoy	Robert Hickmott	Lidari	Ulmann	1:39.7
2015	Turn Me Loose	Opie Bosson	Murray Baker	Bow Creek	Lucky Hussler	1:35.0
2014	Hooked	Craig Williams	John P Thompson	Bull Point	Desert Jeuney	1:34.9
2013	Toydini	Blake Shinn	Guy Walter	Speediness	Sacred Falls	1:36.0
2012	Silent Achiever	James McDonald	Roger James	Rangirangdoo	Solzhenitsyn	1:35.6
2011	Testa My Patience	Craig Newitt	Mick Price	Hawks Bay	He's Remarkable	1:36.7
2010	Sound Journey	Michael Rodd	Mark Kavanagh	Trader	Drumbeats	1:36.7
2009	Rangirangdoo	Corey Brown	Chris Waller	Sound Of Nature	All American	1:34.9
2008	Sea Battle	Michael Rodd	Mark Kavanagh	Conquering	Orange County	1:36.3
2007	Sonic Quest	Danny Nikolic	Lee Freedman	Orange County	Tears I Cry	1:35.9
2006	Flash Trick	Steven King	Colin & Cindy Alderson	New Edge	Rockford Bay	1:37.2
2005	Niconero	Craig Williams	David Hayes	Cargo Cult	Miss Potential	1:39.4
2004	Lad Of The Manor	Brian Johns	Roger Hoysted	Lord Mick	Sir Dex	1:37.0
2003	Rosina Lad	Greg Childs	David Haworth	Walk On Air	Archave	1:38.3
2002	Royal Code	Brett Prebble	David Hall	Weasel Will	Excellerator	1:36.5
2001	Weasel Will	Craig Williams	Nigel Blackiston	Le Zagaletta	Typhoon	1:37.3

BACKGROUND
First run: 1982 (won by Getting Closer). Listed 1982-85. Group 3 1983-96. Group 3 from 1997.
Most recent mare to win: Silent Achiever (2012). Note: Only one mare has won the Crystal Mile.
Most recent 3YO to win: None.
Multiple winners: 1—Weasel Will (2001, 2000).
Fastest time (1600m): Ark Regal (1990) 1:33.20
Notable winners: The United States (2016); Turn Me Loose (2015); Silent Achiever (2012), Rangirangdoo (2009); Niconero (2005); Lad Of The Manor (2004); Le Zagaletta (1999); Rustic Dream (1998); Juggler (1995); Solvit (1992); Keepers (1984); Getting Closer (1982).
Crystal Mile winners won the lead-up races:
Seymour Cup: 1—Turn Me Loose (2015). Note: State Taj (1994) won the 1993 Seymour Cup.
Cameron Handicap: 2—Hooked (2014); Toydini (2013).
Tramway Handicap: 1—Rangirangdoo (2009).
Epsom Handicap: None.
Sir Rupert Clarke Stakes: None.
Toorak Handicap: None.
Crystal Mile winners went on to win in the same preparation:
Cantala Stakes: 2—Turn Me Loose (2015); Dazzling Duke (1985).
Railway Stakes: 1—Getting Closer (season 1982-83)
Kingston Town Classic: 1—Niconero (2006)
Leading winning jockeys: 3 wins Darren Gauci (Holy Roller 1997, Juggler 1995, Ark Regal 1990); Damien Oliver (Le Zagaletta 1999, Rustic Dream 1998, State Taj 1994); Craig Williams (Hooked 2014, Niconero 2005, Weasal Will 2001).
Current winning jockeys: 3 wins Damien Oliver (Le Zagaletta 1999, Rustic Dream 1998, State Taj 1994); Craig Williams (Hooked 2014, Niconero 2005, Weasel Will 2001).
2 wins Brett Prebble (Royal Code 2002, Weasel Will 2000); Michael Rodd (Sound Journey 2010, Sea Battle 2008); Blake Shinn (Lucky Hussler 2017, Toydini 2013).
1 win Opie Bosson (Turn Me Loose 2015); Corey Brown (Rangirangdoo 2009); Grant Cooksley (Solvit 1992); James McDonald (Silent Achiever 2012); Kerrin McEvoy (The United States 2016); Craig Newitt (Testa My Patience 2011).
Leading winning trainers: 2 wins Nigel Blackiston (Weasel Will 2001, 2000); Lee Freedman (Sonic Quest 2007, La Zagaletta 1999); Roger James (Silent Achiever 2012, Carson's Cash 1993); Mark Kavanagh (Sound Journey 2010, Sea Battle 2008); Mick Price (Testa My Patience 2011, Rustic Dream 1998).
Current winning trainers: 2 wins Nigel Blackiston (Weasel Will 2001, 2000); Lee Freedman (Sonic Quest 2007, La Zagaletta 1999); Roger James (Silent Achiever 2012, Carson's Cash 1993); Mark Kavanagh (Sound Journey 2010, Sea Battle 2008); Mick Price (Testa My Patience 2011, Rustic Dream 1998).
1 wins Murray Baker (Turn Me Loose 2015); David Hall (Royal Code 2002); John Hawkes (Holy Roller 1997); David Haworth (Rosina Lad 2003); David Hayes (Niconero 2005); Robert Hickmott (The United States 2016); Moira Murdoch (Solvit 1992); John Sadler (Lochrae 1996); John Thompson (Hooker 2014); Chris Waller (Rangirangdoo 2009); Gai Waterhouse (Juggler 1995); Darren Weir (Lucky Hussler 2017).
Points of interest: Weasel Will won in 2000 and 2001, and also finished second to Royal Code in 2002. Lad Of The Manor (2004) won the Dato Tan Chin Nam Stakes (Feehan, wfa) in 2005 and 2006, over the same track and distance.

MVRC Moonee Valley Gold Cup (2500m)—Moonee Valley
$500,000 Group 2 4YO&Up SWP. October 27, 2018.

YEAR	WINNER	JOCKEY	TRAINER	2ND	3RD	TIME
2017	Who Shot Thebarman	Blake Shinn	Chris Waller	Libran	Cismontane	2:37.3
2016	Grand Marshal	Ben Melham	Chris Waller	Who Shot Thebarman	Pentathlon	2:41.4
2015	The United States	Hugh Bowman	Robert Hickmott	Prince Of Penzance	Bohemian Lily	2:34.4
2014	Prince Of Penzance	Michelle Payne	Darren Weir	Le Roi	Au Revoir	2:36.0
2013	Precedence	Craig Williams	Bart & James Cummings	Shoreham	Gotta Take Care	2:36.9
2012	Vatuvei	Luke Nolen	Peter Moody	Reuben Percival	Ironstein	2:35.7
2011	Americain	Gerald Mosse	Alain De Royer Dupre	Tullamore	Illo	2:36.4
2010	Precedence	Blake Shinn	Bart Cummings	Above Average	Capecover	2:38.9
2009	The Sportsman	Hugh Bowman	Russell Cameron	Irazu	Think Money	2:37.3
2008	Gallopin	James Winks	Danny O'Brien	Baughurst	Ice Chariot	2:36.5
2007	Gallic	Steven Arnold	Graeme Rogerson	Lazer Sharp	Jukebox Johnny	2:36.5
2006	Zipping	Glen Boss	Graeme Rogerson	Show Barry	Gallic	2:38.9
2005	Umbula	Noel Callow	Mick Price	Bazelle	Kindjhal	2:45.1
2004	Another Warrior	Darren Beadman	Alan Bailey	Rizon	Hard To Get	2:37.1
2003	Frightening	Greg Childs	Bart Cummings	Legible	County Tyrone	2:38.5
2002	Thong Classic	Brett Prebble	Pat Carey	Rain Gauge	Mr Prudent	2:40.9
2001	Rain Gauge	Greg Childs	George Hanlon	Spirit Of Westbury	Big Pat	2:37.6

BACKGROUND
First run: 1883 (won by Castaway). Group 3 1979. Group 2 since 1980. Run over 2200m 1900-08 & 1924-32; 2400m 1909, 1934 & 1935; 2000m 1910-18; 2600m 1919-23, 1933 & 1936-94; 2500 from 1995. Set weights and penalties from 1994. Registered name is the Moonee Valley Gold Cup. Run in May 1976-79.

Most recent mare to win: Butternut (1985).

Most recent 3YO to win: C&G—Silvius (1923); Filly—Mirella (1897).

Multiple winners: 5—Precedence (2013, 2010); Valcurl (1946, 1945); Gilltown (1940, 1939); Gladwyn (1915, 1914); Little Bob (1892, 1891).

Fastest time (2500m): The United States (2015) 2:34.43

Notable winners: Who Shot Thebarman (2017); Grand Marshal (2016); The United States (2015); Prince Of Penzance (2014); Americain 2011); Gallic (2007); Zipping (2006); Streak (1999); Istidaad (1996); Kingston Rule (1990); Sydeston (1989); Ideal Centreman (1988); Ngwyni (1977); Red William (1965); Wodalla (1953); Rivette (1939); Shadow King (1930); Royal Charter (1926); Clean Sweep (1990).

Moonee Valley Cup and the state Cups in the same year:
Adelaide Cup: 1—Gallic (2007).
Sydney Cup: 1—Gallic (2007).

Moonee Valley Cup winners also won as lead-up races:
Newcastle Cup: 1—Another Warrior (2004).
The Metropolitan: None.
JRA Cup: 2—Precedence (2010); Rain Gauge (2001).

Moonee Valley Cup and the Melbourne Cup:
Melbourne Cup (same year): 3—Kingston Rule (1990); Wodalla (1953); Blue Spec (1905). Note: Prince Of Penzance (2014) won the Melbourne Cup in 2015; Americain (2011) won the Melbourne Cup in 2010.

Moonee Valley Cup placegetters to win the Melbourne Cup: 7—Prince Of Penzance (2015, second behind The United States); Brew (2000); Tawrrific (1989); Piping Lane (1972); Gatum Gatum (1962); Hi Jinx (1960); Rivette (1939).

Melbourne Cup winners to contest the Moonee Valley Cup since 1980: Prince Of Penzance (2015), Brew (2000), Kingston Rule (1990); Tawrrific (1989). What A Nuisance (1985).

Leading winning jockeys: 4 wins Bill McLachlan (Whito Phast 1920, Gladwyn 1915, Greek Fire 1913, Kerlie 1910); Damien Oliver (Yippyio 2000, Streak 1999, Top Rating 1994, Glastonbury).

3 wins Billy Cook (Valcurl 1945, Gilltown 1940, Dark Chief 1936); Greg Hall (Prince Standaan 1998, Instidaad 1996, Storm 1995); Roy Higgins (Sir Serene 1977, Skint Dip 1971, River Seine 1962)); Ron Hutchinson (Lord Galvin 1957, Pandie Sun 1956, Hoyle 1949); Bobby Lewis (Stand By 1924, Charles Stuart 1906, Clean Sweep 1900); Billy (W.A.) Smith (What's Brewing 1969, Algalon 1964, My Contact 1953); Brent Thomson (Court Of Honour 1997, Ideal Centreman 1988, Triumphal March 1982)

Current winning jockeys: 4 wins Damien Oliver (Yippyio 2000, Streak 1999, Top Rating 1994, Glastonbury 1993).

2 wins Hugh Bowman (The United States 2015, The Sportsman 2009); Blake Shinn (Who Shot Thebarman 2017).

1 win Steven Arnold (Gallic 2007); Glen Boss (Zipping 2006); Noel Callow (Umbula 2005); Ben Melham (Grand Marshal 2016); Gerald Mosse (Americain 2011); Luke Nolen (Vatuvei 2012); Michelle Payne (Prince Of

Penzance 2014); Brett Prebble (Thong Classic 2002); Precedence 2010); Robert Thompson (Reckless Tradition 1986); Craig Williams (Precedence 2013); James Winks (Gallopin 2008).
Leading winning trainers: 6 wins Bart Cummings (Precedence 2013, 2010, Frightening 2003, Kingston Rule 1990, Ngawyni 1977, Holiday Waggon 1975)
3 wins Cecil Godby (Ortelle's Star 1938, Peter Jackson 1933, Purser 1922); Colin Hayes (Triumphal March 1982, Impetus 1968, Pandie Sun 1956); David Hayes (Top Rating 1994, Glastonbury 1993, Al Maheb 1991); Graeme Rogerson (Gallic 2007, Zipping 2006, Donegal Mist 1992).
Current winning trainers: 3 wins David Hayes (Top Rating 1994, Glastonbury 1993, Al Maheb 1991); Graeme Rogerson (Gallic 2007, Zipping 2006, Donegal Mist 1992).
2 wins Chris Waller (Who Shot Thebarman 2017, Grand Marshal 2016).
1 win Clive Balfour (Ideal Centreman 1988); Russell Cameron (The Sportsman 2009); Pat Carey (Thong Classic 2002); Allan Denham (Yippyio 2000); Alain de Royer Dupre (Americain 2011); Lee Freedman (Storm 1995); Robert Hickmott (The United States 2015); Pat Hyland (Prince Standaan 1998); Danny O'Brien (Gallopin 2008); Mick Price (Umbula 2005); Bruce Purcell (King Matthias 1987); Robert Smerdon (Streak 1999); Darren Weir (Prince Of Penzance 2014).

VRC Wakeful Stakes (2000m)—Flemington
$300,000 Group 2 3YO Fillies SWP. November 3, 2018.

YEAR	WINNER	JOCKEY	TRAINER	2ND	3RD	TIME
2017	Luvaluva	Blake Shinn	John Sargent	Glam Guru	Rimraam	2:03.9
2016	Tiamo Grace	Damian Lane	Darren Weir	Sebring Dream	Missrock	2:04.4
2015	Ambience	James McDonald	John O'Shea	Beluga Blue	Muzyka	2:04.7
2014	Thunder Lady	Blake Shinn	John Sargent	Abduction	Fenway	2:03.3
2013	Kirramosa	Tommy Berry	John Sargent	May's Dream	Solicit	2:05.1
2012	Zydeco	Kerrin McEvoy	Anthony Freedman	Maraatib	Transonic	2:02.8
2011	Atlantic Jewel	Michael Rodd	Mark Kavanagh	Rahveel	Dowager Queen	2:04.9
2010	Brazilian Pulse	Craig Williams	Michael Moroney	Placement	Heartsareforlove	2:04.2
2009	Faint Perfume	Michael Rodd	Bart Cummings	Silent Surround	Melito	2:03.2
2008	Rocha	Danny Nikolic	Guy Walter	Miss Scarlatti	Estee	2:05.5
2007	Zarita	Greg Childs	Pat Hyland	Riva San	Katherine Gold	2:05.8
2006	Tuesday Joy	Danny Beasley	Gai Waterhouse	J'adane	Anamato	2:02.7
2005	Serenade Rose	Steven King	Lee Freedman	Astronomia	Zenarta	2:02.5
2004	Hollow Bullet	David Taggart	John McArdle	Storm Alert	Mango Daiquiri	2:02.1
2003	Timbourina	Steven King	Tony Wildman	Special Harmony	Dane Beltar	2:05.5
2002	Hierogram	Darren Beadman	John Hawkes	Its Who Deanie	Lashed	2:02.9
2001	Quays	Craig Williams	Clarry Conners	Gold Lottery	Li Lo Lill	2:01.2

BACKGROUND
First run: 1932 (won by Protea). Group 2 since 1979. Race divided in 1947, 1973 & 1975.
Fastest time (2000m): Quays (2001) 2:01.20
Notable winners: Atlantic Jewel (2011); Faint Perfume (2009); Zarita (2007); Tuesday Joy (2006); Serenade Rose (2005); Grand Archway (1998); Arborea (1993); Richfield Lady (1991); November Rain (1980); How Now (1975); Toltrice (1972); Light Fingers (1964); Indian Summer (1961); Wenona Girl (1960); Evening Peal (1955); True Course (1950); Chicquita (1949); Rainbird (1944); Siren (1935).
Wakeful Stakes winners also won the lead-up races:
Edward Manifold Stakes: 8—Serenade Rose (2005); My Sienna (1999); Richfield Lady (1991); Light Fingers (1964); Indian Summer (1961); Chicquita (1949); Siren (1936); Arachne (1934).
Thousand Guineas: 13—Atlantic Jewel (2011); Arborea (1993); Richfield Lady (1991); Tristanagh (1989); Brava Jeannie (1979); Just Topic (1973); Toltrice (1972); Indian Summer (1961); Wenona Girl (1960); True Course (1950); Chicquita (1949); Nizam's Ring (1947); Sweet Chime (1946).
Wakeful Stakes winners went on to win in the same preparation:
VRC Kennedy Oaks: 35—Kirramosa (2013); Brazilian Pulse (2010); Faint Perfume (2009); Serenade Rose (2005); Hollow Bullet (2004); Grand Archway (1998); Kensington Palace (1997); Saleous (1995); Arborea (1993); Richfield Lady (1991); Tristanagh (1989); Research (1988); Diamond Shower (1986); November Rain (1980); Brava Jeannie (1979); Scomeld (1978); Leica Show (1974); Toltrice (1972); Sanderae (1970); Light Fingers (1964); Indian Summer (1961); Chicola (1958); Evening Peal (1955); True Course (1950); Chicquita (1949); Grey Nurse (1948); Nizam's Ring (1947); Sweet Chime (1946); Three Wheeler (1943); East End (1942); Session (1940); Prairie Moon (1937); Siren (1935); Golden Hair (1933); Protea (1932).
Thousand Guineas & VRC Kennedy Oaks: 10—Arborea (1993); Richfield Lady (1991); Tristanagh (1989); Brava Jeannie (1979); Toltrice (1972); Indian Summer (1961); True Course (1950); Chicquita (1949);

Nizam's Ring (1947); Sweet Chime (1946).
Edward Manifold & Thousand Guineas & VRC Kennedy Oaks: 3—Richfield Lady (1991); Indian Summer (1961); Chicquita (1949).
Wakeful Stakes winners and the Cups:
Melbourne Cup (as 4YO): 3—Light Fingers (Wakeful 1964, Cup in 1965); Evening Peal (Wakeful 1955, Cup in 1956); Rainbird (Wakeful 1944, Cup in 1945).
Caulfield Cup (as 4YO): 2—Imposera (Wakeful 1987, Caulfield Cup 1988); How Now (Wakeful 1975, Caulfield Cup 1976).
Leading winning jockeys: 5 wins Roy Higgins (Sun Sally 1977, Calera 1975, Sanderae 1970, With Respect 1968, Light Fingers 1964).
4 wins Steven King (Serenade Rose 2005, Timbourina 2004; Danendri 1996, Love Comes To Town 1992).
3 wins Jim Cassidy (Tristanagh 1989, Diamond Shower 1986, Heat Of The Moment 1985); Ron Quinton (Our Lafite 1974, La Cassiere 1983, November Rain 1980).
Current winning jockeys: 2 wins Michael Rodd (Atlantic Jewel 2011, Faint Perfume 2009); Blake Shinn (Luvaluva 2017, Thunder Lady 2014); Craig Williams (Brazilian Pulse 2010, Quays 2001).
1 win Stephen Baster (Lolita Star 2000); Tommy Berry (Kirramosa 2013); Opie Bosson (Grand Archway 1998); Damian Lane (Tiamo Grace 2016); James McDonald (Ambience 2015); Kerrin McEvoy (Zydeco 2012); Damien Oliver (Kensington Palace 1997); Brian Werner (Dream Of The Dance 1994).
Leading winning trainers: 14 wins Bart Cummings (Faint Perfume 2009, Danendri 1996, Love Comes To Town 1992, Richfield Lady 1991, Tristanagh 1989, Royal Regatta 1982, Sheraco 1981, Sun Sally 1977, Calera 1975, Leica Show 1974, Sanderae 1970, Glad Rags 1969, With Respect 1968, Light Fingers 1964).
4 wins Neville Begg (Heat Of The Moment 1985, Our Lafite 1984, La Caissiere 1983, November Rain 1980).
Current winning trainers: 3 wins John Sargent (Luvaluva 2017, Thunder Lady 2014, Kirramosa 2013).
2 wins Clarry Conners (Arborea 1993, Research 1988); Lee Freedman (Serenade Rose 2005, Kensington Palace 1997); John Hawkes (Hierogram 2002; Toltrice 1972); Pat Hyland (Zarita 2007, Saleous 1995).
1 win Anthony Freedman (Zydeco 2012); David Hayes (Beachside 1990); Mark Kavanagh (Atlantic Jewel 2011); Robbie Laing (Dream Of The Dance 1994); John McArdle (Hollow Bullet 2004); Mike Moroney (Brazilian Pulse 2010); John O'Shea (Ambience 2015); Graeme Rogerson (Grand Archway 1998); Gai Waterhouse (Tuesday Joy 2006); Darren Weir (Tiamo Grace 2016).
Point of interest: Calera (1975) is the dam of 1987 winner Imposera.

VRC Linlithgow Stakes (1200m)—Flemington
$300,000 Group 2 Open Handicap. November 3, 2018.

YEAR	WINNER	JOCKEY	TRAINER	2ND	3RD	TIME
2017	Rich Charm	Patrick Moloney	Udyta Clarke	Missrock	The Monstar	1:08.9
2016	Illustrious Lad	Anthony Darmanin	Peter Gelagotis	Counterattack	Southern Legend	1:08.3
2015	Eclair Choice	Dom Tourneur	Phillip Stokes	Hot Snitzel	Dothraki	1:09.3
2014	Deep Field	Dwayne Dunn	Michael, Wayne & John Hawkes	Driefontein	In Cahoots	1:11.0
2013	Fontelina	Peter Robl	Anthony Cummings	Spirit Of Boom	Rarefied	1:09.0
2012	Fontelina	Vlad Duric	Anthony Cummings	Spirit Of Boom	Tiger Tees	1:08.8
2011	Sister Madly	Damien Oliver	John Sadler	Rarefied	Temple Of Boom	1:10.4
2010	Whitefriars	Jim Cassidy	Rick Worthington	Beaded	Chasm	1:11.1
2009	Eagle Falls	Damien Oliver	David Hayes	Turffontein	Absolutelyfabulous	1:08.9
2008	Hot Danish	Danny Nikolic	Les Bridge	Fighting Fund	Sunburnt Land	1:10.1
2007	Swick	James Winks	Bart Cummings	Great is Great	Typhoon Zed	1:09.2
2006	Magnus	Luke Nolen	Peter Moody	Undue	Personal Ensign	1:08.9
2005	Glamour Puss	Steven King	Danny O'Brien	Stratum	Cape Of Good Hope	1:08.9
2004	Fastnet Rock	Glen Boss	Paul Perry	Super Impressive	Recurring	1:09.0
2003	Our Egyptian Rain	Nash Rawiller	Grahame Begg	Brief Embrace	Thorn Park	1:09.3
2002	Choisir	Glen Boss	Paul Perry	Falvelon	Belle Du Jour	1:09.3
2001	Belle Du Jour	Patrick Payne	Clarry Conners	Falvelon	Sedation	1:08.8

BACKGROUND
First run: 1908 (won by Pink 'Un). Replaced the VRC Flying Stakes (1200m-1400m, 1868-1907); Group 2 since 1979. Run over 1600m 1908-67.; 1400m 1968-90; 1200m from 1991; Previously known as the The Age Classic, Linlithgow Stakes, Emirates Classic and Lexus Classic. Renamed the Salinger Stakes in 2007, and moved to Derby Day, had various sponsor names since. Weight-For-Age until 2006, since run as a handicap.
Most recent mare to win: Sister Madly (2011).

Most recent 3YO to win: C&G—Fastnet Rock (2004); Filly—Pharein (1999).
Multiple winners: 12—Fontelina (2013, 2012); Redelva (1990, 1988); Scamanda (1976, 1975, 1974); All Shot (1973, 1972); Matrice (1957, 1956); Ellerslie (1952, 1950); High Caste (1941, 1940, 1939 *dead-heat); Ajax (1938, 1937); Chatham (1933, 1932, 1931); Amounis (1929, 1927, 1926); The Night Patrol (1925, 1924); Wolaroi (1918, 1916).
Fastest time (1200m): Toledo (1998) 1:08.10
Notable winners: Magnus (2006); Fastnet Rock (2004); Belle Du Jour (2001); Mahogany (1996); Sequalo (1994); Redelva (1990, 1988); Placid Ark (1987); Campaign King (1986); Scamanda (1976, 1975, 1974); All Shot (1973, 1972); Vain (1969); Star Affair (1965); Star Of Heaven (1964); Wenona Girl (1963); Sky High (1962); Noholme (1959); Matrice (1957, 1956); Royal Gem (1945); High Caste (1941, 1940, 1939 *dead-heat); Ajax (1939, 1938); Chatham (1933, 1932, 1931); Phar Lap (1930); Amounis (1929, 1927, 1926); Violoncello (1922); Popinjay (1911).

Linlithgow Stakes winners won the lead-up races:
Tatt's Lightning Handicap: 2—Deep Field (2014); Whitefriars (2010).
Caulfield Village Stakes: 1—Rich Charm (2017).
Caulfield Sprint: 3—Eclair Choice (2015); Toledo (1998); Tanjian Prince (1992).
Moir Stakes: 5—Our Egyptian Raine (2003); Al Mansour (1997); Sequalo (1994); Placid Ark (1987); Scamanda (1976).

Linlithgow Stakes winners went on to win in Cup week:
VRC Sprint Classic: 6—Glamour Puss (2005); Pharein (1999); Always Welcome (1978); Scamanda (1974); Vain (1969); Star Of Heaven (1964).
Leading winning jockeys: 5 wins Harold Badger (Phoibos 1948, Columnist 1947, Manrico 1939*, Ajax 1938, 1937). 4 wins Ted Bartle (High Caste 1941, 1940, 1939*, Closing Time 1934); Jim Pike (Chatham 1933, Phar Lap 1930, Gothic 1928, Beverage 1910).
3 wins Roy Higgins (Prince Ruling 1980, All Shot 1972, Star Affair 1965); Brent Thomson (Nouvelle Star 1984, Galleon 1982, Always Welcome 1978) Jim Munro (Chatham 1932, Amounis 1929, 1926).
* Dead heat.
Current winning jockeys: 2 wins Glen Boss (Fastnet Rock 2004, Choisir 2002); Damien Oliver (Sister Madly 2011, Eagle Falls 2009); Brett Prebble (Pharein 1999, Toledo 1998).
1 win Larry Cassidy (Al Mansour 1997); Anthony Darmanin (Illustrious Lad 2016); Dwayne Dunn (Deep Field 2014); Vlad Duric (Fontelina 2012); Patrick Moloney (Rich Charm 2017); Luke Nolen (Magnus 2006); Nash Rawiller (Our Egyptian Raine 2003); Dom Tourneur (Eclair Choice 2015); James Winks (Swick 2007).
Leading winning trainers: 4 wins Jack Jamieson (High Caste 1941, 1940, 1939, Closing Time 1934); Maurice McCarten (Noholme 1960, Prince Cortauld 1954, Dickens 1949).
3 wins Colin Hayes (Nouvelle Star 1984, Galleon 1982, Always Welcome 1978); Bob Hoysted (Scamanda 1976, 1975, 1974); Des Judd (Legal Boy 1966, Matrice 1957, 1956); Frank McGrath (Amounis 1929, 1927, 1926); Fred Williams (Chatham 1933, 1932, Greenstead 1920).
Current winning trainer: 2 wins Anthony Cummings (Fontelina 2013, 2012); David Hayes (Eagle Falls 2009, Wrap Around 1991); Paul Perry (Fastnet Rock 2004, Choisir 2002).
1 win Grahame Begg (Our Egyptian Raine 2003); Russell Cameron (Toledo 1998); Udyta Clarke (Rich Charm 2017); Clarry Conners (Belle Du Jour 2001); Mathew Ellerton (Black Bean 2000); Lee Freedman (Mahogany 1996); Peter Gelagotis (Illustrious Lad 2016); David Hall (Pharein 1999); Michael, Wayne, John Hawkes (Deep Field 2014); Wally Mitchell (Placid Ark 1987); Danny O'Brien (Glamour Puss 2005); John Sadler (Sister Madly 2011); Phillip Stokes (Eclair Choice 2015); Rick Worthington (Whitefriars 2010).
Points of interest: Violoncello (1922) had 12 days earlier won the first ever Cox Plate (2040m) at Moonee Valley. In 1930, Phar Lap won the Memsie Stakes (2000m), Melbourne Cup (3200m), The Linlithgow Stakes (1600m) and C.B. Fisher Plate (2400m) on each of the four days of the Melbourne Cup carnival.
Vain (1969) won the Craven A Stakes (1200m) on Derby Day, the Linlithgow on Thursday and backed up to win the Emirates Stakes (George Adams) on Saturday—1200m, 1400m and 1600m. He was injured in the autumn and didn't race again.

Royal Gem won in 1945, finished third in 1946, and second in 1947 and 1948.

VRC Matriarch Stakes (2000m)—Flemington

$300,000 Group 2 4YO&Up Mares SWP. November 10, 2018.

YEAR	WINNER	JOCKEY	TRAINER	2ND	3RD	TIME
2017	Savapinski	Brenton Avdulla	Gai Waterhouse & Adrian Bott	Payroll	Token Of Love	2:01.5
2016	Jessy Belle	Craig Williams	David & Ben Hayes & Tom Dabernig	Sort After	Happy Hannah	2:04.7
2015	Lucia Valentina	Damien Oliver	Kris Lees	Manageress	Casino Dancer	2:04.1
2014	Suavito	Damien Oliver	Nigel Blackiston	Girl In Flight	Amanpour	2:01.7
2013	Girl Gone Rockin'	Dwayne Dunn	Michael, Wayne & John Hawkes	Queenstown	Keep De Rose	2:04.7
2012	Midnight Martini	Michael Rodd	Mark Kavanagh	Lake Sententia	Crafty Irna	2:03.1
2011	Vintedge	Nash Rawiller	Chris Waller	Stole	Skyerush	2:01.2
2010	Well Rounded	Ben Melham	Lee Freedman	Purple	Keep The Peace	2:02.5
2009	Purple	Kerrin McEvoy	Peter Snowden	Moment in Time	Lady Lynette	2:00.1
2008	Bird of Fire	Blake Shinn	Tony Vasil	Tan Tat De Lago	El Daana	2:05.0
2007	Hidden Strings	Blake Shinn	Peter Moody	Sovereign Miss	Danevade	2:03.9
2006	Brom Felinity	Mark Zahra	Jim Mason	Pin Up	Purde	2:02.1
2005	Sutology	Matt Pumpa	Bevan Laming	Storm Alert	Aqua D Amore	2:02.1
2004	Demerger	Corey Brown	Danny O'Brien	Aint Seen Nothin	Full Spec	2:04.8
2003	Sweet Corn	Brett Prebble	Lee Freedman	Sylvaner	Mrs Tendulkar	2:04.4
2002	Damaschino	Danny Nikolic	Roger James	Little Miss Quick	Terrenora	2:00.6
2001	Piper Star	Rhys Mcleod	Roger James	Umaline	Tickle My	2:01.5

BACKGROUND

First run: 1986 (won by Iola). Listed 1995-2000. Group 3 since 2001. Set weights and penalties since 2005. Registered name is the Matriarch Stakes.

Multiple winners: 1—Big Colony (1992, 1991).

Fastest time (2000m): Damaschino (2002) 2:00.69

Notable winners: Lucia Valentina (2015); Sauvito (2014); Demerger (2004); Gold City (1996); Big Colony (1992, 1991).

Matriarch Stakes winners won the following races earlier in the spring:
Tesio Stakes: 2—Suavito (2014); Bird Of Fire (2008).
Cranbourne Cup: 1—Midnight Martini (2012).
Tristarc Stakes: None.
Werribee Cup: 1—Brom Felinity (2006).
Myer Classic: 1—Concordance (1988).

Matriarch Stakes winners went on to win in the same preparation:
Sandown Classic: None. Note: Big Colony (1992, 1991) lost the 1991 Sandown Classic after a positive swab.
Eclipse Stakes: 2—Damaschino (2002); Gold City (1996).

Leading winning jockeys: 2 wins Michael Clarke (French Icing 1989, Iola 1986); Damien Oliver (Lucia Valentina 2015, Suavito 2014); Brett Prebble (Sweet Corn 2003, Flushed 2000); Blake Shinn (Bird Of Fire 2008, Hidden Strings 2007); David Taggart (Big Colony 1992, 1991); Craig Williams (Jessy Belle 2016, Sly Sandra 1999).

Current winning jockeys: 2 wins Damien Oliver (Lucia Valentina 2015, Suavito 2014); Brett Prebble (Sweet Corn 2003, Flushed 2000); Blake Shinn (Bird Of Fire 2008, Hidden String 2007); Craig Williams (Jessy Belle 2016, Sly Sandra 1999).
1 win Brenton Avdulla (Savapinski 2017); Stephen Baster (Laebeel 1998); Corey Brown (Demerger 2004); Dwayne Dunn (Girl Gone Rockin' 2013); Kerrin McEvoy (Purple 2009); Rhys McLeod (Piper Star 2001); Ben Melham (Well Rounded 2010); Nash Rawiller (Vintedge 2011); Michael Rodd (Midnight Martini 2012); Mark Zahra (Brom Felinity 2006).

Leading winning trainers: 2 wins Craig Conron (Big Colony 1992, 1991); Lee Freedman (Well Rounded 2010, Sweet Corn 2003); Colin Hayes (Concordance 1988, Iola 1986); Roger James (Damaschino 2002, Piper Star 2001).

Current winning trainers: 2 wins Craig Conron (Big Colony 1992, 1991); Lee Freedman (Well Rounded 2010, Sweet Corn 2003); Roger James (Damaschino 2002, Piper Star 2001).
1 win Nigel Blackiston (Sauvito 2014); Ken Callaughan (French Icing 1989); Leon Corstens (Laebeel 1998); Michael, Wayne, John Hawkes (Girl Gone Rockin' 2013); David & Ben Hayes & Tom Dabernig (Jessy Belle 2016); Lee Hope (Sly Sandra 1999); Mark Kavanagh (Midnight Martini 2012); Ken Keys (Flushed 2000); Bevan Laming (Sutology 2005); Kris Lees (Lucia Valentina 2015); John Meagher (Gilded Splendour 1993); Danny O'Brien (Demerger 2004); Stuart Padman (Sudden Wonder 1994); Peter Snowden (Purple 2009); Tony Vasil (Bird Of Fire 2008); Chris Waller (Vintedge 2011); Gai Waterhouse & Adrian Bott (Savapinski 2017).

Points of interest: Big Colony (1992, 1991) was first past the post in the 1991 Sandown Classic, but she was subsequently disqualified after a positive swab.
Purple (2009) won the G1 Storm Queen Stakes and G1 Queensland Oaks in the same year.

WATC Lee Steere Stakes (1400m)—Ascot
$250,000 Group 2 3YO&Up WFA. November 10, 2018.

YEAR	WINNER	JOCKEY	TRAINER	2ND	3RD	TIME
2017	Silverstream	Willie Pike	Adam Durrant	Great Shot	Scales Of Justice	1:23.5
2016	Perfect Reflection	Willie Pike	Grant & Alana Williams	Disposition	Tradesman	1:23.0
2015	Black Heart Bart	Glenn Smith	Vaughn Sigley	Magnifisio	Delicacy	1:22.5
2014	Magnifisio	Jason Brown	Jim P Taylor	Fuchsia Bandana	Platinum Rocker	1:23.6
2013	Conservatorium	Joe Bowditch	Gary Kennewell	Checkpoint	Ranger	1:23.8
2012	Luckygray	Shaun O'donnell	Gino Poletti	God Has Spoken	Luke's Luck	1:22.9
2011	Ranger	Willie Pike	Grant Williams	Grand Nirvana	Waratah's Secret	1:22.6
2010	Famous Roman	Shaun O'donnell	Jim P Taylor	Tarzi	For Your Eyes Only	1:24.0
2009	Idyllic Prince	Jason Brown	Jim P Taylor	Tarzi	Spirited One	1:22.5
2008	Marasco	Willie Pike	Fred Kersley	Tarzi	Hartleys Dream	1:22.6
2007	Grasspatch Girl	Peter Knuckey	Tom Widdeson	Mansion House	No Questions	1:22.3
2006	Belle Bizarre	Paul Harvey	Rod Bynder	Hartley's Dream	Wild Target	1:22.4
2005	Avenida Madero	Jason Brown	Jim P Taylor	Covertly	Hartley's Dream	1:21.9
2004	Ellicorsam	Damien Oliver	Sharon Miller	Modem	Mr Sandgroper	1:21.3
2003	Early Express	Peter Hall	Peter Giadresco	Modem	Finito	1:23.3
2002	Hardrada	Jason Whiting	Lou Luciani	Irish Prelude	Finito	1:21.9
2001	Tribula	Stephen Miller	Arthur Mortimer	Fair Alert	Old Comrade	1:25.4

BACKGROUND
First run: 1893 (won by Scarpia). Group 2 since 1979. Run over 1600m 1893-1933 & 1939; 1400m 1938, 1940-77, 1979-84 & since 1993; 1500m 1978 & 1985-92. Previously known as the All-Aged Stakes 1893-1938. Held during the Perth Cup carnival until 1989. Not to be confused with the G3 Sir Ernest Lee Steere Classic (1400m, 3YOs) run in Dec/Jan.
Note: In the past held either late Dec or early Nov which means sometimes two winners in the same year and in some years the race is not run.
Most recent mare to win: Perfect Reflection (2016).
Most recent 3YO to win: C&G—Hardrada (2002); Filly—Denver Dame (1987).
Multiple winners: 7—La Trice (1972, 1971); Railway Boy (1967, 1966); Big Bob (1963, 1962); Cetotis (1936, 1933); Mistico (1920, 1916); Tarquin (1900, 1898, 1897); Scarpia (1895, 1894, 1893).
Fastest time (1400m): Ellicorsam (2004) 1:21.32
Notable winners: Perfect Reflection (2016); Black Heart Bart (2015); Magnifisio (2014); Luckygray (2012); Marasco (2008); Ellicorsam (2004); Umrum (2000); Slavonic (1999); Willoughby (1997); Jacks Or Better (1994); M'Lady's Jewel (1991); Carry A Smile (1989); Sky Filou (1988); Fair Sir (1986); Getting Closer (1982); Iko (1981); Asian Beau (1979); Romantic Dream (1978); Burgess Queen (1977); Millefleurs (1972); Aquanita (1960); Maniana (1956); Gay Gypsy (1938); Einga (1931); Easingwold (1921); Mistico (1920, 1916); Tarquin (1900, 1898, 1897); Scarpia (1895, 1894, 1893).
Lee Steere Stakes winners won the lead-up races:
Farnley Stakes: 2—Idyllic Prince (2009); Master Till (1990).
Birthday Stakes: 2—Black Heart Bart (2015); Welcome Knight (1992).
Northerly Stakes: 4—Silverstream (2017); Black Heart Bart (2015); Ranger (2011); Famous Roman (2010).
Prince Of Wales Stakes: 10—Idyllic Prince (2009); Willoughby (1997); Century Blazer (1995); Jacks Or Better (1994); M'Lady's Jewel (1991); Master Till (1990); Carry A Smile (1989); Argentine Gold (1983); Asian Beau (1979); Burgess Queen (1977).
Asian Beau Stakes: None.
Lee Steere Stakes winners went on to win in the same preparation:
Reeves Stakes: 1—M'Lady's Jewel (1991).
R.J. Peters Stakes: 2—Argentine Gold (1983); Enchanteur (1907).
Scahill Stakes: 4—Conservatorium (2013); Tribula (2001); Willoughby (Lee Steere Dec 1997; Scahill Jan 1998); Burgess Queen (Lee Steere Dec 1977; Scahill Jan 1978).
Winterbottom Stakes: 10—Magnifisio (2014); Ellicorsam (2004); Hardrada (2002); M'Lady's Jewel (1991); Carry A Smile (1989); Sky Filou (1988); Asian Beau (1979); Sherolythe (Winterbottom Nov 1969; Lee Steere Jan 1970); McHarry (Winterbottom 1956; Lee Steere 1957); Chestnut Lady (Winterbottom 1954; Lee Steere 1955).
Note: Magnifisio is the only winner of both races since the Winterbottom was moved to after the Lee Steere.
Kingston Town Classic: 1—Luckygray (2012).
The Lee Steere Stakes and the Railway Stakes:
12—Slavonic (1999); Willoughby (Lee Steere Dec 1997; Railway Jan 1998); Welcome Knight (1992); M'Lady's Jewel (1991); Getting Closer (Lee Steere 1982; Railway 1983); Iko (1981); Asian Beau (1979); Detonator (Lee Steere 1976; Railway 1975); Millefleurs (1972); Big Bob (Lee Steer 1962; Railways 1961); Aquanita (Lee Steere 1960; Railway 1959); Saturate (1912).

Leading winning jockeys: 4 wins Frank "Tiger" Moore (Sherolythe 1970, Big Bob 1963, 1962, Garawind 1949); Reg Treffone (St. Falcon 1949, Westralian 1948, Santheine 1947, Gay Gipsy 1938).
Current winning jockeys: 4 wins Willie Pike (Silverstream 2017, Perfect Reflection 2016, Ranger 2011, Marasco 2008).
3 wins Jason Brown (Magnifisio 2014, Idyllic Prince 2009, Avenida Madero 2005).
2 wins Peter Knuckey (Grasspatch Girl 2007, Willoughby 1997); Shaun O'Donnell (Luckygray 2012, Famous Roman 2010); Damien Oliver (Ellicorsam 2004, Welcome Knight 1992).
1 win Joe Bowditch (Conservatorium 2013); Peter Hall (Early Express 2003); Paul Harvey (Belle Bizarre 2006); Brett Prebble (Slavonic 1999); Glenn Smith (Black Heart Bart 2015); Jason Whiting (Hardrada 2002).
Leading winning trainers: 10 wins Jim "JJ" Kelly (Westralian 1948, Dear Brutus 1942, Einga 1931, Pure Blend 1930, Kongoni 1927, Egyptian Idol 1925, Honneur 1924, Scorpius 1922, Mistico 1920, High Rock 1916)
6 wins George Towton (Tarquin 1900, 1898, 1897, Scarpia 1895, 1894, 1893).
5 wins John Pullen (as private trainer for Paddy Connolly—Tom Castro 1914, Saturate 1912, Jolly Beggar 1910, May King 1907, Lady Agnes 1905).
Current winning trainers: 4 wins Jim Taylor (Magnifisio 2014, Famous Roman 2010, Idyllic Prince 2009, Avenida Madero 2005).
2 wins Grant Williams (Perfect Reflection 2016, Ranger 2011).
1 win Albert Beckett (Wabasso 1993); Adam Durrant (Silverstream 2017); David Harrison (Century Blazer 1995); Peter Giadresco (Early Express 2003); Gary Kennewell (Conservatorium 2013); Fred Kersley (Marasco 2008); Lou Luciani (Hardrada 2002); Leon Macdonald (Umrum 2000); Ted Martinovich (Carry A Smile 1989); Frank Maynard (Denver Dame 1987); Sharon Miller (Ellicorsam 2004); Wally Mitchell (Argentine Gold 1983); Arthur Mortimer (Tribula 2001); Gino Poletti (Luckygray 2012); Mick Price (Slavonic 1999); Ross Price (Welcome Knight 1992); Vaughn Sigley (Black Heart Bart 2015); Tom Widdeson (Grasspatch Girl 2007); Grant & Alana Williams (Perfect Reflection 2016).
Points of interest: Not only is M'Lady's Jewel the only horse to win a Reeves Stakes, Prince Of Wales Stakes, Winterbottom Stakes, Lee Steere Stakes and Railway Stakes, she did it in the one campaign in 1991.
In Melbourne, Easingwold (1921) won the 1923 W.S. Cox Plate at Moonee Valley, and successive G2 Herbert Power Handicaps at Caulfield (1923 & 1924).
Ellicorsam (2004) won the 2006 G1 Robert Sangster Stakes at Morphettville for new trainer Lee Freedman.
Sky Filou (1988) had in the previous spring won the 1987 G1 Salinger Stakes at Flemington.
Millefleurs (1972) was sold to Geoffrey Levett in Victoria, and she won the 1973 G1 Invitation Stakes at Caulfield.
Aquanita (1960) won the equivalent of 11 G1 races. He won the 1962 W.S. Cox Plate at Moonee Valley, two G1 Emirates Stakes (1960 & 1961) at Flemington, two G1 Underwood Stakes (1961 & 1962) and the 1962 G1 Futurity Stakes at Caulfield, and the 1961 Doomben 10,000 at Doomben.

MRC Sandown Guineas (1600m)—Sandown Hillside
$250,000 Group 2 3YO Open SW. November 17, 2018.

YEAR	WINNER	JOCKEY	TRAINER	2ND	3RD	TIME
2017	Villermont	Luke Nolen	Aaron Purcell	Peaceful State	Black Sail	1:37.5
2016	Morton's Fork	Craig Williams	John O'Shea	Ruthven	Jennifer Lynn	1:40.0
2015	Mahuta	Brad Rawiller	Darren Weir	Dal Cielo	Don't Doubt Mamma	1:35.9
2014	Petrology	Nicholas Hall	David Hayes & Tom Dabernig	Stratum Star	Berisha	1:36.7
2013	Paximadia	Kerrin McEvoy	Peter Snowden	Equator	Apollo's Choices	1:37.3
2012	Tatra	Kerrin McEvoy	Peter Snowden	Lunar Rise	Proverb	1:36.7
2011	So Swift	Craig Williams	Bill & Symon Wilde	Niagara	Galah	1:38.8
2010	Pressday	Nash Rawiller	Chris Waller	Chasse	Bigelow	1:42.7
2009	Kidnapped	Kerrin McEvoy	Peter Snowden	Majestic Music	Turf Express	1:36.2
2008	Caymans	Kerrin McEvoy	Peter Snowden	Marveen	Lucky Thunder	1:38.0
2007	Schilling	Damien Oliver	Mick Price	Masked Assassin	Wind Shear	1:38.6
2006	Sender	Darren Gauci	Rodney Douglas	Flame Of Sydney	Wordsmith	1:34.8
2005	Cayambe	Dwayne Dunn	David Hayes	Zigotto	Aztec Smytzer	1:39.4
2004	Binding	Corey Brown	John Hawkes	Barely A Moment	Al Maher	1:42.5
2003	Pay Keys	Brett Prebble	John Hickmott	Ikes Dream	Delzao	1:36.1
2002	Dextrous	Darren Gauci	John Hawkes	Lawsons Storm	Cool Azz	1:35.5
2001	Moon Dragon	Damien Oliver	Lee Freedman	All Courage	Rod To Dance	1:35.8

BACKGROUND
First run: 1957 (won by Orient). Group 2 since 1979. Run over 2100m 1968-69. For fillies only between 1957-67. Run at Caulfield 1957-64.
Most recent filly to win: Cayambe (2002). Note: Eight fillies have won since in the race was for open 3YOs in 1968.

Fastest time (1600m): Scenic Warrior (2000) & Voting (1993) 1:34.60
Notable winners: Pressday (2010); Over (1999); Baryshnikov (1994); Durbridge (1990); Shankhill Lass (1985); Cossack Prince (1982); So Called (1977); Better Draw (1975); Taj Rossi (1973); Abdul (1970); Always There (1968); Light Fingers (1964); Ripa (1963); Indian Summer (1961); Lady Sybil (1960).
Sandown Guineas winners also won the lead-up races:
Poseidon Stakes: 1—Paximadia (2013).
Gothic Stakes: 2—Mahuta (2015); Kidnapped 2009).
Springtime Stakes (Flem 1400m): 1—Binding (2004).
Batman Handicap: 5—Petrology (2014); Pay Keys (2003); Scenic Warrior (2000); Peep On The Sly (1995); Durbridge (1990).
Carbine Club Stakes: 9—Mahuta (2015); Paximadia (2013); Kidnapped (2009); Over (1999); Voting (1993); Shankhill Lass (1985); Brave Salute (1984); Snowing (1979); Shiftman (1974). Note: Schilling (2007) finished second to Zacroona in the Carbine Club Stakes.
Sandown Guineas and the Flemington Classics:
Victoria Derby: 2—Taj Rossi (1973); Always There (1968).
VRC Oaks: 3—Light Fingers (1964); Indian Summer (1961); Lady Sybil (1960).
Leading winning jockeys: 4 wins Roy Higgins (Taj Rossi 1973, Top Flat 1969, Light Fingers 1963, Birthday Card 1962); Kerrin McEvoy (Paximadia 2013, Tatra 2012, Kidnapped 2009, Caymans 2008); Damien Oliver (Schilling 2008, Moon Dragon 2001, Scenic Warrior 2000, Star Video 1991).
Current winning jockeys: 4 wins Kerrin McEvoy (Paximadia 2013, Tatra 2012, Kidnapped 2009, Caymans 2008); Damien Oliver (Schilling 2008, Moon Dragon 2001, Scenic Warrior 2000, Star Video 1991).
2 wins Craig Williams (Morton's Fork 2016, So Swift 2011).
1 win Corey Brown (Binding 2004); Nick Hall (Petrology 2014); Luke Nolen (Villermont 2017); Brett Prebble (Pay Keys 2003); Brad Rawiller (Mahuta 2015); Nash Rawiller (Pressday 2010).
Leading winning trainers: 5 wins Tommy Smith (Stargazer 1989, Shankhill Lass 1985, Snowing 1979, Just A Steal 1978, Orient 1957).
4 wins Peter Snowden (Paximadia 2013, Tatra 2012, Kidnapped 2009, Caymans 2008).
Current winning trainers: 4 wins Peter Snowden (Paximadia 2013, Tatra 2012, Kidnapped 2009, Caymans 2008).
3 wins John Hawkes (Binding 2004, Dextrous 2002, Over 1999).
2 wins Lee Freedman (Moon Dragon 2001, Scenic Warrior 2000); David Hayes (Petrology 2014, Cayambe 2005); John Meagher (Voting 1993, Star Video 1991).
1 win David Hayes & Tom Dabernig (Petrology 2014); John Hickmott (Pay Keys 2003); John O'Shea (Morton's Fork 2016); Paul Perry (Navy Seal 1992); Mick Price (Schilling 2007); Aaron Purcell (Villermont 2017); Chris Waller (Pressday 2010); Darren Weir (Mahuta 2015); Bill & Simon Wilde (So Swift 2011).
Point of interest: Durbridge (1990) is the only Sandown Guineas winner to win an ATC Australian Derby (1991).

MRC Zipping Classic (2400m)—Sandown Hillside
$300,000 Group 2 Open WFA. November 17, 2018.

YEAR	WINNER	JOCKEY	TRAINER	2ND	3RD	TIME
2017	The Taj Mahal	Ben Melham	Robert Hickmott	Almandin	Big Duke	2:30.0
2016	Beautiful Romance	Glyn Schofield	Saeed bin Suroor	Almoonqith	Big Orange	2:29.0
2015	Who Shot Thebarman	James McDonald	Chris Waller	Tall Ship	Do You Remember	2:29.1
2014	Au Revoir	Kerrin McEvoy	Andre Fabre	Epingle	Prince Of Penzance	2:32.0
2013	Sertorius	Ryan Maloney	Jamie Edwards	Epingle	Queenstown	2:30.9
2012	Tanby	Nicholas Hall	Robert Hickmott	Exceptionally	Precedence	2:32.0
2011	Americain	Gerald Mosse	Alain De Royer Dupre	Manighar	Mourayan	2:37.8
2010	Zipping	Nicholas Hall	Robert Hickmott	Exceptionally	Manighar	2:39.4
2009	Zipping	Michael Rodd	Robert Hickmott	Purple	Master O'reilly	2:32.2
2008	Zipping	Michael Rodd	John Sadler	Douro Valley	Red Ruler	2:35.0
2007	Zipping	Steven Arnold	John Sadler	Jukebox Johnny	Baughurst	2:33.7
2006	Gallant Guru	Steven Arnold	Lee Freedman	Casual Pass	Show Barry	2:30.8
2005	Roman Arch	Noel Callow	Robbie Laing	Grey Song	Expunge	2:33.7
2004	Count Ricardo	Blake Shinn	Stephen Theodore	Fantastic Love	Media Puzzle	2:37.9
2003	Legible	Danny Nikolic	Bradley Marzato	Distinctly Secret	Zazzman	2:29.8
2002	Hail	Greg Childs	Bruce Marsh	Hill Of Grace	Grey Song	2:27.9
2001	Sky Heights	Damien Oliver	Colin Alderson	King Keitel	Cinder Bella	2:28.3
2000	Brave Chief	Patrick Payne	John Ledger	Forgotten Hero	Pasta Express	2:24.3

BACKGROUND

First run: 1888 (won by Mara). Group 2 since 1979. WFA since 1999. Run over 2200m 1888-1919.
First run at Sandown in 1965, won by Red William. Also known as the Sandown Classic, Sandown Cup and Williamstown Cup. Registered as the Sandown Classic.
Most recent mare to win: Beautiful Romance (2016).
Most recent 3YO to win: C&G—Count Ricardo (2004); Filly—Eleanor (1902).
Multiple winners: 3—Zipping (2010, 2009, 2008, 2007); Morse Code (1952, 1950); Second Wind (1931, 1930).
Fastest time (2400m): Brave Chief (2000) 2:24.30
Notable winners: Beautiful Romance (2016); Who Shot The Barman (2015); Au Revoir (2014); Americain (2011); Zipping (2010, 2009. 2008, 2007); Roman Arch (2005); Sky Heights (2001); Stylish Century (1991); Sydeston (1989); Arwon (1980); Baghdad Note (1973); Gunsynd (1971); Light Fingers (1966); Sailor's Guide (1957); Shadow King (1933); Amounis (1928); King Ingoda (1922); Richmond Main (1919).
Zipping Classic winners won earlier spring races:
The Bart Cummings: 1—Tanby (2012).
Turnbull Stakes: 1—Zipping (2010).
Bendigo Cup: 1—Sertorius (2013). Note: The Bendigo Cup was run after the Sandown Classic to 2012.
Geelong Cup: 2—Allez Bijoy (1981), Hauberk (1979).
Moonee Valley Cup: 1—Americain (2011).
Lexus Stakes: 4—Fighting Force (1956): My Hero (1953); Howe (1948); Sirius (1944).
Melbourne Cup: 2—Sirius (1944); King Ingoda (1922).
Melbourne Cup (different years): 5—Americain (Cup 2010, Classic 2011); Arwon (Cup 1978, Classic 1980); Baghdad Note (Cup 1970, Classic 1973); Light Fingers (Cup 1965, Classic 1966); Tarcoola (Cup 1893, Classic 1889).
VRC Queen Elizabeth: 1—Gallant Guru (2006).
Zipping Classic winners went on to win in the same preparation:
Eclipse Stakes: 4—What's Brewing (1970); Morse Code (1950, 1952); Manolive (1938).
Note: The Eclipse Stakes is now run on the same day.
Leading winning jockey (from 1965 when first run at Sandown): 4 wins Roy Higgins (Salamander 1978, Gunsynd 1971, General Command 1969, Light Fingers 1966).
Current winning jockeys: 2 wins Nick Hall (Tanby 2012, Zipping 2010); Michael Rodd (Zipping 2009, 2008).
1 win Steven Arnold (Zipping 2007, Gallant Guru 2006); Noel Callow (Roman Arch 2005); Kevin Forrester (Conbituate Lady 1988); Ryan Maloney (Sertorius 2013); James McDonald (Who Shot Thebarman 2015); Kerrin McEvoy (Au Revoir 2014); Ben Melham (The Taj Mahal 2017); Gerald Mosse (Americain 2011); Damien Oliver (Sky Heights 2001); Brett Prebble (Star Binder 1997); Glyn Schofield (Beautiful Romance 2016); Blake Shinn (Count Ricardo 2004).
Leading winning trainers (from 1965 when first run at Sandown): 4 wins Robert Hickmott (The Taj Mahal 2017, Tanby 2012, Zipping 2010, 2009).
3 wins Colin Alderson (Sky Heights 2001, Puckle Harbour 1985, Rich Brother 1984); George Hanlon (Royal Snack 1996, Our Pompeii 1994, Arwon 1980); John Sadler (Zipping 2008, 2007, Pressman's Choice 1990).
Current trainers: 4 wins Robert Hickmott (The Taj Mahal 2017, Tanby 2012, Zipping 2010, 2009); John Sadler (Zipping 2008, 2007, Pressman's Choice 1990).
2 wins Lee Freedman (Gallant Guru 2006, Count Chivas 1995); John Meagher (Star Binder 1997, Tawlord 1993).
1 win Toby Autridge (Al Dwain 1983); Saeed bin Suroor (Beautiful Romance 2016); Cliff Brown (Cheviot 1998); Alain de Royer Dupre (Americain 2011); Jamie Edwards (Sertorius 2013, in partnership with Bruce Elkington); Andre Fabre (Au Revoir 2014); Peter Hurdle (Aerosmith 1999); Robbie Laing (Roman Arch 2005); John Ledger (Brave Chief 2000); Stephen Marsh (Hail 2002); Brian Smith (Pharostan 1986); Stephen Theodore (Count Ricardo 2004); Chris Waller (Who Shot Thebarman 2015).
Points of interest: Big Colony (1991) was first past the post, but was later disqualified over a positive swab. Stylish Century was declared the winner. Aerosmith (1999) survived a protest from Zerpour. In the last 25 years, five horses have won the Sandown Classic after running in the Melbourne Cup. The latest is Zipping (2007), who ran fourth to Efficient at Flemington.
Au Revoir (2014) was trained in France by Andre Fabre.
Americain (2011) was trained in France by Alain de Royer Dupre.
Beautiful Romance (2016) was trained in England by Saeed bin Suroor for Godolphin.
The Taj Mahal (2017) is a northern hemisphere-bred 3YO—bred in Ireland—but races in Australia as a 4YO.
Lloyd Williams has owned or part-owned seven winners of the Zipping Classic—The Taj Mahal (2017); Tanby (2012), Zipping (2007, 2008, 2009, 2010), Legible (2003).

WATC WA Guineas (1600m)—Ascot
$500,000 Group 2 3YO Open SW. November 24, 2018.

YEAR	WINNER	JOCKEY	TRAINER	2ND	3RD	TIME
2017	Perfect Jewel	Willie Pike	Grant & Alana Williams	Achernar Star	Art Series	1:36.6
2016	Variation	Damian Lane	Stephen Miller	Ellicazoom	Ragazzo D'Oro	1:37.0
2015	Man Booker	Jerry Noske	Daniel Morton	Spirit Bird	The Cobbla	1:34.7
2014	Rommel	Steven Parnham	Neville Parnham	Disposition	Say Geronimo	1:36.0
2013	Ihtsahymn	Steven Parnham	Fred Kersley	Miss Rose De Iago	Saint Bro	1:37.6
2012	Academus	Kerrin McEvoy	Peter Snowden	Bippo No Bungus	Darlington Abbey	1:35.9
2011	King Saul	Craig Williams	Trevor Andrews	Caiguna	Red Hot Sax	1:36.1
2010	Playing God	Steven Parnham	Neville Parnham	Lauradane	Hoegaarden	1:36.2
2009	Clueless Angel	Alan Kennedy	Lindsey Smith	Thorn Dancer	The Corporation	1:35.0
2008	Moccasin Bend	Jason Whiting	Lou & Dion Luciani	Locus Standi	Saxon Palace	1:33.7
2007	Megatic	Paul Harvey	Albert Beckett	Perestroika	Moisture	1:35.6
2006	Vain Crusader	Paul Harvey	Trevor Andrews	Real Cheeky	Translate	1:35.8
2005	Cape North	Daniel Staeck	Fred Kersley	Lock The Vault	Geil	1:36.0
2004	Dr John	Willie Pike	Ross Price	Moet Magic	Stormy Nova	1:36.7
2003	River Mist	Peter Knuckey	George Daly	Changing Lanes	Laetare	1:37.3
2002	The Right Money	Paul Harvey	Trevor Andrews	Trimagic	Amphritite	1:36.8
2001	Royal Retrieve	Tom Stubberfield	Neville Parnham	Kentiara	Dexian	1:36.0

BACKGROUND
First run: 1937 (won by Footmark). Group 3 1979-80; Group 2 from 1981. Run at Belmont in 2003.
Most recent filly to win: Perfect Jewel (2017). Note: 13 fillies have won.
Fastest time (1600m): Moccasin Bend (2008) 1:33.70
Notable winners: Variaton (2016); Ihtsahymn (2013); Playing God (2010); Megatic (2007); Summer Beau (1996); Classy Dresser (1992); Importune (1984); Rare Sovereign (1978); Ngawyni (1975); Millefleurs (1972); Norval Boy (1963); Nicopolis (1962); Chestillion (1960); Chestnut Lady (1951); Westralian (1947); True Flight (1939).
WA Guineas and the Karrakatta Plate:
1—Rare Sovereign (Karrakatta 1977; Guineas 1978).
WA Guineas winners also won in same season:
Belgravia Stakes: 17—Perfect Jewel (2017); King Saul (2011); Moccasin Bend (2008); Megatic (2007); The Right Money (2002); So Dashing (1990); Blue Nucleus (1976); Jolly Aster (1966); Baccare (1965); Nicopolis (1962); Chestillion (1960); Queen Of The May (1959); Emporium (1957); Fairflow (1956); Mallant (1955); Raconteur (1952); Jovial Lad (1950).
Fairetha Stakes: 5—Vain Crusader (2006); Royal Retrieve (2001); Tip The Pro (1994); Kaysart (1989); Importune (1984).
Strickland Stakes: 11—Tabharry (1987); Ngawyni (1975); Millefleurs (1972); Jolly Aster (1966); Nicopolis (1962); Chestillion (1960); Raconteur (1952); Chestnut Lady (1951); Jovial Lad (1950); True Flight (1939); Gay Prince (1938).
WA Fillies Championship: 4—Queen Of The May (1959); Chestnut Lady (Guineas Nov 1951, Fillies Mar 1952); Prediction (Guineas Nov 1949. Fillies Mar 1950); Jennie (Guineas Nov 1948, Fillies Mar 1949). Note: Queen Of The May is the only filly to win the double in same campaign/year.
Lee Steere Classic: 1—Classy Dresser (Guineas Nov 1992, Lee Steere Jan 1993).
WA Oaks: 1—Fairflow (Guineas 1956, Oaks 1957). No horses have completed the double since the Oaks was moved from the summer to the autumn in 2002.
WA Derby: 12—Ngawyni (1975); Nicopolis (1962); Chestillion (1960); Raconteur (1952); Jovial Lad (1950); Prediction (1949); Westralian (1947); Cherbourg (1945); Lord Treat (1944); True Flight (1939); Gay Prince (1938); Footmark (1937). Note: No horses have completed the double since the Derby was moved from the summer to the autumn in 2002.
Winterbottom Stakes: 2—Nicopolis (1962), Raconteur (1952).
Railway Stakes: 1—Millefleurs (1972). Note: Kilrickle (1969) won the Railway as a 4YO in 1970 (on protest).
CB Cox Stakes: 1—Ihtsahymn (2013).
Kingston Town Classic: 6—Ihtsahymn (2013); Playing God (2010); Megatic (2007); Old Nick (1998); Summer Beau (1996); Importune (1984).
Belmont Guineas: 1—Variation (2017).
Leading winning jockeys: 5 wins Frank "Tiger" Moore (Millefleurs 1972, Super Sam 1967, Baccare 1965, Nicopolis 1962, Emporium 1957).
4 wins Paul Harvey (Megaton 2007, Vain Crusader 2006, The Right Money 2002, Kalatiara 2000); Frank Treen (Kilrickle 1969, Chestnut Lady 1951, Jovial Lad 1950, Prediction 1949).
Current winning jockeys: 4 wins Paul Harvey (Megaton 2007, Vain Crusader 2006, The Right Money 2002, Kalatiara 2000).

3 wins Steven Parnham (Rommel 2014, Ihtsahymn 2013, Playing God 2010); Willie Pike (Perfect Jewel 2017, Dreamaway Feb 2011, Dr John 2004).
1 win Alan Kennedy (Clueless Angel 2009); Peter Knuckey (River Mist 2003); Damian Lane (Variation 2016); Kerrin McEvoy (Academus 2012); Jerry Noske (Man Booker 2015); Daniel Staeck (Cape North 2005); Craig Williams (King Saul Nov 2011); Jason Whiting (Moccasin Bend 2008).
Leading winning trainers: 3 wins Harold Campbell (Millefleurs 1972, Super Sam 1967, Nicopolis 1962); Ted McAuliffe (Emporium 1957, Jovial Lad 1950, Prediction 1948); Neville Parnham (Rommel 2014, Playing God 2010, Royal Retrieve 2001); Reg Treffone (Rock Drill 1964, Water Power 1961, Queen Of The May 1959).
Current winning trainers: 3 wins Neville Parnham (Rommel 2014, Playing God 2010, Royal Retrieve 2001).
2 wins Trevor Andrews (King Saul Nov 2011, Vain Crusader 2006); Paul Jordan (Devlish Dealer 1999, El Cordero 1993); Fred Kersley (Ihtsahymn 2013, Cape North 2005); Alan Mathews (Kaysart 1989, Importune 1984); Grant Williams (Perfect Jewel 2017, Dreamaway Feb 2011).
1 win Albert Beckett (Megatic 2007); Robert Harvey (Kalatiara 2000); Lou Luciani (Moccasin Bend 2008); Stephen Miller (Variation 2016); Daniel Morton (Man Booker 2015); Ross Price (Dr John 2004); Lindsey Smith (Clueless Angel 2009); Peter Snowden (Academus 2012); Grant & Alana Williams (Perfect Jewel 2017); Chris Willis (Chelsea 1997).
Points of interest: Nicopolis (1962) trained on to be a top-class performer in Melbourne, where he won the 1963 and 1964 G1 Toorak Handicap, and the 1965 G1 Invitation Stakes.
Ngawyni (1975) trained in to be a star galloper for trainer Bart Cummings. In 1977 he won the G1 Australian Cup at Flemington, the G1 Queen Elizabeth Stakes at Randwick, the G2 O'Shea Stakes at Eagle Farm, and the G2 Moonee Valley Cup at Moonee Valley.
Millefleurs (1972) was sold to Geoffrey Levett in Victoria, and she won the 1973 G1 Invitation Stakes at Caulfield.
Raconteur (1952), who also won the 1952 Winterbottom Stakes, went east to win the 1953 Villiers Stakes at Randwick.

ATC Villiers Stakes (1600m)—Randwick
$250,000 Group 2 3YO&Up Quality Handicap. December 15, 2018.

YEAR	WINNER	JOCKEY	TRAINER	2ND	3RD	TIME
2017	Crack Me Up	Jason Collett	Liam Birchley	Cabeza de Vaca	Interlocuter	1:34.9
2016	Sense Of Occasion	Ben Melham	Kris Lees	Dibayani	Sarrasin	1:37.4
2015	Happy Clapper	Brenton Avdulla	Patrick Webster	Tinto	It's Somewhat	1:33.9
2014	Rudy	Luke Tarrant	Helen Page	I'm Imposing	Strawberry Boy	1:36.2
2013	Ninth Legion	Peter Robl	Michael, Wayne & John Hawkes	Limes	Alma's Fury	1:31.4
2012	All Legal	Glyn Schofield	Kevin Moses	Alma's Fury	Darci Be Good	1:35.8
2011	Monton	Hugh Bowman	Ron Quinton	Kontiki Park	King Lionheart	1:36.3
2010	Dances On Waves	Brenton Avdulla	Gerald Ryan	Mentality	Snow Alert	1:35.0
2009	Palacio De Cristal	Peter Wells	Grahame Begg	Parfumier	Spinney	1:34.7
2008	(Dec) Something Anything	Chris Munce	Gary Portelli	Hey Elvis	Rags To Riches	1:36.3
2008	(Jan) Honor In War	Hugh Bowman	Chris Waller	Takeover Target	Alverta	1.21.5
2007	Race not run					
2006	Utzon	Len Beasley	Les Bridge	Anwaar	Spirit of Tara	1:35.2
2005	Aqua D'Amore	Danny Beasley	Gai Waterhouse	Malcolm	Fiery Venture	1.35.4
2004	Ike's Dream	Darren Beadman	John Hawkes	Dante's Paradiso	Sir Dex	1.33.1
2003	On a High	Larry Cassidy	John O'Shea	Mufti	Jeremiad	1.35.8
2002	Boreale	Darren Beadman	John Hawkes	This Manshood	Silver Birch	1.34.8
2001	Carael Boy	Brad Pengelly	Bob Milligan	Space Age	Osca Warrior	1.36.5

BACKGROUND
First run: 1892 (won by Two Up). Group 3 1979-85. Group 2 from 1986. Run over six furlongs 1892–1901. Run over 1600m—1400m in January 2008. Not run in 2007 to El—run twice in 2008, Jan & Dec. Run on the Kensington track (1550m) in 2013.
Most recent mare to win: Palacio de Crystal (2009).
Most rcent 3YO to win: C&G—Hot Diggity (1977); Filly—Ordnance (1895).
Multiple winners: None.
Fastest time (1600m): Ike's Dream (2004) 1:33:13.
Notable winners: Sense Of Occasion (2016); Happy Clapper (2015); Honor In War (Jan 2008); Aqua D'Amore (2005); Referral (1998); Soho Square (1992); Dinky Flyer (1985); Oncidon (1973); Grenoble (1960); Bernborough (1945).
Villiers Stakes winners won the lead-up races:

Tatts Recognition Stakes (Doomben): 2—Crack Me Up (2017); Rudy (2014).
Hawkesbury Ladies' Day Cup: 1—All Legal (2012).
Hawkesbury Gold Cup: 4—Carael Boy (2001); Referral (1998); Shining Wind (1991); Hot Diggity (1977).
Festival Stakes: 4—Monton (2011); Utzon (2006); Ike's Dream (2004); Castanea (1965).
Villiers Stakes and the spring/summer "miles":
Epsom Handicap: None. Note: King's Head (1936) won the 1938 Epsom Handicap and Air Motor (1903) won the 1902 Epsom Handicap.
Cantala Stakes: None.
WATC Railway Stakes: None.
Leading winning jockeys: 4 wins Darren Beadman (Ike's Dream 2004; Boreale 2002; Touch Of Force 1996; Card Shark 1987); Ted Bartle (Rimveil 1940; King's Head 1936; Closing Time 1933; Pavilion 1930).
Current winning jockeys: 3 wins Larry Cassidy (On A High 2003, Referral 1998, Cobbora 1993).
2 wins Brenton Avdulla (Happy Clapper 2015, Dances On Waves 2010); Hugh Bowman (Monton 2011, Honor In War 2008 Jan).
1 win Jason Collett (Crack Me Up 2017); Ben Melham (Sense Of Occasion 2016); Brad Pengelly (Carael Boy 2001); Glyn Schofield (All Legal 2012); Luke Tarrant (Rudy 2014); Peter Wells (Palacio de Cristal 1009).
Leading winning trainer: 7 wins Tommy Smith (Hot Diggity 1977, St. Martin 1975, Americano 1974, Onicdon 1973, Tumberlua 1971, Caesar 1958, Top Ruler 1957).
Current winning trainers: 3 wins John Hawkes (Ninth Legion 2013, Ike's Dream 2004, Boreale 2002).
2 wins Les Bridge (Utzon 2006, Maigret 1967); John O'Shea (On A High 2003, Grey And Gold 2000); Helen Page (Rudy 2014, Spot The Rock 1989).
1 win Alex Aquilina (Aunty Mary 1994); Grahame Begg (Palacio De Crystal 2009); Liam Birchley (Crack Me Up 2017); Bruce Cross (Fine Fantasy 1999); Keith Dryden (Tumble On 1988); Steve Englebrecht (Referral 1998); Lee Freedman (Cobbora 1993): Michael, Wayne, John Hawkes (Ninth Legion 2013); Kris Lees (Sense Of Occasion 2016); Lawrie Mayfield-Smith (Post Elect 1990); John Meagher (Touch Of Force 1996); Bob Milligan (Carael Boy 2001); Kevin Moses (All Legal 2012); Paul O'Sullivan (Arletty 1997); Gary Portelli (Something Anything 2008); Ron Quinton (Monton 2011); Gerald Ryan (Dance On Waves 2010); Chris Waller (Honor In War 2008); Gai Waterhouse (Aqua D'Amore 2005); Pat Webster (Happy Clapper 2015).

WATC Ted Van Heemst Stakes (2100m)—Ascot
$250,000 Group 2 3YO&Up WFA. December 22, 2018.

YEAR	WINNER	JOCKEY	TRAINER	2ND	3RD	TIME
2017	Pounamu	Pat Carbery	Alan Mathews	Material Man	Zarantz	2:16.7
2016	Perfect Reflection	Willie Pike	Grant & Alana Williams	Fathoms Of Gold	Ihtsahymn	2:14.1
2015	Delicacy	Willie Pike	Grant Williams	Black Heart Bart	Bass Strait	2:14.3
2014	Elite Elle	Willie Pike	Grant Williams	Red Blast	Bass Strait	2:14.8
2013	Ihtsahymn	Steven Parnham	Fred Kersley	Kincaple	Rohan	2:11.1
2012	Mr Moet	Daniel Staeck	Adam Durrant	Chester Road	Road Ranger	2:19.8
2011	God Has Spoken	Steven Parnham	Neville Parnham	Kincaple	Ranger	2:09.8
2010	Colour Correct	Paul Harvey	Ross & Clint Price	Admiring	Big Ted	2.08.7
2009	Lords Ransom	Jason Whiting	Adam Durrant	Largo Lad	Dante's Banquet	2:08.8
2008	Gilded Venom	Pat Carbery	Steve Wallace	Annenkov	The Fuzz	2:08.7
2007	Cats Fun	Damien Oliver	Michael Grant	Westerly Breeze	Guyno	2:30.5
2006	DH Daka's Gem/Scenic Shot	Pat Carbery/Damien Oliver	Alan Mathews/Daniel Morton		Ramiro	2:32.5
2005	Early Express	Jason Whiting	Peter Giadresco	Blevvo	Bon Argent	2:29.4
2004	Free At Last	Troy Turner	Alan Mathews	Laetare	Black Tom	2:30.9
2003	Celtus	Peter Knuckey	Lindsey Smith	Higgins Gold	Free At Last	2:32.6
2002	Bold Mirage	Troy Turner	Alan Mathews	Tumeric	Alibi Bay	2:32.3
2001	Never Blue	Paul Harvey	Ross Price	Finito	Lottila Bay	2:32.3

BACKGROUND
First run: 1914 (won by Radnor). Group 2 from 1979. Run over 2400m 1914-1931, 1934-36, 1938-42 & 1952-2007; 1600m 1932-33 & 1937; 2200m 1945-51. Previously known as the Grandstand Plate. Run at Belmont in 2003. Not held 1942 & 1944. Run in January until 1944. Registered as the C.B. Cox Stakes, and known as that until 2015.
Most recent mare to win: Perfect Reflection (2016).
Most recent 3YO to win: C&G—Ihtsahymn (2013). Filly—Old Money (2000). Note: 10 3YOs have won.
Multiple winners: 7—Old Cobber (1999, 1997); Haulpak's Image (1986, 1983); Tropical Chief (1976, 1975); Royal Coral (1966, 1965); Gay Balkan (1941, 1940, 1939); Maple (1928, 1927); Eracre (1926, 1925).

Fastest time (2100m): Gilded Venom (2008) 2:08.7
Notable winners: Pounamu (2017); Perfect Reflection (2016); Delicacy (2015); Mr Moet (2012); Old Money (2000); Dark Ksar (1995); Palatious (1993); Tawrrific (1989); Phizam (1984); Nicholas John (1982); Yashmak (1980); Regimental Honour (1979); Battle Heights (1974); Piping Lane (1972); Royal Coral (1966, 1965); Rack And Ruin (1964); Lady Lucia (1949); Maple (1927, 1926); Eurythmic (1920); Mistico (1917).
Ted Van Heemst Stakes winners also won:
Kingston Town Classic: 3—Pounamu (2017); Ihtsahymn (2013); Early Express (2005).
WA Derby: 8—Delicacy (2015); Old Money (2000); Mirror Magic (1991); Yaringa (Derby Dec 1935); Cox Jan 1936); Hyperion (Dec 1934; Jan 1935); Maple (Dec 1926; Jan 1927); Lilypond (Dec 1923; Jan 1924); Eurythmic (Dec 1919; Jan 1920); Radnor (Dec 1913; Jan 1914).
Perth Cup: 13—Delicacy (Cup 2016); Lords Ransom (2010); Cats Fun (2008); Palatious (1994); Mirror Magic (1992); Saratov (1989); Phizam (1985); Royal Coral (1965); Bay Count (1963); Gay Prince (1939); Lilypond (1924); Jolly Cosy (1923); Eurythmic (1919).
Ted Van Heemst Stakes and the Melbourne Cup:
Tawrrific (1989) and Piping Lane (1972) won the Cox Stakes after winning the Melbourne Cup.
Leading winning jockey: 8 wins Frank "Tiger" Moore (Little Empire 1962, Sparkling Blue 1959, Tribal Ring 1957, Melton Prince 1955, Coronate 1954, Kingsman 1951, Dhostar 1950, Sam Sanatra 1948).
Current winning jockeys: 3 wins Pat Carbery (Pounamu 2017, Gilded Venom 2008, Daka's Gem 2006); Peter Knuckey (Celtus 2003, Old Cobber 1999, 1997); Willie Pike (Perfect Reflection 2016, Delicacy 2015, Elite Belle 2014); Troy Turner (Free At Last 2004, Bold Mirage 2002, Beau Heed 1996).
2 wins Paul Harvey (Colour Correct 2010, Never Blue 2001); Damien Oliver (Cats Fun 2007, Scenic Shot 2006); Steven Parnham (Ihtsahymn 2013, God Has Spoken 2011); Jason Whiting (Lords Ransom 2009, Early Express 2005).
1 win Daniel Staeck (Mr Moet 2012).
Leading winning trainer: 9 wins Jim "JJ" Kelly (Gay Balkan 1941, 1940, 1939, Maikai 1938, Yaringa 1936, Maple 1928, 1927, Eurythmic 1920, New Tipperary 1915).
Current winning trainers: 6 wins Alan Mathews (Pounamu 2017, Daka's Gem 2006, Free At Last 2004, Bold Mirage 2002, Palatious 1993, Mirror Magic 1991).
4 wins Lindsey Smith (Celtus 2003, Old Money 2000, Old Cobber 1999, 1997).
3 wins Grant Williams (Perfect Reflection 2016, Delicacy 2015, Elite Belle 2014).
2 wins Adam Durrant (Mr Moet 2012, Lords Ransom 2009); David Harrison (Haulpak's Image 1986, 1983); Ross Price (Colour Correct 2010, Never Blue 2001).
1 win Lee Freedman (Tawrrific 1989); Peter Giadresco (Early Express 2005); Fred Kersley (Ihtsahymn 2013); Neville Parnham (God Has Spoken 2011); Ross & Clint Price (Colour Correct 2010); Steve Wallace (Gilded Venom 2008); Grant & Alana Williams (Perfect Reflection 2016).

WATC Perth Cup (2400m)—Ascot
$500,000 Group 2 Quality Handicap. January 5, 2019.

YEAR	WINNER	JOCKEY	TRAINER	2ND	3RD	TIME
2018	Material Man	Lucy Warwick	Justin Warwick	Pounamu	Royal Star	2:28.5
2016 (Dec)	Star Exhibit	Jarrad Noske	Geoff Durrant & Jason Miller	Neverland	Tradesman	2:29.4
2016	Delicacy	Peter Hall	Grant Williams	Neverland	Real Love	2:30.0
2015	Real Love	Willie Pike	Adam Durrant	Red Blast	Kirov Boy	2:29.9
2014	Black Tycoon	Damien Oliver	Justin Warwick	God Has Spoken	Ask Me Nicely	2:31.2
2013	Talent Show	Jarrad Noske	Graeme Ballantyne	Mr Moet	Global Flirt	2:29.7
2011 (Dec)	Western Jewel	Kyra Yuill	Grant Williams	God Has Spoken	Senhor Da Gama	2:28.2
2011 (Jan)	Guest Wing	Brad Parnham	Shane Edwards	Guyno	Simply Adorable	2:27.5
2010	Lords Ransom	Alan Kennedy	Adam Durrant	Ma Chienne	Largo Lad	2:30.6
2009	Guyno	Jason Whiting	Lou Luciani	The Fuzz	Ballack	2:25.9
2008	Cats Fun	Damien Oliver	Michael Grant	Exhilerating	Westerly Breeze	3:21.6
2007	Respect	Jason Whiting	Paul Cave	Bay Story	Rossam	3:21.0
2006	Black Tom	Peter Hall	Frank Maynard	Master Minx	Early Express	3:18.8
2005	Crown Prosecutor	Willie Pike	Lindsey Smith	Free At Last	Black Tom	3:21.4
2004	King Canute	Jason Whiting	Lou Luciani	Indigo King	Higgins Gold	3:23.7
2002	Cardinal Colours	Neil Chapman	Michael Miller	Give Me A Chance	Shoeless	3:25.9
2001	Lottila Bay	Pat Carbery	Alan Mathews	Moonrise	King Brian	3:25.6
2000	Lunar Tudor	Jason Brown	Neville Parnham	Victory Morn	Matriculate	3:21.0

BACKGROUND
First run: 1887 (won by First Prince). Group 1 1980-92. Group 2 from 1993. 3200 metres 1887-2008; 2400m from 2009.

Most recent mare to win: Delicacy (2016).
Most recent 3YO to win: C&G—Crying Game (1996). No 3YO filly has won.
Multiple winners: 7—Magistrate (1982, 1981); Fait Accompli (1972, 1970); Fairetha (1959, 1958); Cueesun (1935, Dec 1933,); Artesian (1913, 1911); Scarpia (1894, 1893); Wandering Willie (1892, 1890).
Fastest time (2400m): Guyno (2009) 2:25.90.
Notable winners: Delicacy (2016); Guyno (2009); Cats Fun (2008); Palatious (1994); Phizam (1985); Moss Kingdom (1984); Bianco Lady (1983); Magistrate (1982, 1981); Muros (1977); Dayana (1973); Royal Coral (1966); Eurythmic (1919); Loch Shiel (1909); Blue Spec (1904); Wandering Willie (1892, 1890).
Perth Cup winners have won the lead-up races:
Towton Cup (also known as the Queen's Cup): 4—Real Love (Cup 2015); Cardinal Colours (2002); Linc The Leopard (1988); Ullyatt (1986).
Tattersall's Cup: 9—Black Tycoon (Cup 2014), Cats Fun (2008); Black Top (2006); Crown Prosecutor (2005); Time Frame (1997); Rocket Racer (1987); Phizam (1985); Runyon (1975); Artello Bay (1970).
Cox Stakes: 13—Delicacy (2016); Lords Ransom (Cup 2010); Cats Fun (2008); Palatious (1994); Mirror Magic (1992); Saratov (1989); Phizam (1985); Royal Coral (1965); Bay Count (1963); Gay Prince (1939); Lilypond (1924); Jolly Cosy (1923); Eurythmic (1919).
A.T.A Stakes: 2—Star Exhibit (2016); Ros Reef (Cup 1995). Note: Western Jewel (Cup 2012) won the ATA and the Perth Cup when it was a non-Stakes BM80 Handicap (Non-Stakes from 2005-2014)
The Perth Cup and WA Derby: Note: WA Derby moved to from the spring (before the Perth Cup) to the autumn in 2002.
WA Derby (as a 4YO): 6—Delicacy (2016); Crying Game (Cup 1996); Raconteur (1953); Inveray (1896); Scarpia (1893); Aim (1889).
WA Derby (as a 3YO): 4—Dayana (1973); Lilypond (1923); Eurythmic (1919); Post Town (1907).
Leading winning jockeys 5 wins Frank Treen (Jenark 1969, Resolution 1964, Bay Count 1963, Avarna 1951, Ghurka 1949).
3 wins Bob Morley (Coolbarro 1930, Mercato 1925, Earl Of Seafield 1921); W.A. "Billy" Smith (Artello Bay 1971, Special Reward 1967, Royal Khora 1962); Eric Treffone (Raconteur 1953, Gay Balkan 1938 Dec, Maikai 1938); Bob Trewartha (Mural 1899, Australian 1901, Inveary 1895); Jason Whiting (Guyno 2009, Respect 2007, King Canute 2004); John Wilson (Meliador 1979, Fairetha 1959, 1958).
Current winning jockeys: 3 wins Jason Whiting (Guyno 2009, Respect 2007, King Canute 2004).
2 wins Peter Hall (Delicacy 2016, Black Tom 2006); Damien Oliver (Black Tycoon 2014, Cats Fun 2008); Willie Pike (Real Love 2015, Crown Prosecutor 2005).
1 win Alan Kennedy (Lords Ransom 2010); Jason Brown (Luna Tudor 2000); Pat Carbery (Lollita Bay 2001); Paul Harvey (Crying Game 1996); Peter Knuckey (Field Officer 1993); Jarrad Noske (Talent Show 2013), Brad Parnham (Guest Wing 2011); Lucy Warwick (Material Man 2018); Kyra Yuill (Western Jewel 2012).
Leading winning trainers: 7 wins Jim "JJ"Kelly (Gay Balkan 1939, Maikai 1938, Bonny Note 1931, Coolbarro 1929, Eurythmic 1918, Downing Street 1917, Sparkle 1912)
6 wins Alan Mathews (Tumeric 2003, Lollita Bay 2001, Palatious 1994, Field Officer 1993, Mirror Magic 1992, Word Of Honour 1990); George Towton (Snapshot 1897, Durable 1895, Scarpia 1893, Wandering Willie 1892, The Duke 1891, Telephone 1888).
4 wins Bob Burns (Lucky Escape 1916, Seigneur 1920; Gay Parade 1945, Sydney James 1947); Albert Jordan (Fair's Print 1965, Resolution 1964, Fairetha 1959, 1958); John Pullen (Jolly Beggar 1910, Post Town 1907; May King 1906, Czarovitch 1905).
Current winning trainers: 6 wins Alan Mathews (Tumeric 2003, Lollita Bay 2001, Palatious 1994, Field Officer 1993, Mirror Magic 1992, Word Of Honour 1990).
2 wins Adam Durrant (Real Love 2015, Lords Ransom 2010); Lou Luciani (Guyno 2009, King Canute 2004); Frank Maynard (Black Tom 2006, Moss Kingdom 1984); Justin Warwick (Material Man 2018, Black Tycoon 2014); Grant Williams (Delicacy 2016, Western Jewel 2012).
1 win Paul Cave (Respect 2007); Mick Grant (Cats Fun 2008); Graeme Ballantyne (Talent Show 2013); John Hawkes (Runyon 1975); Michael Miller (Cardinal Colours 2002); Wally Mitchell (Linc The Leopard 1998); Neville Parnham (Luna Tudor 2000); Angela Smith (Time Frame 1997); Lindsey Smith (Crown Prosecutor 2005); Steve Wallace (Heed The Toll 1998).
Points of interest: Eurythmic (1919) won the Caulfield Cup in 1920. Blue Spec (1904) won the 1905 Melbourne Cup.
Telephone (1888) won on protest.
Eurythmic and Rivose (1919) dead-heated.
George Towton trained six winners—he owned and trained them all, and also rode Wandering Willie to win in 1892. He is the only person to own, train and ride a winner.
Big-time owner Paddy Connolly owned seven Perth Cup winners in the early 1900s. He raced his horses in the red and white colours. His winners were: Jolly Cosy 1920, Jolly Beggar 1910, Scorcher 1908, Post Town 1907, May King 1906, Czarowith 1905, Blue Spec 1904.
Bob and Sandra Peters have bred and owned seven winners—Star Exhibit (2016); Delicacy (2016); Real Love (2015), Western Jewel (2012), Lords Ransom (2010), Crown Prosecutor (2005) and Field Officer (1993). In 2016 (Dec), they bred and owned four if the first five placegetters—Star Exhibit (1st), Neverland (2nd), Perfect

Reflection (4th) and Dark Alert (5th).
Fran Gammon (Muros 1977) is the first female trainer to win the Perth Cup; Kay Miller has won it twice (Ros Reef 1995, Ullyatt 1986); Angela Smith (Time Frame 1997); Angela Johnson (Crying Game 1996).
Lucy Warwick (Material Man 201) and Kyra Yuill (Western Jewel 2012) are the only female jockeys to win the Perth Cup. Lucy Warwick's Material Man was trained by her father, Justin Warwick.
Delicacy won with 59kg—a record winning weight for a mare. No mare had won with 55kg or more.

MVRC Australia Stakes (1200m)—Moonee Valley
$200,000 Group 2 Open WFA. January 25, 2019.

YEAR	WINNER	JOCKEY	TRAINER	2ND	3RD	TIME
2018	Thronum	Mark Zahra	David & Ben Hayes & Tom Dabernig	Mr Sneaky	Stellar Collision	1:10.4
2017	Malaguerra	Ben Melham	Peter Galagotis	Black Heart Bart	Sirbible	1:09.2
2016	Holler	Craig Williams	John O'Shea	Churchill Dancer	Rebel Dane	1:10.9
2015	Mourinho	Vlad Duric	Peter Gelagotis	It is Written	Dissident	1:09.9
2014	Richie's Vibe	Damien Oliver	Tony Vasil	Moment Of Change	It Is Written	1:10.9
2013	Sea Lord	Luke Currie	Stephen Brown	Pinwheel	Outlandish Lad	1:10.5
2012	Black Caviar	Luke Nolen	Peter Moody	Zedi Knight	Doubtful Jack	1:09.4
2011	Whitefriars	Jim Cassidy	Rick Worthington	Undeniably	Typhoon Tracy	1.09.6
2010	Black Caviar	Luke Nolen	Peter Moody	Here De Angels	La Rocket	1:10.1
2009	Lucky Secret	Danny Brereton	Tony Vasil	Light Fantastic	Von Costa De Hero	1:11.2
2008	Let Go Thommo	Steven King	Simon Zahra	Maldivian	Casino Prince	1:10.8
2007	El Segundo	Damien Oliver	Colin Little	Cocinero	Super Elegant	1:11.2
2006	California Dane	Noel Callow	Lee Freedman	Virage De Fortune	Casual Pass	1:09.8
2005	Super Elegant	Greg Childs	Tony Vasil	Strikeline	Ruben	1:10.5
2004	Vocabulary	Danny Nikolic	Mick Price	Super Elegant	Confederate Kid	1:11.5
2003	Yell	Darren Gauci	John Hawkes	Libidinious	Pernod	1:10.3
2002	Royal Code	Steven Arnold	David Hall	Intelligent Star	Ustinov	1:11.0
2001	Piavonic	Nash Rawiller	Tony Noonan	Ateates	Le Zagaletta	1:11.8

BACKGROUND
First run: 1988 (won by Special). Listed 1989. Group 3 1990-93. Group 2 since 1994. Also known as the Carlyon Stakes. Registered as the Stanley Wootton Stakes. Run at Flemington in 1995.
Most recent mare to win: Black Caviar (2012).
Most recent 3YO to win: C&G – Holler (2016); Filly – Black Caviar (2010). Note: Eight 3YOs have won; only one filly.
Multiple winners: 1—Black Caviar (2012, 2010).
Fastest time (1200m): Hareeba (1995) 1:08:80.
Notable winners: Malaguerra (2017); Holler (2016); Black Caviar (2012, 2010); El Segundo (2007); Super Elegant (2005); Yell (2003); Flavour (1998); All Our Mob (1996); Hareeba (1995); Schillaci (1993); Redelva (1990); Jet Fighter (1989); Special (1988).
Australia Stakes winners won in the same preparation:
Rubiton Stakes: 2—Super Elegant (2005); Schillaci (1993).
William Reid Stakes: 2—Yell (2003); Hareeba (1995).
Peter Young Stakes: 1—Mourinho (2015).
Orr Stakes: 3—Black Caviar (2012); El Segundo (2007); Yell (2003).
Futurity Stakes: 2—Yell (2003); Schillaci (1993)
Lightning Stakes: 3—Black Caviar (2012); Schillaci (1993); Redelva (1990).
Newmarket Handicap: 1—Special (1988).
Canterbury Stakes: 1—Holler (2016).
Leading winning jockeys: 3 wins Darren Gauci (Yell 2003, Sports 1999, Clang 1997); Damien Oliver (Richie's Vibe 2014, El Segundo 2007, Schillaci 1993).
Current winning jockeys: 3 wins Damien Oliver (Richie's Vibe 2014, El Segundo 2007, Schillaci 1993).
2 wins Luke Nolen (Black Caviar 2012, 2010).
1 win Stephen Arnold (Royal Code 2002); Noel Callow (California Dane 2006); Luke Currie (Sea Lord 2013); Vlad Duric (Mourinho 2015); Ben Melham (Malaguerra 2017); Brett Prebble (Slavonic 2000); Nash Rawiller (Piavonic 2001); Craig Williams (Holler 2016); Mark Zahra (Thronum 2018).
Leading winning trainer 4 wins John Hawkes (Yell 2003, Sports 1999, Flavour 1998, Clang 1997).
3 wins Tony Vasil (Richie's Vibe 2014, Lucky Secret 2009, Super Elegant 2005).

Current winning trainers: 4 wins John Hawkes (Yell 2003, Sports 1999, Flavour 1998, Clang 1997).
3 wins Tony Vasil (Richie's Vibe 2014, Lucky Secret 2009, Super Elegant 2005).
2 wins Lee Freedman (California Dane 2006, Schillaci 1993); Peter Gelagotis (Malaguerra 2017, Mourinho 2015); Mick Price (Vocabulary 2004, Slavonic 2000).
1 win Stephen Brown (Sea Lord 2013); David Hall (Royal Code 2002); David & Ben Hayes & Tom Dabernig (Thronum 2018); Colin Little (El Segundo 2007); Tony Noonan (Plavonic 2001); John O'Shea (Holler 2016); John Sadler (Kenvain 1994); Gai Waterhouse (All Our Mob 1996); Rick Worthington (Whitefriars 2011); Simon Zahra (Let Go Thommo 2008).
Point of interest: Piavonic (2001) is the only Manikato Stakes winner (2001, spring) to win the Stanley Wootton Stakes.

ATC Expressway Stakes (1200m)—Rosehill
$200,000 Group 2 Open WFA. February 2, 2019.

YEAR	WINNER	JOCKEY	TRAINER	2ND	3RD	TIME
2018	Trapese Artist	Tim Clark	Gerald Ryan	Showtime	Addictive Nature	1:10.4
2017	Music Magnate	Kerrin McEvoy	Bjorn Baker	Kuro	Ball Of Muscle	1:09.4
2016	Our Boy Malachi	Tommy Berry	Michael, Wayne & John Hawkes	Solicit	Big Money	1:11.6
2015	Weary	Tommy Berry	Chris Waller	Driefontein	Territory	1:10.6
2014	Appearance	Blake Shinn	Guy Walter	River Lad	Sizzling	1:09.0
2013	Happy Galaxy	Jay Ford	Michael, Wayne & John Hawkes	Skytrain	Centennial Park	1:22.8
2012	Rain Affair	Corey Brown	Joseph Pride	Centennial Park	Shoot Out	1:10.7
2011	Centennial Park	Corey Brown	David Payne	Love Conquers All	Hot Danish	1:10.2
2010	Rangirangdoo	Corey Brown	Chris Waller	Dao Dao	McClintock	1:12.6
2009	Burdekin Blues	Shane Scriven	Barry Baldwin	Gold Trail	Hurried Choice	1:09.7
2008	Paratroopers	Danny Nikolic	Peter Snowden	He's Canny	Sniper's Bullet	1:09.6
2007	Mentality	Darren Beadman	John Hawkes	Fashions Afield	More Than Lucky	1:10.0
2006	Court's In Session	Danny Beasley	Guy Walter	Shania Dane	Primus	1:09.1
2005	Court's In Session	Hugh Bowman	Guy Walter	Our Egyptian Raine	Grand Armee	1:09.5
2004	Sportsman	Christian Reith	Gregory Hickman	Thorn Park	Excellerator	1:08.4
2003	Lonhro	Darren Beadman	John Hawkes	Belle Du Jour	Carael Boy	1:10.7
2002	Ateates	Jim Cassidy	Gary Portelli	Viscount	Caissa	1:11.2
2001	Tie The Knot	Patrick Payne	Guy Walter	Referral	Landsighting	1:10.0

BACKGROUND

First run: 1974 (won by I'm Scarlet). Group 2 since 1979. Run over 1100m 1974-80 & 1997. Run at Warwick Farm 1982, 1983, 1986, 1988, 1989 & 1991; Randwick inner track 1997 & 1998.
Not held in 1990 (abandoned).
Most recent mare to win: Appearance (2014).
Most recent 3YO to win: C&G—Trapeze Artist (2018); Filly—Diamond Shower (1987).
Multiple winners: 1—Court's In Session (2006, 2005).
Fastest time (1200m): Sportsman (2004) 1:08.30
Notable winners: Music Magnate (2017); Appearance (2014); Lonhro (2003); Mr. Innocent (2000); Saintly (1996); Soho Square (1994); Joanne (1992); At Sea (1988); Sir Dapper (1984); Kingston Town (1980); Luskin Star (1978); Zephyr Bay (1975).
Expressway Stakes winners won the lead-up races:
Carrington Stakes: 1—Rain Affair (2012).
Zeditave Stakes: 1—Happy Galaxy (2013).
Australia Stakes: Nil
Expressway Stakes winners went on to win in the same preparation:
Apollo Stakes: 6—Appearance (2014); Rain Affair (2012); Lonhro (2003); Kidman's Cove (1999); At Sea (1988); Diamond Shower (1987).
Challenge Stakes: 4—Rain Affair (2012); Cangronde (1997); Moss Rocket (1995); Groucho (1989).
Canterbury Stakes: 5—Appearance (2014); Kidman's Cove (1999); At Sea (1988); Avon Angel (1986); Sir Dapper (1984).
Chipping Norton Stakes: 2—Lonhro (2003); Tie The Knot (2001).
Futurity Stakes: None.
Orr Stakes: None.

Australian Cup: 1—Saintly (1996).
George Ryder Stakes: 1—Lonhro (2003).
T.J Smith Stakes: 1—Trapeze Artist (2018).
Doncaster Handicap: 1—Rangirangdoo (2010).
Leading winning jockeys: 4 wins Corey Brown (Rain Affair 2012, Centennial Park 2011, Rangirangdoo 2010, Hockney 1998); Malcolm Johnston (Potrero 1991, Avon Angel 1986, Kingston Town 1980, Red Ruffian 1977).
3 wins Darren Beadman (Mentality 2007, Lonhro 2003, At Sea 1988); Jim Cassidy (Ateates 2002, Soho Square 1994, Let's Hurry 1993).
Current winning jockeys: 4 wins Corey Brown (Rain Affair 2012, Centennial Park 2011, Rangirangdoo 2010, Hockney 1998).
2 wins Tommy Berry (Our Boy Malachi 2016, Weary 2015).
1 win Hugh Bowman (Court's In Session 2005); Larry Cassidy (Saintly 1986); Tim Clark (Trapeze Artist 2018); Glen Colless (Mr. Innocent 2000); Jay Ford (Happy Galaxy 2013); Kerrin McEvoy (Music Magnate 2017); Christian Reith (Sportsman 2004); Blake Shinn (Appearance 2014); Robert Thompson (Moss Rocket 1995).
Leading winning trainers: 5 wins John Hawkes (Our Boy Malachi 2016, Happy Galaxy 2013, Mentality 2007, Lonhro 2003, Hockney 1998).
4 wins Guy Walter (Appearance 2014, Court's In Session 2006, 2005, Tie The Knot 2000).
Current winning trainers: 5 wins John Hawkes (Our Boy Malachi 2016, Happy Galaxy 2013, Mentality 2007, Lonhro 2003, Hockney 1998).
2 wins Michael, Wayne & John Hawkes (Our Boy Malachi 2016, Happy Galaxy 2013); Chris Waller (Weary 2015, Rangirangdoo 2010).
1 win Bjorn Baker (Music Magnate 2017); Barry Baldwin (Burdekin Blues 2009); Les Bridge (Sir Dapper 1984); Greg Hickman (Sportsman 2004); David Payne (Centennial Park 2011); Gary Portelli (Ateates 2002); Joe Pride (Rain Affair 2012); Gerald Ryan (Trapeze Artist 2018); John Size (Kidman's Cove 1999).
Point of interest: Mentality (2007) won the 2007 Group 1 Randwick Guineas (1600m).

ATC Breeders' Classic (1200m)—Randwick
$175,000 Group 2 4YO&Up Mares SWP. February 9, 2019.

YEAR	WINNER	JOCKEY	TRAINER	2ND	3RD	TIME
2018	Prompt Response	Blake Shinn	Gai Waterhouse & Adrian Bott	Egyptian Symbol	Danish Twist	1:09.7
2017	In Her Time	Andrew Adkins	Ben Smith	Egyptian Symbol	Flippant	1:10.7
2016	Amicus	Hugh Bowman	Chris Waller	Press Report	I've Got The Looks	1:11.0
2015	Catkins	Hugh Bowman	Chris Waller	Liliburbero	Mihiri	1:09.3
2014	Catkins	Hugh Bowman	Chris Waller	Steps In Time	White Sage	1:10.7
2013	Steps In Time	Jim Cassidy	John O'Shea	Red Tracer	Choice Words	1:10.4
2012	Steps In Time	Jim Cassidy	John O'Shea	Beaded	Red Tracer	1:09.5
2011	More Joyous	Nash Rawiller	Gai Waterhouse	Graceful Anna	No Evidence Needed	1:08.6
2010	Alverta	Tye Angland	Paul Messara	Montana Flyer	Madame Pedrille	1:10.5
2009	Hot Danish	Tim Clark	Les Bridge	Belong To Many	Lustre Lady	1:10.5
2008	Gallant Tess	Jeff Lloyd	David Payne	Flying Alpha	Shirl Pegasus	1:10.0
2007	Pasikatera	Hugh Bowman	Gai Waterhouse	Spinner's Magic	Street Smart	1:09.6
2006	Steflara	Zac Purton	John O'Shea	Wild Queen	Imana	1:09.8
2005	Winning Belle	Chris Munce	Gai Waterhouse	Pentelikon	Imana	1:10.5
2004	Private Steer	Glen Boss	John O'Shea	Irgunette	Forum Floozie	1:08.3
2003	Miss Helterskelter	Lane Moloney	David Payne	Hosannah	Ritual	1:10.6
2002	Gwendolyn	Chris Munce	Max Lees	Another Misty	Poppett	1:11.1
2001	Spinning Hill	Patrick Payne	Guy Walter	Say Good Morning	Corelli	1:09.7

BACKGROUND
First run: 1996 (won by Destruct). Listed:1996-2005. Group 3 2006 & 2007. Group 2 from 2008. Run over 1250m 1997; 1300m 1998; 1180m (Kensington) 2004. Run at Warwick Farm in 2012, Rosehill in 2013.
Fastest time (1200m): Private Steer (2004) 1:08:31.
Multiple winners: 2—Catkins (2015, 2014); Steps In Time (2013, 2012).
Notable winners: Amicus (2016); Catkins (2015, 2014); Steps In Time (2013, 2012); More Joyous (2011); Alverta (2010); Hot Danish (2009); Private Steer (2004); Spinning Hill (2001); Staging (2000).

Breeders' Classic winners went on to win in the same preparation:
Wiggle Stakes: 5—Catkins (2014); Steps In Time (2013, 2012); Hot Danish (2009); Destruct (1996).
Millie Fox Stakes: 1—Catkins (2015).
Emancipation Stakes: 3—Prompt Response (2018); Catkins (2015. 2014).
Birthday Card Stakes: 1—Spinning Hill (2001).
Canterbury Stakes: 1—More Joyous (2011). Note: Hot Danish (2009) Won The Canterbury Stakes In 2010.
Coolmore Classic: 1—Alverta (2010). Note: Steps In Time (2013, 2012) Won The Coolmore In 2014.
Futurity Stakes: 1—More Joyous (2011).
Doncaster Handicap: 1—Private Steer (2004).
Queen Of The Turf Stakes: 2—More Joyous (2011); Arletty (1998).
Sapphire Stakes: 1—Spinning Hill (2001).
Leading winning jockeys: 4 wins Hugh Bowman (Amicus 2016, Catkins 2015, 2014, Pasikatera 2007).
3 wins Chris Munce (Winning Belle 2005, Gwendolyn 2002, Misty Dawn 1997).
Current winning jockeys: 4 wins Hugh Bowman (Amicus 2016, Catkins 2015, 2014, Pasikatera 2007).
1 win Andrew Adkins (In Her Time 2017); Tye Angland (Alverta 2010); Glen Boss (Private Steer 2004); Larry Cassidy (Destruct 1996); Tim Clark (Hot Danish 2009); Grant Cooksley (Arletty 1998); Jeff Lloyd (Gallant Tess 2008); Zac Purton (Steflara 2006); Nash Rawiller (More Joyous 2011); Blake Shinn (Prompt Response 2018).
Leading winning trainers: 4 wins John O'Shea (Steps In Time 2013, 2012, Steflara 2006, Private Steer 2004); Gai Waterhouse (Prompt Response 2018, More Joyous 2011, Pasikatera 2007, Winning Belle 2005).
3 wins Chris Waller (Amicus 2016, Catkins 2015, 2014).
Current winning trainers: 4 wins John O'Shea (Steps In Time 2013, 2012, Steflara 2006, Private Steer 2004); Gai Waterhouse (Prompt Response 2018, More Joyous 2011, Pasikatera 2007, Winning Belle 2005).
3 wins Chris Waller (Amicus 2016, Catkins 2015, 2014);.
2 wins David Payne (Gallant Tess 2008, Miss Helterskelter 2003).
1 win Les Bridge (Hot Danish 2009); Clarry Conners (Staging 2000); John Hawkes (Destruct 1996); Paul Messara (Alverta 2010); Bill Prain (Misty Dawn 1997); Benjamin Smith (In Her Time 2017); Gai Waterhouse & Adrian Bott (Prompt Response 2018).
Point of interest: Spinning Hill (2001) won the 2002 Group 1 Lightning Stakes (1000m) at Flemington.

MRC Autumn Stakes (1400m)—Caulfield
$200,000 Group 2 3YO Open SWP. February 9, 2019.

YEAR	WINNER	JOCKEY	TRAINER	2ND	3RD	TIME
2018	Holy Snow	Michael Dee	Mick Price	Mr So And So	Astoria	1:24.8
2017	Oak Door	Damian Lane	Robert Smerdon	Attention	Knowable	1:23.5
2016	Mahuta	Brad Rawiller	Darren Weir	Sailing By	Snoopy	1:23.4
2015	San Nicasio	Ben Melham	Peter Moody	Zebulon	Firehouse Rock	1:23.6
2014	Thunder Fantasy	Mark Zahra	Anthony Cummings	Rock Hero	Late Charge	1:23.8
2013	Mulaazem	Luke Nolen	Peter Moody	Fiveandahalfstar	Super Cool	1:23.6
2012	Pied A Terre	Mark Zahra	Peter Snowden	Proliferate	Adamantium	1:24.7
2011	Dusty Star	Craig Williams	Peter J Morgan	Under The Eiffel	Eclair Mystic	1:37.2
2010	Denman	Kerrin McEvoy	Peter Snowden	Guru Bob	Most Immediate	1:23.3
2009	Fravashi	Kerrin McEvoy	Peter Snowden	Nicconi	Heart Of Dreams	1:22.8
2008	Light Fantastic	Steven King	Mick Price	Vivacious Spirit	Viatorian	1:23.2
2007	Catechuchu	Craig Williams	David Hayes	Haradasun	Eclair Passion	1:24.7
2006	Apache Cat	Glen Boss	Greg Eurell	God's Own	Empress Lily	1:24.7
2005	Shinzig	Steven King	Chris Waller	Not A Single Doubt	Danehill Express	1:23.4
2004	Special Harmony	Damien Oliver	Lee Freedman	Youth	Dane Fever	1:23.5
2003	Titanic Jack	Patrick Payne	Tony McEvoy	Storm Prince	Step Ahead	1:25.1
2002	Dash For Cash	Greg Childs	Rick Hore-Lacy	Barkada	Zonked	1:24.1
2001	Desert Sky	Greg Childs	Mathew Ellerton	Desert Eagle	Crop	1:25.1

BACKGROUND
First run: 1979 (won by Gondolier). 1979-1986 1200m; from 1987 1400m. Listed 1979-80. Group 3 1981-2007: Group 2 from 2008. Run at Sundown 1979-81, 1987-96.
Most recent filly to win: Catechuchu (2007). Six fillies have won.
Fastest time (1400m): St. Covet (1995); 1:21.70.
Notable winners: Denman (2010); Light Fantastic (2008); Apache Cat (2006); Special Harmony (2004); Titanic Jack (2003); Dash For Cash (2002); Desert Sky (2001); Dignity Dancer (1999); Tarnpir Lane (1997); St. Covet (1995); Canny Lad (1991); King's High (1989); Centaine (1984); Lord Ballina (1983); Pure Of Heart (1982); Deck The Halls (1981).

Autumn Stakes winners also won the lead-up races:
Gold Coast 3YO Guineas: 1—Mahuta (2016).
Zeditave Stakes: 2—Denman (2010); Blaze The Turf (1998).
Manfred Stakes: 1—Denman (2010).
Autumn Stakes winners went on to win in the same preparation:
Kewney Stakes: 2—Special Harmony (2004); Deck The Halls (1981).
C.S. Hayes Stakes: 1—Dash For Cash (2002).
Angus Armanasco Stakes: 1—Special Harmony (2004).
Storm Queen Stakes: 1—Special Harmony (2004).
Autumn Classic: 3—Dignity Dancer (1999); Laranto (1992); King's High (1989).
Alister Clark Stakes: 2—Titanic Jack (2003); Dignity Dancer (1999).
C.F. Orr Stakes: 1—Desert Eagle (2001).
Futurity Stakes: 2—Dash For Cash (2002); Desert Eagle (2001).
Australian Guineas: 5—Light Fantastic (2008); Apache Cat (2006); Dash For Cash (2002); Dignity Dancer (1999); King's High (1989).
Phar Lap Stakes: 1—Apache Cat (2006).
George Ryder Stakes: 1—Pure Of Heart (1982).
Rosehill Guineas: 2—Tarnpir Lane 1997); Deck The Halls (1981).
Leading winning jockeys: 3 wins Jim Cassidy (Dignity Dancer 1999, Canny Lad 1991, The Oval 1990); Greg Childs (Dash For Cash 2002, Desert Sky 2001, Tarnpir Lane 1997); Michael Clarke (Blaze The Turf 1998, King's High 1989, Beach Gown 1986).
Current winning jockeys: 2 wins Kerrin McEvoy (Denman 2010, Fravashi 2009); Craig Williams (Dusty Star 2011, Catechuchu 2007); Mark Zahra (Thunder Fantasy 2014, Pied A Terre 2012).
1 win Glen Boss (Apache Cat 2006); Michael Dee (Holy Snow 2018); Damian Lane (Oak Door 2017); Ben Melham (San Nicosio 2015); Luke Nolan (Mulaazem 2013); Brad Rawiller (Mahuta 2016); Brian Werner (Nick On The Run 1996).
Leading winning trainer: 3 wins Peter Snowden (Pied A Terre 2012, Denman 2010, Fravashi 2009).
Current winning trainers: 3 wins Peter Snowden (Pied A Terre 2012, Denman 2010, Fravashi 2009).
2 wins Greg Eurell (Apache Cat 2006, Nick On The Run 1996); David Hayes (Catechuchu 2007, St. Covet 1995); Mick Price (Holy Snow 2018, Light Fantastic 2008).
1 win Cliff Brown (Tarnpir Lane 1997); Anthony Cummings (Thunder Fantasy 2014); Mathew Ellerton (Desert Sky 2001); John Hawkes (Tolhurst 1980); John Ledger (Blaze The Turf 1998); Colin Little (Testimony 1985); Tony McEvoy (Keep The Faith 2004); Peter Morgan (Dusty Star 2011); Chris Parry (Northern Copy 1987); Mark Riley (Just Juan 1993); Robert Smerdon (Oak Door 2017); Chris Waller (Shinzig 2005); Darren Weir (Mahuta 2016).

MRC Rubiton Stakes (1100m)—Caulfield
$200,000 Group 2 Open WFA. February 9, 2019.

YEAR	WINNER	JOCKEY	TRAINER	2ND	3RD	TIME
2018	Super Cash	Craig Williams	Andrew Noblet	Flamberge	Merchant Navy	1:04.5
2017	Super Cash	Katelyn Mallyon	Andrew Noblet	I Am A Star	Chautauqua	1:02.5
2016	Heatherly	Katelyn Mallyon	Mathew Ellerton & Simon Zahra	Politeness	Just A Bullet	1:02.2
2015	Chautauqua	Dwayne Dunn	Michael, Wayne & John Hawkes	Flamberge	Atmospherical	1:02.3
2014	Lankan Rupee	Craig Newitt	Mick Price	Iconic	First Command	1:02.5
2013	Adebisi	Craig Williams	Desleigh Forster	Rescue Mission	Big Buddie	1:03.3
2012	Eagle Falls	Dwayne Dunn	David Hayes	First Command	Hot Spin	1:03.8
2011	Catapulted	Michael Rodd	Mark Kavanagh	Avenue	Solar Charged	1:02.2
2010	Here De Angels	Michael Rodd	Mark Kavanagh	Lucky Secret	Rostova	1:01.7
2009	Mind Your Head	Mark Pegus	John Ledger	DH Happy Glen/Lucky Secret		1:03.4
2008	Here De Angels	Corey Brown	Lee Freedman	Let Go Thommo	Raid The Royals	1:03.8
2007	Dance The Waves	Brad Stewart	Gillian Heinrich	Barabba Road	Message Bank	1:02.9
2006	Bomber Bill	Vlad Duric	Maureen Harry	Whats The Mail	Live In Vain	0:56.6
2005	Super Elegant	Kelvin Sanderson	Tony Vasil	Truly Wicked	Sensational Spot	1:03.4
2004	Super Elegant	Patrick Payne	Tony Vasil	Ruben	Step Ahead	1:02.3
2003	Super Elegant	Vin Hall	Tony Vasil	Azevedo	Sir Chuckle	1:02.9
2002	Intelligent Star	Stephen Baster	Mick Price	Bomber Bill	Sudurka	1:01.6
2001	DH Appoint/Cullen	Darren Beadman/Patrick Payne	John Hawkes/Graeme Rogerson		Bomber Bill	1:02.4

BACKGROUND

First run: 1989 (Zeditave). Listed: 1989-91. Group 3 from 1982. Run over 1000m until 1997. Run at Sandown (1000m) in 1996 and 2006.
Most recent mare (4YO or older) to win: Super Cash (2018)—the only mare to win. Also won in 2017.
Most recent 3YO to win: Filly—Heatherly (2016); C&G—Al Mansour (1998).
Multiple winners: 4—Super Cash (2018, 2017); Super Elegant (2005, 2004, 2003); Here De Angels (2010, 2008); Schillaci (1995, 1993).
Fastest time (1100m): Intelligent Star (2002) 1:01.86
Notable winners: Chautauqua (2015); Lankan Rupee (2014); Bomber Bill (2006); Super Elegant (2005, 2004, 2003); Miss Pennymoney (2000); Flavour (1999); Al Mansour (1998); Spartacus (1997); Schillaci (1995, 1993); Alannon (1994); Redelva (1991); Zeditave (1989).
Rubiton Stakes winners went on to win in the same preparation:
Lightning Stakes: 2—Schillaci (1993); Zeditave (1989).
Oakleigh Plate: 2—Lankan Rupee (2014); Spartacus (1997).
Newmarket Handicap: 2—Lankan Rupee (2014); Miss Pennymoney (2000).
William Reid Stakes: 4—Miss Pennymoney (2000); Spartacus 91997); Redelva (1991); Zeditave (1989).
TJ Smith Stakes: 2—Chautauqua (2015); Lankan Rupee (2014).
Leading winning jockey: 3 wins Patrick Payne (Super Elegant 2004, Cullen 2001, Schillaci 1995).
Current winning jockeys: 2 wins Dwayne Dunn (Chautauqua 2015, Eagle Falls 2012); Katelyn Mallyon (Super Cash 2017, Heatherly 2016); Damien Oliver (Schillaci 1993, Kingston Heritage 1990); Michael Rodd (Catapulted 2011, Here De Angels 2010); Craig Williams (Super Cash 2018, Adebisi 2013).
1 win Stephen Baster (Intelligent Star 2002); Corey Brown (Here De Angels 2008); Larry Cassidy (Al Mansour 1998); Vlad Duric (Bomber Bill 2006); Craig Newitt (Lankan Rupee 2014); Mark Pegus (Mind Your Head 2009); Brett Prebble (Miss Pennymoney 2000); Nash Rawiller (Flavour 1999); Brad Stewart (Dance The Waves 2007).
Leading winning trainers: 4 wins Lee Freedman (Here De Angels 2008, Schillaci 1995, 1993, Kingston Heritage 1990); John Hawkes (Chautauqua 2015, Appoint 2001, Flavour 1999, Stalk 1996).
Current winning trainers: 4 wins Lee Freedman (Here De Angels 2008, Schillaci 1995, 1993, Kingston Heritage 1990); John Hawkes (Chautauqua 2015, Appoint 2001, Flavour 1999, Stalk 1996).
3 wins Tony Vasil (Super Elegant 2005, 2004, 2003).
2 wins Mark Kavanagh (Catapulted 2011, Here De Angels 2010); Andrew Noblet (Super Cash 2018, 2017); Mick Price (Lankan Rupee 2014, Intelligent Star 2002).
1 win Jim Conlan (Miss Pennymoney 2000); Mathew Ellerton & Simon Zahra (Heatherly 2016); Desleigh Forster (Adebisis 2013); Maureen Harry (Bomber Bill 2006); Michael, Wayne & John Hawkes (Chautauqua 2015); David Hayes (Eagle Falls 2012); Gillian Heinrich (Dance The Waves 2007); Ian Hutchins (Mavournae 1992); John Ledger (Mind Your Head 2009); Graeme Rogerson (Cullen 2001).
Points of interest: 1989 winner Zeditave (The Judge-Summoned) is a half-brother to 1994 winner Alannon (Noalcoholic-Summoned).
Appoint dead-heated with Cullen in 2001.

MRC Blue Diamond Prelude Fillies (1100m)—Caulfield

$200,000 Group 2 2YO Fillies SW. February 9, 2019.

YEAR	WINNER	JOCKEY	TRAINER	2ND	3RD	TIME
2018	Enbihaar	Stephen Baster	David & Ben Hayes & Tom Dabernig	Oohood	Seabrook	1:05.2
2017	Catchy	Craig Williams	David & Ben Hayes & Tom Dabernig	Limestone	Arctic Angel	1:03.6
2016	Samara Dancer	Dom Tourneur	Phillip Stokes	Concealer	Miss Nymeria	1:03.1
2015	Fontiton	Mark Zahra	Robert Smerdon	Miss Gidget	Flamboyant Lass	1:02.8
2014	Earthquake	Damian Browne	Peter Snowden	Eloping	Lumosty	1:03.7
2013	Guelph	Kerrin McEvoy	Peter Snowden	Montsegur	Godiva Rock	1:03.8
2012	Samaready	Craig Newitt	Mick Price	Formidable	Sweetener	1:03.3
2011	One Last Dance	Luke Nolen	Peter Moody	Glissade	Hallowell Belle	1:03.6
2010	Psychologist	Mark Zahra	Tony Vasil	She's Got Gears	Jalsah	1:02.6
2009	Rostova	Steven King	Steve Richards	Corsaire	Rose Darmore	1:04:5
2008	Believe'n'succeed	Stephen Baster	Mark Kavanagh	Sugar Babe	Burgeis	1:03.7
2007	Camarilla	Blake Shinn	John Hawkes	Belcentra	Behind	1:03.7
2006	Nediym's Glow	Noel Callow	Mathew Ellerton	Satin Robes	Anhinga	1:03.4
2005	Doubting	Danny Nikolic	Mick Price	Amarazetti	Street Smart	1:04.2
2004	Alinghi	Damien Oliver	Lee Freedman	Find The Cash	Marie Madelaine	1:03.6
2003	Halibery	Damien Oliver	Mick Price	Rinky Dink	Gaelic Princess	1:03.2
2002	Brief Embrace	Kerrin McEvoy	Peter Moody	Coupe	Romantic Flyer	1:05.2
2001	Faiza	Brett Prebble	John Hawkes	Titanic Rose	Magic Heaven	1:03.2

BACKGROUND

First run: 1982 (won by Formal Invitation). Listed: 1982-85. Group 3 1986-2014. Group 2 from 2015 Run over 1150m in 1996. Run at Sandown in 1996.
Fastest time (1100m): Psychologist 1:02.67.
Notable winners: Catchy (2017); Earthquake (2014); Guelph (2013); Rostova (2009); Camarilla (2007); Doubting (2005); Alinghi (2003); Mannington (2000); Piccadilly Circus (1998); Rose Of Danehill (1997); Merlene (1996); My Flashing Star (1994); Lady Jakeo (1993); Freedom Fields (1992); Courtza (1989); Startling Lass (1988); Midnight Fever (1987); Bounding Away (1986); Love A Show (1983).
Blue Diamond Prelude winners won the lead-up races:
Blue Diamond Preview: 5—Fontiton (2015); One Last Dance (2011); Rostova (2009); Halibery (2003); Midnight Fever (1987).
Blue Diamond Prelude winners went on to win in the same preparation:
Blue Diamond Stakes: 9—Catchy (2017); Earthquake (2014); Samaready (2012); Alinghi (2003); Lady Jakeo (1993); Courtza (1989); Midnight Fever (1987); Bounding Away (1986); Love A Show (1983).
VRC Sires' Produce Stakes: 1—Rostova (2009).
Thoroughbred Breeders Stakes: 1— Nediym's Glow (2006).
Reisling Stakes: 7—Earthquake (2014), Samaready (2012); Alinghi (2004); Rose Of Danehill (1997); Merlene (1996); Startling Lass (1988); Midnight Fever (1987).
Golden Slipper: 3—Merlene (1996); Courtza (1989); Bounding Away (1986).
ATC Sires' Produce: 3—Guelph (2013); Camarilla (2007); Merlene (1996).
ATC Champagne Stakes: 2—Guelph (2013); Bounding Away (1986).
Leading winning jockey: 6 wins Greg Hall (Card Queen 1999, Rose Of Danehill 1997, Merlene 1996, Lady Jakeo 1993, Zedagal 1990, Startling Lass 1988)
Current winning jockeys: 3 wins Stephen Baster (Enbihaar 2018, Believe'n'succeed 2008, Miamore 1995). 2 wins Damien Oliver (Alinghi 2004, Halibery 2003); Mark Zahra (Fontiton 2015, Psychologist 2010). 1 win Damian Browne (Earthquake 2014); Noel Callow (Nediym's Glow 2006); Kevin Forrester (Yachtie 1992); Kerrin McEvoy (Guelph 2013); Craig Newitt (Samaready 2012); Luke Nolen (One Last Dance 2011); Brett Prebble (Faiza 2001); Blake Shinn (Camarilla 2007); Domenic Tourneur (Samara Dancer 2016); Brian Werner (Lochley's Tradition 1986); Craig Williams (Catchy 2017).
Leading winning trainer: 4 wins Lee Freedman (Alinghi 2004, Piccadilly Circus 1998, Rose Of Danehill 1997, Merlene 1996); David Hayes (Enbihaar 2018, Catchy 2017, Freedom Fields 1992, Raise A Rhythm 1991).
Current winning trainers: 4 wins Lee Freedman (Alinghi 2004, Piccadilly Circus 1998, Rose Of Danehill 1997, Merlene 1996); David Hayes (Enbihaar 2018, Catchy 2017, Freedom Fields 1992, Raise A Rhythm 1991). 2 wins John Hawkes (Camarilla 2007, Faiza 2001); Mick Price (Samaready 2012, Halibery 2003); Peter Snowden (Earthquake 2014, Guelph 2013).
1 win Russell Cameron (Mannington 2000); Tom Hughes Jnr (Miamore 1995); David & Ben Hayes & Tom Dabernig (Catchy 2017); Pat Hyland (Card Queen 1999); Mark Kavanagh (Believe'n'succeed 2008); Steve Richards (Rostova 2009); John Sadler (Lady Jakeo 1993); Robert Smerdon (Fontiton 2015); Phillip Stokes (Samara Dancer 2016); Tony Vasil (Psychologist 2010).
Points of interest: Alinghi (2003) went on to win the 2004 Group 1 Newmarket Handicap. Startling Lass (1988) and Midnight Fever (1987) are sisters, by Luskin Star from Trim Girl.

ATC Apollo Stakes (1400m)—Randwick
$250,000 Group 2 3YO&Up WFA. February 16, 2019.

YEAR	WINNER	JOCKEY	TRAINER	2ND	3RD	TIME
2018	Endless Drama	Tye Angland	Chris Waller	Global Glamour	Comin' Through	1:22.4
2017	Winx	Hugh Bowman	Chris Waller	Hartnell	Endless Drama	1:22.5
2016	Winx	Hugh Bowman	Chris Waller	Solicit	Hauraki	1:22.0
2015	Contributer	James McDonald	John O'Shea	Ninth Legion	Weary	1:22.0
2014	Appearance	Blake Shinn	Guy Walter	Speediness	Moriarty	1:21.9
2013	Alma's Fury	Blake Shinn	Paul Murray	Tougher Than Ever	Daneleigh	1:27.3
2012	Rain Affair	Corey Brown	Joseph Pride	Shoot Out	Daneleigh	1:22.3
2011	Melito	Brenton Avdulla	Gerald Ryan	Hot Danish	Centennial Park	1:22.2
2010	Daneleigh	Hugh Bowman	Chris Waller	Rangirangdoo	Palacio De Cristal	1:22.9
2009	Tuesday Joy	Blake Shinn	Gai Waterhouse	Hurried Choice	Gallant Tess	1:25.7
2008	Racing To Win	Hugh Bowman	John O'Shea	Tuesday Joy	Falaise	1:24.3
2007	Desert War	Hugh Bowman	Gai Waterhouse	Mentality	Eremein	1:22.2
2006	Ike's Dream	Darren Beadman	John Hawkes	Shania Dane	Desert War	1:22.2
2005	Grand Armee	Danny Beasley	Gai Waterhouse	Court's In Session	Desert War	1:21.1
2004	Private Steer	Larry Cassidy	John O'Shea	Excellerator	Zanna	1:23.5
2003	Lonhro	Darren Beadman	John Hawkes	Hoeberg	Carael Boy	1:22.5
2002	Ha Ha	Jim Cassidy	Gai Waterhouse	El Mirada	Tie The Knot	1:23.1
2001	Sunline	Greg Childs	Trevor Mckee	Celestial Choir	Referral	1:25.5

BACKGROUND
First run: 1974 (won by Misty Ville). Group 2 from 1979. Run at Warwick Farm 1977, 1978, 1999, 2000-01, 2013; Rosehill from 2006-12; Randwick 1979-98 & 2002-05, from 2014.
Most recent mare to win: Winx (2017).
Most recent 3YO to win: C&G—Key Dancer (1990); Filly—Ha Ha (2002).
Multiple winners: 3—Winx (2017, 2016); Sunline (2001, 2000); Juggler (1997, 1996).
Fastest time (1400m Randwick): Grand Armee (2005) 1:21.06
Notable winners: Winx (2017, 2016); Appearance (2014); Tuesday Joy (2009); Racing To Win (2008); Grand Armee (2005); Private Steer (2004); Lonhro (2003); Ha Ha (2002); Sunline (2001, 2000); Juggler (1997, 1996); Naturalism (1993); Triscay (1991); Beau Zam (1989); Red Anchor (1985); Emancipation (1984).
Apollo Stakes winners won the lead-up races:
Expressway Stakes: 6—Appearance (2014); Rain Affair (2012); Lonhro (2003); Kidman's Cove (1999); At Sea (1988); Diamond Shower (1987).
Apollo Stakes winners went on to win in the same preparation:
Challenge Stakes: 1—Rain Affair (2012).
Chipping Norton Stakes: 10—Winx (2016); Contributer (2015); Tuesday Joy (2009); Grand Armee (2005); Lonhro (2003); Juggler (1996); Pharaoh (1995); Emancipation (1984); Dalmacia (1983); Embasadora (1980).
Canterbury Stakes: 4—Appearance (2014); Kidman's Cove (1999); Quick Flick (1998); At Sea (1988).
George Ryder Stakes: 5—Winx (2016); Daneleigh (2010); Lonhro (2003); Quick Flick (1998); Emancipation (1984).
Doncaster Handicap: 3—Winx (2016); Private Steer (2004); Pharaoh (1995).
Ranvet Stakes: 5—Contributer (2015); Desert War (2007); Grand Armee (2005); Beau Zam (1989); Dalmacia (1983).
Coolmore Classic: 2—Sunline (2000); Emancipation (1984). Note: Appearance (2014) won the Coolmore Classic in 2013; Tuesday Joy (2009) won the Coolmore in 2007; Sunline (2001, 2000) also won the Coolmore in 2002.
All-Aged Stakes: 5—Racing To Win (2008); Private Steer (2004); Sunline (2000); Drawn (1986); Emancipation (1984).
Leading winning jockeys: 5 wins Hugh Bowman (Winx 2017, 2016, Daneleigh 2010, Racing To Win 2008, Desert War 2007).
4 wins Mick Dittman (Naturalism 1993, Triscay 1991, Red Anchor 1985, Scomeld 1979).
Current winning jockeys: 5 wins Hugh Bowman (Winx 2017, 2016, Daneleigh 2010, Racing To Win 2008, Desert War 2007).
3 wins Blake Shinn (Appearance 2014, Alma's Fury 2013, Tuesday Joy 2009).
1 win Tye Angland (Endless Drama 2018); Brenton Avdulla (Melito 2011); Glen Boss (Juggler 1997); Corey Brown (Rain Affair 2012); James McDonald (Contributor 2015).
Leading winning trainer: 7 wins Gai Waterhouse (Tuesday Joy 2009, Desert War 2007, Grand Armee 2005, Ha Ha 2002, Juggler 1997, 1996, Pharaoh 1995).
Current winning trainers: 7 wins Gai Waterhouse (Tuesday Joy 2009, Desert War 2007, Grand Armee 2005, Ha Ha 2002, Juggler 1997, 1996, Pharaoh 1995).
4 wins Chris Waller (Endless Drama 2018, Winx 2017, 2016, Daneleigh 2010).
3 wins John O'Shea (Contributer 2015, Racing To Win 2008, Private Steer 2004).

2 wins John Hawkes (Ike's Dream 2006, Lonhro 2003).
1 win Les Bridge (Drawn 1986); Clarry Conners (Burst 1994); Tim Donnelly (Quick Flick 1988); Lee Freedman (Naturalism 1993); Paul Murray (Alma;s Fury 2013); Graeme Rogerson (Quick Score 1992); Gerald Ryan (Melito 2011); John Size (Kidman's Cove 1999).
Point of interest: Champion Red Anchor retired to stud with an injury after winning the Apollo Stakes in 1985. When Winx won in 2017, it was her 14th consecutive win.

ATC Light Fingers Stakes (1200m)—Randwick
$175,000 Group 2 3YO Fillies SW. February 16, 2019.

YEAR	WINNER	JOCKEY	TRAINER	2ND	3RD	TIME
2018	Alizee	Glyn Schofield	James Cummings	Shumookh	Torvill	1:10.0
2017	Global Glamour	Josh Parr	Gai Waterhouse & Adrian Bott	Foxplay	Spright	1:09.7
2016	Perignon	Tim Clark	Gerald Ryan	Kangarilla Joy	Tempt Me Not	1:09.9
2015	Adrift	Tye Angland	Gai Waterhouse	First Seal	Slightly Sweet	1:09.4
2014	Sweet Idea	Tommy Berry	Gai Waterhouse	Gypsy Diamond	Champagne Cath	1:09.0
2013	Bennetta	James McDonald	Grahame Begg	Ichihara	Dear Demi	1:10.1
2012	Sea Siren	Jim Cassidy	John O'Shea	Streama	Hallowell Belle	1:16.3
2011	Obsequious	Kerrin McEvoy	Peter Snowden	Red Tracer	Parables	1:09.5
2010	More Joyous	Nash Rawiller	Gai Waterhouse	Trim	Sweepstaking	1:09.8
2009	Rock Me Baby	Brad Pengelly	David Payne	Samantha Miss	Glowlamp	1:11.3
2008	Forensics	Rod Quinn	Peter Snowden	Sliding Cube	Seething Duck	1:10.5
2007	Gold Edition	Jim Cassidy	Ron Maund	Montana Sunset	Montmelo	1:09.0
2006	Street Smart	Glenn Lynch	Ron Maund	Regal Cheer	Paulini	1:09.9
2005	Trezevant	Chris Munce	Gai Waterhouse	One in a Million	But I'm Serious	1:10.0
2004	Sharp	Corey Brown	John Hawkes	Generosa	Hinting	1:08.7
2003	Only Glory	Darren Beadman	John O'Shea	Chuckle	Bumptious	1:11.2
2002	Ancient Song	Larry Cassidy	Rado Boljun	Hosannah	Shouq	1:10.9
2001	Lady Mulan	Glen Boss	Bob Thomsen	Maitland Gold	Belle Du Jour	1:09.6

BACKGROUND
First run: 1981 (won by Shaybisc). Listed 1983 & 1985. Group 2 1986. Group 3 1987 & 1990. Group 2 from 1991. Run over 1100m 1997 & 1998; 1180m 2004. Run on Randwick inner track 1997 & 1998.
Fastest time (1200m): Sharp (2004) 1:08.7
Notable winners: Alizee (2018); Global Glamour (2017); Sweet Idea (2014); Sea Siren (2012); More Joyous (2010); Forensics (2008); Gold Edition (2007); Staging (1998); Assertive Lass (1997); Peruzzi (1996); Skating (1993); Whisked (1991); Joanne (1990); Magic Flute (1987); Emancipation (1983).
Spring features and the Light Fingers Stakes:
Flight Stakes: 4—Alizee (2018); Global Glamour (2017); More Joyous (2010); Assertive Lass (1997).
Thousand Guineas: 3—Global Glamour (2017); Whisked (1991); Magic Flute (1987).
Golden Rose: 1—Forensics (2008).
Light Fingers Stakes winners went on to win in the same preparation:
Hobartville Stakes: 1—Shaybisc (1981).
Surround Stakes: 4—More Joyous (2010); Staging (1998); Skating (1993); Office (1992).
Storm Queen Stakes: None.
Australian Oaks: None.
Coolmore Classic: 2—Assertive Lass (1997); Skating (1993).
Queen Of The Turf Stakes: 2—Alizee (2018); Forensics (2008).
Doncaster Handicap: 3—Skating (1993); Magic Flute 1987); Emancipation (1983).
BTC Cup: 1—Sea Siren (2012).
Doomben 10,000: 1—Sea Siren (2012)
Leading winning jockeys: 4 wins Shane Dye (Staging 1998, Assertive Lass 1997, Flight To Fantasy 1995, Office 1992).
3 wins Jim Cassidy (Sea Siren 2012, Gold Edition 2007, Magic Flute 1987).
Current winning jockeys: 2 wins Larry Cassidy (Ancient Song 2002, Camena 2000).
1 win Tye Angland (Adrift 2015); Tommy Berry (Sweet Idea 2014); Glen Boss (Lady Mulan 2001); Corey Brown (Sharp 2004); Tim Clark (Perignon 2016); Grant Cooksley (Gem Of The West 1994); James McDonald (Bennetta 2013); Kerrin McEvoy (Obsequious 2011); Brad Pengelly (Rock Me Baby 2009); Nash Rawiller (More Joyous 2010); Glyn Schofield (Alizee 2018).

Leading winning trainer: 7 wins Gai Waterhouse (Global Glamour 2017, Adrift 2015, Sweet Idea 2014, More Joyous 2010, Trezevant 2005, Assertive Lass 1997, Flight To Fantasy 1995).
Current winning trainers: 7 wins Gai Waterhouse (Global Glamour 2017, Adrift 2015, Sweet Idea 2014, More Joyous 2010, Trezevant 2005, Assertive Lass 1997, Flight To Fantasy 1995).
2 wins John O'Shea (Sea Siren 2012, Only Glory 2003); Gerald Ryan (Perignon 2016, Camena 2000); Peter Snowden (Obsequious 2011, Forensics 2008).
1 win Grahame Begg (Bennetta 2013); Clarry Conners (Staging 1998); James Cummings (Alizee 2018); David Payne (Rock Me Baby 2009); Graeme Rogerson (Skating 1993); John Size (Peruzzi 1996); Gai Waterhouse & Adrian Bott (Global Glamour 2017).
Point of interest: Forensics (2008) is the first Golden Slipper winner to win the Light Fingers.

ATC Hobartville Stakes (1400m)—Rosehill
$400,000 Group 2 3YO Open SW. February 23, 2019.

YEAR	WINNER	JOCKEY	TRAINER	2ND	3RD	TIME
2018	Kementari	Glyn Schofield	James Cummings	Pierata	D'Argento	1:22.4
2017	Man From Uncle	Jason Collett	Anthony Cummings	Echo Effect	Comin' Through	1:24.1
2016	Press Statement	Hugh Bowman	Chris Waller	Defcon	Mount Panorama	1:22.5
2015	Hallowed Crown	Hugh Bowman	Bart & James Cummings	Sweynesse	Kermadec	1:23.7
2014	Dissident	Jim Cassidy	Peter Moody	Atlante	Savvy Nature	1:25.0
2013	Pierro	Nash Rawiller	Gai Waterhouse	Rebel Dane	Proisir	1:24.7
2012	Wild And Proud	Nash Rawiller	Gai Waterhouse	Manawanui	Moment Of Change	1:26.5
2011	Ilovethiscity	Brenton Avdulla	Grahame Begg	Retrieve	Skilled	1:22.5
2010	Monton	Jay Ford	Tim Martin	Shoot Out	Captain Sonador	1:22.9
2009	Mic Mac	Blake Shinn	Greg Eurell	Caymans	Desuetude	1:22.9
2008	Serious Speed	Craig Williams	Leon Macdonald	Murtajill	Turffontein	1:23.4
2007	Mutawaajid	Hugh Bowman	Gai Waterhouse	Gold Edition	Upper Echelon	1:23.3
2006	Racing To Win	Glen Boss	John O'Shea	De Beers	Flying Pegasus	1:22.9
2005	Outback Prince	Hugh Bowman	Anthony Cummings	Eremein	Dance Hero	1:21.9
2004	Impaler	Dale Spriggs	David Atkins	Allgunnadoit	Handsome Ransom	1:23.8
2003	Thorn Park	Darren Beadman	Bob Thomsen	Hydrometer	Shower Of Roses	1:22.5
2002	Lonhro	Rod Quinn	John Hawkes	Athens	Moonflute	1:23.6
2001	Sir Clive	Len Beasley	John Size	Debrief	Fourdee	1:26.4

BACKGROUND
First run: 1925 (won by Amounis). Group 2 from 1979. Warwick Farm before 2002; Rosehill 2006. Not held in 1980 when switched from spring to the autumn.
Most recent filly to win: Serious Speed (2008). Note: 10 fillies have won.
Fastest time (1400m): Shaftesbury Avenue (1990) 1:21:40.
Notable winners: Kementari (2018); Press Statement (2016); Dissident (2014); Pierro (2012); Racing To Win (2006); Lonhro (2002); Nothin' Leica Dane (1996); Danewin (1995); Shaftesbury Avenue (1990); Sir Dapper (1984); Marscay (1983); Imagele (1973); Baguette (1970); Todman (1957); Shannon (1944); Flight (1943).
Hobartville Stakes winners also won the lead-up races:
Royal Sovereign Stakes: 4 – Mutawaajid (2007); Lonhro (2002); Danewin (1995); Shaftesbury Avenue (1990). Note: The Royal Sovereign Stakes has been run after the Hobartville since 2014.
Light Fingers Stakes: 1—Shaybisc (1981).
Eskimo Prince Stakes: 2—Kementari (2018); Man From Uncle (2017).
Phar Lap Stakes: 4—Thorn Park (2003); Monet's Cove (1997); Merry Ruler (1987); Imagele (1974).
Hobartville Stakes winners went on to win in the same preparation:
Canterbury Stakes: 1—Pierro (2013).
Hobartville Stakes & Australian Guineas: None.
Randwick Guineas: 16—Kenemtari (2018); Hallowed Crown (2015); Dissident (2014); Ilovethiscity (2011); Fairway (2000); Arena (1999); High Regard (1988); Rare Form (1982); Rosie Heir (1975); Imagele (1973); Garcon (1966); Fair Summer (1965); Martello Towers (1959); Todman (1957); Pride Of Egypt (1954); Hadrian (1935). Note: The Randwick Guineas was known as the Canterbury Guineas until 2006.
George Ryder Stakes: 1—Pierro (2013)
Rosehill Guineas: 17—Danewin (1995); Imagele (1973); Fair Summer (1965); Wenona Girl (1960); Martello Towers (1959); Pride Of Egypt (1954); Hydrogen (1951); Careless (1950); Prince Standard (1946); Hall Stand (1942); High Caste (1939); Aeolus (1938); Hadrian (1935); Silver King (1934); Bronze Hawk (1932); Mollison (1928); Amounis (1925).
Phar Lap Stakes: 4—Thorn Park (2003); Monet's Cove (1997); Merry Ruler (1987); Imagele (1974).

Australian Derby: 4—Fairway (2000); Imagele (1973); Martello Towers (1959); Magnificent (1945).
Royal Sovereign Stakes & Hobartville Stakes: 4 – Mutawaajid (2007); Lonhro (2002); Danewin (1995); Shaftesbury Avenue (1990). Note: The Royal Sovereign Stakes has been run after the Hobartville since 2014.
Leading winning jockeys: 6 wins Billy Cook (Pride Of Egypt 1954, San Domenico 1948, Temeraire 1947; Hall Stand 1942, Bronze Hawk 1932, Toper 1929).
5 wins Darby Munro (Hydrogen 1951, Shannon 1944, All Love 1941, Caesar 1937, Hadrian 1935).
Current winning jockeys: 4 wins Hugh Bowman (Press Statement 2016, Hallowed Crown 2015, Mutawaajid 2007, Outback Prince 2005)
2 wins Nash Rawiller (Pierro 2013, Wild And Proud 2012).
1 win Brenton Avdulla (Ilovethiscity 2011); Glen Boss (Racing To Win 2006); Corey Brown (Arena 1999); Jason Collett (Man From Uncle 2017); Jay Ford (Monton 2010); Glyn Schofield (Kementari 2018); Blake Shinn (Mic Mac 2009); Dale Spriggs (Impaler 2004); Craig Williams (Serious Speed 2008).
Leading winning trainers: 7 wins Tommy Smith (Chanteclair 1986, Imagele 1973, Fairy Walk 1971, Rajah 1968, Great Exploits 1967, Garcon 1966, Chastise 1949).
4 wins Maurice McCarten (Farnworth 1964, Young Brolga 1961, Wenona Girl 1960, Todman 1957); Gai Waterhouse (Pierro 2013, Wild And Proud 2012, Mutawaajid 2007, Nothin' Leica Dane 1996).
Current winning trainers: 4 wins Gai Waterhouse (Pierro 2013, Wild And Proud 2012, Mutawaajid 2007, Nothin' Leica Dane 1996).
2 wins James Cummings (Kementari 2018, Hallowed Crown 2015; the latter in partnership with Bart Cummings); John Hawkes (Lonhro 2002, Arena 1999); Paul Perry (Clearly Chosen 1994, Navy Seal 1993).
1 win Les Bridge (Sir Dapper 1984); Anthony Cummings (Man From Uncle 2017); Greg Eurell (Mic Mac 2009); Leon Macdonald (Serious Speed 2008); Tim Martin (Monton 2010); Chris Waller (Press Statement 2016).
Points of interest: Racing To Win (2006) went on to win the 2006 Group 1 Doncaster Handicap (1600m) at Randwick.
Maurice McCarten trained four winners of the Hobartville (see above) and rode three winners (Gold Rod 1936, Ammon Ra 1931, Veilmond 1930).

ATC Silver Slipper Stakes (1100m)—Rosehill
$250,000 Group 2 2YO Open SW. February 23, 2019.

YEAR	WINNER	JOCKEY	TRAINER	2ND	3RD	TIME
2018	Sunlight	Tim Clark	Tony McEvoy	Estijaab	Gongs	1:03.5
2017	She Will Reign	Ben Melham	Gary Portelli	Veranillo	Showtime	1:04.7
2016	Astern	Hugh Bowman	John O'Shea	Defcon	Mount Panorama	1:04.1
2015	Headwater	Blake Shinn	Michael, Wayne & John Hawkes	Voilier	Mishani Honcho	1:04.3
2014	Mossfun	James McDonald	Michael, Wayne & John Hawkes	Press Report	Risen From Doubt	1:06.2
2013	Sweet Idea	Jim Cassidy	Gai Waterhouse	Whiskey Allround	Charlie Boy	1:06.3
2012	Pierro	Nash Rawiller	Gai Waterhouse	Hussousa	Kyria	1:06.8
2011	Satin Shoes	Hugh Bowman	Clarry Conners	Elite Falls	Straight Gold	1:03.4
2010	Chance Bye	Kathy O'Hara	Michael Tubman	Ambers Waltz	Zutara	1:04.2
2009	Melito	Danny Nikolic	Gerald Ryan	Sunday Rose	Onemorenomore	1:03.8
2008	Amelia's Dream	Nash Rawiller	Gai Waterhouse	Hips Don't Lie	Glowlamp	1:02.9
2007	Shaft	Darren Beadman	John Hawkes	Husson Lightning	Murtajill	1:04.0
2006	Plagiarize	Darren Beadman	John Hawkes	Boom Time Savings	Five Ways	1:04.0
2005	Domesday	Darren Beadman	John Hawkes	Flying Pegasus	Dr Green	1:04.0
2004	Ballybleue	Glen Boss	Anthony Cummings	Dane Shadow	Esther	1:04.0
2003	Hasna	Chris Munce	Gai Waterhouse	Polar Success	Legally Bay	1:04.0
2002	Victory Vein	Danny Beasley	Bede Murray	Chuckle	Air Of Grace	1:05.2
2001	Excellerator	Jim Cassidy	Gai Waterhouse	Ha Ha	Donna Natalia	1:03.1

BACKGROUND
First run: 1963 (won by Eskimo Prince). Group 2 since 1979. Run over 4½ furlongs 1963-83, except in 1970 when run over 5 furlongs at Canterbury. Run over 1100m at Canterbury 1991. Not held in 1997.
Most recent filly to win: Sunlight (2018).
Fastest time (1100m): Amelia's Dream (2008) 1:02:90.
Notable winners: Sunlight (2018); She Will Reign (2017); Astern (2016); Mossfun (2014); Amelia's Dream (2008); Hasna (2003); Victory Vein (2002); Excellerator (2001); Strategic (1994); Triscay (1989); Show County (1988); Black Shoes (1980); Luskin Star (1976); Eskimo Prince (1963).

Silver Slipper Stakes winners also won the lead-up races:
Magic Millions Classic Gold Coast: 1—Sunlight (2018).
Widden Stakes: 5—Mossfun (2014); Satin Shoes (2011); Triscay (1989); Rainbeam (1975); Topmost (1967);
Silver Slipper Stakes winners went on to win in the same preparation:
Skyline Stakes: 4—Strategic (1994); Kenfair (1992); Show County (1988); Pre Catelan (1985).
Todman Stakes: 2—Pierro (2012); Luskin Star (1977).
Golden Slipper Stakes: 6—She Will Reign (2017); Mossfun (2014); Pierro (2012); Luskin Star (1976); Baguette (1969); Eskimo Prince (1963).
Kindergarten Stakes: 3—Astern (2016); Plagiarize (2006); Show County (1989).
ATC Sires Produce Stakes: 7—Pierro (2012); Hasna (2003); Victory Vein (2002); Luskin Star (1977); Sovereign Slipper (1971); Baguette (1969); Eskimo Prince (1963).
Champagne Stakes: 6—Pierro (2012); Hasna (2003); Victory Vein (2002); Triscay (1989); Luskin Star (1976); Baguette (1969).
Leading winning jockey: 5 wins Darren Beadman (Shaft 2007, Plagiarize 2006, Domesday 2005, Strategic 1994, Honey Be Quick 1990).
3 wins Jim Cassidy (Sweet Idea 2013, Excellerator 2001, Iglesia 1998); Peter Cook (Ballook 1987, Mersing 1978, Rainbeam 1975).
Current winning jockeys: 2 wins Hugh Bowman (Astern 2016, Satin Shoes 2011); Nash Rawiller (Pierro 2012, Amelia's Dream 2008).
1 win Glen Boss (Ballybleue 2004); Corey Brown (French Braids 2000); Tim Clark (Sunlight 2018); James McDonald (Mossfun 2014); Ben Melham (She Will Reign 2017); Kathy O'Hara (Chance Bye 2010); Blake Shinn (Headwater 2015).
Leading winning trainer: 7 wins John Hawkes (Headwater 2014, Mossfun 2014, Shaft 2007, Plagiarize 2006, Domesday 2005, Clang 1995, Strategic 1994).
6 wins Jack Denham (Passmore 1999, Iglesia 1998, Triscay 1989, Maizcay 1986, Vaindarra 1981, Jewel Thief 1972).
Current winning trainers: 7 wins John Hawkes (Headwater 2015, Mossfun 2014, Shaft 2007, Plagiarize 2006, Domesday 2005, Clang 1995, Strategic 1994).
5 wins Gai Waterhouse (Sweet Idea 2013, Pierro 2012, Amelia's Dream 2008, Hasna 2003, Excellerator 2001).
2 wins Michael, Wayne & John Hawkes (Headwater 2015, Mossfun 2014).
1 win Clarry Conners (Satin Shoes 2011); Anthony Cummings (Ballybleue 2004); Tony McEvoy (Sunlight 2018); John O'Shea (Astern 2016); Gary Portelli (She Will Reign 2017); Gerald Ryan (Melito 2009); Michael Tubman (Chance Bye 2010).
Points of interest: Millward (1996) won the Group 1 VRC Sires' Produce Stakes (1400m) at Flemington in March, 1996. Amelia's Dream (2008) broke down after winning by 6.5lens in record time.

ATC Millie Fox Stakes (1300m)—Rosehill
$175,000 Group 2 3YO&Up Fillies & Mares SWP. February 23, 2019.

YEAR	WINNER	JOCKEY	TRAINER	2ND	3RD	TIME
2018	Daysee Doom	Andrew Adkins	Ron Quinton	Girl Sunday	Foxplay	1:16.8
2017	In Her Time	Josh Parr	Ben Smith	Euro Angel	Daysee Doom	1:17.6
2016	First Seal	Blake Shinn	John P Thompson	Telepathic	I've Got The Looks	1:16.4
2015	Catkins	Hugh Bowman	Chris Waller	Plucky Belle	Avoid Lightning	1:16.4
2014	Red Tracer	Nash Rawiller	Chris Waller	A Time For Julia	Lucky Lago	1:19.2
2013	Red Tracer	Nash Rawiller	Chris Waller	Risk Aversion	Ladys Angel	1:19.6
2012	Red Tracer	Hugh Bowman	Chris Waller	Crafty Irna	Older Than Time	1:20.5
2011	Montana Flyer	Tommy Berry	Gai Waterhouse	Graceful Anna	Jersey Lily	1:16.3
2010	Montana Flyer	Blake Shinn	Gai Waterhouse	Chakvetadze	Subtle Cove	1:16.8
2009	Neroli	Kerrin McEvoy	Peter Snowden	Pravana	Belong To Many	1:16.3
2008	November Flight	Tye Angland	Garry White	Absolutelyfabulous	Swissac	1:16.4
2007	A Country Girl	Zac Purton	Barbara Joseph	Pasikatera	Spinner's Magic	1:16.6
2006	Wild Queen	Jamie Innes	Gai Waterhouse	Steflara	Regal Cheer	1:17.2
2005	Tivoli Dancer	Darren Beadman	Kevin Moses	Lil Elsa	Johan's Toy	1:10.0
2004	Seances	Corey Brown	John Hawkes	In A Bound	Recurring	1:09.7
2003	Gentle Genius	Len Beasley	Tony Wildman	Snow Hero	Ancient Song	1:09.8
2002	Triko	Larry Cassidy	Ken Callaughan	Vita	Pirouettes	1:11.2
2001	Nanny Maroon	Darryl Mclellan	Paul Englebrecht	Stella Maree	Poppett	1:08.9

BACKGROUND

First run: 1996 (won by Chlorophyll). Listed 1998-2006. Group 3 2007-16. Group 2 from 2017. Run over 1200m 1996-2005.
Most recent 3YO to win: Tivoli Dancer (2005)
Multiple winners: 2—Red Tracer (2014, 2013, 2012); Montana Flyer (2011, 2010).
Fastest time (1300m): Montana Flyer (2011) & Neroli (2009) 1:16:30
Notable winners: Daysee Doom (2018); First Seal (2016); Catkins (2015); Red Tracer (2014, 2013, 2012); Montana Flyer (2011, 2010); Dashing Eagle (1997); Chlorophyll (1996).
Millie Fox Stakes winners won the lead-up races:
Breeders' Classic: 2—In Her Time (2017); Catkins (2015).
Millie Fox Stakes winners went on to win in the same preparation:
Emancipation Stakes: 1—Catkins (2015).
Coolmore Classic: 2—Daysee Doom (2018); Chlorophyll (1996).
Queen Of The Turf Stakes: 1—Neroli (2009).
Birthday Card Stakes: 1—Verdict Declared (2000).
Leading winning jockeys: 2 wins Hugh Bowman (Catkins 2015, Red Tracer 2012); John Marshall (Dashing Eagle 1997, Chlorophyll 1996); Nash Rawiller (Red Tracer 2014, 2013); Blake Shinn (First Seal 2016, Montana Flyer 2010).
Current winning jockeys: 2 wins Hugh Bowman (Catkins 2015, Red Tracer 2012); Nash Rawiller (Red Tracer 2014, 2013); Blake Shinn (First Seal 2016, Montana Flyer 2010).
1 win Andrew Adkins (Daysee Doom 2018); Tye Angland (November Flight 2008); Tommy Berry (Montana Flyer 2011); Corey Brown (Seances 2004); Larry Cassidy (Triko 2002); Kevin Forrester (Just Like Crystal 1998); Jamie Innes (Wild Queen 2006); Kerrin McEvoy (Neroli 2009); Josh Parr (In Her Time 2017); Zac Purton (A Country Girl 2007).
Leading winning trainer: 4 wins Chris Waller (Catkins 2015, Red Tracer 2014, 2013, 2012).
Current winning trainers: 4 wins Chris Waller (Catkins 2015, Red Tracer 2014, 2013, 2012).
3 wins Gai Waterhouse (Montana Flyer 2011, 2010, Wild Queen 2006).
2 wins Barbara Joseph (A Country Girl 2007, Verdict Declared 2000); Ron Quinton (Daysee Doom 2018, Wynciti 1999).
1 win Paul Englebrecht (Nanny Maroon 2001); John Hawkes (Seances 2004); Benjamin Smith (In Her Time 2017); Peter Snowden (Neroli 2009); John Thompson (First Seal 2016); Garry White (November Flight 2008).

MRC Peter Young Stakes (1800m)—Caulfield
$200,000 Group 2 Open WFA. February 23, 2019.

YEAR	WINNER	JOCKEY	TRAINER	2ND	3RD	TIME
2018	Gailo Chop	Mark Zahra	Darren Weir	Single Gaze	Hartnell	1:48.2
2017	Stratum Star	Mark Zahra	Darren Weir	Humidor	The United States	1:48.2
2016	Bow Creek	Damien Oliver	John O'Shea	Fenway	Mourinho	1:48.6
2015	Mourinho	Vlad Duric	Peter Gelagotis	Happy Trails	Akzar	1:48.0
2014	Fiorente	Damien Oliver	Gai Waterhouse	Mourayan	Star Rolling	1:50.0
2013	Foreteller	Dwayne Dunn	Chris Waller	Mr Moet	Budriguez	1:50.9
2012	Lucas Cranach	Nash Rawiller	Anthony Freedman	Illo	Manighar	1:48.8
2011	Heart Of Dreams	Damien Oliver	Mick Price	Precedence	Spacecraft	1:48.8
2010	La Rocket	Stephen Baster	Dale Sutton	Heart Of Dreams	Miss Maren	1:49.0
2009	Theseo	Nash Rawiller	Gai Waterhouse	Baughurst	Zarita	1:47.8
2008	Princess Coup	Damien Oliver	Mark Walker	Sirmione	Douro Valley	1:51.0
2007	Pompeii Ruler	Craig Newitt	Mick Price	Marasco	Aqua D'Amore	1:49.2
2006	Our Smoking Joe	Noel Callow	Lee Freedman	Lad Of The Manor	Vroom Vroom	1:50.2
2005	Elvstroem	Nash Rawiller	Tony Vasil	Makybe Diva	Casual Pass	1:49.5
2004	Lonhro	Darren Gauci	John Hawkes	Sound Journey	Mummify	1:50.9
2003	Northerly	Patrick Payne	Fred Kersley	Fields Of Omagh	Mr Casanova	1:51.8
2002	Northerly	Damien Oliver	Fred Kersley	Old Comrade	Piper Star	1:49.2
2001	Cent Home	David Walker	Jim Wallace	Giovana	Kaapstad Way	1:47.1

BACKGROUND

First run: 1900 (won by Parthian). Group 2 from 1979. Run over 1200m in 1979; 1600 1982-87; 2000m in 1995. Run at Flemington in 1996. Registered as the St. George Stakes. Run as Peter Young Stakes from 2013.
Most recent mare to win: Princess Coup (2008).

Most recent 3YO to win: C&G—Ashbah (1977); Filly—Tranquil Star (1941).
Multiple winners: 13—Northerly (2003, 2002); Istadaad (1999, 1997); Durbridge (1995, 1994); Vo Rogue (1989, 1988); Leilani (1976, 1975); Rain Lover (1970, 1969); Dhaulagiri (1962, 1961); Lord (1960, 1959); Comic Court (1951, 1950); Tranquil Star (1945, 1944, 1941); High Caste (1942, 1940); Black Duchess (1929,1928); The Hawk (1925, 1924).
Fastest time (1800m): Cent Home (2001) 1:47:19.
Notable winners: Gailo Chop (2018); Stratum Star (2017); Fiorente (2014); Princess Coup (2008); Elvstroem (2005); Lonhro (2004); Northerly (2003, 2002); Dane Ripper (1998); Let's Elope (1992); Vo Rogue (1989, 1988); Hyperno (1981); Leilani (1976, 1976); Rain Lover (1970, 1969); Tobin Bronze (1967); Light Fingers (1966); Sometime (1963); Lord (1960, 1959); Redcraze (1957); Delta (1952); Comic Court (1951, 1950); Flight (1946); Tranquil Star (1945, 1944, 1941); High Caste (1942, 1940); Ajax (1939); Phar Lap (1931); Amounis (1930); Heroic 91927); Easingwold (1923); Eurythmic (1922); Desert Gold (1918); Comedy King (1911); Wakeful (1902); Clean Sweep (1901).
Peter Young Stakes winners won the lead-up races:
Australia Stakes: 1—Mourinho (2015).
Orr Stakes: 17—Elvstroem (2005); Lonhro (2004); Let's Elope (1992); Vo Rogue (1989, 1988); Lawman (1982); Leilani (1975); Winfreux (1968); Tobin Bronze (1967); Aquanita (1963); Lord (1960, 1959); Comic Court (1951); Attley (1947); Flight (1946); High Caste (1940); Whittier (1926).
Carlyon Cup: 1—Gailo Chop (2018).
Peter Young Stakes winners went on to win in the same preparation:
Australian Cup: 12—Fiorente (2014); Pompeii Ruler (2007); Lonhro (2004); Northerly (2003); Istidaad (1999); Dane Ripper (1998); Durbridge (1994); Let's Elope (1992); Vo Rogue (1989); Hyperno (1981); Leilani (1975); Gay Icarus (1971).
Orr Stakes & Australian Cup: 4—Lonhro (2004); Let's Elope (1992); Vo Rogue (1989); Leilani (1975).
Blamey Stakes: 11—Racer's Edge (1996); Durbridge (1995, 1994); Vo Rogue (1989, 1988); Hyperno (1981); Sobar (1974); Gay Icarus (1971); Tobin Bronze (1967); Dhaulagiri (1962, 1961).
Ranvet Stakes: 9—Gailo Chop (2018); Foreteller (2013); Theseo (2009); Hyperno (1981); Minuetto (1980); Redcraze (1957); Ammon Ra (1932); The Hawk (1925); Artilleryman (1920);
The Peter Young Stakes and the Melbourne Cup (same season):
Melbourne Cup winners to win the Peter Young Stakes in the following autumn: 11—Fiorente (2014); Let's Elope (1992); Rain Lover (1970, 1969); Light Fingers (1966); Delta (1952); Phar Lap (1931); Comic Court (1951); Artilleryman (1920); Comedy King (1911); Clean Sweep (1901).
Leading winning jockeys: 5 wins Jim Pike (Phar Lap 1931, Amounis 1930, The Hawk 1925, 1924, Jolly Beggar 1914).
4 wins Harold Badger (Sun Valley 1843, High Caste 1940, Ajax 1939, Farndale 1935); Roy Higgins (Lawman 1982, Leilani 1976, 1975, Light Fingers 1966); Geoff Lane (Dhaulagiri 1962, 1961, Lord 1960, 1959); Bobby Lewis (Artilleryman 1920, Patrobas 1917, Cyklon 1916, Alawa 1910); Damien Oliver (Fiorente 2014, Heart Of Dreams 2011, Princess Coup 2008, Northerly 2002); Jack Purtell (Cromis 1954, Comic Court 1951, 1950, Attley 1947).
Current winning jockeys: 4 wins Damien Oliver (Fiorente 2014, Heart Of Dreams 2011, Princess Coup 2008, Northerly 2002).
3 wins Nash Rawiller (Lucas Cranach 2012, Theseo 2009, Elvstroem 2005).
2 wins Cyril Small (Vo Rogue 1989, 1988); Mark Zahra (Gailo Chop 2018, Stratum Star 2017).
1 win Stephen Baster (La Rocket 2010); Noel Callow (Our Smoking Joe 2006); Dwayne Dunn (Foreteller 2013); Vlad Duric (Mourinho 2015); James McDonald (Bow Creek 2016); Craig Newitt (Pompeii Ruler 2007).
Leading winning trainers: 7 wins Bart Cummings (Dane Ripper 1998, Let's Elope 1992, Hyperno 1981, Ashbah 1977, Leilani 1976, 1975, Light Fingers 1966).
5 wins Jack Holt (Young Idea 1937, Heroic 1927, Easingwold 1923, Eurythmic 1922, Mistico 1919).
4 wins Colin Hayes (King's High 1990, Mrs. Fiztherbert 1986, Minuetto 1980, Unaware 1978); James Scobie (Hua 1938, Cyklon 1916, Alawa 1910, Clean Sweep 1901).
Current winning trainers: 3 wins Lee Freedman (Our Smoking Joe 2006, Durbridge 1995, 1994).
2 wins Fred Kersley (Northerly 2003, 2002); Mick Price (Heart Of Dreams 2011, Pompeii Ruler 2007); Gai Waterhouse (Fiorente 2014, Theseo 2009); Darren Weir (Gailo Chop 2018, Stratum Star 2017).
1 win Mat Ellerton (Royal Voyage 2000); Anthony Freedman (Lucas Cranach 2012); Peter Gelegotis (Mourinho 2015); John Hawkes (Lonhro 2004); John Meagher (Star Of The Realm 1993); John O'Shea (Bow Creek 2016); Tony Vasil (Elvstroem 2005); Chris Waller (Foreteller 2013); Mark Walker (Princess Coup 2008); Wayne Walters (Torbek 1985).
Points of interest: Vo Rogue (1989, 1988) was first past the post in 1990, but lost on protest to King's High. Hyperno and Little Brown Jug dead-heated for first in 1981.

MRC Caulfield Autumn Classic (1800m)—Caulfield
$200,000 Group 2 3YO Open SW. February 23, 2019.

YEAR	WINNER	JOCKEY	TRAINER	2ND	3RD	TIME
2018	Valiant Spirit	Regan Bayliss	Daniel Williams	Astoria	Mr So And So	1:49.4
2017	Farson	Stephen Baster	Gai Waterhouse & Adrian Bott	Cliff Hanger	Captain Rhett	1:49.4
2016	Tally	Craig Williams	John O'Shea	Flying Light	Top Ravine	1:49.1
2015	Alpine Eagle	Damien Oliver	Tony McEvoy	Minnesinger	Firehouse Rock	1:48.4
2014	Vilanova	Craig Newitt	Chris Waller	Countersnip	Alpha Beat	1:51.0
2013	Super Cool	Michael Rodd	Mark Kavanagh	Fiveandahalfstar	Subiaso	1:49.8
2012	Upbeat	Blake Shinn	Anthony Cummings	Flashy Fella	Ethiopia	1:50.0
2011	Folding Gear	Ben Melham	Lee & Shannon Hope	Elusive King	Almindoro	1:48.1
2010	Extra Zero	Glen Boss	David Hayes	Absolute Faith	Money Rocks	1:50.6
2009	Stokehouse	Craig Williams	David Hayes	Excelltastic	Zapurple	1:49.7
2008	Brom Brom	Brad Rawiller	Colin & Cindy Alderson	Allanthus	Buca Di Bacco	1:51.4
2007	Ambitious General	Damien Oliver	Peter Moody	Danever	Furio	1:48.9
2006	Spinney	Darren Beadman	John Hawkes	Silver Ninja	Cinderella Man	1:48.1
2005	Renewable	Danny Nikolic	Graeme Rogerson	Stella Grande	Dizelle	1:50.1
2004	Elvstroem	Damien Oliver	Tony Vasil	Delzao	Strafed	1:49.1
2003	Natural Blitz	Nash Rawiller	Doug Harrison	Glefti	Gallic	1:49.4
2002	Don Eduardo	Damien Oliver	Lee Freedman	Royal Code	All Courage	1:49.4
2001	Fubu	Vin Hall	Cliff Brown	Neptunes Journey	Inspire	1:47.5

BACKGROUND
First run: 1957 (won by Lord Gavin). Listed 1979-88. Group 3 1989-90. Group 2 since 1991. Run over 2000 1957-70 & 1972-86. Originally known as the Stanley Plate (1957-1986), run over 2000m (except 1971 when 1800m).
Most recent filly to win: Triscay (1991).
Fastest time (1800m): Waikikamukau (1994) 1:47.30
Notable winners: Elvstroem (2004); Natural Blitz (2003); Don Eduardo (2002); Pins (2000); Dignity Dancer (1999); Gold Guru (1998); Hurricane Sky (1995); Redding (1993); Triscay (1991); Stylish Century (1990); King's High (1989); Myocard (1987); Gurner's Lane (1982).
Victoria Derby and the Autumn Classic:
Victoria Derby (spring) & Autumn Classic (February): 4—Elvstroem (2005); Redding (1993); Stylish Century (1991); King's High (1989).
Autumn Classic winners won the lead-up races:
Alister Clark Stakes: 4—Tally (2016); Spinney (2006); Pins (2000); Dignity Dancer (1999). Note: Tally (2016) & Spinney (2006) won the double after the Alister Clarke was moved to be run before the Autumn Classic in 2005.
Autumn Classic winners went on to win in the same preparation:
Australian Guineas: 4—Pins (2000); Dignity Dancer (1999); Gold Guru (1998); King's High (1989).
Australian Cup: 1—Super Cool (2013).
Rosehill Guineas: Nil
ATC Australian Derby: 4—Don Eduardo (2002); Gold Guru (1998); Myocard (1987); Double Century (1979).
Leading winning jockey: 4 wins Damien Oliver (Alpine Eagle 2015, Ambitious General 2007, Elvstroem 2004, Don Eduardo 2002).
Current winning jockeys: 4 wins Damien Oliver (Alpine Eagle 2015, Ambitious General 2007, Elvstroem 2004, Don Eduardo 2002).
1 win Stephen Baster (Farson 2017); Regan Bayliss (Valiant Spirit 2018); Glen Boss (Extra Zero 2010); Kevin Forrester (Admiral Lincoln 1983); Ben Melham (Folding Gear 2011); Craig Newitt (Vilanova 2014); Brad Rawiller (Brom Brom 2008); Nash Rawiller (Natural Blitz 2003); Michael Rodd (Super Cool 2013); Blake Shinn (Upbeat 2012); Craig Williams (Tally 2016, Stokehouse 2009).
Leading winning trainer: 7 wins Geoff Murphy (Normandy Bay 1986, Tri-Flow 1984, Admiral Lincoln 1983, Gurner's Lane 1982, Royal Guardsman 1971, Pharaon 1967, Blue Era 1962).
Current winning trainers: 2 wins David Hayes (Extra Zero 2010, Stokehouse 2009); John Hawkes (Spinney 2006, Waikikamukau 1994).
1 win Cindy Alderson (Brom Brom 2008, in partnership with her father Colin); Cliff Brown (Fubu 2002); Clarry Conners (Pins 2000); Anthony Cummings (Upbeat 2012); Lee Freedman (Don Eduardo 2002); Robbie Griffiths (Silver Glade 1997); Doug Harrison (Natural Blitz 2003); Lee & Shannon Hope (Folding Gear 2011); Mark Kavanagh (Super Cool 2013); Leon Macdonald (Gold Guru 1998); Tony McEvoy (Alpine Eagle 2015); John O'Shea (Tally 2016); Graeme Rogerson (Renewable 2005); Gerald Ryan (Hurricane Sky 1995); Tony Vasil (Elvstroem 2004); Chris Waller (Vilanova 2014); Gai Waterhouse & Adrian Bott (Farson 2017); Daniel Williams (Valiant Spirit 2018).

Points of interest: Gurner's Lane (1982) won the 1982 Caulfield and Melbourne Cup double.
Double Century (1979) won the Sydney Cup in the same campaign.
Mick Mallyon won the race in 1963 on Soldate and 16 years later on Double Century (1979).

MRC Angus Armanasco Stakes (1400m)—Caulfield
$200,000 Group 2 3YO Fillies SW. February 23, 2019.

YEAR	WINNER	JOCKEY	TRAINER	2ND	3RD	TIME
2018	Summer Sham	Daniel Moor	Danny O'Brien	Palazzo Vecchio	Miss Wahoo	1:23.3
2017	Savanna Amour	Joao Moreira	John & Chris Meagher	Ellicazoom	Oregon's Day	1:22.9
2016	Catch A Fire	Damian Lane	David Hayes & Tom Dabernig	Mossin' Around	Pasadena Girl	1:23.5
2015	Sabatini	Nicholas Hall	Lee & Shannon Hope	Fontein Ruby	Samartested	1:23.2
2014	Spirits Dance	Chad Schofield	Peter Moody	Marianne	Metaphorical	1:23.5
2013	Meliora	Luke Nolen	Peter Moody	Members Joy	Red Fez	1:23.3
2012	Shopaholic	Glen Boss	Danny O'Brien	Soft Sand	Cute Emily	1:23.4
2011	Pinker Pinker	Dwayne Dunn	Greg Eurell	Sayahailmary	Sistine Angel	1:21.4
2010	Set For Fame	Luke Nolen	Peter Moody	Gigas	Irish Lights	1:22.5
2009	Gold Water	Nash Rawiller	Gai Waterhouse	Gallica	Miss Scarlatti	1:35.9
2008	Zarita	Greg Childs	Pat Hyland	Pleasantsundaygirl	El Daana	1:37.9
2007	Miss Finland	Craig Williams	David Hayes	Causeway Lass	Kisumu	1:36.6
2006	Serenade Rose	Steven King	Lee Freedman	Doubting	Fanciful Bella	1:34.8
2005	Ballet Society	Steven King	Pat Hyland	Astrodame	Glen Shian	1:36.8
2004	Special Harmony	Damien Oliver	Lee Freedman	Deep In The Woods	Demerger	1:38.6
2003	La Bella Dama	Danny Nikolic	Mick Price	Lashed	Dextrous	1:36.2
2002	Elegant Fashion	Greg Childs	Tony McEvoy	Li Lo Lill	Moon Dragon	1:36.7
2001	Rose Archway	Eddie Cassar	Clarry Conners	St Therese	Ponton Flyer	1:35.9

BACKGROUND
First run: 1976 (won by Better Draw). Group 3 from 1980. Run over 1400m 1984-97, from 2010. 1600m 1998-2012. Run at Sandown in 1996. Originally known as the Tranquil Star Stakes (1976-1995).
Fastest time (1400m): Pinker Pinker (2011) 1:21:40.
Notable winners: Pinker Pinker (2011); Set For Fame (2010); Zarita (2008); Miss Finland (2007); Serenade Rose (2006); Special Harmony (2004); Rose Archway (2001); Rose O'War (1999); Champagne (1998); Northwood Plume (1995); Shackle (1987); Delightful Belle (1985); Richebourg (1984); Brett's Honour (1977); Better Draw (1976).
The VRC Oaks and the Armanasco Stakes:
VRC Oaks (Nov) & Armanasco Stakes (Feb): 4—Miss Finland (2007); Serenade Rose (2006); Special Harmony (2004); Northwood Plume (1995).
Angus Armanasco Stakes winners won the lead-up races:
Kevin Hayes Stakes: 3—Sabatini (2015); Spirits Dance (2014); Set For Fame (2010).
The Vanity: 3—Shopaholic (2012); Ballet Society (2005); Rose O'War (1999).
Matron Stakes: 1—Pinker Pinker (2011).
Armanasco Stakes winners went on to win in the same preparation:
Kewney Stakes: 6—Zarita (2008); Ballet Society (2005); Special Harmony (2004); Elegant Fashion (2002); Northwood Plume (1995); Bravita (1980).
MV Fillies Classic: None. Note: Special Harmony (2004), Elegant Fashion (2002) and Champagne (1998) won the double when the Armanasco was run before the MV Fillies Classic (1500m), which then was run over 2040m.
Australasian (Schwepps) Oaks: 1—Zarita (2008).
Storm Queen Stakes: 5—Miss Finland (2007); Serenade Rose (2006); Special Harmony (2004); Champagne (1998); Northwood Plume (1995).
ATC Australian Oaks: 2—Serenade Rose (2006); Rose Archway (2001).
Leading winning jockeys: 3 wins Steven King (Serenade Rose 2006, Ballet Society 2005, Cheval Place 1997); Damien Oliver (Special Harmony 2004, Rose O'War 1999, Tessuti 1991); Greg Childs (Zarita 2008, Elegant Fashion 2002, Champagne 1988); Harry White (Golden Unicorn 1988, Rogue's Delight 1982, Tynia 1981).
Current winning jockeys: 3 wins Damien Oliver (Special Harmony 2004, Rose O'War 1999, Tessuti 1991).
2 wins Luke Nolen (Meliora 2013, Set For Fame 2010).
1 win Glen Boss (Shopaholic 2012); Dwayne Dunn (Pinker Pinker 2011); Nick Hall (Sabatini 2015); Damian Lane (Catch A Fire 2016); Daniel Moor (Summer Sham 2018); Joao Moreira (Savanna Amour 2017); Nash Rawiller (Gold Water 2009); Chad Schofield (Spirits Dance 2014); Craig Williams (Miss Finland 2007).
Leading winning trainers: 8 wins Lee Freedman (Serenade Rose 2006, Special Harmony 2004, Rose O'War

1999, Cheval Place 1997, Northwood Plume 1995, Party Time 1994, Tessuti 1991, Shackle 1987).
4 wins Colin Hayes (Deira 1990, Delightful Belle 1985, Bravita 1980, Pushy 1978).
Current winning trainers: 8 wins Lee Freedman (Serenade Rose 2006, Special Harmony 2004, Rose O'War 1999, Cheval Place 1997, Northwood Plume 1995, Party Time 1994, Tessuti 1991, Shackle 1987).
2 wins David Hayes (Catch A Fire 2016, Miss Finland 2007); Pat Hyland (Zarita 2008, Ballet Society 2005); Danny O'Brien (Summer Sham 2018, Shopaholic 2012).
1 win Clarry Conners (Rose Archway 2001); Craig Conron (Big Jamaica 1993); David Hayes & Tom Dabernig (Catch A Fire 2016); Greg Eurell (Pinker Pinker 2011); Lee & Shannon Hope (Sabatini 2015); Bevan Laming (I Am A Ripper 2000); Laurie Laxon (Champagne 1998); Tony McEvoy (Elegant Fashion 2002); John & Chris Meagher (Savanna Amour 2017); Mick Price (La Bella Dame 2003); Gai Waterhouse (Gold Water 2009).
Point of interest: Party Time and Sovereign Appeal dead-heated for first in 1994.
Pinker Pinker (2011) won the G1 Cox Plate (2040m) later that year.

ATC Skyline Stakes (1200m)—Warwick Farm
$175,000 Group 2 2YO C&G SW. March 2, 2019.

YEAR	WINNER	JOCKEY	TRAINER	2ND	3RD	TIME
2018	Santos	Tim Clark	Gai Waterhouse & Adrian Bott	Spin	Legend Of Condor	1:11.1
2017	Diamond Tathagata	Glyn Scbofield	Mark Newnham	Coruscate	Single Bullet	1:14.2
2016	Good Standing	Hugh Bowman	James Cummings	Lionhearted	Souchez	1:09.0
2015	Exosphere	James McDonald	John O'Shea	Odyssey Moon	Wolf Cry	1:10.6
2014	Valentia	Tommy Berry	Gai Waterhouse	Mr Bogart	Modoc	1:11.4
2013	All The Talk	Brenton Avdulla	Gary Portelli	Octane Flyer	Dothraki	1:09.7
2012	Ashokan	Jim Cassidy	John O'Shea	Raceway	Collect	1:10.9
2011	Uate	Nash Rawiller	Kris Lees	Hot Snitzel	Flight Of Pegasus	1:09.7
2010	Hinchinbrook	Hugh Bowman	Gerald Ryan	Brightexpectations	Pressday	1:08.8
2009	Manhattan Rain	Nash Rawiller	Gai Waterhouse	The Mikado	Romanus	1:10.3
2008	All American	Brad Rawiller	David Hayes	Over the Wicket	Dubai To Sydney	1.11.2
2007	Murtajill	Jim Cassidy	Tim Martin	Husson Lightning	Pistols	1.09.6
2006	Casino Prince	Jim Cassidy	Anthony Cummings	Empire's Choice	My Middi	1.11.1
2005	Snitzel	Glen Boss	Gerald Ryan	Stratum	Paratroopers	1:10.0
2004	Dance Hero	Chris Munce	Gai Waterhouse	Fastnet Rock	Econsul	1:10.7
2003	Kusi	Corey Brown	John Hawkes	Face Value	Resistor	1:10.0
2002	Choisir	Len Beasley	Paul Perry	Emerging Star	Charlie Bub	1:10.3
2001	Viscount	Rod Quinn	John Hawkes	Excellerator	Shags	1:10.3

BACKGROUND
First run: 1979 (won by Top Hat Joe). Listed 1980-86. Group 3 1987-2013. Group 2 from 2014.
Run Canterbury 1979-1995, 2000-2005; Rosehill 1979, 1981, 1997 & 1998; Warwick Farm 2011, 2013, 2015, from 2019. Run at Randwick 2006-18.
Fastest time (1200m, Randwick): Hinchinbrook (2010) 1:08.87.
Notable winners: Exosphere (2015); Hnchinbrook (2010); Manhattan Rain (2009); All American (2008); Casino Prince 2006); Snitzel (2005); Dance Hero (2004); Choisir (2002); Viscount (2001); Shogun Lodge (1999); Prowl (1998); Guineas (1997); Strategic (1995); Star Watch (1998); Sir Dapper (1983).
Skyline Stakes winners won the lead-up races:
Breeders' Plate: 5—Murtajill (2007); Snitzel (2005); Choisir (2002); Show County (1999); Pre Catelan (1986). Note: The Breeders' Plate Is Run In The Spring.
Canonbury Stakes: 4—Hinchinbrook (2010); Kootoomootoo (1999); Shogun Lodge (1999); Strategic (1995). Note: Only Hinchinbrook (2010) has won the double since the Canonbury was moved from December to February.
Silver Slipper Stakes: 4—Strategic (1994); Kenfair (1992); Show County (1989); Pre Catelan (1986). Note: Kenfair (1992), Show County (1989) and Pre Catelan (1986). All won the Silver Slipper Stakes when it was run during the spring carnival.
Blue Diamond Stakes & Skyline Stakes: 1—Kusi (2003).
Skyline Stakes winners went on to win in the same preparation:
Todman Stakes: None.
Pago Pago Stakes: 3—Shogun Lodge (1999); Strategic (1995); Big Dreams (1991).
Golden Slipper Stakes: 5—Dance Hero (2004); Prowl (1998); Guineas (1997); Star Watch (1988); Sir Dapper (1983).
ATC Sires Produce Stakes: 3— Manhattan Rain (2009); Dance Hero (2004); Viscount (2001).
Champagne Stakes: 2—Dance Hero (2004); Viscount (2001).
Leading winning jockeys: 3 wins Jim Cassidy (Ashokan 2012, Murtajill 2007, Casino Prince 2006);

Wayne Harris (Big Dreams 1991, Timothy 1985, Cosmic Delight 1980).
Current winning jockeys: 2 wins Hugh Bowman (Good Standing 2016, Hinchinbrook 2010); Nash Rawiller (Uate 2011, Manhattan Rain 2009).
1 win Brenton Avdulla (All The Talk 2013); Tommy Berry (Valentia 2014); Glen Boss (Snitzel 2005); Corey Brown (Kusi 2003); Larry Cassidy (Guineas 1997); Tim Clark (Santos 2018); James McDonald (Exosphere 2015); Brad Rawiller (All American 2008); Glyn Schofield (Diamond Tathagata 2017).
Leading winning trainers: 5 wins Gai Waterhouse (Santos 2018, Valentia 2014, Manhattan Rain 2009, Dance Hero 2004, Allez Glen 1993).
4 wins John Hawkes (Kusi 2003, Viscount 2001, Guineas 1997, Strategic 1995).
Current winning trainers: 5 wins Gai Waterhouse (Santos 2018, Valentia 2014, Manhattan Rain 2009, Dance Hero 2004, Allez Glen 1993).
4 wins John Hawkes (Kusi 2003, Viscount 2001, Guineas 1997, Strategic 1995).
2 wins John O'Shea (Exosphere 2015, Ashokan 2012); Gerald Ryan (Hinchinbrook 2010, Snitzel 2005).
1 win Les Bridge (Sir Dapper 1983); Clarry Conners (Prowl 1998); Anthony Cummings (Casino Prince 2006); James Cummings (Good Standing 2016); David Hayes (All American 2008); Kris Lees (Uate 2011); Mick Mair (Dr Zachary 2013); Tim Martin (Murtajill 2007); Mark Newnham (Diamond Tathagata 2017); Paul Perry (Choisir 2002); Gary Portelli (All The Talk 2013); Gai Waterhouse & Adrian Bott (Santos 2018).
Point of interest: Two Golden Slipper winners have been placed in the Skyline: Stratum (2nd to Snitzel, 2005) and Inspired (2nd to Hula Drum, 1984).

ATC Sweet Embrace Stakes (1200m)—Warwick Farm
$175,000 Group 2 2YO Fillies SW. March 2, 2019.

YEAR	WINNER	JOCKEY	TRAINER	2ND	3RD	TIME
2018	Seabrook	Hugh Bowman	Mick Price	Fiesta	Into The Abyss	1:10.9
2017	One More Honey	Jay Ford	John Thompson	Arctic Angel	Teaspoon	1:12.2
2016	Scarlet Rain	Kathy O'Hara	Gai Waterhouse	In The Vanguard	Tale Of Choice	1:09.5
2015	Always Allison	Glyn Schofield	Chris Waller	Speak Fondly	Tibrogargan Miss	1:10.7
2014	Believe Yourself	Jason Collett	Gerald Ryan	Twirl	Tetsuko	1:11.2
2013	Romantic Moon	James McDonald	John O'Shea	Thump	Greytfilly	1:10.0
2012	Jade Marauder	Hugh Bowman	Chris Waller	Valerio	Kyria	1:11.2
2011	Shared Reflections	Nash Rawiller	Gai Waterhouse	Streama	Pane In The Glass	1:09.5
2010	Crystal Lily	Damien Oliver	Mathew Ellerton & Simon Zahra	Ambers Waltz	Zutara	1:09.0
2009	Headway	Chris Munce	Peter Moody	Lovemelikearock	Horizons	1:11.1
2008	Stripper	Jeff Lloyd	David Payne	Glowlamp	Samantha Miss	1:11.0
2007	Chinchilla Rose	Stathi Katsidis	Steele Ryan	Vecchia Roma	Moonboat	1:10.1
2006	Universal Queen	Danny Beasley	Bede Murray	Tuesday Joy	Pure Energy	1:11.4
2005	Carry On Cutie	Jim Cassidy	Graeme Rogerson	Media	Flion Fenena	1:10.5
2004	Burning Sands	Jim Cassidy	Graeme Rogerson	All Knowledge	Written By Xaar	1:11.9
2003	Legally Bay	Rod Quinn	John Hawkes	How Funny	Bella Corona	1:10.0
2002	Victory Vein	Danny Beasley	Bede Murray	Chuckle	Calaway Gal	1:09.9
2001	Ha Ha	Brian York	Gai Waterhouse	Moonflute	Palais	1:11.0

BACKGROUND
First run: 1979 (won by Ingenue). Listed 1979-86. Group 3 1987-2012. Group 2 from 2013.
Run Canterbury 1979-1995, 2000-2005; Rosehill 1979, 1981, 1997 & 1998; Warwick Farm 2011, 2013, 2015, from 2019. Run at Randwick 2006-18.
Fastest time (1200m, Randwick): Scarlet Rain (2016) 1:09.52
Notable winners: Seabrook (2018); Crystal Lily (2010); Headway (2009); Universal Queen (2006); Victory Vein (2002); Ha Ha (2001); Skating (1992); Black Shoes (1981); Dark Eclipse (1980).
Sweet Embrace Stakes winners won the lead-up races:
MRC Chairman's Stakes: 2—Crystal Lily (2010); Headway (2009).
Blue Diamond Preview: 1—Crystal Lily (2010).
Blue Diamond Stakes: 1—Black Shoes (1981).
Silver Slipper Stakes: 2—Victory Vein (2002); Black Shoes (1981). Note: Blacks Shoes (1981) won the 1980 Silver Slipper Stakes when it was run during the spring carnival.
Sweet Embrace Stakes winners went on to win in the same preparation:
Reisling Stakes: 1—Purpose (1983).
Magic Night Stakes: 3 —Victory Vein (2002); Countess Christie (1999); Dark Eclipse (1980).
Golden Slipper Stakes: 3—Crystal Lily (2010); Ha Ha (2001); Dark Eclipse (1980).

ATC Sires Produce Stakes: 1—Victory Vein (2002).
Champagne Stakes: 3—Seabrook (2018); Carry On Cutie (2005); Victory Vein (2002).
Leading winning jockey: 3 wins Jim Cassidy (Carry On Cutie 2005, Burning Sands 2004, Paklani 1990).
Current winning jockeys: 2 wins Hugh Bowman (Serabrook 2018, Jade Marauder 2012).
1 win Larry Cassidy (Rock Review 1993); Glen Colless (Dynamic Love 2000); Jason Collett (Believe Yourself 2014); Grant Cooksley (Skating 1992); Jay Ford (One More Honey 2017); Jeff Lloyd (Stripper 2008); James McDonald (Romantic Moon 2013); Kathy O'Hara (Scarlet Rain 2016); Damien Oliver (Crystal Lily 2010); John Powell (Rubicall 1998); Nash Rawiller (Shared Reflections 2011); Glyn Schofield (Always Allison 2015).
Leading winning trainers: 4 wins Gai Waterhouse (Scarlet Rain 2016, Shared Reflections 2011, Ha Ha 2001, Shadowy Outline 1994).
3 wins Colin Hayes (Scollata 1988, Postage Due 1987, Vain Display 1984); Graeme Rogerson (Carry On Cutie 2005, Burning Sands 2004, Skating 1992).
Current winning trainers:
4 wins Gai Waterhouse (Scarlet Rain 2016, Shared Reflections 2011, Ha Ha 2001, Shadowy Outline 1994).
3 wins Graeme Rogerson (Carry On Cutie 2005, Burning Sands 2004, Skating 1992).
2 wins Barry Lockwood (Rock Review 1993, Shadea 1991); Chris Waller (Always Allison 2015, Jade Marauder 2012).
1 win Mathew Ellerton & Simon Zahra (Crystal Lily 2010); John Hawkes (Legally Bay 2003); Peter Moody (Headway 2009); David Payne (Stripper 2008); Mick Price (Seabrook 2018); John O'Shea (Romantic Moon 2013); Gerald Ryan (Believe Yourself 2014); Steele Ryan (Chinchilla Rose 2007); John Thompson (One More Honey 2017); John Wallace (Dynamic Love 2000).
Point of interest: Two fillies have won the Golden Slipper after being placed in the Sweet Embrace: Calaway Gal (3rd to Victory Vein, 2002); Bint Marscay (2nd to Rock Review, 1993).

ATC Guy Walter Stakes (1400m)—Warwick Farm
$175,000 Group 2 4YO&Up Mares SWP. March 2, 2019.

YEAR	WINNER	JOCKEY	TRAINER	2ND	3RD	TIME
2018	Dixie Blossoms	Christian Reith	Ron Quinton	Raiment	Francaletta	1:22.6
2017	Dixie Blossoms	Tim Clark	Ron Quinton	Zanbagh	Flippant	1:26.5
2016	Solicit	Kerrin McEvoy	Gerald Ryan	Zanbagh	Peeping	1:20.3
2015	Danesiri	Christian Reith	John P Thompson	Cosmic Endeavour	Mahara	1:22.2
2014	Catkins	Hugh Bowman	Chris Waller	Sharnee Rose	Dear Demi	1:23.4
2013	Steps In Time	Nash Rawiller	John O'Shea	Streama	Pear Tart	1:21.6
2012	Steps In Time	Jim Cassidy	John O'Shea	Foxstar	Ladys Angel	1:23.6
2011	Jersey Lily	Tim Clark	Les Bridge	Graceful Anna	Turnstiles	1:22.2
2010	Dane Julia	Glyn Schofield	Lee Freedman	Bejewelled	Messenger	1:23.7
2009	Hot Danish	Tim Clark	Les Bridge	Absolutelyfabulous	Mary's Grace	1:21.4
2008	Hot Danish	Tim Clark	Les Bridge	Like Me Wild	Hairy	1:23.6
2007	Doubting	Jay Ford	Anthony Cummings	Grey Stream	Shirl Pegasus	1:22.6
2006	Bhandara	Hugh Bowman	Guy Walter	Prisoner Of Love	Pekalan	1:23.0
2005	Danni Martine	Glen Boss	Guy Walter	Golden Weekend	Hec Of A Party	1:23.7
2004	Gold Lottey	Len Beasley	John O'Shea	Hennessy Waltz	Lucinda	1:24.4
2003	Forum Floozie	Darren Beadman	John Hawkes	Size Her Up	Brecon Rose	1:22.8
2002	Youhadyourwarning	Corey Brown	John Hawkes	Veloce	Card Queen	1:23.0
2001	Corelli	Mark Newhman	Mario Caltabiano	Say Good Morning	Sorrento	1:26.8

BACKGROUND
First run: 1996 (won by Destruct). Listed 1996-2014. Group 3 2015; Group 2 from 2016. Run at Randwick 1996-2018. Registered as the Wiggle Quality Handicap.
Most recent 3YO to win: Stella Maree (2000): The only 3YO to win.
Multiple winners: 3—Dixie Blossoms (2018, 2017); Steps In Time (2013, 2012); Hot Danish (2009, 2008).
Fastest time (1400m): Solicit (2016) 1:20.34
Notable winners: Dixie Blossoms (2018, 2017); Solicit (2016), Catkins (2014); Steps In Time (2013, 2012); Hot Danish (2009, 2008); Danni Martine (2005); Gold Lottey (2004); Forum Floozie (2003); Bonanova (1999).
Guy Walter Stakes winners won the lead-up races:
Breeders' Classic: 5—Catkins (2014); Steps In Time (2013, 2012); Hot Danish (2009); Destruct (1996).
Guy Walter Stakes winners went on to win in the same preparation:
Emancipation Stakes: 1—Catkins (2014).
Coolmore Classic: 1—Danni Martine (2005).

Dark Jewel Classic: 1—Stella Maree (2000).
Tatt's Tiara: 1—Bonanova (1999).
Leading winning jockey: 4 wins Tim Clark (Dixie Blossoms 2017, Jersey Lily 2011, Hot Danish 2009, 2008).
Current winning jockeys: 4 wins Tim Clark (Dixie Blossoms 2017, Jersey Lily 2011, Hot Danish 2009, 2008).
2 wins Glen Boss (Danni Martine 2005, Timeless Winds 1997); Hugh Bowman (Catkins 2014, Bhandara 2006); Christian Reith (Dixie Blossoms 2018, Danesiri 2015).
1 win Corey Brown (Youhadyourwarning 2002); Grant Cooksley (Destruct 1996); Jay Ford (Doubting 2007); Kerrin McEvoy (Solicit 2016); Nash Rawiller (Steps In Time 2013); Glyn Schofield (Dane Julia 2010).
Leading winning trainer: 3 wins Les Bridge (Jersley Lily 2011, Hot Danish 2009, 2008); John Hawkes (Flying Floozie 2003, Youhadyourwarning 2002, Destruct 1996).
Current winning trainers: 3 wins Les Bridge (Jersley Lily 2011, Hot Danish 2009, 2008); John Hawkes (Flying Floozie 2003, Youhadyourwarning 2002, Destruct 1996); Ron Quinton (Dixie Blossoms 2018, 2017, Timeless Winds 1997).
2 wins John O'Shea (2013, 2012).
1 win Grahame Begg (Bonanova 1999); Mario Caltabiano (Corelli 2001); Anthony Cummings (Doubting 2007); Lee Freedman (Dane Julia 2010); Gerald Ryan (Solicit 2016); John Thompson (Danesiri 2015); Chris Waller (Catkins 2014).

ATC Challenge Stakes (1000m)—Randwick
$500,000 Group 2 3YO&Up WFA. March 9, 2019.

YEAR	WINNER	JOCKEY	TRAINER	2ND	3RD	TIME
2018	Redzel	Kerrin McEvoy	Peter & Paul Snowden	Jungle Edge	Super Too	0:55.7
2017	English	Blake Shinn	Gai Waterhouse & Adrian Bott	Redzel	Supido	0:59.9
2016	English	Tommy Berry	Gai Waterhouse	Kinglike	Boss Lane	0:56.5
2015	Miracles Of Life	Hugh Bowman	Peter & Paul Snowden	Va Pensiero	Rubick	0:56.7
2014	Villa Verde	James McDonald	Anthony Cummings	Snitzerland	Famous Seamus	0:57.3
2013	Snitzerland	Corey Brown	Gerald Ryan	Decision Time	Howmuchdoyouloveme	0:56.1
2012	Rain Affair	Corey Brown	Joseph Pride	Satin Shoes	Neeson	1:03.7
2011	Hay List	Glyn Schofield	John Mcnair	Keen Commander	Solar Charged	0:56.8
2010	De Lightning Ridge	Glyn Schofield	Joseph Pride	Dorf Command	Stryker	0:55.9
2009	Olonona	Tim Clark	John O'Shea	Hoystar	Fantene	0:56.9
2008	Hurried Choice	Jeff Lloyd	David Payne	Keen Commander	German Chocolate	0:57.3
2007	Spark Of Life	Zac Purton	Allan Denham	Whoever	Biscayne Bay	0:56.8
2006	Snitzel	Craig Newitt	Gerald Ryan	Spark of Life	Media	0:56.8
2005	Impaler	Dale Spriggs	David Atkins	Snippetson	Charge Forward	0:56.2
2004	Star Of Florida	Patrick Payne	Pat Duff	Mistegic	Majestic Fiesta	0:56.3
2003	Star Of Florida	Patrick Payne	Pat Duff	Snowland	Fair Embrace	0:56.5
2002	Bomber Bill	Damien Oliver	Russell Cameron	Mistegic	Ateates	0:56.5
2001	Pimpala Prince	Shane Treweek	Gordon Yorke	Ateates	Notoire	0:59.2

BACKGROUND
First run: 1906 (won by The Pet). Group 2 from 1979. Run over 6 furlongs until 1963, 1100m in 2012. Until 1979 was a handicap. Run at Randwick before 2002; Warwick Farm 2003-06. Returned to Randwick 2007. Run at Rosehill (1100m) in 2012. Run in January before 2003.
Most recent mare (4YO & over) to win: English (2017).
Most recent 3YO to win: Filly—English (2016); C&G—Snitzel (2006).
Multiple winners: 10—English (2017, 2016); Star Of Florida (2004, 2003); Cangronde (1998, 1997); At Sea (1987, 1986, 1985); Razor Sharp (1984, 1983, 1982); Gay Gauntlet (1969, 1967); San Domenico (1950, 1949); Felbeam (1946, 1945); High Caste (1942, 1940); Golden Hop (1914, 1913).
Fastest time (1000m): Redzel (2018) 0:55.73 (track record)
Notable winners: Redzel (2018); English (2017, 2016); Miracles Of Life (2015), Hay List (2011); Snitzel (2006); Bomber Bill (2002); Easy Rocking (2000); Snippets (1988); At Sea (1987, 1986, 1985); Razor Sharp (1984, 1983, 1982); Zephyr Bay (1975); Wenona Girl (1963); San Domenico (1950, 1949); High Caste (1942, 1940); The Hawk (1925).
Challenge Stakes winners also won (Note: moved from January to March in 2003):
Carrington Stakes: 8—Rain Affair (2012); Classic Magic (1994); Lightning Bend (1991); Snippets (1988); At Sea (1987, 1986, 1985); Gay Gauntlet (1969).
Expressway Stakes: 5—Rain Affair (2012); Cangronde (1997); Moss Rocket (1995); Groucho (1989); Zephyr Bay (1975). Note: Run after the Expressway from 2003.

Apollo Stakes: 1—Rain Affair (2012).
Challenge Stakes winners went on to win in the same preparation:
The Galaxy: 2—Snippets (1988); Playbill (1972).
Robert Sangster Stakes: 1—Miracles Of Life (2015).
T.J. Smith Stakes: 1—Ab Initio (1999).
All-Aged Stakes: 2—English (2016), The Hawk (1925).
BTC Cup: None.
Stradbroke Handicap: None.
Leading winning jockeys: 6 wins George Moore (Gay Gauntlet 1967, The Tempest 1964, Rush Bye 1962, Gili 1961, Dubbo 1958, Brazier 1947).
5 wins Billy Cook (Gay Vista 1955, Gay Monarch 1958, Felbeam 1946, Yaralla 1944, Caesar 1941); Ron Quinton (At Sea 1985, Acamar 1980, Farlara 1971, Biarritz Star 1970, Dawn Boy 1968).
4 wins Ted Bartle (High Caste 1942, 1940, Captivation 1933, Greenline 1928); Arthur Ward (Apple Bay 1956, Tarien 1954, San Domenico 1950, 1949).
Current winning jockeys: 2 wins Corey Brown (Snitzerland 2013, Rain Affair 2012); Glyn Schofield (Hay List 2011, De Lightning Ridge 2010);
1 win Tommy Berry (English 2016); Hugh Bowman (Miracles Of Life 2015); Larry Cassidy (Ab Initio 1999); Tim Clark (Olonana 2009); Jeff Lloyd (Hurried Choice 2008); James McDonald (Villa Verde 2014); Kerrin McEvoy (Redzel 2018); Craig Newitt (Snitzel 2006); Damien Oliver (Bomber Bill 2002); Zac Purton (Spark Of Life 2007); Blake Shinn (English 2017).
Leading winning trainers: 6 wins Tommy Smith (Christole 1979, The Tempest 1964, Rush Bye 1962, Dubbo 1958, Apple Bay 1956, Tarien 1954).
4 wins Fred Cush (Gay Monarch 1948, Felbeam 1946, 1945, Yaralla 1944); Maurice McCarten (Wenona Girl 1963, Huntly 1959, My Kingdom 1957, Donegal 1951).
Current winning trainers: 3 wins Gai Waterhouse (English 2017, 2016, Light Up The World 1996).
2 wins Joe Pride (Rain Affair 2012, De Lightning Ridge 2010); Gerald Ryan (Snitzerland 2013, Snitzel 2006); Peter & Paul Snowden (Redzel 2018, Miracles Of Life 2015).
1 win David Atkins (Impaler 2005); Russell Cameron (Bomber Bill 2002); Anthony Cummings (Villa Verde 2014); Allan Denham (Spark Of Life 2007); Pat Duff (Star Of Florida 2004, 2003); Bill Farrow (Spanish Mix 1993); John McNair (Hay List 2011); John O'Shea (Olonana 2009); David Payne (Hurried Choice 2008); Ron Quinton (Easy Rocking 2000); Gai Waterhouse & Adrian Bott (English 2017); Pat Webster (Ab Initio 1999); Gordon Yorke (Pimpala Prince 2001).
Points of interest: The leading jockey Ron Quinton (five wins) also trained Easy Rocking (2000) to win this race.
Maurice McCarten trained four winners and also rode Whitta to win in 1929.
James Barden trained three winners and rode Neith to win in 1909.

ATC Reisling Stakes (1200m)—Randwick
$300,000 Group 2 2YO Fillies SW. March 9, 2019.

YEAR	WINNER	JOCKEY	TRAINER	2ND	3RD	TIME
2018	Estijaab	Brenton Avdulla	Michael, Wayne & John Hawkes	Pure Elation	Sister Sledge	1:09.1
2017	Frolic	Tommy Berry	Michael Freedman	She Will Reign	Villa Carlotta	1:13.5
2016	French Fern	Blake Shinn	David Payne	Quick Feet	Moqueen	1:10.6
2015	English	Blake Shinn	Gai Waterhouse	Ottoman	Fireworks	1:10.1
2014	Earthquake	Kerrin McEvoy	Peter Snowden	Mossfun	Alpha Fun	1:10.7
2013	Overeach	Tommy Berry	Gai Waterhouse	Villa Verde	Spurrendous	1:10.7
2012	Samaready	Craig Newitt	Mick Price	Hussousa	Meidung	1:12.0
2011	Elite Falls	Jim Cassidy	John O'Shea	Satin Shoes	Fast And Sexy	1:12.3
2010	Military Rose	Michael Rodd	Gillian Heinrich	Obsequious	Solar Charged	1:11.7
2009	More Joyous	Darren Beadman	Gai Waterhouse	Melito	So Anyway	1:11.4
2008	Hips Don't Lie	Craig Williams	David Hayes	Anatomica	Love And Kisses	1:10.2
2007	Press The Button	Glen Boss	David Hayes	Hurried Choice	Sleek Chasis	1:10.5
2006	Pure Energy	Greg Childs	Ron Maund	Boom Time Savings	Gold Edition	1:11.6
2005	Fashions Afield	Chris Munce	Gai Waterhouse	Mnemosyne	Poetic Genius	1:11.8
2004	Alinghi	Damien Oliver	Lee Freedman	Crimson Reign	Ballybleue	1:09.7
2003	Polar Success	Danny Beasley	Graeme Rogerson	Hasna	Dorky	1:10.3
2002	Fatoon	Len Beasley	Clarry Conners	Kidman	Brief Embrace	1:11.2
2001	Regal Kiss	Patrick Payne	Leon Macdonald	Faiza	True Jewels	1:09.9

BACKGROUND

First run: 1973 (won by Favourite Girl). Group 3 1980-85. Group 2 since 1986. Called the Reisling Slipper Trial before 2005, and the Perfect Vision Stakes. Run at Rosehill 1973-2014. Run at Canterbury in 2008. Registered as the Reisling Slipper Trial.

Fastest time (1200m): Estijaab (2018) 1:09:10.

Notable winners: English (2015); Earthquake (2014); Overreach (2013); Samaready (2012); More Joyous (2009); Fashions Afield (2005); Alinghi (2004); Polar Success (2003); Belle Du Jour (2000); Merlene (1996); Burst (1992); Triscay (1990); Midnight Fever (1987); Magic Flute (1986); Hartshill (1974).

Reisling Stakes winners also won the lead-up races:

Widden Stakes: 5—Overreach (2013); Manana (1998); Triscay (1990); Magic Flute (1986); Shaybisc (1980).

Blue Diamond Stakes: 4—Earthquake (2014); Samaready (2012); Alinghi (2004); Midnight Fever (1987).

Kindergarten Stakes: 1—Belle Du Jour (2000).

Inglis Classic: 1—Frolic (2017).

Sweet Embrace Stakes: 1—Purpose (1983).

Reisling Stakes winners went on to win in the same preparation:

Golden Slipper Stakes: 7—Estijaab (2018); Overreach (2013); Polar Success (2003); Belle Du Jour (2000); Merlene (1996); Burst (1992); Hartshill (1974).

ATC Sires' Produce Stakes: 4—Fashions Afield (2005); Merlene (1996); Burst (1992); Shaybisc (1980).

ATC Champagne Stakes: 2—Burst (1992); Triscay (1990).

Leading winning jockeys: 2 wins Lenny Beasley (Fatoon 2002, Belle Du Jour 2000); Tommy Berry (Frolic 2017, Overreach 2013); Jim Cassidy (Elite Falls 2011, Magic Flute 1986); Mick Dittman (Triscay 1990, Vaindarra 1982); Shane Dye (Burst 1992, Bold Promise 1991); Kevin Langby (Spanish Yacht 1978, Hartshill 1974); Chris Munce (Fashions Afield 2005, Ginzano 1995); Damien Oliver (Alinghi 2004, Star Of Nouvelle 1993); Blake Shinn (French Fern 2016, English 2015).

Current winning jockeys: 2 wins Tommy Berry (Frolic 2017, Overreach 2013); Damien Oliver (Alinghi 2004, Star Of Nouvelle 1993); Blake Shinn (French Fern 2016, English 2015).

1 win Brenton Avdulla (Estijaab 2018); Glen Boss (Press The Button 2007); Corey Brown (Moment's Pleasure 1994); Larry Cassidy (Manana 1998); Kerrin McEvoy (Earthquake 2014); Craig Newitt (Samaready 2012); Michael Rodd (Military Rose 2010); Craig Williams (Hips Don't Lie 2008).

Leading winning trainers: 5 wins Jack Denham (Triscay 1990, Startling Lass 1988, Vaindarra 1982, Bianca 1976, Inner Magic 1975).

4 wins Clarry Conners (Fatoon 2002; Belle Du Jour 2000, Let's Rock Again 1999, Burst 1992); Gai Waterhouse (English 2015, Overreach 2013, More Joyous 2009, Fashions Afield 2005).

Current winning trainers: 4 wins Clarry Conners (Fatoon 2002; Belle Du Jour 2000, Let's Rock Again 1999, Burst 1992); Gai Waterhouse (English 2015, Overreach 2013, More Joyous 2009, Fashions Afield 2005).

3 wins Lee Freedman (Alinghi 2004, Rose Of Danehill 1997, Merlene 1996); David Hayes (Hips Don't Lie 2008, Press The Button 2007, Star Of Nouvelle 1993).

2 wins John Hawkes (Estijaab 2018, Manana 1998).

1 win Michael Freedman (Frolic 2017); Michael, Wayne & John Hawkes (Estijaab 2018); Gillian Heinrich (Military Rose 2010); Dianne Lumsden (Ginzano 1995); Leon Macdonald (Regal Kiss 2001); David Payne (French Fern 2016); John O'Shea (Elite Falls 2011); Mick Price (Samaready 2012); Graeme Rogerson (Polar Success 2003); Peter Snowden (Earthquake 2014).

Points of interest: Beach Gown (1985) is the dam of Rose Of Danehill (1997).

Bold Promise (1991) is the dam of Merlene (1996).

Midnight Fever (1987) and Startling Lass (1988) are sisters—by Luskin Star from Trim Girl.

ATC Todman Stakes (1200m)—Randwick

$300,000 Group 2 2YO C&G SW. March 9, 2019.

YEAR	WINNER	JOCKEY	TRAINER	2ND	3RD	TIME
2018	Aylmerton	Andrew Adkins	Jean Dubois	Ef Troop	Tchaikovsky	1:08.8
2017	Gunnison	Blake Shinn	Peter & Paul Snowden	Invader	Veranillo	1:13.4
2016	Kiss And Make Up	Kerrin McEvoy	Gai Waterhouse	Capitalist	Weatherly	1:09.5
2015	Vancouver	Tommy Berry	Gai Waterhouse	Furnaces	Headwater	1:08.8
2014	Ghibellines	Kerrin McEvoy	Peter Snowden	Unencumbered	Cornrow	1:10.6
2013	Criterion	Craig Williams	David Payne	Fast 'n' Rocking	Havana	1:10.7
2012	Pierro	Nash Rawiller	Gai Waterhouse	Epaulette	Shelford	1:12.1
2011	Smart Missile	Glen Boss	Anthony Cummings	Sepoy	Foxwedge	1:09.9
2010	Masquerader	Michael Rodd	David Payne	Decision Time	Carved In Stone	1:11.4
2009	Real Saga	Darren Beadman	Michael, Wayne & John Hawkes	Phelan Ready	Purdey	1:11.5
2008	Krupt	Hugh Bowman	Matthew Smith	Related	Typhoon Fury	1:10.6
2007	Meurice	Hugh Bowman	Gai Waterhouse	Zizou	Shaft	1:11.1
2006	Diego Garcia	Larry Cassidy	Gai Waterhouse	Just Mambo	My Middi	1:11.6
2005	Written Tycoon	Nash Rawiller	Grahame Begg	Domesday	Flying Pegasus	1:12.0
2004	Charge Forward	Darren Beadman	John O'Shea	Dane Shadow	Samboy	1:10.3
2003	Exceed And Excel	Hugh Bowman	Tim Martin	Untouchable	Niello	1:10.6
2002	Snowland	Chris Munce	Gai Waterhouse	Yell	Takas	1:10.7
2001	Royal Courtship	Brian York	Gai Waterhouse	Viscount	Mistegic	1:09.9

BACKGROUND

First run: 1973 (won by Imagele). Group 3 1980-85. Group 2 from 1986. Run as two divisions 1975-76. Before 2005 was the Todman Slipper Trial. Run at Rosehill 1973-2014. Run at Canterbury in 2008. Registered as the Todman Slipper Trial.
Fastest time (1200): Aylmerton (2018) 1:08.84
Notable winners: Vancouver (2015); Criterion (2013); Pierro (2012); Exceed And Excel (2003); Snowland (2002); General Nediym (1997); Octagonal (1995); Tierce (1991); Marauding (1987); Crown Jester (1981); Luskin Star (1977); Imagele (1973).
Todman Stakes winners and the Blue Diamond Stakes (run at Caulfield in Feb):
No Blue Diamond Stakes winner has won the Todman Stakes. Sepoy (2011, 2nd behind Smart Missile) and Let's Get Physical (1985, 2nd behind Asarka) are the closest to achieving the double.
Todman Stakes winners won the Sydney lead-up races:
Breeders' Plate: 7—Vancouver (2015); Pierro (2012); Smart Missile (2011); Real Saga (2009); Charge Forward (2004); Luskin Star (1977); Blue And Gold (1976).
Canonbury Stakes: 3—Vancouver (2015); Snowland (2001); Asarka (1985).
Skyline Stakes: None.
Black Opal Stakes: 1—Criterion (2013).
Silver Slipper Stakes: 2—Pierro (2012); Luskin Star (1976). Moved from spring to early autumn in 1998.
Todman Stakes winners went on to win in the same preparation:
Golden Slipper Stakes: 5—Vancouver (2015); Pierro (2012); Tierce (1991); Marauding (1987); Luskin Star (1977).
ATC Sires Produce Stakes: 5—Pierro (2012); Align (1999); Octagonal (1995); Tierce (1991); Luskin Star (1977).
Champagne Stakes: 6—Pierro (2012); Meurice (2007); Tierce (1991); Full And By (1988); Luskin Star (1977); Rose Heir (1975).
Leading winning jockeys: 3 wins Darren Beadman (Real Saga 2009, Charge Forward 2004, Flavour 1996); Hugh Bowman (Krupt 2008, Meurice 2007, Exceed And Excel 2003); Mick Dittman (General Nediym 1997, Auranch 1990, Mercury 1989).
Current winning jockeys: 3 wins Hugh Bowman (Krupt 2008, Meurice 2007, Exceed And Excel 2003).
2 wins Grant Cooksley (Octagonal 1995, Clan O'Sullivan 1992); Kerrin McEvoy (Kiss And Make Up 2016, Ghibellines 2014); Nash Rawiller (Pierro 2012, Written Tycoon 2005).
1 win Andrew Adkins (Aylmerton 2018); Tommy Berry (Vancouver 2015); Glen Boss (Smart Missile 2011); Michael Cahill (Great Crusader 2000); Larry Cassidy (Diego Garcia 2006); Michael Rodd (Masquerader 2010); Blake Shinn (Gunnison 2017); Craig Williams (Criterion 2013).
Leading winning trainers: 7 wins Gai Waterhouse (Kiss And Makeup 2016; Vancouyver 2015, Pierro 2012, Meurice 2007, Diego Garcia 2006, Snowland 2002; Royal Courtship 2001).
6 wins John Hawkes (Real Saga 2009, Align 1999; Flavour 1996, Octagonal 1995, Pauillac 1994, Justice Prevails 1993).
Current winning trainers: 7 wins Gai Waterhouse (Kiss And Makeup 2016; Vancouver 2015, Pierro 2012, Meurice 2007, Diego Garcia 2006, Snowland 2002; Royal Courtship 2001).

6 wins John Hawkes (Real Saga 2009, Align 1999; Flavour 1996, Octagonal 1995, Pauillac 1994, Justice Prevails 1993).
2 wins David Payne (Criterion 2013, Masquerader 2010); Peter Snowden (Gunnison 20127, Ghibellines 2014).
1 win Clarry Conners (Tierce 1991); Anthony Cummings (Smart Missile 2011); Jean Dubois (Aylmerton 2018); Michael, Wayne & John Hawkes (Real Saga 2009); Tim Martin (Exceed And Excel 2003); John Meagher (County 1984); Michael Nolan (Laurie's Lottery 1998); Matthew Smith (Krupt 2008); John O'Shea (Charge Forward 2004); Peter & Paul Snowden (Gunnison 2017).
Points of interests: Five colts/geldings have finished second in the Todman Stakes and won the Golden Slipper—Capitalist (2016); Sepoy (2011); Phelan Ready (2009); Marscay (1982) and Sir Dapper (1983).

VRC A.V. Kewney Stakes (1400m)—Flemington
$200,000 Group 2 3YO Fillies SW. March 9, 2019.

YEAR	WINNER	JOCKEY	TRAINER	2ND	3RD	TIME
2018	Bella Martini	Dwayne Dunn	Michael, Wayne & John Hawkes	Shokora	Palazzo Vecchio	1.22.3
2017	I Am A Star	Dean Yendall	Shane Nicholls	Ellicazoom	Kenedna	1:22.4
2016	Badawiya	Craig Newitt	Mick Price	Don't Doubt Mamma	Egypt	1:22.9
2015	Wawail	Michael Walker	David Hayes & Tom Dabernig	Sabatini	Vezalay	1:23.2
2014	Solicit	Damian Lane	Mathew Ellerton & Simon Zahra	Marianne	Suavito	1:22.6
2013	Flying Snitzel	Craig Williams	Gerald Ryan	Norzita	Red Fez	1:22.9
2012	Empress Rock	Steven Arnold	Bart Cummings	Assertive Eagle	Bliss Street	1:22.5
2011	Do Ra Mi	Michael Walker	Peter Moody	Brazilian Pulse	Divorces	1:22.2
2010	Faint Perfume	Michael Rodd	Bart Cummings	Response	No Evidence Needed	1:23.3
2009	Gallica	Damien Oliver	Mick Price	Gold Water	Lamarr	1:36.3
2008	Zarita	Greg Childs	Pat Hyland	Absolut Glam	Bashful Girl	1:36.7
2007	Anamato	Craig Newitt	David Hayes	Catechuchu	Flame Of Sydney	1:35.2
2006	Doubting	Danny Nikolic	Mick Price	Serenade Rose	Empress Lily	1:37.8
2005	Ballet Society	Steven King	Pat Hyland	Kylikwong	Astrodame	1:35.1
2004	Special Harmony	Damien Oliver	Lee Freedman	Country Lodge	Sky Cuddle	1:35.5
2003	Lashed	Damien Oliver	Graeme Rogerson	Umaris	Tarcoola Diamond	1:36.2
2002	Elegant Fashion	Scott Seamer	Tony McEvoy	Bridal Hill	Gold Lottey	1:34.9
2001	Ponton Flyer	Damien Oliver	Tom Hughes Jnr	St Therese	Flying Spice	1:35.2

BACKGROUND
First run: 1952 (won by Great Field). Group 2 from 1980. Run over 2000m 1952-84. 1600 1985-2009. 1400m from 2010. Set weights and penalties until 1997. Run at Caulfield in 2007. Registered as the A.V. Kewney Stakes.
Fastest time (1400m): Do Ra Mi (2011) 1:22.21
Notable winners: I Am A Star (2017); Faint Perfume (2010); Gallica (2009); Zarita (2008); Anamato (2007); Special Harmony (2004); Sunline (1999); Northwood Plume (1995); Tristalove (1994); Mannerism (1991); Deck The Halls (1981); How Now (1976); Cap d'Antibes (1975); Sanderae (1971);Gay Poss (1970); Mintaway (1960); Wiggle (1959); Waltzing Lady (1954).
Kewney Stakes (autumn) and the spring features:
Edward Manifold Stakes: 6—Badawiya (Kewney 2016); Gallica (2009); Special Harmony (2004); Rose Of Danehill (1998); Mintaway (1960); Wiggle (1959).
Thousand Guineas: 3—Gallica (Kewney 2009); Special Harmony (2004); Northwood Plume (1995);
Wakeful Stakes: 8—Faint Perfume (Kewney 2010); Zarita 2008); Sun Sally (1978); How Now (1976); Love Aloft (1974); Sanderae (1971); Sandara (1957); Just Caroline (1953).
Myer Classic: 1—I Am A Star (Kewney 2017).
VRC Oaks: 6—Faint Perfume (Kewney 2010); Special Harmony (2004); Northwood Plume (1995); Sanderae (1971); Mintaway (1960); Waltzing Lady (1954).
Kewney Stakes winners won the lead-up races:
The Vanity 3—Solicit (2014); Ballet Society (2005); Tennessee Vain (1988).
MV Fillies Classic: 2—Empress Rock (2012); Anamato (2007). Note: Special Harmony (2004), Elegant Fashion (2002) and Sunline (1999) won the double when the Kewney was run before the MV Fillies Classic (1500m), which then was run over 2040m.
Armanasco Stakes: 6—Zarita (2008); Ballet Society (2005); Special Harmony (2004); Elegant Fashion (2002); Northwood Plume (1995); Bravita (1980).
Kewney Stakes winners went on to win in the same preparation:

Australasian Oaks: 6—Gallica 2009); Zarita (2008); Anamato (2007); Tristalove (1994); Mannerism (1991); Send Me An Angel (1987).
SA Oaks: None.
Storm Queen Stakes: 4—Faint Perfume (2010); Special Harmony (2004); Northwood Plume (1995); Tennessee Vain (1988).
ATC Australian Oaks: 7—How Now (1976); Gossiper (1972); Gay Poss (1970); Lowland (1968); Dual Quest (1966); Gay Satin (1958); Sandara (1957).
Leading winning jockeys: 7 wins Roy Higgins (Deck The Halls 1981, Sun Sally 1978, Cap d'Antibes 1975, Gossiper 1972, Sanderae 1971, Gay Poss 1970, Lowland 1968); Damien Oliver (Gallica 2009, Special Harmony 2004, Lashed 2003, Ponton Flyer 2001, Northwood Plume 1995, Orsay 1993, Mannerism 1991).
Current winning jockeys: 7 wins Damien Oliver (Gallica 2009, Special Harmony 2004, Lashed 2003, Ponton Flyer 2001, Northwood Plume 1995, Orsay 1993, Mannerism 1991).
2 wins Craig Newitt (Badawiya 2016, Anamato 2007); Michael Walker (Wawail 2015, Do Ra Mi 2011); Craig Williams (Flying Snitzel 2013, Umaline 2000).
1 win Steven Arnold (Empress Rock 2012); Dwayne Dunn (Bella Martini 2018); Kevin Forrester (Tarare 1992); Damian Lane (Solicit 2014); Michael Rodd (Faint Perfume 2010); Dean Yendall (I Am A Star 2017).
Leading winning trainers: 10 wins Bart Cummings (Empress Rock 2012, Faint Perfume 2010, Tristalove 1994, Reganza 1990, More Rain 1983, Sun Sally 1978, Cap d'Antibes 1975, Sandarae 1971, Gay Poss 1970, Lowland 1968).
7 wins Colin Hayes (Send Me An Angel 1987, Mapperley Heights 1984, Voli Dream 1982, Bravita 1980, In Pursuit 1977, How Now 1976, Love Aloft 1974).
Current winning trainers: 4 wins Lee Freedman (Special Harmony 2004, Rose Of Danehill 1998, Northwood Plume 1995, Mannerism 1991).
3 wins David Hayes (Wawail 2015, Anamato 2007, Orsay 1993); Mick Price (Badawiya 2016, Gallica 2009, Doubting 2006).
2 wins Pat Hyland (Zarita 2008, Ballet Society).
1 win Jim Conlan (Regal Crown 1997); Mathew Ellerton & Simon Zahra (Solicit 2014); John Griffiths (Imperial Regina 1986); Michael, Wayne & John Hawkes (Bella Martini 2018); David Hayes & Tom Dabernig (Wawail 2015); Tom Hughes Jnr (Ponton Flyer 2001); Tony McEvoy (Elegant Fashion 2002); Shane Nicholls (I Am A Star 2017); Graeme Rogerson (Lashed 2003); Gerald Ryan (Flying Snitzel 2013).
Point of interest: Deck The Halls (1981) won the 1981 Rosehill Guineas in the same preparation.

VRC Sires' Produce Stakes (1400m)—Flemington
$200,000 Group 2 2YO Open SW. March 9, 2019.

YEAR	WINNER	JOCKEY	TRAINER	2ND	3RD	TIME
2018	Not A Single Cent	Mark Zahra	Aaron Purcell	Seberate	Akkadian	1:23.4
2017	Sircconi	Linda Meech	Peter Morgan	Aspect	Feng Chu	1:22.7
2016	Seaburge	Mark Zahra	David Hayes & Tom Dabernig	Detective	Revolving Door	1:23.7
2015	Jameka	Nicholas Hall	Ciaron Maher	Lazumba	Sampeah	1:24.6
2014	Zululand	Stephen Baster	David Hayes	Awesome Rock	Marcado	1:24.3
2013	Twilight Royale	Michael Rodd	Bjorn Baker	Shamus Award	Great Esteem	1:23.3
2012	All Too Hard	Dwayne Dunn	Michael, Wayne & John Hawkes	Pronto Pronto	Road Trippin	1:22.5
2011	Running Tall	Ben Melham	Danny O'Brien	Decircles	Grand Britannia	1:24.2
2010	Shamrocker	Glen Boss	Danny O'Brien	Willow Creek	Yosei	1:23.5
2009	Rostova	Steven King	Steve Richards	Bombay Sling	Gathering	1:23.4
2008	Von Costa De Hero	Craig Williams	David Hayes	Carnero	Burgeis	1:23.7
2007	Incumbent	Damien Oliver	Graeme Rogerson	Marching	Below Zero	1:22.8
2006	De Lago Mist	Paul Gatt	David Hayes	Ulfah	Danever	1:22.4
2005	Danger Looms	Brad Rawiller	John McArdle	Under The Floor	Ferocity	1:22.8
2004	Barely A Moment	Greg Childs	Tony McEvoy	Big Poppa Pump	Kylikwong	1:24.2
2003	Winestock	Brett Prebble	Terry O'Sullivan	Fresh Boy	Hammerbeam	1:23.6
2002	Pillaging	Patrick Payne	Lee Freedman	Delago Brom	Tom Coureuse	1:22.2
2001	Spectatorial	Patrick Payne	Mathew Ellerton	Tuscanos	Valkyrian	1:25.3

BACKGROUND
First run: 1862 (won by Musidora). Group 1 1979-2004. Run over 1600m 1862-63; 1200m 1864-1919. Run at Caulfield in 2007. Not held 1866-1873.
Most recent filly to win: Jameka (2015).

Fastest time (1600m Flemington): Pillaging (2002) 1:22.23
Notable winners: Jameka (2015); All Too Hard (2013); Shamrocker (2010); Testa Rossa (1999); Blevic (1994); Canny Lad (1990); Kaapstad (1987); Grosvenor (1982); Full On Aces (1981); Mighty Kingdom (1979); Desirable (1976); Lord Dudley (1975); Imagele (1973); Century (1972); Vain (1969); Storm Queen (1966); Citius (1965); Pago Pago (1963); Wenona Girl (1960); Tulloch (1957); High Caste (1939); Young Idea (1935); Mollison (1928); Wolaroi (1916); Sweet Nell (1903); Newminster (1875); Musidora (1862).
Sires' Produce Stakes winners won the early autumn races in Melbourne:
Talindert Stakes: 2—All Too Hard (2012); Spectatorial (2001);
Blue Diamond Prelude: 3—Rostova (f 2009); Millward (g 1997); Brave Show (c 1983).
Blue Diamond Stakes: 3—Street Café (1984); Lord Dudley (1975); Tolerance (1971).
Sires' Produce Stakes winners and the Sydney Triple Crown:
Golden Slipper: 5—Canny Lad (1990); Full On Aces (1981); Vain (1969); Storm Queen (1966); Pago Pago (1953).
ATC Sires' Produce: 20—Full On Aces (1981); Desirable (1976); Wenona Girl (1960); Tulloch (1957); Pure Fire (1952); True Course (1950); Nuffield (1938); Gold Rod (1936); Young Idea (1935); Kuvera (1932); Mollison (1928); Royal Feast (1927); Thrice (1917); Beverage (1910); Autonomy (1892); Stromboli (1891); Titan (1890); Abercorn (1887); Warwick (1883); His Lordship (1878).
ATC Champagne Stakes: 20—Vain (1969); Storm Queen (1966); Knave (1955); True Course (1950); All Love (1941); High Caste (1939); Young Idea (1935); Kuvera (1932); Mollison (1928); Rampion (1926); Thrice (1917); Wolaroi (1916); Woorak (1914); Aurum (1897); Coil (1896); Autonomy (1892); Volley (1888); Warwick (1883); Grand Prix (1880); His Lordship (1878).
Leading winning jockey: 7 wins Roy Higgins (Bold Zest 1977, Lord Dudley 1975, Skyjack 1974, Imagele 1973, Century 1972, Tolerance 1971, Storm Queen 1966).
5 wins Tom Hales (Titan 1890, Volley 1888, Abercorn 1887, Monte Christo 1885, Petrea 1879); Bobby Lewis (Isa 1921, Thrice 1917, Eleanor 1902, United States 1901, Finland 1900); Bill Williamson (Pure Fire 1952, Usage 1951, True Course 1950, Iron Duke 1949, Delina 1944).
Current winning jockeys: 2 wins Mark Zahra (Not A Single Cent 2018, Seaburge 2016).
1 win Stephen Baster (Zululand 2014); Glen Boss (Shamrocker 2010); Dwayne Dunn (All Tar Hard 2012); Paul Gatt (De Lago Mist 2006); Nick Hall (Jameka 2015); Linda Meech (Sircconi 2017); Ben Melham (Running Tall 2011); Damien Oliver (Incumbent 2007); Brett Prebble (Winestock 2003); Brad Rawiller (Danger Looms 2005); Michael Rodd (Twilight Royale 2013); Craig Williams (Von Costa De Hero 2008).
Leading winning trainers: 7 wins Tom Payten (Antonius 1906, Coil 1896, Autonomy 1892, Stromboli 1891, Titan 1890, Volley 1888, Abercorn 1887); James Scobie (Hua 1937, Mother Goose 1908, Thrice 1917, Isa 1921,Sweet Nell 1903, Eleanor 1902, United States 1901); Tommy Smith (Wonder Dancer 1988Mighty Kingdom 1979, Imagele 1973, Flying Fable 1968, Jan's Image 1962, Travel Boy 1959, Tulloch 1957).
5 wins Bart Cummings (Bold Zest 1977, Lord Dudley 1975, Skyjack 1964, Century 1972, Storm Queen 1966); David Hayes (Seaburge 2016, Zululand 2014, Von Costa De Hero 2008, De Lago Mist 2006, Blevic 1994).
Current winning trainers: 5 wins David Hayes (Seaburge 2016, Zululand 2014, Von Costa De Hero 2008, De Lago Mist 2006, Blevic 1994).
3 wins Lee Freedman (Incumbent 2007, Pillaging 2002, Coup De Grace 1998).
2 wins John Hawkes (All Too Hard 2012, Preserve 2000); Tony McEvoy (Barely A Moment 2004, Spectatorial 2001); Danny O'Brien (Running Tall 2011, Shamrocker 2010); Gerald Ryan (My Duke 1996, Lochrae 1995).
1 win Bjorn Baker (Twilight Royale 2013); David Hayes & Tom Dabernig (Seaburge 2016); Michael, Wayne, John Hawkes (All Too Hard 2012); Ciaron Maher (Jameka 2015); John McArdle (Danger Looms 2005); Peter Morgan (Sircconi 2017); Aaron Purcell (Not A Single Cent 2018); Terry O'Sullivan (Winestock 2003); Steve Richards (Rostova 2009); Ken Sweeney (Not Related 1991).

Point of interest: Park Lane (1964) was first past the post, but lost on protest to Boeing Boy.

SAJC Adelaide Cup (3200m)—Morphettville
$400,000 Group 2 Quality Handicap. March 11, 2019.

YEAR	WINNER	JOCKEY	TRAINER	2ND	3RD	TIME
2018	Fanatic	Michael Walker	David & Ben Hayes & Tom Dabernig	Ormito	Poppiholla	3:25.2
2017	Annus Mirabilis	Regan Bayliss	Stuart Webb	Double Bluff	Master Of Arts	3:24.2
2016	Purple Smile	Stephen Baster	David Hayes & Tom Dabernig	Tunes	Real Love	3:24.1
2015	Tanby	Dean Holland	Mick Cerchi	Taiyoo	Renew	3:25.5
2014	Outback Joe	Chad Schofield	Nigel Blackiston	Black Tycoon	Base	3:22.0
2013	Norsqui	Chris Symons	Walter Mcshane	Waratone	Dame Claire	3:24.4
2012	Rialya	Shayne Cahill	Lloyd Kennewell	Drunken Sailor	Norsqui	3:23.3
2011	Muir	Darren Gauci	Robert Hickmott	Saddler's Story	Macedonian	3:23.4
2010	Capecover	Steven Arnold	Patrick Payne	Kerdem	Itstheone	3:28.8
2009	Zavite	Nash Rawiller	Anthony Cummings	Kerdem	Banana Man	3:22.7
2008	Lacey Underall	Dwayne Dunn	Dan O'Sullivan	Cefalu	Tails Of Triomphe	3:22.0
2007	Gallic	Steven Arnold	Graeme Rogerson	Lacey Underall	Exalted Time	3:20.9
2006	Exalted Time	Clare Lindop	Jim Smith	Tubular Bells	Ista Kareem	3:25.1
2005	Demerger	Blake Shinn	Danny O'Brien	Envoy	Intriguing	3:21.9
2004	Pantani	Kevin Forrester	Robbie Laing	Danestorm	Bel Air	3:27.5
2003	Pilage 'N Plunder	Steven King	John Keirnan	Nautilism	Odysseus	3:28.4
2002	The A Train	Stephen Baster	Cliff Brown	Homewrecker	Silver Baron	3:29.3
2001	Apache King	Peter Mertens	Russell Cameron	Native Jazz	Bel Air	3:29.7

BACKGROUND

First run: 1864 (won by Falcon). Group 1 from 1980-2006. Group 2 from 2007. Run over 2600m 1884-1944. Run at Flemington in 1885; Victoria Park 1980 & 2000. Not held 1886-88 & 1942-43.

Most recent mare to win: Fanatic (2018). Note: Since 1940 only seven mares have won the Adelaide Cup, the others are: Lacey Underall (2008); Demerger (2005); French Resort (1996); Laelia (1971); Jamagne (1964); and Pushover (1956).

Most recent 3YO to win: C&G – The Hind (1998); Filly – Laelia (1971). Note: 23 3YOs have won (10 since 1920).

Multiple winners: 6—Our Pompeii (1994, 1993); Lord Reims (1989, 1988, 1987); Tavel (1973, 1970); Peerless Fox (1951, 1050); Eye Glass (1912., 1911); Cowra (1887, 1886).

Fastest time (3200m): Grand Scale (1976) 3:20:50.

Notable winners: Zavite (2009); Gallic (2007); Our Pompeii (1994, 1993); Subzero (1992); Lord Reims (1989, 1988, 1987); Mr. Lomondy (1986); Just a Dash (1981); Hyperno (1978); Reckless (1977); Rain Lover (1968); Fulmen (1967); Wynette (1924); King Ingoda (1923); Malua (1884).

Adelaide Cup winners won the lead-up races:
Lord Reims Stakes: 17—Apache King (2001); Cronus (1997); French Resort (1996); Lord Reins (1989, 1988); Moss Kingdom (1984); Yashmak (1980); Phar Ace (1974); Tavel (1970); Fulmen (1967); Far Away Places (1961); Suzumi (1931); Altimeter (1928); Spearer (1926); Stralia (1925); Port Admiral (1894); Vakeel (1893).
Birthday Cup: 3—Rialya (2012); Exalted Time (2006); Cheong Sam (1962).
South Australian Derby: 2—Our Pompeii (1993); Subzero (1992). Note: Vakeel (SA Derby 1892, Adelaide Cup 1893) won the Derby when it was conducted in the spring.
SA Fillies Classic: None.
Australasian Oaks: None.

Adelaide Cup winners and the other cups:
Melbourne Cup: 5—Subzero (1992); Just A Dash (1981); Rain Lover (1968); King Ingoda (Melbourne 1922; Adelaide 1923); Malua (1884).
Caulfield Cup: 3— Lord Reims (Adelaide 1989, 1988, 1987; Caulfield 1987); Mr. Lomondy (1986); Wynette (Adelaide Cup 1924; Caulfield Cup 1923).
Sydney Cup: 2—Reckless (1977 when Adelaide Cup was run after the Sydney Cup);
Gallic (2007 when the Adelaide Cup was moved from May (after the Sydney Cup) to March in 2006.
Brisbane Cup (same year): 3—Amarant (1983); Reckless (1977); Fulmen (1967). Note: Sanctus (Adelaide 1948; Brisbane 1949).

Leading winning jockeys: 3 wins Denny Boase (First Water 1880, Totalizator 1881, Vakeel 1893); Des Coleman (Dealer's Choice 1982, Far Away Placed 1961, Borgia 1857); John Letts (Amarant 1983, Grand Scale 1976, Rain Lover 1968); Bobby Lewis (Green Cap 1917, Eye Glass 1912, 1911); Roy "Mick" Medhurst (Beau Cheval 1947, Apostrophe 1940, Suzumi 1931); Ted Preston (Peerless Fox 1951, 1950, Little Tich 1946); Alan Wilson (Romany Rye 1932, Altimeter 1928, King Ingoda 1923).

Current winning jockeys: 2 wins Steven Arnold (Capecover 2010, Gallic 2007); Stephen Baster (Purple Smile 2016, The A Train 2002).

1 win Regan Bayliss (Annus Mirabilis 2017); Shayne Cahill (Rialya 2012); Michael Carson (Scrupulous 1995); Grant Cooksley (Lord Reins 1989); Dwayne Dunn (Lacey Underall 2008); Kevin Forrester (Pantani 2004); Jason Holder (French Resort 1996); Dean Holland (Tanby 2015); Clare Lindop (Exalted Time 2006); Damien Oliver (Sheer Kingston 1999); Nash Rawiller (Zavite 2009); Chad Schofield (Outback Joe 2014); Blake Shinn (Demerger 2005); Chris Symons (Norsqui 2013); Michael Walker (Fanatic 2018).
Leading winning trainers: 6 wins John Hill (Spinaway 1907, Sojourner 1903, Totalizator 1881, First Water 1880, Cowra 1867, 1866). James Scobie (Temptation 1930, King Ingoda 1923, Green Cap 1917, Eye Glass 1912, 1911, Paul Pry 1898).
4 wins Bart Cummings (Mr Lomondy 1986, Laelia 1971, Tavel 1970, Fulmen 1967); George Hanlon (Our Pompeii 1994, 1993, Amarant 1983, Gnapur 1969); Colin Hayes (Water Boatman 1990, Yashmak 1980, Wine Taster 1972, Cheong Sam 1962).
Current winning trainers: 2 wins David Hayes & Tom Dabernig (Fanatic 2018, Purple Smile 2016).
1 win Nigel Blackiston (Outback Joe 2014); Cliff Brown (The A Train 2002); Russell Cameron (Apache King 2001); Mick Cerchi (Tanby 2015); Lee Freedman (Subzero 1992); David Hall (Sheer Kingston 1999); David & Ben Hayes & Tom Dabernig (Fanatic 2018); Robert Hickmott (Muir 2011); Roger James (Cronus 1997); John Kiernan (Pillage 'N Plunder 2003); Robbie Laing (Pantani 2004); Lloyd Kennewell (Rialya 2012); Frank Maynard (Moss Kingdom 1984); Walter McShane (Norsqui 2013); Patrick Payne (Capecover 2010); Dan O'Sullivan (Lacey Underall 2008); Graeme Rogerson (Gallic 2007); Robert Smerdon (Bohemiath 2000); Stuart Webb (Annus Mirabilis 2017).
Points of interests: The Adelaide Cup was moved from May to March in 2006 (won by Exalted Time). Clare Lindop (Exalted Time 2006) is the only female jockey to win the Adelaide Cup.
Patrick Payne rode Our Pompeii to win in 1994 and trained Capeover (2010).
Ted Power owned, trained and rode Warpaint to win in 1896.
Jim Cummings trained Storm Glow to win the 1955 Adelaide Cup; his son Bart trained four winners (see leading winning trainers) and Bart's son, Anthony, trained Zavite to win in 2009.

MVRC Alister Clark Stakes (2040m)—Moonee Valley
$200,000 Group 2 3YO Open SW. March 15, 2019.

YEAR	WINNER	JOCKEY	TRAINER	2ND	3RD	TIME
2018	Cliff's Edge	Jamie Mott	Darren Weir	Levendi	Belfast	2:06.3
2017	Hardham	Luke Nolen	David Brideoake	Ruthven	Farson	2:05.7
2016	Tally	Craig Williams	John O'Shea	Palentino	Hardern	2:08.3
2015	Chill Party	Patrick Moloney	Tom Hughes (Jnr)	Stratum Star	Maastricht	2:06.1
2014	Pheidon	Damien Oliver	Gai Waterhouse	Cadillac Mountain	Surge Ahead	2:06.6
2013	Philippi	Luke Nolen	Michael Kent	Sheer Talent	Gerontius	2:05.6
2012	Highly Recommended	Luke Nolen	Peter Moody	Ethiopia	Sangster	2:08.6
2011	Domesky	Craig Williams	Michael Kent	Coldens Choice	Folding Gear	2:06.6
2010	Linton	Michael Rodd	Robert Hickmott	Take The Rap	Offhanded	1:39.4
2009	Pre Eminence	Craig Newitt	Mick Price	Eagle Falls	Definitive	1:37.1
2008	Sound Journey	Damien Oliver	Mick Price	Playwright	Schilling	1:35.8
2007	Casino Prince	Damien Oliver	Anthony Cummings	Furio	Ambitious General	1:36.3
2006	Spinney	Darren Beadman	John Hawkes	Langarza	Bonny Laird	1:36.7
2005	Lieutenant	Darren Gauci	John Hawkes	Volitant	Renewable	1:38.9
2004	Speedy King	Brett Prebble	Graham Woolston	Confectioner	Strafed	1:37.8
2003	Titanic Jack	Patrick Payne	Tom Hughes Jnr	Tycoon Ruler	Regicide	1:37.7
2002	Royal Code	Steven Arnold	David Hall	Ebony Night	Mr Trickster	1:38.2
2001	Mr Murphy	Damien Oliver	Lee Freedman	Diamond Dane	Fubu	1:31.0

BACKGROUND
First run: 1939 (won by Amiable). Group 2 since 1979. Run as a handicap 1939-74. Run as an open age race until 1986. 3YO only since 1987. Run over 1600m 1939-47 & 1963-86; 2040m 1987-97; 1500m 2001. Run at Flemington (2000m) in 1995.
Fastest time (Strathayr 2040m): Philippi (2013) 2:05.61
Most recent filly to win: Tristalove (1994).
Notable winners (since 3YO race from 1987): Linton (2010); Casino Prince (2007); Titanic Jack (2003); Mr. Murphy (2001); Pins (2000); Dignity Dancer (1999); Zonda (1998); Blevic (1995); Tristalove (1994); Naturalism (1992); Durbridge (1991); Zabeel (1990); Bar Landy (1989); Flotilla (1988); Vo Rogue (1987).
Alister Clark Stakes winners won the lead-up races:
Alister Clark & Autumn Classic: 4—Tally (2016); Spinney (2006); Pins (2000); Dignity Dancer (1999). Note: Tally (2016) & Spinney (2006) won the double since the Alister Clarke was moved to run before the Autumn Classic in 2005.

Alister Clark Stakes winners went on to win in the same preparation:
Australian Guineas: 5—Mr. Murphy (2001); Pins (2000); Dignity Dancer (1999); Zabeel (1990); Flotilla (1988).
Note: Zabeel (1990) and Flotilla (1988) won the double when the Alister Clark (2040m) was run after the Guineas.
Rosehill Guineas: 1—Naturalism (1992).
Tulloch Stakes: 2—Philippi (2013); Durbridge (1991);
ATC Australian Derby: 2—Naturalism (1992); Durbridge (1991).
Leading winning jockeys: 4 wins Scobie Breasley (St Fairy 1947, Tranquil Star 1942, Zonda 1942, Pure Gold 1941); Roy Higgins (My Brown Jug 1981, Leica Show 1976, Sir Dane 1965, Aquanita 1962); Geoff Lane (Dhaulagiri 1961, Stormy Passage 1960, Baron Boissier 1958, Glitzern 1956); Damien Oliver (Pheidon 2013, Sound Journey 2008, Casino Prince 2007, Mr Murphy 2001).
Current winning jockeys: 4 wins Damien Oliver (Pheidon 2013, Sound Journey 2008, Casino Prince 2007, Mr Murphy 2001).
2 wins Luke Nolen (Hardham 2017, Highly Recommended 2012); Craig Williams (Tally 2016, Domesky 2011).
1 win Steven Arnold (Royal Code 2002); Vin Coglan (Zonda 1998); Patrick Moloney (Chill Party 2015); Jamie Mott (Cliff's Edge 2018); Craig Newitt (Pre Eminence 2009); Brett Prebble (Speedy King 2004); Michael Rodd (Linton 2010); Cyril Small (Vo Rogue 1987); Brian Werner (Lockley's Tradition 1986).
Leading winning trainers: 3 wins Bart Cummings (Tristalove 1994, Leica Show 1976, Stormy Passage 1960); John Hawkes (Spinney 2006, Lieutenant 2005, Toltrice 1974); Tommy Hughes Snr (My Evita 1983, Cyron 1970, Heroic Stone 1968); Tony Lopes (Bowl King 1966, St. Joel 1955, Chicquita 1951).
Current winning trainers: 3 wins John Hawkes (Spinney 2006, Lieutenant 2005, Toltrice 1974).
2 wins Anthony Cummings (Casino Prince 2007, Flak Jacket 1997); Lee Freedman (Mr. Murphy 2001, Naturalism 1992); Tom Hughes Jnr (Chill Party 2014, Titanic Jack 2003); Mick Price (Pre Eminence 2009, Sound Journey 2008).
1 win David Brideoake (Hardham 2017); Clarry Conners (Pins 2000); David Hall (Royal Code 2002); David Hayes (Blevic 1995); Robert Hickmott (Linton 2010); Roger James (Zonda 1998); Mick Kent (Domesky 2011); John Meagher (Scenic Royale 1996); John O'Shea (Tally 2016); Gai Waterhouse (Pheidon 2013); Darren Weir (Cliff's Edge 2018).
Points of interest: Blevic (1995) survived a protest. He is the only Victoria Derby winner to win the Alister Clark in the autumn.
When Pins (2000) and Dignity Dancer (1999) won the Alister Clark, it was the middle race of a Triple Crown promotion with the Autumn Classic and the Australian Guineas. Both these 3YOs completed the Triple Crown.

VRC Blamey Stakes (1600m)—Flemington
$200,000 Group 2 3YO&Up Open SWP. March 16, 2019.

YEAR	WINNER	JOCKEY	JOCKEY	2ND	3RD	TIME
2018	Humidor	Mark Zahra	Darren Weir	Cool Chap	Helluva Street	1:36.2
2017	Palentino	Mark Zahra	Darren Weir	Tosen Stardom	Harlem	1:35.4
2016	He Or She	Craig Williams	David Hayes & Tom Dabernig	The United States	Stratum Star	1:34.9
2015	Suavito	Damien Oliver	Nigel Blackiston	Sertorius	Kourkam	1:36.9
2014	Lidari	Luke Nolen	Peter Moody	Foundry	Sertorius	1:38.1
2013	DH Budriguez/ Puissance De Lune	Craig Williams/Glen Boss	David Jolly/Darren Weir	Wall Street		1:36.3
2012	Green Moon	Craig Williams	Robert Hickmott	Pied A Terre	Wall Street	1:35.8
2011	Whobegotyou	Damien Oliver	Mark Kavanagh	Dao Dao	Fanjura	1:36.5
2010	Lord Tavistock	Jason Waddell	Andrew R Campbell	Vigor	Dao Dao	1:36.3
2009	Largo Lad	Chris Symons	David Hayes	Playright	Just Look	1:38.1
2008	The Fuzz	Vlad Duric	David Hayes	Barlinnie	Orange County	1:36.9
2007	Apache Cat	Damien Oliver	Greg Eurell	Bon Hoffa	Molotov	1:37.7
2006	Rosden	Adrian Paterson	Roslyn Day	Great Is Great	Roman Arch	1:33.8
2005	Grey Song	Steven Arnold	Tom Hughes Jnr	Roman Arch	Gallic	1:33.9
2004	Gold Wells	Damien Oliver	Danny O'Brien	Lord Erin	Pretorius	1:36.2
2003	Walk On Air	Danny Nikolic	Colin Alderson	Mr Murphy	Mr Magoo	1:35.1
2002	Tears Royal	Peter Mertens	Grant Dalziel	Weasel Will	Consular	1:37.2
2001	Market Price	Vin Hall	Tony McEvoy	Emission	Second Coming	1:37.4

BACKGROUND
First run: 1955 (won by Prince Cortauld). Group 2 since 1980. Run over 2000m 1955-72. WFA 1955-80, 1987-97. Handicap 1981-86. Run at Caulfield in 2007.
Most recent mare to win: Suavito (2015).

Most recent 3YO to win: Filly – Surround (1977); C&G – Lord Dudley (1976). Note: Only four 3YOs have won the Blamey. Tobin Bronze (1966) and But Beautiful (1959) are the others.
Multiple winners: 7—Durbridge (1995, 1994); Better Loosen Up (1991, 1990); Vo Rogue (1989, 1988); Hyperno (1981, 1980); Tobin Bronze (1967, 1966); Dhaulagiri (1962, 1961); Sailor's Guide (1958, 1957).
Fastest time (1600m Flemington): Rosden (2006) 1:33.85
Notable winners: Humidor (2018); Palentino (2017); Green Moon (2012); Apache Cat (2007); Oliver Twist (2000); Durbridge (1995, 1994); Prince Salieri (1993); Shiva's Revenge (1992); Better Loosen Up (1991, 1990); Vo Rogue (1989, 1988); Hyperno (1981, 1980); Surround (1977); Lord Dudley (1976); Sobar (1974); Gunsynd (1973); Gay Icarus (1971); Tobin Bronze (1967, 1966); Sir Dane (1965); Dhaulagiri (1962, 1961); Sailor's Guide (1958, 1957); Rising Fast (1956); Prince Cortauld (1955).
Blamey Stakes winners won the preceding races in that autumn:
Carlyon Cup: 4—Budriguez (2013); Apache Cat (2007); Thackeray (1999); Trissaro (1983).
Orr Stakes: 6—Vo Rogue (1988-89); Surround (1977); Fileur (1969); Tobin Bronze (1967); Rising Fast (1956); Prince Cortauld (1955).
Futurity Stakes: 1—Suavito (2015);
Peter Young Stakes: 11—Racer's Edge (1996); Durbridge (1995, 1994); Vo Rogue (1989, 1988); Hyperno (1981); Sobar (1974); Gay Icarus (1971); Tobin Bronze (1967); Dhaulagiri (1962, 1961).
Australian Cup: 5—Better Loosen Up (1991); Vo Rogue (1989); Kip (1982); Lord Dudley (1976); Gay Icarus (1971). Note 1: Only Better Loosen Up (1991) and Vo Rogue (1988) has won the double since the Australian Cup was weight-for-age.
Melbourne Cup (same year): 1—Green Moon (2012).
Leading winning jockeys: 6 wins Harry White (Lord Of Camelot 1986, Trissaro 1983, Hyperno 1981, 1980, Lord Dudley 1976, Gunsynd 1973).
5 wins Damien Oliver (Suavito 2015, Whobegotyou 2011, Apache Cat 2007, Gold Wells 2004, Oliver Twist 2000).
Current winning jockeys: 5 wins Damien Oliver (Suavito 2015, Whobegotyou 2011, Apache Cat 2007, Gold Wells 2004, Oliver Twist 2000).
3 wins Craig Williams (He Or She 2016, Budriguez 2013, Green Moon 2012).
2 wins Cyril Small (Vo Rogue (1989, 1988); Mark Zahra (Humidor 2018, Palentino 2017).
1 win Steven Arnold (Grey Song 2005); Glen Boss (Puissance de Lune 2013); Vlad Duric (The Fuzz 2008); Luke Nolen (Lidari 2014); Chris Symons (Largo Lad 2009); Jason Waddell (Lord Tavistock 2010).
Leading winning trainers: 5 wins Bart Cummings (Shiva's Revenge 1992, Trissaro 1983, Hyperno 1981, 1980, Lord Dudley 1976); David Hayes (He Or She 2016, Largo Lad 2009, The Fuzz 2008, Better Loosen Up (1991, 1990).
Current winning trainers: 5 wins David Hayes (He Or She 2016, Largo Lad 2009, The Fuzz 2008, Better Loosen Up (1991, 1990).
3 wins Darren Weir (Humidor 2018, Palentino 2017, Puissance de Lune 2013).
2 wins Lee Freedman (Durbridge 1995, 1994).
1 win Nigel Blackiston (Suavito 2015); Andrew Campbell (Lord Tavistock 2010); Grant Dalziel (Tears Royal 2002); Roslyn Day (Rosden 2006); Greg Eurell (Apache Cat 2007); John Hawkes (Thackeray 1999); David Hayes & Tom Dabernig (He Or She 2016); Tom Hughes Jnr (Grey Song 2005); David Jolly (Budriguez 2013); Mark Kavanagh (Whobegotyou 2011); Tony McEvoy (Market Price 2001); Danny O'Brien (Gold Wells 2004); Michael Pateman (Willoughby 1998); Gerald Ryan (Racer's Edge 1996).
Points of interest: Prior to 2000, the Blamey Stakes (1600m) was run before the Peter Young Stakes (1800m). No horse has won the double since the positions were reversed.
Vo Rogue (1989, 1988) finished third to Better Loosen Up in 1990, and second the same horse in 1991.
Puissance De Lune & Budriguez dead-heated in 2013.

ATC Phar Lap Stakes (1500m)—Rosehill

$175,000 Group 2 3YO Open SW. March 16, 2019.

YEAR	WINNER	JOCKEY	TRAINER	2ND	3RD	TIME
2018	Unforgotten	Jason Collett	Chris Waller	Holy Snow	Hiyaam	1:29.1
2017	Foxplay	Kerrin McEvoy	Chris Waller	Zenalicious	Comic Set	1:30.5
2016	Hattori Hanzo	Noel Callow	Michael Kent	Man Of Choice	Believe	1:29.9
2015	Winx	Tommy Berry	Chris Waller	Hauraki	Supara	1:30.2
2014	Traitor	Brenton Avdulla	Michael, Wayne & John Hawkes	Define	Guelph	1:29.4
2013	Toydini	Blake Shinn	Guy Walter	Ninth Legion	Force Command	1:28.9
2012	Colorado Claire	James McDonald	John O'Shea	Rekindled Alliance	Wild And Proud	1:32.2
2011	Blackie	Corey Brown	Michael Kent	Fast Clip	Sworn To Secrecy	1:30.0
2010	Tickets	Luke Nolen	Peter Moody	Al Dhafra	Descarado	1:29.6
2009	Heart Of Dreams	Damien Oliver	Mick Price	Whobegotyou	Predatory Pricer	1:29.9
2008	Acey Ducey	Darren Beadman	Grahame Begg	Voice Commander	Our Mosstique	1:32.1
2007	Just Mambo	Glen Boss	John O'Shea	Raheeb	Amory Lane	1:31.7
2006	Apache Cat	Craig Williams	Greg Eurell	Racing To Win	Wasp	1:30.6
2005	Shania Dane	Corey Brown	John Hawkes	Al Maher	Svenska	1:32.1
2004	Only Words	Rod Quinn	John Hawkes	Kingside	Skittles	1:28.5
2003	Thorn Park	Glen Boss	Bob Thomsen	Sportsman	Bumptious	1:28.6
2002	Arlington Road	Jim Cassidy	Gai Waterhouse	Ugachaka	Gordo	1:30.5
2001	Maitland Gold	Chris Munce	Albert Stapleford	Star Satire	Glenrowan	1:27.9

BACKGROUND

First run: 1973 (won by Toltrice). Group 2 since 1979. Run at Canterbury in 2008.
Most recent filly to win: Unforgotten (2018).
Fastest time (1500m): Maitland Gold (2001) 1:27:80.
Notable winners: Unforgotten (2018); Foxplay (2017); Winx (2015); Apache Cat (2006); Thorn Park (2003); Mr. Innocent (1999); Brave Warrior (1995); Arborea (1994); Luskin Star (1978); Imagele (1974); Toltrice (1973).
Phar Lap Stakes winners won earlier in their preparation:
Hobartville Stakes: 4—Thorn Park (2003); Monet's Cove (1997); Merry Ruler (1987); Imagele (1974).
Australian Guineas: 1—Apache Cat (2006).
Phar Lap Stakes winners went on to win in the same preparation:
Rosehill Guineas: 2—Solar Circle (1990); Imagele (1973).
George Ryder Stakes: None.
Doncaster Handicap: None.
Tulloch Stakes: 3—Northern Drake (1998); Periscope (1986); Prince Frolic (1985).
Australian Oaks: 1—Unforgotten (2018).
Leading winning jockey: 3 wins Kevin Langby (Cheyne Walk 1976, Knight Reign 1975, Imagele 1974).
Current winning jockeys: 2 wins Glen Boss (Just Mambo 2007, Thorn Park 2003); Corey Brown (Blackie 2011, Shania Dane 2005).
1 win Brenton Avdulla (Traitor 2014); Tommy Berry (Winx 2015); Noel Callow (Hattori Hanzo 2016); Jason Collett (Unforgotten 2018); Grant Cooksley (Northern Drake 1998); James McDonald (Colorado Claire 2012); Kerrin McEvoy (Foxplay 2017); Luke Nolen (Tickets 2010); Damien Oliver (Heart Of Dreams 2009); Blake Shinn (Toydini 2013); Craig Williams (Apache Cat 2006).
Leading winning trainers: 5 wins John Hawkes (Traitor 2014, Shania Dane 2005, Only Words 2004, Encores 1996, Toltrice 1973).
4 wins Tommy Smith (Private Thoughts 1981, Cheyne Walk 1976, Knight Reign 1975, Imagele 1974)
Current winning trainers: 5 wins John Hawkes (Traitor 2014, Shania Dane 2005, Only Words 2004, Encores 1996, Toltrice 1973).
3 wins Chris Waller (Unforgotten 2018, Foxplay 2017; Winx 2015).
2 wins Michael Kent (Hattori Hanzo 2016, Blackie 2011); John O'Shea (Colorado Claire 2012, Nittan's Crown 2007).
1 win Clarry Conners (Arborea 1994); Greg Eurell (Apache Cat 2006); Michael, Wayne & John Hawkes (Traitor 2014); Mick Price (Heart Of Dreams 2009); Graeme Rogerson (Kaaptive Edition 1993); John Size (Lord Essex 2000); Gai Waterhouse (Arlington Road 2002).
Points of interest: Imagele (1974) is the only Phar Lap Stakes winner to win the Australian Derby. He did it when the Derby was run the previous spring before it moved to the autumn in 1977.

ATC Ajax Stakes (1500m)—Rosehill
$175,000 Group 2 3YOY&Up Quality Handicap. March 16, 2019.

YEAR	WINNER	JOCKEY	TRAINER	2ND	3RD	TIME
2018	Comin' Through	Michael Walker	Chris Waller	Tom Melbourne	Radipole	1:28.5
2017	It's Somewhat	William Buick	John O'Shea	New Tipperary	Testashadow	1:31.0
2016	It's Somewhat	Sam Clipperton	John O'Shea	Excess Knowledge	Dances On Stars	1:28.1
2015	Burbero	Brodie Loy	Bjorn Baker	Ninth Legion	San Diego	1:29.7
2014	Messene	James McDonald	Michael, Wayne & John Hawkes	Weary	Malavio	1:28.1
2013	Havana Rey	Glyn Schofield	Bjorn Baker	Riva De Lago	Monton	1:29.6
2012	Niagara	Tommy Berry	Gai Waterhouse	Star Of Octagonal	Alma's Fury	1:28.8
2011	Pureness	Glen Boss	Gai Waterhouse	Mentality	Lebrechaun	1:30.4
2010	Brilliant Light	Jay Ford	Kerry Parker	Centennial Park	Mentality	1:28.5
2009	Soho Flyer	Corey Brown	Anthony Cummings	Marching	Chasm	1:28.7
2008	All Silent	Jeff Lloyd	Grahame Begg	Friday Creek	Bobadah	1:29.2
2007	High Cee	Zac Purton	Bart Cummings	Danleigh	The Free Stater	1:29.7
2006	Malcolm	Darren Beadman	John Hawkes	Lantwin	Utzon	1:28.7
2005	River To The Sea	Dale Spriggs	Diane Poidevin-Laine	Daniel's The Man	This Manshood	1:27.8
2004	True Glo	Damien Oliver	Lee Freedman	Gordo	So Assertive	1:28.7
2003	Grand Armee	Jim Cassidy	Gai Waterhouse	Lord Essex	Carael Boy	1:28.4
2002	Mowerman	Corey Brown	John Hawkes	Make Me A Miracle	Gordo	1:27.9
2001	Galiano	Craig Agnew	Paul O'Sullivan	Palladium Star	Emission	1:27.7

BACKGROUND
First run: 1974 (won by Tontonan). Listed 1979-83. Group 3 1984-2005. Group 2 from 2006. Run over 1200m at Randwick 1974. Run over 1200m 1975-78; 1400m 1979-84. Known as STC 50th Anniversary Stakes 1993; Konica Stakes 1996; Parramatta Leagues Club Stakes 1998-2002.
Most recent mare to win: Sea Pictures (1986).
Most recent 3YO to win: C&G—Niagara (2012); Filly—Lowan Star (1980).
Multiple winners: 3—It's Somewhat (2017, 2016); Confiscate (1999, 1998); Catalan Opening (1997, 1996).
Fastest time (1500m): Soho Square (1993) 1:27:30.
Notable winners: It's Somewhat (2017, 2016); All Silent (2008); Grand Armee (2003); Catalan Opening (1996 & 97); Poetic King (1994); Soho Square (1993); From The Planet (1991); Vite Cheval (1984); Lowan Star (1980); Tontonan (1974).
Ajax Stakes winners also won the lead-up races:
Canterbury Stakes: None.
Newcastle Newmarket Handicap: 1—Solo Flyer (2009).
Canberra National Sprint: 1—Messene (2014).
Apollo Stake: None.
Ajax Stakes winners went on to win in the same preparation:
Doncaster Prelude (Royal Parma Stakes): 2—Brilliant Light (2010); Alderson (1992)
George Ryder Stakes: None.
Sellwood Stakes: 1—It's Somewhat (2016).
Doncaster Handicap: 4—It's Somewhat (2017); Grand Armee (2003); Vite Cheval (1984); Tontonan (1974).
Leading winning jockeys: 3 wins Darren Beadman (Malcolm 2006, Catalan Opening 1997, Mac's Treasure 1987); Glen Boss (Pureness 2011, Protara's Bay 1995, Poetic King 1994); Jim Cassidy (Grand Armee 2003, Soho Square 1993, Sea Pictures 1986); Larry Cassidy (Confiscate 1999, 1998, Catalan Opening 1996).
Current winning jockeys: 3 wins Glen Boss (Pureness 2011, Protara's Bay 1995, Poetic King 1994); Larry Cassidy (Confiscate 1999, 1998, Catalan Opening 1996).
2 wins Corey Brown (Solo Flyer 2009, Mowerman 2002).
1 win Tommy Berry (Niagara 2012); William Buick (It's Somewhat 2017); Michael Cahill (Normal Practice 2000); Sam Clipperton (It's Somewhat 2016); Jay Ford (Brilliant Light 2010); Jeff Lloyd (All Silent 2008); Brodie Loy (Burbero 2015); James McDonald (Messene 2014); Damien Oliver (Tru Glo 2004); Zac Purton (High Cee 2007); Glyn Schofield (Havana Rey 2013); Michael Walker (Comin' Through 2018).
Leading winning trainers: 5 wins Bart Cumming (High Cee 2007, Catalan Opening 1997, 1996, Lloyd Boy 1979, Tontonan 1974); John Hawkes (Messene 2014, Malcolm 2006, Mowerman 2002; Confiscate 1999, 1998).
4 wins Brian Mayfield-Smith (Sea Pictures 1986, C'est Si Bon 1983, Winter's Dance 1982, Tiger Town 1977); Gai Waterhouse (Niagara 2012, Pureness 2011, Grand Armee 2003, Protara's Bay 1995).
3 wins Tommy Smith (Lowan Star 1980, Wayne's Bid 1976, Helmsman 1975).
Current winning trainers: 5 wins John Hawkes (Messene 2014, Malcolm 2006, Mowerman 2002; Confiscate 1999, 1998).
4 wins Gai Waterhouse (Niagara 2012, Pureness 2011, Grand Armee 2003, Protara's Bay 1995).
2 wins Bjorn Baker (Burbero 2015, Havana Rey 2013); Lee Freedman (Tru Glo 2004, Poetic King 1994); John

O'Shea (It's Somewhat 2017, 2016).
1 win Anthony Cummings (Solo Flyer 2009); Michael, Wayne & John Hawkes (Messene 2014); Kerry Parker (Brilliant Light 2010); Paul O'Sullivan (Galiano 2001); Diane Poidevin-Laine (River To The Sea 2005); Chris Waller (Comin' Through 2018); Danny Williams (Normal Practice 2000).
Point of interest: Tontonan (1974) carried 57.5kg to win as a 3YO.

MVRC Sunline Stakes (1600m)—Moonee Valley
$200,000 Group 2 3YO&Up Fillies & Mares WFA. March 22, 2019.

YEAR	WINNER	JOCKEY	TRAINER	2ND	3RD	TIME
2018	Spanish Reef	Mark Zahra	Ken Keys	Samovare	Flying Jess	1:35.3
2017	I Am A Star	Dean Yendall	Shane Nichols	French Emotion	First Seal	1:36.6
2016	Miss Rose De Lago	James McDonald	Danny O'Brien	Noble Protector	Metaphorical	1:35.0
2015	Noble Protector	Craig Williams	Robert Smerdon	Girl In Flight	Marianne	1:36.5
2014	Text'n Hurley	Craig Williams	Colin Little	Bippo No Bungus	You're So Good	1:36.8
2013	Spirit Song	Craig Williams	Aaron Purcell	Lights Of Heaven	Goldslick	1:35.7
2012	Spirit Song	Nash Rawiller	Aaron Purcell	Lady Lynette	Raspberries	1:38.5
2011	Nakaaya	Craig Newitt	Mick Price	Lady Lynette	Platinum Passion	1:37.5
2010	Zarita	Steven Arnold	Pat Hyland	Princess Marizza	Silvercitymiss	1:39.6
2009	Subtle Cove	Damien Oliver	Jason Coyle	Youthful High	Fifth Avenue Lady	1:37.7
2008	Laura's Charm	Steven Arnold	Patrick Payne	Illinois Girl	Wayne's Gold	1:37.8
2007	Like It Is	Craig Williams	Darren Weir	Laura's Charm	Brockman's Lass	1:37.4
2006	Candy Vale	Peter Mertens	Pat Carey	Plans	Holy Bounty	1:37.6
2005	Beautiful Gem	Damien Oliver	Lee Freedman	Umber	Charmed Lady	1:30.3
2004	Sylvaner	Nash Rawiller	Barry James	La Sirenuse	Love's Here	1:37.9
2003	Tickle My	Steven King	Bruce Purcell	Kayano	White Mist	1:38.0
2002	Spurn	Steven Arnold	Robert Smerdon	Tickle My	It's Platonic	1:37.0
2001	Flushed	Noel Callow	Ken Keys	Calm Smytzer	Shelbourne Lass	1:40.3

BACKGROUND
First run: 1977 (won by Princess Veronica). Listed 1981-90. Group 3 1991-94. WFA since 1988. For Fillies & Mares until 2006. Run over 1500m in 2005. Run at Flemington in 1995. Registered name is the Diamond Jubilee Stakes.
Most recent 3YO filly to win: I Am A Star (2017), before that Rockets Galore (1991). Note: five fillies have won the Sunline.
Multiple winners: 1—Spirit Song (2013, 2012).
Fastest time (1600m): Rockets Galore (1991) 1:34:20.
Notable winners: I Am A Star (2017); Spirit Song (2013, 2012); Zarita (2010); Beautiful Gem (2005); Sylvaner (2004); Rose O'War (2000); Excited Angel (1993); Acushla Marie (1992); Boardwalk Angel (1989); Bianco Flyer (1988); Just Landed (1979).
Moonee Valley mares' features:
Stocks Stakes (spring) & Sunline Stakes (autumn): 1—Princess Veronica (1977).
Sunline Stakes winners won the lead-up races:
Mannerism Stakes: 1—Spurn (2002).
Matron Stakes: 3—Spanish Reef (2018); Spirit Song (2012); Like It Is (2007).
Kewney Stakes: 1—I Am A Star (2017).
Sunline Stakes winners went on to win in the same preparation:
Easter Cup: 1—Princess Veronica (1977).
Coolmore Classic: 1—Acushla Marie (1992).
Goodwood Handicap: 1—Boardwalk Angel (1989).
Leading winning jockeys: 4 wins Craig Williams (Noble Protector 2015, Text'n Hurley 2014, Spirit Song 2013, Like It Is 2007).
3 wins Steven Arnold (Zarita 2010, Laura's Charm 2008, Spurn 2002); Steven King (Tickle My 2003, Excited Angel 1993, Rockets Galore 1991); Damien Oliver (Subtle Cove 2009, Beautiful Gem 2005, Snap 1995).
Current winning jockeys: 4 wins Craig Williams (Noble Protector 2015, Text'n Hurley 2014, Spirit Song 2013, Like It Is 2007).
3 wins Steven Arnold (Zarita 2010, Laura's Charm 2008, Spurn 2002); Damien Oliver (Subtle Cove 2009, Beautiful Gem 2005, Snap 1995).
2 wins Nash Rawiller (Spirit Song 2012, Sylvaner 2004).
1 win Noel Callow (Flushed 2001); Wayne Davis (Acushla Marie 1992); James McDonald (Miss Rose De Lago

2016); Craig Newitt (Nakaaya 2011); Mark Zahra (Spanish Reef 2018); Dean Yendall (I Am A Star 2017).
Leading winning trainer: 3 wins Colin Hayes (Bianco Flyer 1988, Mrs. Fitzherbert 1985, Princess Veronica 1977).
Current winning trainers: 2 wins Lee Freedman (Beautiful Gem 2005, Rose O'War 2000); Ken Keys (Spanish Reef 2018, Flushed 2001); Aaron Purcell (Spirit Song 2013, 2012); Bruce Purcell (Tickle My 2003, Vonanne 1999); Robert Smerdon (Noble Protector 2015, Spurn 2002).
1 win Clive Balfour (Kalimna Queen 1983); Pat Carey (Candy Vale 2006); Jim Conlan (Excited Angel 1993); Jason Coyle (Subtle Cove 2009); Pat Hyland (Zarita 2010); Barry James (Sylvaner 2004); Gary Lamb (Silver Satellite 1987); Colin Little (Text'n Hurley 2014); John Meagher (Rockets Galore 1991); Shane Nichols (I Am A Star 2017); Danny O'Brien (Miss Rose De Lago 2016); Patrick Payne (Laura's Charm 2008); Mick Price (Nakaaya 2011); John Sadler (Prefer An Angel 1997); Ken Sweeney (Not Related 1994); Tony Vasil (Marathon Star 1990); Darren Weir (Like It Is 2007).

ATC Tulloch Stakes (2000m)—Rosehill
$175,000 Group 2 3YO C&G SW. March 30, 2019.

YEAR	WINNER	JOCKEY	TRAINER	2ND	3RD	TIME
2018	Levendi	Mark Zahra	Peter Gelogotis	Astoria	Weather With You	2:04.1
2017	Jon Snow	Damian Lane	Murray Baker & Andrew Forsman	Prized Icon	Captain Duffy	2:09.8
2016	Old North	James McDonald	John O'Shea	Torgersen	Multifacets	2:01.9
2015	Hauraki	James McDonald	John O'Shea	Omeros	Merion	2:03.1
2014	Gallatin	Nash Rawiller	Peter Snowden	Singing Flame	Best Case	2:07.5
2013	Philippi	Luke Nolen	Michael Kent	Hippopus	Sir Denzel	2:05.0
2012	Polish Knight	Brenton Avdulla	Michael, Wayne & John Hawkes	Iggi Pop	Rekindled Alliance	2:01.7
2011	Fast Clip	Nash Rawiller	Gai Waterhouse	I Think I Do	Shootoff	2:03.8
2010	Count Encosta	Brenton Avdulla	John P Thompson	Descarado	Maluckyday	2:03.9
2009	Harris Tweed	Hugh Bowman	Murray & Bjorn Baker	Dr Doutes	Old Jock	2:07.2
2008	Book Of Kells	James Winks	Bart Cummings	Rios	Prince De Galles	2:08.0
2007	Tipungwuti	Dwayne Dunn	Mark Kavanagh	Pacino	Carnegie House	2:01.8
2006	Manton	Darren Beadman	John Hawkes	Sepia	Goldtown	2:02.1
2005	Stella Grande	Damien Oliver	Lee Freedman	Roving Owl	King Johny	2:03.0
2004	Starcraft	Glen Boss	Garry Newham	Strafed	Delzao	2:01.6
2003	Natural Blitz	Kerrin McEvoy	Doug Harrison	Platinum Scissors	So Assertive	2:00.9
2002	Prince Of War	Scott Seamer	Graeme Rogerson	Valedict	My Tally	2:02.0
2001	Zareyev	Brian York	Gai Waterhouse	Universal Prince	Off Guard	2:00.7

BACKGROUND
First run: 1973 (won by Longfella). Group 2 since 1979. Run over 1850m 1973-78. Known as the Carringbush Cup 1987-89.
Fastest time (2000m): Peep On The Sly (1996); Durbridge (1991) 2:00:30.
Notable winners: Levendi (2018); Jon Snow (2017); Hauraki (2015); Harris Tweed (2009); Starcraft (2004); Shogun Lodge (2000); Northern Drake (1998); Ivory's Irish (1995); Mahogany (1994); Durbridge (1991); Ming Dynasty (1977); Balmerino (1976); Longfella (1973).
Tulloch Stakes winners won the lead-up races:
Alister Clark Stakes: 2—Philippi (2013), Durbridge (1991),
Adelaide Guineas: 1—Tipungwuti (2007).
Chipping Norton Stakes: 1—Starcraft (2004).
Hobartville Stakes: None.
Phar Lap Stakes: 3—Northern Drake (1998); Periscope (1986); Prince Frolic (1985).
Tulloch Stakes winners have gone on to win in the same preparation:
ATC Australian Derby: 7—Levendi (2018); Jon Snow (2017); Starcraft (2004); Ivory's Irish (1995); Mahogany (1994); Durbridge (1991); Prolific (1984). Note: Since Starcraft in 2004, five Tulloch Stakes winners have finished second in the ATC Australian Derby—Hauraki (2015), Philippi (2013), Polish Knight (2012), Harris Tweed (2009), Stella Grande (2005).
Tulloch Stakes: None.
Leading winning jockey: 3 wins Malcolm Johnston (Mighty Willem 1988, Hermod 1983, Career 1979).
Current winning jockeys: 2 wins Brenton Avdulla (Polish Knight 2012, Count Encosta 2010); Larry Cassidy (Lease 1999, Ivory's Irish 1995); James McDonald (Old North 2016, Hauraki 2015); Nash Rawiller (Gallatin 2014, Fast Clip 2011)

1 win Glen Boss (Starcraft 2004); Hugh Bowman (Harris Tweed 2009); Grant Cooksley (Northern Drake 1998); Dwayne Dunn (Tipungwuti 2007); Damian Lane (Jon Snow 2017); Kerrin McEvoy (Natural Blitz 2003); Luke Nolen (Philippi 2013); Damien Oliver (Stella Grande 2005); James Winks (Book Of Kells 2008); Mark Zahra (Levendi 2018).

Leading winning trainers: 5 wins Bart Cummings (Book Of Kells 2008, Ivory's Irish 1995, Prolific 1984, Ming Dynasty 1977, Asgard 1975).
4 wins Murray Baker (Jon Snow 2017, Harris Tweed 2009, The Bill 1993, Our Palliser 1987).
3 wins John Hawkes (Polish Knight 2012, Manton 2006, Lease 1999); Tommy Smith (Career 1979, Mansingh 1975, Longfella 1973)

Current winning trainers:
4 wins Murray Baker (Jon Snow 2017, Harris Tweed 2009, The Bill 1993, Our Palliser 1987).
3 wins John Hawkes (Polish Knight 2012, Manton 2006, Lease 1999).
2 wins Lee Freedman (Stella Grande 2005, Mahogany 1994); John O'Shea (Old North 2016, Hauraki 2015); Graeme Rogerson (Prince Of War 2002, Heroes Return 1997); Gai Waterhouse (Fast Clip 2011, Zareyev 2001).
1 win Bjorn & Murray Baker (Harris Tweed 2009); Peter Gelogotis (Levendi 2018); Doug Harrison (Natural Blitz 2003); Michael, Wayne & John Hawkes (Polish Knight 2012); Mark Kavanagh (Tipungwuti 2007); Mick Kent (Philippi 2013); Brian Smith (Balmerino 1976); Peter Snowden (Gallatin 2014); John Thompson (Count Encosta 2010).

Points of interest: Golden Slipper winner Luskin Star ran second to Lefroy in the 1978 Tulloch Stakes. Mahogany (1994) is the only Victoria Derby winner to win the Tulloch Stakes.

ATC Emancipation Stakes (1500m)—Rosehill
$175,000 Group 2 3YO&Up Fillies & Mares SWP. March 30, 2019.

YEAR	WINNER	JOCKEY	TRAINER	2ND	3RD	TIME
2018	Prompt Response	Damien Oliver	Gai Waterhouse & Adrian Bott	Oregon's Day	Dixie Blossoms	1:31.1
2017	Zanbagh	Hugh Bowman	John P Thompson	Daysee Doom	Dixie Blossoms	1:34.5
2016	Zanbagh	Blake Shinn	John P Thompson	Supara	Amicus	1:28.4
2015	Catkins	James McDonald	Chris Waller	Amanpour	Gypsy Diamond	1:29.2
2014	Catkins	Hugh Bowman	Chris Waller	Sharnee Rose	Angel Of Mercy	1:31.9
2013	Skyerush	Blake Shinn	Guy Walter	Floria	Cathay Lady	1:35.4
2012	Skyerush	Blake Shinn	Guy Walter	Fibrillation	Divorces	1:35.3
2011	Sworn To Secrecy	Brenton Avdulla	John O'Shea	Skyerush	Shannara	1:39.4
2010	Sacred Choice	Michael Rodd	Joseph Pride	Gold Water	Strawberry Field	1:35.1
2009	Amberino	Damien Oliver	John Moloney	Bernicia	Reggie	1:38.3
2008	Kosi Bay	Damien Oliver	Bart Cummings	Translate	Camarilla	1:37.4
2007	Hot Danish	Tim Clark	Les Bridge	Kosi Bay	More Than Lucky	1:37.1
2006	Fantasia	Hugh Bowman	Guy Walter	Octapussy	Villa Bled	1:34.5
2005	Perfect Promise	Blake Shinn	Grahame Begg	Uprize	Tui Song	1:37.0
2004	Hec of a Party	Glen Boss	Gai Waterhouse	Zanna	In a Bound	1:35.9
2003	Faith Hill	Jim Cassidy	Ron Quinton	Moon Dragon	Barawin	1:38.2
2002	Miss Zoe	Kerrin McEvoy	Les Bridge	Sibyl	Call Me Lily	1:36.0
2001	Heather	Larry Cassidy	John Hawkes	Poppett	More Haste	1:37.1

BACKGROUND
First run: 1985 (won by Aspirations). Listed 1985-95. Group 3 1996-98. Group 2 from 1999. Handicap before 1998. 1600m 1985-2013. Run at Randwick 1985-2013.
Most recent 3YO filly to win: Hot Danish (2007).
Fastest time (1500m): Zanbagh (2016) 1:28.43.
Multiple winners: 3—Zanbagh (2017, 2016); Catkins (2015, 2014); Skyerush (2013, 2012).
Notable winners: Prompt Response (2018); Catkins (2015); Sacred Choice (2010); Hot Danish (2007); Perfect Promise (2005); Beat The Fade (2000); Staging (1999); Romanee Conti (1992); Ice Cream Sundae (1991).
Emancipation Stakes winners won the lead-up races:
Aspiration Quality: 1—Sacred Choice (2010)
Breeders' Classic: 2—Prompt Response (2018); Catkins (2015).
Coolmore Classic: None.
Millie Fox Stakes: 1—Catkins (2015).
South Pacific Classic: None.
Queen Of The Turf Stakes: 1 – Romanee Conti (1992). Note: The Queen Of The Turf was run before the Emancipation Stakes until 2013.

Doncaster Prelude (Royal Parma Stakes): 1—Skyerush (2013).
Emancipation Stakes winners went on to win in same preparation:
Queen Of The Turf Stakes: None. Note: The Queen Of The Turf was run before the Emancipation Stakes until 2013.
Leading winning jockeys: 6 wins Shane Dye (Staging 1999, Almazyoon 1997, Vital Consent 1995, Romanee Conti 1992, Twining 1989, Balmoral 1988).
4 wins Blake Shinn (Zanbagh 2016, Skyerush 2013, 2012, Perfect Promise 2005).
Current leading jockeys: 4 wins Blake Shinn (Zanbagh 2016, Skyerush 2013, 2012, Perfect Promise 2005);
3 wins Damien Oliver (Prompt Response 2018, Amberino 2009, Kosi Bay 2008).
2 wins Hugh Bowman (Zanbagh 2017, Fantasia 2006).
1 win Brenton Avdulla (Sworn To Secrecy 2011); Glen Boss (Hec Of A Party 2004); Larry Cassidy (Heather 2001); Tim Clark (Hot Danish 2007); James McDonald (Catkins 2015); Kerrin McEvoy (Miss Zoe 2002); Michael Rodd (Sacred Choice 2010).
Leading winning trainers: 4 wins Guy Walter (Skyerush 2013, 2012, Fantasia 2006, Star County 1996).
3 wins Bart Cummings (Kosi Bay 2008, Beat The Fade 2000, Vital Consent 1995).
Current winning trainers: 3 wins Gai Waterhouse (Prompt Response 2018, Hec Of A Party 2004, Almazyoon 1997).
2 wins Les Bridge (Hot Danish 2007, Miss Zoe 2002); John Hawkes (Heather 2001, Ausmart 1994); Laurie Laxon (Palia 1998, Romanee Conti 1992); John Thompson (Zanbagh 2017, 2016); Chris Waller (Catkins 2015, 2014).
1 win Clarry Conners (Staging 1999); Lee Freedman (Perfect Promise 2005); Max Hinton (Top Dance 1990); Garry Kirkup (Ice Cream Sundae 1991); John Moloney (Amberino 2009); John O'Shea (Sworn To Secrecy 2011); Joe Pride (Sacred Choice 2010); Ron Quinton (Faith Hill 2003); Brian Smith (Clavell's Girl 1987); Gai Waterhouse & Adrian Bott (Prompt Response 2018).
Point of interest: Perfect Promise (2005) began racing in South Africa.

ATC Chairman's Handicap (2600m)—Randwick

$300,000 Group 2 3YO&Up Quality Handicap. April 6, 2019.

YEAR	WINNER	JOCKEY	TRAINER	2ND	3RD	TIME
2018	Sir Charles Road	Blake Shinn	Lance O'Sullivan & Andrew Scott	Ventura Storm	Peribsen	2:41.5
2017	Big Duke	Craig Williams	Darren Weir	Aloft	Rock On	2:52.4
2016	Libran	Brenton Avdulla	Chris Waller	Alegria	Cafe Society	2:48.1
2015	Tremec	Brenton Avdulla	John P Thompson	Sir John Hawkwood	Grand Marshal	2:49.4
2014	The Offer	Tommy Berry	Gai Waterhouse	Tremec	Hippopus	2:51.6
2013	Tremec	Craig Newitt	John P Thompson	Blood Brotha	Aliyana Tilde	2:44.4
2012	Permit	Corey Brown	Chris Waller	Older Than Time	Nextanix	2:41.9
2011	Once Were Wild	Nash Rawiller	Gai Waterhouse	Anudjawun	C'est Le Guerre	2:43.4
2010	Jessicabeel	Craig Williams	John O'Shea	No Wine No Song	Harris Tweed	2:44.6
2009	Divine Rebel	Kerrin McEvoy	Michael Moroney	Ice Chariot	Common Objective	2:45.9
2008	No Wine No Song	Damien Oliver	Kevin Moses	Sky Biscuit	Resolution	2:49.8
2007	No Wine No Song	Michael Rodd	Kevin Moses	Prince Arthur	Magic Instinct	2:48.1
2006	Fooram	Darren Beadman	John O'Shea	Three Chimneys	Cross Bar	2:45.0
2005	Philosophe	Dwayne Dunn	Jim Conlan	Padfoot Charlie	County Tyrone	2:51.1
2004	Mummify	Danny Nikolic	Lee Freedman	County Tyrone	Saturday Fever	2:47.7
2003	Grey Song	Steven King	Tommy Hughes	Honor Babe	County Tyrone	2:32.4
2002	Henderson Bay	Darryl Mclellan	Neville Mcburney	Homewrecker	Asia	2:29.7
2001	Steel Phoenix	Darren Beadman	John Size	Giovana	Wellington	2:32.0

BACKGROUND

First run: 1979 (won by Lady Dignitas). Group 3 1979-2001. Group 2 since 2002. Run over 2400m 2000-03.
Most recent mare to win: Once Were Wild (2011).
Most recent 3YO to win: C&G – None; Filly – None.
Multiple winners: 3—Tremec (2015, 2013); No Wine No Song (2008, 2007); Steel Phoenix (2001, 1999).
Fastest time (2600m): Permit (2012) 2:41:97.
Notable winners: The Offer (2014); No Wine No Song (2007-08); Mummify (2004); Henderson Bay (2002); Linesman (1997); Te Akau Nick (1993); Round The World (1988); Marooned (1986); What A Nuisance (1984).
Chairman's Handicap winners also won the lead-up races:
Randwick City Stakes: 4—Libran (2016); No Wine No Song (2008); Steel Phoenix (2001); Bianco Lady (1982).
Manion Cup: 7—Big Duke (2017); Libran (2016); The Offer (2014); Permit (2012); Fooram (2006); Pravda (2000); Marooned (1986).
Chairman's Handicap winners went on to win in the same preparation:
Sydney Cup: 6—No Wine No Song (2008); Henderson Bay (2002); Linesman (1997); King Aussie (1990); Major Drive (1987); Marooned (1986).
Queen Elizabeth Stakes: None.
Leading winning jockey: 3 wins Jim Cassidy (Demerit 1992, King Aussie 1990, Marooned 1986).
Current winning jockeys: 2 wins Larry Cassidy (Linesman 1997, Spiritual Star 1995).
2 wins Brenton Avdulla (Libran 2016, Tremex 2015); Craig Williams (Big Duke 2017, Jessicabeel 2010).
1 win Tommy Berry (The Offer 2014); Dwayne Dunn (Philosophe 2005); Kerrin McEvoy (Divine Rebel 2009); Craig Newitt (Tremec 2013); Damien Oliver (No Wine No Song 2008); Nash Rawiller (Once Were Wild 2011); Michael Rodd (No Wine No Song 2007); Blake Shinn (Sir Charles Road 2018).
Leading winning trainers: 4 wins Gai Waterhouse (The Offer 2014, Once Were Wild 2011, Linesman 1997, Te Akau Nick 1993).
Current winning trainers: 4 wins Gai Waterhouse (The Offer 2014, Once Were Wild 2011, Linesman 1997, Te Akau Nick 1993).
2 wins John Meagher (Major Drive 1987, What A Nuisance 1984); Kevin Moses (No Wine No Song 2008, 2007); John O'Shea (Jessicabeel 2010, Fooram 2006); John Size (Steel Phoenix 2001, 1999); John Thompson (Tremec 2015, 2013); Chris Waller (Libran 2016, Permit 2012).
1 win Jim Conlan (Philosophe 2005); Lee Freedman (Mummify 2004); Tom Hughes Jnr (Grey Song 2003); Michael Moroney (Divine Rebel 2009); Lance O'Sullivan & Andrew Scott (Sir Charles Road 2018); Paul O'Sullivan (Pravda 2000); Robert Pearse (Joss Sticks 1998); Steve Richards (Cornwall King 1996); Darren Weir (Big Duke 2017); Garry White (Prizaan 1991).

Point of interest: Grey Song (2003) survived a protest from Honor Babe.

WATC Karrakatta Plate (1200m)—Ascot
$500,000 Group 2 2YO Open. SW. April 6, 2019.

YEAR	WINNER	JOCKEY	TRAINER	2ND	3RD	TIME
2018	Valour Road	Aaron Mitchell	Simon A Miller	Lady Cosmology	Lordhelpmerun	1:10.4
2017	Lucy Mae	Shaun Mc Gruddy	Ted Martinovich	Achernar Star	Debellatio	1:10.3
2016	Whispering Brook	Peter Knuckey	Simon A Miller	Spangled Impact	Saul's Special	1:11.1
2015	Lucky Street	Paul Harvey	Trevor Andrews	Mystic Maid	Showy Chloe	1:10.6
2014	Hobart Jones	Jason Brown	Vern Brockman	Vitalism	Jezpark	1:11.4
2013	Ms Funovits	Glen Boss	John Sadler	Trichologist	Camporella	1:10.7
2012	Luke's Luck	Sean Mc Gruddy	Trevor Andrews	Keeper Quiet	Miss Solis	1:11.2
2011	Night War	Pat Carbery	Simon A Miller	Benny's Halo	Rebel Call	1:11.5
2010	Motion Pictures	Troy Turner	David Casey	Miss Gai Flyer	Absolute Pleasure	1:10.3
2009	Gold Rocks	Pat Carbery	Peter Giadresco	Wolfe Dream	Dontrocktheboat	1:10.4
2008	Brava Fortune	Brad Arnham	Neville Parnham	Grand Nirvana	Pegase	1:10.7
2007	Roman Time	Willie Pike	Fred Kersley	Scenic Blast	Jestatune	1:10.5
2006	Canny Jack	Jason Whiting	George Daly	Oroya Gold	Paris Petard	1:10.3
2005	No Questions	Peter Knuckey	Shane A Edwards	Hantu	Ripped	1:11.9
2004	Redwoldt	Jason Whiting	Lou Luciani	Metaldale	Refemme	1:11.5
2003	Diffraction	Peter Knuckey	George Daly	Shout From Maroof	Yarraman	1:10.5
2002	Confront	Lucas Camilleri	John Price	Zoometric	Femme	1:11.0
2001	Born Priceless	Daniel Staeck	Lou Luciani	Brocky's Dream	Classic Cut	1:11.7

BACKGROUND
First run: 1900 (won by Willie). Group 2 1979-84 & since 1999. Group 1 1985-98. Not held in 1901, 1993 & 1997. Run over 1000m 1900-78. Run at Belmont in 2005. Run pre-Christmas prior to 1994, and in 1996.
Most recent filly to win: Lucy Mae (2017).
Fastest time (1200m): Bomber Bill (1998) & Highpak (1989) 1:10.10
Notable winners: Bomber Bill (1998); Jacks Or Better (1994); Umatilla (1990); Top Post (1982); Burgess Queen (1976); Vain Prince (1973); Par Avion (1968); Lady Orator (1955); Gay Gipsy (1933); Easingwold (1920); Eurythmic (1919); Jolly Beggar (1908).
Karrakatta Plate winners also won the lead-up races:
Magic Millions (Perth): 3—Valour Road (2018); Lucy Mae (2017); Lucky Street (2015).
Gimcrack Stakes: 4—Whispering Brook (2016); Hold That Smile (1988); Scornvale (1983); Elegant Shell (1978).
Perth Stakes: 5—Lucky Street (2015); Canny Jack (2006); Redwoldt (2004); Metal Master (2000); Bomber Bill (1998).
Perth Stakes & Karrakatta & WA Sires' Produce: 1—Bomber Bill (1998).
Supremacy Stakes: 4—Whispering Brook (2016); Elegant Shell (1978); Top Post (1982); Burgess Queen (1976).
Karrakatta Plate winners went on to win in the same preparation:
WA Sires' Produce Stakes: 15—Whispering Brook (2016); Luke's Luck (2012); Motion Pictures (2010); Brava Fortune (2008); Roman Time (2007); Bomber Bill (1998); Rare Sovereign (Karrakatta 1977, Sires' 1978); Haze (Karrakatta 1965; Sires' 1966); Nanna Tale (Karrakatta 1964; Sires' 1965); Ruby (Karrakatta 1940; Sires' 1941); Loyalist (Karrakatta 1938; Sires' 1939); Riveret (Karrakatta 1931; Sires' 1932); Dawn Of Youth (Karrakatta 1927; Sires' 1928); Eurythmic (Karrakatta 1918; Sires' 1919); Welkin Queen (Karrakatta 1914; Sires' 1915).
Karrakatta Plate winners as 3YOs and older:
WA Oaks: 2—Queen Of The Nile (Karrakatta 1958, Oaks 1960); Copper Beech (Karrakatta 1951, Oaks 1953).
WA Derby: 5—Lady Orator (Karrakatta 1955, Derby 1956); Easingwold (Karrakatta 1920, Derby 1921); Eurythmic (Karrakatta 1918, Derby 1919); Jolly Beggar (Karrakatta 1909, Derby 1909); Thorina (Karrakatta 1907; Derby 1908).
Railway Stakes: 4—Jacks Or Better (Karrakatta 1994; Railway 1995); La Trice (Karrakatta 1967, Railway 1968); Gay Gipsy (Karrakatta 1933; Railway 1936); Jolly Odd (Karrakatta 1924; Railway 1927).
Leading winning jockeys: 6 wins Frank Treen (Elegant Shell 1978, Sans Sabre 1970, Astra Vista 1961, Spherical 1957, Copper Beech 1951, Barlowerie 1947).
5 wins Frank "Tiger" Moore (Solid Gold 1971, Tricar 1969, Haze 1965, San Vista 1956, Churinga 1946)
Current winning jockeys:
3 wins Peter Knuckey (Whispering Brook 2016, No Questions 2005, Diffraction 2003).
2 wins Pat Carbery (Night War 2011, Gold Rocks 2009); Shaun Mc Gruddy (Lucy Mae 2017, Luke's Luck 2012); Troy Turner (Motion Pictures 2010, Daney Boy 1995); Jason Whiting (Canny Jack 2006, Redwoldt 2004).
1 win Glen Boss (Ms Funovits 2013); Jason Brown (Hobart Jones 2014); Lucas Camilleri (Confront 2002); Paul Harvey (Lucky Street 2015); Aaron Mitchell (Valour Road 2018); Brad Parnham (Brava Fortune 2008); Daniel Staeck (Born Priceless 2001); Craig Staples (Bomber Bill 1998); Willie Pike (Roman Time 2007).
Leading winning trainers: 7 wins Jim (J.J.) Kelly (Beaufiler 1937, Gay Balkan 1936, Three Stripes 1928,

Kongoni 1925, Honneur 1922; Eurythmic 1918, Bardeur 1915).
4 wins Paddy Bolger (Lucky Beggar 1912, Jolly Beggar 1908, Hurley Burley 1903, San Toy 1902); Ted McAuliffe (Astra Vista 1961, Hyperical 1954, Copper Beech 1951, Barlowerie 1947)
Current winning trainers: 3 wins Hec McClaren (Bomber Bill 1998, Umah 1997, Alabama Whirly 1996); Simon Miller (Valour Road 2018, Whispering Brook 2016, Night War 2011).
2 wins Trevor Andrews (Lucky Street 2015, Luke's Luck 2012); Lou Luciani (Redwoldt 2004, Born Priceless 2001); Ted Martinovich (Lucy Mae 2017, Hold That Smile 1988); Frank Maynard snr (Parlez Doux 1987, Burgess Queen 1976); Brian Mueller (Scornvale 1983, Elegant Shell 1978).
1 win Vern Brockman (Hobart Jones 2014); David Casey (Motion Pictures 2010); Peter Giadresco (Gold Rocks 2009); Fred Kersley (Roman Time 2007); Frank Maynard jnr (Lady Kariba 1991); John McNair (Highpak 1989); John Meagher (Daney Boy 1995); Neville Parnham (Brava Fortune 2008); John Price (Confront 2002); John Sadler (Ms Funovits 2013).
Points of interest: Paklani (1989) was won in front of Highpak but was later disqualified due to a positive swab. Dead-heats for first: His Double & Honneur (1922); Jolly Beggar & Blue Moon (1908). Easingwold (1920) won the 1923 Cox Plate at Moonee Valley. Eurythmic (1918) won the Perth Cup (1919) and Caulfield Cup (1920). Entrepreneurial Pat Connolly owned seven winners—Lace Girl (1923); His Double (1922); Green Lord (1916); Miss Bob (1911); Louvima (1909); Jolly Beggar (1908); Thorina (1907)

ATC Arrowfield 3YO Sprint (1200m)—Randwick
$500,000 Group 2. 3YO Open SW. April 13, 2019.

YEAR	WINNER	JOCKEY	TRAINER	2ND	3RD	TIME
2018	Catchy	Joao Moreira	David & Ben Hayes & Tom Dabernig	Showtime	I Am Excited	1:10.2
2017	Derryn	Mark Zahra	David & Ben Hayes & Tom Dabernig	Global Glamour	Impending	1:12.6
2016	Japonisme	Hugh Bowman	Chris Waller	Counterattack	Takedown	1:10.3
2015	Delectation	Hugh Bowman	Chris Waller	Bring Me The Maid	Rekindled Power	1:11.7
2014	Sidestep	Kerrin McEvoy	Peter Snowden	Bounding	In Cahoots	1:10.2
2013	Rebel Dane	Jason Collett	Gary Portelli	Urquidez	Taxmeifyoucan	1:10.7
2012	Hot Snitzel	Hugh Bowman	Gerald Ryan	Manawanui	Moment Of Change	1:08.9
2011	Master Harry	Tim Clark	Peter Moody	Audacious Spirit	Skilled	1:10.2
2010	Shoot Out	Kerrin McEvoy	John Wallace	More Than Great	Viking Legend	1:10.7
2009	Youthful Jack	Robert Thompson	Allan Denham	Over the Wicket	Desuetude	1:11.3
2008	El Cambio	Hugh Bowman	Peter Snowden	Kingda Ka	Solo Flyer	1:10.3
2007	Mutawaajid	Hugh Bowman	Gai Waterhouse	Sniper's Bullet	Mearas	1:09.5
2006	Flying Pegasus	Michael Rodd	David Payne	Racing To Win	De Beers	1:10.0
2005	Dance Hero	Chris Munce	Gai Waterhouse	Eremein	Star Cat	1:10.0
2004	Exceed and Excel	Corey Brown	Tim Martin	Ambulance	Impaler	1:08.2
2003	Athelnoth	Hugh Bowman	Tiger Holland	Planchet	Charlie Bub	1:10.1
2002	Lonhro	Rod Quinn	John Hawkes	Viking Ruler	Shags	1:11.0
2001	Assertive Lad	Chris Munce	Gai Waterhouse	Continum	Century Kid	1:09.9

BACKGROUND
First run: 1979 (won by Acamar). Group 3 1981-95. Group 2 from 1996. Run over 1100m 1997 & 1998 on Randwick Kensington track. Run over 1180m in 2004 on Randwick Kensington. Held in February until 2014. The initial race in 1979, known as the Sovereign Stakes, was for open 3YOs and won by the filly Acamar; not held in 1980 and from 1981-2013 for colts and geldings. Open 3YO from 2014. Registered as the Royal Sovereign Stakes.
Fillies to win: Catchy (2018); Achmar (1979).
Fastest time (1200m): Exceed And Excel (2004) 1:08.27.
Notable winners: Catchy (2018); Japonisme (2016); Shoot Out (2010); Dance Hero (2005); Exceed And Excel (2004); Lonhro (2002); Assertive Lad (2001); Guineas (1998); Catalan Opening (1996); Danewin (1995); Coronation Day (1993); Shaftesbury Avenue (1990); Hula Chief (1986); Best Western (1982).
(Note: the move of the Royal Sovereign Stakes (Arrowfield 3YO Sprint) from February to April in 2014, means that there is no longer any relevance to the old lead-up races).
Arrowfield 3YO Sprint winners also won in same preparation:
Hobartville Stakes: 4—Mutawaajid (2007); Lonhro (2002); Danewin (1995); Shaftesbury Avenue (1990).
Liverpool City Cup: 1—All Archie (1991).
Randwick Guineas: 1—Shoot Out (2010).
Lightning Stakes: 1—Hula Chief (1986).

Newmarket Handicap: 1—Exceed And Excel (2004).
Canterbury Stakes: 2—Dance Hero (2005); Chimes Square (1985).
Phar Lap Stakes: 1—Trench Digger (1981).
Darby Munro Stakes: 3—Derryn (2017); Sidestep (2014); Sovereign State (1997).
Ajax Stakes: 1—Catalan Opening (1997).
Doncaster Handicap: 2—Assertive Lad (2001); Hula Chief (1986).
Australian Derby: 1—Shoot Out (2010).
BRC Classic: 1—El Cambio (2008).
Gold Coast Guineas: 1—El Cambio (2008).
Doomben Cup: 1—Danewin (1995).
Arrowfield 3YO Sprint winners won in the spring of the same year:
Missile Stakes: 2—Dance Hero (2005); Lonhro (2002).
Chelmsford Stakes: 1—Lonhro (2002).
George Main Stakes: 1—Shaftesbury Avenue (1990).
Caulfield Stakes: 2—Lonhro (2002); Danewin (1995).
Mackinnon Stakes: 2—Lonhro (2002); Danewin (1995).
Leading winning jockeys: 5 wins Hugh Bowman (Japonisme 2016, Hot Snitzel 2012, El Cambio 2008, Mutawaajid 2007, Athelnoth 2003); Jim Cassidy (Rouslan 1994, Coronation Day 1993, Big Dreams 1992, Imperial Baron 1987, Chimes Square 1985).
Current winning jockeys: 5 wins Hugh Bowman (Japonisme 2016, Hot Snitzel 2012, El Cambio 2008, Mutawaajid 2007, Athelnoth 2003).
2 wins Kerrin McEvoy (Sidestep 2014, Shoot Out 2010).
1 win Glen Boss (Catalan Opening 1996); Corey Brown (Exceed And Excel 2004); Larry Cassidy (Hire 2000); Tim Clark (Master Harry 2011); Jason Collett (Rebel Dane 2013); Joao Moreira (2018); Michael Rodd (Flying Pegasus 2006); Robert Thompson (Youthful Jack 2009); Mark Zahra (Derryn 2017).
Leading winning trainers: 3 wins John Hawkes (Lonhro 2002, Hire 2000, Guineas 1998); Gai Waterhouse (Mutawaajid 2007, Dance Hero 2005, Assertive Lad 2001); Bart Cummings (Catalan Opening 1996, Shaftesbury Avenue 1990, Best Western 1982).
Current winning trainers: 3 wins John Hawkes (Lonhro 2002, Hire 2000, Guineas 1998); Gai Waterhouse (Mutawaajid 2007, Dance Hero 2005, Assertive Lad 2001).
2 wins David & Ben Hayes & Tom Dabernig (Catchy 2018, Derryn 2017); Peter Snowden (Sidestep 2014, El Cambio 2008).
1 win Allan Denham (Youthful Jack 2009); Tim Martin (Exceed And Excel 2004); Peter Moody (Master Harry 2011); David Payne (Flying Pegasus 2006); Gary Portelli (Rebel Dane 2013); Gerald Ryan (Hot Snitzel 2012); John Wallace (Shoot Out 2010); Chris Waller (Japonisme 2016).

Point of interest: Dance Hero (2005) and Guineas (1998) had won the Golden Slipper Stakes.

ATC Sapphire Stakes (1200m)—Randwick
$300,000 Group 2 3YO&Up Fillies & Mares. SWP. April 13, 2019.

YEAR	WINNER	JOCKEY	TRAINER	2ND	3RD	TIME
2018	Quilista	Damian Lane	Darren Weir	Ravi	White Moss	1:09.3
2017	Secret Agenda	Damien Oliver	Mick Price	Missrock	Artistry	1:13.2
2016	Two Blue	Paul King	Kristen Buchanan	Secret Agenda	Brook Road	1:10.8
2015	Avoid Lightning	Tim Clark	Les Bridge	Griante	Fine Bubbles	1:12.1
2014	Cosmic Endeavour	Tommy Berry	Gai Waterhouse	Avoid Lightning	Belle De Coeur	1:10.7
2013	Arinosa	Brenton Avdulla	Chris Waller	Miss Stellabelle	Forarainyday	1:10.5
2012	Atlantic Jewel	Michael Rodd	Mark Kavanagh	Mid Summer Music	Ladys Angel	1:08.9
2011	Hurtle Myrtle	Damien Oliver	Matthew Smith	Kimillsy	Marquardt	1:10.6
2010	Renaissance	Josh Parr	Peter Snowden	Beaded	Jersey Lily	1:10.5
2009	Court	Glyn Schofield	Clarry Conners	Belong To Many	Cajou	1:10.8
2008	Belong to Many	James Winks	Barbara Joseph	Tenant's Tiara	Fritz's Princess	1:11.1
2007	Fire Song	Michael Rodd	Graeme Rogerson	Whoever	Splashing Out	1:12.9
2006	Coolroom Candidate	Zac Purton	Keith Dryden	Imana	Shalimar Sky	1:10.6
2005	Glamour Puss	Steven King	Danny O'Brien	With My	Wild Queen	1:12.0
2004	Recurring	Kerrin McEvoy	Gerald Ryan	Fair Embrace	Cataclysm	1:10.4
2003	Fatoon	Greg Childs	Clarry Conners	Provokes	Miss Helterskelter	1:11.4
2002	Fair Embrace	Damien Oliver	Graeme Rogerson	Spinning Hill	Hot Riff	1:09.2
2001	Spinning Hill	Patrick Payne	Guy Walter	Nanny Maroon	Marlina	1:10.3

BACKGROUND

First run: 1998 (won by Coolroom Candidate). Listed 1998-2001. Group 3 2002-05. Group 2 from 2006.
Most recent 3YO filly to win: Atlantic Jewel (2012).
Multiple winners: 1—Spinning Hill (2001, 2000).
Fastest time (1200m): Atlantic Jewel (2012) 1:08.96
Notable winners: Secret Agenda (2017); Cosmic Endeavour (2014); Atlantic Jewel (2012); Hurtle Myrtle (2011); Glamour Puss (2005); Spinning Hill (2001, 2000).
Sapphire Stakes winners also won the lead-up races:
Birthday Card Stakes: 3—Quilista (2018); Arinosa (2013); Spinning Hill (2001).
Canterbury Stakes: None.
Robert Sangster Stakes: 1—Secret Agenda (2017).
Sapphire Stakes winners went on to win in the same preparation:
T.J.Smith Stakes: None. Note: Spinning Hill (2000 & 2001) won the 2003 T.J. Smith Stakes.
Research Stakes: 1 – Spinning Hill (2000).
Dane Ripper Stakes: 2—Cosmic Endeavour (2014); Hurtle Myrtle (2011).
BTC Classic: 1—Court (2005).
Tatt's Tiara: 1—Cosmic Endeavour (2014).
All Aged Stakes: 1—Atlantic Jewel (2012).
Leading winning jockey: 3 wins Shane Dye (Spinning Hill 2000, Snippets' Lass 1999; What Can I Say 1998); Damien Oliver (Secret Agenda 2017, Hurtle Myrtle 2011, Fair Embrace 2002).
Current winning jockeys: 3 wins Damien Oliver (Secret Agenda 2017, Hurtle Myrtle 2011, Fair Embrace 2002). 2 wins Michael Rodd (Atlantic Jewel 2012, Fire Song 2007).
1 win Brenton Avdulla (Arinosa 2013); Tommy Berry (Cosmic Endeavour 2014); Tim Clark (Avoid Lightning 2015); Damian Lane (Quilista 2018); Kerrin McEvoy (Recurring 2004); Zac Purton (Coolroom Candidate 2006); Glyn Schofield (Court 2009); James Winks (Belong To Many 2008).
Leading winning trainers: 2 wins Clarry Conners (Court 2009, Fatoon 2003); Graeme Rogerson (Fire Song 2007, Fair Embrace 2002); Guy Walter (Spinning Hill 2001, 2000).
Current winning trainers: 2 wins Clarry Conners (Court 2009, Fatoon 2003); Graeme Rogerson (Fire Song 2007, Fair Embrace 2002).
1 win Les Bridge (Avoid Lightning 2015); Kristen Buchanan (Two Blue 2016); Keith Dryden (Coolroom Candidate 2006); Barbara Joseph (Belong To Many 2008); Mark Kavanagh (Atlantic Jewel 2012); Danny O'Brien (Glamour Puss 2005); Mick Price (Secret Agenda 2017); Gerald Ryan (Recurring 2004); Matthew Smith (Hurtle Myrtle 2011); Peter Snowden (Renaissance 2010); Jenny Vance (What Can I Say 1998); Chris Waller (Arinosa 2013); Gai Waterhouse (Cosmic Endeavour 2014); Darren Weir (Quilista 2018).

ATC Percy Sykes Stakes (1200m)—Randwick
$600,000 Group 2 2YO Fillies SWP. April 13, 2019.

YEAR	WINNER	JOCKEY	TRAINER	2ND	3RD	TIME
2018	Pure Elation	Michael Walker	Peter & Paul Snowden	Fiesta	Outback Barbie	1:10.0
2017	Shoals	Mark Zahra	Lee & Anthony Freedman	Formality	Serena Bay	1:13.7
2016	Missrock	Hugh Bowman	Robbie Laing	Prompt Response	Spright	1:11.0
2015	Ottoman	Sam Clipperton	John O'Shea	Calaverite	Lake Geneva	1:12.4
2014	Eloping	Stephen Baster	Peter Morgan & Craig Widdison	Ygritte	Shaumari	1:10.8
2013	Everage	Nathan Berry	Craig Carmody	Little Miss Smiley	Major Conquest	1:13.4
2012	Single Style	James McDonald	Gary Portelli	Driefontein	Meidung	1:10.5
2011	Streama	Hugh Bowman	Guy Walter	Charm's Honour	Houston Benefactor	1:13.1
2010	Golden Millennium	Jay Ford	Anthony Cummings	Boto Vermelho	Parables	1:10.2
2009	Readyor	Rod Quinn	Jack Denham	Amarantha	Tallow	1:13.1
2008	Shoboard	Larry Cassidy	Pat Webster	Strawberry Field	Silent But Deadly	1:12.6
2007	Sliding Cube	Jamie Innes	Gai Waterhouse	Gamble Me	Mega Lass	1:11.1
2006	Catechuchu	Craig Williams	David Hayes	Heat Of The Fire	Admirelle	1:10.6
2005	Blizzardly	Darryl McLellan	Gai Waterhouse	Regal Cheer	Heart Strings	1:12.3
2004	Strawberry Storm	Len Beasley	Graeme Rogerson	Sweet Ransom	Monsoon Wedding	1:11.5
2003	Bella Corona	Darren Beadman	Robert Pearse	Shamekha	Danish Magic	1:12.0
2002	Before Too Long	Larry Cassidy	Gary Portelli	Verstak	Cirque De Soleil	1:10.2
2001	Allez France	Jim Cassidy	Gai Waterhouse	Miss Bussell	Breezer	1:10.8

BACKGROUND

First run: 1960 (won by Primrose Lane). Run over 1200m 1960-69, 1972-83, since 1986; over 1400m 1970-71, 1984-85. Run in two divisions in 1976 & 1984. Listed from 1979-2013, Group 3 2014-16. Group 2 from 2016. Registered as the Keith Mackay Handicap. Also known as the Royal Randwick Stakes (2014-15) and the Percy Sykes Stakes from 2016.

Fastest time (1200m, Randwick): Snapshots (1997) and Gay Rosalind (1980): 1:09.60.

Notable winners: Shoals (2017); Eloping (2014); Streama (2011); Sliding Cube (2007); Katima (1999); Flitter (1992); Rhythmic Charm (1990); Magic Flute (1986); Dinky Flyer (1984); Lady Eclipse (1983); I Like Diamonds (1982); Charity (1979); Impede (1978); Favoured (1973); Kiss Me Cait (1971); Tumberlua (1970); Candy Floss (1966); April Wonder (1962).

Percy Sykes Stakes winners also won in the same autumn/winter campaign:

VRC Thoroughbred Breeders' Stakes: 2—Shoals (2017); Red Cat (1977).

Blue Diamond Preview: 1—Eloping (2014).

Riesling Stakes: 2—Ginzano (1995); Magic Flute (1986).

Magic Night Stakes: 1—Lady Eclipse (1983)

AJC Sires' Produce Stakes: 1—Rhythmic Charm (1990).

AJC Champagne Stakes: 3—Lady Eclipse (1983); I Like Diamonds (1982); Charity (1979);

BRC Champagne Classic: 1—Ginzano (1995)

Leading winning jockeys: 4 wins George Moore (Kiss Me Cait 1971, Tumberlua 1970, Candy Floss 1966, Cymbal 1961).

3 wins Darren Beadman (Bella Corona 2003, Flitter 1992, The Cloisters 1987); Larry Cassidy (Shoboard 2008, Before Too Long 2002, Emotive 1998); Mick Dittman (Rhythmic Charm 1990, Dazzling Flyer 1989, Paris Weekend 1988); Ron Quinton (Stater 1984 (Div 1), I Like Diamonds 1982, Gay Rosalind 1980); Ray Selkrig (Surre Queen 1967, Lone 1965, April Wonder 1962).

Current winning jockeys: 3 wins Larry Cassidy (Shoboard 2008, Before Too Long 2002, Emotive 1998).

2 wins Hugh Bowman (Missrock 2016, Streama 2011).

1 win Stephen Baster (Eloping 2014); Glen Boss (Law Of Logic 1996); Sam Clipperton (Ottoman 2015); Grant Cooksley (Snapshots 1997); Jay Ford (Golden Millennium 2010); Jamie Innes (Sliding Cube 2007); James McDonald (Single Style 2012); Michael Walker (Pure Elation 2018); Craig Williams (Catachuchu 2006); Mark Zahra (Shoals 2017).

Leading winning trainers: 8 wins Tommy Smith (Paris Weekend 1988, Charity 1979, Impede 1978, La Stupenda 1975, Kiss Me Cait 1971, Tumberlua 1970, Candy Floss 1966, Cymbal 1961).

4 wins Neville Begg (Stater 1984, I Like Diamonds 1982, Gay Rosalind 1980, Obelia 1969); Gai Waterhouse (Sliding Cube 2007, Blizzardly 2005, Allez France 2001, Actress 2000.)

Current winning trainers: 4 wins Gai Waterhouse (Sliding Cube 2007, Blizzardly 2005, Allez France 2001, Actress 2000.)

2 wins Clarry Conners (Snapshots 1997, Alouette 1994); David Hayes (Catechuchu 2006, Dangerous Seam 1991); Gary Portelli (Single Style 2012, Before Too Long 2002);

1 win Craig Carmody (Everage 2013); Anthony Cummings (Golden Millennium 2010); Lee & Anthony Freedman (Shoals 2017); John Hawkes (Emotive 1998); Robbie Laing (Missrock 2016); Jim Lee (Zipella 1985); Dianne Lumsden (Ginzano 1995); John Meagher (Miss Prospect 1993); Peter Morgan & Craig Widdison (Eloping 2014); John O'Shea (Ottoman 2015); Robert Pearse (Bella Corona 2003); Graeme Rogerson (Strawberry Storm 2004); Peter & Paul Snowden (Pure Elation 2018); Pat Webster (Shoboard 2008).

W.A.T.C. Derby (2400m)—Ascot
$400,000 Group 2 3YO Open SW. April 13, 2019.

YEAR	WINNER	JOCKEY	TRAINER	2ND	3RD	TIME
2018	Action	Willie Pike	Grant & Alana Williams	Like A Butterfly	Media Baron	2:29.9
2017	Gatting	Matthieu Autier	Darren Mcauliffe	Very Tempting	Chill The Champers	2:30.3
2016	Arcadia Dream	Willie Pike	Grant Williams	Who Dat Singa	Culverin	2:31.3
2015	Delicacy	Willie Pike	Grant Williams	Keysbrook	Boom Time	2:38.2
2014	Respondent	Willie Pike	Grant Williams	Ihtsahymn	Real Love	2:29.5
2013	Mystic Prince	Ben Melham	Grant Williams	Moreish	Desert Glow	2:31.4
2012	Rohan	Glenn Smith	Vaughn Sigley	Flashy Fella	The Social Network	2:34.5
2011	Dreamaway	Willie Pike	Grant Williams	Playing God	Rio Dane	2:30.7
2010	Chartreux	Brad Rawiller	David Hayes	Bridgestone	Brother Mak	2:27.9
2009	Marcus Maximus	Luke Nolen	Peter Moody	Berlioz	Phenomenons	2:31.2
2008	Grand Journey	Willie Pike	David Brideoake	Yuro	Star Encounter	2:28.8
2007	Guyno	Jason Whiting	Lou Luciani	Ballack	Original Lovalover	2:29.0
2006	Catsfun	Willie Pike	Michael Grant	Raise A Call	Scenic Shot	2:29.7
2005	Plastered	Paul Harvey	Lindsey Smith	Royal Drive	Master Minx	2:31.3
2004	Mr Sandgroper	Paul King	David Edwards	Fatal Attraction	Crown Prosecutor	2:36.2
2003	Shirazamatazz	Daniel Staeck	Fred Kersley	Conspirator	Golden Prospect	2:32.8
2002	Honor Lap	Paul King	George Daly	Lord Mason	Storm Fille	2:31.5
2001	Not Held					

BACKGROUND
First run: 1888 (won by Harridan). Group 1 1979 & 1991, from 1993 (Dec, won by Firing Range). Group 2 1992 and May 1993. Run twice in 1993—May (Beaujolais Boy) and December (Firing Range). Switched to April in 2004. Not held in 1987.
Most recent filly to win: Arcadia Dream (2016). Note: 28 fillies have won the WATC Derby.
Fastest time (2400m): Firing Range (Dec 1993) 2:27.80
Notable winners: Dreamaway (2011); Plastered (2005); Crying Game (1995); Beaux Art (1994); Heroicity (1992); Belele (1989); Joindre (1986); National Gallery (1984); Mighty Kingdom (1989); Stormy Rex (1977); Ngawyni (1975); Bottled Sunshine (1974); Asgard (1973); Dayana (1972); Nicopolis (1962); Lady Orator (1956); Raconteur (1952); Gay Prince (1938); Easingwold (1921); Eurythmic (1919); Jolly Beggar (1909).
WA Derby winners won the following races earlier in the season:
WA Champion Fillies: 6—Dreamaway (2011); Kim Angel (Derby Dec 1998, Fillies Mar 1999); Kev's Folly (1964); Lady Orator (1956); Prediction (Derby Dec 1949, Fillies March 1950); Lady Lucia (Derby Dec 1946; Fillies Mar 1947).
WA Guineas: 12—Ngawyni (1975); Nicopolis (1962); Chestillion (1960); Raconteur (1952); Jovial Lad (1950); Prediction (1949); Westralian (1947); Cherbourg (1945); Lord Treat (1944); True Flight (1939); Gay Prince (1938); Footmark (1937). Note: No horses have completed the double since the Derby was moved from the summer to the autumn in 2002.
Ascot 1000 Guineas (first run 2010): 2—Delicacy (2015); Dreamaway (2011).
Natasha Stakes: 4—Arcadia Dream (2016); Delicacy (2015); Dreamaway (2011); Grand Journey (2008).
WA Oaks: 6—Delicacy (2015); Dreamaway (2011); Grand Journey (2008); Honor Lap (2002); Old Money (2000); Beaux Art (1994).
J.C. Roberts Stakes: 4—Respondent (2014); Rohan (2012); Crying Game (1995); The Bukhra (Roberts 1987; Derby 1988).
Strickland Stakes: 14—Ngawyni (1975); Nicopolis (1972); Chestillion (1960); Lady Orator (1956); Raconteur (1952); Jovial Lad (1950); True Flight (1939); Gay Prince (1938); Yaringa (1935); Maple (1926); Huette (1924); Lilypond (1923); Easingwold (1921); Honeydew (1902). Note: No horse has completed the double since both races were moved to the autumn in 2004.
Perth Cup (as 3YOs—WA Derby moved from Boxing Day to April in 2004): 9—Crying Game (1996); Dayana (1973); Raconteur (1953); Lilypond (1923); Eurythmic (1919); Post Town (1907); Inveray (1896); Scarpia (1893); Aim (1889).
Kingston Town Classic: 3—Rant And Rave (1985); Mighty Kingdom (1979); Stormy Rex (1977).
Note: No horse has completed the double since the Derby was moved to the autumn in 2004.
Melvista Stakes (from 2004 when Derby moved to March): 4—Gatting (2017); Cats Fun (2006); Plastered (2005); Mr Sandgroper (2004).
WA Derby winners went on to win:
Australasian Oaks: 1—Delicacy (2015).
SA Derby: 1—Delicacy (2015).
Perth Cup (as 4YOs since 2003): None. Since the Derby was moved from December to April in 2004, Cats Fun (2006) and Guyno (2007) have gone on to win the Perth Cup as 5YOs.

Leading winning jockeys:
7 wins Frank "Tiger" Moore (Surrender 1969, Hidalios 1968, Baccare 1965, Nicopolis 1962, Little Empire 1959, Nhargo 1957, Just Peter 1953); Willie Pike (Action 2018, Delicacy 2015, Respondent 2014, Dreamaway 2011, Grand Journey 2008, Cats Fun 2006).
6 wins Frank Treen (Sir Chatary 1967, Redacre 1966, Chestillion 1960, Smart Chief 1951, Jovial Lad 1950, Prediction 1949).
4 wins Bobby Morley (Lord Treat 1944, Isle Of Astur 1931, Second Wind 1928, Maple 1926); Mark Sestich (Hot Jules 1997, Heroicity 1992, Belele 1989, Rare Flyer 1982).
Current winning jockeys: 7 wins Willie Pike (Action 2018, Arcadia Dream 2016, Delicacy 2015, Respondent 2014, Dreamaway 2011, Grand Journey 2008, Cats Fun).
3 wins Paul Harvey (Plastered 2005, Kim Angel 1998, Crying Game 1995).
1 win Matthieu Autier (Gatting 2017); Jason Brown (Old Money 2000); Kevin Forrester (Old Currency 1983); Ben Melham (Mystic Prince 2013); Luke Nolen (Markus Maximus 2009); Shaun O'Donnell (Beaujolais Boy 1993, May); Brad Rawiller (Chartreux 2010); Glenn Smith (Rohan 2012); Daniel Staeck (Shirazamatazz 2003); Jason Whiting (Guyno 2007).
Leading winning trainers: 6 wins Jim (JJ) Kelly (Westralian 1947, Gay Prince 1938, Yaringa 1935, Second Wind 1928, Maple 1926, Eurythmic 1919); Grant Williams (Action 2018, Arcadia Dream 2016, Delicacy 2015, Respondent 2014, Mystic Prince 2013, Dreamaway 2011).
4 wins Bart Cummings (Stormy Rex 1977; Bottled Sunshine 1974; Asgard 1973; Dayana 1972); George Towton (Ormuz 1899, Tarquin 1898, Florrie 1895, Scarpia 1893).
Current winning trainers: 6 wins Grant Williams (Action 2018, Arcadia Dream 2016, Delicacy 2015, Respondent 2014, Mystic Prince 2013, Dreamaway 2011).
2 wins Lindsey Smith (Plastered 2005, Old Money 2000).
1 win David Brideoake (Grand Journey 2008); Michael Grant (Cats Fun 2006); David Hayes (Chartreux 2010); Paul Jordan (Hot Jules 1997); Fred Kersley (Shirazamatazz 2003); Lou Luciani (Guyno 2007); Alan Mathews (Mirror Magic 1991); Darren Mcauliffe (Gatting 2017); Joe Miller (Voile d'Or 1999); Wally Mitchell (Chipolata 1990); Ross Price (Firing Range 1993, Dec.); Vaughn Sigley (Rohan 2012); Angela Timpeley (Crying Game 1995); Paula Wagg (Kim Angel 1998); Grant & Alana Williams (Action 2018).
Points of interest: Carbine (by Tremando) who won in 1894 is not to be mistaken with the famous Carbine (by Musket) who won the 1890 Melbourne Cup.
Eurythmic (1919) went on to win the 1920 Caulfield Cup, 1920 Cox Plate and 1921 Sydney Cup, as well as three Caulfield Stakes and three Memsie Stakes.
Easingwold (1921) won the 1923 Cox Plate.
The champion filly Delicacy (2015) won six Stakes races on the trot, including three Group 1s. They were: LR WA 1000 Guineas (Ascot, 1800m), LR Natasha Stakes (Ascot, 2200m), G3 WA Oaks (Ascot, 2400m), G1 WA Derby (Ascot, 2400m), G1 Australasian Oaks (Morphettville, 2000m) and the G1 SA Derby (Morphettville, 2500m).
Bob and Sandra Peters bred and owned four consecutive WA Derby winners from 2013-16, and also Action (2018). They also bred and raced Dreamaway (2011).

BRC Victory Stakes (1200m)—Eagle Farm
$200,000 Group 2 3YO&Up WFA. April 27, 2019.

YEAR	WINNER	JOCKEY	TRAINER	2ND	3RD	TIME
2018	Impending	Damian Browne	James Cumming	Most Important	I Am Excited	1:10.0
2017	Music Magnate	Jeff Lloyd	Bjorn Baker	Hopfgarten	Miss Cover Girl	1:13.2
2016	Fell Swoop	Jay Ford	Matthew Dale	Didntcostalot	Artlee	1:09.0
2015	Srikandi	Damian Browne	Ciaron Maher	Ball Of Muscle	Dances On Stars	1:09.6
2014	Temple Of Boom	Tegan Harrison	Tony Gollan	Spirit Of Boom	Snitzerland	1:09.0
2013	Buffering	Damian Browne	Robert Heathcote	Spirit Of Boom	Albrecht	1:08.5
2012	Not held					
2011	Buffering	Larry Cassidy	Robert Heathcote	Atomic Force	Azzaland	1:13.0
2010	Ghetto Blaster	Stathi Katsidis	Gillian Heinrich	The Jackal	Albert The Fat	1:09.6
2009	Swiss Ace	Ken Pope	Mick Mair	Sniper's Bullet	Red Element	1:09.7
2008	Swiss Ace	Ken Pope	Mick Mair	Atapi	Dance The Waves	1:09.8
2007	Mitanni	Shane Scriven	John Wallace	Anwaar	Tellem	1:09.7
2006	All Bar One	Glen Colless	Gillian Heinric	Falaise	Impaler	1:08.5
2005	Wager	Danny Beasley	Gai Waterhouse	Deuxieme	Dezigna	1:21.9
2004	Only Words	Rod Quinn	John Hawkes	Our Egyptian Raine	Defier	1:25.8
2003	Tit For Taat	John Powell	Wayne Herbert	Scenic Peak	Mr Bureaucrat	1:21.5
2002	Mr Bureaucrat	Alan Robinson	Warwick Hailes	Salgado	Faiza	1:23.3
2001	Make Mine Magic	Glen Colless	Alan Bailey	Play Station	Camarena	1:20.8

BACKGROUND

First run: 1980 (won by Golden Rhapsody). Run as a handicap 1980-88. WFA since 1989. Listed in 1980. Group 3 from 1981-91. Group 2 from 1992. Run over 1810m 1980-83, 1988. 2100 (abt) 1984-87, 1989. 1400m from 1990. 1200m from 2006. Not held in 2012. Run at the Gold Coast 2015-16. Doomben in 2013, 2018. Meeting abandoned in 1996 due to rain. Previously known as the QTC International Cup, QTC The XXXX, Coca Cola Stakes and the Sir Byrne Hart Stakes.

Most recent filly/mare to win: Wager (3YO filly, 2005); Srikandi (mare, 2015). Note: Seven fillies/mares have won.

Most recent 3YO to win: C&G—Swiss Ace (2008); Filly—Wager (2005).

Fastest time (1200m Eagle Farm): All Bar One (2006) 1:08.50

Notable winners: Impending (2018); Music Magnate (2017); Srikandi (2015); Buffering (2013, 2011); Swiss Ace (2009, 2008); Tit For Taat (2003); Summer Beau (1998); Rough Habit (1991); Joindre (1987).

Victory Stakes winners also won the lead-up races:
Gold Coast Summer Cup: 1—Mitanni (2007).
Chief De Beers Quality: 1—Swiss Aace (2008)
Weetwood Handicap (Toowoomba): 1—Swiss Ace (2008).
Eye Liner Stakes (Ipswich): None.

Victory Stakes winners went on to win in the same preparation:
Stradbroke Handicap: 2—Srikandi (2015); Rough Habit (1991). Note: Rough Habit also won the Stradbroke in 1992.
Doomben 10,000: None.
Kingsford Smith Stakes: 1—Impending (2018).
Doomben Cup: 3—Mr. Bureaucrat (2002); Rough Habit (1991); Golden Rhapsody (1980).
Queensland Derby: 1—Handy Proverb (1986). Note: Rough Habit (1991) won the Derby in 1990.

Leading jockeys: 3 wins Damian Browne (Impending 2018, Srikandi 2015, Buffering 2013).
2 wins Glen Colless (All Bar One 2006, Make Mine Magic 2001); Shane Dye (Let's Hurry 1994, Majestic Boy 1992); Ken Pope (Swiss Ace 2009, 2008); Neil Williams (Roipeka 1984, Home Maid 1983).

Current winning jockeys: 3 wins Damian Browne (Impending 2018, Srikandi 2015, Buffering 2013).
2 wins Glen Colless (All Bar One 2006, Make Mine Magic 2001); Ken Pope (Swiss Ace 2009, 2008).
1 win Glen Boss (Roulette 1999); Opie Bosson (Cheiron 2000); Larry Cassidy (Buffering 2011); Jay Ford (Fell Swoop 2016); Tegan Harrison (Temple Of Boom 2014); Jeff Lloyd (Music Magnate 2017); John Powell (Tit For Taat 2003).

Leading winning trainers: 2 wins Robert Heathcote (Buffering 2013, 2011); Gillian Heinrich (Ghetto Blaster 2010, All Bar One 2006); Mick Mair (Swiss Ace 2009, 2008); Brian Mayfield-Smith (Joindre 1987, Handy Proverb 1986); Bruce McLachlan (Chortle 1993, Noble Clubs 1990).

Current winning trainers: 2 wins Robert Heathcote (Buffering 2013, 2011); Gillian Heinrich (Ghetto Blaster 2010, All Bar One 2006); Mick Mair (Swiss Ace 2009, 2008).
1 win Bjorn Baker (Music Magnate 2017); Barry Baldwin (Roulette 1999); Bruce Brown (Noble Lad 1985); James Cummings (Impending 2018); Matthew Dale (Fell Swoop 2016); Tim Donnelly (Quick Flick 1997); Warwick Hailes (Mr. Bureaucrat 2002); John Hawkes (Only Words 2004); Wayne Herbert (Tit For Taat 2003); Tony Gollan (Temple Of Boom 2014); Laurie Laxon (Finezza Belle 1988); Ciaron Maher (Srikandi 2015); Bruce Marsh (Cheiron 2000); Paul Perry (Home Maid 1983); John Wallace (Mitanni 2007); Gai Waterhouse (Wager 2005); John Wheeler (Rough Habit 1991).

GCTC A.D. Hollindale Stakes (1800m)—Gold Coast
$358,000 Group 2 3YOY&Up WFA. May 4, 2019.

YEAR	WINNER	JOCKEY	TRAINER	2ND	3RD	TIME
2018	Oregon's Day	Jim Byrne	Mick Price	Tom Melbourne	Man Of His Word	1:46.8
2017	It's Somewhat	Tye Angland	John O'Shea	Single Gaze	Maurus	1:48.5
2016	Leebaz	Michael Cahill	Michael, Wayne & John Hawkes	Hauraki	Volkstok'n'Barrell	1:48.1
2015	Leebaz	Jim Byrne	Michael, Wayne & John Hawkes	Sir Moments	I'm Imposing	1:47.9
2014	Streama	Blake Shinn	Guy Walter	Mr O'Ceirin	Precedence	1:53.1
2013	Lights Of Heaven	Luke Nolen	Peter Moody	Foreteller	Transporter	1:49.5
2012	Shez Sinsational	Opie Bosson	Allan Sharrock	Lights Of Heaven	Mawingo	1:56.0
2011	My Kingdom Of Fife	Nash Rawiller	Chris Waller	Glass Harmonium	Scenic Shot	1:52.2
2010	Metal Bender	Hugh Bowman	Chris Waller	Road To Rock	Gold Water	1:49.5
2009	Fulmonti	Joe Bowditch	Chris Jordan	Izonit	Sir Slick	1:48.1
2008	Scenic Shot	Glen Colless	Daniel Morton	Spinney	Stormhill	1:49.9
2007	Coalesce	Darren Beadman	John Hawkes	Dracs Back	Desert War	1:47.4
2006	Above Deck	Mark Zahra	Jim Conlan	Vouvray	Roman Arch	1:49.1
2005	Platinum Scissors	Danny Beasley	Gai Waterhouse	Roman Arch	Devastating	1:52.4
2004	This Manshood	Jim Cassidy	Tim Martin	St Basil	Pentastic	1:45.9
2003	Bush Padre	Michael Rodd	Lee Freedman	Boreale	Cheverny	1:49.9
2002	Mr Bureaucrat	Alan Robinson	Warwick Hailes	Kaapstad Way	My Special Scorpio	1:50.9
2001	Shogun Lodge	Glen Boss	Bob Thomsen	Camarena	Go Flash Go	1:47.3

BACKGROUND
First run: 1989 (won by Eye Of The Sky). Listed 1991 & 1992. Group 3 1993-95. Group 2 from 1996.
Previous known as the Southport Cup.
Most recent mare to win: Oregon's Day (2018). Note: Five mares have won.
Most recent 3YO to win: C&G—Shogun Lodge (2000). No 3YO filly has won.
Multiple winners: 3—Leebaz (2016, 2015); Shogun Lodge (2001, 2000); Rough Habit (1992, 1991).
Fastest time (1800m): Oregon's Day (2018) 1:46.83
Notable winners: It's Somewhat (2017); Streama (2014); Metal Bender (2010); Scenic Shot (2008); Shogun Lodge (2001, 2000); Might And Power (1998); Danewin (1995); Durbridge (1994); Rough Habit (1992, 1991).
Hollindale Cup and the Melbourne/Sydney autumn features:
Australian Cup: 1—Durbridge (1994).
Ranvet Stakes: Nil
The BMW: 1—Might And Power (1998).
Doncaster Handicap: 1—It's Somewhat (2017).
Queen Elizabeth Stakes: 4—My Kingdom Of Fife (2011); Might And Power (1998); Durbridge (1994); Rough Habit (1992).
Hollindale Stakes winners went on to win in the same preparation:
Doomben Cup: 10—Streama (2014); Metal Bender (2010); Above Deck (2006); Bush Padre (2003); Mr. Bureaucrat (2002); Might And Power (1998); Danewin (1995); Durbridge (1994); Rough Habit (1992, 1991). Note: Rough Habit also won the Doomben Cup in 1993 (after finishing second in the Hollindale). Eye Of The Sky won the Hollindale in 1989, and the Doomben Cup in 1990.
Eagle Farm Cup (O'Shea Stakes): 1 – Scenic Shot (2008). Note: Rough Habit won the Hollindale in 1991 & 1992, and the Eagle Farm Cup in 1995.
Brisbane Cup: None.
Queensland Derby: None. Note: No 3YO has won the double, but Super Slew (1996) finished second to Valance in the Qld Derby. Summer Beau (1997) finished third to Yippyio in the Qld Derby. Rough Habit (1991 & 1992) is the only horse to win both races. He won the Qld Derby in 1990.
Hollindale Stakes and Cox Plate:
1—Might And Power (1998).
Leading winning jockey: 4 wins Jim Cassidy (This Manhood 2004, Rough Habit 1992, 1991, Hunter 1990).
Current winning jockeys: 2 wins Jim Byrne (Oregon's Day 2018, Leebaz 2015); Larry Cassidy (Super Slew 1996, Corndale 1993).
1 win Tye Angland (It's Somewhat 2017); Glen Boss (Shogun Lodge 2001); Opie Bosson (Shez Sinsational 2012); Joe Bowditch (Fulmonti 2009); Hugh Bowman (Metal Bender 2010); Michael Cahill (Leebaz 2016); Vinnie Colgan (Melora 1999); Glen Colless (Scenic Shot 2008); Luke Nolen (Lights Of Heaven 2013); Nash Rawiller (My Kingdom Of Fife 2011); Michael Rodd (Bush Padre 2003); Blake Shinn (Streama 2014); Mark Zahra (Above Deck 2006).

Leading winning trainers: 3 wins John Hawkes (Leebaz 2016, 2015, Coalesce 2007); Bob Thomsen (Shogun Lodge 2001, 2000, Danewin 1995).
Current winning trainers: 3 wins John Hawkes (Leebaz 2016, 2015, Coalesce 2007).
2 wins Lee Freedman (Bush Padre 2003, Durbridge 1994); Chris Waller (My Kingdom Of Fife 2011, Metal Bender 2010); John Wheeler (Rough Habit 1992, 1991).
1 win Jim Conlan (Above Deck 2006); Clarry Conners (Super Slew 1996); Warwick Hailes (Mr. Burearcrat 2002); Michael, Wayne, John Hawkes (Leebaz 2016, 2015); Roger James (Melora 1999); Chris Jordan (Fulmonti 2009); Tim Martin (This Manshood 2004); Daniel Morton (Scenic Shot 2008); John O'Shea (It's Somewhat 2017); Mick Price (Oregon's Day 2018); Allan Sharrock (Shez Sinsational 2012); Gai Waterhouse (Platinum Scissors 2005).
Point of interest: In the one year Might And Power (1998) dominated at middle-distance weight-for-age. He won the The BMW, AJC Queen Elizabeth Stakes, Hollindale Stakes, Doomben Cup, Yalumba Stakes, Cox Plate and VRC Queen Elizabeth Stakes. (He was beaten by Gold Guru in the Ranvet Stakes).

SAJC Euclase Stakes (1200m)—Morphettville
$250,000 Group 2 3YO Open SW. May 4, 2019.

YEAR	WINNER	JOCKEY	TRAINER	2ND	3RD	TIME
2018	I'll Have A Bit	Chris Parnham	John McArdle	She's So High	Viridine	1:09.1
2017	Sweet Sherry	Noel Callow	Brent Stanley	Fuhryk	So You Too	1:09.9
2016	Faatinah	Matt Neilson	David Hayes & Tom Dabernig	Sooboog	Demonstrate	1:09.8
2015	Nicoscene	Mark Zahra	Lee & Anthony Freedman	Tudor	We've Got This	1:10.6
2014	Miracles Of Life	Dean Yendall	Daniel Clarken	Jazz Song	Classy Jack	1:11.0
2013	Lonhspresso	Ben Melham	Darren Weir	Essay Raider	Shamal Wind	1:10.4
2012	Go The Knuckle	Shayne Cahill	Mark Minervini	Satin Shoes	Snitzem	1:10.2
2011	Shrapnel	Michael Rodd	Mark Kavanagh	Happy Trails	General Truce	1:08.8
2010	Majestic Music	Clare Lindop	Leon Macdonald	Sister Madly	Happy Hippy	1:10.9
2009	Champagne Harmony	Steven King	Mark Kavanagh	Cerberus Gal	Very Discreet	1:09.1
2008	Diplomatic Force	Jason Benbow	Wayne Nichols	Vivacious Spirit	Royal Asscher	1:08.7
2007	Universal Queen	Corey Brown	Lee Freedman	Pencelaron	Nediyms Glow	1:08.2
2006	Magically	Steven King	Mick Price	Amyjaye Power	Swish Trish	1:09.7
2005	Honalee	Matt Neilson	Mark Kavanagh	Stormy Nova	Cocinero	1:08.7
2004	Danabaa	Danny Nikolic	Mark Kavanagh	Shablec	Ellicorsam	1:08.4
2003	Toast Of The Coast	Kerrin McEvoy	Tony Vasil	Super Groove	Prosperous Bid	1:10.0
2002	Troubles	Brian Park	Robert Smerdon	The Big Chill	Zip Zip Aray	1:10.2
2001	Ateates	Paul Harvey	Russell Cameron	Miss Power Bird	Romilada	1:09.4

BACKGROUND
First run: 1981 (won by Apollo's Flame). Listed 1981-85; Group 3 1986-90. Group 2 since 1991. Previously known as the Great Western Plate, Carrington Blush Plate, Angas Brut Classic, Yallambee Classic, Sportingbet Stakes, Ubet Stakes, William Hill Stakes. Registered as the Euclase Stakes.
Most recent filly to win: I'll Have A Bit (2018). Note: 10 fillies have won, all since 1999.
Fastest time (1200m): Universal Queen (2007) 1:08.29
Notable winners: Miracles Of Life (2014); Universal Queen (2007); Never Undercharge (1993); Euclase (1991); Rechabite (1990); Vitalic (1989).
Euclase Stakes winners also won in the same preparation:
Robert Sangster Stakes: 1—Universal Queen (2007): Note now run on the same day.
Goodwood Hcp: None.
RA Lee Stakes: 1—Majestic Music (2010).
McKay Stakes: 1—Euclase (1991). Note: Now run on the same day in May.
Leading winning jockeys: 2 wins Steven King (Champagne Harmony 2009, Magically 2006); Matthew Neilson (Faatinah 2016, Honalee 2005).
Current winning jockeys: 2 wins Matthew Neilson (Faatinah 2016, Honalee 2005).
1 win Jason Benbow (Diplomatic Force 2008); Corey Brown (Universal Queen 2007); Shayne Cahill (Go The Knuckle 2012); Noel Callow (Sweet Sherry 2017); Paul Harvey (Ateates 2001); Clare Lindop (Majestic Music 2010); Kerrin McEvoy (Toast Of The Coast 2003); Ben Melham (Lonhspresso 2013); Damien Oliver (Blazing Reality 1997); Chris Parnham (I'll Have A Bit 2018); Nash Rawiller (Show No Motion 1998); Michael Rodd (Shrapnel 2011); Dean Yendall (Miracles Of Life 2014); Mark Zahra (Nicoscene 2015).
Leading winning trainers: 4 wins Mark Kavanagh (Shrapnel 2011, Champagne Harmon 2009, Honalee 2005, Danabaa 2004).
3 wins Lee Freedman (Nicoscene 2015, Universal Queen 2007, Honour The Name 2000).

Current winning trainers: 4 wins Mark Kavanagh (Shrapnel 2011, Champagne Harmon 2009, Honalee 2005, Danabaa 2004).
3 wins Lee Freedman (Nicoscene 2015, Universal Queen 2007, Honour The Name 2000).
2 wins Robert Smerdon (Troubles 2002, Close Your Eyes 1999); Tony Vasil (Toast Of The Coast 2003, Elegancy 1994).
1 win Daniel Clarken (Miracles Of Life 2014); Lee and Anthony Freedman (Nicoscene 2015); David Hayes & Tom Dabernig (Faatinah 2016); John Hawkes (Mighty Manitou 1983); Leon Macdonald (Majestic Music 2010); John McArdle (I'll Have A Bit 2018); Mark Minervini (Go The Knuckle 2012); Tony Noonan (Show No Emotion 1998); Chris Parry (Northern Copy 1987); Gary Portelli (Ateates 2001); Mick Price (Magically 2006); Graeme Rogerson (Masked Party 1996); Brent Stanley (Sweet Sherry 2017); Darren Weir (Lonhspresso 2013).
Point of interest: Three horses have won the Euclase Stakes and also backed up by winning the Goodwood as a 4YO—Sword (11996, 1995); Euclase (1991 & 1992); Mighty Avenger (1984 & 1985).
I'll Have A Bit (2018) won at SP of $151.00.

SAJC Queen Of The South Stakes (1600m)—Morphettville
$175,000 Group 2 3YO&Up Fillies & Mares SWP. May 4, 2019.

YEAR	WINNER	JOCKEY	TRAINER	2ND	3RD	TIME
2018	French Emotion	Ben Melham	Chris Waller	Tahanee	Shenandoah	1:36.4
2017	Amelie's Star	Damian Lane	Darren Weir	Have Another Glass	Miles Of Krishnan	1:36.1
2016	Into The Mist	Jason Holder	Tony McEvoy	Atlantis Dream	Rocket Commander	1:36.3
2015	Atlantis Dream	Nicholas Hall	Darren Weir	Let's Make Adeal	Marianne	1:36.7
2014	Tango's Daughter	Dean Yendall	Mick Price	Floria	Vivi Veloce	1:39.0
2013	Star Of Giselle	Brad Rawiller	Mathew Ellerton & Simon Zahra	Danish Spy	Lake Sententia	1:39.5
2012	So Pristine	Luke Nolen	Peter Moody	Little House	Blue Ribbon	1:39.1
2011	Goon Serpent	Nicholas Hall	David Jolly	Lady Lynette	Ocean Challenger	1:36.4
2010	Returntosender	Mark Zahra	Peter Moody	Marchelle Belle	Amberino	1:36.8
2009	Bird Of Fire	Daniel Moor	Tony Vasil	Amberino	Autumn Jeuney	1:37.3
2008	Trick Of Light	Steven King	Michael Kent	Bellini Rose	Cuban Girl	1:36.0
2007	Cinque Cento	Steven Arnold	Peter Moody	Isanami	Subsequential	1:35.7
2006	Open Cut	Darren Beadman	Leon Macdonald	Holy Bounty	Lotto Rock	1:36.8
2005	Hidden Strings	Danny Nikolic	Ken Keys	Llanga	Fairessa	1:35.1
2004	Jameela	Steven King	Tony McEvoy	Infinite Grace	Ruling Eyes	1:35.8
2003	Sylvaner	Nash Rawiller	Barry James	Devonshire	Tickle My	1:38.3
2002	Sylvaner	Brett Prebble	Barry James	Tyrolean	Its Platonic	1:37.7
2001	Lady Marion	Stephen Baster	Dean Lawson	Calm Smytzer	Bumbelina	1:36.5

BACKGROUND
First run: 1980 (won by Golden Kingdom). Listed 1980-84; Group 3 1985-86; Group 2 from 1987. Previously known as the Coolmore Classic, Sedgwick Stakes and Marsh Classic. Run over 1500m in 1980 & 1981.
Most recent 3YO filly to win: Tango's Daughter (2014). Note: 12 3YO fillies have won.
Fastest time (1600m): Shavano Miss (1991) 1:34:50.
Multiple winners: 3—Sylvaner (2003, 2002); Shavano Miss (1993, 1992); Memphis Blues (1990, 1989).
Notable winners: Spectrum (1998); Miss Tessla (1997); Our Marquis (1995); Shavano Miss (1991 & 1992); Canny Lass (1986); Casey Belle (1984); Rose Of Kingston (1982).
Queen Of The South winners also won the lead-up races:
Mannerism Stakes: 2—Star Of Giselle (2013); Memphis Blues (1990).
Nischke Stakes: 2—Tango's Daughter (2014); Shavano Miss (1991).
MVRC Sunline Stakes: None. Note: Sylvaner won the Sunline Stakes (2004) after winning the Queen Of The South (2002 & 2003).
Queen Of The South winners went on to win in the same preparation:
Goodwood Hcp: 1—Spectrum (1998).
Doomben Cup: 1—Cinque Cento (2007).
Leading winning jockey: 3 wins Steven King (Trick Of Light 2008, Jameela 2004, Miss Tessla 1997).
Current winning jockeys: 2 wins Matt Gatt (La Zoffany 2000, Noircir 1999); Nicholas Hall (Atlantis Dream 2015, Goon Serpent 2011).
1 win Steven Arnold (Cinque Cento 2007); Stephen Baster (Lady Marion 2001); Jason Holder (Into The Mist 2016); Damian Lane (Amelie's Star 2017); Ben Melham (French Emotion 2018); Daniel Moor (Birds On Fire 2009); Luke Nolen (So Pristine 2012); Brett Prebble (Sylvaner 2002); Brad Rawiller (Star Of Giselle 2013);

Nash Rawiller (Sylvaner 2003); Dean Yendall (Tango's Daughter 2014); Mark Zahra (Returntosender 2010).
Leading winning trainer: 5 wins Colin Hayes (Memphis Blues 1990, 1989, Star Style Girl 1985, Casey Belle 1984, Corona Miss 1983).
Current winning trainers: 2 wins Russell Cameron (Shavano Miss 1992, 1991); Barry James (Sylvaner 2003, 2002); Tony McEvoy (Into The Mist 2016, Jameela 2004); Darren Weir (Amelie's Star 2017, Atlantis Dream 2015).
1 win Jim Conlan (La Zoffany 2000); Mathew Ellerton & Simon Zahra (Star Of Giselle 2013); Lee Freedman (Miss Tessla 1997); John Hawkes (Ausmart 1994); Pat Hyland (Saleous 1996); David Jolly (Goon Serpent 2011); Michael Kent (Trick Of Light 2008); Ken Keys (Hidden Strings 2005); Laurie Laxon (Our Marquise 1995); Leon Macdonald (Open Cut 2006); Mick Price (Tango's Daughter 2014); John Sadler (Goboet 1987); Tony Vasil (Bird Of Fire 2009); Chris Waller (French Emotion 2018).
Points of interest: No filly has won the Angus Armanasco Stakes (Caulfield) and the Moonee Valley Fillies Classic (Moonee Valley) and a Queen of The South Stakes.
No Queen Of The South winner has also won a Centaurea Stakes or a Laelia Stakes in the same season. Sylvaner (2003, 2002) won the Laelia Stakes in 2001.

BRC Champagne Classic (1200m)—Doomben
$175,000 Group 2 2YO Open SW. May 11, 2019.

YEAR	WINNER	JOCKEY	TRAINER	2ND	3RD	TIME
2018	Zousain	Kerrin McEvoy	Chris Waller	Mishani Hustler	Blue Book	1:10.8
2017	Tangled	Kerrin McEvoy	Chris Waller	All Too Huiying	Italia Bella	1:11.8
2016	Winning Rupert	Jeff Lloyd	Bjorn Baker	Attention	Souchez	1:09.5
2015	Blueberry Hill	Larry Cassidy	Liam Birchley	Wicked Intent	Pepperano	1:09.9
2014	Brazen Beau	Nash Rawiller	Chris Waller	Looks Like The Cat	Shaumari	1:09.7
2013	Vo Heart	Eddie Wilkinson	Darryl Hansen	Vilanova	Global Dream	1:12.1
2012	Sizzling	Chris Munce	Kelso Wood	Academus	Dances On Stars	1:09.9
2011	Free Wheeling	Hugh Bowman	Peter Snowden	Dr Ichi	Hot Snitzel	1:10.5
2010	Pressday	Nash Rawiller	Chris Waller	Spirit Of Boom	Buffering	1:09.9
2009	Funtantes	Larry Cassidy	Robert Heathcote	Trim	Impulsive Dream	1:09.7
2008	Court	Jim Byrne	Clarry Conners	Captain Fantastic	Cat D'Antibes	1:10.8
2007	Keiki	Damien Oliver	Gai Waterhouse	Key Bar Nights	Diamond Deck	1:10.2
2006	Gold Edition	Glen Lynch	Ron Maund	Ghetto Blaster	Silent Power	1:09.3
2005	Virage de Fortune	Jim Byrne	Bruce Mclachlan	Kincharm	Well Noted	1:10.3
2004	Golden Fox	Scott Seamer	Trevor Whittington	Star Shiraz	Our Sweet Dreams	1:10.3
2003	Shamekha	Jim Cassidy	Gai Waterhouse	In Top Swing	Sir Success	1:10.8
2002	Lovely Jubly	David Thosby	Brett Prebble	Yell	Verstak	1:10.5
2001	Dolce Veloce	Larry Cassidy	Clarry Conners	Dutch Harry	Jar Jar Binks	1:09.8

BACKGROUND
First run: 1982 (won by Peand). Listed 1982-86. Not held in 1988. Group 3 from 1987-2006.
Also known as the Moet And Chandon Classic; Coca Cola Bottlers' Classic and the Coca Cola Classic.
Most recent filly to win: Blueberry Hill (2015).
Fastest time (1200m): Gold Edition (2006) 1:09.36.
Notable winners: Brazen Beau (2014); Sizzling (2012); Pressday (2010); Gold Edition (2006); Virage de Fortune (2005); Shamekha (2003); Lovely Jubly (2002); Flavour (1996); Chief De Beers (1994)—all winners at Group 1 level.
Champagne Classic winners also won:
Magic Millions 2YO Classic: 2—Lovely Jubly (2002); Bold Promise (1991).
Champagne Classic winners went on to win in the same preparation:
BRC Sires' Produce Stakes: 4—Sizzling (2012); Pressday (2010); Virage de Fortune (2005); Lovely Jubly (2002).
JJ Atkins Stakes (TJ Smith Classic): 3—Sizzling (2012); Pressday (2010); Lovely Jubly (2002).
Leading winning jockeys: 4 wins Larry Cassidy (Blueberry Hill 2015, Funtantes 2009, Dolce Veloce 2001, Flavour 1996);
3 wins Gavan Duffy (Chief De Beers 1994, Swifty Roman 1985, Peand 1982).
Current winning jockeys: 4 wins Larry Cassidy (Blueberry Hill 2015, Funtantes 2009, Dolce Veloce 2001, Flavour 1996).
2 wins Jim Byrne (Court 2008, Virage De Fortune 2005); Kerrin McEvoy (Zousain 2018, Tangled 2017); Nash Rawiller (Brazen Beau 2014, Pressday 2010).
1 win Hugh Bowman (Free Wheeling 2011); Michael Cahill (Alpine Express 1999); Glen Colless (Electrifying 1998); Jeff Lloyd (2016); Glen Lynch (Gold Edition 2006); Damien Oliver (Keiki 2007); Brett Prebble (Lovely Jubly 2002); Eddie Wilkinson (Vo Heart 2013).

Leading winning trainer: 5 wins Clarry Conners (Court 2008, Alpine Express 1999, Electrifying 1998, Staging 1997, Ginzano).
Current winning trainers: 5 wins Clarry Conners (Court 2008, Alpine Express 1999, Electrifying 1998, Staging 1997, Ginzano).
4 wins Chris Waller (Zousain 2018, Tangled 2017, Brazen Beau 2014, Pressday 2010).
2 wins Rob Heathcote (Funtantes 2009, Chenar 2000); Gai Waterhouse (Keiki 2007, Shamekha 2003); Kelso Wood (Sizzling 2012, Swiftly Roman 1985).
1 win Bjorn Baker (Winning Rupert 2016); Liam Birchley (Blueberry Hill 2015); Darryl Hansen (Vo Heart 2013); John Hawkes (Flavour 1996); Peter Snowden (Free Wheeling 2011); Trevor Whittington (Golden Fox 2004).
Point of interest: 15 fillies have won the Champagne Classic.

BRC The Roses (2000m)—Doomben
$175,000n Group 2 3YO Fillies SW. May 19, 2019.

YEAR	WINNER	JOCKEY	TRAINER	2ND	3RD	TIME
2018	Youngstar	Kerrin McEvoy	Chris Waller	Another Dollar	Highway	2:04.7
2017	Kenedna	John Allen	Darren Weir	Oklahoma Girl	Perilous Love	2:08.0
2016	Kebede	Jim Byrne	Matthew Dunn	Sebring Sally	Imposing Lass	2:02.5
2015	Bohemian Lily	Blake Shinn	Gai Waterhouse	Col 'n' Lil	Whatalovelyday	2:04.0
2014	Arabian Gold	Blake Shinn	David Vandyke	Tinto	Tornado Miss	2:03.0
2013	Dear Demi	Luke Nolen	Clarry Conners	Gondokoro	Vaquera	2:05.3
2012	Invest	Peter Mertens	Clarry Conners	Miss Artistic	Scorpio Queen	2:04.1
2011	Scarlett Lady	James McDonald	Graeme & Debbie Rogerson	Savannah's Choice	Divorces	2:04.0
2010	Marheta	Mark Zahra	Michael Moroney	Femina Fashion	Dariana	2:03.5
2009	Awesome Planet	Jim Cassidy	Graeme Rogerson	Ekstreme	Purple	2:04.3
2008	Heavenly Glow	Robert Thompson	Allan Denham	Pentacity	Miss Maren	2:05.5
2007	Lasoron	Darren Beadman	Bryan Guy	My Ladys Chamber	Eskimo Queen	2:03.0
2006	Gaze	Darren Beadman	Roger James	Upstaged	Zenarta	2:03.5
2005	Cinque Cento	Justin Sheehan	Tony Wildman	Ponte Piccolo	Fiery Sunset	2:04.0
2004	Natural Woman	Greg Childs	Bruce Mclachlan	Charmview	Imana	2:04.3
2003	The Jewel	Greg Childs	Hec Anderton	Crianca	Domielle	2:04.9
2002	Palidamah	Jason Taylor	Noel Doyle	Faiza	Quays	2:01.9
2001	Ethereal	Scott Seamer	Sheila Laxon	Life Is Beautiful	Dandify	2:04.3

BACKGROUND
First run: 1996 (won by Ballare). Listed race 2000-02. Group 3 2003-2013. Run as 1615m quality handicap 1996-98. Run over 2020m from 1999 (won by Episode) to 2012. 2000m from 2013. Formerly known as the Doomben Roses.
Fastest time (2000m): Kebede (2016) 2:02.55
Notable winners: Youngstar (2018); Dear Demi (2013); Heavenly Glow (2008); Episode (1999); Ethereal (2001); The Jewel (2003); Cinque Cento (2005); Gaze (2006).
The Roses and the Sydney autumn 3YO fillies features:
Adrian Knox Stakes: 1—Arabian Gold (2014).
Storm Queen Stakes: 1—Heavenly Glow (2008).
AJC Australian Oaks 1—Heavenly Glow (2008).
The Roses winners won the lead-up races:
Australasian Oaks: 2—Invest (2011); Episode (1999).
South Australian Oaks: 1—Episode (1999).
Gold Coast Bracelet: 1—Bohemian Lily (2015).
Manawatu Breeders' Stakes: 2—Scarlett Lady (2011); Awesome Planet (2009).
Doomben Roses winners went on to win in the same preparation:
Queensland Oaks: 3—Youngstar (2018); Scarlett Lady (2011); Ethereal (2001).
Leading winning jockeys: 2 wins Darren Beadman (Lasoron 2007, Gaze 2006); Greg Childs (Natural Woman 004, The Jewel 2003); Blake Shinn (Bohemian Lily 2015, Arabian Gold 2014).
Current winning jockeys: 2 wins Blake Shinn (Bohemian Lily 2015, Arabian Gold 2014).
1 win John Allen (Kenedna 2017); Jim Byrne (Kebede 2016); Michael Cahill (Avilde 2000); Vinnie Coglan (Melora 1998); James McDonald (Scarlett Lady 2011); Kerrin McEvoy (Youngstar 2018); Luke Nolen (Dear Demi 2013); Damien Oliver (Episode 1999); Jason Taylor (Palidamah 2002); Robert Thompson (Heavenly Glow 2008); Mark Zahra (Marheta 2010).

Leading winning trainers: 2 wins Clarry Conners (Dear Demi 2013, Invest 2012); Roger James (Gaze 2006, Melora 1998); Graeme Rogerson (Scarlett Lady 2011, Awesome Planet 2009); Gai Waterhouse (Bohemian Lily 2015; Ballare 1996).
Current winning trainers: 2 wins Clarry Conners (Dear Demi 2013, Invest 2012); Roger James (Gaze 2006, Melora 1998); Graeme Rogerson (Scarlett Lady 2011, Awesome Planet 2009); Gai Waterhouse (Bohemian Lily 2015; Ballare 1996).
1 win Hec Anderton (The Jewel 2003); Allan Denham (Heavenly Glow 2008); Noel Doyle (Palidamah 2002); Matt Dunn (Kebede 2016); David Hall (Episode 1999); John Hawkes (Avilde 2000); Bryan Guy (Lasoron 2007); Sheila Laxon (Ethereal 2001); Graeme & Debbie Rogerson (Scarlett Lady 2011); David Vandyke (Arabian Gold 2014); Chris Waller (Youngstar 2018); Darren Weir (Kenedna 2017).
Points of interest: Dear Demi (2013) won the 2012 G1 VRC Oaks.
Ethereal (2001) went on the in the same year as a 4YO to win the Caulfield Cup and Melbourne Cup double.
Cinque Cento (2005) and Gaze (2006) went on to quinella the 2007 Doomben Cup.
The Jewel (2003) ran second to Zagalia in the Queensland Oaks. Episode (1999) ran second to Miss Danehill in the Queensland Oaks.
The Jewel (2003) had previously finished 2nd to Bramble Rose in the NZ Oaks (2400m) at Trentham.

BRC Sires' Produce (1400m)—Eagle Farm
$250,000 Group 2 2YO Open SW. May 26, 2019.

YEAR	WINNER	JOCKEY	TRAINER	2ND	3RD	TIME
2018	Lean Mean Machine	Corey Brown	Chris Waller	Zousain	Boomsara	1:19.9
2017	Melody Belle	Opie Bosson	Stephen Autridge & Jamie Richards	Taking Aim	Pierata	1:25.6
2016	Attention	Blake Shinn	Peter & Paul Snowden	Dreams Aplenty	Nikitas	1:19.0
2015	Look To The Stars	Luke Tarrant	Clarry Conners	Blueberry Hill	Cylinder Beach	1:19.5
2014	Time For War	Tye Angland	Gerald Ryan	Brazen Beau	Looks Like The Cat	1:18.7
2013	Zoustar	Jim Cassidy	Chris Waller	Vilanova	Bound For Earth	1:20.5
2012	Sizzling	Chris Munce	Kelso Wood	Academus	Dances On Stars	1:26.3
2011	Hot Snitzel	Hugh Bowman	Gerald Ryan	Playtime	Mahisara	1:23.3
2010	Pressday	Jim Cassidy	Chris Waller	Jesse's Girl	Levi's Choice	1:23.4
2009	Shoot Out	Dan Griffin	John Wallace	Impulsive Dream	Carrara	1:25.9
2008	Fravashi	Corey Brown	Peter Snowden	Rockdale	Cat D Antibes	1:26.2
2007	Masked Assassin	Luke Nolen	Peter Moody	Diamond Deck	Kyros	1:24.6
2006	Danleigh	Michael Rodd	Bob Thomsen	Gold Edition	Upper Echelon	1:23.4
2005	Virage De Fortune	Greg Childs	Bruce Mclachlan	Upilio	Testafiable	1:21.5
2004	Star Shiraz	Glen Boss	Rex Lipp	Midnight City	Rule Of Engagement	1:22.3
2003	Ambulance	Scott Galloway	John Hawkes	Sir Dex	Bushland	1:23.6
2002	Lovely Jubly	Brett Prebble	David Throsby	Sir Breakfast	Saddlers Silk	1:21.4
2001	Juanmo	Glen Colless	Alan Bailey	Counter Agent	Jar Jar Binks	1:21.9

BACKGROUND
First run: 1916 (won by Lord Vindex). Group 2 1980-86; from 2006. Group 1 1987-2005. Not held 1942-45 & 1988. Abandoned due to weather in 1999. Run at Doomben 2012-16, 2018 (1350m).
Most recent filly to win: Melody Belle (2017). Note: 20 fillies have won.
Fastest time (Eagle Farm 1400m): Lovely Jubly (2001) 1:21.40
Notable winners: Melody Belle (2017); Zoustar (2013); Sizzling (2012); Hot Snitzel (2011); Pressday (2010); Shoot Out (2009); Danleigh (2006); Mahogany (1993); Slight Chance (1992); Red Anchor (1984); Luskin Star (1977); Fine And Dandy (1959); Tulloch (1957); Prince Morvi (1953); Spear Chief (1937); Lough Neagh (1931); High Syce (1927).
BRC Sires' Produce Stakes winners also won as 2YOs:
Magic Millions 2YO Classic: 1—Lovely Jubly (2002).
Golden Slipper: 2—Luskin Star (1977); Fine And Dandy (1959).
ATC Sires' Produce Stakes: 6—Zephyr Zip (1979); Karaman (1978); Luskin Star (1977); Fine And Dancy (1959); Man Of Iron (1958); Tulloch (1957).
ATC Champagne Stakes: 5—Dracula (1998); True Version (1985); Red Anchor (1984); Luskin Star (1977); Rajah (1968).
Manawatu Sires' Produce Stakes (Awapuni NZ): 1—Melody Belle (2017).
BRC Sires' Produce Stakes winners won the lead-up races:
ATC Baillieu Handicap: 1—Attention (2016).
Gold Coast Ken Russell Memorial: 2—Sizzling (2012); Hot Snitzel (2011).

Champagne Classic: 4—Sizzling (2012); Pressday (2010); Virage de Fortune (2005); Lovely Jubly (2002).
BRC Sires' Produce Stakes winners went on to win in the same preparation:
JJ Atkins Stakes (TJ Smith Classic): 11—Sizzling (2012); Lovely Jubly (2002); Juanmo (2001); Anthems (1996); Mahogany (1993); Slight Chance (1992); Flotilla (1987); Royal Paree (1980); Zephyr Zip (1979); Luskin Star (1977); Romantic Dream (1976).
Champagne Classic & JJ Atkins: 2—Sizzling (2012); Lovely Jubly (2002).
Leading winning jockeys: 4 wins George Moore (Rajah 1968, Todwana 1964, Man Of Iron 1958, Tulloch 1957).
3 wins Colin O'Neill (Mr Consistency 1970, Heroic Isle 1969, Joliffe 1962); Jack Thompson (Fine And Dandy 1959, Duchesne 1956, Malarno 1955); Edward Tucker (Soft Step 1933, Wee Glen 1925, Ardglen 1923).
Current winning jockeys: 2 wins Corey Brown (Lean Mean Machine 2018, Fravashi 2008); Grant Cooksley (Shame 1995, Aragen 1994).
1 win Tye Angland (Time For War 2014); Glen Boss (Star Shiraz 2004); Opie Bosson (Melody Belle 2017); Hugh Bowman (Hot Snitzel 2011); Larry Cassidy (Dracula 1998); Glen Colless (Juanmo 2001); Scott Galloway (Ambulance 2003); Daniel Griffin (Shoot Out 2009); Brett Prebble (Lovely Jubly 2002); Luke Nolen (Masked Assassin 2007); Michael Rodd (Danleigh 2006); Blake Shinn (Attention 2016); Luke Tarrant (Look To The Stars 2015); Robert Thompson (Romantic Dream 1976).
Leading winning trainers: 5 wins Eric Kirwan (Star Of The Knight 1982, Zephyr Zip 1979, Heroic Isle 1969, Prince Gauntlet 1967, Kiwanis 1963); Tommy Smith (Zahedi 1973, Merry Minstrel 1972, Rajah 1968, Tulloch 1957, Sea Sovereign 1952).
4 wins George Benn (Todwana 1964, Refulgent 1960, Malarno 1955, Thurlow 1954); John Hawkes (Ambulance 2003, Dracula 1998, Anthems 1996, Shame 1995); Harry Plant (Fine And Dancy 1959, Man Of Iron 1958, Coniston 1950, Auto Buz 1935); Bill Tucker jnr (Real Step 1948, Seven Fifty 1938, Spear Chief 1937, Soft Step 1933).
Current winning trainers: 4 wins John Hawkes (Ambulance 2003, Dracula 1998, Anthems 1996, Shame 1995).
3 wins Chris Waller (Lean Mean Machine 2018, Zoustar 2013, Pressday 2010).
2 wins Gerald Ryan (Time For War 2014, Hot Snitzel 2011).
1 win Stephen Autridge & Jamie Richards (Melody Belle 2017); Clarry Conners (Look At The Stars 2015); Lee Freedman (Mahogany 1993); Rex Lipp (Star Shiraz 2004); Bruce Marsh (Mr Shannon 1986); Peter Snowden (Fravashi 2008); John Wallace (Shoot Out 2009); Kelso Wood (Sizzling 2012).
Points of interest: Mahogany (1993) and Red Anchor (1984) went on to win the Victoria Derby in the spring. Zoustar (2013) went on to win the 2013 Golden Rose and 2013 Coolmore Stud Stakes in the following spring. The Tucker family had a significant influence on Queensland racing. Bill "Old Bill" Tucker trained two winners of the Sires' Produce (Wee Glen 1925, Ardglen 1923); his son Bill "Young Bill" trained four winners (see leading winning trainers); another son Edward (Georgie) rode three winners (see leading winning jockeys); and another son A.E. "Macker" trained Royal Flavour to win the Sires' in 1928.

BRC PJ O'Shea Stakes (2200m)—Eagle Farm
$250,000 Group 2 3YO&Up WFA. June 1, 2019.

YEAR	WINNER	JOCKEY	TRAINER	2ND	3RD	TIME
2018	Egg Tart	Leith Innes	Chris Waller	Tradesman	Megablast	2:20.7
2017	Single Gaze	Kathy O'Hara	Nick Olive	Rudy	High Church	2:19.2
2016	Not run (abandoned)					
2015	Werther	Jim Byrne	Andrew Campbell	Moriarty	Epingle	2:17.2
2014	Moriarty	Nash Rawiller	Chris Waller	Mr O'Ceirin	Floria	2:16.3
2013	Quintessential	Damian Browne	John Sargent	Manighar	Voila Ici	2:19.5
2012	Lights Of Heaven	Luke Nolen	Peter Moody	Scenic Shot	Ginga Dude	2:19.0
2011	Glass Harmonium	Lisa Cropp	Michael Moroney	Shoot Out	Scenic Shot	2:15.1
2010	Triple Honour	Larry Cassidy	Chris Waller	Raffaello	Newport	2:14.3
2009	Scenic Shot	Shane Scriven	Daniel Morton	Mirkola Lass	Fulmonti	2:20.9
2008	Scenic Shot	Glen Colless	Daniel Morton	Rampant Lion	Dougs Mate	2:19.2
2007	Pentathon	Jason Taylor	John Wheeler	Gaze	Grand Zulu	2:17.9
2006	Mahtoum	Steven King	Kim Moore	Art Success	Gorgeous George	2:30.7
2005	Natural Blitz	Michael Cahill	Doug Harrison	Zumanity	Regal Punch	2:30.0
2004	Pentastic	Nash Rawiller	David Hall	Maze	Another Warrior	2:28.7
2003	Maguire	Chris Munce	John Collins	County Tyrone	Grey Song	2:30.5
2002	Hey Pronto	Brian York	Gai Waterhouse	Freemason	Prized Gem	2:28.1
2001	Yippyio	Darren Beadman	Allan Denham	Citi Habit	King Keitel	2:25.6

BACKGROUND

First run: 1947 (won by Sir John). Group 2 from 1980. Run over distances from 1600m to 2400m. 2200m 1969-83, from 2007. 2400m from 1984 to 2007. Not held 1942-45. Replaced the Queen's Plate and the Royal Stakes (from 1887-1946). Registered as the Eagle Farm Cup. Run as the Eagle Farm Cup 2010-15. Not run in 2016 (abandoned due to the state of the track); run at Doomben 2017; Sunshine Coast 2018.
Most recent mare to win: Egg Tart (2018).
Most recent 3YO to win: Werther (2015). No 3YO filly has won the O'Shea Stakes.
Multiple winners: 9—Roman Consul (1970, 1969); Striking Force (1967, 1966); Tulloch (1961, 1960); Redcraze (1957, 1956); Lough Neagh (1937, 1936); Fairy Bob (1922, 1921); Bandon Lad (1913, 1912); Cabin Boy (1899, 1898); Babel (1896, 1895).
Fastest time (2200m): Roman Consul (1970) 2:13:10.
Notable winners: Werther (2015); Glass Harmonium (2011); Triple Honour (2010); Scenic Shot (2009, 2008); Yippyio (2001); Intergaze (1998); The Phantom Chance (1996); Rough Habit (1995); Belmura Lad (1979); Balmerino (1976); Baghdad Note (1973); Tails (1972); Tulloch (1961, 1960); Sailor's Guide (1958); Redcraze (1957, 1956); Hydrogen (1953); Russia (1947); Lough Neagh (1937, 1936); Fitz Grafton (1905).
O'Shea Stakes and the Melbourne/Sydney autumn features:
Australian Cup: 1—Ngawyni (1977).
The BMW: 2—Tails (1972); Striking Force (1966).
O'Shea Stakes winners and the Brisbane winter carnival features:
Hollindale Stakes: 1—Scenic Shot (2008). Note: Rough Habit won the Hollindale in 1991-92, and the O'Shea in 1995.
Doomben Cup: 2—Scenic Shot (2009); Lord Hybrow (1988). Note: Scenic Shot (2009) and Lord Hybrow (1988) are the only horses to win the Doomben Cup, Eagle Farm Cup and Brisbane Cup in the same year.
Chairman's Handicap: 1—Quintessential (2013).
Brisbane Cup: 18—Lights Of Heaven (2012); Scenic Shot (2009); Yippyio (2000); Shuzohra (1990); Lord Hybrow (1988); Four Crowns (1981); Balmerino (1976); Fair Patten (1965); Tulloch (1961); Redcraze (1956); Hydrogen (1953); Good Idea (1946); Spear Chief (1939); Lough Neagh (1936); Venerable (1919); Bunting (1917); Plunder (1908); Fitz Grafton (1905).
O'Shea Stakes and the Melbourne spring:
Caulfield Cup: 1—Redcraze (O'Shea 1957 & 1956; Cup 1956).
Cox Plate: 4—The Phantom Chance (O'Shea 1996, Cox 1993); Tulloch (O'Shea 1961 & 1960, Cox 1960); Redcraze (O'Shea 1957 & 1956, Cox 1957); Hydrogen (O'Shea 1953, Cox 1953 & 1952).
Melbourne Cup: 2—Baghdad Note (O'Shea 1973, Cup 1970); Russia (O'Shea 1947, Cup 1946).
Note: Russia is the only horse to complete the double in the same season.
Leading winning jockeys: 4 wins George Moore (Bluelough 1971, Count Radiant 1964, Tulloch 1961, Persist 1950); Neville Sellwood (Tulloch 1960, Caesar 1959, Sailor's Guide, Hydrogen 1953).
Current winning jockeys: 2 wins Nash Rawiller (Moriarty 2014, Pentastic 2004).
1 win Damian Browne (Quintessential 2013); Jim Byrne (Werther 2015); Michael Cahill (Natural Blitz 2005); Larry Cassidy (Triple Honour 2010); Glen Colless (Scenic Shot 2008); Leith Innes (Egg Tart 2018); Luke Nolen (Lights Of Heaven 2012); Kathy O'Hara (Single Gaze 2017); Justin P Stanley (Ken's Joy 2000); Jason Taylor (Pentathon 2007).
Leading winning trainer: 15 wins Tommy Smith (Iko 1980, Tod Bay 1978, Passetreul 1974, Bluelough 1971, Roman Consul 1970, 1969, Fair Patton 1965, Count Radiant 1964, Oakland 1963, Tulloch 1961, 1960, Caesar 1959, Redcraze 1957, 1956, Persist 1950).
Current winning trainers: 3 wins Chris Waller (Egg Tart 2018, Moriarty 2014, Triple Honour 2010); John Wheeler (Pentathon 2007, The Phantom Chance 1996, Rough Habit 1995).
2 wins Daniel Morton (Scenic Shot 2009, 2008).
1 win Andrew Campbell (Werther 2015); Rod Craig (Intergaze 1998); Steve Gulliver (Pakaraka Star 1997); David Hall (Pentastic 2004); Doug Harrison (Natural Blitz 2005); John Hawkes (Spring Thaw 1991*); David Hayes (Dark Ksar 1993); Ron Leemon (Godarchi 1984); Bruce Marsh (Shamrock 1982); Nick Olive (Single Gaze 2017); Helen Page (Magnolia Hall 1991*); John Sargent (Quintessential 2013); Michael Moroney (Glass Harmonium 2011); Gerald Ryan (Sharscay 1999); Brian Smith (Balmerino 1976); Kim Waugh (Mahtoum 2006); Gai Waterhouse (Hey Pronto 2002).
* dead heat
Point of interest: Magnolia Hall and Spring Thaw dead-heated for first in 1991.

BRC Moreton Cup (1300m)—Eagle Farm
$175,000 Group 2 Quality Handicap. June 1, 2019.

YEAR	WINNER	JOCKEY	TRAINER	2ND	3RD	TIME
2018	The Monstar	Skye Bogenhuber	Brett Cavanough	Platinum Angel	Calanda	1:12.5
2017	Deploy	Tim Clark	Gerald Ryan	Dothraki	Perfect Dare	1:09.1
2016	Spill The Beans	Tim Clark	Gerald Ryan	Federal	Stratum Star	1:17.8
2015	Ball Of Muscle	Glyn Schofield	Joseph Pride	That's A Good Idea	Kuro	1:08.4
2014	Sacred Star	Timothy Bell	Tony Pike	Masthead	Bennetta	1:17.1
2013	Galah	Kerrin McEvoy	Peter Snowden	Conservatorium	Griffon	1:17.6
2012	Celtic Dancer	Timothy Bell	Noel Doyle	Belltone	Joint Chiefs	1:20.9
2011	Varenna Miss	Dwayne Dunn	Tony Noonan	Phelan Ready	Zingaling	1:16.1
2010	Catapulted	Damien Oliver	Mark Kavanagh	Border Rebel	Ego's Dare	1:15.1
2009	Ortensia	Craig Williams	Tony Noonan	Maxison	Mr Baritone	1:19.1
2008	Chinchilla Rose	Stephen Baster	Steele Ryan	Black Ink	Easy Rocker	1:19.3
2007	Nova Star	Michael Rodd	Kelly Schweida	Rasmussen	Son Of Dane	1:17.6
2006	Messiaen	Jason Holder	Ray Mccali	Consular	Spuruson	1:16.5
2005	Sir Breakfast	Danny Nikolic	Liam Birchley	Beautiful Gem	All Bar One	1:08.7
2004	Falkirk	Scott Galloway	Paul O'sullivan	Patpong	Bomber Bill	1:08.8
2003	Into The Night	Scott Seamer	Keith Dryden	Bomber Bill	Polygram	1:10.6
2002	Pembleton	Brian York	John Morrisey	Maitland Gold	Machtig Mini Panis	1:09.2
2001	Century Kid	Len Beasley	Graeme Rogerson	Super Impressive	Federal Agent	1:08.1

BACKGROUND

First run: 1979 (won by Famoso Gris). Group 3 1979-83. Group 2 from 1984. Meetings abandoned on 1988 and 1999 due to rain. Previously known as the Katie's Cup, Westfield Cup, Ansett Cup, Qantas Cup & QTC Cup. Run over 1300m in 1996 and 2006. Not held in 1999. Run at Doomben (1200m) in 2017.
Most recent mare to win: Varenna Miss (2011). Note: Only three mares have won.
Most recent 3YO to win: C&G—Spill The Beans (2016); Filly—Ortensia (2009).
Multiple winners: None.
Fastest time (1300m): Hareeba (1996) 1:15:00.
Notable winners: Ortensia (2009); Hareeba (1996); Schillaci (1992); Rechabite (1990); Vitalic (1989); My Gold Hope (1982); Tulip Town (1981).
QTC Cup winners won the lead-up races:
Hawkesbury Guineas: 1—Spill The Beans (2016).
Gold Coast Prime Minister's Cup: 1—Celtic Dancer (2012).
Glenlogan Park Stakes: 1—Ortensia (2009).
Kingsford Smith (BTC) Cup: None.
Doomben 10,000: None. Note: My Axeman (1983) won the Doomben 10,000 before finishing second in the QTC Cup to Nosey Parker. Buck's Pride (1993), Barossa Boy (1991) and Daybreak Lover (1986) were runner-up in both races.
QTC Cup winners went on to win in the same preparation:
Stradbroke Handicap: None. Note: Daybreak Lover (1986) was runner-up in the QTC Cup before winning the Stradbroke Hcp. Mr. Magic (1982) and Gentle James (1979) finished second in both races.
Leading winning jockeys: 2 wins Tim Clark (Deploy 2017, Spill The Beans 2016); Damien Oliver (Catapulted 2010, Schillaci 1992); Graham Watson (Bellzevir 1994, Tolai 1987).
Current winning jockeys: 2 wins Tim Clark (Deploy 2017, Spill The Beans 2016); Damien Oliver (Catapulted 2010, Schillaci 1992).
1 win Stephen Baster (Chinchilla Rose 2008); Skye Bogenhuber (The Monstar 2018); Corey Brown (Celestial Choir 1997); Michael Cahill (Gallopini 2000); Dwayne Dunn (Varenna Miss 2011); Grant Cooksley (Overpitch 1993); Scott Galloway (Falkirk 2004); Jason Holder (Messiaen 2006); Kerrin McEvoy (Galah 2014); Michael Rodd (Nova Star 2007); Glyn Schofield (Ball Of Muscle 2015);l Craig Williams (Ortensia 2009).
Leading winning trainer: 2 wins Tony Noonan (Varenna Miss 2011, Ortensia 2009).
Current winning trainers: 2 wins Tony Noonan (Varenna Miss 2011, Ortensia 2009); Gerald Ryan (Deploy 2017, Spill The Beans 2016).
1 win Liam Birchley (Sir Breakfast 2005); Brett Cavanough (The Monstar 2018); Noel Doyle (Celtic Dancer 2012); Keith Dryden (Into The Night 2003); Lee Freedman (Schillaci 1992); David Hall (Gallopini 2000); John Hawkes (Overpitch 1993); Mark Kavanagh (Catapulted 2010); Ron McCall (Messiaen 2006); John Morrisey (Pembleton 2002); Paul O'Sullivan (Falkirk 2004); Helen Page (Celestial Choir 1997); Tony Pike (Sacred Star 2014); Joe Pride (Ball Of Muscle 2015); Graeme Rogerson (Century Kid 2001); Steele Ryan (Chinchilla Rose 2008); John Sadler (Scandinavia 1998); Kelly Schweida (Nova Star 2007); Peter Snowden (Galah 2014).
Points of interest: The highest winning weight is Hareeba (60kg) in 1996. Schillaci carried 59kg in 1992, while My Gold Hope, a mare, lumped 59kg to win in 1982.
In 2004, Patpong was first across the line, but lost on protest to Falkirk.

BRC Queensland Guineas (1600m)—Eagle Farm
$350,000 Group 2 3YO Open SW. June 8, 2019.

YEAR	WINNER	JOCKEY	TRAINER	2ND	3RD	TIME
2018	Sambro	Michael Walker	Chris Waller	Seaway	Magnufighter	1:38.0
2017	Salsonic	Hugh Bowman	Jason Coyle	Volpino	Niccanova	1:34.8
2016	Tsaritsa	Joao Moreira	Chris Waller	Denmagic	Sold For Song	1:36.9
2015	Jabali	Jim Byrne	Mick Price	Bachman	Merion	1:34.6
2014	Sir Moments	Timothy Bell	Steven O'dea	Liberty's Choice	Ryker	1:22.9
2013	Sizzling	Chris Munce	Kelso Wood	Dances On Stars	Lucky Hussler	1:24.2
2012	Pear Tart	Jeff Lloyd	John P Thompson	Free Wheeling	Stradon	1:26.1
2011	Torio's Quest	Hugh Bowman	Brett Partelle	Benny's Buttons	Spot The Rock	1:35.4
2010	Rothesay	Blake Shinn	Gerald Ryan	Launay	Fifteen Carat	1:33.7
2009	Express Air	Craig Williams	Rex Lipp	Marveen	La Etoile	1:39.8
2008	Turffontein	Danny Nikolic	Anthony Cummings	Royal Discretion	Pepperwood	1:40.4
2007	Sequential Charm	Stathi Katsidis	Rex Lipp	J Adane	Danleigh	1:35.5
2006	Nova Star	Michael Rodd	Kelly Schweida	Fashions Afield	Funlove	1:36.5
2005	Saxon	Scott Seamer	Gerald Ryan	Hit The Road	Special Times	1:35.9
2004	Winning Belle	Glen Boss	Gai Waterhouse	Toulouse Lautrec	Little Punc	1:40.3
2003	True Glo	Craig Newitt	Lee Freedman	Sportsman	King Of Them All	1:33.3
2002	Regent Street	Steven King	Gerald Ryan	Galroof	Deuxienne	1:35.6
2001	Heroism	Stathi Katsidis	Kaye Tinsley	Yoruba	Pimpala Player	1:34.3

BACKGROUND
First run: 1896 (won by College Cap). Run in October 1896-1983. Transferred to May in 1984.
Not run 1942-45 & 1983. Meeting abandoned in 1996 due to rain. Group 3 1979-87; Group 2 since 1988.
1400m 2012-2014. Run at Doomben in 2016-18.
Most recent filly to win: Tsaritsa (2016). Note: 19 fillies have won the Guineas.
Fastest time (1600m): True Glo (2003) 1:33.30.
Notable winners: Turffontein (2008); Yippyio (1997); Paris Lane (1994); Triscay (1991); Cole Diesel (1989); Planet Ruler (1988; Zephyr Zip (1979); Dalrello (1973); Charlton Boy (1971); Maybe Lad (1965); Spear Chief (1937); Lough Neagh (1931); High Syce (1927); Lord Acre (1916); Fitz Grafton (1903); Boreas (1898).
Queensland Guineas winners won the lead-up races:
BRC Classic: None.
Doomben Classic: 1—Saxon (2005).
Lord Mayor's Cup: 1—Rothesay (2010).
Queensland Guineas winners went on to win in the same preparation:
Queensland Derby: 21—Camarena (1999); Yippyio (1997); Confidence (1963); Booklink (1956); Blue Slipper (1948); Sefiona (1947); Spearace (1939); Spear Chief (1937); Lough Neagh (1931); Bernfield (1929); High Syce (1927); Ardglen (1923); Kingslot (1922); Lordacre (1916); Flaxen (1908); Euroa (1907); Alexis (1905); Joyance (1904); Fitz Grafton (1903); Balfour (1902); Boreas (1898).
Queensland Oaks: 1—Triscay (1991).
Grand Prix: Nil: Note: Make Mine Magic (2000), who finished third in the Guineas behind Magnifier, is the only Guineas placegetter to win the Grand Prix.
Stradbroke Handicap: 2—Fitz Grafton (1903); Boreas (1998): Note: Syceonelle (1920) won the Stradbroke as a 4YO in 1921. Some Cure (1932) ran second in the Stradbroke to Credence.
Tatts Tiara: 1—Peart Tart (2012).
Leading winning jockeys: 6 wins Graham Cook (Cloud Pink 1980, Zephyr Zip 1979, Spinneli 1974, Paola Pisani 1969, Lord Kearsey 1966, Countwood 1959); E. "Georgie" Tucker (Soft Step 1933, Irish Smile 1930, High Syce 1927, Ardglen 1923, Ladamond 1921, Delinacre 1914).
4 wins Russell Maddock (Aboukir 1955, Coniston 1950, Sefiona 1947, Maytown 1946); Colin O'Neill (Waminda 1970, Flying Ace 1968, Confidence 1963, Persian King 1962).
Current winning jockeys: 2 wins Glen Boss (Winning Belle 2004, Camarena 1999); Hugh Bowman (Salsonic 2017, Torio's Quest 2011).
1 win Jim Byrne (Jabali 2015); Scott Galloway (Magnifier 2000); Jeff Lloyd (Pear Tart 2012); Joao Moreira (Tsaritsa 2016); Craig Newitt (True Glo 2003); Michael Rodd (Nova Star 2006); Blake Shinn (Rothesay 2010); Michael Walker (Sambro 2018).
Leading winning trainers: 5 wins William Noud (High Syce 1927, Mountain Song 1924, Koatanui 1912, Flaxen 1908, Grattan 1901).
4 wins Fred Best (Spinnelli 1974, Flying Ace 1968, Persian King 1962, Book Link 1956); Watty Blacklock (Lordacre 1916, Balfour 1902, Araxes 1900, Boreas 1898); Bill Tucker Jnr (Bold Step 1940, Seven Fifty 1938, Spear Chief 1937, Soft Step 1933); Gerald Ryan (Rothesay 2010, Saxon 2005, Regent Street 2002; Magnifier 2000).
Current winning trainers: 4 wins Gerald Ryan (Rothesay 2010, Saxon 2005, Regent Street 2002; Magnifier 2000).

2 wins Lee Freedman (True Glo 2003, Paris Lane 1994); Chris Waller (Sambro 2018, Tsaritsa 2016).
1 win Jason Coyle (Salsonic 2017); Anthony Cummings (Turffontein 2008); Garry Frazer (Turridu 1995); Rex Lipp (Sequential Charm 2007); John Morrisey (Camarena 1999); Steve O'Dea (Sir Sir Moments 2014); Brett Partelle (Torio's Quest 2011); Mick Price (Jabali 2015); Kelly Schweida (Nova Star 2006); John Thompson (Pear Tart 2012); Kaye Tinsley (Heroism 2001); Gai Waterhouse (Winning Belle 2004).

BRC Brisbane Cup (2400m)—Eagle Farm
$300,000 Group 2 Quality Handicap. June 8, 2019.

YEAR	WINNER	JOCKEY	TRAINER	2ND	3RD	TIME
2018	Sedanzer	Tim Clark	Gai Waterhouse & Adrian Bott	Anton En Evant	Kiwia	2:18.3
2017	Chocante	Jim Byrne	Stephen Marsh	Single Gaze	Pemberley	2:15.0
2016	Benzini	Rosie Myers	Adrian & Harry Bull	Sir John Hawkwood	Junoob	2:31.6
2015	Jetset Lad	Paul Hammersley	Brian Smith	Sense Of Occasion	Epingle	2:15.0
2014	Floria	Kerrin McEvoy	Peter Moody	Moriarty	Zephyron	2:25.6
2013	Moriarty	Nash Rawiller	Chris Waller	Quintessential	Zennista	2:29.1
2012	Lights Of Heaven	Luke Nolen	Peter Moody	Dance With Her	Mawingo	2:29.6
2011	Tullamore	Chris Munce	Gai Waterhouse	Glass Harmonium	De Fine Lago	2:27.5
2010	Crossthestart	Chris Munce	Bevan & Richard Laming	Scouting Wide	Ekstreme	2:27.5
2009	Scenic Shot	Shane Scriven	Daniel Morton	Ready To Lift	Tinseltown	2:34.6
2008	Viewed	Damien Oliver	Bart Cummings	Fulmonti	Sky Biscuit	2:35.9
2007	Newport	Alan Robinson	Paul Perry	Lilakyn	Ice Chariot	2:28.1
2006	Art Success	Tony Pattillo	John Collins	Gorgeous George	Sculptor	3:22.4
2005	Portland Singa	Larry Cassidy	Neville Mcburney	Shamrock Shore	Regal Punch	3:20.8
2004	Danestorm	Michael Walker	Jim Conlan	Pentastic	Upsetthym	3:20.2
2003	Piachay	Glen Boss	David Hall	County Tyrone	Homewrecker	3:22.5
2002	Prized Gem	Michael Rodd	Murray Baker	Majestic Avenue	Nauders	3:24.6
2001	Star Covet	Jason Taylor	Pam Webber	Citi Habit	Karasi	3:17.4

BACKGROUND
First run: 1866 (won by Forester over 3600m). 3200m 1867-2006 except for 1883 & 1888 when 2800m. Run over 2400m 1946 (when called the Victory Cup) & from 2007. Run at Eagle Farm in 1871. Group 1 until 2007 when downgraded to Group 2. Run at Doomben (2200m) in 2015 & 2017-18.
Most recent mare to win: Sedanzer (2018).
Most recent 3YO to win: C&G – Balmerino (1976); Filly – Queen's Road (1982).
Multiple winners: 5—Desert Chill (1997, 1995); Fair Patton (1965, 1964); Spear Chief (1939, 1938); St. Valorey (1934, 1932); Fitz Grafton (1905, 1904).
Fastest Time (Eagle Farm 2400m): Floria (2014) 2:25.69.
Notable winners: Scenic Shot (2009); Viewed (2008); Prized Gem (2002); Reckless (1977); Balmerino (1976); Igloo (1974); Mode (1972); Tulloch (1961); Macdougal (1959); Hydrogen (1953); Spear Chief (1939, 1938); Fitz Grafton (1905, 1904).
Brisbane Cup winners also won in the same Qld winter campaign:
Lord Mayor's Cup (first run in 2012): 1—Moriarty (2013); Chairman's Handicap: 2—Crossthestart (2010); Art Success (2006).
Doomben Cup: 2—Scenic Shot (2009); Lord Hybrow (1988).
Eagle Farm Cup (PJ O'Shea Stakes): 18—Lights Of Heaven (2012); Scenic Shot (2009); Yippyio (2000); Shuzohra (1990); Lord Hybrow (1988); Four Crowns (1981); Balmerino (1976); Fair Patten (1965); Tulloch (1961); Redcraze (1956); Hydrogen (1953); Good Idea (1946); Spear Chief (1939); Lough Neagh (1936); Venerable (1919); Bunting (1917); Plunder (1908); Fitz Grafton (1905).
Queensland Derby: 2—Fitz Grafton (season 1903-04); Tridentate (1892-93). Note: No horse has won the Queensland Derby-Brisbane Cup double since the Derby was moved from the spring to the winter in 1973.
Brisbane Cup and the Melbourne Cup:
2—Viewed (2008); Macdougal (1959). Note: Reckless (1977) won the Sydney, Adelaide and Brisbane Cups before finishing second to Gold And Black in the Melbourne Cup.
Leading winning jockeys: 5 wins Chris Munce (Tullamore 2011, Crossthestart 2010, Desert Chill 1997, 1995, Grooming 1992).
4 wins Maurice McCarten (Spear Chief 1939, 1938, St. Valorey 1934, Trainer 1930); Johnno Stone (Fightaway 1909, Haidee 1907, Scorcher 1906, Jessie 1903).
Current winning jockeys: 2 wins Larry Cassidy (Portland Singa 2005, Yippyio 2000); Damien Oliver (Viewed 2008, Sheer Kingston 1999).
1 win Glen Boss (Piachay 2003); Jim Byrne (Chocante 2017); Tim Clark (Sedanzer 2018); Kevin Forrester

(Dupain 1996); Paul Hammersley (Jetset Lad 2015); Kerrin McEvoy (Floria 2014); Rosie Myers (Benzini 2016); Luke Nolen (Lights Of Heaven 2012); Nash Rawiller (Moriarty 2013); Michael Rodd (Prized Gem 2002); Jason Taylor (Star Covet 2001); Michael Walker (Danestorm 2004).
Leading winning trainers: 7 wins *James McGill (Lyndhurst 1890, Lancer 1885, Mozart 1883, Proctor 1882, Lord Clifden 1881, Sunrise 1877, North Australian 1867).
6 wins Tommy Smith (Chiamare 1984, Igloo 1974, Royal Shah 1971, Fair Patton 1965, Tulloch 1961, Redcraze 1956).
5 wins Bill Tucker snr (Trainer 1930, Seremite 1923, Grichka 1922, Venerable 1919, Demeranthis 1916).
*James McGill was a pioneer owner-trainer who ran a private stable where he employed trainers. Fitz Grafton (1905, 1904), his best-known horse, was officially trained by H. Bert McGill, although James McGill is often credited as being the trainer.
Current winning trainers: 2 wins Bevan Laming (Desert Chill 1997, 1995); Peter Moody (Floria 2014, Lights Of Heaven 2012); Gai Waterhouse (Sedanzer 2018, Tullamore 2011).
1 win Murray Baker (Prized Gem 2002); Adrian & Harry Bull (Benzini 2016); John Collins (Art Success 2006); Jim Conlan (Danestorm 2004); Allan Denham (Yippyio 2000); David Hall (Piachay 2003); Bruce Marsh (Marlon 1986); Stephen Marsh (Chocante 2017); John Meagher (Sheer Kingston 1999); Daniel Morton (Scenic Shot 2009); Paul Perry (Newport 2007); Graeme Rogerson (Just A Dancer 1991); Brian Smith (Jetset Lad 2015); Chris Waller (Moriarty 2013); Gai Waterhouse & Adrian Bott (Sedanzer 2018); Pam Webber (Star Covet 2001); Simon Wilde (Crossthestart 2010).
Points of interest: Strathearn and The Dean dead-heated for first in 1878. The only dead-heat since the photo finish camera was introduced was in 1969 (Sandy's Hope and Bobalex, third to Galleon King).
Carbine (by Tamerlane) who won the Brisbane Cup in 1875 is not the same Carbine (by Musket) in the Australian Hall of Fame. Fitz Grafton is the only horse to win a Stradbroke Handicap (as a 2YO in 1903) and a Brisbane Cup (1904 & 1905). He also won the Queensland Derby in the spring of 1903.
Maurice McCarten rode four winners (see leading winning jockeys) and trained Putuko to win in 1952.

BRC Dane Ripper Stakes (1400m)—Eagle Farm
$200,000 Group 2 Open Fillies & Mares SWP. June 8, 2019.

YEAR	WINNER	JOCKEY	TRAINER	2ND	3RD	TIME
2018	Invincibella	James McDonald	Chris Waller	Prompt Response	Moss Trip	1:21.5
2017	Prompt Response	Tommy Berry	Gai Waterhouse & Adrian Bott	My True Love	Bonny O'Reilly	1:19.2
2016	Cradle Me	Zac Purton	David Pfeiffer	Artistry	Jessy Belle	1:24.1
2015	Hazard	James McDonald	Lee & Anthony Freedman	Catkins	Bound For Earth	1:19.3
2014	Cosmic Endeavour	Tommy Berry	Gai Waterhouse	Driefontein	Belle De Coeur	1:22.8
2013	Red Tracer	Nash Rawiller	Chris Waller	Floria	Arctic Flight	1:22.7
2012	Red Tracer	Hugh Bowman	Chris Waller	Forfeiture	Alltherightmoves	1:26.0
2011	Hurtle Myrtle	Brenton Avdulla	Matthew Smith	Zero Rock	Pontiana	1:23.9
2010	Set For Fame	Luke Nolen	Peter Moody	Acquired	Wealth Princess	1:22.5
2009	Chinchilla Rose	Craig Williams	Steele Ryan	Bird of Fire	Jacqueline Rouge	1:25.4
2008	Vietnam	Glen Colless	Liam Birchley	Seconde	Quizzical Lady	1:25.2
2007	Rosa's Spur	Craig Williams	Rod Northam	J Adane	Storm Signal	1:22.9
2006	Countess Bathory	Kevin Forrester	John Wallace	Freeroller	Love And Money	1:22.2
2005	Our Sweet Moss	Michael Cahill	Gerald Ryan	Mardi Gras	Wasimah	1:16.0
2004	Ta Ta Tatiana	Jim Byrne	Joe Cleary	With My	Secret Gift	1:15.8
2003	Recurring	Kerrin McEvoy	Gerald Ryan	Mon Mekki	Golden Snitch	1:16.4
2002	Princess Clang	Michael Rodd	Kaye Tinsley	Here For Glory	Juanmo	1:15.7
2001	China Amber	Scott Seamer	Glenn Wilkins	Dynamic Love	Past Blast	1:15.7

BACKGROUND
First run: 1992 (won by Blushing Bijou). Handicap from 1992-2001. Listed: 2002-05. Group 3 from 2006-09. Group 2 from 2010. Run over 1300m 1994-2005; 1400m from 2006. Run at Doomben (1350m) in 2015 & 2017-18.
Most recent 3YO filly to win: Prompt Response (2017).
Multiple winners: Red Tracer (2013, 2012).
Fastest time (1400m): Countess Bathory (2006) 1:22.22
Notable winners: Cosmic Endeavour (2014); Red Tracer (2013, 2012); Hurtle Myrtle (2011); Set For Fame (2010); Recurring (2003), Seawinne (1994).
Dane Ripper Stakes winners won the lead-up races:
Angus Armanasco Stakes: 1—Set For Fame (2010).
Millie Fox Stakes: 2—Red Tracer (2013, 2012).
Sapphire Stakes: 2—Cosmic Endeavour (2014); Hurtle Myrtle (2011).

Inglis 3YO Guineas: 1—Cosmic Endeavour (2014).
Bright Shadow Quality: 1—Vietnam (2008).
Dane Ripper Stakes winners went on to win in the same preparation:
Tatt's Tiara: 2—Cosmic Endeavour (2014); Tripping (1996).
Leading winning jockey: 2 wins Tommy Berry (Prompt Response 2017, Cosmic Endeavour 2014); James McDonald (Invincibella 2018, Hazard 2015); Craig Williams (Chinchilla Rose 2009, Rosa's Spur 2007).
Current winning jockeys: 2 wins Tommy Berry (Prompt Response 2017, Cosmic Endeavour 2014); James McDonald (Invincibella 2018, Hazard 2015); Craig Williams (Chinchilla Rose 2009, Rosa's Spur 2007).
1 win Brenton Avdulla (Hurtle Myrtle 2011); Hugh Bowman (Red Tracer 2012); Jim Byne (Ta Ta Tatiana 2004); Michael Cahill (Our Sweet Moss 2005); Larry Cassidy (Tripping 1996); Glen Colless (Vietnam 2008); Kevin Forrester (Countess Bathory 2006); Kerrin McEvoy (Recurring 2003); Luke Nolen (Set For Fame 2010); Zac Purton (Cradle Me 2016); Nash Rawiller (Red Tracer 2013); Michael Rodd (Princess Clang 2002).
Leading winning trainers: 3 wins Gerald Ryan (Our Sweet Moss 2005, Recurring 2003, Blushing Bijou 1992); Chris Waller (Invincibella 2018, Red Tracer 2013, 2012).
2 wins Gai Waterhouse (Prompt Response 2017; Cosmic Endeavour 2014).
Current winning trainers: 3 wins Gerald Ryan (Our Sweet Moss 2005, Recurring 2003, Blushing Bijou 1992); Chris Waller (Invincibella 2018, Red Tracer 2013, 2012).
2 wins Gai Waterhouse (Prompt Response 2017; Cosmic Endeavour 2014).
1 win Liam Birchley (Vietnam 2008); Danny Bougoure (Belle Salieri 1997); Geoff Burns (Annunciation 2000); Joe Cleary (Ta Ta Tatiana 2004); Clarry Conners (Tripping 1996); Lee & Anthony Freedman (Hazard 2015); Peter Moody (Set For Fame 2010); Michael Nolan (Grouse Lane 1999); Rod Northam (Rosa's Spur 2007); David Pfieffer (Cradle Me 2016); Steele Ryan (Chinchilla Rose 2009); Matthew Smith (Hurtle Myrtle 2011); John Wallace (Countess Bathory 2006); Gai Waterhouse & Adrian Bott (Prompt Response 2017).
Points of Interest: Red Tracer (2013, 2012) went on to win the 2013 G1 Myer Classic at Flemington.
Hurtle Myrtle (2011) went on to win the 2011 G1 Myer Classic at Flemington.

Group 1 winning jockeys

Leading jockeys all time
(Australian G1s—
to July 31, 2018):

Wins	Jockey
109	Damien Oliver
105	George Moore
98	Jim Cassidy
92	Roy Higgins
89	Shane Dye
86	Mick Dittman
81	Glen Boss
79	Darren Beadman
75	Hugh Bowman
75	Neville Sellwood
64	Tom Hales
64	Bobby Lewis
63	Darby Munro
60	Harry White
57	Kerrin McEvoy
56	Nash Rawiller
55	Jim Pike
52	Peter Cook
50	Bill Cook
46	Corey Brown
45	Steven King
44	Craig Williams
43	Chris Munce

Current jockeys
(Australian G1s only—
to July 31, 2018):

Wins	Jockey
109	Damien Oliver
81	Glen Boss
75	Hugh Bowman
57	Kerrin McEvoy
56	Nash Rawiller
46	Corey Brown
44	Craig Williams
36	Luke Nolen
34	Larry Cassidy
33	Craig Newitt
32	Michael Rodd
26	Danny Nikolic
23	James McDonald
23	Brad Rawiller
22	Dwayne Dunn

Wins	Jockey
19	Steven Arnold
19	Grant Cooksley
19	Blake Shinn
18	Tommy Berry
18	Glyn Schofield
16	Brett Prebble
15	Ben Melham
13	Stephen Baster
13	Damian Browne
12	Paul Harvey
11	Tim Clark
11	Damian Lane
11	Mark Zahra
10	Tye Angland
10	Zac Purton
8	Jay Ford
7	Nick Hall
6	Brenton Avdulla
6	Danny Miller
6	Willie Pike
6	Cyril Small
5	Jim Byrne
5	Noel Callow
5	Kevin Forrester
5	Michelle Payne
5	Robert Thompson
5	Michael Walker
5	David Walsh
4	Opie Bosson
4	Luke Currie
4	Vlad Duric
4	Paul King
4	Joao Moreira
4	Chad Schofield
4	James Winks
4	Dean Yendall
3	Regan Bayliss
3	Jason Brown
3	Michael Cahill
3	Pat Carbery
3	Michael Dee
3	Clare Lindop
3	Shaun O'Donnell
3	Steven Parnham
3	Josh Parr
3	Christian Reith
3	Jason Whiting
3	Eddie Wilkinson
2	Tony Allan

Wins	Jockey
2	John Allen
2	Joe Bowditch
2	Michael Carson
2	Sam Clipperton
2	Glen Colless
2	Peter Hall
2	Jason Holder
2	Leith Innes
2	Jeff Lloyd
2	Rhys McLeod
2	Ryan Moore
2	Kathy O'Hara
2	Simon Price
2	Daniel Staeck
2	Dom Tourneur
2	Douglas Whyte
1	Andrew Adkins
1	Jason Benbow
1	Nikita Beriman
1	Darryl Bradley
1	Lucas Camilleri
1	Jordan Childs
1	Harry Coffey
1	Wayne Davis
1	Pat Farrell
1	Paul Gatt
1	Paul Hammersley
1	Dean Holland
1	Yasunari Iwata
1	Peter Knuckey
1	Christophe Lemaire
1	Glenn Lynch
1	Katelyn Mallyon
1	Linda Meech
1	Gerald Mosse
1	Jake Noonan
1	Chris O'Brien
1	Cory Parish
1	Ken Pope
1	Jonathan Riddell
1	Jamie Spencer
1	Blake Spriggs
1	Craig Staples
1	Lauren Stojacovic
1	Jason Taylor
1	Troy Turner
1	Peter Wells
1	Brian Werner
1	Ryan Wiggins

Footnote: Pattern racing was introduced in the 1979-80 season. Racing In Australia has allotted historical Group 1 wins restrespectively to races that were given original Group 1 status in 1979-80. The one exception is the Merson Cooper Stakes which was widely regarded as Victoria's premier 2YO race in the autumn before a seamless transition to the G1 Blue Diamond Stakes in 1980. The Merson Cooper Stakes returned three years later as a new Group 3 race at Sandown in late spring. Racing In Australia regards winners of the Merson Cooper Stakes before 1980 to deserve Group 1 status.

Group 1 winning trainers

Leading trainers all time
(Australian G1s—
to July 31, 2018):

Wins	Trainer
246*	Bart Cummings**
243	Tommy Smith
139*	Gai Waterhouse
125*	Lee Freedman
111*	John Hawkes
91	Colin Hayes
84	Chris Waller
74	James Scobie
73*	David Hayes
71	Tom Payten
59	Jack Denham
56	Jack Holt
54	Maurice McCarten
53	Peter Moody
47	Geoff Murphy
42	Frank McGrath
41*	Peter Snowden
39	Angus Armanasco
38	Neville Begg
38	Walter Hickenbottom
37	Clarry Conners
36	George Hanlon
36	Guy Walter
34	Mick Price
30	Darren Weir
29	Brian Mayfield-Smith
29*	Graeme Rogerson
28	John O'Shea

*includes G1s won in partnership.
**includes two wins in partnership with grandson James Cummings, and one Merson Cooper Stakes.

Current trainers
(Australian G1s—
to July 31, 2018):

Wins	Trainer
139*	Gai Waterhouse
125*	Lee Freedman
111*	John Hawkes
84	Chris Waller
73*	David Hayes
53	Peter Moody
41*	Peter Snowden
37	Clarry Conners
34	Mick Price
30	Darren Weir

29	Graeme Rogerson
28	John O'Shea
24	Michael Moroney
21*	Murray Baker
21	Mark Kavanagh
19	Kris Lees
19	John Wheeler
18	Anthony Cummings
18	Greg Eurell
17	Gerald Ryan
16	Danny O'Brien
16	Tony Vasil
15	Michael, Wayne & John Hawkes
15	John Meagher
13	Grahame Begg
13*	David Hayes & Tom Dabernig
13	Robert Hickmott
12*	Leon Corstens
12*	Leon Macdonald
12	Robert Smerdon
12	Peter & Paul Snowden
11	Allan Denham
11	Fred Kersley
11	Joe Pride
10	Les Bridge
10*	Anthony Freedman
10	Robert Heathcote
10	Ciaron Maher
9*	James Cummings
9*	Mathew Ellerton
9	Greg Eurell
9	David Hall
9	David & Ben Hayes & Tom Dabernig
9	Paul Perry
8	Rod Craig
8	Lindsey Smith
7	Trevor Andrews
7	Russell Cameron
7	Wally Mitchell
7	Frank Ritchie
7	John Sadler
6	Pat Hyland
6	Joe Janiak
6	Colin Little
6	Buster O'Malley
6	David Payne
6	John Thompson
6	Bruce Wallace
6	Gai Waterhouse & Adrian Bott
5	Cliff Brown
5	Jim Conlan
5	Roger James
5	Robbie Laing
5	Laurie Laxon
5	Tim Martin

5	Noel Mayfield-Smith
5	Tony McEvoy
5	Daniel Morton
5	Ron Quinton
5	Grant Williams
4	Nigel Blackiston
4	Danny Bougoure
4	Pat Carey
4	Bryan Guy
4	Sheila Laxon
4	Alan Mathews
4	Frank Maynard snr
4	Barry Miller
4	Gary Portelli
4	Brian Smith
3	Murray Baker & Andrew Forsman
3	Albert Beckett
3	Gary Carson
3	Shaun Dwyer
3	Mathew Ellerton & Simon Zahra
3	Garry Frazer
3	Lee & Anthony Freedman
3	Peter Gelagotis
3	Tony Gollan
3	Tom Hughes Jnr
3	Gary Hennessy
3	Mick Kent
3	Jim Lee
3	Bruce Marsh
3	Hec McClaren
3	Clinton McDonald
3	John Size
3	Phillip Stokes
3	John Symons
3	John Wallace
3	Stuart Webb
3	Pat Webster
2*	Stephen Autridge
2*	Bjorn Baker
2	Tracey Bartley
2	Stan Bates
2	Paul Beshara
2	David Brideoake
2	Vern Brockman
2	Ray Brock
2*	Trent Busuttin
2	Shane Clarke
2	Marc Conners
2	Jason Coyle
2	Lee Curtis
2	Mikel Delzangles
2	Henry Dwyer
2	Steve Farley
2	Warwick Hailes
2	Greg Hickman

Current trainers (cont)

Wins	Trainer
2	Con Karakatsanis
2	Rex Lipp
2	Lou Luciani
2	Roberta Maguire
2	Ted Martinovich
2	John McArdle
2	Stephen McKee
2	John McNair
2	Paul Messara
2	Joe Miller
2	Paul O'Sullivan
2	Tony Pike
2	Gino Poletti
2	Ross Price
2	Aaron Purcell
2	Steve Richards
2	Mark Riley
2	John Sargent
2	Kelly Schweida
2	Benjamin Smith
2	David Vandyke
2	Kerry Walker
2	Wayne Walters
2	Dermot Weld
2	Kelso Wood
1	Katrina Alexander
1	Charlie Appleby
1	Stephen Autridge & Jamie Richards
1	Alan Bailey
1	Andrew Balding
1	Barry Baldwin
1	Murray & Bjorn Baker
1	John Bary
1	Darren Beadman
1	Bill Borrie
1	Barry Brook
1	Bruce Brown
1	Paddy Busuttin
1	Trent Busuttin & Natalie Young
1	Paul Butterworth
1	Michael Campbell
1	Graeme Clarke
1	Daniel Clarken
1	John Collins
1	Pat Conroy
1	Leon & Troy Corstens
1	Bruce Cross
1	Stuart Dodd
1	Tim Donnelly
1	Noel Doyle
1	Alain de Royer Dupre
1	Adam Durrant
1	Peter Eggleston
1	Jamie Edwards
1	Steve Englebrecht
1	Peter Giadresco
1	Michael Grant
1	Robbie Griffiths
1	David Harrison
1	Ian Harrison
1	Mick Hewson
1	Bernie Howlett
1	Liam Howley
1	Tom Hogan
1	Wez Hunter
1	Peter Hurdle
1	Brian Jenkins
1	Paul Jenkins
1	David Jolly
1	Richard Jolly
1	Gwenda Johnstone
1	Paul Jordan
1	Barbara Joseph
1	Kazuhiro Kato
1	Sylvia Kay
1	Wendy Kelly
1	Lloyd Kennewell
1	John Kiernan
1	Bevan Laming
1	Matt Laurie
1	Ron Leemon
1	Donna Logan
1	Jeff Lynds
1	Mick Mair
1	Kenny Mann
1	Jim Mason
1	Frank Maynard Jnr
1	Natalie McCall
1	Peter McGregor
1	Peter McKenzie
1	Steve McKinnon
1*	Jason McLachlan
1	Gary Moore
1	Kim Moore
1	Kevin Moses
1	Moira Murdoch
1	Shane Nichols
1	Andrew Noblet
1	Tony Noonan
1	Aidan O'Brien
1	Joseph O'Brien
1	Nick Olive
1	Terry O'Sullivan
1	Kerry Parker
1	Michael Pateman
1	Eden Petrie
1	Ross Price
1	Robert Priscott
1	Rhys Radford
1	Steven Ryan
1	John Salanitri
1	Andrew Scott
1	Grant Searle
1	John Shoard
1	Bill Smart
1	Matthew Smith
1	Jake Stephens
1	Katsuhiko Sumii
1	Saeed bin Suroor
1	Tomoyuki Umeda
1	Jim Taylor
1	Angela Timpeley
1	Paula Wagg
1	Mark Walker
1	Jason Warren
1	Bruce Watkins
1	Antoine de Watrigant
1	Pam Webber
1	Colin Webster
1	Allan Williams
1	Andreas Wohler
1	Chris Wood

*includes G1s won in partnership.

Footnote: Pattern racing was introduced in the 1979-80 season. Racing In Australia has allotted historical Group 1 wins restrespectively to races that were given original Group 1 status in 1979-80. The one exception is the Merson Cooper Stakes which was widely regarded as Victoria's premier 2YO race in the autumn before a seamless transition to the G1 Blue Diamond Stakes in 1980. The Merson Cooper Stakes returned three years later as a new Group 3 race at Sandown in late spring. Racing In Australia regards winners of the Merson Cooper Stakes before 1980 to deserve Group 1 status.

NSW Metropolitan Jockeys' Premierships

SEASON	JOCKEY	WINS	SEASON	JOCKEY	WINS
2017-18	Brenton Avdulla	92	1962-63	George Moore	106½
2016-17	Hugh Bowman	83	1961-62	George Moore	85
2015-16	James McDonald	89½	1960-61	Athol Mulley	64½
2014-15	Hugh Bowman	96	1959-60	Neville Sellwood	87
2013-14	James McDonald	72	1958-59	Ray Selkrig	67
2012-13	Nash Rawiller	77	1957-58	George Moore	83
2011-12	Hugh Bowman	93½	1956-57	George Moore	83
2010-11	Nash Rawiller	93	1955-56	Jack Thompson	68
2009-10	Nash Rawiller	90	1954-55	Arthur Ward	66
2008-09	Hugh Bowman	98	1953-54	Neville Sellwood	76½
2007-08	Blake Shinn	79	1952-53	Neville Sellwood	63
2006-07	Darren Beadman	162	1951-52	Neville Sellwood	63
2005-06	Darren Beadman	152	1950-51	Arthur Ward	43
2004-05	Darren Beadman	143	1949-48	Neville Sellwood	66
2003-04	Darren Beadman	115½	1948-49	Neville Sellwood	65½
2002-03	Darren Beadman	141	1947-48	Jack Thompson	60½
2001-02	Corey Brown	106	1946-47	Billy Cook	42
2000-01	Brian York	111½	1945-46	Athol Mulley	57
1999-00	Larry Cassidy	103	1944-45	Jack Thompson	34½
1998-99	Larry Cassidy	119	1943-44	Jack Thompson	46½
1997-98	Larry Cassidy	139½	1942-53	Billy Cook	27
1996-97	Shane Dye	94	1941-42	Billy Cook	60
1995-96	Darren Beadman	115	1940-41	Jack Thompson (a)	106½
1994-95	Darren Beadman	128	1939-40	Billy Cook	124½
1993-94	Kevin Moses	102	1938-39	Maurice McCarten	87½½
1992-93	Kevin Moses	113	1937-38	Ted Bartle	93½
1991-92	Kevin Moses	88½	1936-37	Andy Knox	83
1990-91	Shane Dye	106	1935-36	Andy Knox	96½
1989-90	Mick Dittman	75	1934-45	Andy Knox	82½½
1988-89	Mick Dittman	74	1933-34	Jack O'Sullivan	68½
1987-88	John Marshall	86	1932-33	Jim Simpson	59½
1986-87	Malcolm Johnston	92½	1931-32	Billy Cook	64
1985-86	Jim Cassidy	82	1930-31	Billy Cook	56½
1984-85	Mick Dittman	83½	1929-30	Ted Bartle	72
1983-64	Ron Quinton	80	1928-29	Ted Bartle	59½½½
1982-83	Ron Quinton	80	1927-28	Ted Bartle	50½½½½
1981-82	Ron Quinton	84½	1926-27	Stan Davidson	58½
1980-81	Ron Quinton	99½	1925-26	Jim Munro	60½
1979-80	Ron Quinton	89½	1924-25	Jack Toohey	48
1978-79	Ron Quinton	104½	1923-24	Jack Toohey	44
1977-78	Malcolm Johnston	115	1922-23	Jack Toohey	52½½
1976-77	Ron Quinton	93	1921-22	William Johnstone	52
1974-75	Kevin Langby	107	1920-21	Jack Toohey	36½½½½
1973-74	Kevin Langby	121	1919-20	William Lillyman	41
1972-73	Kevin Langby	86	1918-19	Loyal Walker	29½
1971-72	Kevin Langby	104½	1917-18	Ken Bracken/Loyal Walker	27
1970-71	Des Lake	75	1916-17	Charles Barden*	29
1969-70	Ron Quinton	78½	1915-14	Albert Wood	27
1968-69	George Moore	87	1914-15	William Lillyman	25
1967-68	George Moore	74	1913-14	Bill McLachlan	24
1966-67	George Moore	86	1912-13	Geoffrey Pinn	23
1965-66	George Moore	105	*apprentice		
1964-65	George Moore	112			
1963-64	George Moore	84			

In A Nutshell

Leading winning jockeys

TITLES	JOCKEY
10	George Moore
7	Darren Beadman, Ron Quinton
6	Billy Cook, Neville Sellwood

Current winning jockeys

TITLES	JOCKEY
4	Hugh Bowman
3	Larry Cassidy, Nash Rawiller
2	James McDonald
1	Brenton Avdulla, Corey Brown, Blake Shinn

Record season

SEASON	JOCKEY	YEAR
2006-07	Darren Beadman	162

NSW Metropolitan Apprentices Premierships

SEASON	JOCKEY	WINS
2017-18	Rachel King	38
2016-17	Andrew Adkins	36
2015-16	Rory Hutchings	33
2014-15	Winona Costin	41
2013-14	Sam Clipperton	27
2012-13	Sam Clipperton	27
2011-12	Chad Schofield	39
2010-11	Josh Adams	43
2009-10	Tommy Berry	47
2008-09	Daniel Ganderton	45
2007-08*	Peter Wells	25
2006-07	Tye Angland	59
2005-06	Tim Clark	33
2004-05	Kathy O'Hara	24
2003-04	Jay Ford	43
2002-03	Ron Stewart	23
2001-02	Robbie Brewer	29
2000-01	Scott Pollard	29
1999-00	Hugh Bowman	56½
1998-99	Mitch Newman	19
1997-98	Bobby El'Issa	29
1995-96	Craig Agnew	47
1993-94	Corey Brown	46
1992-93	Darryl McLellan	56
1991-92	Aaron Kennedy	42
1990-91	Jeff Wilson	33
1989-90	Matthew Privato	45
1988-89	Shane Edmonds	29
1987-88	Mark Peters	25
1986-87	Craig Carmody	34
1985-86	Tracey Bartley	28
1984-85	Darren Beadman	33
1983-64	John Nisbett	38½
1982-83	Darren Beadman	48
1981-82	Steven Jeffries	40½
1980-81	Wayne Harris	89
1979-80	Wayne Harris	56
1978-79	Wayne Harris	73
1977-78	Mark de Montfort	47
1976-77	Malcolm Johnston	67½
1974-75	Malcolm Johnston	65
1973-74	Allan Denham	51½
1972-73	Kevin Moses	27
1971-72	John Duggan	44
1970-71	Gerald Shinn	46½
1969-70	John Duggan	44
1968-69	Denis McClune	38
1967-68	Steven Spinks	42
1966-67	Ron Quinton	28
1965-66	Steven Spinks	41
1964-65	Neil Campton/Kevin Langby	18
1963-64	Bernie Goddard	29
1962-63	David Royle	17
1961-62	Dorian Osborne	26
1960-61	Hilton Cope	40
1959-60	Keith Smith	35
1958-59	Bernie Howlett	25
1957-58	Mel Schumacher	36
1956-57	Geoff Howard	12
1955-56	Frank Leman	15
1954-55	Ted Lee	17
1953-54	Bill Toohey	17
1952-53	Bob Faux	11
1951-52	Bobby Reed	24
1950-51	Ray Selkrig	23
1949-48	Ray Selkrig	24
1948-49	Ray Selkrig	29
1947-48	Fred Walker	13
1946-47	Tommy Mullane	16½
1945-46	George Podmore	18
1944-45	Ted Doon	15
1943-44	George Moore	11
1942-43	Jack Thompson	20½
1941-42	Jack Thompson	42½
1940-41	Jack Thompson	106½
1939-40	Jack Thompson	39
1938-39	William Lappin	87
1937-38	Stan Neale	29
1936-37	Harold Hanley	24
1935-36	Harold Hanley	30

*Winning numbers affected by racing's closure in NSW & Queensland due to Equine Influenza.

In A Nutshell

Leading jockeys

TITLES	JOCKEY
4	Jack Thompson
3	Wayne Harris, Ray Selkrig

Record season

SEASON	JOCKEY	WINS
1980-81	Wayne Harris	89

QLD Metropolitan Jockeys' Premierships

SEASON	JOCKEY	WINS	SEASON	JOCKEY	WINS
2017-18	Jeff Lloyd	108	1963-62	Colin O'Neill/Arthur Lister	30
2016-17	Jeff Lloyd	137	1962-63	Arthur Lister	27
2015-16	Jeff Lloyd	80	1961-62	Colin O'Neill (a)	28
2014-15	Jim Byrne	71	1960-61	Terry Ramsay (a)	40½
2013-14	Tim Bell	58	1959-60	Russell Maddock	41
2012-13	Michael Cahill	86	1958-59	Russell Maddock	43
2011-12	Chris Munce	103	1957-58	Jim Standfield	56
2010-11	Chris Munce	79½	1956-57	Jim Standfield	50
2009-10	Stathi Katsidis	72	1955-56	Russell Maddock	38
2008-09	Shane Scriven	51	1954-55	Russell Maddock	53
2007-08*	Jim Byrne	46	1953-54	Noel Best	37
2006-07	Glen Colless	62	1952-53	Jim Standfield	56
2005-06	Glen Colless	59	1951-52	Noel Best	60
2004-05	Stathi Katsidis	75	1950-51	Russell Maddock	51
2003-04	Stathi Katsidis	58	1949-50	Russell Maddock	35½
2002-03	Zac Purton (a)	59	1948-49	Russell Maddock	44
2001-02	Michael Rodd (a)	74	1947-48	Bruce McLean	36
2000-01	Scott Seamer	91	1946-47	Russell Maddock	32
1999-00	Glen Colless	68	1945-46	Billy Briscoe	82½
1998-99	Jim Byrne	65	1944-45	Billy Briscoe	47
1997-98	Jim Byrne	72½	1943-44	Billy Briscoe	34
1996-97	Michael Pelling	64	1942-43	Edwin (Ted) Fordyce	39½
1995-96	Michael Pelling	75	1941-42	George Moore (a)	56
1994-95	Michael Pelling	54	1940-41	Billy Briscoe	66½½½
1993-92	Chris Munce	73	1939-40	Billy Briscoe	54
1992-93	Brian York	74	1938-39	Billy Briscoe	82½
1991-92	Chris Munce	86	1937-38	Billy Briscoe	51
1990-91	Michael Pelling	64½	1936-37	Billy Briscoe	87½½
1989-90	Chris Munce (a)	56	1935-36	Billy Hill	50½½
1988-89	Brian York	65	1934-35	Fred Shean	60
1987-88	Brian York	88	1933-34	Tom Spencer	77½
1986-87	Ken Russell	92	1932-33	Billy Hill	63½½
1985-86	Neil Williams	74	1931-32	Fred Shean	50½
1984-85	Neil Williams	86	1930-31	Billy Hill	48
1983-64	Neil Williams	92	1929-30	John Conquest	37
1982-83	Graham Cook	69	1928-29	Billy Hill	46
1981-82	Gavan Duffy	84	1927-28	Arthur Davis	44½
1980-81	Gavan Duffy	87	1926-27	Arthur Davis	44½
1979-80	Mick Dittman	97½	1925-26	John Conquest	44
1978-79	Mick Dittman	71	1924-25	John Conquest	46
1977-78	Mick Dittman	97	1923-24	John Conquest	30
1976-77	Mick Dittman	88½	1922-23	Des O'Connor	30
1975-76	Graham Cook	57	1921-22	Billy Hill	42
1974-75	Graham Cook	74	1920-21	Billy Hill	39
1973-74	Mick Dittman	65½	1919-20	Arthur Davis	60
1972-73	Graham Cook	53½	1918-19	Georgie Tucker	40
1971-72	Doug Messingham	64	1917-18	"Parkie" O'Neill	38½
1970-71	Colin O'Neill	41	1916-17	Arthur Davis	41½
1969-70	Colin O'Neill	45	1916-17	Arthur Davis	N/A 41½
1968-69	Colin O'Neill	50	*apprentice		
1967-68	Len Hill	34			
1966-67	Tony Erhart (a)	46			
1965-66	Len Hill/Arthur Sanders	28			
1964-65	Arthur Lister	32			

In A Nutshell

Leading winning jockeys

TITLES	JOCKEY
8	Billy Briscoe, Russell Maddock
6	Billy Hill
5	Mick Dittman, Chris Munce, Colin O'Neill

Current winning jockeys

TITLES	JOCKEY
4	Jim Byrne
3	Glen Colless, Jeff Lloyd
1	Michael Cahill, Zac Purton, Michael Rodd

Record season

SEASON	JOCKEY	WINS
2016-17	Jeff Lloyd	137

QLD Metropolitan Apprentice Premierships

SEASON	JOCKEY	WINS
2017-18	Jag Guthmann-Chester	23
2016-17	Tiffani Brooker	50
2015-16	James Orman	70
2014-15	Luke Tarrant	57
2013-14	Tegan Harrison	43
2012-13	Tegan Harrison	44
2011-12	Tim Bell	56
2010-11	Justin Wood	20
2009-10	Michael Hellyer	22
2008-09	Brent Evans	30
2007-08*	Mandy Radecker	23
2006-07	Ric McMahon	29
2005-06	Ric McMahon	40
2004-05	Gavin McKeon	26
2003-04	Adam Best	30
2002-03	Zac Purton	59
2001-02	Michael Rodd	74
2000-01	Daniel Griffin	28
1999-00	Justin Stanley	43
1998-99	Brad Stewart	24
1997-98	Brad Stewart	29
1996-97	Mark Lister	28
1995-96	Alan Russell	31
1994-95	Alan Russell	33
1993-92	Alan Russell	37
1992-93	Neil Day	33
1991-92	Shane Shield	30½
1990-91	Jim Byrne	54
1989-90	Chris Munce	56
1988-90	Michael Boyce	43
1987-88	Chris Munce	36
1986-87	Dave Murphy	43
1985-86	Ray McGrath	31
1984-85	Neil Williams	86
1983-84	Neil Williams	92
1982-83	Shane Scriven	27
1981-82	Ben Saunders	20
1980-81	Mark Lynch	34
1979-80	Gary Palmer	86
1978-79	Michael Pelling	53½
1977-78	Michael Pelling	62
1976-77	Gary Palmer	46
1975-76	Garry Legg	38
1974-75	Rod Smyth	18
1973-74	Rod Smyth	21
1972-73	Mick Dittman	43
1971-72	Mick Dittman	50
1970-71	Mick Dittman	25
1969-70	Mick Dittman	30
1968-69	Larry Olsen	19
1967-68	J Andrews	24
1966-67	Tony Erhart	46
1965-66	Tony Erhart	24
1964-65	Len Hill	26
1963-64	Tony Erhart	22
1962-63	Les Harris	26
1961-62	Colin O'Neill	28
1960-61	Terry Ramsey	40½
1959-60	Darryl Sippel	25
1958-59	Merv Wrigley	32
1957-58	Gary Rashleigh	32
1956-57	Mel Schumacher	27
1955-56	Dan Jamieson	23
1954-55	Mel Schumacher	30
1953-54	William Barnes	19
1952-53	Bert Freeman	23
1951-52	Billy Johnson	16
1950-51	Cecil Markey	32
1949-50	Cecil Markey	32
1948-49	Jim Standfield	16
1947-48	Noel Best	30½
1946-47	Don Genn	24
1945-46	J Page	10

In A Nutshell

Leading jockeys

TITLES	JOCKEY
4	Mick Dittman
3	Tony Erhart, Alan Russell

Record season

SEASON	JOCKEY	WINS
1983-84	Neil Williams	92

SA Metropolitan Jockeys' Premierships

SEASON	JOCKEY	WINS	SEASON	JOCKEY	WINS
2017-18	Jamie Kah	63	1966-67	Bob Cox	90
2016-17	Jamie Kah	53	1965-66	John Miller	52
2015-16	Jason Holder	53	1964-65	John Stocker	50½
2014-15	Clare Lindop	55	1963-64	Bob Cox	58½
2013-14	Dom Tourneur	50	1962-63	Jim Johnson	50½
2012-13	Jamie Kah*	41	1961-62	Jim Johnson	52
2011-12	Matthew Neilson	58	1960-61	Bill Pyers	61
2010-11	Paul Gatt	50	1959-60	Bill Pyers	57
2009-10	Chad Lever	45	1958-59	Jim Johnson	55
2008-09	Chad Lever	46	1957-58	Jim Johnson	41
2007-08	Clare Lindop	50	1956-57	Bill Pyers	51½
2006-07	Paul Gatt	53	1955-56	Bill Pyers	44
2005-06	Paul Gatt	48	1954-55	Bill Pyers	62
2004-05	Clare Lindop	37	1953-54	Bill Pyers	61
2003-04	Paul Gatt	42½	1952-53	Bill Pyers	59½
2002-03	Jason Holder	60½	1951-52	Bill Pyers	47½
2001-02	Travis Creek	48	1950-51	Bill Pyers	43
2000-01	Dwayne Dunn	48	1949-50	Steve Dodd	30
1999-00	Dwayne Dunn	60½½	1948-49	Mick Medhurst	34½
1998-99	Simon Price/Paul Gatt*	41	1947-48	Mick Medhurst	26½
1997-98	Dwayne Dunn	49	1946-47	Hezekiah Bastian	38
1996-97	Steven Arnold	51½	1945-46	Darrol Graetz	30½
1995-96	Jason Holder	72	1944-45	Hezekiah Bastian	39
1994-95	Steven Arnold	48	1943-44	Herbert Raven	26
1993-94	Gary Clarke	37	1942-43	No racing this season	
1992-93	Simon Price	44	1941-42	Mick Medhurst	28
1991-92	Not Available	n/a	1940-41	Hezekiah Bastian	34
1990-91	Not Available	n/a	1939-40	Bob Carling	35½
1989-90	Not Available	n/a	1938-39	Mick Medhurst	33
1988-89	Not Available	n/a	1937-38	Mick Medhurst	36
1987-88	Jim Courtney	50	1936-37	Hezekiah Bastian	34
1986-87	Jim Courtney	40	1935-36	Hezekiah Bastian	36
1985-86	Jim Courtney	51	1934-35	Mick Medhurst	25½
1984-85	Jim Courtney	61	1933-34	Mick Medhurst	22
1983-64	John Letts	62½	1932-33	Mick Medhurst	25
1982-83	John Letts	61½	1931-32	Mick Medhurst	29
1981-82	John Letts	68	1930-31	Paddy Slattery	27
1980-81	Jim Courtney	66	1929-30	Ned Wright	18½
1979-80	John Letts	62	1928-29	Mick Medhurst	29½
1978-79	John Letts	78½	1927-28	Fred Cameron	21
1977-78	John Letts	68½	1926-27	Mick Medhurst	38½
1976-77	Jim Courtney	70	1925-26	Mick Medhurst	37½
1975-76	Jim Courtney	75	1924-25	Mick Medhurst	30½
1974-75	Mick Goreham	66	1923-24	Ben Matson	23
1973-74	John Letts	75½	1922-23	Mick Medhurst	21
1972-73	John Letts	73½	1921-22	Jack Sing	23
1971-72	Glen Pretty	75	*apprentice		
1970-71	Mick Goreham	46			
1969-70	Mick Goreham	40			
1968-69	Bob Cox	58½			
1967-68	Mick Goreham	59			

In A Nutshell
Leading winning jockeys

TITLES	JOCKEY
14	Mick Medhurst
9	Bill Pyers
8	Jim Courtney, John Letts

Current winning jockeys

TITLES	JOCKEY
5	Paul Gatt
3	Dwayne Dunn, Jason Holder, Jamie Kah, Clare Lindop
2	Steven Arnold, Chad Lever, Simon Price
1	Matthew Neilson, Dom Tourneur

Record season

SEASON	JOCKEY	WINS
1978-79	John Letts	78½

Tasmanian Metropolitan Jockeys' Premierships

SEASON	JOCKEY	WINS
2017-18	Craig Newitt	78
2016-17	David Pires	78
2015-16	David Pires	68
2014-15	David Pires	72
2013-14	Brendon McCoull	80
2012-13	Brendon McCoull	73
2011-12	Steve Maskiell	64½
2010-11	Brendon McCoull	46
2009-10	Brendon McCoull	25
2008-09	Steve Maskiell/Brendon McCoull	20
2007-08	Brendon McCoull	71
2006-07	Brendon McCoull	87
2005-06	Brendon McCoull	109
2004-05	Brendon McCoull	83
2002-03	Brendon McCoull	85
2001-02	Craig Newitt*	61
2000-01	Kelvin Sanderson	61½
1999-00	Brendon McCoull	70
1998-99	Brendon McCoull	59½
1997-98	Brendon McCoull	90
1996-97	Brendon McCoull	59
1995-96	Bev Buckingham	64
1994-95	Bev Buckingham	108½
1993-94	Steve Maskiell	67
1992-93	Steve Maskiell	93
1991-92	Steve Maskiell	79
1990-91	Bruce MacDonald	76
1989-90	William Burt	76
1988-89	Garry Glover/Anthony Skeoch	51
1987-88	Steve Maskiell	82
1986-87	Steve Maskiell	61½
1985-86	Steve Maskiell	66
1984-85	Garry King	58
1983-84	Max Baker	64
1982-83	Max Baker	50
1981-82	Bev Buckingham	62½
1980-81	Max Baker	62
1979-80	Max Baker	58
1978-79	Geoff Prouse	45
1977-78	Geoff Prouse	58
1976-77	Brian Pulbrook	45
1975-76	Geoff Prouse	57
1974-75	Anthony Skeoch	54
1973-74	Geoff Prouse	60
1972-73	Max Baker	50
1971-72	Geoff Prouse	51
1970-71	Max Baker	59
1969-70	Max Baker	70
1968-69	Max Baker	49
1967-68	Max Baker	51
1966-67	Geoff Prouse	46
1965-66	Brian Pulbrook	46
1964-65	Garry King	35
1963-64	Garry King	46
1962-63	Geoff Prouse	35
1961-62	Eddie Cox	41
1960-61	Eddie Cox	63
1959-60	Eddie Cox	51
1958-59	Eddie Cox	58
1957-58	Eddie Cox	62½
1956-57	Eddie Cox	57
1955-56	Eddie Cox	48
1954-55	Eddie Cox	64½
1953-54	Eddie Cox	54
1952-53	Eddie Cox	70
1951-52	Eddie Cox	58
1950-51	Eddie Cox	53½
1949-50	Eddie Cox	42
1948-49	Eddie Cox	37
1947-48	Eddie Cox	23
1946-47	Eddie Cox	30
1945-46	Eddie Cox	22
1944-45	Bill Cox	31
1943-44	Bill Cox	28
1942-43	Bill Cox	28
1941-42	Don McDonnell	41
1940-41	Don McDonnell	38½
1939-40	Don McDonnell	25
1938-39	Vin Fitzgibbon	27½
1937-38	James O'Mara	30
1936-37	Harold Coutts	23½
1935-36	Jack Connelly	33
1934-35	Tas Wood	22½
1933-34	Tas Wood	21
1932-33	Tas Wood	24
1931-32	Harold Coutts	32
1930-31	William Bevis	30½
1929-30	William Bevis	36
1928-29	William Bevis	20½
1927-28	William Bevis	24
1926-27	William Bevis	32
1925-26	William Bevis	33
1924-25	Hugh Stuart	28½
1923-24	Bobby Grinham	29
1922-23	Bobby Grinham	29
1921-22	Ted Webster	31½
1920-21	Hugh Stuart	28
1919-20	Vincent Hillyard	34

*apprentice

In A Nutshell

Leading winning jockeys

TITLES	JOCKEY
17	Eddie Cox
14	Brendon McCoull
9	Max Baker

Current winning jockeys

TITLES	JOCKEY
14	Brendon McCoull
3	David Pires
2	Craig Newitt

Record season

SEASON	JOCKEY	WINS
2005-06	Brendon McCoull	109

Victorian Metropolitan Jockeys' Premierships

SEASON	JOCKEY	WINS	SEASON	JOCKEY	WINS
2017-18	Craig Williams	63	1955-56	Bill Williamson	45
2016-17	Craig Williams	77	1954-55	Jack Purtell	45
2015-16	Craig Williams	70	1953-54	Bill Williamson	67½
2014-15	Damien Oliver	60	1952-53	Bill Williamson	48
2013-14	Damien Oliver	59	1951-52	Bill Williamson	51
2012-13	Glen Boss	65	1950-51	Jack Purtell	64
2011-12	Luke Nolen	74	1949-50	Jack Purtell	59½
2010-11	Luke Nolen	71	1948-49	Jack Purtell	48
2009-10	Luke Nolen	66	1947-48	Harold Badger	46
2008-09	Damien Oliver/Craig Williams	71	1946-47	Jack Purtell	43½
2007-08	Craig Williams	86	1945-46	Scobie Breasley	52½
2006-07	Craig Williams	94	1944-45	Scobie Breasley	53½
2005-06	Craig Williams	70	1943-44	Scobie Breasley	23
2004-05	Nick Ryan*	83	1942-43	Harold Badger	22½
2003-04	Damien Oliver	77	1941-42	Harold Badger	57½
2002-03	Kerrin McEvoy	62	1940-41	Harold Badger	51½
2001-02	Damien Oliver	91	1939-40	Harold Badger	52½
2000-01	Brett Prebble	86½	1938-39	Harold Badger	48½
1999-00	Brett Prebble	99½	1936-37	Bill Elliot	53½
1998-99	Damien Oliver	90½	1935-36	Harold Skidmore	45
1997-98	Greg Childs	77½	1934-35	Harold Skidmore	53
1996-97	Steven King	64½	1933-34	Harold Skidmore*	52½
1995-96	Darren Gauci	61½	1932-33	Bill Duncan	37½
1994-95	Damien Oliver	81½	1931-32	Bill Duncan	38½
1993-94	Damien Oliver	66	1930-31	Bill Duncan	47½
1992-93	Damien Oliver*	63	1929-30	Bill Duncan	31
1991-92	Greg Childs	69	1928-29	Jack O'Brien*	27
1990-91	Damien Oliver*	71	1927-28	Bill Duncan	54
1989-90	Michael Clarke	83	1926-27	Bill Duncan	49½
1988-89	Michael Clarke	79	1925-26	Bill Duncan	41
1987-88	Michael Clarke	75	1924-25	Bill Duncan	57
1986-87	Michael Clarke	85	1923-24	Frank Dempsey	34
1985-86	Darren Gauci*	70	1922-23	Bill Duncan	30
1984-85	Darren Gauci*	62	1921-22	Vic Sleigh*	32
1983-84	Darren Gauci*	65	1920-21	Bill Duncan	35
1982-83	Brent Thomson	52	1919-20	Bill Duncan	38
1981-82	Brent Thomson	59½	1918-19	Frank Dempsey	33½
1980-81	Harry White	63½	1917-18	Frank Bullock	38
1979-80	Brent Thomson	63	1916-17	Bobby Lewis	39½
1978-79	Harry White	51½	1915-16	Frank Dempsey*	47
1977-78	Roy Higgins	48	1914-15	Pat Kelly	45
1976-77	Roy Higgins	56	1913-14	Joe Killorn	27
1975-76	Roy Higgins	41	1912-13	Bob Harris	25
1974-75	Roy Higgins	56½	1911-12	Bobby Lewis	25
1973-74	Harry White	48	1910-11	Cyril Bolton	34
1972-73	Roy Higgins	57	1909-10	Cyril Bolton	40
1971-72	Roy Higgins	75	1908-09	Cyril Bolton	46
1970-71	Roy Higgins	63	1907-08	Eddie Turner	31
1969-70	Roy Higgins	53	1906-07	Fred Burn	26
1968-69	Roy Higgins	45	1905-06	Norman Godby	27
1967-68	Harry White	49½	1904-05	Billy Minter	30
1966-67	Jim Johnson	63	1903-04	Brownie Carslake	38
1965-66	Roy Higgins	45	1902-03	Billy Minter	40
1964-65	Roy Higgins	58	1901-02	Pat Kelly	44
1963-64	Alan Burton	29½	1900-01	Bobby Lewis	35
1962-63	Bill Smith	27	1899-00	Walter Burn	31
1961-62	Jack Purtell	32½	*Apprentice		
1960-61	Jack Purtell	48½			
1959-60	Geoff Lane*	44			
1958-59	Ron Hutchison	49½			
1957-58	Bill Williamson	53			
1956-57	Bill Williamson	58½			

In A Nutshell

Leading winning jockeys

TITLES	JOCKEY
11	Roy Higgins, Bill Duncan
10	Damien Oliver
7	Jack Purtell, Craig Williams
6	Harold Badger, Bill Williamson
4	Michael Clarke, Darren Gauci

Current winning jockeys

TITLES	JOCKEY
10	Damien Oliver
7	Craig Williams
3	Luke Nolen
2	Brett Prebble
1	Glen Boss, Steven King, Kerrin McEvoy

Record season

SEASON	JOCKEY	WINS
1999-00	Brett Prebble	99½

Victorian Metropolitan Apprentice Premierships

SEASON	JOCKEY	WINS
2017-18	Ethan Brown	49
2016-17	Beau Mertens	73
2015-16	Dylan Dunn	33
2014-15	Patrick Moloney	42
2013-14	Katelyn Mallyon	31
2012-13	Chad Schofield	41
2011-12	Katelyn Mallyon	23
2010-11	Jake Noonan	37
2009-10	Jason Maskiell	52
2008-09	Nicholas Hall	33
2007-08	Sebastian Murphy	51
2006-07	Sebastian Murphy	51
2005-06	Ben Melham	43
2004-05	Nick Ryan	83
2003-04	Nick Ryan	50
2002-03	Craig Newitt	59
2001-02	Reece Wheeler	33
2000-01	Vin Hall	49
1999-00	Luke Nolen	34
1998-99	Matt Gatt	45
1997-98	Aaron Spiteri	37½
1996-97	Brett Prebble	44
1995-96	Brett Prebble	39
1994-95	Brett Prebble	30
1993-94	Patrick Payne	40
1992-93	Damien Oliver	61
1991-92	Damien Oliver	48
1990-91	Damien Oliver	71
1989-90	Steven King	42
1988-89	Steven King	33
1987-88	Simon Marshall	45½
1986-87	Len Maund	43
1985-86	Darren Gauci	70
1984-85	Darren Gauci	62
1983-84	Darren Gauci	65
1982-83	Darren Gauci	40
1981-82	Malcolm Pay	37
1980-81	Mark Riley	22
1979-80	Brendan Clements	37
1978-79	Dale Short	38
1977-78	Wayne Treloar	37½
1976-77	Wayne Treloar	25
1975-76	Wayne Treloar	30
1974-75	Robert Heffernan/Wayne Treloar	16
1973-74	Norm Waymouth	23
1972-73	Stan Aitken	35½
1971-72	Pat Trotter	16
1970-71	Stan Aitken	29
1969-70	Terry Finger	16
1968-69	Gary Gath	18
1967-68	Lee Hope	14
1966-67	Paul Jarman	25
1965-66	Paul Jarman	33
1964-65	Paul Jarman	18
1963-64	Jim Courtney/Harry White	22
1962-63	Rod Dawkins	22
1961-62	Peter Wallen	20
1960-61	Rod Scarlett	17
1959-60	Denis MacGregor	17
1958-59	Geoff Lane	43½
1957-58	Geoff Lane	41½
1956-57	Geoff Lane	32
1955-56	Geoff Lane	37
1954-55	Geoff Lane	23
1953-54	Brian Gilders	18
1952-53	Ray Ball	13½
1951-52	Norm Dickens	13
1950-51	Bob Irons	11½
1949-50	Ron Lindsay	9
1948-49	Doug Barclay	13
1947-48	Doug Barclay	12
1946-47	Ron Hutchinson/Des Snart	12½
1945-46	Ron Hutchinson	13
1944-45	Tommy Hoppo	13½
1943-44	Harry F. White	9½
1942-43	Harry McCloud	12
1941-42	Harry McCloud/Ken Smith	14
1940-41	Tom Unkovich	13
1939-40	Tommy Griffiths (Jack Purtell finished his time in May when on 26 winners)	19
1938-39	Vic Hartnett	12½
1937-38	Clyde McLauchlan	15½
1936-37	Stan Burgoine	9
1935-36	Ted Preston	18
1934-35	Herbert Moran	17
1933-34	Harold Skidmore	37½
1932-33	Harold Skidmore	29
1931-32	Harold Skidmore	35
1930-31	Harold Skidmore	N/A
1929-30	Arthur Dewhurst	14½
1928-29	Arthur Dewhurst	22½
1927-28	Jack O'Brien	13½
1926-27	Alex Fullarton	20
1925-26	Alex Fullarton	19
1924-25	Hezekiah "Kiah" Bastian	13
1923-24	Roy Cooper	23
1922-23	Tim Simmons	23
1921-22	Vic Sleigh	32
1920-21	Vic Sleigh	10
1919-20	George May (Bill Duncan rode 27½ as apprentice to end of Jan 1920)	13
1918-19	Billy Duncan	N/A
1917-18	Billy Duncan	9
1916-17	Frank Dempsey	39
1915-16	Frank Dempsey	47
1914-15	Frank Dempsey	12
1913-14	N/A	
1912-13	N/A (Bob Harris won the senior title with 25 wins, 23 as apprentice)	

In A Nutshell

Leading jockeys
TITLES	JOCKEY
5	Geoff Lane
4	Darren Gauci, Harold Skidmore, Wayne Treloar
3	Frank Dempsey, Paul Jarman, Damien Oliver

Record season
SEASON	JOCKEY	WINS
2004-04	Nick Ryan	83

Fact: Frank Dempsey (1915-16) is the first apprentice to win the Victorian Metropolitan Jockeys' title.

Victorian Metropolitan Jockeys' Premierships (jumps)

SEASON	JOCKEY	WINS	SEASON	JOCKEY	WINS
2018	(in progress)		1961-62	Glen Bilney	9
2017	John Allen	13	1960-61	Trevor Jones	10
2016	John Allen	14	1959-60	Peter Riley	10
2015	Steve Pateman	13	1958-59	Brian Smith	11
2014	Steve Pateman	15	1957-58	Brian Smith	13½
2013	Steve Pateman	22	1956-57	Brian Smith	15
2012	Steve Pateman	27	1955-56	Brian Smith	15
2011	Steve Pateman	27	1954-55	Ron Lindsay	12
2010	Steve Pateman	14	1953-54	Brian Smith	15
2009	Steve Pateman	16	1952-53	Ron Hall	9
2007-08	Craig Durden/Steve Pateman	5	1951-52	Brian Smith	10
2006-07	Steve Pateman	7	1950-51	Brian Smith	12
2005-06	Craig Durden	8	1949-50	Brian Smith	10
2004-05	Craig Durden	7	1948-49	Brian Smith	9
2003-04	Brad McLean	8	1947-48	Ron Hall	9
2002-03	Craig Durden	7	1946-47	Ron Hall	10
2001-02	Brett Scott	8	1945-46	Ron Hall	9½
2000-01	Craig Durden	14	1944-45	Laurie Meenan	15
1999-00	Willie Harnett	7	1943-44	Laurie Meenan	7
1998-99	Craig Durden	12	1942-43	Laurie Meenan	9
1997-98	Brett Scott	7	1941-42	Laurie Meenan	22
1996-97	Ricky Maund	8	1940-41	Laurie Meenan/Stan McKee	22½
1995-96	Adrian Garraway	7	1939-40	Laurie Meenan	21
1994-95	Adrian Garraway	8	1938-39	Ron Sweetnam	14
1993-94	Craig Durden	11	1937-38	Alex Fullarton	23
1992-93	Jamie Evans	17	1936-37	Alex Fullarton	11
1991-92	Brian Constable	7	1935-36	Alex Fullarton	14½½
1990-91	Brian Constable	11	1934-35	Alex Fullarton	13½
1989-90	Laurie Paltridge	11	1933-34	L Jack Hynes	16½
1988-89	Nick Harnett	10	1932-33	Alex Fullarton	14
1987-88	Nick Harnett	9	1031-32	Bob Inkson	16
1986-87	Nick Harnett	10	1930-31	Bob Inkson	19
1985-86	Peter Delaney	11	1929-30	Bill Howson	16V
1984-85	Nick Harnett	11	1928-29	Bob Inkson	19
1983-84	Nick Harnett	7	1927-28	Tom Butler	13
1982-83	Nick Harnett	13	1926-27	Frank Leonard	16
1981-82	Grant Ace	9	1925-26	Patrick Dinsdale	10
1980-81	Paul Hely	8	1924-25	Patrick Dinsdale	20
1979-80	Kevin Wynne	7	1923-24	Collie Boyd	13
1978-79	Paul Hely	14	1922-23	Collie Boyd	15
1977-78	Paul Hely	11	1921-22	Collie Boyd	19
1976-77	Michael Laurence	14	1920-21	Collie Boyd	11
1975-76	Neville Rantall	9	1919-20	Herbert Thompson	15
1974-75	Matt Van Strien	19	1918-19	Collie Boyd	N/A
1973-74	Gary Carson	10	1917-18	Wilfred McLean	16
1972-73	Ron J Hall Jnr	15	1916-17	Bob Amson	27
1971-72	Kelvin Bourke	12	1915-16	N/A	
1970-71	Ted Byrne	14	1914-15	Archie Hawkins	15
1969-70	Tom McGinley	15	1913-14	Archie Hawkins	N/A
1968-69	Ted Byrne	12	1912-13	Archie Hawkins	N/A
1967-68	Tom McGinley	9			
1966-67	Tassie Kitchin	7			
1965-66	Tom McGinley/Tom Doyle	9			
1964-65	Ted Byrne	10			
1963-64	Ted Byrne	15			
1962-63	Ted Byrne	9			

In A Nutshell

Leading winning jockeys

TITLES	JOCKEY
9	Steven Pateman, Brian Smith
6	Craig Durden, Nick Harnett, Laurie Meenan
5	Collie Boyd, Ted Byrne, Alex Fullarton

Current winning jockeys

TITLES	JOCKEY
9	Steven Pateman
2	John Allen
1	Brad McLean

Record seasons

SEASON	JOCKEY	WINS
2011-12	Steven Pateman	27
2010-11	Steven Pateman	27
1916-17	Bob Amson	27

Note: after 2007-08 includes all jumps races in Victoria, and held annually.

WA Metropolitan Jockeys' Premierships

SEASON	JOCKEY	WINS
2017-18	Willie Pike	130
2016-17	Willie Pike	109
2015-16	Willie Pike	135
2014-15	Willie Pike	80
2013-14	Willie Pike	77
2012-13	Willie Pike	67
2011-12	Willie Pike	72
2010-11	Willie Pike	80½
2009-10	Paul Harvey	58½
2008-09	Willie Pike	86
2007-08	Paul Harvey	76
2006-07	Willie Pike	91
2005-06	Paul Harvey	88
2004-05	Paul Harvey	72
2003-04	Paul Harvey	65½
2002-03	Paul Harvey	103
2001-02	Paul Harvey	82
2000-01	Jason Brown	72
1999-00	Paul Harvey	116½
1998-99	Paul Harvey	112
1997-98	Paul Harvey	67
1996-97	Paul Harvey	114
1995-06	Paul Harvey	83½
1994-95	Stephen Miller	56½
1993-94	Troy Turner	53
1992-93	Peter Knuckey	57
1991-92	Mark Sestich	60
1990-92	Mark Sestich	60½
1989-90	Mark Sestich	62
1988-89	Mark Sestich	50
1987-88	Ian Albuino	52
1986-87	Rod Kemp	72
1985-86	Rod Kemp	86
1984-85	Rod Kemp	130
1983-84	Rod Kemp	137
1982-83	Ian Albuino	107½
1981-82	Ian Albuino	108
1980-81	Rod Kemp	123½
1979-80	Mark Grisby	125
1978-79	John Wilson	103
1977-78	Gerry Donnelly	99
1976-77	David Brosnan	95
1975-76	Laurie Millington	74
1974-75	David Brosnan	95
1973-74	Rod Staples	93
1972-73	David Brosnan*	86
1971-72	Rod Kemp	90
1970-71	Ross Cherry	85
1969-70	Ross Cherry	58
1968-69	Ross Cherry	70
1967-68	Ross Cherry	74
1966-67	Keith Mifflin	57
1965-66	Frank Moore	54
1964-65	Peter Moran*	50
1963-64	Frank Treen	64½
1962-63	Frank Treen	52
1961-62	Frank Moore	62
1960-61	Keith Moxham	86
1959-60	Keith Moxham	63
1958-59	Keith Moxham	57
1957-58	Keith Moxham	54
1956-57	Frank Treen	53
1955-56	Frank Treen	58
1954-55	Frank Treen	50
1953-54	Frank Moore	54
1952-53	Frank Treen	50
1951-52	Frank Treen	52
1950-51	Frank Moore	54
1949-50	Eric Treffone	49
1948-49	Frank Moore	43
1947-48	Eric Treffone	49
1946-47	Frank Moore	49
1945-46	Roy Percival	49
1944-45	Eric Treffone	22
1943-44	Eric Treffone	19
1942-53	Eric Treffone	29
1941-42	Colin Tulloh	37
1940-41	Jackie Meyers	28
1939-40	Eric Treffone	53
1938-39	Eric Treffone	59
1937-38	Eric Treffone	61
1936-37	Neil Huthison	47
1935-36	Steve Dodd	47
1934-35	Johnny Corry	47
1933-34	Johnny Corry	36
1932-33	Angus Armanasco	60
1931-32	Bob Morley	69
1930-31	Angus Armanasco	40
1929-30	Angus Armanasco*	50
1928-29	Bob Morley	40
1927-28	Bob Morley	50
1926-27	Arthur Cooper	46
1925-26	Bob Morley	42
1924-25	Neville Percival	58
1923-24	Sam Bowler	41
1922-23	Neville Percival	62
1921-22	George Leonard	38
1920-21	Wally Sibbritt	50
1919-20	Sam Bowler	49
1918-19	Sam Bowler	52

*apprentice

In A Nutshell

Leading winning jockeys

TITLES	JOCKEY
12	Paul Harvey
10	Willie Pike
8	Eric Treffone
7	Frank Treen

Current winning jockeys

TITLES	JOCKEY
12	Paul Harvey
10	Willie Pike
1	Jason Brown, Peter Knuckey, Troy Turner

Record season

SEASON	JOCKEY	WINS
1983-84	Rod Kemp	137

WA Metropolitan Apprentice Premierships

SEASON	JOCKEY	WINS	SEASON	JOCKEY	WINS
2017-18	Tayla Stone	31	1979-80	Craig Coombe	50
2016-17	Randy Tan	27	1978-79	Mark Grisby	97
2015-16	Clint Johnston-Porter	41	1977-78	David Rudland	55
2014-15	Lucy Warwick	65½	1976-77	Gerry Donnelly	73
2013-14	Jerry Noske	29	1975-76	Gerry Donnelly	60
2012-13	Ben Paterson	34	1974-75	Gerry Donnelly	67
2011-12	Ryan Hill	35	1973-74	Ian Albuino	45
2010-11	Kyra Yuill	56	1972-73	David Brosnan	86
2009-10	Ben Kennedy	26	1971-72	Rod Kemp	90
2008-09	Jarrad Noske	37	1970-71	Harry Wulff	37
2007-08	Alan Kennedy	29	1969-70	Rod Staples	34
2006-07	Jessica Hill	21	1968-69	Tommy Pike	23
2005-07	Brad Parnham	36	1967-68	Laurie Millington	23
2004-05	Dion Luciani	40	1966-67	Peter Moran	28
2003-04	William Pike	48½	1965-66	Danny Miller	37
2002-03	Takahide Ikenushi	33	1964-65	Peter Moran	50
2001-02	Neil Chapman	31	1963-64	Ross Cherry	31
2000-01	Alana Sansom	50½	1962-63	Ron Sibley	39
1999-00	Clint Harvey	33	1961-62	Keith Mifflin	59
1998-99	Daniel Staeck	41	1960-61	Les Burgess	31
1997-98	Daniel O'Heare	46½	1959-60	Ray Oliver	59
1996-97	Troy Morrissey	27	1958-59	Ray Oliver	28
1995-96	Peter Farrell	34	1957-58	Jim Taylor	30
1994-95	Troy Turner	20	1956-57	Jim Taylor	18
1993-94	Troy Turner	53	1955-56	Johnny Wilson	29
1992-93	Peter Knuckey	57	1954-55	Don McClymans	22
1991-92	Peter Knuckey	54	1953-54	Johnny Wilson	29
1990-91	Chad Davies	30½	1952-53	Colin Clune	30
1989-90	Shaun O'Donnell	40	1951-52	Sheldon Geyer	15
1988-89	Mark Grantham	43	1950-51	William Bodger	16
1987-88	Jason Oliver	40	1949-50	Les Pearson	27
1986-87	Tim Stubberfield	82	1948-49	Peter McKay	15
1985-86	Lannie Bell	62	1947-48	Frank Treen	17
1984-85	Lisa Harris	66	1946-47	Frank Treen	14
1983-64	Alan Hughes	59			
1982-83	Jason Taylor	83			
1981-82	Craig Wake	76			
1980-81	Peter Barnett	85½			

In A Nutshell

Leading jockeys

TITLES	JOCKEY
3	Gerry Donnelly
2	Peter Knuckey, Peter Moran, Ray Oliver, Jim Taylor, Frank Treen, Troy Turner

Record season

SEASON	JOCKEY	WINS
1978-79	Mark Grisby	97

NSW Metropolitan Trainers' Premierships

SEASON	TRAINER	WINS
2017-18	Chris Waller	189
2016-17	Chris Waller	152
2015-16	Chris Waller	169
2014-15	Chris Waller	143½
2013-14	Chris Waller	158½
2012-13	Chris Waller	167½
2011-12	Chris Waller	124½
2010-11	Chris Waller	117
2009-10	Peter Snowden	97
2008-09	Gai Waterhouse	83½
2007-08	Gai Waterhouse	70
2006-07	John Hawkes	152
2005-06	John Hawkes	134
2004-05	Gai Waterhouse	118
2003-04	John Hawkes	113
2002-03	Gai Waterhouse	156
2001-02	Gai Waterhouse	137
2000-01	Gai Waterhouse	153
1999-00	John Hawkes	112
1998-99	John Hawkes	97
1997-98	John Hawkes	116½
1996-97	Gai Waterhouse	104½
1995-96	John Hawkes	93
1994-95	John Hawkes	97
1993-94	John Hawkes	85
1992-93	Jack Denham	81½
1991-92	Vic Thompson	80
1990-91	Jack Denham	81½
1989-90	Bart Cummings	77
1988-89	Tommy Smith	88
1987-88	Brian Mayfield-Smith	86
1986-87	Brian Mayfield-Smith	98½
1985-86	Brian Mayfield-Smith	99
1984-85	Tommy Smith	102½
1983-64	Tommy Smith	109
1982-83	Tommy Smith	81½
1981-82	Tommy Smith	111½
1980-81	Tommy Smith	126
1979-80	Tommy Smith	133
1978-79	Tommy Smith	146
1977-78	Tommy Smith	154½
1976-77	Tommy Smith	127
1975-76	Tommy Smith	156
1974-75	Tommy Smith	153
1973-74	Tommy Smith	125
1972-73	Tommy Smith	139
1971-72	Tommy Smith	141½
1970-71	Tommy Smith	123½
1969-70	Tommy Smith	141
1968-69	Tommy Smith	102
1967-68	Tommy Smith	143
1966-67	Tommy Smith	116
1965-66	Tommy Smith	88
1964-65	Tommy Smith	101
1963-64	Tommy Smith	93
1962-63	Tommy Smith	107
1961-62	Tommy Smith	82
1960-61	Tommy Smith	71
1959-60	Tommy Smith	69
1958-59	Tommy Smith	74
1957-58	Tommy Smith	85
1956-57	Tommy Smith	61
1955-56	Tommy Smith	54
1954-55	Tommy Smith	57
1953-54	Tommy Smith	46
1952-53	Tommy Smith	54
1951-52	Maurice McCarten	36
1950-51	Maurice McCarten	38
1949-48	Maurice McCarten	30
1948-49	Maurice McCarten	31
1947-48	Braden Payten	32½
1946-47	J. Bill McCurley	19½
1945-46	Braden Payten	34
1944-45	Braden Payten	21
1943-44	Braden Payten	22½
1942-53	Braden Payten/Frank Dalton	13
1941-42	Braden Payten	33½
1940-41	Braden Payten	46
1939-40	Alf Papworth	34½
1938-39	George Price	29
1937-38	Jack King	34½
1936-37	Jack King	35½
1935-36	Jack King	37½
1934-45	Jack King	38
1933-34	Jack Jamieson	25½
1932-33	Frank McGrath	24½
1931-32	George Price	30½
1930-31	Elver Walker	20½
1929-30	William Booth	29
1928-29	George Price	22½½½
1927-28	George Price	17½½
1926-27	Bill Kelso	N/A
1925-26	George Price	23
1924-25	George Price	22
1923-24	William Booth	24½
1922-23	William Booth	31
1921-22	William Booth	21
1920-21	William Booth	21
1919-20	Fred Williams	25½
1918-19	William Booth	15
1917-18	William Booth	21
1916-17	William Booth	16
1915-17	William Booth	15
1914-15	Bill Kelso	16
1913-14	James Barden/Mark Thompson/Paddy Nolan	12
1912-13	Elver Walker	10
1911-12	Paddy Nolan	13

In A Nutshell

Leading winning trainers

TITLES	TRAINERS
34	Tommy Smith
9	William Booth, John Hawkes
8	Chris Waller
7	Braden Payten, Gai Waterhouse

Current winning trainers

TITLES	TRAINERS
9	John Hawkes
8	Chris Waller
7	Gai Waterhouse
1	Peter Snowden

Record season

SEASON	TRAINERS	WINS
2017-18	Chris Waller	189

QLD Metropolitan Trainers' Premierships

SEASON	TRAINER	WINS
2017-18	Tony Gollan	90
2016-17	Tony Gollan	77
2015-16	Tony Gollan	87½
2014-15	Tony Gollan	79
2013-14	Tony Gollan	57
2012-13	Rob Heathcote	70
2011-12	Rob Heathcote	63½
2010-11	Rob Heathcote	62½
2009-10	Rob Heathcote	55
2008-09	Rob Heathcote	46
2007-08	Barry Baldwin	41
2006-07	Bryan Guy	45½
2005-06	Alan Bailey	45
2004-05	John Hawkes	58
2003-04	Alan Bailey	47
2002-03	Alan Bailey	50
2001-02	Gerald Ryan	66
2000-01	Gerald Ryan	61
1999-00	John Hawkes	53
1998-99	Alan Bailey	38
1997-98	Barry Baldwin	40
1996-97	John Hawkes	36
1995-96	Bruce McLachlan	48
1994-95	Bruce McLachlan	65
1993-94	Bruce McLachlan	51
1992-93	Bruce McLachlan	64
1991-92	Bruce McLachlan	45
1990-91	Bruce McLachlan	48
1989-90	Bruce McLachlan	60
1988-87	Bruce McLachlan	51
1987-88	Bruce McLachlan	78
1986-87	Bruce McLachlan	49
1985-86	Bruce McLachlan	64
1984-85	Bruce McLachlan	49
1983-64	Jim Atkins	48
1982-83	Bruce McLachlan	37½
1981-82	Bruce McLachlan	54
1980-81	Bruce McLachlan	65
1979-80	Henry Davis	46
1978-79	Bruce McLachlan	43
1977-78	Henry Davis	52
1976-77	Henry Davis	42
1975-76	Henry Davis	41
1974-75	Jim Griffiths	47
1973-74	Jim Atkins	42
1972-73	Jim Atkins	35½
1971-72	Jim Atkins	44½
1970-71	Alby Pratt	49
1969-70	Roy Dawson	35½
1968-69	Fred Best	30
1967-68	Fred Best	30
1966-67	Fred Best	21
1965-66	Fred Best	33
1964-65	Fred Best	20
1963-64	Roy Dawson	20
1962-63	Fred Best	30
1961-62	Neil Strong	18
1960-61	Fred Best	19
1959-60	Fred Best	25
1958-59	Fred Best	31
1957-58	Fred Best	37
1956-57	Fred Best	36
1955-56	Fred Best	25
1954-55	Fred Best	N/A
1953-54	Fred Best (Frank Kennedy)	25
1952-53	Fred Best (Mick Kenny)	29
1951-52	Fred Best (Best)	31
1950-51	Mick Kenny (George Anderson)	20
1949-50	Jim Douglas (Douglas)	25
1948-49	Jim Douglas (Douglas)	21
1947-48	Jim Douglas (George Anderson)	16
1946-47	George Anderson (Anderson)	22
1945-46	Jim Douglas (Harry Plant)	21
1944-45	Jim Shean (Con Doyle)	20
1943-44	Jim Douglas (Douglas)	34
1942-43	Bill Reynolds (Reynolds)	23
1941-42	Jim Douglas (Roley Wall)	20
1940-41	Clive Morgan/Bill Shean (Bill A Tucker)	22
1939-40	George Anderson (Walter Neale)	22
1938-39	George Anderson/Peter Venaglia (Venaglia)	21
1937-38	Jim Douglas (Bill A Tucker)	26
1936-37	George Anderson (Anderson)	33
1935-36	George Anderson (Anderson)	35
1934-35	Jim Douglas (Douglas)	27
1933-34	George Anderson (Bill A Tucker)	25
1932-33	Bill A Tucker (Tucker)	30
1931-32	Charlie McLoughlin (McLoughlin)	23
1930-31	George Anderson (Anderson)	20
1929-30	Bill J Tucker (Tucker)	20
1928-29	George Anderson (Anderson)	22
1927-28	George Anderson (Billy Noud)	20
1926-27	Fred Stanfield (Walter Neale)	16
1925-26	Billy Noud (Noud)	26
1924-25	Billy Noud (Noud)	24
1923-24	Billy Noud (Noud)	23
1922-23	Bill J Tucker (Tucker)	25
1921-22	Bill J Tucker/Billy Noud (Vic Bergstrom)	22
1920-21	Vic Bergstrom (John Booth)	34
1919-20	Bill J Tucker (Jack Kahl)	25
1918-19	Bill J Tucker (Tucker)	24
1917-18	Albert Carr (Carr)	20
1916-17	Jack Kahl (Watty Blacklock)	20
1915-16	Jack Kahl/John Stone (Bill J Tucker)	18
1916-17	Watty Blacklock/Bill Noud (Bill J Tucker)	17

In A Nutshell

Leading winning trainers

TITLES	TRAINERS
16	Fred Best, Bruce McLachlan
9	George Anderson
8	Jim Douglas
5	Tony Gollan, Rob Heathcote. Bill J Tucker
4	Jim Atkins, Alan Bailey, Henry Davis, Billy Noud

Current winning trainers

TITLES	TRAINERS
5	Tony Gollan, Rob Heathcote
3	John Hawkes
2	Barry Baldwin, Gerald Ryan
1	Bryan Guy

Record season

SEASON	TRAINERS	WINS
2017-18	Tony Gollan	90

Note: Before 1955 the Brisbane Trainers' Premiership was awarded to the trainer who earned the most prizemoney for the season. Records for leading trainers pre-1955 display the trainer with the most wins and the trainer with the most prizemoney (in brackets).

SA Metropolitan Trainers' Premierships

SEASON	TRAINER	WINS
2017-18	Tony McEvoy	52
2016-17	Leon Macdonald & Andrew Gluyas	49
2015-16	Phillip Stokes	50
2014-15	Phillip Stokes	36
2013-14	Phillip Stokes	55
2012-13	Tony McEvoy	34
2011-12	Tony McEvoy	44
2010-11	Mark Kavanagh	36
2009-10	Mark Kavanagh	44
2008-09	David Hayes	44
2007-08	David Hayes	59
2006-07	David Hayes	60½
2005-06	David Hayes	63
2004-05	Tony McEvoy	54
2003-04	Tony McEvoy	75
2002-03	Tony McEvoy	68
2001-02	Tony McEvoy	46
2000-01	Leon Macdonald	32
1999-00	Peter Hayes	49½½
1998-99	Peter Hayes	72
1997-98	Peter Hayes	65
1996-97	Peter Hayes	55
1995-96	Peter Hayes	N/A
1994-95	David Hayes	N/A
1993-94	David Hayes	N/A
1992-93	David Hayes	N/A
1991-92	David Hayes	N/A
1990-91	David Hayes	N/A
1989-90	Colin Hayes	N/A
1988-89	Colin Hayes	N/A
1987-88	Colin Hayes	110
1986-87	Colin Hayes	76
1985-86	Colin Hayes	94½
1984-85	Colin Hayes	136
1983-64	Colin Hayes	89
1982-83	Colin Hayes	68
1981-82	Colin Hayes	100
1980-81	Colin Hayes	111
1979-80	Colin Hayes	76
1978-79	Colin Hayes	55½
1977-78	Colin Hayes	55
1976-77	Colin Hayes	104
1975-76	Colin Hayes	112
1974-75	Colin Hayes	70
1973-74	Colin Hayes	71
1972-73	Bart Cummings	77
1971-72	Colin Hayes	80
1970-71	Bart Cummings	74
1969-70	Bart Cummings	48
1968-69	Bart Cummings	58
1967-68	Bart Cummings	73
1966-67	Colin Hayes	62
1965-66	Bart Cummings	78
1964-65	Colin Hayes	67½
1963-64	Grahame Heagney	59
1962-63	Colin Hayes	59
1961-62	Colin Hayes	63
1960-61	Colin Hayes	55
1959-60	Colin Hayes	60
1958-59	Roy Dini	49
1957-58	Colin Hayes	34
1956-57	Colin Hayes	37
1955-56	Colin Hayes	26
1954-55	George Jesser	22
1953-54	Jack Plews	26
1952-53	Jack Plews	20
1951-52	Jack Plews	18
1950-51	Jack Plews	24
1949-50	Jack Brett	16½
1948-49	Jack Plews	19
1947-48	Ike Reid	19
1946-47	Jack Brett	17
1945-46	Jack Brett	23
1944-45	George Bates	24
1943-44	Ab Macdonald	20
1942-43	(No racing)	
1941-42	Sam Evans	13
1940-41	Sam Evans	22
1939-40	George Bates/Ike Reid	19
1938-39	Harry Butler	18
1937-38	Ike Reid	22
1936-37	Jack Tait	16
1935-36	George Jesser	20
1934-35	Sam Evans	21
1933-34	Ike Reid	22
1932-33	George Bates/Jim Cummings	14
1931-32	Jim Cummings	13
1930-31	Ike Reid	N/A
1929-30	Harry Butler	18
1928-29	Harry Butler	27
1927-28	Harry Butler	17
1926-27	Harry Butler	19
1922-23	Ike Reid	18

In A Nutshell

Leading winning trainers

TITLES	TRAINERS
27	Colin Hayes
9	David Hayes
7	Tony McEvoy
6	Bart Cummings

Current winning trainers

TITLES	TRAINERS
9	David Hayes
7	Tony McEvoy
3	Phillip Stokes
2	Mark Kavanagh, Leon Macdonald*
1	Leon Macdonald & Andrew Gluyas

* includes wins in partnership

Record season

SEASON	TRAINERS	WINS
1984-85	Colin Hayes	136

Tasmanian Metropolitan Trainers' Premierships

SEASON	TRAINER	WINS
2017-18	Scott Bruton	69
2016-17	Scott Bruton	96
2015-16	Scott Bruton	70
2014-15	Scott Bruton	56½
2013-14	David & Scott Brunton	68
2012-13	David & Scott Brunton	78
2011-12	David & Scott Brunton	75½
2010-11	David & Scott Brunton	92
2009-10	David & Scott Brunton	78
2008-09	Charlie Goggin	60
2007-08	John Blacker	46
2006-07	David Brunton	68
2005-06	David Brunton	57
2004-05	John Blacker	63
2003-04	Charlie Goggin	60
2002-03	Charlie Goggin	57
2001-02	Charlie Goggin	60
2000-01	Charlie Goggin/John Blacker	54
1999-00	Charlie Goggin	67
1998-99	Charlie Goggin	68
1997-98	Charlie Goggin	65
1996-97	Charlie Goggin	47
1995-96	Barry Campbell	52
1994-95	Charlie Goggin	47
1993-94	Charlie Goggin	63
1992-93	Charlie Goggin	52
1991-92	Charlie Goggin	60
1990-91	Alan Stubbs	73
1989-90	Alan Stubbs	62½
1988-89	Alan Stubbs	62
1987-88	Alan Stubbs	46
1986-87	Michael Trinder	59½
1985-86	Michael Trinder	59
1984-85	Len Dixon	N/A
1983-84	Michael Trinder	51
1982-83	Graeme McCulloch	45
1981-82	Graeme McCulloch	55
1980-81	Graeme McCulloch	46
1979-80	Graeme McCulloch	42
1978-79	Alan Stubbs	29
1977-78	Alan Stubbs	39
1976-77	Maurie Long	38
1975-76	Alan Stubbs	32
1974-75	Bill Wells	44
1973-74	Alan Stubbs	34
1972-73	Mal Gerrard	43
1971-72	Mal Gerrard	40
1970-71	Mal Gerrard	34
1969-70	Mal Gerrard	62
1968-69	Mal Gerrard	32
1967-68	Brian Lomasney	32
1966-67	Brian Lomasney	28
1965-66	Brian Lomasney	42
1964-65	Jack Stubbs	42
1963-64	Jack Stubbs	31
1962-63	Bill Wells	29
1961-62	Eric Devine	29
1960-61	Eric Connelly	32
1959-60	Andy Robertson	28
1958-59	Bill Wells	19
1957-58	Bert Quarry	23
1956-57	Andy Robertson	26
1955-56	Jim Brooker	29
1954-55	Andy Robertson	32
1953-54	Alex Grant	31
1952-53	Alex Grant	43
1951-52	Len Quinn	32½
1950-51	Len Quinn	26½
1949-50	Dick Morley	32
1948-49	Andy Robertson	25
1947-48	Bob Campbell	15½
1946-47	Dick Morley	27½
1945-46	Mick Conway	19
1944-45	Dick Morley	32
1943-44	Dick Morley	27
1942-43	Dick Morley	28
1941-42	Dick Morley	28
1940-41	Harry Ligerwood	25½
1939-40	Dick Pitt	17
1938-39	Bert Cook	20
1937-38	Alex Grant	19
1936-37	Dick Pitt	21½
1935-36	Dick Pitt	19
1934-35	William Southerwood	14½
1933-34	George Cann	22½
1932-33	William Sullivan/Arthur Hodgetts	16
1931-32	Ben McKenna	12½
1930-31	William Southerwood	16
1929-30	George Cann	30
1928-29	George Cann	12½
1927-28	Ben McKenna	17
1926-27	Joseph Greig	25
1925-26	William Sullivan	29
1924-25	William Sullivan	39
1923-24	William Southerwood	24
1922-23	William Sullivan	37
1921-22	William Sullivan	26
1920-21	William Sullivan	38
1919-20	William Sullivan	45

In A Nutshell

Leading winning trainers

TITLES	TRAINERS
13	Charlie Goggin
9	Scott Brunton*
7	David Brunton*, Alan Stubbs, William Sullivan
6	Dick Morley

* includes wins in partnership

Current winning trainers

TITLES	TRAINERS
13	Charlie Goggin
9	Scott Brunton*
7	David Brunton*
5	David & Scott Brunton
4	Graeme McCulloch
3	Michael Trinder
2	John Blacker

* includes wins in partnership

Record season

SEASON	TRAINERS	WINS
2016-17	Scott Brunton	96

Victorian Metropolitan Trainers' Premierships (flat)

SEASON	TRAINER	WINS
2017-18	Darren Weir	153
2016-17	Darren Weir	137
2015-16	Darren Weir	106
2014-15	Darren Weir	79
2013-14	Darren Weir	86
2012-13	Peter Moody	69
2011-12	Peter Moody	91
2010-11	Peter Moody	103½
2009-10	Peter Moody	82
2008-09	Lee Freedman	65
2007-08	David Hayes	95
2007-06	David Hayes	103
2005-06	Lee Freedman	115
2004-05	Lee Freedman	81
2003-04	Lee Freedman	82
2002-03	Tony McEvoy	67
2001-02	Lee Freedman	59
2000-01	Peter Hayes	46
1999-00	Peter Hayes	68
1998-99	Peter Hayes	70
1997-98	Lee Freedman	94½
1996-97	Lee Freedman	81
1995-96	David Hayes	62½
1994-95	David Hayes	82½
1993-94	David Hayes	74
1992-93	David Hayes	84
1991-92	David Hayes	93½
1990-91	David Hayes	77
1989-90	Colin Hayes	87
1988-89	Colin Hayes	68
1987-88	Colin Hayes	61½
1986-87	Colin Hayes	71
1985-86	Colin Hayes	52½
1984-85	Colin Hayes	66
1983-84	Colin Hayes	57
1982-83	Colin Hayes	57
1981-82	Colin Hayes	67½
1980-81	Colin Hayes	71½
1979-80	Colin Hayes	71
1978-79	Colin Hayes	45½
1977-78	Colin Hayes	47
1976-77	Geoff Murphy	45½
1975-76	Bart Cummings	44
1974-75	Bart Cummings	57½
1973-74	Angus Armanasco	41
1972-73	Angus Armanasco	44
1971-72	Angus Armanasco	38½
1970-71	Bart Cummings	41½
1969-70	Bart Cummings	42
1968-69	Bart Cummings	37½
1967-68	Angus Armanasco	26½
1966-67	Des Judd	26
1965-66	Angus Armanasco/Des Judd	18
1964-65	Angus Armanasco	26
1963-64	Angus Armanasco	23
1962-63	Brian Courtney	26
1961-62	Brian Courtney	46
1960-61	Brian Courtney	29½
1959-60	Fred Hoysted	27
1958-59	Phil Burke	27½
1957-58	Fred Hoysted	37
1956-57	Roy Shaw	20.3
1955-56	Theo Lewis/Fred Hoysted	33
1954-55	Des Judd	37½
1953-54	Fred Hoysted	34
1952-53	Theo Lewis	30
1951-52	Fred Hoysted	41
1950-51	Fred Hoysted	27
1949-50	Fred Hoysted	32½
1948-49	Fred Hoysted	26
1947-48	Fred Hoysted	39
1946-47	Fred Hoysted	25
1945-46	Fred Hoysted	21
1944-45	Lou Robertston	21
1943-44	Lou Robertson	24
1942-43	Fred Hoysted	22
1941-42	Harold Freedman	25
1940-41	Fred Hoysted	32½
1939-40	Stan Murphy	26
1938-39	Bill Burke	28
1937-38	Jack Holt/Fred Hoysted	28
1936-37	Harold Freedman	21½
1935-36	Fred Hoysted	29
1934-35	Fred Hoysted	45
1933-34	Jack Holt	25½
1932-33	Fred Hoysted	36½
1931-32	Jack Holt	26½
1930-31	Jack Holt	25
1929-30	Jack Holt	30
1928-29	Lou Robertson	20½
1927-28	Jack Holt	22
1926-27	Bill Burke	22
1925-26	Jack Holt	24
1924-25	Jack Holt	22
1923-24	Jack Holt	30
1922-23	Jack Holt/Harry McCalman	19
1921-22	Cecil Godby	31½
1920-21	Jack Holt	34
1919-20	Jack Holt	29½
1918-19	Jack Holt	43

In A Nutshell

Leading winning trainers

TITLES	TRAINERS
17	Fred Hoysted
13	Colin Hayes, Jack Holt
8	David Hayes

Current winning trainers

TITLES	TRAINERS
8	David Hayes
7	Lee Freedman
5	Darren Weir
1	Tony McEvoy

Record season

SEASON	TRAINERS	WINS
2017-18	Darren Weir	153

Victorian Metropolitan Trainers' Premierships (jumps)

SEASON	TRAINER	WINS
2018	(in progress)	
2017	Darren Weir	13
2016	Darren Weir	19
2015	Eric Musgrove	20
2014	Eric Musgrove/Patrick Payne	12
2013	Ciaron Maher	12
2012	Patrick Payne	12
2011	Eric Musgrove	14
2010	Eric Musgrove	13
2009	Eric Musgrove	13
2007-08	David Hayes/Chris Hyland	4
2006-07	Robbie Lang	6
2005-06	Eric Musgrove	7
2004-05	Eric Musgrove	5
2003-04	David Brideoake	9
2002-03	Tony Rosolini	6
2001-02	Eric Musgrove	7
2000-01	Jim Houlahan	9
1999-00	Robert Smerdon	4
1998-99	Jim Houlahan	11
1997-98	Jim Houlahan	5
1996-97	Eric Musgrove	8
1995-96	Eric Musgrove	8
1994-95	Eric Musgrove	7
1993-94	Jim Houlahan	10
1992-93	Jim Houlahan	7
1991-92	Eric Musgrove	10
1990-91	Eric Musgrove	11
1989-90	Jim Houlahan	9
1988-89	Jim Houlahan	7
1987-88	Jim Houlahan	9

SEASON	TRAINER	WINS
1986-87	Eric Musgrove	11
1985-86	Rick Hore-Lacy	4
1984-85	Rick Hore-Lacy	8
1983-84	Kath Smith	5
1982-83	Bruce Purcell	5
1981-82	Mark Houlahan	7
1980-81	Ted Harvey	4
1979-80	Jack Winder	5
1978-79	Kath Smith	5
1977-78	Mark Houlahan	7
1976-77	Mark Houlahan	4
1975-76	Mark Houlahan	4
1974-75	Mark Houlahan	12
1973-74	Theo Howe	9
1972-73	Les Cole/Tom Hughes	6
1971-72	Theo Howe	10
1970-71	Theo Howe/Ron Maund	5
1969-70	Theo Howe/George McCormick	7
1968-69	Theo Howe	7
1967-68	Ray McClaren	6
1966-67	Des McCormick	8
1965-66	George McCormick	5
1964-65	Des McCormick/Ray McLaren/ George Hanlon	5
1963-64	Des McCormick	8
1962-63	Des McCormick	7
1961-62	Jim McDonald	6
1960-61	Harry Bird/Des McCormick	6
1959-60	Alex Fullarton	9

In A Nutshell

Leading winning trainers

TITLES	TRAINERS
14	Eric Musgrove
9	Jim Houlahan
5	Mark Houlahan, Theo Howe, Des McCormick

Current winning trainers

TITLES	TRAINERS
14	Eric Musgrove
2	Patrick Payne, Darren Weir
1	David Brideoake, David Hayes, Chris Hyland, Robbie Laing, Ciaron Maher, Bruce Purcell, Tony Rosolini, Robert Smerdon.

Record season

SEASON	TRAINERS	WINS
2015	Eric Musgrove	20

Note: after 2007-08, the jumps program was held annually and all wins, metro and provincial, are counted. There are no winners on record from 1918–19 through to 1958–59.

WA Metropolitan Trainers' Premierships

SEASON	TRAINER	WINS
2017-18	Adam Durrant	71
2016-17	Grant & Alana Williams	74
2015-16	Adam Durrant	67
2014-15	Adam Durrant	69½
2013-14	Adam Durrant	77
2012-13	Adam Durrant	53
2011-12	Adam Durrant	47
2010-11	Neville Parnham	54
2009-10	Adam Durrant	56
2008-09	Neville Parnham	76
2007-08	Neville Parnham	45
2006-07	Neville Parnham	48½
2005-06	Neville Parnham	55
2004-05	Neville Parnham	69
2003-04	Neville Parnham	47
2002-03	Neville Parnham	33
2001-02	Neville Parnham	44
2000-01	Neville Parnham	43
1999-00	Neville Parnham	42
1998-99	Neville Parnham	56
1997-98	Lou Luciani	42½
1996-97	Lou Luciani	59½
1995-96	Lou Luciani	32
1994-95	Lou Luciani	53
1993-94	Lou Luciani	54
1992-93	Frank Maynard	32
1991-92	Lou Luciani/Neville Parnham	27
1990-91	Lou Luciani	43
1989-90	Wally Mitchell	32
1988-89	Lou Luciani	39
1987-88	Frank Maynard	38
1986-87	Buster O'Malley	55
1985-86	Frank Maynard	43
1984-85	Frank Maynard	57
1983-64	Frank Maynard	55
1982-83	Frank Maynard	52½
1981-82	Neville Pateman	63
1980-81	Neville Pateman	62½
1979-80	Vern Brockman	63
1978-79	Len Pike	74
1977-78	Len Pike	97
1976-77	Len Pike	101
1975-76	Len Pike	80
1974-75	Barry Mueller	40
1973-74	Bill Dillon	33
1972-73	Neville Pateman	44
1971-72	Jim Scott	42
1970-71	Paul Graham	36
1969-70	Paul Graham	39
1968-69	Paul Graham	29
1967-68	Ab Jordan	30
1966-67	Ted Parnham	26
1965-66	Len Pike	29
1964-65	Ab Jordan	30
1963-64	Ab Jordan	43½
1962-63	Jock Campbell	34
1961-62	Bob Burns	45
1960-61	Ab Jordan	36
1959-60	Ab Jordan	59
1958-59	Bill Purvis	34
1957-58	Ab Jordan	35
1956-57	Jock Campbell	25
1955-56	Bert Allpike	23
1954-55	Bob Burns	23
1953-54	Ted Parnham	22
1952-53	Jack Thomas	21
1951-52	Jock Campbell	22
1950-51	Jock Campbell	22
1949-48	Jock Campbell	27
1948-49	Jock Collinson	24½
1947-48	Jock Collinson	23½
1946-47	Ted McAuliffe	26
1945-46	Jock Collinson	45
1944-45	Jock Collinson	22
1943-44	Jock Collinson	14
1942-53	Eric O'Malley	11
1941-42	Fred J. Kersley	18
1940-41	Jock Campbell	31
1939-40	Fred J. Kersley	17
1938-39	Jim Kelly	24
1937-38	Jim Kelly	24
1936-37	Jim Cockell	28
1935-36	Jock Anderson	29
1934-35	Jock Anderson/Jock Campbell	20
1933-34	Bob Burns	33
1932-33	Jim Kelly	28
1931-32	Jim Kelly	27
1930-31	Vic Pinkus	22
1929-30	Jim Kelly	31
1928-29	Bob Burns	30
1927-28	Bob Burns	33
1926-27	Bob Burns	47
1925-26	Bob Burns	36
1924-25	Bob Burns	33
1923-24	Bob Burns	23
1922-23	Bob Burns	28
1921-22	Charlie Norton	28
1920-21	Bob Burns	34
1919-20	Tom Tighe	27
1918-19	Jim Kelly	21

In A Nutshell

Leading winning trainers

TITLES	TRAINERS
13	Neville Parnham
10	Bob Burns
8	Lou Luciani
7	Adam Durrant

Current winning trainers

TITLES	TRAINERS
13	Neville Parnham
8	Lou Luciani
7	Adam Durrant
6	Frank Maynard snr, Neville Pateman
1	Vern Brockman, Wally Mitchell, Barry Mueller, Grant & Alana Williams

Record seasons

SEASON	TRAINERS	WINS
1976-77	Len Pike	101